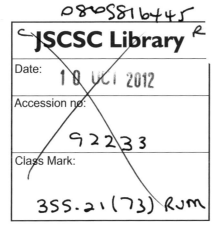

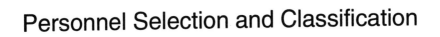

Personnel Selection and Classification

Personnel Selection and Classification

Edited by

Michael G. Rumsey
Clinton B. Walker
Army Research Institute

James H. Harris
Human Resources Research Organization

LAWRENCE ERLBAUM ASSOCIATES, PUBLISHERS
1994   Hillsdale, New Jersey   Hove, UK

Lawrence Erlbaum Associates, Inc., Publishers
365 Broadway
Hillsdale, New Jersey 07642

Cover design by Mairav Salomon-Dekel

Library of Congress Cataloging-in-Publication Data

Personnel selection and classification / edited by Michael G. Rumsey,
    Clinton B. Walker, James H. Harris.
        p. cm.
    Chiefly papers presented at a conference sponsored by the U.S.
Army.
    Includes bibliographical references and index.
    ISBN 0-8058-1644-5 (alk. paper)
    1. United States—Armed Forces—Personnel management—
Congresses. 2. United States—Armed Forces—Recruiting, en-
listment, etc.—Congresses. I. Rumsey, Michael G. II. Walker,
Clinton B. III. Harris, James H. (James Harry), 1944– .
UB323.P47 1994
355.6'1'0973—dc20   94-7161
                                                        CIP

Books published by Lawrence Erlbaum Associates are printed on
acid-free paper, and their bindings are chosen for strength and dura-
bility.

Printed in the United States of America
10 9 8 7 6 5 4 3 2 1

CONTENTS

Foreword: Selection and Classification for the Army of the Future

Major General Fred Gorden[1]
U.S. Army

I want to explain to you my expectations concerning the Army of the future. The Army is engaged in downsizing the force while maintaining its mission readiness. Questions about how to recruit, select, classify, and retain officers, noncommissioned officers, and soldiers for the Army will still be the principal personnel management concerns after this process is complete.

In military terms, we say that the Army of the future should be deployable, lethal, and versatile. For two of these dimensions—lethality and versatility—selection and classification research is particularly relevant. Selection affects lethality by supplying soldiers who can be trained to operate our weapons systems effectively. However, it is in the area of versatility that I think selection and classification can make a particularly strong impact. Versatility translates into creativity in leadership, not only in our commissioned and noncommissioned officers, but also in our new soldiers.

Besides having deployability, lethality, and versatility, the future force will need a balanced structure. This balance will be in terms of special operating forces (SOF), light forces, and heavy forces. It will be a capabilities-based force, which will provide versatility to respond to many types of crises and conflicts. Notice that I did not say respond to threats, but to crises and conflicts.

---

[1] Major General Gorden was the first speaker at the Selection and Classification conference. At the time of the conference, he was the Army's Director of Military Personnel Management (DMPM). The DMPM is responsible for policies relating to enlisted and officer accessions, recruiting, retention, and professional development, among other things. Principal sponsorship for all Army research in selection and classification belongs to DMPM.

Among Major General Gorden's previous assignments, he was Commandant of Cadets at the United States Military Academy and the Commanding General of the 25th Infantry Division in Hawaii. He has been awarded two Distinguished Service Medals and the Legion of Merit, as well as numerous other decorations and badges. Although his remarks are in the context of the U.S. Army's personnel system, they apply to the broader world of employment where workplaces and work are evolving, often in unanticipated ways.

Now, let's look at the larger context. A peacekeeping role has emerged for our Army. That effort could consist primarily of special operating forces and light forces. What does that mean with regard to our soldiers? Recall that we have been training them at the National Training Center,[2] where they have been conditioned to respond to a wartime situation. But some of these same soldiers will be put suddenly into a quite different environment. This environment may in some respects be very similar to that which our peacekeeping forces find today in the Sinai, but will perhaps be more challenging and complicated. I say that because the situation in the Sinai has developed over time and the duties and responsibilities associated with that have generally stabilized over that time. However, what we face in the future may be more akin to what happened in Los Angeles in 1992 than to anything for which our soldiers have been traditionally trained.

So we expect a much more complex, dynamic, and uncertain environment in the future. Selecting those who can handle uncertainty may be the greatest challenge that we have.

Now, what does this mean? Let me contrast it with my personal history in the Army. I graduated from West Point in 1962. The summer before, as part of the Cadet Training Program, I had gone to Europe in late July and early August of 1961. What happened then? The Berlin Wall went up.

At my graduation from West Point, the speaker was President Kennedy. He spoke of wars of national liberation, of warfare by proxy, and of the Green Berets, then an emerging institution in the Army.

Later on that summer, before I joined my unit, the Cuban Missile Crisis put substance into President Kennedy's speech. As the 1960s progressed, events in Southeast Asia and Latin America further confirmed these words.

I was a product of a period in which the threats and training requirements were well defined. I don't know what the graduation speakers at West Point will say about the world today, except that it is changing and uncertain. And when we get to the uncertainty part, there's nothing to anchor on except that great word. You researchers need to help me select, classify, and train the Gordens of the future to deal adaptively with the spectrum of situations that will face our country. The challenge we face is to determine what kind of research will enable us to select the persons who will be able to act and lead effectively in the emerging uncertain world.

---

[2] A U.S. military installation where intact, fully equipped combat units carry out engagement exercises against a resident opposing force.

PREFACE

Some might question the need for major new research undertakings in selection and classification. Indeed, if selection and classification are viewed as the conduct of routinized test development, validation, and application, such doubts might be justified.

But a much broader view of the subject guided the U.S. Army Research Institute (ARI) Selection and Classification Conference, which was held May 27–28, 1992, at the headquarters of the Human Resources Research Organization (HumRRO) in Alexandria, Virginia. This book presents the edited papers from that conference.

The view guiding this meeting was that many basic issues have not been resolved. In this view, the world of work is seen as complex and multidimensional, and the domain of predictor testing as encompassing all individual characteristics that relate to this world. This view brings together a wide range of topics in selection and classification research, including cognitive psychology, personality theory, interest assessment, psychometric theory, job analysis, organizational psychology, decision theory, and performance measurement.

This broader perspective opens up a panorama of research opportunities and needs. We grouped these topics into three major areas for the conference: (a) conceptualizing and measuring job performance, (b) conceptualizing and measuring individual differences, and (c) operational models for selection and classification decisions.

Historically, performance measurement in selection and classification research relied mostly on ratings or operational performance measures. Researchers seldom had the resources to develop research-only job sample measures. However, during the 1980s, the Joint-Service Job Performance Measurement/Enlistment Standards (JPM) Project (Wigdor & Green, 1991) made hands-on job sample measurement a central focus.

The Army's Project A (Campbell & Zook, 1990; Project A, 1990) was included in the JPM Project but also extended beyond it. Project A (Improving the Selection, Classification, and Utilization of Army Enlisted Personnel) showed the value of using comprehensive, systematic multiple measures for developing a multidimensional model of performance. This model is one indication of a growing understanding of the complexity of job performance and of the need to take this complexity into account in designing, conducting, and interpreting selection and classification research. This and other performance measurement issues, such as the changing nature of work and the problems associated with assessing individual contributions by team members, were addressed by speakers in this conference.

Relative to the field of performance measurement, the field of individual difference measurement is mature. In particular, cognitive testing has had a long successful history. But the measurement of individual differences is not confined to a single approach. Since the 1980s, great progress has occurred in conceptualizing and developing personality, biographical, psychomotor, and spatial measures; questions about how these might best be used in a selection and classification context are far from resolved. Recently, a variety of new approaches have surfaced that, if they live up to their proponents' claims, could revolutionize aptitude measurement. Again, in this conference many of the emerging issues in individual differences were put forward.

Although there is considerable agreement on what many of the major issues are in measuring performance and individual differences, in the area of decision models agreement is much harder to find. Is classification still important, or has validity generalization made this concept obsolete? What is the purpose of classification research? How should the capabilities of decision models be researched? What questions should receive the most emphasis?

Until some of those basic questions are answered, progress may be difficult. But ultimately this may be the area that offers opportunities for the most dramatic breakthroughs. Classification research, which for many years has not received much attention, is undergoing a revival. The complexity of the issues poses formidable challenges. In the conference, speakers reviewed major recent developments in the area and explored the implications.

The chapters in this volume come at a particularly important time in the history of selection and classification. Businesses and government, particularly the military, are downsizing. When the job must be done with fewer people, the selection of those people takes on greater significance. It also becomes important to ensure that those individuals chosen are placed in positions that make best use of their skills. Downsizing also tends to reduce the total number of separate occupations, meaning that individuals must often be capable of performing a wider variety of roles.

Selection and classification has become particularly important for the Army, which sponsored this conference, and the other military Services. Not only are they downsizing, but they are taking on a greater variety of missions that require a wider range of individual aptitudes. How best to identify persons who can operate effectively under these circumstances poses new challenges for selection and classification research.

This, then, was the environment in which the selection and classification conference was held. It was an environment marked by turbulence in terms of the concepts being addressed and the world context in which research applications were to take place. The conference was designed to both capture this turbulence and attempt to reduce it to some reasonable order. The desired outcome: Research topics, strategies, and concepts that the Army and other organizations and researchers could incorporate into their research planning and execution. In two lively days of paper presentations, discussants' comments, and group discussion, this outcome was achieved.

This book is both more and less than a transcript of the conference; more, in that three chapters have been added to broaden the content; less, in that the group discussion has been summarized. However, we believe that this volume conveys the spirit and vision that emerged during this conference and that promise to energize selection and classification research for years to come.

An endeavor such as this requires the labors of many organizations and individuals. We are grateful for the fiscal support that brought about the conference and this book. That support was provided by a Scientific Services Agreement between the U.S. Army Research Office, Battelle, and ARI. We owe a particular debt of gratitude to Ms. Marty Carson and Ms. Pam O'Quinn for typesetting and illustrations and Ms. Lola M. Zook for her service as the coordinating editor. We wish particularly to thank and acknowledge the participants in the conference who made its success a reality. Finally, we wish to thank our respective organizations, ARI and HumRRO, for their continuing encouragement and unstinting support throughout the period of the conference and the preparation of this volume.

Michael G. Rumsey
Clinton B. Walker
James H. Harris

REFERENCES

Campbell, J. P., & Zook, L. M. (Eds.).(1990). *Building and retaining the Career Force: New procedures for accessing and assigning Army enlisted personnel - Annual Report, 1990 fiscal year* (Tech. Rep. No. 952). Alexandria, VA: U.S. Army Research Institute for the Behavioral and Social Sciences.

Project A: The U.S. Army Selection and Classification Project [Special issue] (1990). *Personnel Psychology, 43*.

Wigdor, A. K., & Green, B. F. (Eds.).(1991). *Performance assessment for the workplace* (Vols. 1–2). Washington, DC: National Academy Press.

Part I

Conceptualizing and Measuring

Performance

CHAPTER

1

JOB ANALYSIS FOR THE FUTURE

Michael A. Campion
Purdue University

This chapter is based on two premises. First, our science has knowledge about how jobs are designed that is relevant to developing selection and classification systems, but is not currently measured in most job analysis studies. Future research should explore the value of including job design measures in job analysis studies.

Second, most current job analysis studies do not specifically consider requirements for teamwork, and thus do not provide a basis for reflecting those requirements in subsequent selection and classification systems. Future research should explore the value of examining teamwork more explicitly in job analysis studies.

This chapter draws on recent research on job and teamwork design conducted by the author and his colleagues in order to derive propositions for changes in future job analysis studies conducted to develop selection and classification systems.

ANALYZING JOB DESIGN

The theoretical background for the author's research on job design comes from a variety of different academic disciplines. This interdisciplinary perspective is briefly described first. Then propositions for job analysis research are derived and discussed. Finally, measurement is addressed, including instrumentation and sources of information used in past studies.

Interdisciplinary Framework

The author's research has attempted to consider a variety of models of job design. Each of these models is derived from a different academic discipline, and each has a different set of intended outcomes. Four models are fairly inclusive of the major schools of thought, even though they may not be exhaustive. The four models and their outcomes are briefly described here, summarized in Table 1.1, and documented in previous articles (Campion, 1985, 1988, 1989; Campion & Berger, 1990; Campion, Kosiak, & Langford, 1988; Campion & McClelland, 1991, 1993; Campion & Medsker, 1992; Campion & Stevens, 1991; Campion & Thayer, 1985, 1987, 1989; Campion & Wong, 1991; Wong & Campion, 1991).

First, a mechanistic model comes from classic industrial engineering. It provides recommendations based on scientific management, time and motion study, and work simplification (Barnes, 1980; Gilbreth, 1911; Neibel, 1992; Taylor, 1911). It is oriented toward human resource efficiency and flexibility outcomes such as staffing ease, low training requirements, reduced mental skills, and low compensation requirements.

Second, a motivational model comes from organizational psychology. It provides recommendations based on job enrichment and enlargement (Herzberg, 1966), characteristics of motivating jobs (Hackman & Lawler, 1971; Hackman & Oldham, 1980), theories of work motivation (Mitchell, 1976; Steers & Mowday, 1977), and psychological principles from sociotechnical approaches (Cherns, 1976; Englestad, 1979; Rousseau, 1977). It represents an encompassing collection of recommendations intended to enhance the motivational nature of jobs, and it has been associated with affective outcomes such as satisfaction, intrinsic motivation, and involvement, as well as behavioral outcomes such as performance, customer service, and low turnover.

Third, a perceptual-motor model comes from experimental psychology. It provides recommendations based on human factors engineering (McCormick, 1976; Van Cott & Kinkade, 1972), skilled performance (Welford, 1976), and human information processing (Fogel, 1967; Gagne, 1962). It is oriented toward reducing demands on human mental capabilities and limitations, primarily with regard to lowering attention and concentration requirements of jobs. It has been shown to be related to reliability outcomes (e.g., reduced errors and accidents) and positive user reactions (e.g., reduced mental overload, fatigue, and stress, and favorable attitudes toward the workstation and equipment).

Fourth, a biological model comes from work physiology (Astrand & Rodahl, 1977), biomechanics (Tichauer, 1978), and ergonomics (Grandjean, 1980). This model attempts to minimize physical stress and strain on the worker, and it has been associated with less physical effort and fatigue, more comfort, and fewer aches, pains, and health complaints.

Although there are some similarities in the recommendations made for proper job design by the different disciplines, there are also considerable differences and even some direct conflicts. Such differences mean that each model has costs as well as benefits. The costs are the lost benefits of the other models. The most central conflict is between the mechanistic and perceptual-motor models on the one hand, which both generally recommend design features that minimize mental demands, and the motivational model on the other hand, which gives the opposite

TABLE 1.1
Interdisciplinary Models of Job Design

Model/Discipline Base (example references)	Illustrative Recommendations	Illustrative Benefits	Illustrative Costs
MECHANISTIC/ Classic industrial engineering (Barnes, 1980; Gilbreth, 1911; Taylor, 1911)	i-specialization i-simplification i-repetition i-automation d-spare time	d-training d-staffing difficulty d-making errors d-mental overload and fatigue d-mental skills and abilities d-compensation	d-satisfaction d-motivation i-absenteeism i-boredom
MOTIVATIONAL/ Organizational psychology (Hackman & Lawler, 1971; Hackman & Oldham, 1980; Herzberg, 1966)	i-variety i-autonomy i-significance i-skill usage i-participation i-feedback i-recognition i-growth i-achievement	i-satisfaction i-motivation i-involvement i-performance d-absenteeism d-turnover i-customer service i-catching errors	i-training i-staffing difficulty i-making errors i-mental overload and fatigue i-stress i-mental skills and abilities i-compensation
PERCEPTUAL-MOTOR/ Experimental psychology, human factors (Fogel, 1967; McCormick, 1976; Welford, 1976)	i-lighting quality i-display and control quality d-information processing requirements i-user friendly equipment	d-making errors d-accidents d-mental overload and fatigue d-stress d-training d-staffing difficulty d-compensation d-mental skills and abilities i-positive attitudes toward equipment	i-boredom d-satisfaction

(Continued)

TABLE 1.1
(Continued)

Model/Discipline Base (example references)	Illustrative Recommendations	Illustrative Benefits	Illustrative Costs
BIOLOGICAL/ Physiology, biomechanics, ergonomics (Astrand & Rodahl, 1977; Grandjean, 1980; Tichauer, 1978)	d-strength requirements d-endurance requirements i-seating comfort i-postural comfort d-environmental stressors	d-physical abilities d-physical fatigue d-aches & pains d-medical incidents	i-financial costs i-inactivity

Note. Benefits and costs based on findings in previous interdisciplinary research (Campion, 1988, 1989; Campion & Berger, 1990; Campion & McClelland, 1991, 1993; Campion & Thayer, 1985). Table adapted from Campion and Medsker (1992).
Key: i = increased, d = decreased.

advice by recommending design features that enhance mental demands. Therefore, the motivational model may create costs in terms of staffing difficulty, increased training requirements, greater likelihood of errors, more overload, more stress, and increased compensation requirements. The mechanistic and perceptual-motor models may create costs in terms of less satisfaction and motivation, greater boredom, and higher turnover. The biological model is fairly independent because it reflects physical demands, but it may also have costs in terms of financial requirements for changing equipment and environments, as well as the potential for inadequate physical activity.

Propositions for Job Analysis

Proposition 1. Including measures of job design in future job analysis studies may help identify potential costs (negative outcomes) from the job that could subsequently be used as criteria for the selection system. For example, jobs poorly designed on the perceptual-motor model would be expected to have potential costs in terms of errors, mental overload, accidents, and stress. Minimizing these outcomes could then become the focus of future selection systems. Not only could they become the criteria for empirical validation studies, but they might suggest the abilities or attributes on which to focus the predictors (e.g., information-handling capacity, quality orientation, safety awareness, stress tolerance).

Likewise, for jobs high on the mechanistic or perceptual-motor models, there could be costs in terms of reduced satisfaction and motivation and increased boredom. When jobs are designed in such a manner that these costs are likely, the selection systems could be oriented to help counteract them. Affective outcomes like satisfaction are usually ignored as validation criteria, despite their relationships with a host of important behavioral outcomes (e.g., turnover, unionism). Again, in this way selection systems can compensate for poorly designed jobs. Jobs well designed on the motivational model, which is the only model taught in most business and management schools (see typical human resources textbooks such as Heneman, Schwab, Fossum, & Dyer, 1989; or Milkovich & Boudreau, 1991), are likely to have higher mental ability requirements, greater training needs, and some of the same costs associated with the poor perceptual-motor design already described (e.g., errors and overload). This may suggest that a selection system based on cognitive abilities is needed, and it may also suggest modifications to existing systems such as raising cutting scores and using training criteria for validation. Finally, jobs poorly designed on the biological model may have costs in terms of physical demands and requirements. Physically demanding jobs have special implications for selection system development and validation that are not well understood by most behavioral scientists (Campion, 1983).

Proposition 2. Individual differences identified in job design research may be worth exploring as experimental predictors and should, thus, be considered in future job analysis studies. Research within the motivational model of job design has identified higher-order needs as potential moderators of employee reactions to enriched jobs (Hackman & Lawler, 1971). Those with more higher-order needs respond more positively to enriched work. Research within the interdisciplinary perspective on job design has expanded this notion into preferences or tolerances for all four job design models. Thus, employees may differ with respect to their preferences or tolerances for motivational work (e.g., challenging, mentally demanding, working without supervision), mechanistic work (e.g., routine, repetitive), perceptual-motor work (e.g., fast-paced, complicated, stressful), and biological work (e.g., physically demanding, environmental stressors). There is evidence that these individual differences moderate reactions to the various models of job design to some degree (Campion, 1988; Campion & McClelland, 1991, 1993).

These individual differences have not been examined in previous selection research to the author's knowledge, but may offer a fruitful avenue to explore. They are personality oriented and, thus, might be difficult to use in a selection context due to susceptibility to faking. However, a variety of approaches could be explored to overcome this potential problem (e.g., disguise question purpose, control for social desirability, use biodata measures).

Proposition 3. Anticipated changes in jobs, as well as jobs not yet developed, can be analyzed in terms of job design, and such information can have implications for the development or modification of selection systems. As noted above and in Table 1.1, staffing ease or difficulty is an outcome of job design that has been identified in previous research. This outcome derives from the industrial engineering concept of "utilization level," defined as the proportion of employees who can perform the job. In traditional industrial engineering, the goal is to design jobs that can be performed by all potential employees who might be assigned to them.

In personnel selection vernacular, jobs with high utilization levels usually have low mental ability requirements; they can be easily staffed because of the wide range of competence that can be accommodated. Therefore, changes in jobs that increase staffing difficulty suggest a corresponding increase in the need for a selection system based on mental abilities or a need for a modification of the current system (e.g., raising the cutting score or expanding the applicant pool). Job design measures are especially useful for forecasting these changes in selection systems because they require less information to use than do the traditional job analysis systems, which require specific information on tasks and skills. These measurement issues will be addressed later in the chapter.

Proposition 4. Interdependence among tasks on the same job has been shown to predict ability requirements in job design research and, thus, should potentially be examined in future job analysis studies. Task interdependence is the degree to which the inputs, processes, or outputs of some tasks in a given job depend on the inputs, processes, or outputs of other tasks in the job. Research has shown that interdependence among tasks is related to the motivational value of a job and to the job's ability requirements (Wong & Campion, 1991). Interdependence among tasks has a unique effect on ability requirements beyond the effects of job design. The importance of task-level analysis in order to understand ability requirements has long been reported in job analysis research, but this study would suggest that interdependencies among the tasks are also important to consider in order to more fully understand ability requirements, and should be included in future job analysis studies.

Proposition 5. Changing the job should be considered as an alternative to changing the selection and placement systems. The implicit assumption that jobs are fixed and technologically determined and, thus, human resource systems must be adapted to them, is incorrect. Jobs are inventions (Davis & Taylor, 1979). Typically, they reflect the values of the era in which they were constructed (e.g., mechanistic design earlier in the century, motivational design after that, and team design most recently). Jobs are not immutable givens but are subject to change and modification. Thus, they can be changed to increase the need for selection systems (e.g., typically by applying the motivational model), or jobs can be designed to decrease the need for selection systems (e.g., typically by applying the mechanistic and perceptual-motor models). If it is too difficult to find an adequate number of employees with the needed abilities, perhaps changing the jobs to reduce their ability requirements should be considered.

Measurement of Job Design

Several instruments have been developed to measure the four interdisciplinary models of job design. The original study (Campion & Thayer, 1985) used an analysis instrument that was completed based on observation (contained in Campion, 1985). It was very detailed in terms of including explanations of each of the job design recommendations, but it was somewhat oriented toward blue-collar jobs. Subsequent research developed a self-report version (contained in Campion, 1988; Campion & Medsker, 1992) because many jobs and situations preclude the use of observational measures. The self-report version can also be used on the entire range of blue- and white-collar jobs.

More recent research has further modified the self-report instrument to make it easier to complete (e.g., changed items to first person, adopted singular format similar to the survey format familiar to employees, simplified several questions). That instrument is described in Campion and McClelland (1991, 1993) and is available from the author. The self-report version of the instrument has been used with analysts and supervisors, as well as incumbents.

All three versions of the instrument have demonstrated adequate psychometric qualities, including internal consistency; interrater reliability and agreement among and between incumbents, managers, and analysts; and convergent and discriminant validity with other popular measures of job design (Campion, Kosiak, & Langford, 1988). All three versions have also demonstrated substantial relationships with the wide range of costs and benefits described above, both in cross-sectional research (that avoids common methods variance, such as Campion, 1988; Campion & Thayer, 1985) and quasi-experimental research (Campion & McClelland, 1991, 1993).

Two other instruments have been developed that might have value in future job analysis studies. First, a measure of the preferences for and tolerances of different types of work is contained in Campion and Medsker (1992), and evidence of the moderating effect of these individual differences is contained in Campion (1988) and Campion and McClelland (1991, 1993). Second, a measure of interdependencies among tasks is contained along with evidence of its validity in Wong and Campion (1991).

In summary, measures of job design are easy to use and would logically fit in a job analysis questionnaire. They provide information on the nature of the jobs that is different from that obtained by traditional job analysis measures. They can identify likely costs and benefits of jobs without having to measure the outcomes directly. This is especially useful for developing selection systems for jobs that do not yet exist.

Also, job design measures may be somewhat easier to complete than normal job analysis questionnaires when the jobs do not yet exist or when potential changes in jobs are being evaluated. This is because they do not require knowledge of specific details about tasks and skills, but instead require only an assessment of the nature of the future job in terms of more general dimensions (e.g., amount of autonomy, repetition, information processing, physical stressors). Furthermore, job incumbents do not have to provide judgments if they are not available, because the instruments can be completed by a range of other subject matter experts (e.g., analysts and managers).

ANALYZING TEAMWORK REQUIREMENTS

Organizing employees into work teams is an extremely popular management strategy in organizations today, including the military (e.g., Salas, Dickinson, Converse, & Tannenbaum, 1992). Such work designs may have implications for selection and classification systems. Two recent studies conducted by the author and his colleagues suggest that future job analysis studies should examine teamwork requirements.

Staffing Teams

Campion and Medsker (1993) reviewed a wide range of areas of literature in order to delineate dimensions for designing effective work teams, including social psychology (McGrath, 1984; Steiner, 1972), sociotechnical theory (Cummings, 1978; Pasmore, Francis, & Haldeman, 1982), industrial engineering (Davis & Wacker, 1987; Majchrzak, 1988), and organizational psychology (Gladstein, 1984; Hackman, 1987; Shea & Guzzo, 1987; Sundstrom, De Meuse, & Futrell, 1990). They derived 19 dimensions, and then validated them in a field setting against three effectiveness criteria: productivity, employee satisfaction, and management judgments of effectiveness.

Three of the 19 dimensions are relevant to staffing work teams. First, there should be membership heterogeneity. According to the team literature, members should have a variety of different skills and experiences, so that the team can take on a range of tasks and so that the members can learn from each other. Second, the team size should be appropriate. Teams should be staffed to the smallest number of members needed to do the work. Teams should be large enough to accomplish the work assigned to them, but teams that are too large require excessive coordination, and employees may feel less involved in very large teams. Third, teams should be staffed with employees who prefer to work in teams. As noted previously, employees' preferences for types of work can influence their reactions to their jobs. Some employees prefer to work in teams, others prefer to work alone, and this should be considered when staffing.

The research on work teams is not as clear as these recommendations may sound, however. For example, membership should not be excessively heterogeneous, because conflict and communication breakdowns can result. Most of the research on team size has been conducted in laboratory settings, so the generalizability of the findings to field settings is unknown. Also, very little research has been done on the issue of work preferences for team settings. Therefore, research on the correctness of these work team staffing recommendations is needed, and the following proposition is presented: *Proposition 6*—Future job analysis studies might consider the degree of team-oriented work required so that team staffing recommendations can be examined.

Knowledge, Skills, and Abilities (KSAs) Required for Teamwork

Research in progress is attempting to identify the KSAs required for teamwork (Stevens, 1992). The focus of this research is on those KSAs that are unique to the team-oriented situation itself, rather than technical or other KSAs that would be needed by those performing the job even if they were not in a team. The focus is also on KSAs, rather than personality or dispositions required to work in a team. Finally, the focus is on formal, task-performing teams, especially those of a semi-autonomous nature. Based on an extensive review of the work team literature, two core dimensions of teamwork KSAs were identified, each consisting of several categories as listed in Table 1.2.

Table 1.2
Knowledge, Skill, and Ability Requirements for Teamwork

I. Directing and controlling skills	II. Interpersonal skills
A. Planning and goal setting skills	A. Conflict resolution skills
B. Task coordination skills	B. Collaborative problem-solving skills
C. Self-monitoring skills	C. Communication skills
D. Participation skills	

Note: See Stevens (1992) for listings of specific skills and detailed explanations.

Subsequent research will validate these KSAs in terms of their relationships with teamwork effectiveness, but the following proposition still seems warranted: *Proposition 7*—Future job analysis studies might attempt to assess the KSAs required for teamwork. The list of dimensions in Table 1.2 might be a place to start such an assessment.

SUMMARY AND CONCLUSIONS

The chapter started with the premise that future job analysis studies could be improved by considering recent findings from research on job and work team design. Based on research conducted by the author and his colleagues, seven propositions were forwarded for future job analysis research.

REFERENCES

Astrand, P. O., & Rodahl, K. (1977). *Textbook of work physiology: Physiological bases of exercise* (2nd ed.). New York: McGraw-Hill.

Barnes, R. M. (1980). *Motion and time study: Design and measurement of work* (7th ed.). New York: Wiley.

Campion, M. A. (1983). Personnel selection for physically demanding jobs: Review and recommendations. *Personnel Psychology, 36*, 527-550.

Campion, M. A. (1985). The multimethod job design questionnaire (MJDQ). *Psychological Documents, 15*(1) (Ms. No. 2695).

Campion, M. A. (1988). Interdisciplinary approaches to job design: A constructive replication with extensions. *Journal of Applied Psychology, 73*, 467-481.

Campion, M. A. (1989). Ability requirement implications of job design: An interdisciplinary perspective. *Personnel Psychology, 42*, 1-24.

Campion, M. A., & Berger, C. J. (1990). Conceptual integration and empirical test of job design and compensation relationships. *Personnel Psychology, 43*, 525-553.

Campion, M. A., Kosiak, P. L., & Langford, B. A. (1988, August). *Convergent and discriminant validity of the multimethod job design questionnaire.* Paper presented at the meeting of the American Psychological Association, Anaheim, CA.

Campion, M. A., & McClelland, C. L. (1991). Interdisciplinary examination of the costs and benefits of enlarged jobs: A job design quasi-experiment. *Journal of Applied Psychology, 76*, 186-198.

Campion, M. A., & McClelland, C. L. (1993). Follow-up and extension of the interdisciplinary costs and benefits of enlarged jobs. *Journal of Applied Psychology, 76*, 339-351.

Campion, M. A., & Medsker, G. J. (1992). Job design. In G. V. Salvendy (Ed.), *Handbook of industrial engineering* (pp. 845-881). New York: Wiley.

Campion, M. A., & Medsker, G. J. (1993). Relations between work group characteristics and effectiveness: Implications for designing effective work groups. *Personnel Psychology, 46*, 823-850.

Campion, M. A., & Stevens, M. J. (1991). Neglected questions in job design: How people design jobs, influence of training, and task-job predictability. *Journal of Business and Psychology, 6*, 169-191.

Campion, M. A., & Thayer, P. W. (1985). Development and field evaluation of an interdisciplinary measure of job design. *Journal of Applied Psychology, 70*, 29-34.

Campion, M. A., & Thayer, P. W. (1987). Job design: Approaches, outcomes, and trade-offs. *Organizational Dynamics, 15*(3), 66-79.

Campion, M. A., & Thayer, P. W. (1989). How do you design a job? *Personnel Journal, 68*(1), 43-44, 46.

Campion, M. A., & Wong, C. S. (1991). Improving efficiency and satisfaction through job design: An interdisciplinary perspective. In J. W. Jones, B. D. Steffy, & D. W. Bray (Eds.), *Applied psychology in business: The manager's handbook.* Lexington, MA: Lexington Books.

Cherns, A. (1976). The principles of socio-technical design. *Human Relations, 29,* 783-792.

Cummings, T. G. (1978). Self-regulating work groups: A socio-technical synthesis. *Academy of Management Review, 3,* 625-634.

Davis, L. E., & Taylor, J. C. (Eds.). (1979). *Design of jobs* (2nd ed.). Santa Monica, CA: Goodyear.

Davis, L. E., & Wacker, G. L. (1987). Job design. In G. Salvendy (Ed.), *Handbook of human factors* (pp. 431-452). New York: Wiley.

Englestad, P. H. (1979). Socio-technical approach to problems of process control. In L. E. Davis & J. C. Taylor (Eds.), *Design of jobs* (2nd ed., pp. 184-205). Santa Monica, CA: Goodyear.

Fogel, L. J. (1967). *Human information processing.* Englewood Cliffs, NJ: Prentice-Hall.

Gagne, R. M. (1962). Human functions in systems. In R. M. Gagne (Ed.), *Psychological principles in system development* (pp. 35-73). New York: Holt, Rinehart & Winston.

Gilbreth, F. B. (1911). *Motion study: A method for increasing the efficiency of the workman.* New York: Van Nostrand.

Gladstein, D. L. (1984). Groups in context: A model of task group effectiveness. *Administrative Science Quarterly, 29,* 499-517.

Grandjean, E. (1980). *Fitting the task to the man: An ergonomic approach.* London: Taylor & Francis.

Hackman, J. R. (1987). The design of work teams. In J. W. Lorsch (Ed.), *Handbook of organizational behavior* (pp. 315-342). Englewood Cliffs, NJ: Prentice-Hall.

Hackman, J. R., & Lawler, E. E. (1971). Employee reactions to job characteristics [Monograph]. *Journal of Applied Psychology, 55,* 259-286.

Hackman, J. R., & Oldham, G. R. (1980). *Work redesign.* Reading, MA: Addison-Wesley.

Heneman, H. G., Schwab, D. P., Fossum, J. A., & Dyer, L. D. (1989). *Personnel/human resource management* (4th ed.). Homewood, IL: Irwin.

Herzberg, F. (1966). *Work and the nature of man.* Cleveland: World.

Majchrzak, A. (1988). *The human side of factory automation.* San Francisco: Jossey-Bass.

McCormick, E. J. (1976). *Human factors in engineering and design* (4th ed.). New York: McGraw-Hill.

McGrath, J. E. (1984). *Groups: Interaction and performance.* Englewood Cliffs, NJ: Prentice-Hall.

Milkovich, G. T., & Boudreau, J. W. (1991). *Human resource management* (6th ed.). Homewood, IL: Irwin.

Mitchell, T. R. (1976). Applied principles in motivation theory. In P. Warr (Ed.), *Personal goals in work design* (pp. 163-171). New York: Wiley.

Neibel, B. W. (1992). Time study. In G. Salvendy (Ed.), *Handbook of industrial engineering* (2nd ed., pp. 1599-1638). New York: Wiley.

Pasmore, W., Francis, C., & Haldeman, J. (1982). Socio-technical systems: A North American reflection on empirical studies of the seventies. *Human Relations, 35,* 1179-1204.

Rousseau, D. M. (1977). Technological differences in job characteristics, employee satisfaction, and motivation: A synthesis of job design research and socio-technical systems theory. *Organizational Behavior and Human Performance, 19,* 18-42.

Salas, E., Dickinson, T. L., Converse, S. A., & Tannenbaum, S. I. (1992). Toward an understanding of team performance and training. In R. W. Swezey & E. Salas (Eds.), *Teams: Their training and performance.* Norwood, NJ: Ablex.

Shea, G. P., & Guzzo, R. A. (1987). Groups as human resources. In K. M. Rowland & G. R. Ferris (Eds.), *Research in human resources and personnel management* (Vol. 5, pp. 323-356). Greenwich, CT: JAI Press.

Steers, R. M., & Mowday, R. T. (1977). The motivational properties of tasks. *Academy of Management Review, 2,* 645-658.

Steiner, I. D. (1972). *Group process and productivity*. New York: Academic Press.

Stevens, M. J. (1992). *Individual level knowledge, skill, and ability requirements for group-based work design systems*. Doctoral dissertation in progress, Purdue University, West Lafayette, IN.

Sundstrom, E., De Meuse, K. P., & Futrell, D. (1990). Work teams: Applications and effectiveness. *American Psychologist, 45*, 120-133.

Taylor, F. W. (1911). *The principles of scientific management*. New York: Norton.

Tichauer, E. R. (1978). *The biomechanical basis of ergonomics: Anatomy applied to the design of work situations*. New York: Wiley.

Van Cott, H. P., & Kinkade, R. G. (Eds.). (1972). *Human engineering guide to equipment design* (rev. ed.). Washington, DC: U.S. Government Printing Office.

Welford, A. T. (1976). *Skilled performance: Perceptual and motor skills*. Glenview, IL: Scott Foresman.

Wong, C. S., & Campion, M. A. (1991). Development and test of a task level model of motivational job design. *Journal of Applied Psychology, 76*, 825-837.

CHAPTER

2

JOBS AND ROLES: ACCEPTING AND COPING WITH THE CHANGING STRUCTURE OF ORGANIZATIONS

Daniel R. Ilgen
Michigan State University

This chapter was prepared for a conference on selection and classification. Yet the conference began not with a discussion of selection and classification models and practices but with a discussion of the nature of jobs and their measurement. Does it seem strange or, perhaps, somewhat misguided, that we led off such a conference with a discussion of jobs when selection and classification were our primary concerns? Obviously not—none of the participants questioned this order because we all share the same underlying view of selection and classification.

It is accepted that the logical starting point for a discussion of selection and classification is an understanding of the domain of jobs with known characteristics. From knowledge of the jobs and job structure, we develop criteria for successful job performance on the one hand, and we identify our individual difference characteristics on the other. Then we attempt to match people to the jobs in ways that will optimize or at least satisfy some criteria of organizational effectiveness.

Nothing I have said is new to any of you. Yet, I want to add that, in my opinion, fundamental changes are taking place in today's organizations that are shaking the jobs and job structure foundation on which selection and classification models rest. I believe these changes have major implications for how we think about selection and classification. I raise some of these issues in this chapter. Unfortunately, I have more questions than answers. However, I hope that in raising the questions, I can stimulate some thought both about the issues themselves, and, if you agree with them, about reactions to them.

Once I have addressed some of the contemporary issues affecting selection and classification, I turn to my primary task—that of discussing the nature of what we typically call *jobs*. I will describe a construal of jobs that John Hollenbeck and I presented in the second volume of the most recent edition of the *Handbook of Industrial and Organizational Psychology* (Dunnette & Hough, 1991).

We called it job-role differentiation (JRD). But, before I describe JRD, I want to step back and look at a critical assumption of our selection and classification models in general and what I believe are some major trends in the nature of work in our society today that are impacting on that assumption.

SELECTION AND CLASSIFICATION

Basic Assumption

A necessary condition for personnel selection and classification is some degree of stability. For selection, stability is needed both in the individual difference characteristics of the applicants (predictors) and in the behavioral requirements or dimensions of the jobs. For classification, the network or structure of jobs must have some level of stability, for it represents the category system into which individuals are sorted/classified. Our classification models assume that the jobs in the total set of jobs into which people are to be assigned can be described on some dimensions, and that the job demands remain as described over the time period for which the classification system operates. The length of this time period varies as a function of many organizational factors, but it is safe to say that its length is typically measured in years. From a practical utility standpoint, the costs of developing and validating selection and classification systems in large organizations demand that the systems remain in place for a few years in order to be cost effective.

The underlying model, whether dealing with a subset of the applicant pool (in the case of selection) or all members of the pool (for classification), is a predictive model. In all cases, there is a set of predictors mapped onto applicants and a set of criteria, typically job performance. Jobs in these models are the environments in which the models are applied. In the case of selection, the jobs are constants, controlled by holding them constant at one. For classification, jobs are variables; they are incorporated into the model, but, once entered, each job is assumed to remain constant over the time period for which the predictive system is in place. Thus, in both cases, it is assumed that the jobs remain constant in order for the predictive models to be used and/or evaluated.

Changing Jobs and Job Systems

In the last 10 years, a number of changes across a large variety of organizations have reduced the stability of jobs and job systems. At one level these changes have shortened the time period over which jobs have remained constant. At a more fundamental level, the changes have reduced the extent to which work is organized around stable job systems. Six factors are briefly mentioned next as having contributed to instability in jobs and job systems.

Mergers, Acquisitions, and Downsizing. During the 1980s, there was a great deal of buying, selling, and combining of previously free-standing organizations into conglomerates. Frequently the acquiring and merging of organizations led to the creation of a single organization or modifications of all of the initial organizations. In either case, there were often major changes in the structure and nature of jobs in all the organizations involved in the mergers. Jobs were dropped, redefined, and altered. The mergers and acquisitions often resulted in a smaller set of jobs than there was when the two or more organizations existed separately.

In addition, economic pressures, automation, and other changes frequently created conditions that led to the downsizing of corporations, and, with the downsizing, major structural changes in the nature of jobs in the corporation (Kozlowski, Chao, Smith, & Hedlund, 1993; Tomasko, 1990). Greenberg (1988), in a survey for the American Management Association, reported that 66% of the firms with over 5,000 employees reduced their work force in the 1980s. Often the reduction in the work force required redefinitions of jobs, and frequently the redefinitions expanded the numbers of duties and responsibilities associated with particular jobs (Kozlowski et al., 1993).

Regardless of the nature of the changes in positions, selection and classification systems needed to be adjusted to the new structures. The need for major adjustments was exacerbated by the fact that some organizations were bought and sold several times during the decade and faced the need to modify these systems on several occasions.

Decline/Shift in Union Activity. Two trends in union activity arose in the 1980s and are apparent at present. The first is a general decline in the power of unions. This is evidenced by the drop in numbers of workers represented by unions and by the very visible failures of some unions when confronting management. This trend began with the air traffic controllers' strike that was broken by President Reagan, who refused to hire back striking union members when a settlement was reached. More recently, the ending of the strike against Caterpillar Company in the spring of 1992 with the union members going back to work without a contract is further evidence for the general trend.

A second trend related to unions is stylistic. There has been movement away from competition with management to a mode of cooperation. Cooperation is in the form of joint union-management activities where union members and management worked together to attempt to deal with problems facing the effectiveness and competitiveness of the organization as a whole, which was seen as important for both groups.

Both trends have similar effects on the structure of jobs. In a competitive labor-management environment where unions are strong, the tendency is to create and maintain relatively rigid job structures. In such structures, the duties and responsibilities of job holders are clearly specified and job incumbents are expected to adhere strictly to the duties and responsibilities outlined in their job descriptions. In general, such structures allow for the creation of jobs with titles that can be explicitly addressed in collective bargaining agreements between unions and organizations. They also guide disagreements as to duties and responsibilities, such as may be the case when a grievance is addressed. Once jobs are addressed explicitly in contracts, it is likely that this exerts some force on an organization to maintain the jobs in the structure during business downturns.

With decreasing power of the unions and a more cooperative stance toward management, the pressure to maintain rigid job structures for union employees has been reduced. One effect of this reduced pressure for clearly specified job systems is greater flexibility in job descriptions and in job systems as a whole.

Integrated Manufacturing. Largely in response to the need for manufacturing firms to remain competitive in a global economy, major changes have occurred in manufacturing processes. These changes have been described under such headings as integrated manufacturing, just-in-time inventory control, advanced manufacturing technology, and total quality management, to name several.

Dean and Snell (1991) made a compelling argument for the fact that these processes have substantial impacts on human resource management issues and vice versa. In particular, they argued that these manufacturing processes, most of which focus on technological issues, cannot function if the people who carry them out operate in highly structured job systems. Integration across space, time, and informational systems is required in all of these modern systems, in order to create cross-functional problem solving and collaboration. Rigid demarcations among duties, responsibilities, and knowledge bases of people in the systems, particularly at the boundaries between positions or jobs, interfere with the effectiveness of integrated manufacturing systems (Dean & Snell, 1991). Thus, jobs in these systems tend to become less differentiated. Over time, job incumbents are often required to perform behaviors that overlap with those that previously may have been defined as part of another job.

Teams and Teamwork. Over the last 10 years, interest in organizing work around teams rather than around individuals has accelerated exponentially. This trend has been documented in scholarly reviews (Bettenhausen, 1991; Levine & Moreland, 1990), edited books directed toward teams and teamwork (Goodman, 1986; Hackman, 1990), and the popular press, such as the cover stories of *Time, Business Week*, and *Fortune*, all in 1990 (see "The Right Stuff," "Here Comes GM's Saturn," and "Who Needs a Boss?").

One of the key features of organizing work around teams is that task responsibilities are mapped onto teams (work groups) rather than onto individual persons who comprise the teams. Within the team there are tasks to be done, and the tasks are often performed by individuals. However, these tasks are not allocated to specific individuals in a formal sense. Team members are expected, over time, to learn multiple tasks assigned to the team and to be able to fill in for others on various tasks. As a result, the link of people to specific jobs is broken to a greater degree when work is organized by teams rather than by individuals.

Americans With Disabilities Act. The Americans With Disabilities Act (ADA) of 1990 specifies that persons with disabilities must be considered for jobs that they may be able to perform well if some modifications are made in either the selection requirements, the job, or both. In the case of selection requirements, the ADA addresses those cases for which an applicant's disability may lower his or her performance on the methods used for screening applicants but not on the job itself. With respect to the job, it is concerned with features of a job that may not be central to the successful performance of critical job tasks but may affect noncritical ones and exclude a disabled person from being appointed to the job. If it is economically feasible to change the job so that the disabled person can perform the job successfully, such changes must be made on a case-by-case basis. As of this writing, it is too early to tell the effects of this law on human resource management practices, but it is reasonable to anticipate that these effects will be major.

At one level, the Americans With Disability Act will affect the specific practices related to the way that people with designated disabilities are treated with respect to selection and classification. I would suggest, however, that there is the potential for a more fundamental shift due to this law. I believe that it will force a system-level perspective on the selection or classification problem. When an employer is confronted with a person with a designated disability, no longer will the approach be to assess the needs of the individual and fit that individual into a job with known characteristics. Rather, the task will begin at a higher level of abstraction. Consideration must be given to the need to address the purpose or function of the person-job couplet and ask whether the tasks previously assigned to persons, technology, or whatever can be redistributed within the person's constraints and the technology's capabilities to accomplish the goals of the couplet.

In essence, the Act is an invitation for individualizing jobs, at least for a subset of the applicant pool—those with disabilities. The result is that, by law, strict adherence to a rigid job structure with clearly defined duties, responsibilities, tasks, and procedures for accomplishing those tasks is being brought into question. What the long-term effect will be is not clear at this time, but it is reasonable to conclude that the effect on the job system will be in the destabilizing rather than the stabilizing direction.

Work Force 2000. Based on an analysis of demographic data, it is clear that a number of dramatic changes are taking place in the work force. By the year 2000, it is projected that the work force will be growing at a slower rate than it is at present, with a substantial decrease in the number of young workers entering the work force (Goldstein, 1990). In addition, this work force will be more diverse in terms of gender, age, and ethnicity (Fullerton, 1985). These changes are predicted to have many effects on human resource management practices (Cascio & Zammuto, 1987).

Selection and classification most certainly will not be immune. We can expect labor shortages and the prospect, across the spectrum of jobs, of creating a diverse work force that mirrors more closely the ethnic and gender mix of the population from which it (the work force) is selected. It is reasonable to expect that the luxury of low selection ratios and the total freedom to eliminate quickly those candidates from an applicant pool who fail to meet one or more of the standards set by the organization will be more restricted. Furthermore, as employment is viewed more from a societal than an organizational perspective, classification and placement along with other human resource practices, such as training, replace selection by definition. The alterations in the work force and workplace practices are in the direction of this type of change.

Conclusion. The purpose of introducing these conditions was to support my contention that we need to question our assumption that organizations provide us with stable jobs and job structures on which to build our selection and classification models. I do not mean to imply that all the conditions just mentioned are relevant to all organizations. To my knowledge, the Army is not bothered by threats of a leveraged buy-out. Nor do I want to imply that, all of a sudden, there is so much change and so much instability that jobs and job systems are disappearing rapidly, and, therefore, it is no longer reasonable to do selection and classification the way that it was done before. Clearly this is not the case.

At the same time, if our purpose is to ask where we need to go from here and what are some of the future issues we need to address, then I think it is imperative that we give some thought to what appear to many to be changes in the nature of work that are likely to have selection and classification implications. Lowered stability on job structures is one of those changes, in my opinion.

JOB-ROLE DIFFERENTIATION

If indeed jobs are less stable than they were in the past and our current models of selection and classification are based on the assumption of stable jobs, there are a number of ways to address the issue of instability. One of these is to reexamine the way that jobs are defined and consider modifying the definition to be more open to change. The potential effects of such changes would have to be explored in terms of their affects on selection and classification. This is the approach that I propose. In particular, I propose a view of jobs, which John Hollenbeck and I labeled as job-role differentiation, as one way that might allow us to deal with the flexible nature of jobs.

Job-role differentiation[1] (JRD) developed when we undertook the task of writing a chapter on jobs and roles for the second edition of the *Handbook of Industrial and Organizational Psychology* (Dunnette & Hough, 1991). Initially, we naively expected to describe the work on jobs, and the work on roles, and then compare and contrast the two of them. We soon discovered that although the literatures of the two domains were separate, the lack of conceptual clarity in both domains produced constructs that were confusing at best and hopelessly intertwined at worst.

Our solution was to force the two domains farther apart than those working in either domain would probably like and then to try to bring them back together. The result was what we labeled job-role differentiation. It is described next. The discussion begins by defining jobs and roles separately and continues by bringing the two back together. It is the combination of job and role that represents JRD.

Jobs. For purposes of JRD, a job was defined as "a set of task elements grouped together under one job title and designated to be performed by a single individual" (Ilgen & Hollenbeck, 1991, p. 173). In addition, we made four assumptions about jobs for purposes of differentiating them from roles.

The first assumption was that jobs were created by agents acting for the organization in order to accomplish tasks believed to be necessary for accomplishing of the organization's goals. Using Blau and Scott's (1962) notion of "primary beneficiaries," it was argued that persons acting as agents for the primary beneficiaries of the organization (agents such as managers, engineers, production supervisors) established jobs for the purpose of meeting the organization's goals.

Second, jobs were described as "objective" in the sense that a shared consensus exists among organizational members aware of the jobs and the elements that comprise them. No claim was made that a shared comparison implied that jobs were "real" in any positivistic sense. The shared consensus was often evident in larger organizations by the existence of formal job descriptions typically recorded

---

[1] Much of the material on jobs and roles was initially developed with John Hollenbeck in a chapter in the second volume of the *Handbook of Industrial and Organizational Psychology*, edited by Marvin D. Dunnette and Leatta Hough (see Ilgen & Hollenbeck, 1991). This section is primarily descriptive of the Ilgen and Hollenbeck ideas expressed in that chapter, in which the contributions of John Hollenbeck were substantial; the order of authorship in that chapter was not meant to imply differences in effort or ideas.

in some written form. The formal nature of job systems was labeled their bureaucratic characteristic.

Third, jobs were said to exist independent of the job incumbents. The descriptions of the job elements exist regardless of the persons who hold the jobs. That is not to say that any person can occupy any job. Job requirements usually identify a set of knowledges, skills, and abilities necessary for success-fully fulfilling the job responsibilities. But within the set of persons who meet the qualifications, it was assumed that the tasks making up the job were invariant. As people move in and out of jobs, it was assumed that the job itself remained constant until it was formally redefined by representatives of the organization.

Finally, it was assumed that jobs were quasi-static. The activities and responsibilities that make up a job do not change on a day-to-day basis. This does not mean that jobs are immutable. However, it was assumed that jobs maintained their central characteristics for a reasonable amount of time until some formal change in the job or job system.

Task elements of jobs possessing the above characteristics were labeled established task elements. Established task elements are highly similar, but not identical, to Pepinsky and Pepinsky's (1961) "official task," McGrath and Altman's (1966) "tasks qua tasks," Roby and Lanzetta's (1958) "objective tasks," and Hackman's (1969) "defined tasks." These elements were less similar to what is often labeled task elements in the job design or job analysis literatures.

Roles. Whereas jobs were arbitrarily defined by Ilgen and Hollenbeck (1991) as objective, bureaucratic, quasi-static, and created for prime beneficiaries, the authors clearly recognized that jobs exist in environments that are subjective, personal, and dynamic. In addition, these environments are often populated by diverse constituencies—so diverse that agents of prime beneficiaries do not and cannot represent the needs and interests of all organizational members who hold the jobs. Just as is the case for the prime beneficiaries, the members who hold the jobs also have a great deal at stake in the way that the jobs are defined and performed. The definition of jobs offered previously fails to capture many of the interests of the latter constituencies as well as the subjective, personal, and dynamic conditions that exist in the organizations in which jobs are imbedded. The definition of a job is incomplete.

To address the incompleteness, it was proposed that the set of established task elements defining a job be expanded to include emergent task elements. Emer-gent task elements are, by definition, subjective, personal, dynamic, and specified by a variety of social constituencies other than the prime beneficiary. They are similar to what others have called "private tasks" (Pepinsky & Pepinsky, 1961), "subjective tasks" (Roby & Lanzetta, 1958), and "redefined tasks" (Hackman, 1969). They are also socially defined. The total set of emergent task elements constitute what has typically been described as a role.

Job-Role Differentiation (JRD).
JRD separated work roles from jobs by
relegating established task elements to
jobs and emergent ones to roles, and then
combining the two into a single set. Fig.
2.1 illustrates the combined set. The
authors suggested that the boundaries of
a job could be relatively precisely defined
by limiting the job elements to those that
are formally established. Roles, on the
other hand, were believed to have less
precise boundaries that could not be
established independent of the job
incumbent. The role incumbent's role
includes task elements that are either self-
generated or thrust on him or her by other
people in the social network in which the

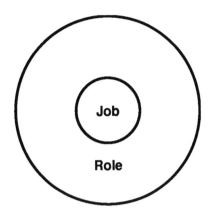

FIG. 2.1. An illustration of
job-role differentiation.

role is enacted. Given the complexities and changing nature of social networks,
the exact nature of the elements comprising the role set at any one time is less
precise than that of the elements comprising the job.

One feature of JRD as illustrated in Fig. 2.1 needs to be highlighted. Job
elements are nested within roles. This nesting occurs as the JRD is created for
and by incumbents. Ilgen and Hollenbeck (1991) adopted the role-making model
of Graen (Graen, 1976; Graen & Cashman, 1975; Graen & Scandura, 1987). This
is a developmental view. It assumes that job incumbents are assigned to jobs
that are described by the established job elements. These jobs exist in social and
technical systems in which the social relationships exist between the newly
arrived job incumbent, his or her supervisor, and relevant others in the social
setting.

From the time the new job incumbent is placed on the job, he or she begins
to establish the emergent job elements through interactions with others. This
process of establishing the role elements is an active and dynamic one in which,
according to Graen and Scandura (1987), the job incumbent builds his or her role
through a negotiation process with those in his or her role set. The process is
a very active one early in the job incumbent's time on the job and becomes less
active as the emergent elements become established.

The proportions of the total JRD allocated to jobs and allocated to roles in
Fig. 2.1 are not meant to represent any general distribution of jobs and roles
within JRD. In some cases, such as those where the job is very standardized
with little freedom to vary across persons, very little may be devoted to roles.
In others, there may be a great deal of individualization, thus loading the JRD
very heavily in the role area as compared to the job. An example of the latter
might be that of professor, where the position has some common "job" elements

but much of the total position behavior is shaped to the special skills of the faculty member.

An observation that can be made from Fig. 2.1 is that JRD may be seen as nothing more than what a job incumbent would typically describe as his or her job (i.e., JRD is just a new label for an old construct). At one level, Ilgen and Hollenbeck (1991) would agree. It is true the elements that they sorted into categories of established and emergent elements could be combined in other fashions, and have been in a number of job descriptive taxonomies. However, by explicitly recognizing the two sets, it can be argued that a number of problems with job descriptions and job analyses become more apparent.

For example, typical job-analytic techniques that rely on interviews of job incumbents or even experts face the problem of variance in descriptions across job incumbents for the same job. When the persons from whom the information is gathered do not agree, the problem becomes one of deciding how to treat the disagreement. Often it is treated as measurement error and the common core of elements about which the individuals agree is considered the job elements. Yet, from a JRD perspective, if it is accepted that jobs are made or created by a social interaction, then the disagreement is likely to contain, along with measurement error, valid differences in the role component of the jobs.

Under such conditions, depending on the use to which the job analysis is to be put, these differences should be treated differently and not necessarily relegated to error variance. In particular, the strategy of "trimming" the job description by limiting it to the common core of behaviors or dimensions that fit all persons assigned to the job classification and dropping off those that are not shared by all or most would be suspect from a JRD perspective. In the latter case, the nature of the uniqueness may be very important.

One final point about the job elements in the role set compared to the job set is that they differ primarily in origin rather than in nature. That is to say, identical behaviors may be part of the job set in one job and the role set in another. In the former case, those who define jobs for the organization specify that the elements are part of the job for all incumbents who hold it. In the latter, the elements are not specified by the formal description; they emerge as part of negotiations between the job incumbents and others in the worksite. One exception to the nature of the elements is that, because the role elements are socially constructed, socially referenced elements may be more likely to appear in the role set than the job set.

The focus in separating jobs from roles, up to this point, has been on the difference in the nature of the elements that comprise the two sets. There is, however, another major difference between jobs and roles. It is in the primary orientation of the approach to each. For jobs, the focus is on the elements that comprise the jobs (McCormick, 1979). Efforts are made to create taxonomic systems that are useful for the purposes to which they are to be put and to develop measurement systems for assessing jobs with respect to the taxonomic system. The utility of the job system is judged against the ability of the elements of the taxonomy to be useful in the human resource functions for which the system is to be used—selection, training, classification, job design and redesign, and so forth. By contrast, the role literature focuses on the process by which the elements are generated rather than the final structures that result from the process. Thus, for example, Graen and Scandura (1987) developed a model for the interaction process between a supervisor and a subordinate over the time period from the subordinate's joining the organization to the point at which that person's role becomes stable or relatively routine. Little or no attention is paid to the actual content of the role in the sense of the particular duties and responsibilities that emerge from the role development and mutual negotiation process that eventually leads to the definition of the role.

JRD and Flexible/Changing Jobs. Earlier in this chapter it was argued that, in today's organizations, jobs themselves are less stable over time and are often less firmly specified than they were in the past. From a JRD perspective, both of these conclusions can be interpreted as a change in the ratio of the role to the job elements in what is commonly called a job (and called the JRD by Ilgen and Hollenbeck, 1991). In terms of Fig. 2.1, this means that the area of the circle representing roles is expanding at the expense of that reserved for job elements.

However, even in times of rapid change, it is unlikely that the job core of most jobs disappears. Rather, the role portion simply occupies a greater proportion of the whole. Therefore, a JRD perspective implies that, in times of change, attention needs to shift toward a concern for role elements and an understanding of the implications of role processes as they relate to the use of job data in selection and classification.

IMPLICATIONS OF JRD FOR SELECTION AND CLASSIFICATION

Role Behaviors: Identification and Measurement

It is assumed that, for purposes of selection and classification, clustering job elements into those related to jobs and those related to roles as described by JRD does not alter the necessity to identify and measure elements that fall into each set. For our purposes here, I accept the current state of the art for measuring job elements. I believe that reports of the Army's Project A (Campbell, 1990) have demonstrated some excellent ways to address these measurement issues.

Measuring role elements, on the other hand, is likely to prove much more difficult for a number of reasons, stemming primarily from the fact that role elements are socially constructed. Because these elements emerge from a social process, they are likely to contain more social variables than job elements. Experience has shown that we are less capable of measuring performance on social variables than on individual task-focused ones. Leadership, sensitivity, initiative, responsiveness, and other socially referenced behaviors have been around a long time. Yet, developing clear definitions of these constructs and then developing good measures of them have been problematic. Even under the control offered by assessment center methods, we find that situations rather than individuals predict more variance in performance measures of these character-istics (Sackett & Dreher, 1982; Turnage & Muchinsky, 1982).

On the other hand, it was encouraging that two of the common dimensions that emerged in Project A, from the careful identification and description of a job population and the systematic selection of elements from it, were variables of the type we have been discussing (effort and leadership, and personal discipline) although one of them (personal discipline) was not very easily predicted from a set of common predictors (McHenry, Hough, Toquam, Hanson, & Ashworth, 1990). These social variables were, however, predictable from personality variables (McHenry et al., 1990). Careful work on criterion specification and the use of multiple measures, as was done in this case, is an important model to follow for further work.

This discussion assumes that role elements are not unlike job elements, so the problem of measuring them is one of applying the same general procedures to the somewhat different class of elements. There is, however, a more difficult problem with role elements that stems from a fundamental difference between them and job elements. This is due to the fact that role elements are, by defini-tion, socially determined on at least a somewhat idiosyncratic basis. They evolve out of the interaction of the job incumbent with others in his or her work setting. Thus, behavior in this domain is, at least in part, jointly determined. Yet, for selection and classification purposes, measures of the behavior are mapped back onto an individual, the job incumbent. Such a mapping process is bound to be less precise than is the case for job elements because of the inability to standard-ize the job experience with the same degree of precision for role elements as is possible for many of the elements that will fall in the job domain of JRD.

Finally, one subset of the role elements has been ignored in previous job analytic and criterion development work. These elements are behaviors that Graen (Graen, 1976; Graen & Cashman, 1975; Graen & Scandura, 1987) called role negotiation behaviors. Role negotiation behaviors are behaviors that involve the creation of the role elements that get defined into the job incumbent's job.

The position taken in the JRD approach is that these are very critical behaviors. They are the basis for much of the within-job variance regarding the nature of role elements. It is suggested that the size and nature of the set of these elements have a major impact on job performance for many types of jobs. In fact, the number of elements is often an indicator of the role incumbent's performance. Two individuals both holding jobs with the same job classification yet differing in terms of the amount or number of activities attributed to each job may lead to the inference that the two are performing their roles differently and in such a way as to favor the one whose job has more elements in it (i.e., is more "demanding").

At this point, we know very little about the nature of role negotiation behaviors. These behaviors are just beginning to appear as a focus of interest in the literature (e.g., Graen & Scandura, 1987). In addition, our methods of job analyses tend to overlook these. For the most part, job analyses begin with jobs that exist and then try to measure their characteristics. In such cases, most of the jobs in the sample are held by incumbents who have moved beyond the initial stages of employment when role negotiation activity is greatest and, thus, are holding negotiated JRDs.

If one then tries to summarize job descriptions across a pool of jobs, all with the same classification, one of two things occurs. For those behaviors that were negotiated by all or most incumbents and therefore appear as shared, the negotiated behaviors become part of the job. For those that are relatively uniquely negotiated among different individuals in the sample, the job analyst is faced with a decision about what to do with the lack of consistency within the job classification. A typical solution is to eliminate these inconsistent ones from the job description, thus dropping these types of negotiated ones.

In both the inclusion and exclusion case, the critical behaviors that go on during negotiation are never captured. Future work from a JRD perspective needs to focus attention on the actual behaviors that drive the negotiation process in an attempt to understand factors that influence persons' performance at negotiating their own jobs.

Predictors and Impact Over Time

As described, JRD is a dynamic model of jobs with the elements of a job being viewed as created by the job incumbent from the moment he or she is placed in the job. Core job elements are embellished by a set of role elements that are negotiated and developed by the job incumbent in interaction with others in his or her social environment. This process never ends, although there are periods (often long periods) in which little effort may be put forth to change the job and/or in which little effort is required to maintain a steady state. Nevertheless, the model places a premium on the need to be cognizant of the amount and nature of change over time and the potential for future change in what is considered a person's job.

Those interested in the affects of human abilities on performance have had a longstanding concern in the influence of abilities on task (job) performance over time. The extent and nature of the changing impact of abilities on job performance as the job incumbent gains more experience on the job is particularly important for selection and classification decisions. For both decisions, individual difference measures are obtained at one point and time and a decision regarding the assignment (or rejection) of a person to a position is made at about that same time. However, the person's placement in the position and his or her performance in it often extend for a long period of time into the future, beyond the point at which the initial decision was made. Ideally, inferences made from the initial measures of individual differences will validly predict the person's performance well into the future. Thus, if the predictability of individuals changes over time, knowledge of the nature and causes of these changes is critical for the effectiveness of predicting job performance.

Although some have investigated a wide range of human abilities with respect to the prediction of performance over time as persons gain experience on the task/job (e.g., Fleishman, 1960; Fleishman & Hempel, 1955), most attention has been paid to cognitive abilities and, specifically, general mental ability (Schmidt, Hunter, Outerbridge, & Goff, 1988) and cognitive abilities represented by college/graduate entrance examinations (e.g., Humphreys, 1960, 1968; Humphreys & Tabor, 1973).

Findings from empirical studies that have tracked the effect of cognitive abilities on performance as a function of experience on the job or task have been inconsistent. The correlation between cognitive abilities and performance has been found to increase, stay the same, or decrease over time (Schmidt et al., 1988), although the preponderance of the support favors a decrease in predictability (Alvares & Hulin, 1972, 1973; Hulin, Henry, & Noon, 1990; Humphreys, 1960, 1968) or little change (Schmidt et al., 1988). Explanations for change (or the lack thereof) in predictability over time have argued for the stability of general mental ability (Schmidt et al., 1988), a change in skills and abilities over time (Alvares & Hulin, 1972, 1973), and the changing nature of task demands with experience (Fleishman, 1960).

Although it is beyond the scope of this paper to review and critique thoroughly the literature on the stability or instability of ability predictors of job or task performance over time, two observations are relevant to our discussion of JRD. First, past work has focused almost entirely on elements of tasks and jobs that would be described as jobs by Ilgen and Hollenbeck (1991).

Second, the job elements themselves are considered to be stable. In some cases, it is quite likely that these demands were indeed stable. For example, in the work by Schmidt et al. (1988), data from military samples were collected for the jobs of cook, supply specialist, armor crewman, and armor repairman. For these jobs, it is quite likely that job elements did not change appreciably over the time period studied, and the elements of importance are likely to be job-type rather than role-type. Furthermore, when criteria that were likely to vary in their emphasis on job and role elements were compared over time by Schmidt et al., the two criteria most closely related to job elements (work sample and job knowledge measure) showed no change over time, whereas supervisory ratings (criteria likely to capture more role elements) did vary in their predictability over time. Supervisory ratings were better predicted in the earlier months than in later months.

In other cases, as in the "job" of being a student in the work of Humphreys (1968), it seems likely that the elements faced by a freshman may have been somewhat different from those faced by seniors, and role-type elements are likely to be a major part of this job. Perhaps the fact that Schmidt et al. (1988) concluded that prediction from general mental ability measures is stable over time and Humphreys concluded that it is not may have been due, in part, to the stability of the job elements and differences in the proportion of role elements in the jobs studied.

Hulin et al. (1990) clearly demonstrated that decreases in validities over time in their sample of validity studies from a wide range of studies were not due to criterion restriction in range or to unreliability; corrections for both did not alter the pattern of validities over time. To the two typical explanations for validity decreases, changing abilities and changing ability requirements over time, the authors offered a third. This was that social factors in the work groups in which persons perform create performance norms. The norms in the setting then affect performance, and the more that such norms influence performance the less influence the ability factor has. It was not possible to test a norm effect in the Hulin et al. data.

To this list, the JRD view would offer a fourth explanation. This is that performance at later times is based on a job (using the common definition of the whole set of activities or what is labeled JRD in Fig. 2.1). Thus, performance has a smaller proportion of the activities that were relevant at Time 1 and captured by the ability measures taken at that time. This explanation remains possible along with the other three offered by Hulin et al. (1990) without arguing that it is an alternative explanation. That is to say, it is not necessary to take the strong position that the presence of any one explanation negates the possibility of others.

Recently, Ackerman (1987, 1989) provided an intriguing information-processing view of changes in skill and ability effects on performance over time. Ackerman (1987) viewed human abilities as resources that individuals bring to tasks. Tasks were seen to vary in the nature and amount of resources they demand from task performers. With experience at the tasks, demands for human resources change as some activities that initially demanded a great deal of the performer's attention become routinized and are processed automatically (without awareness). Empirical work by the author supported the changing of resource demands as behaviors shift from conscious control to automatic processing with experience. Finally, Kanfer combined a resource-focused view of work motivation with Ackerman's skill acquisition model to offer a more complete view of job performance over time (Kanfer & Ackerman, 1989).

Combining JRD with Kanfer and Ackerman's changing resource model of skill acquisition recognizes the complexity of jobs and the fact that the boundary of what comprises the job itself is often changing. Kanfer and Ackerman ignored role elements in jobs by concentrating their research on a job heavily loaded with job elements, that of air traffic controller in a simulated setting where role making is not allowed. Yet, their model clearly allowed for dealing with role elements. Ilgen and Hollenbeck (1991), on the other hand, provided little detail with respect to the nature of ability and motivational characteristics important to role and job elements or the nature of the dynamic process by which such abilities may operate.

Interesting implications of the combination of the two are that skill acquisition for role elements may be quite different from that of job elements but share the same fundamental processes. For example, it is likely that role elements, since they are created through the interaction of the job incumbent in the social setting, are less likely to be as stable as are job elements. Hence, routinization effects are less and the mix of automatic to controlled processing different from that in job elements. Clearly, far more space could be devoted to developing such a combined model than can be given here. However, a JRD perspective on jobs leads me to expect that such developments could be quite valuable.

CONCLUSION

I began this chapter with a caution: The fundamental assumption of stability in the structure of jobs in organizations over time is being brought into question. The foundation on which selection and classification are based is shifting. I then presented a model of jobs and roles, job-role differentiation (JRD), described in the chapter by Ilgen and Hollenbeck in the *Handbook of Industrial and Organizational Psychology* (1991). This was followed by a few suggestions regarding the implications of a JRD point of view with respect to adjusting our view of selection and classification when the structure of jobs within organizations is shifting over time and over people.

Such adjustments can be viewed along a continuum from minor to major. At the least-change extreme, the sum total of job and role elements can simply be seen as relatively similar clusters of what is typically called job dimensions. The selection and classification task is simply identifying a set of predictors of the elements. The predictor set would be expanded somewhat to include individual difference variables more commonly labeled personality, along with the more typical skill and ability predictors. The criterion set would include behaviors related to role making as well as the final set of role and job elements.

At the other end of the continuum would be the recognition of JRDs that differed a great deal within a single job classification due to large role components. In this case, it would not be sufficient to simply make minor changes in the standard selection model. Interestingly, the innovative genius of Cronbach and Gleser (1955) may also serve us well for these kinds of situations as well. In their discussion of adaptive treatments, they suggested that adaptations could be made to the task/job as well as to the person in order to create a better fit of people to jobs. Most of the work to date on adaptive treatments has focused on training as a way to change people to fit jobs. However, it is also possible to think of adaptive treatment in terms of fitting jobs to people.

Thus, one might envision using tests and other measures to discover the skills, abilities, and temperaments of people that might lead them to build certain kinds of roles in the JRD. As individuals are brought into the system, the system itself would be modified in order to fit the kinds of people that are interested in it. The focus would consider both the system and the individual as somewhat flexible and fluid as the two are brought together. In a sense, knowledge about the applicant could be used by the supervisor to guide the role-making process and create the kind of position or job that would have unique contributions of both the applicant and the social system into which he or she were placed.

As selection and classification move toward the latter position, the approach to staffing organizations shifts from that of selection and classification to that of placement and classification. It seems probable that the "reject" option is less likely to be exercised with an adaptive treatment perspective. This condition is hardly likely to be of concern. From one perspective, the restricted option is becoming more and more the reality of many organizations, if for no other reason than the anticipated nature of the future work force (see earlier comments under Work Force 2000). From another standpoint, that of society in general, selection never was an issue, assuming full employment is an issue. There is no repository for low g individuals. Therefore, shifting models away from selection to placement and classification is not only a desirable goal, it is the only goal.

In conclusion, one final point needs emphasis. Although I believe that the changes I suggested are having influence on the way that we need to see jobs and the way that selection and classification are considered, I am not throwing up my arms in despair. Not at all. A lot is known about selection and classification. Project A has demonstrated that criteria can be measured in ways that we had not seen before and that the generalizable nature of validities can be integrated with the specificity of job families. Validity generalization research in a wide variety of settings has shown that general mental abilities are very useful for predicting performance. I am suggesting not revolution but evolution—evolution where conditions at time $t + 1$ are the accumulations of knowledge from time t, $t - 1$, and so on.

Yet, at the same time, to count on more stability in the nature of jobs than we can reasonably expect in the total domain of jobs as we build our models is equally unreasonable. It is unreasonable in two ways. First, we may apply our models to situations which they do not fit by assuming a degree of stability that is not there. The alternative is to narrow the domain of jobs to which we apply our models. That will work in the short run. We can always define out of our universe those conditions for which our models do not apply. This is fine as long as there remains a large and relevant pool of conditions for which our methods do apply. But if the relevant pool shrinks to the point that the interesting things are happening somewhere else, we are left with little to contribute.

As psychologists we are very good at developing good tools and at paying careful attention to our designs and analyses. I would have it no other way. I believe that is one of our greatest strengths. Yet, we need to think ahead to avoid missing some potential problems; thus, the caution. Our methods are no better than the validity of the assumptions on which they are based. In the case of selection and classification, the assumption I question is that of the stability of jobs and job systems. By addressing potential impacts of changing systems, at this point, I believe we can adjust our models to cope with such changes.

ACKNOWLEDGMENTS

Work on this chapter was supported, in part, by Grant No. N00014-90-J-1786 from the Office of Naval Research. Although the support for this work is gratefully acknowledged, the ideas expressed herein are those of the author and not necessarily endorsed by the supporting agency. I also wish to thank John Hollenbeck, Steve W. J. Kozlowski, and Neal Schmitt for their willingness to listen and discuss some of these ideas, and for their thoughtful comments on earlier drafts of this chapter.

REFERENCES

Ackerman, P. L. (1987). Individual differences in skill learning: An integration of psychometric and information processing perspectives. *Psychological Bulletin, 102*, 3-27.

Ackerman, P. L. (1989). Within task intercorrelations of skilled performance: Implications for predicting individual differences. *Journal of Applied Psychology, 74*, 360-364.

Alvares, K. M., & Hulin, C. L. (1972). Two explanations of tempera changes in ability-skill relationships: A literature review and theoretical analysis. *Human Factors, 14*, 295-308.

Alvares, K. M., & Hulin, C. L. (1973). An experimental evaluation of temporal decay in the prediction of performance. *Organizational Behavior and Human Performance, 9*, 169-185.

Bettenhausen, K. L. (1991). Five years of groups research: What we have learned and what needs to be addressed? *Journal of Management, 17*, 345-381.

Blau, P. M., & Scott, R. W. (1962). The nature and types of formal organizations. In P. M. Blau (Ed.), *Formal organizations: A comparative approach* (pp. 40-58). New York: Chandler.

Campbell, J. P. (1990). An overview of the Army selection and classification project (Project A). *Personnel Psychology, 43*, 231-240.

Cascio, W. F., & Zammuto, R., Jr. (1987). *Societal trends and staffing policies.* Denver: University of Colorado.

Cronbach, L. J., & Gleser, G. C. (1955). *Psychological tests and personnel decisions.* Urbana: University of Illinois Press.

Dean, J. W., Jr., & Snell, S. A. (1991). Integrated manufacturing and job design: Moderating effects of organizational inertia. *Academy of Management Journal, 34*, 776-804.

2. JOBS AND ROLES

Dunnette, M. D., & Hough, L. M. (Eds.). (1991). *Handbook of industrial and organizational psychology* (Vol. 2). Palo Alto, CA: Consulting Psychologists Press.

Fleishman, E. A. (1960). Abilities at different stages of practice in rotary pursuit performance. *Journal of Experimental Psychology, 60*, 162-171.

Fleishman, E. A., & Hempel, W. E., Jr. (1955). The relationship between abilities and improvement with practice in a visual discrimination reaction task. *Journal of Experimental Psychology, 49*, 301-312.

Fullerton, H. N., Jr. (1985). The 1995 labor force: BLS' [Bureau of Labor Statistics'] latest projections. *Monthly Labor Review, 117*, 17-25.

Goldstein, I. L. (1990). Training system issues in the year 2000. *American Psychologist, 45*, 134-144.

Goodman, P. S. (Ed.) (1986). *Designing effective workgroups*. San Francisco: Jossey-Bass.

Graen, G. B. (1976). Role making processes within complex organizations. In M. D. Dunnette (Ed.), *Handbook of industrial and organizational psychology* (pp. 1201-1245). Chicago: Rand McNally.

Graen, G. B., & Cashman, J. (1975). A role making model of leadership in formal organizations: A developmental approach. In J. G. Hunt & L. L. Larson (Eds.), *Leadership frontiers* (pp. 143-166). Kent, OH: Kent University Press.

Graen, G. B., & Scandura, T. A. (1987). Toward a psychology of dyadic organizing. In L. L. Cummings & B. M. Staw (Eds.), *Research in organizational behavior, 9*, 175-208.

Greenberg, E. R. (1988, November). Downsizing and worker assistance: Latest AMA survey results. *Personnel*, 49-53.

Hackman, J. R. (1969). Toward understanding the role of tasks in behavioral research. *Acta Psychological, 31*, 97-128.

Hackman, J. R. (Ed.). (1990). *Groups that work (and those that don't)*. San Francisco: Jossey-Bass.

Here comes GM's Saturn (1990, April). *Business Week*, pp. 56-62.

Hulin, C. L., Henry, R. A., & Noon, S. L. (1990). Adding a dimension: Time as a factor in the generalization of predictive relationships. *Psychological Bulletin, 107*, 328-340.

Humphreys, L. G. (1960). Investigations of simplex. *Psychometrika, 25*, 313-323.

Humphreys, L. G. (1968). The fleeting nature of prediction of college academic success. *Journal of Educational Psychology, 59*, 375-380.

Humphreys, L. G., & Tabor, T. (1973). Postdiction study of the Graduate Record Examination and eight semesters of college grades. *Journal of Educational Measurement, 10*, 179-184.

Ilgen, D. R., & Hollenbeck, J. R. (1991). The structure of work: Jobs and roles. In M. D. Dunnette & L. M. Hough (Eds.), *Handbook of industrial and organizational psychology* (Vol. 2, pp. 165-208). Palo Alto, CA: Consulting Psychologists Press.

Kanfer, R., & Ackerman, P. L. (1989). Motivation and cognitive abilities: An integrative/aptitude-treatment interaction approach to skill acquisition [Monograph]. *Journal of Applied Psychology, 74*, 657-690.

Kozlowski, S. W. J., Chao, G. T., Smith, E. M., & Hedlund, J. (1993). Organizational downsizing: Strategies, interventions, and research implications. In C. L. Cooper & I. T. Robertson (Eds.), *International review of industrial and organizational psychology: 1993*, pp. 263-331). London: Wiley.

Levine, J. M., & Moreland, R. L. (1990). Progress in small group research. *Annual Review of Psychology, 41*, 585-634.

McCormick, E. J. (1979). *Job analysis: Methods and applications*. New York: Amacom.

McGrath, J. E., & Altman, I. (1966). *Small group research: A synthesis and critique of the field*. New York: Holt, Rinehart, & Winston.

McHenry, J. J., Hough, L. M., Toquam, J. L., Hanson, M. A., & Ashworth, S. (1990). Identifying optimal predictor composites and testing for generalizability across jobs and performance factors. *Personnel Psychology, 43*, 335-354.

Pepinsky, H. P., & Pepinsky, P. N. (1961). Organization, management strategy and team productivity. In L. Petrillo & B. M. Bass (Eds.), *Leadership and interpersonal behavior*. New York: Holt.

The right stuff (1990, October). *Time*, pp. 74-84.

Roby, T. B., & Lanzetta, J. T. (1958). Considerations in the analysis of group tasks. *Psychological Bulletin, 55*, 88-101.

Sackett, P. R., & Dreher, G. F. (1982). Constructs and assessment center: Some troublesome empirical findings. *Journal of Applied Psychology, 67*, 401-410.

Schmidt, F. L., Hunter, J. E., Outerbridge, A. N., & Goff, S. (1988). Joint relation of experience and ability with job performance: Test of three hypotheses. *Journal of Applied Psychology, 73*, 46-57.

Tomasko, R. M. (1990). *Downsizing: Reshaping the corporation for the future*. New York: AMACOM.

Turnage, J. J., & Muchinsky, P. M. (1982). Transitional variability in human performance in assessment centers. *Organizational Behavior and Human Performance, 30*, 174-200.

Who needs a boss? (1990, May). *Fortune*, pp. 52-60.

ALTERNATIVE MODELS OF JOB PERFORMANCE AND THEIR IMPLICATIONS FOR SELECTION AND CLASSIFICATION

John P. Campbell
University of Minnesota

Developing selection and classification systems, or evaluating their effects, requires some identification of the goals that are to be served by the system. From this perspective, one major overall goal seems to be to make selection and classification decisions in such a way that aggregate individual performance is improved, maximized, or optimized. Making this goal operational requires the use of one or more specific measures of performance. By design or by default, the choice of specific criterion measures for performance assessment is guided by a model or theory of what performance is. Consequently, the objectives of this paper are to:

1. Provide a label and a brief description for each of a set of alternative ways one could think about, or model, job performance for purposes of selection/classification criterion measurement. The set of alternative models to be described is meant to include all possible alternatives. Sometimes a particular point of view is made explicit by the proponents for it, and sometimes it must be inferred from what they actually do. However, nothing major should have been left out. If something seems to be missing, it is because of either the author's faulty knowledge or his faulty descriptions, for which there will most likely be penalties.

2. Outline the circumstances under which a particular model might be more appropriate than the others, particularly with regard to the distinctions among differing subgoals for selection and classification.

3. Outline the principal measurement implications of the different models, particularly for selection and classification research. Although this paper is not about the pros and cons of specific measurement methods, a major reason for having a model, or theory, of performance is to guide the search for, or the construction of, observable measures.

Performance is one of the most abused words in the English language, particularly during election years, when it takes on strange and sometimes amazing meanings or, more accurately perhaps, no meaning at all. However, enough of the political commentary and on to the performance of individuals in organizations, where there are more than enough variations in meaning to keep us arguing for a long time. In fact, everyone is invited to do as we did once (Campbell, McCloy, Oppler, & Sager, 1992) and go through the literature in applied psychology and personnel management and note the number and variety of phenomena to which the term *performance* has been attached. It's a bit scary. How can we make sense of such helter-skelter? The textbook answer is to appeal to theory—in this case, theories about the nature of performance.

ALTERNATIVE MODELS OF PERFORMANCE

In the context of job performance, there seem to be at least eight reasonably distinct points of view, most of which are useful for some purpose, but a few (one?) of which are not. Each of these eight is described in the subsections that follow, in varying degrees of detail.

Performance Is One Thing (The Classic Model)

This model says simply that the general factor will account for almost all the relevant true score covariances among observed measures. Correlation matrices that appear otherwise do so because of differential reliabilities, the influence of method-specific variance, or other kinds of contamination. The goal of measurement is to obtain the best possible measure of the general factor. Further, the best possible measure is an "objective" indicator of an individual's overall contribution that is maintained by the organization itself; but approximations are also useful, so long as they have a significant correlation with the general factor and do not introduce any large new sources of contamination. This certainly seemed to be what Robert Thorndike (1949) had in mind when he coined the terms *immediate, intermediate,* and *ultimate criteria.*

The reasons for identifying this as the classic model of performance are as follows. First, for most of this century the single criterion measure has dominated in personnel research. Further, in the scientific/professional literature, the term *job performance* is virtually always used in the singular, with no explicit or implicit conditionals. When discussing whether or not job performance can be changed by this or that treatment, predicted by a particular ability, or measured better or worse by a particular method, the implication is clearly that there is one general thing to be changed, predicted, or measured.

This unidimensional model would seem to be a major source of the criterion problem, because the search for reliable, uncontaminated, and objective indicators that significantly reflect the general factor, or ultimate criterion, has generally been a failure. Good ones seem never to be found. A very undesirable fallback position is to use supervisory ratings, which are seen by this model as subjective, contaminated with halo error, and full of information-processing errors.

Multiple Factor Models

The model used in the Army's Project A (Campbell, 1990) and the Career Force project (J. Campbell, McHenry, & Wise, 1990) is much different than the classic unidimensional view. We have attempted to expand what we learned in these projects and have described a multiple factor model of performance that is meant to be applicable to virtually any job. Much of what follows is taken from J. Campbell et al. (1992).

This model assumes that performance is genuinely multidimensional and is composed of a number of basic distinguishable components such that some people could perform well on one component but, relatively speaking, not as well on others. That is, while the true intercorrelations among the factors are probably not zero, they are significantly less than unity.

The substantive nature of each factor is defined to be synonymous with individual behavior or action. Performance is something that people actually do and can be observed. By definition, it includes only those actions or behaviors that are relevant for the organization's goals and that can be scaled (measured) in terms of each individual's proficiency (i.e., level of contribution). Performance is what the organization hired you to do, and do well. Performance is not the consequence(s) or result(s) of action, it is the action itself.

Admittedly, this distinction is troublesome in at least one major respect. That is, behavior is not always observable (e.g., cognitive behavior—as in solving a math problem) and can be known only by its effects (e.g., producing a solution after much thought). However, solutions, statements, or answers that are produced as a result of covert cognitive behavior and are totally under the control of the individual are included as actions that can be defined as performance. In general, a strict definition of "observable behavior" is epistomologically difficult. Without getting too esoteric about it all, the argument is simply that performance consists of goal-relevant actions that are under the control of the individual, regardless of whether they are cognitive, motor, psychomotor, or interpersonal. Consequently, writing a job-relevant memo falls within the definition, if the availability of resources such as a word processor is a constant across individuals, while the number of pieces produced does not, unless such an outcome is under the complete control of the individual.

For this model, it is axiomatic that job performance is not one thing. A job, any job, is a very complex activity; and, for any job, there are a number of major performance components that are distinguishable in terms of their determinants and covariation patterns with other variables. Some possible examples of performance components are: giving emergency first aid (police officer), planning and designing undergraduate courses (university faculty), driving safely under hazardous conditions (truck operator), rewarding sales personnel for appropriate actions (sales supervisor), and using rules of separation efficiently (air traffic controller).

At the highest level of generality we have hypothesized that there are eight basic components of performance. For reference purposes, they are shown as Table 3.1. Not every job would include all eight factors, and some factors, such as Factor 1, would have more subfactors than others, thus offering more potential differential prediction.

TABLE 3.1
A Proposed Taxonomy of Higher-Order Performance Components

1.   **Job-specific task proficiency**

The first factor reflects the degree to which the individual can perform the core substantive or technical tasks that are central to his or her job. They are the job-specific performance behaviors that distinguish the substantive content of one job from another. Constructing custom kitchens, doing word processing, designing computer architecture, driving a city bus through Chicago traffic, and directing air traffic are all categories of job-specific task content. Individual differences in how well such tasks are executed is the focus of this performance component.

2.   **Non-job-specific task proficiency**

This factor reflects the situation that in virtually every organization, but perhaps not all, individuals are required to perform tasks or execute performance behaviors that are not specific to their particular job. For example, in research universities with PhD programs, the faculty must teach classes, advise students, make admission decisions, and serve on committees. All faculty must do these things, in addition to practicing chemistry, psychology, economics, or electrical engineering. In the military services this factor is institutionalized as a set of common tasks (e.g., first aid, basic navigation, using NBC equipment) for which everyone is responsible.

3.   **Written and oral communication task proficiency**

Many jobs in the work force require the individual to make formal oral or written presentations to audiences that may vary from one to tens of thousands. For those jobs, the proficiency with which one can write or speak, independent of the correctness of the subject matter, is a critical component of performance.

(continued)

TABLE 3.1
Continued

4.   **Demonstrating effort**

The fourth factor is meant to be a direct reflection of the consistency of an individual's effort day by day, the frequency with which people will expend extra effort when required, and the willingness to keep working under adverse conditions. It is a reflection of the degree to which individuals commit themselves to all job tasks, work at a high level of intensity, and keep working when it is cold, wet, or late.

5.   **Maintaining personal discipline**

The fifth component is characterized by the degree to which negative behavior, such as alcohol and substance abuse at work, law or rules infractions, and excessive absenteeism, is avoided.

6.   **Facilitating peer and team performance**

Factor 6 is defined as the degree to which the individual supports his or her peers, helps them with job problems, and acts as a de facto trainer. It also encompasses how well an individual facilitates group functioning by being a good model, keeping the group goal directed, and reinforcing participation by the other group members. Obviously, if the individual works alone, this component will have little importance. However, in many jobs, high performance on this factor would be a major contribution toward the goals of the organization.

7.   **Supervision/leadership**

Proficiency in the supervisory component includes all the behaviors directed at influencing the performance of subordinates through face-to-face interpersonal interaction and influence. Supervisors set goals for subordinates, they teach them more effective methods, they model the appropriate behaviors, and they reward or punish in appropriate ways. The distinction between this factor and the preceding one is a distinction between peer leadership and supervisory leadership. While modeling, goal setting, coaching, and providing reinforcement are elements in both factors, the belief here is that peer versus supervisor leadership implies significantly different determinants.

8.   **Management/administration**

The eighth and last factor is intended to include the major elements in management that are distinct from direct supervision. It includes the performance behaviors directed at articulating goals for the unit or enterprise, organizing people and resources to work on them, monitoring progress, helping to solve problems or overcome crises that stand in the way of goal accomplishment, controlling expenditures, obtaining additional resources, and representing the unit in dealings with other units.

By this model, understanding and being able to measure job performance depends on having some understanding of the organizational goals to which the individual is supposed to contribute; otherwise, job behavior could not be scaled in terms of the level of performance represented. For example, for air traffic controllers, consider the implications of individual actions directed at the two goals of maximizing air traffic safety and maximizing efficiency of air traffic movement at the same time. What do these joint goals imply about the actions that would constitute high performance and the actions that would constitute low performance? Closer to home, what are, or should be, the goals of one's family? Family members are always judging each other in terms of their contribution to the family's goals. Some families consider them explicitly, others do not; but goals are always there, if only by default. Depending on the family's goals, a particular action can be judged as good performance or bad performance. In the job setting, both confusion and trouble could result if either the formal employment contract or the informal psychological contract incorporates goals that are different than those against which performance is actually judged (Rousseau, 1989; Schein, 1970).

Within this model, performance is to be distinguished from both effectiveness and productivity. Effectiveness refers to the evaluation of the results of performance. By definition, the variance in a measure of effectiveness is controlled by more than the actions of the individual. Dollar amount of sales is the obvious example. An implication of this distinction is that rewarding or punishing individuals on the basis of effectiveness may be unfair and counterproductive. As an indicator of performance, effectiveness is by definition contaminated. This is not to argue that results are not important. They most certainly are. Ultimately, the organization needs to know the sources of variation in performance and the sources of variation in effectiveness. Effectiveness is the bottom line, and organizations cannot exist without it. By defining performance this way this model simply argues the point that if the research questions deal with predictor validities, or training effects, or any other strategy focused on the individual, then the dependent variable should not be something that the individual cannot influence.

The usually agreed-on definition of productivity (Mahoney, 1988) is the ratio of effectiveness (output) to the cost of achieving that level of effectiveness (input). Its primary use is as a relative index of how well a group, organization, or industry is functioning. Depending on which inputs are used in the denominator, it is possible to talk about the productivity of capital, the productivity of technology, or the productivity of labor. That is, total productivity has its subcomponents.

For the sake of completeness, utility is defined as the value of a particular level of performance, effectiveness, or productivity. That is, we can talk about the utility of performance, the utility of effectiveness, or the utility of productivity.

In terms of the consistency between the measurement operations and the definition of performance, this model allows only three, or possibly four, primary measurement methods. First, the model strongly implies that ratings (expert judgments) should remain as an important method since they can be constructed to conform directly to the specified definition. The principal worry about ratings has always been that, no matter how they are constructed, there may still be significant contamination by systematic variance unrelated to the performance of the person being assessed. Thinking of performance rating as a sequence of observation, sampling, encoding, storage, retrieval, evaluation, differential weighting, and composite scoring shows it to be a very complex cognitive process that allows many opportunities for entry of both unsystematic variance and contamination (Cooper, 1981; DeNisi, Cafferty, & Meglino, 1984; Ilgen & Feldman, 1983). As with any criterion measure, the overall problem is to estimate the proportion of observed variance accounted for by (a) the latent variable, (b) general method variance, (c) measure-specific method variance, (d) other systematic contamination, and (e) unreliability. It has been difficult to assess the effect of nonrelevant sources of variation on the accuracy of job performance ratings. However, the model clearly implies that it is inappropriate to infer that the variance in ratings that does not overlap with the variance in other measures of performance (e.g., job samples) is "error variance."

Although ratings generally have a bad press, the overall picture is not as bleak as might be expected, given all the ways the true score variance can be contaminated. One advantage of ratings, assuming that they share at least some variance with the latent variable, is that their content can be directly linked to the measurement objectives by straightforward content validation methods (e.g., critical incident sampling combined with retranslation procedures). Also, if they are used with care, their reliabilities are usually respectable (i.e., .50-.60) and can be improved considerably by using more than one rater; and they are as predictable as are objective effectiveness measures (Nathan & Alexander, 1988; Schmitt, Gooding, Noe, & Kirsch, 1984). Additional faith is restored by the fact that the more thorough attempts to use the method have produced credible results (C. Campbell et al., 1990), and over a number of studies, the largest source of variance in ratings is in fact the performance of the ratee (Landy & Farr, 1980). Any procedure can be made to look bad by poor implementation, and no method should be made a victim of its most inexpert users. However, it is also true that we still have much to learn about the determinants of ratings.

The second measurement method is the standardized job sample, in which the task content of the job is simulated, or actually sampled intact, and presented to the assessee in a standardized format under standardized conditions. The content validity of the method can also be determined directly, but for reasons to be discussed later it may not reflect the influence of all relevant determinants of performance variance.

A third method would consist of direct task observation and measurement as it occurs in the job setting. This is what Sackett, Zedeck, and Fogli (1988) were fortunate enough to have in their study of supermarket checkout personnel. However, except in rare instances, using this method would ordinarily require rather expensive observational or recording techniques; and for complex positions, the difficulties in observation might be insurmountable.

In general, the fourth measurement method is a bit dangerous, but it may sometimes be possible to specify outcomes of performance that are virtually under the complete control of the individual.

The Results Model

Rather than worry too much about the degree to which the individual has control over specific indicators of results, one could take the opposing view and be very explicit about making the bottom line synonymous with performance. The appropriate performance measures would then be indicators of the quantity, quality, or value of whatever the individual was supposed to produce—for example, the number of service calls for a repair person; total amount of insurance in force for insurance sales personnel; number of student class hours, number of PhDs produced, or number of publications for an academic; or meeting (but not exceeding) recruiting goals for a military recruiter.

The results model is an implicit part of the frequent argument that objective measures are better than subjective measures and that high-performing people are people who get results. The upside of this argument is that specific objective goals attached to powerful reward contingencies do in fact motivate people to achieve those goals (Ilgen & Klein, 1988; Kanfer, 1990). The downside is that such indicators aren't readily available for all jobs, they suffer from varying degrees of contamination, and they may indeed reinforce undesired behavior, as when recruiters compromise test results or when academics trying not to perish only do research that is quick and cheap and then publish the same thing several times.

Finally, in the construct validity sense, the results model seems not to make a distinction between the latent variable, or performance construct, and the observable measure. The measure is the variable. Performance is nothing more, or less, than the sum of scores on the available indicators. In that sense, such a theory of performance is very much in the tradition of radical behaviorism and is reminiscent of the statement that intelligence is what intelligence tests measure.

The Success Model

There are a number of classic studies in management selection (e.g., Bray, R. Campbell, & Grant, 1974) that adopt a view of performance that we might call the "success model." It is really a combination of the "one-thing" and "results" models. By implication, success is unidimensional and refers to the overall level of rewards an individual has received for being effective. The two primary indicators of success are the rate at which the individual has been promoted and the salary or compensation level that has been reached. In longitudinal studies, these indicators have yielded substantial correlations with a previously administered test battery or assessment center ratings, even though the risks of contamination are considerable. Users of these two indicators usually attempt to deal with their noncomparability across organizations and cohorts by various adjustments such as standardizing salary within type of organization, correcting for inflation, and controlling promotion rates for the number of levels in the organization.

Using data from the archives of a large personnel management consulting firm, Joy Fisher-Hazucha recently completed a dissertation (1991) that examined the covariance structure of three variables she called *performance, success*, and *jeopardy*. Jeopardy referred to the estimated probability that the individual could lose his or her job. Success, as measured by a composite of salary and organization level, had a negative correlation with jeopardy. That is, the people judged to be in greatest danger tended to be people who were the most successful. The correlations with performance depended on which component of performance was at issue. Success was associated with technical accomplishment, but jeopardy tended to be related to what might be described as the leadership/supervision performance component. Loosely speaking, these two performance components correspond to Factor 1 (Core Technical Performance) and Factor 3 (Effort and Leadership) in the Project A taxonomy, or to Factor 1 and Factor 5 in Table 3.1. The sample was composed almost entirely of people with management responsibilities, and the prototypic high-success/high-jeopardy individual was a scientifically trained R&D manager who rose quickly based on technical accomplishment but who did not perform the face-to-face leadership tasks very well. The observed correlations of cognitive ability tests and personality and interest measures with the three criterion measures were consistent with this picture.

To cite at least one military example, the performance indicator used in the RAND model (Armor, Fernandez, Bers, & Schwarzbach, 1982) is a type of success model within this framework. That is, the performance index is taken as the number of months after advanced individual training that an individual has been in service and has maintained a Skills Qualification Test (SQT) score of 70 or better. In fact, the index is referred to as "successful man-months of service." The Project A criterion array (C. Campbell et al., 1990) also included one success measure. It is an index obtainable from the Enlisted Master File that reflects whether the individual has been promoted at a slower or faster rate than the average for the people in the same cohort. Interestingly, in the Project A performance modeling analysis this indicator loaded highest on the factor called "Maintaining Personal Discipline."

The National Research Council (NRC) Model

A very explicit model of performance has been incorporated in the final report of the National Research Council's (NRC) Committee on the Performance of Military Personnel (Green & Wigdor, 1991). The committee chose to define performance as the proficiency with which the individual can do the technical tasks, or has mastered the substantive content, of the job. The content of performance was delineated in this way for the specific purpose of accentuating the differences in content across jobs so as to enhance classification decisions. The intent was to exclude performance components that might be common to virtually all jobs (e.g., being supportive of one's peers).

The measurement task then becomes one of enumerating the full population of substantive or technical tasks and assessing an individual's performance on this population of tasks under standardized conditions. Since no measurement method can deal with the entire population of tasks, tasks must be sampled. For the NRC committee, the sampling method of choice is stratified random sampling. The strata are things like the major job content categories (e.g., teaching versus research for academics or field techniques versus weapons maintenance for infantrymen) and task criticality, as judged by subject matter experts (SMEs). Once the strata are identified, the tasks are sampled randomly within strata. This method is contrasted (unfavorably) with the more commonly used procedure, in which the representativeness of the task sample is judged by SMEs and/or the management.

For the Committee on the Performance of Military Personnel, the measurement method of choice is the standardized job sample, commonly referred to as the hands-on measure. That is, replicas of actual job tasks are constructed at a test site and administered in a standardized manner to everyone in the sample. The committee places great importance on the job sample method as the only appropriate way, in the military at least, to assess how well an individual can actually do something. All other measurement methods are viewed as "surrogates."

The Critical Task Model

The logic of the NRC Committee on the Performance of Military Personnel can be carried one step further in terms of maximizing the distinctiveness of performance across jobs. That is, instead of sampling representatively from the population of all substantive tasks making up a job, another alternative would be to identify a much smaller number of only the most critical tasks (perhaps only one) in each job. Further, the most critical tasks would be chosen so as to maximize the degree to which task content is different across jobs.

This would deliberately stack the deck in favor of classification, but if the total group to be assigned was first selected on the basis of predicted scores for the performance components held in common by most jobs, it would be a reasonable model to use. The Army has used such a model in developing a specialized predictor battery for the TOW gunner (Grafton, Czarnolweski, & Smith, 1989). The Marine Corps' Job Performance Measurement Project (Felker et al., 1991) defined troubleshooting certain equipment malfunctions as the most critical task for a number of specialties, and measured performance on it with a longer than usual hands-on simulation. One advantage of dealing with just a small number of critical tasks is that each task can be measured more reliably.

The Critical Deficiency Model

If there are critical task accomplishments that can differentiate jobs, perhaps there are also critical task failures, and they may not represent two ends of the same continuum. That is, the reasons for failure may not be simply a very low score on the determinants of success. An explicit example of this model may not exist anywhere, but it seems at least implicit in jobs where certain individual errors can be very serious or even catastrophic, such as airline pilot or school bus driver; or for jobs where the concern is really for avoiding certain performance deficiencies rather than achieving particularly high levels of performance. For example, job analysis might establish a number of critical errors to be avoided, and if the existing base rates for such errors were sufficiently high to obtain useful research data, the selection/classification system could be designed to make job assignments that would reduce the probabilities of such errors.

However, whether such a model has greater relevance for selection or for classification is an interesting research question. It is not too difficult to think of substantively based errors across jobs that would have different skill and ability determinants such that classification would be enhanced (airline pilot versus air traffic controller). It is also possible to think of instances in which the error determinants might be much the same across a range of jobs.

Performance as Attrition

Attrition, or turnover as it's known in the private sector, has a long history as a criterion variable in selection research, particularly in the military services. However, while the military services tend to account for attrition via the economic cycle and with stable individual differences such as interests (Abrahams, Neumann, & Githens, 1968), temperament (White, Nord, & Mael, 1990), and high school graduation status, the private sector worries about the economic cycle and things that happen to the individual after he or she enters the organization (Mobley, Griffith, Hand, & Meglino, 1979). That is, much of the blame for turnover is placed on compensation and benefit practices, training opportunities, or management practices, as when, for example, the individual feels underrewarded, excessively stressed, underutilized, or that some other part of the formal or informal employment contract has been broken.

There is evidence for the validity of both points of view. However, both are hindered by a lack of information concerning the latent structure of attrition itself. Everyone seems to agree that there are different kinds of attrition and that the different kinds have different antecedents. Further, almost every organization at least gives lip service to recording reasons for why people leave. However, the list of reasons is usually idiosyncratic to the organization and the reasons that are recorded may not always be what they seem.

Ideally, we need both a basic taxonomy of types of attrition that would be used by everyone and methods of capturing attrition data that avoid the criterion contamination to which operational data are often subjected. Neither exists at the moment and all existing studies of predicting attrition suffer from criterion contamination to some extent.

CHOICES AMONG MODELS

It would be a mistake to assume that there is one best model for thinking about performance or, conversely, that they are all equally useful. But what else can be said beyond, "it depends"? The following points, while not earthshaking, are perhaps worth repeating.

Research Versus Appraisal

In general, collecting performance information for the purpose of operational performance appraisal is a very different context than collecting such data for research purposes, and the difference has very little to do with the specific theory of performance or measurement method being used. It has everything to do with the reward contingencies that operate on those who provide the data. For good and sufficient reasons it may not be a wise strategy, in the operational setting, to attempt to estimate an individual's true performance score as closely as possible. If you do that, people may never get promoted, or it might play havoc with the salary structure. In the operational setting, it also makes a difference whether the appraisal is being done for evaluative (e.g., salary or promotion) or feedback (e.g., coaching) reasons. If it is the latter, then the one-factor and results-oriented models are not very helpful. Very general feedback is of little use for instructional purposes and using distal results as feedback information will not seem very relevant to the individual (Ilgen, Fisher, & Taylor, 1979).

The context of measuring performance for research purposes makes it more likely that the measurement system will try to estimate the individual's true performance score. There is everything to gain and little to lose by doing so.

However, the specific sources of variation in the true score that should be allowed to operate or that should be controlled are a function of the particular research goal. For example, they would be different for selection/classification research, training evaluation, or the evaluation of alternative supervision/ leadership strategies.

The Research Objectives

We (J. Campbell et al., 1992) have argued elsewhere that for ongoing performance in a job setting there are three, and only three, direct determinants of the variation in performance across people. Following the general literature in psychology they are referred to as declarative knowledge, proceduralized knowledge and skill, and motivation.

Declarative knowledge is simply knowledge about facts and things. Specifically, it represents an understanding of a given task's requirements (e.g., general principles for equipment operation) (Anderson, 1985; Kanfer & Ackerman, 1989). Procedural knowledge and skill is attained when declarative knowledge (knowing what to do) has been successfully combined with knowing how to do it (modified from Anderson, 1985; Kanfer & Ackerman, 1989).

As a direct determinant of performance, motivation is defined as a combined effect from three choice behaviors: (a) choice to expend effort; (b) choice of level of effort to expend; and (c) choice to persist in the expenditure of that level of effort. These are the traditional representations for the direction, amplitude, and duration of volitional behavior. The important point is that the most meaningful way to talk about motivation as a direct determinant of behavior is as one or more of these three choices.

Accounting for individual differences in knowledge, skill, and choice behavior encompasses a very large number of research topics that are not to be discussed here. From the trait perspective, almost a century of research has produced taxonomic models of abilities, personality, interests, and personal histories. Another major research tradition has focused on the instructional treatment. At least three major types of such treatments are relevant in the job performance content—formal education, job-relevant training (formal and informal), and previous experience. The possible antecedents of motivation, or choice behavior, are specified by the various theories of motivation. For example, an operant model stipulates that the reinforcement contingency is the most important determinant of the choices people make. Cognitive expectancy models say that certain specific thoughts (e.g., self-efficacy, instrumentality, valence) govern these three choices. Other models might see such choices as a function of certain stable predispositions, such as the need for achievement. For example, perhaps certain kinds of people virtually always come to work on time and always work hard. A schematic representing these points is shown in Fig. 3.1.

$$PC_i^* = f\,[\quad \begin{array}{c}\text{Declarative}\\ \text{Knowledge}\\ \text{(DK)}\end{array} \quad x \quad \begin{array}{c}\text{Procedural}\\ \text{Knowledge}\\ \text{and Skill}\\ \text{(PKS)}\end{array} \quad x \quad \begin{array}{c}\text{Motivation]}\\ \text{(M)}\end{array}$$

Declarative Knowledge (DK)	Procedural Knowledge and Skill (PKS)	Motivation (M)
- Facts	- Cognitive skill	- Choice to
- Principles	- Psychomotor	perform
- Goals	skill	- Level of
- Self-knowledge	- Physical skill	effort
	- Self-manage-	- Persistence
	ment skill	of effort
	- Interpersonal	
	skill	

$_i = 1,2 \ldots k$ performance components

*Predictors of Performance Determinants***

DK $= f$ [(Ability, personality, interests), (Education, training, experience), (Aptitude/treatment interactions)]

PKS $= f$ [(Ability, personality, interests), (Education, training, practice, experience), (Aptitude/treatment interactions)]

M $= f$ (Whatever independent variables are stipulated by your favorite motivation theory)

Note: This entire schema can be repeated for educational performance, training performance, and laboratory task performance.
* Obviously, performance differences can also be produced by situational effects such as the quality of equipment, degree of staff support, or nature of the working conditions. For purposes of this model of performance, these conditionals are assumed to be held constant (experimentally, statistically, or judgmentally).
** Individual differences, learning, and motivational manipulations can only influence performance by increasing declarative knowledge, procedural knowledge and skill, or the three choices.

FIG. 3.1. Determinants of job performance components.

A few general points should be noted. Performance will not occur unless there is a choice to perform at some level of effort for some specified time. Consequently, motivation is always a determinant of performance, and a relevant question for virtually any personnel selection problem is how much of the variance in choice behavior can be accounted for by stable predispositions measurable at the time of hire, and how much is a function of the motivating properties of the situation or the trait/situation interaction.

Also, performance that is not simply trial and error cannot occur unless there is some threshold level of procedural skill. There may also be a very complex interaction between procedural skill and motivation. For example, the higher the skill level, the greater the tendency to choose to perform, but skill level may have no relationship with the choice of effort level. That is, the three choices may be controlled by different antecedents.

Another reasonable assumption is that declarative knowledge is a prerequisite for procedural skill (Anderson, 1985). That is, before being able to use the procedural skills that are necessary for task performance one must know what should be done. However, this point is not without controversy (Nissen & Bullmer, 1987) and it may indeed be possible to master a skill without first acquiring the requisite declarative knowledge. Two examples that come to mind are modeling the social skills of your parents or modeling the final form of an expert skier without really knowing what you are trying to do. Nevertheless, given the current findings in cognitive research, the distinction is a meaningful one. Performance could suffer because procedural skill was never developed or because declarative knowledge was never acquired or because one or the other has decayed. Also, some data suggest that different abilities account more for individual differences in declarative knowledge than for individual differences in procedural skills (Ackerman, 1988). At this point, the major implication is still that performance is directly determined only by some combination of these three elements.

Notice that there are now two levels of performance determinants, direct and indirect. Changes in selection/classification systems, changes in training and development programs, changes in management or leadership strategies, or other kinds of interventions are all indirect determinants that can only affect performance by changing one or more of the three direct determinants (i.e., knowledge, skill, the three choices). It is also true that in the real world there are a large number of physical or environmental constraints that could operate to restrict the range of performance differences across individuals. Conversely, performance differences could be accentuated by applying the constraints differentially, such as by giving some people better equipment than others. Such constraints are sources of contamination, not determinants of performance, and must be controlled for in some way.

If the research goal is to determine the validity of selection and classification procedures, then the validation sample should be as homogeneous as possible in terms of the individuals' post-selection experiences (e.g., training programs or quality of supervision) or in terms of the performance constraints under which each person must currently operate. Any systematic mean differences in true performance scores produced by differential experiences not under the individual's control constitute criterion contamination and, for validation purposes, lower the estimate of validity artifactually.

Also, the criterion measure should allow all three determinants of performance to operate. This should be reason enough to be wary of the standardized job sample as the sole source of criterion information. It purposely controls for much of the influence of the motivational determinant. However, the rank order of individuals may change a great deal when performance on the job sample is compared to performance on the very same tasks in the job setting.

Perhaps the best available estimate of this latter correlation was obtained in the Sackett et al. (1988) study of supermarket checkout personnel. As luck would have it, the computerized recording system kept exactly the same scores on the same tasks over the course of a workday as were obtained from the standardized job sample. The reliabilities of both the job sample scores and real-time scores were high (.81-.85), but the correlation between them was much lower (.31). By comparison, for the Project A data, if the average correlation (across MOS) between the first tour hands-on (job sample) measures and the single rating of overall performance is corrected to the same level of reliability as the variables in the Sackett et al. study, the mean intercorrelation is about .30. That is, when corrected for differences in reliability, the correlation between standardized and naturally occurring job sample measures is about the same as the correlation between a standardized job sample and a single rating of overall performance.

If the research goal is not the validation of selection and classification procedures but the evaluation of the effectiveness of specific skills training programs, then the measurement goal is quite different. In such a context, the motivational determinants should be controlled. The research goal is to find out whether people have, in fact, mastered the skills. Choosing to actually use the skills back on the job is a separate issue. Lack of transfer should not be blamed on lack of mastery if the training program is, in fact, not guilty.

By similar reasoning, if the research goal is to evaluate the effects of new supervisory practices that are hypothesized to work because they influence subordinate motivation, then it is knowledge and skill that should be held constant by the measurement procedure. It would be undesirable to confound changes in subordinate motivation with changes in skill if the objective is to evaluate the supervisor as a motivator.

The moral of the story is that, insofar as possible, the performance measures used as validation criteria should control for unwanted sources of variation and allow the relevant determinants to operate.

The Goals of Selection and Classification

One final consideration is the variety of alternative goals that might be adopted for selection and classification itself. Certainly attempting to maximize aggregate performance and attempting to minimize attrition are two relatively different goals, and they have different implications for criterion measurement. However, it is also possible to talk about maximizing performance on different components of performance or about minimizing different components of attrition. For some components, the specific determinants may be different enough across jobs, or MOS, to make classification worthwhile (e.g., see Johnson, Zeidner, & Scholarios, 1990), but for others it may not. This could be as true for attrition as it is for performance. Also, the nature of differential prediction across subgroups (e.g., race or gender) may be different for different performance components.

The questions of (a) how to make choices or trade-offs among selection/classification goals (e.g., should the system emphasize increasing technical performance or reducing attrition, and to what degree?) or (b) how to combine information from multiple criterion components to make selection/classification decisions are not defined away by any of the models. The multiple factor models simply make them more explicit. The unifactor models resolve these issues by default before any analysis is ever done.

SUMMARY

A set of eight alternative models of job performance have been briefly reviewed. Given the measurement goal of providing criteria for evaluating selection and classification procedures, some of the models seem much more useful than others. For example, the unifactor models cover up too much information in unknown ways. The models that emphasize bottom-line results (or effectiveness) advocate a measurement method that is by definition contaminated, probably to an unknown extent. The critical task model and the multiple factor models have much to recommend them if a multiple-stage selection and classification strategy is possible, as it seems to be in all military services. However, using these models effectively requires a good research base that indicates which components are common across assignments and which are distinctive. Finally, the multiple factor and National Research Council models highlight the need to carefully consider the sources of variation that should influence criterion scores and those that should not. Insofar as possible, the criterion construction procedure should produce measures that allow the appropriate determinants to operate.

REFERENCES

Abrahams, N. M., Neumann, I., & Githens, W. H. (1968). *The SVIB in predicting NROTC officer retention.* San Diego: U.S. Naval Personnel Research and Development Center.

Ackerman, P. L. (1988). Determinants of individual differences during skill acquisition: Cognitive abilities and information processing. *Journal of Experimental Psychology: General, 117,* 288-318.

Anderson, J. R. (1985). *Cognitive psychology and its implications* (2nd ed.). New York: W. H. Freeman.

Armor, D., Fernandez, R., Bers, K., & Schwarzbach, D. (1982). *Recruit aptitudes and Army job performance* (R-2874-MRAL). Santa Monica, CA: RAND Corp.

Bray, D. W., Campbell, R. J., & Grant, D. L. (1974). *Formative years in business.* New York: Wiley.

Campbell, C. H., Ford, P., Rumsey, M. G., Pulakos, E. D., Borman, W. C., Felker, D. B., De Vera, M. V., & Riegelhaupt, B. J. (1990). Development of multiple job performance measures in a representative sample of jobs. *Personnel Psychology, 43*(2), 277-300.

Campbell, J. P. (1990). An overview of the Army Selection and Classification Project (Project A). *Personnel Psychology, 43*(2), 231-239.

Campbell, J. P., McCloy, R. A., Oppler, S. H., & Sager, C. E. (1992). A theory of performance. In N. Schmitt & W. Borman (Eds.), *New developments in selection and placement.* San Francisco: Jossey-Bass.

Campbell, J. P., McHenry, J. J., & Wise, L. L. (1990). Modeling job performance in a population of jobs. *Personnel Psychology, 43*(2), 313-333.

Cooper, W. H. (1981). Conceptual similarity as a source of illusory halo in job performance ratings. *Journal of Applied Psychology, 66,* 302-307.

DeNisi, A. S., Cafferty, T. P., & Meglino, B. M. (1984). A cognitive view of the performance appraisal process: A model and research propositions. *Organizational Behavior and Human Performance, 33,* 360-396.

Felker, D. B., Crafts, J. L., Bowler, E. C., Martin, M. F., Hilburn, B. G., McGarvey, D., & Rose, A. M. (1991). *Developing and administering job performance measures for three USMC occupational areas* (Mechanical Maintenance Final Report). Washington, DC: American Institutes for Research.

Fisher-Hazucha, J. (1991). Success, jeopardy, and performance: Contrasting managerial outcomes and their predictors. Unpublished doctoral dissertation, University of Minnesota, Minneapolis.

Grafton, F., Czarnolweski, M. Y., & Smith, E. P. (1989). *Relationship between Project A psychomotor and spatial tests and TOW2 gunnery performance: A preliminary investigation* (Selection and Classification Technical Area Working Paper WP-RS-89-1). Alexandria, VA: U.S. Army Research Institute.

Ilgen, D. R., & Feldman, J. M. (1983). Performance appraisal: A process focus. In B. M. Staw & L. L. Cummings (Eds.), *Research in Organizational Behavior* (Vol. 5, pp. 141-197). Greenwich, CT: JAI Press.

Ilgen, D. R., Fisher, C. D., & Taylor, M. S. (1979). Consequences of individual feedback on behavior in organizations. *Journal of Applied Psychology, 64,* 349-371.

Ilgen, D. R., & Klein, H. J. (1988). Individual motivation and performance: Cognitive influences on effort and choice. In J. P. Campbell & R. J. Campbell (Eds.), *Productivity in organizations.* San Francisco: Jossey-Bass.

Johnson, C. D., Zeidner, J., & Scholarios, D. (1990). *Improving the classification validity of the ASVAB through the use of alternative test selection indices* (IDA Paper P-2427). Alexandria, VA: Institute for Defense Analysis.

Kanfer, R. (1990). Motivation theory and industrial/organizational psychology. In M. D. Dunnette (Ed.), *Handbook of Industrial and Organizational Psychology* (2nd ed., Vol. I). Palo Alto, CA: Consulting Psychologists Press.

Kanfer, R., & Ackerman, P. L. (1989). Motivation and cognitive abilities: An integrative-aptitude-treatment interaction approach to skill acquisition. *Journal of Applied Psychology, 74,* 657-690.

Landy, F. J., & Farr, J. L. (1980). Performance rating. *Psychological Bulletin, 87,* 72-107.

Mahoney, T. A. (1988). Productivity defined. The relativity of efficiency, effectiveness, and change. In J. P. Campbell & R. J. Campbell (Eds.), *Productivity in organizations*. San Francisco: Jossey-Bass.

Mobley, W. H., Griffith, R. W., Hand, H. H., & Meglino, B. M. (1979). Review of the conceptual of the employee turnover process. *Psychological Bulletin, 86*, 493-522.

Nathan, B. R., & Alexander, R. A. (1988). A comparison of criteria for test validation: A meta analytic investigation. *Personnel Psychology, 41*, 517-536.

Nissen, M. J., & Bullmer, P. (1987). Attentional requirements of learning: Evidence from performance measures. *Cognitive Psychology, 19*, 1-32.

Rousseau, D. M. (1989). *Psychological contracts in recruitment*. Paper presented at the Society of Industrial and Organizational Psychology, Boston.

Sackett, P. R., Zedeck, S., & Fogli, L. (1988). Relations between measures of typical and maximum job performance. *Journal of Applied Psychology, 73*, 482-486.

Schein, E. H. (1970). *Organizational psychology* (2nd ed.). Englewood Cliffs, NJ: Prentice-Hall.

Schmitt, N., Gooding, R. Z., Noe, R. A., & Kirsch, M. (1984). Meta-analysis of validity studies published between 1964 and 1982 and the investigation of study characteristics. *Personnel Psychology, 37*, 407-422.

Thorndike, R. L. (1949). *Personnel selection: Test and measurement techniques*. New York: Wiley.

White, L. A., Nord, R., & Mael, F. A. (1990). *Setting enlistment standards on the ABLE to reduce attrition*. Paper presented at the Army Science conference, Washington, DC.

Wigdor, A. K., & Green, B. F. (Eds.) (1991). *Performance assessment for the workplace: Report of the Committee on the Performance of Military Personnel, National Research Council*. Washington, DC: National Academy Press.

4

ORGANIZATIONAL CITIZENSHIP BEHAVIOR AND THE GOOD SOLDIER

Dennis W. Organ
Indiana University

The term *organizational citizenship behavior* (OCB) is of uncertain lineage. I cannot say for sure whether it was my invention or was suggested by Tom Bateman or Ann Smith when one or the other was a doctoral student at Indiana University. But the purpose of the term, that is, its referent, was never in doubt. It was seized upon to denote a class of job behaviors that are separate from in-role productivity but were presumed to be affected by a participant's job satisfaction.

THEORY AND RESEARCH ON OCB: THE EARLY STUDIES

In 1977, I published in the *Academy of Management Review* a paper intended to provide a rationale for, and thus some respectability to, the then-battered hypothesis that satisfaction causes performance. At that time, there was scant empirical basis to support such a "conventional wisdom" view. In brief, I argued that the empirical tests of the hypothesis dealt with too narrow a concept of performance. We should not expect an attitude (such as job satisfaction) to have much to do with conventional measures of productivity, because the latter—to the extent that it can vary—is more a function of ability than attitude.

And, in truth, productivity often does not vary appreciably, due to constraints imposed by technology, work flow interdependence, and exogenous determinants of the actual amount of work to do be done. Finally, one must reckon with the costs of translating dissatisfaction into low productivity. Whereas that no doubt can and does happen occasionally, more generally even dissatisfied participants would not wish to incur the sanctions (verbal reprimands, probation status, discharge) invited by low productivity.

I suggested that we look at the more discretionary work behaviors that contribute to a group's or organization's effectiveness, particularly those not likely to be constrained by ability, but rather by intent. Thus, one might expect the more satisfied employees to be more likely to do those things that are valued by supervisors and management officials, but that are not enforceable job requirements and not contractually rewarded by the organization. At that time I had no coherent category system for describing or defining such "things." I simply offered some examples, such as lending a hand to a hard-pressed co-worker, helping to orient a new hire, cooperating actively (as opposed to dragging one's feet) with management to implement new methods of operation, exhibiting attendance and punctuality beyond the required norm, observing the intent or spirit of rules rather than their minimal literal rendering, making constructive suggestions for improvements, and "rolling with the punches" so as to tolerate periodic inconveniences when they arise rather than making a fuss about them.

The rationale I offered for why a satisfied person would more likely exhibit such behaviors took essentially the form of the rule of reciprocity, that is, a basic equity notion. When people are satisfied, presumably they have received treatment they appreciate and would choose to return the favor. To reciprocate, they would choose those behaviors of which they are capable, that are not constrained by the situation, that are volitional, and that they have reason to believe their benefactors (i.e., management, the supervisor) would appreciate. In sum, when managers say they believe that satisfaction causes performance, they are not obtuse; they simply include more in their notion of performance than industrial psychologists had hitherto been wont to measure. Implicitly, they are thinking in terms of a gratitude hypothesis that has some basis in social psychological theory.

The Bateman and Organ Study (1983)

To this point I engaged in the craft of devil's advocacy rather than self-consciously designing a program of research. But when one says something in print, some readers will take it seriously, as did a doctoral student, Tom Bateman. He set forth in his dissertation (the findings of which were reported in Bateman & Organ, 1983) at Indiana University to develop a measure of what he called "nonquantitative performance"—what we now call OCB—to see how it would correlate with job satisfaction.

His measure was an ungainly one that has been much improved on, so it is not included in the appendix. But using that measure in a cross-lagged panel design with 77 nonacademic university employees (rated by their supervisors), he found a correlation of .41 between "nonquantitative performance" and job satisfaction; the static correlations were the same .41 at two testings six weeks apart. Moreover, initial job satisfaction correlated .43 with the performance measure taken six weeks later. This was a substantially higher correlation than had generally been found between job satisfaction and traditional (in-role) performance measures.

At some point between the time of this study and that of the next one I will report, the term *OCB* came into usage to describe these discretionary, volitional contributions that go beyond in-role productivity. I wish to call attention right now, however, to two considerations essential to interpreting the larger program of research.

First, note that all of this came about from the idea of "finding something that will correlate with job satisfaction." In other words, we did not start out with OCB as a phenomenon to be understood and explained in its own right, but as a candidate to restore to respectability the satisfaction causes performance hypothesis.

Second, and this will become more obvious later in this chapter, OCB in its origins had a managerial bias. The emphasis was on contributions, of course, but grounded in the kind of contributions that supervisors and managers would appreciate. The point is that had we started out otherwise, we might have allowed for some forms of OCB that are not born of satisfaction (indeed, might well arise from some form of dissatisfaction) and for others that managers might not appreciate so keenly.

The Smith, Organ, and Near Study (1983)

As noted previously, the measure used by Bateman, while acceptable for an exploratory look at the issue of interest, presented no grounds for complacency: It did not yield an interpretable factor structure, it included some items of questionable relevance, and it might well have included a few items constituting, in effect, a hidden measure of satisfaction. Ann Smith, another doctoral student at Indiana University, set forth with OCB as the focus, hoping to identify other antecedent variables in addition to job satisfaction, and to craft an improved OCB measure.

Smith began by interviewing first-line supervisors at several firms in the Bloomington (IN) area. She asked them to identify employee behaviors they valued, but could not demand, coerce, or reward in a tangible fashion (such as with increased pay or benefits or better working conditions). From these she fashioned a scale of 16 items (see the appendix to this chapter). She then showed these items to a group of 67 managerial and professional people enrolled in an evening MBA class, asking them to think of an individual who had worked for them and to rate that person on each of the items.

Factor analysis of the responses revealed two dimensions that were readily interpretable. The first factor we called *Altruism*, because the items comprising it referred to helping a specific person (either a co-worker or the supervisor) in a direct way. The second factor we labeled *Generalized Compliance*, and it captured the more impersonal forms of reliable, conscientious behavior, such as punctuality, attendance, not wasting time, and observing the rules. In later writings, I chose the term *Conscientiousness* to denote this factor, feeling that the word *compliance* connoted a servile posture.

In every study using Smith's items or some larger version of them, we have found at least two such dimensions—Altruism and Conscientiousness—to emerge from the analysis. In some instances, attendance-related items dropped out onto a third factor separate from the other conscientiousness items. Empirically, then, we have a basis for distinguishing at least two dimensions of OCB that have rather clear and straightforward conceptual meaning. We speculated early on, at least intuitively, that these different forms of OCB might well have different determinants, whether from a motivational or a personality standpoint.

The main part of Smith's study involved 422 employees of two large banks in a major metropolitan area. As predicted, job satisfaction correlated significantly with both Altruism and Conscientiousness (.33 and .29, respectively). (Incidentally, every study of which I am aware that has looked at job satisfaction and these two OCB factors has found Altruism to relate more strongly with satisfaction than did Conscientiousness, a point addressed later in the chapter.) Contrary to hypothesis, neither work group interdependence nor the respondent's "belief in a just world" had any reliable association with either Altruism or Conscientiousness. The personality trait neuroticism indirectly related to altruism through the former's correlation with job satisfaction. Net of satisfaction, education level, and small town/rural background accounted for a modest portion of the variance in Altruism.

Interestingly, while job satisfaction correlated significantly with Conscientiousness, the best-fitting path model predicting this factor of OCB did not show satisfaction to be a direct effect. The direct determinants were, rather, supervisory supportiveness, small town/rural background, and the four-item "lie scale" located in the short form of the Eysenck Personality Inventory (Eysenck, 1958).

The predictive power of the lie scale at first seemed like a quirky finding. It could not be dismissed as an artifact of common method variance, because OCB ratings came from the supervisor. Our initial interpretation was that the lie scale, because of the patent social desirability content of the items, captured something like a need for approval, which indeed makes some sense as a predictor of generally conscientious behavior.

Alternatively, responses to the lie scale might not be lies at all, or any other kind of artifact, but genuinely descriptive accounts of how a person tries to act—that is, lawfully, politely, dependably, conscientiously. Further, a number of articles have appeared since that time suggesting that scales intended to reflect socially desirable responding actually provide something of substance; they are not merely a means of checking for the existence of some artifact or bias, but a plausible index of a stable personality trait.

The Williams Study (1989)

Larry Williams conducted a dissertation research project (findings eventually reported in Williams & Anderson, 1991) that provided additional construct validity for the OCB measures. He mixed items defining altruism, conscientious-ness, and in-role performance in a larger scale. This scale was distributed to a large number of full-time employees enrolled in an evening MBA program. Subjects were asked to rate themselves on the OCB and in-role performance items; in addition, each subject was asked to take additional copies to a co-worker and to his or her immediate superior for independent ratings of the subject—thus providing three independent sources of measurement of a group of subjects' in-role performance, altruism, and conscientiousness.

Williams found that for all three sources of ratings, confirmatory factor analysis resulted in a three-factor solution. All items loaded on their appropriate factors. These results strongly support the assumption that raters distinguish OCB from in-role performance (i.e., performance that meets job requirements and/or qualifies contractually for system rewards) and that they distinguish altruism and conscientiousness from each other, as well as from in-role performance.

OCB: SATISFACTION, FAIRNESS, AND AFFECT

As noted at the outset, our work on OCB originated with the intent of finding a variation or dimension of performance that would associate with job satisfaction. We appear to have succeeded in doing that, at least to some degree. At least 15 studies at Indiana and elsewhere have tested, among other hypotheses, the notion that job satisfaction relates to OCB, and the findings are invariably positive—Athough with varying levels of magnitude. The median correlation to date hovers around .30, which of course leaves much OCB unaccounted for, but comfortably exceeds the .14 that Vroom (1964) reported (and with which later meta-analyses basically agreed with) as the median correlation of satisfaction with traditional performance measures.

Recent work on OCB has sought to explain why there is a robust empirical connection with job satisfaction. Space does not permit a detailed account of this work. Suffice it to say that we have tried, first, to sort out the affective versus cognitive components presumably underlying job satisfaction as a measured attitude; and second, to explore the possibility that common causes—anotably dispositional (i.e., personality) variables—perhaps underlie the covariance between satisfaction and OCB.

Originally, our guiding hunch was that people contribute OCB out of a sense of reciprocity or fairness. We soon became aware, however, of a growing body of research in social psychology (much of this work done by Alice Isen, e.g., Isen & Baron, 1991) demonstrating that mood state has much to do with many forms of prosocial behavior, such as helping a stranger, donating to a worthy cause, sharing resources with friends, and the like. On the face of it, OCB has much in common with the episodic prosocial behavior studied by the social psychologist in naturalistic settings. Thus, the correlation between job satisfaction and OCB would be consistent not only with a cognitive (perceived fairness) basis for OCB, but also with an affective basis.

Sorting out the relative importance of cognitive versus affective determinants of OCB is of interest for at least three reasons. To begin with, a growing body of empirical work now indicates that satisfaction measures—whether having to do with work, life, or community—tell us more about the cognitive assessments of the respondent than about the happiness or feelings of the person (Campbell, 1976). The presumption, then, is that job satisfaction scores reflect more of the variance in people's assessments of the workplace than of their characteristic mood state (Organ & Near, 1985). If so, and if the basis for OCB is affective mood state, then the job satisfaction-OCB correlations would understate the magnitude of the effect of mood on OCB.

Further, the work of David Watson (e.g., Watson & Clark, 1984; Watson & Tellegen, 1985) offers a compelling view of affectivity as a dispositional variable. While certainly not denying that situational factors influence mood states, Watson's research and analysis indicate that personality has much to do with whether an employee tends characteristically toward a good or bad mood at work. Therefore, if mood state is the predominant influence on OCB, we would be led toward thinking of OCB as largely determined by temperament or disposition—with obvious implications for the personnel selection and placement process.

On the other hand, if we were to conclude that OCB has less to do with mood than with participants' perceptions of fair treatment, we would be less concerned with selection than with managing in a fashion that meets consensually shared criteria of equity. We would manage not so much to "keep people happy" as to "give them a fair shake."

Thus, Organ and Konovsky (1989) sought to compare cognitive and affective factors in terms of their respective abilities to account for variance in OCB. In their field study of over 200 professional and clerical employees of two hospitals, they found only cognitive assessments to account for unique variance in OCB. Positive and negative affective mood states added nothing to the regression equation once cognitive appraisals had been entered. Conversely, cognitions (essentially those pertaining to fairness in pay and work conditions) contributed significantly to variance explained in OCB after the affective measures had been entered.

Organ and Konovsky, noting this apparent discrepancy with social psychological studies of mood and prosocial behavior, suggested that sustained OCB over long periods of employment is of a different character than one-shot, hit-and-run episodes of helping a stranger or contributing to a charity. They argued that OCB is a set of controlled behaviors, susceptible to thoughtful and deliberate intentions arising from perceptions of fair treatment.

In a separate study, Farh, Podsakoff, and Organ (1990) used three scales to comprise a factor corresponding to perceived leader fairness, and found that job satisfaction had no relation to OCB once the leader fairness factor was taken into account. Much of the work at Indiana University has proceeded from this point to assume that fairness perceptions strongly influence OCB, and takes as its major task that of ferreting out how various aspects of fairness—i.e., distributive justice, procedural justice, interactional justice—compare in their relation to OCB.

In contrast to the conclusions reached at Indiana, the work of Jennifer George and others at Texas A&M University still argues for the importance of affective states in determining OCB. George (1991) maintained that the Organ and Konovsky study used a measure of affect that led respondents to focus on too long a time period—in effect, producing a measure of trait rather than state affectivity, and thus understating the role of affect in OCB. George, using what she contended is the proper measure of affective states, reported a strong connection between mood and the measure of OCB.

What we have, then, is a controversy of sorts regarding the importance of affective mood state as it bears on OCB.

OCB AND DISPOSITION

Regardless of the position one takes on the affect versus cognitions (i.e., mood state versus perceived fairness) debate, there is abundant reason for pursuing the trail of dispositional determinants of OCB. If one grants major importance to mood state, the case for OCB as dispositional becomes almost presumptive, given the well-established case for negative and positive affectivity as traits. Even if one discounts the role of temporary mood state, however, the fact remains that something in job satisfaction robustly correlates with OCB, and there is now persuasive evidence that much (maybe even half) of the variance in measured job satisfaction is dispositional in nature (e.g., Arvey, Bouchard, Segal, & Abraham, 1989; Staw, Bell, & Clausen, 1986).

Thus, any trait or traits—whether affectively toned or not—that reliably relate to satisfaction could well account for the observed correlation between satisfaction and OCB. Indeed, even if perceptions of fairness comprise the critical influence on OCB, one could argue that such perceptions derive in considerable degree from dispositional differences. Finally, the correlations found between job satisfaction and OCB leave much of the variance in OCB unexplained, so it could be that traits having nothing to do with satisfaction might well explain additional variance.

At Indiana, we have turned to the work of McCrae and Costa (1987) on the Big Five factor model of personality to inform our search for dispositional linkages to OCB. Two of the Big Five dimensions would seem to have obvious relevance for OCB. One, agreeableness, pertains to the ease or difficulty one has in getting along with other people, or how good-natured one is with respect to interpersonal relations. We would expect persons scoring high in this dimension, first of all, to generally report higher satisfaction with work and especially with the people with whom they work. Also, whether or not this is a consequence of the preceding statement, we would expect the more agreeable person to render more OCB in the forms that help specific individuals.

Another of the Big Five, conscientiousness, has more in common with one of our OCB dimensions than just the label. The items that load on this factor have to do with reliability, dependability, neatness, punctuality, discipline, and the like. These adjectives define something like a personal code for adhering to certain standards in one's conduct, and they do not seem to be anchored in face-to-face interaction or the give-and-take relationships with others. We thought this would be good predictor of the like-named form of OCB, and we also speculated that it might well predict job satisfaction. After all, work organizations often stress the importance of such characteristics in people.

We undertook a study (Organ & Lingl, 1992) to test whether these two dimensions of dispositional differences could account for OCB, and, if so, whether they do so in a fashion mediated by job satisfaction or independently of satisfaction or both. Furthermore, we took the occasion to try to go beyond the the original two-factor version of OCB to look at additional factors described in Organ (1988a, 1988b, 1990). We composed items aimed at describing courtesy, or the things people do to help prevent problems from arising for other people; sportsmanship, the degree to which people bear occasional inconveniences without fuss; and civic virtue, or how well people keep up with developments in the organization and bear some responsibility for governance and constructive political involvement in the issues affecting the organization. (See the appendix for a description of this five-factor measurement version.)

As it happened, our first try along these lines met with some disappointment. We were given access to only 99 employees in two manufacturing facilities in two different countries. Doing the best we could with what we had—recognizing the limited statistical power for doing the analyses we had in mind—the results were nonetheless of interest. First, and of less interest, the OCB items did not fit a neat five-factor model. The most parsimonious and interpretable model showed something like the usual altruism factor; a conscientiousness factor that actually picked up some of the civic virtue and courtesy items; and a smaller factor (four items) defined by attendance, promptness, and use of time.

Of more substantive interest, the agreeableness dispositional dimension had a strong relationship with satisfaction, particularly satisfaction with co-workers and supervision. However, it had no direct relation to OCB once satisfaction was held constant. On the other hand, the conscientiousness dispositional factor had a strong negative relationship with satisfaction with co-workers and supervisors. In retrospect, this makes some sense. Conscientious people have high standards and often try to enforce them on others; they can be critical of people who don't readily accept those standards, and the result could be more strained relations with people at work and all that this implies. But when this negative effect on satisfaction is held constant, conscientiousness had a positive connection with the Conscientiousness factor of OCB.

Previously, we had always found stronger correlations between satisfaction and Altruism than we had found between satisfaction and Conscientiousness. The results of the study of disposition and OCB offer an explanation of why this should happen. If satisfaction affects OCB positively, then anything that simultaneously affects satisfaction negatively but OCB positively will act to lower the overall zero correlation between satisfaction and OCB. In other words, the dispositional variable Conscientiousness acts as a suppressor variable when the more impersonal form of OCB is regressed on satisfaction.

In a follow-up study (Konovsky & Organ, 1992) of personality, satisfaction, perceived fairness, and OCB, we obtained access to a much larger group, permitting much greater statistical power (over 400 respondents). Again, we sought to distinguish five categories of OCB, and this time did so successfully. In addition to a satisfaction measure, we had a separate measure of perceived fairness. In addition to agreeableness and conscientiousness from the Big Five model, we used Huseman, Hatfield, and Miles' (1985) scale designed to measure equity sensitivity.

We found that agreeableness accounted for unique variance in fairness perceptions; however, none of the personality measures added to the substantial variance in satisfaction explained by fairness. Fairness explained unique variance in sportsmanship and courtesy; satisfaction accounted for unique variance in Altruism; and Conscientiousness as a personality factor explained unique variance in the Conscientiousness form of OCB. None of the intended predictors —personality, fairness, or satisfaction—could account for a reliable portion of the variance in civic virtue. [Another study done as a doctoral dissertation at Indiana University and subsequently published by Moorman (1991) also failed to explain a statistically significant amount of variance in civic virtue.]

The clear thrust of the combined studies is that Conscientiousness accounts for certain elements in OCB, and does so independently of any connection to fairness or satisfaction. The findings support and extend those of earlier studies in granting a pivotal role to perceived fairness—which directly affects two of the OCB factors, and indirectly (via satisfaction) explains an appreciable portion of the variance in a third OCB factor.

We also have just completed two studies with students (one study experimental, one cross-sectional) on Type A behavior syndrome (TABS), time pressure, and OCB. Without going into the details, it may be noted that, contrary to what some might have guessed, we found no evidence that TABS has any negative effect on OCB. In fact, we saw rather an indication that one dimension of TABS—described as an achievement-striving subscale of TABS— appears to relate positively to at least the conscientiousness form of OCB, especially under conditions of time pressure. This finding suggests that the achievement-striving dimension of the Jenkins Activity survey (Jenkins, Zyzanski, & Rosenman, 1979) taps a construct analogous to the Conscientiousness dimension of the Big Five.

CONCLUSION

For ease of exposition I have limited my report to the work directly associated with Indiana University. Of necessity, this account omits much independent and important work at other institutions that has, in fact, informed some of our work. Overall, I believe much of the work done elsewhere—while using different nomenclature, such as "extra-role behavior" and "prosocial organization behavior" —has produced results consistent with those described in this narrative.

A major exception to the preceding statement, as indicated earlier, is that the work of Jennifer George assigns more importance to the role of positive and negative mood state than we have found supportable at Indiana University. What I think we are seeing here is another form of the debate that has for many years reverberated among students of human behavior. The basic underlying question is: Do people act primarily on the basis of their feelings or their beliefs?

Of course, to the extent that feelings and beliefs are concordant with each other, the answer may not be of practical importance. But the work of Zajonc (1980) suggests that feeling and beliefs are not as coincident as once assumed, and even suggests that they are controlled by systems somewhat independent of each other. It will be interesting to see if future work on OCB can address this question more directly.

The work on OCB as it has evolved at Indiana University has not gone without criticisms, some of them well grounded. As noted earlier, the development of our measures of OCB was almost certainly biased by the intent to find a type of performance that correlated with job satisfaction. But to take OCB on its own terms—contributions to organizational effectiveness beyond those mandated by job requirements or contractually rewarded by the system—one would almost certainly have to allow for contributions that come from people who are in some sense dissatisfied—that is, critical of the system and/or its leaders, practices, policies. We have yet to correct for this oversight.

Also, again as noted earlier, the seeds of our development of measures of OCB gave it a managerial bias. Operationally, OCB has come to measure "what managers appreciate." This defines away the contributions to the larger organization that supervisors or managers don't covet. Some contributions might come from actions that make managers unhappy because such actions are implicitly critical of management, make the manager's job more difficult, or otherwise threaten management's interest. Managers are well placed to see the bigger picture of organizational effectiveness, but it is not their exclusive prerogative to say what constitutes effectiveness, nor are their views perfectly correlated with those of stockholders, customers, and other stakeholder groups.

In truth, the work on OCB has proceeded on an article of faith, to wit, that we can identify some discretionary behaviors that contribute to organizational effectiveness. Of course, we and everyone else are hard pressed to provide a comprehensive operational definition of organizational effectiveness. Even if we could, we would still be hard pressed to prove that a certain set of behaviors brought about that effectiveness. Still, it would be nice to have even suggestive data beyond the anecdotal level that OCB is associated with convincing indicators of effectiveness.

Not surprisingly, we have met with arguments that much of what we have been measuring as OCB does not even fit the definition. The charge is that such things as good attendance, punctuality, keeping up with the issues, perhaps even training new employees and offering suggestions, are usually expected by those with whom or for whom one works. Our position has consistently been yes, to some extent they are job requirements (formally or otherwise), but only up to some minimally enforceable levels; going beyond those levels becomes OCB.

Thus, we readily admit to some imperfections in methods and measures, as well as incompleteness in conceptual framework. We hope to improve on some of these things; we can surely expect that others will have the incentive to do so.

Briefly to note the influence that the work on OCB has had, I would say that first of all we are now seeing in the research on organizational behavior and human resource management (OB/HRM) a more complex conceptualization, measurement, and interpretation of performance. Instead of narrowly defined productivity measures or global performance ratings, we see increasing attempts to get at the variety of ways in which people contribute to organizational effectiveness, some of which the system does not often take formal account.

Second, I think we have in some small way restored some credibility to managers who contend that job satisfaction is important because it can affect a person's performance. To this extent, we have provided a corrective to the view of some that satisfaction doesn't matter, and we have made a case for why managing for satisfaction isn't just a humanistic add-on. Third, along with some other recent research programs, we have begun to restore to prominence the agenda for research on dispositional determinants of behavior at work.

Ultimately, I think an extension of this work will be shown to have serious implications for HR practices, such as reward systems, appraisal, and selection. Just to cite one example, the much-maligned selection interview, even if of doubtful incremental validity for predicting technical excellence or in-role productivity, might well contribute to recognizing person-specific attributes that predict OCB. Indeed, my impression is that the work that has gone into the Army's Project A (Campbell, 1990) has, independent of the work at Indiana University, suggested quite a bit along these lines. This convergence strongly reinforces my confidence in the value of what we have been doing.

APPENDIX

A.   Two-Factor Measure of Organizational Citizenship Behavior

Altruism

1.   Helps other employees with their work when they have been absent.
2.   Volunteers to do things not formally required by the job.
3.   Takes the initiative to orient new employees to the department even though it is not part of his or her job description.
4.   Helps others when their work loads increase (assists others until they get over the hurdles).
5.   Assists me [the supervisor] with my duties.
6.   Makes innovative suggestions to improve the overall quality of the department.

Conscientiousness

1.   Exhibits punctuality in arriving at work on time in the morning and after lunch and breaks.
2.   Takes undeserved work breaks. (r)*
3.   Exhibits attendance at work beyond the norm.
4.   Gives advance notice if unable to come to work.
5.   Spends a great deal of time in personal telephone conversations. (r)
6.   Does not take unnecessary time off work.
7.   Does not take extra breaks.
8.   Does not spend a great deal of time in idle conversation.

B.   Proposed Five-Factor Measure of Organizational Citizenship Behavior

Altruism

1.   Helps others who have been absent.
2.   Helps others who have heavy work loads.
3.   Helps orient new people even though it is not required.
4.   Shares personal property when necessary to help others who have work-related problems.
5.   Willingly gives of his or her time to help others who have work-related problems.
6.   Is someone to whom co-workers often turn for help on the job.

Conscientiousness

1. Is always punctual.
2. Attendance at work is above the norm.
3. Takes undeserved breaks. (r)
4. Maintains a clean workplace.
5. Follows company rules, regulations, and procedures.
6. Spends a lot of time in idle conversation. (r)

Courtesy

1. Is mindful of how his or her behavior affects other people's jobs.
2. Respects the rights and privileges of others.
3. Respects other people's rights to common or shared resources.
4. Informs others of what he or she is doing in order to prevent unanticipated problems.
5. Is courteous in his or her interactions with others.
6. Tries to avoid creating problems for co-workers.

Sportsmanship

1. Always finds fault with what the organization is doing. (r)
2. Tends to make "mountains out of molehills." (r)
3. Consumes a lot of time complaining about trivial matters. (r)
4. Constantly talks about wanting to quit his or her job. (r)
5. Always focuses on what's wrong with his or her situation rather than the positive side of it. (r)
6. Expresses resentment with any new changes in the department. (r)

Civic Virtue

1. Reads and keeps up with organization announcements, messages, memos, etc.
2. Attends and participates in meetings regarding the organization.
3. Keeps abreast of developments in the company.
4. Keeps abreast of changes in the organization.
5. Takes an active role in workplace governance.
6. Demonstrates concern about the image of the company.

* (r) = reversed scoring

REFERENCES

Arvey, R. D., Bouchard, T. J., Jr., Segal, N. L., & Abraham, L. M. (1989). Job satisfaction: Environmental and genetic components. *Journal of Applied Psychology, 74,* 187-192.

Bateman, T. S., & Organ, D. W. (1983). Job satisfaction and the good soldier: The relationship between affect and employee "citizenship." *Academy of Management Journal, 26,* 587-595.

Campbell, A. (1976). Subjective measures of well-being. *American Psychologist, 31,* 117-124.

Campbell, J. P. (1990). An overview of the Army Selection and Classification Project (Project A). *Personnel Psychology* (Special Issue), *43*(2), 231-239.

Eysenck, H. J. (1958). A short questionnaire for the measurement of two dimensions of personality. *Journal of Applied Psychology, 42,* 14-17.

Farh, J., Podsakoff, P. M., & Organ, D. W. (1990). Accounting for organizational citizenship behavior: Leader fairness and task scope versus satisfaction. *Journal of Management, 16,* 705-722.

George, J. M. (1991). State or trait: Effects of positive mood on prosocial behaviors at work. *Journal of Applied Psychology, 76,* 299-307.

Huseman, R. C., Hatfield, J. D., & Miles, E. W. (1985). Test for individual perceptions of job equity: Some preliminary findings. *Perceptual and Motor Skills, 61,* 1055-1064.

Isen, A. M., & Baron, R. A. (1991). Positive affect as a factor in organizational behavior. In L. L. Cummings, & B. M. Staw, (Eds.), *Research in Organizational Behavior* (Vol. 13, pp. 1-53). Greenwich, CT: JAI Press.

Jenkins, C. D., Zyzanski, S. J., & Rosenman, R. H. (1979). *Manual for the Jenkins Activity Survey.* New York: Psychological Corporation.

Konovsky, M. A., & Organ, D. W. (1992). *Personality, satisfaction, and fairness: Sorting out their linkages with organizational citizenship behavior.* Unpublished manuscript, Tulane University, New Orleans.

McCrae, R. R., & Costa, P. T., Jr. (1987). Validation of the five-factor model of personality across instruments and observers. *Journal of Personality and Social Psychology, 52,* 81-90.

Moorman, R. H. (1991). Relationship between organizational justice and organizational citizenship behaviors: Do fairness perceptions influence employee citizenship? *Journal of Applied Psychology, 76,* 845-855.

Organ, D. W. (1977). A reappraisal and reinterpretation of the satisfaction-causes-performance hypothesis. *Academy of Management Review, 2,* 46-53.

Organ, D. W. (1988a). *Organizational citizenship behavior: The Good Soldier syndrome.* Lexington, MA: Lexington Books.

Organ, D. W. (1988b). A restatement of the satisfaction-performance hypothesis. *Journal of Management, 14,* 547-557.

Organ, D. W. (1990). The motivational basis of organizational citizenship behavior. In B. M. Staw, & L. L. Cummings (Eds.), *Research in Organizational Behavior* (Vol. 12, pp. 43-72). Greenwich, CT: JAI Press.

Organ, D. W., & Konovsky, M. (1989). Cognitive versus affective determinants of organizational citizenship behavior. *Journal of Applied Psychology, 74,* 157-164.

Organ, D. W., and Lingl, A. (1992). *Personality, satisfaction, and organizational citizenship behavior.* Paper presented as part of symposium, Academy of Management meetings, Las Vegas.

Organ, D. W., & Near, J. P. (1985). Cognition vs. affect in measures of job satisfaction. *International Journal of Psychology, 20,* 241-253.

Smith, C. A., Organ, D. W., & Near, J. P. (1983). Organizational citizenship behavior: Its nature and antecedents. *Journal of Applied Psychology, 68,* 653-663.

Staw, B. M., Bell, N. E., & Clausen, J. A. (1986). The dispositional approach to job attitudes: A lifetime longitudinal test. *Administrative Science Quarterly, 31,* 56-77.

Vroom, V. H. (1964). *Work and motivation*. New York: Wiley.

Watson, D., & Clark, L. A. (1984). Negative affectivity: The disposition to experience aversive emotional states. *Psychological Bulletin, 96*, 465-490.

Watson, D., & Tellegen, A. (1985). Toward a consensual structure of mood. *Psychological Bulletin, 98*, 219-235.

Williams, L. J., & Anderson, S. E. (1991). Job satisfaction and organizational commitment as predictors of organizational citizenship and in-role behaviors. *Journal of Management, 17*, 601-617.

Zajonc, R. B. (1980). Feeling and thinking: Preferences need no inferences. *American Psychologist, 35*, 151-176.

CHAPTER

5

SELECTING AND CLASSIFYING FUTURE NAVAL OFFICERS: THE PARADOX OF GREATER SPECIALIZATION IN BROADER ARENAS

Jack E. Edwards
Robert F. Morrison
Navy Personnel Research and Development Center

If a civilian organization needs to take a new direction, it has the luxury of seeking a chief executive officer or president from outside the organization. Bringing in outside leadership offers a prime opportunity to redirect an organization's course and establish new procedures and processes that would never have been possible under either the prior leader or a subordinate successor of that leader. The branches of the military have no such luxury. With but few exceptions (e.g., physicians), all officers accept commissions at the lowest level and must have "their tickets punched" in a variety of assignments at each career step. This career progression requires moving through sequential selection boards (for promotions and assignments) to increasingly higher levels of leadership. Thus, decisions made today in selecting, classifying, and assigning officer candidates will be felt continuously for the next 35 years as today's officer candidates attain successively higher positions in the military.

Many changes occur in any organization during a 20- to 35-year career. Thus, there is little wonder why the military spends billions of dollars each year for training. Similarly, learning by doing presents another common method for adapting to gradual changes. In the military, the training and experiential adaptation process will generally be slow because of (a) many military traditions, (b) government regulations (e.g., women in combat exclusion), and (c) selective reinforcement and discipline administered by leaders who have been members of the same organization for most, if not all, of their adult lives. The limitations on changing officers once they have been selected and commissioned hint at the need for effective initial selection. Because some officers will possess characteristics that are more appropriate for some roles and assignments, classification for subsequent assignments, roles, and missions is also important.

CURRENT CONSTRAINTS ON OFFICER SELECTION
AND CLASSIFICATION RESEARCH

At least four assumptions are key to selecting and classifying officers and officer candidates. First, people possess characteristics that are relatively stable across time. Second, these characteristics can be identified and measured. Third, these characteristics are useful in making inferences about an individual's future work-related behaviors. Fourth, some of these characteristics are relevant for predicting performance at multiple levels in the hierarchy, including four-star admiral. Current officer-candidate selection systems (e.g., Edwards, Burch, & Abrahams, 1990) adequately predict grade point average and military course grades at the U. S. Naval Academy or across colleges/universities participating in the Naval Reserve Officers Training Corps. These selection systems do less well in predicting longer-term (e.g., extending service beyond the minimum obligation) and more military-oriented (e.g., probability of promotion) criteria.

In part, these prediction problems are caused by the range restriction that results from the rigorous competition for military academy appointments and reserve officer training corps scholarships. Another, possibly larger, less tractable problem is encountered when data supplied by high school seniors are used to predict subsequent officer behavior. For instance, inferences about which applicants will extend beyond an initial obligation require predictions nine to thirteen years (one year for the selection process, four years at an academy or university, four to six years of initial obligation, and in some instances two additional years for training in special skills for positions such as jet pilot) from the time of application. Further, these individuals are still maturing in their knowledge, skills, abilities, and other characteristics (KSAOs). In essence, predictions are made for a length of time that is equivalent to 50% to 75% of the years that the applicants had been alive when they applied. No other organization puts new leaders/"managers" through a minimum of four years of training before seeking a return on investment.

Predicting promotion potential using the original selection measures is made even more difficult because of a criterion problem. From commissioning through the rank of lieutenant commander, the Navy's promotion system is based primarily on the time that an officer and his or her cohort group have been commissioned. In the first nine years, an officer's progress from ensign to lieutenant is on a specific schedule with an insignificant number selected early or passed over for promotion. Even around the 10-year point, where the officer is reviewed for promotion to lieutenant commander, only about 5% to 10% of the cohort group (that has not resigned from the Navy) fail to be promoted and very few are selected early or late. Thus, until the 14-year point, the ratio of promoted to nonpromoted officers is so high that any validity studies using this bimodal criterion with its extreme base rate cannot improve on one that would identify every officer as promotable.

These long-range prediction problems are magnified when they are combined with changing military missions and, hence, changing officer roles. Borman (1991) warned researchers about the prediction problems caused by changing job requirements. He stated, "Researchers should keep in mind the possibility that job requirements could change sufficiently over time to alter the patterns of validities for predictors of job performance" (p. 277).

Borman's conclusion suggests that a first step in developing new technology for future officer selection and classification is anticipating the changes that will occur. Once those changes are anticipated, selection and classification researchers still face another major concern—how to translate the new or anticipated requirements of the job into person characteristics. For the most part, researchers and practitioners continue to use job-analysis methods that have been available for decades. Massive efforts such as the current review of the *Dictionary of Occupational Titles (DOT)* (Department of Labor, 1992) offer one vehicle for examining and improving current job-analysis methods. One duty of the DOT advisory panel is to "Advise on [the] appropriateness of [the] methodologies of occupational analysis used to identify, classify, define, and describe jobs in the DOT" (p. 10,588).

Because adequate job-analysis information is basic to any well-designed personnel system, improving technology in this area should advance our ability to operationalize, measure, and predict criteria related to officer behavior. While some effort to improve basic job-analysis technology is taking place, no progress has been made on more accurate methods for translating tasks into person characteristics—the basis for developing selection and classification instruments. The use of subject matter experts' judgments needs to be supplanted by new, more accurate techniques.

In the next section, we attempt to anticipate future officer roles, the reasons for the new or altered roles, and general conclusions regarding the selection and classification technology that will be required. This information should furnish personnel researchers who are unfamiliar with military situational concerns with an opportunity to provide input about needs and technologies that we have not anticipated. Although we frequently mention only Naval officers, much of our discussion also pertains to military officers in general. We talk about only Naval officers in some sections for two reasons. First, we are most familiar with that group. Second, differences in missions, officer roles, and so forth may limit the generalizability for some of our conclusions. In the last section, new and adapted technologies for future officer selection and classification are discussed.

CHANGING OFFICER ROLES AND THE SOURCES
OF THOSE CHANGES

Changing Mission

The most significant factor affecting officer roles is the collapse of the Soviet Union. That result, along with other factors (e.g., the Federal budget deficit), has led to calls for massive Department of Defense budget/force reductions and the need to reassess the missions of the various branches of the military. More specifically, the primary mission of the U.S. military formerly was to be prepared to fight a single well-identified enemy using well-developed plans to either counter a nuclear attack or wage a protracted war. Now, military leaders will have more limited resources, but they must be prepared to intervene against multiple smaller opponents in briefer, intense, conventional actions (e.g., Grenada, Panama, and Iraq). The nature and location of these enemies are, however, subject to change (e.g., Iraq changes from friend to enemy). Therefore, battle plans may be less thorough and require coordination of resources from many countries. These battle plans could place U.S. forces as equal participants in, rather than the leaders of, a coalition.

This greater uncertainty as to the nature, location, and so forth of future interventions might require officers who are very different from today's leaders. Rather than basing strategy on battle plans that have been refined over years, today's and tomorrow's leaders might need to be more adaptable and have a more well-rounded set of military experiences. As a result, new emphasis might need to be placed on designing officer-career paths and selecting and classifying officers for anticipated missions, roles, and assignments.

In addition to changing from fighting a single well-identified enemy to many less well-identified enemies, military missions are also being expanded into some areas that are qualitatively different from prior missions. Thus, it must be questioned how current officer selection and classification systems need to be modified to obtain officers who would excel in these new missions and roles. Sinaiko (1992) reported that, in a presentation at the 1991 Armed Forces and Military Service in a Democratic Society conference in Moscow, Colonel Frank Pinch (Director of Condition of Service, Canadian Forces) suggested

> that professional military forces are moving toward the same values, norms, and management practices of the larger society, and he distinguished two opposing concepts. The traditional view of military organizations has been that they are masculine, authoritarian in structure, centered on obligations to the group, homogeneous, and with unlimited liability of their members. In contrast, Pinch referred to a "modern" military concept, characterized as more open to changes and ideas, overlapping civilian society, and providing service in return for monetary

reward. Failure to conform to those norms will lead to withdrawal of public support for the military. (Sinaiko, 1992, p. 14)

General Vigelik Eide (Norway, Chairman of NATO's Military Committee), in another session of the same conference, provided some indications of the roles that will lead to the modern military discussed by Colonel Pinch. General Eide noted, "New military roles will include peacekeeping, relief, arms control, crisis management, and providing early warnings to the political arms of NATO" (quoted from Sinaiko, 1992, p. 11).

Perhaps the most discussed new mission of the U.S. military is drug interdiction. Already more than $1 billion in military spending is devoted to the drug war (Matthews, 1992). Traditionally, this mission has been under the almost exclusive purview of civilian agencies. Responsibilities found in this new mission often use KSAOs that were required for similar military roles (e.g., commanding an airborne platform that monitors flight traffic). Other military roles for the same drug-interdiction activities might require other little-used or, as yet, undeveloped KSAOs. For example, officers aboard ships coordinating interdiction activities with U.S. Coast Guard ships may need supplemental KSAOs. If supplemental KSAOs are necessary, specialty-specific tests and other selection and classification technology might need to be developed. This new technology could help to identify the officers who have the highest probabilities for success in the new roles/assignments that emerge from the changing military missions.

Assignment Issues

Unlike civilian organizations, the military does not allow its officers (managers) to remain in a single location or assignment for the individual's entire career. Instead, the military assigns individuals to a variety of jobs. For example, in a 20-year career, Navy aviators will probably have flying assignments for less than 50% of their careers (Steigman, 1992). Given that officers may be away from their primary specialties for so long, selection and classification of officers to secondary specialties provide opportunities for personnel researchers to increase military readiness.

In essence, each new officer assignment involves at least three selection or classification decisions: which officer characteristics are most needed (i.e., job-analysis information), which officers possess relevant characteristics (i.e., preliminary selection decisions), and which officer-to-assignment pairings result in the best overall fit of the officer pool to the assignment pool (i.e., classification) when several officers are simultaneously being assigned to several billets (i.e., positions). To enhance such decision making, the Navy needs new technology to help officers themselves, selection boards, and detailers more effectively and efficiently match officers' KSAOs to the Navy's needs. This selection and classification technology, however, needs to be designed with anticipated future Navy assignments and roles in mind.

In general, military officers have traditionally functioned as leaders, managers, trainers, coaches, students, and liaisons. In the future, all these roles should continue to be important. The relative importance of these roles will, however, probably change depending on an officer's rank and assignment. For instance, as a Naval officer progresses through the grade of lieutenant commander to commander, KSAOs involving the day-to-day technology used in a mission become less important, and planning and interpersonal KSAOs become more important. At this transition stage in an officer's career, prior cross-specialty, cross-service, and multinational assignments should begin to pay significant dividends. Such assignments provide an officer with a broader appreciation of the needs and problems faced by leaders who must coordinate their activities with other units outside their own specialty, branch of the military, or country.

Assignments Outside an Officer's Specialty, Across Services, and to Multinational Forces. One significant change in officer careers will probably be a changing perception about the importance of liaison assignments. Previously, assignments to billets that crossed specialties within the Navy made it difficult for the officers to stay competitive for promotions and subsequent assignments within their own community (i.e., "out of sight, out of mind"). Officers who had such assignments, however, reported that these types of billets materially enhanced their tactical proficiency. Likewise, joint-duty assignments across U.S. Services were not career enhancing until Congress passed the Goldwater-Nichols Act requiring joint duty.

The decreasing Department of Defense budget may encourage even more cross-Service assignments. For example, the Interservice Training Review Organization studies enlisted training (e.g., air traffic controllers) that is given by more than one military Service or federal agency (Philpott, 1992). If officer training that is common across Services/federal agencies is treated similarly, it may become feasible to design job-sample tests and job-specific aptitude instruments for selection to such training programs. Services and agencies jointly underwriting the research and development costs of such technology would greatly lessen previous cost-benefit concerns. The cost would be less per Service or agency, and the larger potential population of assessees would provide greater returns on investment and more personnel research opportunities.

International officer-liaison billets previously suffered from some of the concerns listed for the cross-specialty and cross-Service assignments. As the U.S. military pulls back from overseas bases (Philpott, 1992), the role of the officer who has liaison responsibilities with the military of another country will be increasingly important. The importance of such billets is suggested by the coordination that was required in Operation Desert Storm. Future officer liaison roles will include representing the U.S. military (not only at the highest levels of leadership) in U.S.-led international exercises/war games/expeditionary forces (e.g., future Desert Storms); other-led international exercises/war games/expeditionary forces (e.g., the impact of a Franco-German joint force); NATO/SEATO [e.g., a recent agreement that will place a U.S. division under a non-U.S. commander for the first time in NATO history (Jolidon, 1992)]; United Nations peace-keeping forces; and personnel exchange programs with foreign militaries.

Our interviews with commanding officers of Naval surface ships revealed that their liaison activities have expanded greatly since the end of Operation Desert Storm. Now, upon entry into a foreign port, members of the crew are frequently expected to meet with high-level military and civilian personnel as well as with their peers. In addition to the formal exchange of courtesies, these meetings have resulted in additional exchanges regarding methods of operation, tactics, and strategy.

Together, these liaison-role considerations suggest a need for new technology to measure interpersonal skills. Such skills are especially needed in unfamiliar situations that may require adaptation to conflicting cultural values. Also, these considerations suggest a need to develop technology for assessing whether officers can take an "other"-oriented perspective. Finally, technology is needed to assess an officer's potential to thrive in a foreign culture. (These technologies would also be very useful in identifying enlisted personnel to be assigned to foreign installations. Additionally, the technologies would transfer readily to industry where the same types of problems are present.)

As proportionally more of the U.S. military is drawn back into the United States, and as the U.S. military relies increasingly on access agreements to facilities in foreign countries (Fernandez, 1992), less social support and other amenities of home will be available overseas. As a result, personality assessment and adjustment technology should be explored. Better identification of officers and enlisted personnel who show promise for foreign assignments will both decrease costs associated with reassignments before the end of a foreign tour of duty and increase the goodwill with host countries.

Assignments to Government and Other Civilian Staffs. Several easily recognized assignments place officers in high-visibility liaison positions, for example, presidential, congressional, and embassy staff work. Some change in the role of officers at embassies might occur as the need for attaches in military intelligence wanes and other military-liaison activities increase.

A potential new area of expertise for military officers could be working with civilian regulatory organizations. With base closings comes a need to prepare the property for non-military use. News reports are already documenting the costs of cleanup activities at bases such as Fort Ord. These resulting cleanups require special skills not now emphasized by the military. To answer this concern, the military could develop a proven subspecialty in environmental science. Officers in that subspecialty would have roles beyond those of environmental cleanup. They could also serve as liaison with occupational hygiene specialists to minimize future contamination. Similarly, officers from the Navy's nuclear power program could work closely with nuclear regulatory organizations that monitor civilian installations. Already, the Navy somewhat reluctantly serves as a major personnel-acquisition pipeline for such organizations.

Because officers (especially those in the Navy) spend most of their work time with other military personnel, assignments that routinely deal with civilians present problems for some officers. This situation is not surprising given that most officers have never worked full time in an organization other than a branch of the armed services. Many senior Navy officers report that they find it difficult to manage civilians. One common concern is that the officers are not familiar with civilian personnel policies. Also, officers may face more situations in which they must deal with contractors/consultants/buyers. For example, an officer may be part of a contract proposal-development, negotiation, or evaluation team. Different skills might be required for each part of the contract process. To handle some of its procurement problems, the Navy developed an officer subspecialty for materiel professionals. Still, purchasing major weapons systems requires technical expertise from the officers in the community that will be using the new technology.

These potential changes in assignments that require frequent interactions with civilians and professional/technical specialists echo the earlier call for advances in the technology used to determine the personnel specifications of jobs, identify and operationalize criteria, and develop selection systems. The appropriate characteristics of the officers who would manage programs and technical organizations effectively are quite different from those of officers who effectively manage line operations personnel and activities (Morrison & Vosburgh, 1987).

Assignments: Contrasting Navy Unrestricted Line Officers (URLs) to Restricted Line Officers (RLs) and Staff Officers. If the drawdown affects support functions more than operations, many support roles may be privatized to save the remaining military billets for "warriors." As recently as 1984 (University of San Diego, 1984), the Navy's "tooth" (warriors or URLs) to "tail" (RLs and staff officers) ratio was nearly 40:60. This figure should move closer to 50:50 as the drawdown continues. The less technical/specialized shore-based support roles will continue to be performed by the URL officers since they need a respite from their operational duties at sea.

In an interview for *Navy Times* (Steigman, 1992), Captain Steve McDermaid, Director of Naval Aviation Personnel Plans and Requirements, noted that the selection boards for prospective commanding officers and captains look at the entire career of aviators, not just the officers' skills in the cockpit. These boards must also consider aviators' "tours in the Pentagon, joint tours with other Services, advanced schooling and shipboard tours in nonflying jobs, including navigator or operations officer aboard an aircraft carrier or with a battle group staff" (Steigman, 1992, p. 14). All of the nonflying billets may result in prospective commanding officers and captains flying for only 8 of their 22 years in the Navy. For the near term, the length of flying assignments may be shortened even further to clear the backlog in the aviation pipeline; some new pilots must wait 20 months after completing flight training before obtaining a flying assignment (Steigman, 1992).

The job-relatedness of assignments for some other URLs is in marked contrast to that for aviators. At the other extreme are the officers in the submarine community. The joint-Service-tour requirement is frequently waived for submarine officers. The need for two crews for each submarine and the shorter but much more frequent periods underway require more time assigned to and deployed in submarines.

The officer communities also vary widely in terms of their use of simulators in training. For example, the aviation community makes extensive use of available simulators, whereas the general URL and surface warfare officer communities make little use of them. In the communities that have simulators, this technology could be included in the selection processes, especially during the period before commissioning. A parallel for using simulators as selection technology is found in civilian organizations. Often, employees are selected using job-sample tests. In a transfer of the job-sample test technology, competency tests could be developed to allow a trainee to select out of a training module when a minimum proficiency level is reached. Psychometric and test development methods could supplement the instructional technologies of training.

Simulators also could be used to select aviators for specific missions. "In several years, said [Captain Robert W.] Hechtman [Assistant Chief of Naval Personnel for Training], a pilot aboard an aircraft carrier will be able to sit down at a simulator 'and do a mission rehearsal wearing his helmet and holding a flight stick in his hand.' The simulator will duplicate what the pilot will experience only hours later" (Philpott, 1992). Scores on such simulations combined with other mission-relevant KSAOs (e.g., calmness under stress) could then be used to determine who would be selected for a given mission in aircraft, tanks, and so forth. Simulators will become increasingly important as the introduction of new systems slows. Upgrading existing material will continue to introduce new, higher technology but at a slower, continuous rate.

Materially Modified Organizational Philosophy

The Navy's new emphasis on total quality leadership (TQL) has implications for all levels of officer and enlisted leadership. As a result, new officer assessment technology is needed to measure citizenship, teamwork (rather than peer competition), customer-orientation (rather than allegiance to the bureaucratic or hierarchical organization), and the ability to adapt to the constantly changing external world.

According to the TQL philosophy, authority and responsibility for an objective are shared with individuals who are intimately involved with the work process. Junior officers and enlisted personnel are being empowered to perform activities and make decisions that were previously reserved for more senior leaders.

In another departure from the previous method of conducting business, leaders are supposed to emphasize continuous improvement rather than crisis management. Paradoxically, this change from results orientation to process orientation might not occur because tour lengths for commanding officers, executive officers, and some department head jobs have been decreased. A shorter tour combined with the need to gain visibility by solving a significant problem during the tour (to remain competitive for future promotions and prime assignments) might work against the move from a results orientation. Another potential constraint on limiting the creation of crises (for leaders to cope with) is that such crises help to prepare the officers for the constant unforeseen situations that are inherent in the fog of actual war.

This change in philosophy should lead to a reevaluation of the personnel specifications used in the initial selection of officer candidates to the various commissioning programs. Although assessing temperament type is not part of the U.S. Naval Academy selection process, Roush (1989) found that midshipmen for the graduating class of 1992 had the following characteristics: 59% were higher on extroversion (e.g., emphasizes people and things) than on introversion (e.g., emphasizes concepts and ideas); 53% were higher on sensing (e.g., emphasizes facts and reality) than on intuition (e.g., emphasizes the big picture); 77% were higher on thinking (e.g, emphasizes logic and objectivity) than on feeling (e.g., emphasizes values and tactfulness); and 61% were higher on judging (e.g., emphasizes structure and planning) than on perceiving (e.g., emphasizes flexibility and spontaneity). Roush also reported that midshipmen with feeling and intuition preferences resigned during their first year at a significantly higher rate than their thinking and sensing peers. These findings suggest that the Navy may be attracting and retaining officer candidates who have temperaments (i.e., personality factors) that do not mesh with the Navy's new TQL philosophy.

The significance of Roush's findings becomes more apparent when they are considered in light of Hogan and Hogan's (1992) article synthesizing literature from personality and leadership research. Hogan and Hogan concluded that the personality traits that allow a person to obtain promotions in the military (and in civilian organizations) can be detrimental in a crisis. They posited that the individuals who attain promotions are ambitious, assertive, and conforming rather than creative, innovative, visionary, or strategic thinkers. They also suggested

that these traditional military leadership styles may not be appropriate in combat
and crises because combat situations require innovative problem solving.

In summary, the development of new technology for selecting leaders seems
warranted given the move to a new Navy organizational philosophy, the findings
of Hogan and Hogan (1992) and Roush (1989), and the suggestion that more
creative problem solving (and less long-range, strategic planning) might be
required in future missions against undetermined enemies. One method for
conducting this research and development would be to use a construct validation
approach, rather than attempting to support any current theory of leadership.
That is, personnel researchers conducting military leadership research should
spend much time investigating the hypothetical characteristics (underlying
leadership) that could then be operationalized.

Changing Characteristics of the Personnel Being Led

Tomorrow's military will have fewer personnel than does today's military. As
a result, the military can become more selective if the number of applicants
remains constant. This lower selection ratio, in turn, translates into enlisted
personnel who will be better educated and brighter (i.e., higher standardized test
scores) than are their peers of today. If this set of circumstances emerges as
suggested, the higher quality of enlisted personnel should contribute significantly
to implementation of the TQL philosophy and its emphasis on sharing authority
and responsibility with subordinates.

Another significant change in personnel will be women moving into
nontraditional and operational billets (e.g., fighter pilot) at both the officer and
enlisted levels. This change may present some interesting dilemmas in foreign
(e.g., Arab) lands that do not support equal rights for women. This issue could
be especially problematic for women in command or liaison billets. The
question becomes how to provide women with equal opportunities in foreign
lands where the foreign cultures do not support equal rights for women and men.

A third important difference in tomorrow's Navy pertains to the racial and
ethnic group representation of those being led. As the non-Hispanic White
population becomes a smaller portion of the U.S. population, cultural differences
should become an increasingly visible concern. Even though the military has
always been viewed as one of the greatest equal opportunity employers, new
strides will need to be made to address the concerns of minorities.

Many officer selection and classification issues raised in regard to assignment
to multinational forces are equally relevant here. In particular, officers will need
to possess interpersonal skills and the ability to see points of view from the
perspectives of other cultures. Also, the military will need to search for ways
to combine classification and training technologies so that minority officers will
spread more evenly through the various specialty areas. For example, African-
American Naval officers are currently overrepresented in the surface community

and underrepresented in the submarine and aviation communities. A more representative officer corps at the specialty level would provide greater role models for enlisted personnel and junior officers across the military.

"NEW" METHODS OF CLASSIFYING MIDSHIPMEN

The information in the previous section contained speculation regarding new and modified roles for future officers and the technology that would be needed to select and classify officers for those roles. The information contained in this section will return to more contemporary considerations regarding needed officer selection and classification technology. This section differs from the prior section in another way as well. The preceding section considered personnel from officer candidates to senior officers. This section deals almost exclusively with officer candidates and, to a lesser degree, newly commissioned officers.

Some of the "new" methods are new only in the sense that they have not been used previously with officer staffing. Other methods/procedures, however, will require technology that is not currently available.

Assessment Centers

The military has made extensive use of hardware simulations (e.g., cockpit and submarine simulators) for training because of their general utility, increased safety over actual operational equipment, and cheaper cost. Many similar benefits could be derived if the military provided additional funding for human-resource simulators to classify officer candidates during the early stages of their training/careers. In particular, the success of assessment centers in private-sector organizations would suggest that creating military versions would be beneficial. (Ironically, the idea for assessment centers relied heavily on the military's initial development of such technology during the World War II evaluation of candidates for the Office of Strategic Services.) Using civilian research as a base, the military could develop simulations that are high in both psychological and physical fidelity.

Compared to other assessment techniques, assessment centers have tradition-ally been more expensive. For the Navy, the per-assessee cost could be minimized. Because the Navy brings aboard more than 2,000 officers each year, the per-assessee cost of developing simulation exercises would be drastically cut. Also, the personnel costs in terms of lost productivity would be eliminated since officer candidates are not fully functioning members of the organization until after commissioning. As a result, assessees could be sent to assessment centers during their one month of active duty between the freshman and sophomore years. The assessment centers would not replace the first summer cruise; instead, they would be a supplement to the cruise.

To use the time most efficiently, written supplements (e.g., specialized aptitude tests, interest inventories, and biographical data forms) could be administered at the academy or college before the officer candidate attends the assessment center. Further cost saving (relative to the civilian sector) could be obtained by having the Navy's assessment centers in three locations (San Diego, Norfolk, and Mayport/Jacksonville/King's Bay) that have access to diverse fleet resources and adequate berthing to process all 2,000 of the officer candidates each summer. (If a flow of 2,000 assessees is too large to process each summer in the three regional centers, the per-summer number of assessees could be halved. All of the U.S. Naval Academy midshipmen could be assessed on weekends during the regular academic year.)

In summary, the per-assessee costs would be lower than civilian costs because more assessees would be processed, no mission-specific time would be lost, and housing and meal facilities would already be available. In addition, the logistics problems caused by arranging the first summer cruise would be lessened.

While officer candidates are at the "assessment centers," they could also receive realistic job previews (RJPs) for the various officer careers. Currently, summer cruises appear to serve more as recruiting efforts than as RJPs. A change toward RJPs may better aid midshipmen in their career/officer-community decisions and help them toward satisfactory, successful Naval careers. There is growing evidence (see Baron & Greenberg, 1990) that individuals who receive RJPs are more likely to have higher satisfaction and lower turnover than are individuals who have standard previews that are glowing and, in many cases, misleading.

Computerized Testing

Computers present assessment capabilities previously not available with paper-and-pencil assessment. Already, computer-assessment technology is used in enlisted personnel selection and classification (e.g., Alderton & Larson in this volume).

The computer might offer an important new technology for assessing the ability of pilots and naval flight officers (NFOs) to use the head's up/down displays that are becoming increasing prevalent in the military aviation. By developing computer-based aptitude tests to measure three-dimensional perception and judgment, training cost could be decreased. The savings would be the result of a decrease in training accidents and the elimination of potential pilot trainees who are relatively deficient in this aptitude. One aspect of the three-dimensional assessment that might be particularly useful is moving depth-perception gathered at various rates of speed. Such technology might be useful in determining the type of aircraft that would be assigned to a pilot.

Reaction-time measures could be paired with the three-dimensional perception/judgment assessment and other computer-based assessment technology. This technology could, thus, measure reaction time while the prospective pilots or NFOs were concentrating on accomplishing other tasks. The multitasking is important, because pilots and NFOs continuously monitor numerous instruments while performing the various tasks required by the mission.

Identification of potential officers (and enlisted personnel) for the cryptographic and intelligence communities might also be enhanced by computerized tests of pattern recognition. Current paper-and-pencil tests assess simple, unidimensional tasks such as recognizing whether a set of numbers or letters is similar to another set of numbers or letters. The computer (possibly connected to a videodisc) would allow various other types of pattern recognition (e.g., picture recognition, identification of changes in pictures, and monitoring transmissions for words or phrases). Further, the computer offers the ability to intersperse extraneous or distractor information. This additional advantage provides an opportunity to measure something more than short-term memory (e.g., the measurement of the higher mental processes required in pattern recognition).

SUMMARY

Current officer-candidate/midshipmen selection systems are effective in predicting behavior in the source program. These selection systems perform less adequately when predicting later performance as an officer. Also, there are no systematic decision aids for officers to use in classifying themselves into communities (occupational groups). A third concern is the lack of selection or classification technologies for identifying officers to be retrained or reclassified to new communities as job and community requirements change over a 20- to 35-year career.

In addition to overcoming these concerns, future officer selection and classification technologies will need to consider a changing world environment and the accomplishment of missions with fewer human and less fiscal resources. The new selection and classification technologies must be designed to consider new military missions and officer roles such as (a) a shift from focusing on a single major enemy to diverse missions, (b) greater interactions with personnel from other branches of the U.S. military and from international forces, and (c) more emphasis on secondary officer specialties.

These mission and role changes will require officers to be very adaptive to changes in tasks, technologies, and the world. For example, as the officers spend increasing time in liaison roles, negotiation and persuasion skills will become more important and directing skills will be less needed. Similarly, the change to a total quality leadership style of management will require teamwork, customer orientation, assimilating diverse cultures, and so forth, in contrast to peer competition, allegiance to the organization's bureaucratic structure, representing a coherent set of cultural values, and so forth. This shift means that the abilities of the entire officer force may need to change, and the selection standards for midshipmen may need to be modified.

RECOMMENDATIONS

- New technology should be developed to aid in the translation of job analysis information into person characteristics.

- New technologies, such as assessment centers, computer-based tests, or decision aids, should be developed and introduced to help classify officers more effectively into their occupational fields, both at the start of their careers and as they change fields later on.

- Procedures that will forecast future Naval assignments and roles need to be developed and tested.

- A new technology should be developed to identify potential senior officers who can move most effectively from a functional to a global perspective (and live in a new culture).

- Entry standards for officer candidates/midshipmen should be reviewed to ensure that they are consistent with the impending changes in the Navy's leadership philosophy.

ACKNOWLEDGMENTS

The opinions expressed in this paper are those of the authors, are not official, and do not necessarily reflect the views of the Navy Department. Funding for this research was provided by the Office of Naval Technology (Program Element 62233N, Work Unit Number RM33M20.11—Classification of Officers and Midshipmen). The authors wish to thank David Alderton and Marie Thomas for comments on earlier drafts of this document.

REFERENCES

Baron, R. A., & Greenberg, J. (1990). *Behavior in organizations: Understanding and managing the human side of work.* Boston: Allyn and Bacon.

Borman, W. C. (1991). Job behavior, performance, and effectiveness. In M. D. Dunnette & L. M. Hough (Eds.), *Handbook of industrial and organizational psychology* (pp. 271-326). Palo Alto, CA: Consulting Psychologists Press.

Department of Labor, Employment and Training Administration (1992, March). Part IV: Interim report of the Advisory Panel for the Dictionary of Occupational Titles. *Federal Register, 57*(59), 10,588-10,599.

Edwards, J. E., Burch, R. L., & Abrahams, N. M. (1990, November). Validation of the Naval Reserve Officers Training Corps quality index. In J. W. Tweeddale (Chair), *The Naval Reserve Officers Training Corps (NROTC) scholarship selection system.* symposium conducted at the annual conference of the Military Testing Association, Orange Beach, AL.

Eide, V. (1991, November). *NATO: Policy and strategy under the conditions of the democratization of societal relations.* Paper presented at the conference of the Armed Forces and Military Service in a Democratic Society, Moscow, Russia.

Fernandez, W. (1992, April 29). Cheney: Permanent bases less crucial now. *Singapore Straits Times,* pp. 1-2.

Hogan, R., & Hogan, J. (1992, April). *The necessary and sufficient conditions for emergent and effective leadership.* Paper presented at the Psychology in the Department of Defense symposium, Colorado Springs.

Jolidon, L. (1992, April 30). Marching into the future: Military plans for a smaller, more mobile force. *USA Today,* p. 4.

Matthews, W. (1992, April 6). Military gains in war on drugs: But drug epidemic remains unabated, Corps general says. *Navy Times,* p. 24.

Morrison, R. F., & Vosburgh, R. M. (1987). *Career development for engineers and scientists.* New York: Van Nostrand Reinhold.

Philpott, T. (1992, April 27). Special report. *Navy Times,* pp. 9-16.

Pinch, F. (1991, November). *Social change and individual rights in the Canadian military.* Paper presented at the conference on the Armed Forces and Military Service in a Democratic Society, Moscow, Russia.

Roush, P. E. (1989). MBTI type and voluntary attrition at the United States Naval Academy. *Journal of Psychological Type, 18,* 72-79.

Sinaiko, H. W. (1992, January 16). *Report of a conference: The Armed Forces and Military Service in a Democratic Society.* Unpublished manuscript, Smithsonian Institution, Washington, DC.

Steigman, D. S. (1992, March 23). From deck to desk: Cutbacks slow pilots' takeoff. *Navy Times,* pp. 12-14.

University of San Diego (1984). *Proceedings: Volume 1. Group reports. Tri-service career research workshop.* San Diego, CA: Author.

CHAPTER

6

TOWARD A BROADER CONCEPTION OF JOBS AND JOB PERFORMANCE: IMPACT OF CHANGES IN THE MILITARY ENVIRONMENT ON THE STRUCTURE, ASSESSMENT, AND PREDICTION OF JOB PERFORMANCE

Kevin R. Murphy[1]
Colorado State University

The chapters presented by Campion (1), Ilgen (2), Campbell (3), Organ (4), and Edwards and Morrison (5) raise a variety of issues and imply a number of challenges to researchers interested in measuring and predicting job performance in the military. In this paper, I comment on each of the preceding papers, and attempt to highlight both the unique issues raised in each paper and the communalities. In particular, I discuss the implications of these papers for conceptualizing and predicting job performance. Taken together, these papers present some fundamental challenges to present conceptions of job analysis and job performance measurement, and they suggest several vital areas of future research for the military in the next several decades.

IMPLICATIONS OF RESEARCH ON JOBS, ROLES, AND PERFORMANCE

In thinking about the papers in this section, it is useful to group the issues they raise into two broad categories, job oriented and person oriented. Four papers focus primarily on understanding the various job and role requirements of military jobs, although several of these papers also raise questions about the types of individuals who are most likely to succeed in the changing military

---

[1] The author served as the discussant for Session One, "Conceptualizing and Measuring Performance," at the S & C Conference.

environment. For example, Ilgen discussed the nature of jobs and roles, and their interrelationships. Organ described a critical category of extra-role behaviors (organizational citizenship) that contribute substantially to the effectiveness of the work group. Campbell discussed various models of job performance, and noted that performance may mean many different things to different researchers or personnel specialists. Campion noted that there are a number of bases for designing or describing jobs, and suggested that a proactive, multidisciplinary approach to job design is called for. The Edwards and Morrison chapter, on the other hand, was primarily person oriented, in the sense that it attempted to describe the types of persons most likely to perform well in evolving military jobs and the difficulties faced in trying to develop officers who are likely to function effectively in the changing military environment.

Thinking About the Job: Job-Oriented Research

Because of recent and upcoming changes in the roles, resources, size, and mission of the American military, it is likely that the structure of work in the Army and other Services will change dramatically over the next 10 to 20 years. Future forces will be smaller and more flexible, and they will be asked to function in a number of roles (e.g., peacekeeping, relief) that require different skills than are emphasized in current training and doctrine. Research on the nature of jobs and job performance is therefore especially timely, and suggests a number of challenges for the future.

Jobs, Roles, and Extra-Role Behavior. Ilgen drew a distinction between job elements and role elements. Job elements are objective (in the sense that there is clear consensus about what constitutes a job requirement), are defined independent of the person occupying the job or the context in which the job exists, and are relatively static. Ilgen and Hollenbeck (1991) referred to these as established requirements; written job descriptions usually capture the key job elements.

Role elements, in contrast, are subjective, dynamic, and largely defined by the context. These role elements are the aspects of the job that evolve as a result of the social role-making process, in which members of work groups or units develop a shared understanding about how jobs and tasks will be performed and allocated. Ilgen and Hollenbeck (1991) referred to these as emergent requirements. These role elements may change as people move in and out of work groups, and as people's conceptions of the job and its relationships to other jobs change. Most job analyses and job descriptions focus on task elements, and may treat role elements (which constitute a key part of the informal job description) as a source of error on instability in the analysis.

The distinction between a job and a position is important for understanding the relationships between job and role elements, and the implications of the job-role distinction. Ilgen and Hollenbeck (1991) defined a job as a set of task elements grouped together under one job title and designated to be performed by a single individual (p. 173). A position is the job held by a specific individual. The job description for secretary may define the tasks that are expected of all secretaries, but the actual tasks performed by each secretary might vary considerably. Positions that have the same job title differ to the extent that they contain differing role elements.

Ilgen noted that it is impossible to fully understand a job if one focuses solely on job elements, in part because no person's job is completely captured in a job description; the real description of any job (or position) contains both job and role elements. Further, he noted that role elements are context dependent, in the sense that the informal description of a job evolves over the course of a set of social relationships with other members of the organization. A notion that some aspects of the job are informally defined, and that this definition depends on the social context of work, is neither new nor controversial. It does, however, carry a number of implications for conducting and interpreting job analyses.

It is important to determine the degree to which the definition of a job is context dependent. Suppose, for example, that the role elements that are involved in a job are totally context dependent, and are likely to change with any change in personnel, tasks, or work methods [Murphy (1989) noted that such changes might also affect job elements]. If role elements are totally context dependent, the task of the job analyst might be totally hopeless. If fundamental aspects of the job change frequently (and unpredictably), there may be little point in attempting to describe or document jobs. Suppose, on the other hand, that once role elements evolve, they are highly stable, and that the informal description of a particular position in an organization does not change over time or with changes in personnel or methods. The job analyst's task is still a difficult one; individuals who have the same job title might have very different informal job descriptions, and it might be necessary to conduct analyses at the level of the position rather than the job.[2] However, if role elements are reasonably stable, it should be feasible to carry out thorough analyses of positions and jobs.

Although the research on roles reviewed by Ilgen (and by Ilgen & Hollenbeck, 1991) emphasized the fluid nature of role requirements, I believe that it is unlikely that the role elements present in most jobs are so unstable as to preclude meaningful job analysis. I cannot offer compelling evidence to support this conclusion, but I can cite both logical arguments and experience to argue for the relative stability of role elements.

---

[2] The Americans With Disabilities Act may require that analyses be conducted at the level of the position rather than the job, particularly if the description of what an individual actually does varies considerably for individuals holding the same job title.

To begin with, it is important to keep in mind the pervasive influence of tradition in virtually all organizational activities. Once a set of role elements has been negotiated between the original holder of a position and his or her co-workers and superiors, a precedent has been set that can easily outlive any of the members of the original role set. The fact that things have always been done this way is the most compelling (and sometimes the only) argument for a wide array of organizational structures and practices. My own experience in various organizations is that changes in personnel (which ought to open the way for renegotiating role elements) have relatively little effect on the fundamental definitions of the various positions in a work group, and that even with total turnover in personnel, role relations tend to be highly stable.

As Ilgen noted, jobs vary in the extent to which job elements (i.e., elements that are present in all positions) versus role elements define the actual work performed. If we symbolize the proportion of all performance elements that are common across positions (i.e., job elements) as p_{job} and the proportion of the elements that are potentially unique to each position (i.e., role elements) as p_{role} (where $p_{role} = 1 - p_{job}$), then it seems likely that p_{role} provides a surrogate measure of job complexity. That is, simple jobs should also be relatively uniform in their descriptions and performance requirements, and should have relatively few true role elements. More complex jobs offer more latitude for negotiation, as well as more ambiguity in their job descriptions. It has been widely observed that jobs in the American workplace are becoming more complex, which implies that the relative importance of role elements in defining the true nature of a position should also increase.

If p_{role} is, in fact, increasing as jobs become more complex, the task of recruiting, selecting, placing, and training new employees will also become more complex. The traditional models for all of these tasks assume that the job is a fixed target—that is, that the fundamental nature of the job does not change greatly over time or across positions. If this assumption is incorrect, it might be both critically important and extremely difficult to continuously tailor personnel systems to the changing requirements of each position in the organization. More fundamentally, as p_{role} increases, it will become increasingly important to conduct analyses at the position level rather than at the job level, and to frequently update such analyses.

Organ described a program of research on extra-role behavior, in particular those behaviors labeled as organizational citizenship. Whereas Ilgen noted that most jobs include informally defined requirements that extend beyond a person's job description, Organ reminded us that many individuals go beyond the requirements (either formal or informal) of their jobs to aid their co-workers and to take on responsibilities that they could avoid without risking sanction. Although these behaviors are neither required nor sufficiently rewarded, they are critical to the survival and effectiveness of organizations.

Organ distinguished organizational citizenship behaviors (OCBs) from job and role elements in terms of their antecedents. In particular, OCBs are thought to be the result of one's orientation to the job and the organization.   Such a distinction is relatively easy to make as long as the job and role requirements of a position are well defined and well understood. However, if jobs are becoming more complex and more fluid (which implies the need for frequent negotiation of role requirements and considerable variability in role requirements among individuals with nominally identical jobs), the distinction between role requirements and OCBs may become increasingly hard to draw. For example, if the nature of my job is constantly up in the air, it is reasonable to believe that I will attempt to define a more narrow set of role requirements if I am dissatisfied with the job or the organization than if I am highly satisfied and committed.

Ilgen suggested that the total domain of performance-relevant behaviors that are expected or required (in the sense that sanctions will be applied if they are not carried out) can be broken down into job and role elements. Organ suggested that this total domain must be expanded to include extra-role behaviors, since these behaviors tend to enhance the effectiveness and productivity of the individuals and work groups involved. Although Organ distinguished OCBs from role elements in terms of the role of intent (versus ability) as a key antecedent, it might be more useful to distinguish the two in terms of how these behaviors are controlled. Job and role requirements are enforced through externally administered rewards and sanctions, whereas OCBs are not usually directly rewarded (although individuals who engage in many OCBs may be more likely to receive promotions), nor is their absence sanctioned.

Although I prefer definitions of job and role requirements versus OCBs in terms of their consequences (including the consequences of not exhibiting the behavior) to definitions in terms of antecedents (e.g., ability versus intent), the role of attitudes toward the job and the organization is obviously critical in determining whether OCBs occur, and is also important in understanding the generalizability of civilian research to the military context.   In military organizations, especially in their combat-related arms, the distinction between role requirements and OCBs may be difficult to draw.

In the civilian sector, it is usually easy to draw a distinction between work and nonwork environments, but the same is not always true in military environments. Consider the crew of a submarine on extended patrol. Although individuals are assigned to duty and off-duty shifts, it is essentially impossible to leave the work environment. Behaviors such as staying with a task after your shift has ended or helping members of your work group (who are also bunkmates) with tasks that are not in your job description may have different implications on a submarine than in a factory, where a clean break between work and nonwork is easier to establish.   The fact that many military jobs are performed in an environment in which it is not possible (or easy) to leave work when the day is done may mean that the line between role requirements and OCBs cannot be easily drawn.

There are some private-sector analogs of the type of military job described above, in which the time spent at work is only a small part of a total environment defined by the organization. I am speaking here of large manufacturing organizations in Japan, which sometimes provide housing, medical care, recreation, and even marital advice to their members. Like the Services, these organizations go to great lengths to build esprit de corps, and this high level of commitment appears to be a key determinant of their success. Also, like the Services, these organizations encourage and expect behavior that in most American private- and public-sector organizations is considered exceptional—that is, organizational citizenship. Finally, unlike most civilian organizations in this country, it is unlikely that someone who is not a good citizen will thrive in either the Services or in this type of Japanese organization.

Defining Job Performance. Personnel researchers and practitioners frequently talk about performance as if it was simple, unidimensional (e.g., good versus poor performance), and well understood. Campbell reminded us that nothing could be further from the truth. The definition of performance depends in part on who is asking and why. Performance has been measured or defined in terms of behaviors, results, success, retention, the acquisition and demonstration of skill and job knowledge, advancement, and so on. In comparing the various models of job performance, the question is not which model is right, but which is most useful for what purposes.

Campbell described the performance model that structured much of the performance research in Project A. This model starts with the simple premise that performance is behavior (it is something that people do) that is relevant to important goals. Thus, linking back to the Ilgen and Organ papers, job elements, role elements, and OCBs might all be part of performance. Campbell then went on to make two potentially profound statements. First, he hypothesized that performance in most jobs might be represented in terms of eight basic components or facets (e.g., job-specific task proficiency, demonstrating effort). Second, he hypothesized that if situational constraints (e.g., availability of materials and supplies) are controlled, each of the major components of performance can be represented as a function of declarative knowledge (DK), procedural knowledge and skill (PKS), and motivation (M).

The hypothesis that performance in all jobs can be represented in terms of the same eight general facets has clear implications for job classification and for personnel placement. In essence, this hypothesis represents performance on any job in terms of a 1 x 8 vector (i.e. performance in each of eight facets), where each of the elements could vary (across jobs) in terms of its importance and in terms of the specific content of the facets. For example, one aspect of performance is supervision and leadership. Both the relevance of this factor and the specific type of supervision and leadership (e.g., shop-floor supervision versus military leadership versus management) might vary, but the element of leadership would be present in the vector of facets describing performance in any job.

Suppose, for the moment, that the content factor were not important (i.e., that supervision or military leadership or management were all pretty much the same thing). In that case, the only thing that would distinguish performance in one job from performance in another would be the relative importance of the eight facets. Jobs in which the importance weights for the facets were similar would have similar performance determinants, and the problem of classification and placement would be trivially easy. Suppose, on the other hand, that the content factor was absolutely critical, and that there was no cross-job similarity in the determinants of performance on a given facet (e.g, if supervision were completely different from military leadership, which was completely different from leadership as a manager). In this case, classification and placement might be hopeless (even though the same eight facets underlie performance in all jobs), because the components of performance in different jobs would be similar in name only.

The preceding paragraph points up the importance of understanding the importance of job content in defining performance. If the eight factors are truly universal, in the sense that an individual who performs well on one facet in Job A will also perform well on that facet (given sufficient training and freedom from constraints) in Jobs B, C, and so on, the theory described in Campbell's chapter should provide a fundamental basis for classification and placement. If they are truly unique, in the sense that there is no cross-job transfer in performance on each facet, the theory may lead to the conclusion that job classification and placement is a waste of time and resources.

The assertion that performance on each facet can be described as a function of declarative knowledge, procedural knowledge and skill, and motivation (i.e., Performance = f [DK * PKS * M]) is hardly controversial, especially if the terms of the equation are translated into everyday language. In essence, Campbell said that performance is a function of knowing what to do, being able to do it, and being willing to do it; when the concept is expressed in these terms, one can hardly disagree. What makes his performance equation potentially profound is that it is likely to significantly broaden the meaning of the terms *declarative knowledge* and *procedural skill and knowledge*. These terms are common in the cognitive and educational literatures [see Lohman's chapter in this volume (10) and Lord & Maher (1991) for recent reviews], but they are almost always applied to performance on relatively simple, well-defined tasks. In Campbell's model, major performance dimensions included ones that are highly interpersonal (e.g., facilitating peer and task performance) as well as ones that seem to relate to basic personality or character traits (e.g., maintaining personal discipline). What are the declarative and procedural knowledge bases that lead to personal discipline or support for one's work team? I am not sure I can answer this question, but I suspect that the eventual answer will include things that are traditionally classified as attitudes, values, and personality traits. In any case, it is clear that declarative knowledge and procedural knowledge and skill have broader meanings here than in the cognitive and educational literatures where these terms are usually encountered.

Although Campbell did not explicitly link his two major hypotheses (i.e., that performance is always made up of the same eight facets and that it is determined by the same three general classes of variables), they are clearly compatible, and this link may be important for understanding cross-job consistency in performance. For example, suppose you wanted to predict whether performance in the area of maintaining personal discipline was likely to be consistent across jobs. One strategy would be to determine the specific DK, PKS, and M factors that seemed to underlie performance in this area, and determine whether they were reasonably consistent. In the case of personal discipline, one might expect that the declarative knowledge and procedural knowledge and skill required to carry out these behaviors are reasonably consistent across settings.[3] It is quite possible, however, that the motivational factors that lead to good or poor performance in this area vary widely, and that individuals who do quite well in some environments might experience severe disciplinary problems in others (Murphy, 1993). In general, cross-job consistency in each of the major facets of performance might be defined and investigated in terms of the similarity of the DK, PKS, and M factors involved in good or poor performance.

Designing and Analyzing Jobs. Campbell noted that there are many ways to conceptualize job performance. Campion's chapter conveyed a similar theme, that there are a variety of ways of designing and analyzing jobs. In a number of influential papers, he identified four distinct disciplinary bases for designing and analyzing jobs: (a) biological, which involves applications of physiology and ergonomics to job design; (b) mechanistic, which is an extension of classic industrial engineering; (c) perceptual/motor, which applies experimental psychology and human factors engineering to job design; and (d) motivational, which is an outgrowth of organizational psychology. Each disciplinary base leads to different conclusions about what constitutes a good job, and leads to different recommendations for designing jobs.

While Campion emphasized the disciplinary bases, assumptions, and costs and benefits of different schools of thought regarding job design, there are other ways

---

[3] The Services (especially the Navy) have adopted training programs as a response to reports of sexual harassment of female officers, enlisted personnel, and cadets, which suggests that they believe that problems in this area are due to deficiencies in declarative or procedural knowledge.

of thinking about the four models that might help to illustrate both the implications of his analysis and the difficulties in generalizing this work to the military context. Table 6.1 represents ways of mapping Campion's four models either to a set of key constructs or to the organizational levels and occupational groups in which these constructs are likely to be most relevant.

TABLE 6.1
Constructs, Levels, and Occupational Groups
Most Relevant to Models of Job Design

Model	Key Constructs	Most Applicable
Biological	Ergonomic load, Physical stress	Unskilled labor
Mechanistic	Routine work	Semi-skilled labor
Perceptual/ motor	Motor control, Visual information processing	Skilled labor, craft work
Motivational	Choice	Service jobs, managerial jobs

In the civilian work force, the four models of job design match very nicely with the level or complexity of the job. The simplest jobs are most likely to be designed with physical demands in mind, the next most complex with the need to tolerate relatively routine and repetitive work in mind, the next most complex with perceptual and motor skills in mind, and the most complex with motivational constructs in mind. For example, in designing and analyzing a manager's job, relatively little thought will be given to physical or motor demands, or to tolerance for boredom (except to minimize these factors), but considerable thought will be given to designing a job that is likely to be the source of satisfaction and commitment to the organization. The implication of all of this is that different disciplinary bases (and perhaps different individuals) will be involved in designing the structure of work at different levels of most organizations.

One of the many differences between the civilian and military sectors is that the traditional breakdown into unskilled (and physically demanding) labor, semi-skilled work, skilled labor, and management is not as rigid in the military as in the civilian sector, which implies that military job design and analysis must take the multidisciplinary perspective called for in Campion's chapter. Unlike their civilian counterparts, military supervisors and managers (i.e., noncoms and officers) do not always make a clean break from the types of physically demanding or technical work that is present in the lower ranks. It would be almost bizarre to design physical fitness standards for civilian managers, but highly sensible to do so for some combat officers (e.g., airborne or light infantry officers might face the same physical demands as privates). In the civilian sector, career progress almost always means increasing removal from the technical side of work, with increasing emphasis on general management. In the military, officers and senior noncoms might be expected and required to stay highly involved in technical training throughout much of their careers. Thus, unlike the civilian sector, personnel planners might have to take several of the disciplinary bases outlined by Campion into account in designing jobs at virtually any level in the military.

Each of the disciplinary bases identified by Campion highlights the importance of specific constructs for designing and understanding jobs. In the military, job design may involve assessments of most or all of the key constructs identified in Table 6.1. One implication is that it may be more difficult in the military than in the civilian sector to determine whether a particular job is well designed. As more constructs become relevant to defining a well-designed job, the task of creating such a job is likely to become more complex.

The traditional bias in personnel and human resource management is to treat the job as a fixed entity and either: (a) recruit and select people who fit the job, or (b) change people (e.g., through training or socialization) to increase the extent to which they fit the requirements of the job. Campion noted that it may often make more sense to consider changing the job to fit the people. In the section that follows, I comment on the problems (and opportunities) involved in identifying the types of people who are most likely to succeed in the changing military environment, and return to this suggestion as one way to maximize the likelihood that the military will, in fact, be able to find and develop the sorts of people needed to fulfill its future missions.

Thinking About the People: Person-Oriented Research

In both the civilian and military environments, there are indications that jobs are becoming more fluid, in the sense that job and role requirements are less well defined, and more difficult, in the sense that successful performance will require higher levels of both ability and effort. A person-oriented approach to understanding job performance addresses characteristics of persons that are likely to contribute to success in a changing military environment, and explores structural and environmental barriers to the selection and development of individuals who are most likely to succeed. Personnel selection researchers have long devoted attention to those characteristics of individuals that are likely to be critical for success, and they have mainly focused on cognitive variables such as ability, skill, and knowledge. The changing nature of jobs in both the civilian and military sector suggests that dispositional and motivational variables might become increasingly important, which may substantially change the nature of the questions addressed by personnel selection researchers. Several chapters in this volume (both in this section and in others) outline how an increasing focus on the noncognitive determinants of performance may change personnel research and application.

Cognitive Versus Dispositional Influences on Performance. If you ask personnel psychologists what variable is most critical to success on the job, the answer is likely to be g, or general mental ability (for a recent statement of this position, see Ree & Earles, 1992; for more general background, see a special issue of *Journal of Vocational Behavior*, 1986, Vol. 29, No. 3). The conventional wisdom is that g is ubiquitous, in the sense that it is relevant to performance in virtually all jobs, and that it is unique, in the sense that it is the best single predictor of performance.

Although g may be the best single predictor of performance, this does not necessarily imply that cognitive abilities represent the most important class of predictors. Rather, there are a number of dispositional and motivational variables that are likely to be critically important to successful performance in a wide range of jobs, perhaps more important than g. Like g, the importance of dispositional and motivational variables may increase as jobs become more complex or less well defined. Going back to Campbell's performance model, variables such as self-efficacy [Bandura's chapter in this volume (15) reviews research on self-efficacy] are clearly relevant to the motivational component of performance, and are likely to have a critical role in the acquisition of job knowledge and skill (Ackerman, 1987, 1989; Schmidt & Hunter, 1992). Individuals who are unmotivated and who believe that they will be ineffective are less likely to make substantial efforts to acquire new knowledge and skills, and thus may create a self-fulfilling prophecy, in which their unwillingness to acquire new knowledge (because of self-limiting beliefs) makes them less effective in their future performance.

The job-oriented chapters discussed earlier clearly suggest that jobs in both the civilian and military sectors are likely to become more demanding and less well defined. If this is true, the jobs of the future will pose heavy demands in both the cognitive and noncognitive realms. That is, such jobs will require both different types and levels of ability and different orientations than the more static jobs of the past. An increasing emphasis on dispositional and motivational factors poses several challenges for researchers and practitioners.

Dispositional and motivational variables differ from cognitive abilities in a number of ways, all of which can affect the types of questions that have been or might be framed in personnel selection research. First, we may need to shift our thinking from a univariate to a multivariate focus. Because virtually all cognitive abilities and skills are related to g, it is easy to fall into the habit of thinking in univariate terms (e.g., the relationship between ability and performance might be summarized with a single validity coefficient). The same is not true for noncognitive attributes; the statement that personality traits or motivational variables are relevant for understanding performance immediately leads to the question of which traits or variables. Second, research on dispositional and motivational antecedents of performance may lead us to consider a wider range of criteria. Although there are often questions about the specific measures, there is usually little controversy over the constructs that should be involved in validating ability measures (e.g. performance, training success). Different noncognitive attributes might be related to very different outcome variables.

Third, the relationships between dispositional and motivational variables and job performance may be more complex than has been the case for cognitive variables. In the cognitive domain, more is usually better, in the sense that ability typically shows a linear relationship with performance. The same is not true for dispositional or motivational attributes; individuals might have too little of, too much of, or the wrong mix of any of a number of noncognitive attributes to function effectively in particular jobs or organizational settings.

Advances in Assessment. Edwards and Morrison addressed advancements in assessment methods that might be useful in identifying individuals likely to succeed in the future military environment. They focused on fairly intensive methods of assessment, such as the assessment center. The assessment center method has a long and highly successful history (this method originated in the military), and it may prove quite useful in the military of the future. In thinking about advances in assessment, it is critical to distinguish between advances in how we measure versus advances in what we measure. The greatest possible contribution that methods such as the assessment center may make is to refocus our assessment methods toward a wider range of variables than are assessed by traditional standardized tests.

Although increasing the range of variables that are included in future assessment activities may indeed help, I believe that advances in assessment methods will in the end make only a minor contribution to future selection and assessment. First, existing assessment methods are relatively effective, and it is possible that there is a ceiling that limits how much more can be gained by assessing individual differences of any kind. I have no idea whether we are approaching this ceiling, but it would be naive to think that job performance will ever be completely predictable on the basis of individual difference variables. I am not sure whether better assessment methods will, in the long run, significantly affect the quality of military selection decisions. Second, the environment in which the military exists may place some limits on the effectiveness of even the best candidates, which implies that the incremental gain in better selection might be small.

Environmental Limits. Edwards and Morrison described seven characteristics of the military organization of the future that can be expected to affect the selection and development of military officers. These characteristics may be summarized as follows:

- Less clearly defined missions.
- Smaller, with fewer resources.
- Changing philosophy.
- Changing demographics.
- Multiple roles over an officer's career.
- Increasing number of boundary roles.
- Long, relatively inflexible process for developing senior officers.

These seven characteristics can be subsumed under four general themes. First, the philosophy, mission, and resources of the military are changing. Second, there are substantial changes in the demographic characteristics of officers and enlisted personnel. Third, officers will be expected to take on a number of different roles over their careers, many of which will represent liaison or boundary roles. Finally, the process of developing a Naval officer (similar comments apply to the other Services) is a relatively long and inflexible one.

The first six characteristics listed previously suggest that military officers must be highly flexible and tolerant of ambiguity. However, the process used to develop officers is long and inflexible. It is reasonable to speculate that officers who are most likely to succeed in the changing environment described by the first six characteristics will find the developmental environment for officers (which can span 10 to 20 years) to be troublesome. One of the great strengths of military organizations is the reliance on tradition to build identification with the organization and its values and norms. Indeed, the military resembles the classic description of a stodgy, bureaucratic organization (e.g., extreme hierarchical differentiation, high reliance on rules and established procedures, low tolerance for diversity). By most accounts, the Navy is particularly traditional in its organization. Unfortunately, this orientation may be one of the worst for developing flexible officers who function well in ill-defined environments. I believe that the Services will face a tremendous challenge in retaining what is good about a traditional orientation while at the same time creating ways of developing officers for an uncertain future.

KEY THEMES AND IMPLICATIONS

The research presented in the papers in this section suggests a variety of avenues for investigating and conceptualizing the nature and structure of jobs in the future military. Several chapters point to the increasing complexity and unpredictability of the work environment, and point to challenges that personnel planners are likely to face over the next 10 to 20 years. In particular, I believe that this research (together with the research on Project A and the body of relevant civilian research on jobs and job performance) helps to clearly identify the types of individuals likely to succeed in the future. Unfortunately, it might be difficult to recruit and select such individuals. In the final section of this paper, I consider both barriers and opportunities provided by the unique structure and nature of the military that are likely to influence their success in identifying, recruiting, and developing such individuals, together with the implications of these barriers and opportunities for future personnel research.

What Characteristics Do We Want, and How Do We Get Them?

Based on what is known about the changing military environment, about the nature of jobs and roles in the military, and about the determinants of job performance in a variety of jobs, there are four characteristics that appear to be critical for success in the military of the future. First, future recruits, enlisted personnel, and officers must be flexible, in the sense that they must be willing and able to adapt to changing environments, tasks, missions, and so on. Second, they must be smart, in the sense that they must have the cognitive ability needed to acquire and apply job knowledge and skills. Third, they must be committed. That is, they must be motivated to attain the goals of the organization. Fourth, they must be confident, in the sense that they must be willing to attempt and to persist at difficult tasks.

All of these characteristics might be described in terms of a variety of more specific cognitive abilities, personality traits, values, temperaments, and so on, and instruments are available to assess many of them. Note, however, that these characteristics are not merely individual difference variables; rather, some of them (e.g., commitment, confidence) are likely to represent an interaction of the individual with his or her environment. I return to this point shortly.

It is certainly useful to know what sort of people you want, but it is also depressing to know that everyone else wants exactly the same sort of person. The changes in the military work environment mirror changes that are occurring in civilian environments, and it is likely that the four characteristics noted here will be seen as critical in virtually all sectors. As a result, the competition for persons who are flexible, smart, committed, and confident is likely to be intense, and it is unlikely that any organization will succeed in attracting such individuals without a concerted effort to compete for their services. One implication is that recruitment may be a more important determinant of overall success than selection may be. It is unlikely that there is a large pool of people who possess all of the desired characteristics, and organizations that succeed in recruiting these individuals are most likely to prosper in an unstable environment.

At least three of the desired characteristics (i.e., flexibility, commitment, and confidence) are likely to be influenced by organizational variables, ranging from training to reward systems. Given the high degree of competition for persons who possess all of the desired characteristics, it seems wise to invest more resources in interventions designed to increase flexibility, commitment, and confidence, and fewer resources in the selection of individuals who already possess these characteristics. For example, commitment to an organization is thought to represent some interaction between one's values, preferences, and so on and one's experiences in the organization (Dawis & Lofquist, 1984; Hulin, 1991). I believe that the Services would benefit by assessing values, by including this information in their selection decisions, and by changing assignments and work environments to maximize the match (given the constraints of organizational mission requirements) between the values of the people involved and the reward structure of work.

Organizational Barriers and Sources of Opportunity

Several characteristics of the military are likely either to present unique barriers to recruiting, selecting, and developing individuals with the characteristics most likely to lead to success in the future, or to provide unique opportunities for achieving these goals. It is important to consider these organizational characteristics when evaluating the generalizability of research and theory developed in the civilian sector to the problems that will be faced by the military in the future.

Barriers to Success. Several characteristics of military organizations are likely to impede the military's ability to attract and develop the types of individuals who are most likely to cope well with the changing military environment. First, the military represents a relatively tall and rigid organization. Manufacturing and service organizations seem to be moving to relatively flat structures, with few levels of authority, flexible assignment structures, and substantial downward delegation of decision making. Military organizations have elaborate structures of rank, as well as relatively entrenched assignment structures (e.g., separate structures for combat versus support specialties), and it is unlikely that these features will change within the foreseeable future. Second, the military is a relatively insulated community, in the sense that movement into and out of the military is highly regulated, making career flexibility potentially more restricted in military than in nonmilitary organizations. Third, as noted earlier, the structure of military organizations is highly bureaucratic, with a heavy emphasis on rules, procedures, written codes, and so on. Fourth, it is an environment in which both risk taking and innovation are, on the whole, discouraged. There are certainly examples of highly risky or innovative officers and enlisted personnel, but the bias in military organizations worldwide is clearly conservative and risk averse.

The characteristics just listed present serious barriers to the attraction, selection, and retention of highly flexible individuals; on the whole, rigid, tradition-bound, bureaucratic organizations are not the ideal place to find or develop flexibility. Does this mean that the military should imitate the private sector and move toward flatter, more loosely organized structures? The answer is probably no. Although the structure of the military is probably not optimal for developing flexibility, it is a highly adaptive one for a variety of other purposes, including the task of turning large number of 18- to 20 year-olds into responsible and capable members of a large and complex organization.

Opportunities. Three special features of the Services substantially increase the likelihood that they will be able to attract and develop individuals with the desirable characteristics noted at the beginning of this section. First, it is reasonable to expect a level of commitment to the organization and its mission that is not common in the civilian work force. Military officers and enlisted personnel, particularly those who have chosen the military as a career, appear to identify strongly with their branch of the Service, and are likely to take their missions quite seriously. Furthermore, the Services have developed a wide range of socialization activities, traditions, rituals, symbols, and so on that are designed to increase a sense of loyalty, commitment, and identification with the Service and the unit. The ability to develop relatively high levels of commitment is a potentially critical advantage of military over civilian organizations.

Second, the Services are uniquely attractive to a large number of individuals who possess all of the characteristics required for success, but who may be artificially excluded from advancement in the civilian world. In particular, the Services have a well-deserved reputation as one of the best avenues for advancement among racial and ethnic minorities. Talented members of several groups that are underrepresented in civilian sector organizations have good reason to believe that their opportunities to compete fairly for advancement and success are greater in the military than in the civilian sector (particularly the private sector). There is evidence of parallel progress in the selection and promotion of qualified female enlisted personnel and officers. The Services appear to do very well in attracting highly qualified females into a variety of fields, in part because of the appearance of greater fairness in personnel policies and practices in the Services. Recent changes in policies that provide females with greater access to combat-oriented assignments will probably further increase the attractiveness of military careers for females.

Third, the Services have both the ability and the willingness to thoroughly assess candidates. Despite the demonstrated utility of systematic personnel selection and placement, many civilian organizations appear unwilling to make the investment required to select well. The military has consistently supported personnel research, and is the leading player in a variety of applied testing programs. For example, the Armed Services vocational testing and counseling systems (e.g., ASVAB, CAT-ASVAB, the Student Testing Program) are highly sophisticated, and are considerably larger in scope than any of their competitors. On the whole, the military seems poised to take maximum advantage of technical developments in selection and placement.

Implications for Personnel Research. Industrial and organizational (I/O) psychologists have traditionally treated topics such as selection, placement, job analysis, and so on as aspects of I psychology, while treating topics such as organizational socialization, organizational structure, and interactions between the organization and its environment as aspects of O psychology. Unfortunately, I and O psychology seem to co-exist, but rarely cooperate. I believe that future research and thinking regarding selection and placement in the military must take into account both the I and the O sides of our fields. In particular, it is time for personnel researchers to more carefully consider aspects of the organization and its environment similar to those outlined in this section when thinking about selection and placement.

Future research on selection and placement must take into account the ways in which the mission, resources, and demographics of the organization are likely to affect the structure of work and the determinants of performance. Military jobs are becoming more fluid and unpredictable, and we need to broaden our future thinking about what variables are most relevant in designing a system for the selection and classification of future recruits. The time for treating the job (and its performance requirements) as a fixed, stable, and simple entity is quickly drawing to a close, and personnel planners will need to go beyond the narrow disciplinary boundaries of traditional I psychology in designing jobs and evaluating job performance in the military of the future.

REFERENCES

Ackerman, P. L. (1987). Individual differences in skill learning: An integration of psychometric and information-processing perspectives. *Psychological Bulletin, 102,* 3-27.

Ackerman, P. L. (1989). Individual differences in skill acquisition. In P. L. Ackerman, R. J. Sternberg & R. Glaser (Eds.), *Learning and individual differences* (pp. 164-217). New York: Freeman.

Dawis, R. V., & Lofquist, L. H. (1984). *A psychological theory of work adjustment.* Minneapolis: University of Minneapolis Press.

Hulin, C. (1991). Adaptation, persistence, and commitment in organizations. In M. Dunnette and L. Hough (Eds.), *Handbook of industrial and organizational psychology* (2nd ed., Vol. 2, pp. 445-505). Palo Alto, CA: Consulting Psychologists Press.

Ilgen, D. R. & Hollenbeck, J. R. (1991) The structure of work: Jobs and roles. In M. Dunnette & L. Hough (Eds.), *Handbook of industrial and organizational psychology* (2nd ed., Vol. 2, pp. 165-208). Palo Alto, CA: Consulting Psychologists Press.

Journal of Vocational Behavior (1986), Vol. 29, No. 3.

Lord, R. G., & Maher, K. J. (1991). Cognitive theory in industrial and organizational psychology. In M. Dunnette & L. Hough (Eds.), *Handbook of industrial and organizational psychology* (2nd ed., Vol. 2, pp. 1-62). Palo Alto, CA: Consulting Psychologists Press.

Murphy, K. R. (1989). Is the relationship between cognitive ability and job performance stable over time? *Human Performance, 2,* 183-200.

Murphy, K. R. (1993). *Honesty in the workplace.* Pacific Grove, CA: Brooks/Cole.

Ree, M. J., & Earles, J. A. (1992). Intelligence is the best predictor of job performance. *Current Directions in Psychological Science, 1,* 86-89.

Schmidt, F. L. & Hunter, J. E. (1992). Development of a causal model of processes determining job performance. *Current Directions in Psychological Science, 1,* 89-92.

Part II

Conceptualizing and Measuring

Individual Differences

CHAPTER

7

COGNITIVE ABILITIES TESTING: AN AGENDA FOR THE 1990s

Patrick C. Kyllonen
Armstrong Laboratory

This chapter is concerned with what Carroll (1992) called "the dimensional analysis of cognitive abilities," that is, the study of the ways in which individuals differ cognitively. Over the past several years, I and other members of the Learning Abilities Measurement Program (LAMP) research team[1] have developed a framework for measuring cognitive abilities and an actual computerized test battery constructed from that framework. We have called this the Cognitive Abilities Measurement (CAM) framework and battery (Kyllonen, in press). We have administered the CAM battery in a number of different studies along with various learning tasks. Some of the learning tasks have been fairly simple, laboratory tasks lasting 30 minutes to an hour. Others have been quite complex and elaborate computerized tutorials, lasting from 10 to 30 hours and administered over several days. The domains have been primarily technical, cognitive ones—computer programming, electronics troubleshooting, electricity principles, statistics, graph reading—but have also included learning to fly an aircraft.

The purpose of these studies has been to examine the degree to which performance on the CAM battery can predict success on the learning tasks. More specifically, the question has been this: Can a test battery constructed on the basis of cognitive theory predict success on learning tasks more accurately than can a more conventional test battery, such as the Armed Services Vocational Aptitude Battery (ASVAB), constructed on some other, less theoretical, more empirical basis?

---

[1] Team members include William Tirre, Valerie Shute, Scott Chaiken, Joshua Hurwitz, Raymond Christal, Dan Woltz (now at the University of Utah), Lisa Gawlick, and the programming staff, Richard Walker, Janice Hereford, Cynthia Garcia, Henry Clark, Terilee Perdue, Terri Simmons, Joanne Hall, Brent Townsend, and Karen Raouff. Others who have contributed to the project are William Alley (Technical Director of our division), John Tangney (of the Air Force Office of Scientific Research, a major sponsor), Linda Sawin, James Earles, and Lonnie Valentine (Branch Chief).

What have we found? Not surprisingly, performance on the CAM battery predicts performance on the learning tasks fairly accurately. More importantly, CAM battery performance predicts learning success more accurately than does ASVAB battery performance. There are some problems with these results (e.g., the CAM battery takes more time to administer than does the ASVAB), but for the most part we interpret them positively. At worst we are on the right track; at best we have achieved major success. We are pleased enough to have invested in a more thorough and long-term validation of the CAM battery.[2]

The purpose of this chapter is to review some of the principles and empirical findings that have guided the development of the CAM battery. I also will discuss where research on the battery is headed, including several significant new projects just under way or about to begin. The chapter is organized into two major sections, what abilities should be measured (theory issues), and how they should be measured (interface issues).

WHAT ABILITIES SHOULD BE MEASURED? THEORY ISSUES

A prerequisite to developing a battery of cognitive abilities tests is determining what abilities to measure. Ideally, one would know the "total domain of cognitive abilities," as Carroll (1992) put it, then experiment with different methods for measuring those abilities. Unfortunately, the field has not matured to the point of being able to specify the abilities set, and so a crucial first step is to decide what ought to be measured, that is, what the dimensions of cognitive abilities are. During the early days of the project, we examined extant abilities frameworks, such as the hierarchical frameworks (Gustafsson, 1989), the top-down taxonomic framework of Guilford (1967), and the newer frameworks inspired by developments in cognitive psychology (Hunt, Frost, & Lunneborg, 1973; Sternberg, 1977). All these frameworks have their strengths and weaknesses, known by most students of the field, but none was exactly what we needed for our purposes. We conceived our goal not as simply finding or producing a new abilities framework, but as finding or producing a framework that could guide the development of an aptitude test battery that would be an improvement over the currently used ASVAB for personnel selection and classification.

We adopted several guiding principles. One was that the framework should be closely connected to, even guided by, cognitive psychology. The advantages

---

[2] We are now conducting a more elaborate study with a reduced-size CAM battery, comparable to the ASVAB in length. In this more elaborate study, we are examining the correlation between CAM battery performance and success in actual operational Air Force technical training, which lasts for weeks and even months, depending on the course. We determine training success from a wide variety of learning indicators, performance scores, classroom performance, and the like. We expect to have data to report in about two years.

to this are clear—if the framework is tied to cognitive psychology, then advances in cognitive psychology (findings, models, etc.) should lead directly to advances in the abilities framework. Being guided by cognitive psychology does not mean being impervious to correlational data; in fact, a second principle was that the framework should be grounded in correlational data and models derived from the framework should be supportable by factor analysis. Finally, a third principle was that the framework should be broad and comprehensive, even if, initially anyway, at the expense of being deep. That is, a battery based on the framework ought to sample a wide range of cognitive abilities, rather than probe into the intricacies of a small set of them. We envisioned ourselves conducting a "breadth-first search" of the abilities space. The thinking was, let's get the broad strokes of what it is we want to measure—we'll fill in the subtleties and the details later.

The CAM Taxonomy

Consider two ways to go about constructing a theory of cognitive abilities—top down (theory driven, confirmatory) and bottom up (data driven, exploratory). The bottom-up approach is what Thurstone (1938) used when he adminstered 56 various abilities tests to University of Chicago students, factor analyzed the resulting correlation matrix, then submitted the list of factors extracted as his primary mental abilites model of intelligence. The top-down approach is what Guilford (1967) used in his structure of intellect work. Guilford proposed a taxonomy, or set of dimensions (products, operations, and content) along which tests vary, created a set of tests according to taxonomic specifications, then tested the degree to which the factors specified by the taxonomy coincided with those suggested by the data.

These two approaches are complementary, and ultimately they should converge in identifying ability dimensions. But the approaches are different, and each has its strengths and weaknesses. Conclusions drawn from the bottom-up approach are as interesting as the tests selected to be factor analyzed. The top-down approach is only as useful as the quality of the theory underlying it. The bottom-up approach provides data, for which any fully adequate theory of intelligence ultimately must account, but in its pure form does not test hypotheses as much as generate them (e.g., the hypothesis that there is a spatial ability or a general ability). The top-down approach provides testable hypotheses, but only in domains previously worked out.

The CAM framework is inspired by both approaches. From the top-down perspective, the CAM framework borrows from what might called the "consensus model of human information processing." This is the view that the human cognitive architecture consists of a short-term or working memory, which contains the contents of processing at any given moment, and two long-term memories, one containing declarative knowledge and the other containing procedural knowledge, which contain previously stored results of processing.

Declarative memory can be augmented with new declarative knowledge as a result of declarative learning mechanisms (e.g., association, strengthening), and procedural memory can be augmented through the action of procedural learning mechanisms.

From the bottom-up perspective, the CAM framework reflects the empirical finding, observed over decades of correlational research, that abilities are sensitive to the content of the tests that measure those abilities. Factor analysts, at least since Thurstone (1938), have repeatedly found evidence for separate verbal, quantitative, and spatial factors. However, content and process have typically been confounded in these analyses. Thus, the reasoning factor is often a quantitative reasoning factor, and the verbal factor is often a verbal knowledge factor, where knowledge and reasoning, respectively, are confounded with content. However, the potential separability of content and process was clearly demonstrated in a multidimensional scaling reanalysis of Thurstone's (1938) primary mental abilities data by Snow, Kyllonen, and Marshalek (1984) (see also Kyllonen, in press).

We believe that this two-dimensional process (working memory, processing speed, declarative knowledge, procedural knowledge, declarative learning, procedural learning) by content (verbal, quantitative, spatial) taxonomy provides an adequate starting point for constructing a comprehensive model of human abilities. Most important, from the standpoint of this chapter, the taxonomy helps organize the research that needs to be done to achieve that goal. Research can be divided into that associated with extending the taxonomy (adding process rows or domain columns) and that associated with improving the measurement of the factors already specified by the taxonomy. Given this central, anchoring role for the CAM taxonomy, it is useful to quickly review evidence to date for its viability.

CAM Taxonomy: A "Test"

There are various levels at which an abilities taxonomy, such as CAM, can be considered useful. At a fairly weak level, the taxonomy (actually, an abilities list) can serve as a heuristic for generating ideas on how to organize existing abilities tests and on how to create new ones. Educational Testing Service's Kit of Cognitive Refererence Tests (Ekstrom, French, & Harman, 1976) is organized around this kind of taxonomy. Many extant theories of human abilities seem to be operating at about this level. At an intermediate level of usefulness, the taxonomy can generate specific models of ability organization that can then be tested against data. For example, from the CAM taxonomy one can derive row and column models (there is an ability factor associated with each row and each column in the CAM taxonomy) and cell-factor models (there is a factor associated with each cell in the CAM taxonomy). It is at this level that interesting comparisons among alternative models of abilities organizations can be made. Still more powerful taxonomies are constructed as subfactors within factors can be identified. For example, where CAM might include a working memory factor, a further refinement would be the identification of working memory subfactors such as an executive factor or an attention allocation factor.

In our initial test of the CAM concept, we assembled a battery of tests (which we now refer to as the CAM battery, version 1) by combing the literature for cognitive tasks that nicely conformed to the definitions of the CAM taxonomy's rows and columns. That is, we sought good exemplars of working-memory tests, processing-speed tests, and so on in the verbal, quantitative, and spatial domains (CAM factor definitions can be found in Kyllonen, in press, and in Kyllonen & Christal, 1989). Fig. 7.1 shows the taxonomy (note that declarative and procedural learning rows are missing; these were added only in later versions of the CAM taxonomy and battery). Grey rectangles indicate tests selected. There were three tests for each cell, with the exception of the Procedural Knowledge cells, where there were either one or two, and the Declarative Knowledge cells, where there were no Quantitative or Spatial Knowledge tests.

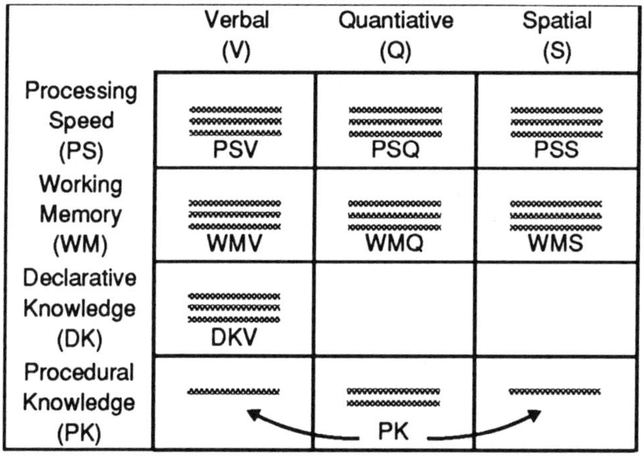

	Verbal (V)	Quantiative (Q)	Spatial (S)
Processing Speed (PS)	PSV	PSQ	PSS
Working Memory (WM)	WMV	WMQ	WMS
Declarative Knowledge (DK)	DKV		
Procedural Knowledge (PK)		PK	

FIG. 7.1. Cognitive Abilities Measurement (CAM) taxonomy (version 1). Gray bars represent tests (e.g., there are three Processing Speed-Verbal, or PSV tests).

We administered all the tests to more than 300 paid volunteers recruited from the local area as part of a larger experiment examining the relationship between test performance and learning computer programming (for details, see Kyllonen, 1993; Shute & Kyllonen, 1990).

The data from the tests allowed us to compute a 25 x 25 matrix of test-score correlations. We analyzed this matrix using confirmatory factor analysis procedures to test various models of those scores. Models included cell-factor and row-and-column models, hierarchical g and flat models, one (g)-factor, three (content)-factor, four (process)-factor models, and so on. From the standpoint of the viability of the CAM taxonomy, there were two critical findings. First, single-factor, content-only-factor, and process-only-factor models did not fit the data as well as did process-plus-content-factor models. This finding implicates both CAM's content and process dimensions, and provides support for the CAM taxonomic framework.

The second finding was that not only were CAM's factors found necessary, but they behaved correlationally in a way one would expect if the taxonomic framework were viable. Fig. 7.2 shows an idealized multidimensional scaling (MDS) solution for the factor intercorrelation matrix generated from the nonhierarchical (flat) cell-factor model, which was one of the models that best fitted the data (a hierarchical variant on this model, which included a *g* factor, fitted the data equally well; the flat variant described here is used to make the subsequent arguments, not to argue for or against the necessity of *g*). The actual MDS solution is close to this idealized one, but the idealized one may be easier to follow. Correlations among factors are listed on the double-headed arrow lines connecting the factors (numbers in the circles are correlations with ASVAB-g).

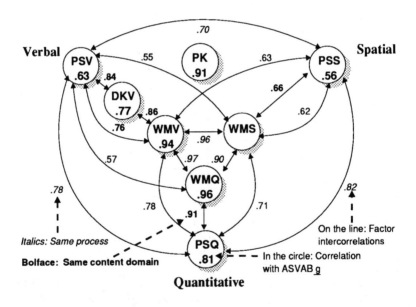

FIG. 7.2. Organization of human abilities. Idealized multidimensional scaling solution of cell factor intercorrelation matrix. Coefficients within circles are correlations with ASVAB *g*. Coefficients on the double-headed arrows are cell-factor correlations.

From the organization of the CAM taxonomy, one should expect several correlational outcomes. First, same-*process* factors should correlate more highly with each other than with different-process factors. Fig. 7.2 shows that, indeed, the working-memory factors correlated more highly with each other than they did with other factors. The processing-speed factors also correlated more highly with each other than they did with other factors, except in some cases where they shared content. Second, same-*content* factors should correlate more highly with each other than they should with different-content factors. For example, quantitative processsing speed (PSQ) correlated more highly with quantitative working memory (WMQ), than it did with the two different-content working-memory factors. Both these correlational outcomes are consistent with what one would expect if the taxonomic organization were correct.

Two other features of Fig. 7.2 are worth noting in passing. Each factor circle includes a number which is the correlation of that factor with ASVAB *g*. Note that the working-memory factors were very highly correlated with g, a finding consistent with other studies of their relationship (Kyllonen & Christal, 1990). Also note that the working-memory factors were most highly correlated with *g*, followed by the knowledge factors, then the processing-speed factors. This has been described elsewhere as the complexity continuum of the radex (Marshalek, Lohman, & Snow, 1977; see also Snow, Kyllonen, & Marshalek, 1984).

CAM Taxonomy: Further Developments

The data from CAM version 1 (hereafter, CAM-1) provided what we believed was a useful proof of the viability of the CAM process *x* content concept, but there were several glaring inadequacies that we have subsequently begun to address. One of these, mentioned previously, was the confounding of knowledge and learning factors, both declarative and procedural. CAM-1 included one procedural-knowledge row and one declarative-knowledge row. In the current CAM taxonomy and battery (CAM-4), there are now separate declarative-knowledge, declarative-learning, procedural-knowledge, and procedural-learning rows (see Fig. 7.3). Second, missing cells and missing cell entries in the CAM-1 battery have now been filled. For example, CAM-1 included no declarative-knowledge tests in the quantitative or spatial domains. We now have developed these. Also, CAM-1 included only one or two procedural-knowledge tests in each domain; these cells now include three tests each. Third, and perhaps most interesting theoretically, additional structure has been imposed on the CAM taxonomy in the form of paradigm relationships across columns and part-task-whole-task relationships (part-whole links) across rows. It is to this particular point that the remainder of this section is addressed.

Paradigms

A criticism that could be leveled against the proof of the CAM concept work described previously is that test type or paradigm is confounded with CAM cell.

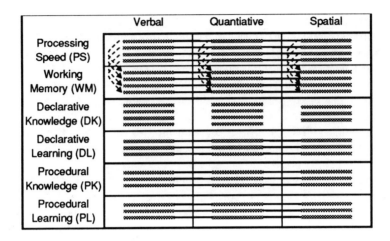

	Verbal	Quantiative	Spatial
Processing Speed (PS)			
Working Memory (WM)			
Declarative Knowledge (DK)			
Declarative Learning (DL)			
Procedural Knowledge (PK)			
Procedural Learning (PL)			

FIG. 7.3. CAM taxonomy (version 4). Grey bars represent tests. Lines connecting gray bars represent shared paradigm (across columns). Dotted arrows represent part-whole relationships between tests (across rows).

That is, within a given CAM cell there are certain types of tests and within other CAM cells there are other types of tests. This is a kind of testing method confound. The implication is that the finding that the test correlation data were consistent with a cell-factor model is ambiguous. Such a finding could be due either to process x content factors or to test-type factors generating the data. One way to remove or at least minimize this confound is to hold the testing method, or paradigm, constant across columns.

To illustrate the paradigm concept, consider the reading span test of working memory capacity (Daneman & Carpenter, 1980), which is one of the more popular tests of its type appearing in the cognitive literature. In one variant of this test, the subject reads a sentence, memorizes the last word in the sentence, reads another sentence, memorizes the last word in that sentence, and then is asked to recall the last words of the two sentences. If the subject successfully remembers both last words, he or she is asked to read three sentences in a row before beginning the recall of last words and, if successful, is moved up to four sentences, and so on. The subject's reading span score is the number of sentences that he or she can read successively and still recall all the last words. In a variant on this task (based on Turner & Engle, 1989), the subject is asked to memorize a random word (not the last word) presented between sentences.

The CAM-4 battery includes what we have called a "processing-span" paradigm with verbal, quantitative, and spatial variants. The verbal test is like the one described previously, except that for group testing purposes, we have subjects verify sentences ("Monkeys are animals that live in trees, true or false?") rather than simply read those sentences. In the quantitative variant of the processing-span test, rather than verify sentences, subjects verify arithmetic expressions (e.g., "6 + 3 - 4 = 5, true or false?") and attempt to memorize digits (e.g., "4") inserted between expressions. In the spatial variant, subjects verify spatial-form equations (e.g., "A part of a figure + another part of the figure = the whole figure, true or false?") and attempt to memorize partially filled matrices inserted between equations.

Three other paradigms have been developed for the working-memory row, including a running-span paradigm, a value-assignment paradigm, and a "four-term ordering" paradigm. Similar paradigms have been developed for the processing-speed row, the declarative- and procedural-learning rows, and the procedural knowledge row (declarative-knowledge tests are not now organized by paradigm). Fig. 7.3 indicates paradigm commonality with links connecting the grey rectangles that represent tests.

The key point is that paradigms in CAM-4 are now crossed rather than confounded factors and their effect in producing variance in scores can be estimated and removed from the content and process factors of interest. This enables a superior test of the CAM taxonomy concept, as well as providing less contaminated factor scores. Because the variance associated with paradigms can be estimated, the estimation of paradigm factors can be a useful tool in evaluating the goodness of paradigms. The goodness of a paradigm, per se, can be evaluated independently of the goodness of a particular test (domain variant of the paradigm), which is obviously useful for battery development.

Part-Whole Links

Method confounding across columns is pretty obvious, as is its solution, the positing and use of paradigm factors, but a second, less obvious confounding occurs over rows. That is, within a particular domain (e.g., verbal), the tests in one particular cell (e.g., the processing-speed cell) are different from the tests in another cell (e.g., the working-memory cell). Thus test type is confounded with process as well as content. The solution to this problem is not as obvious as is the solution to column confounding, in that paradigm seems to be necessarily more integrally bound with the processing factors than it does with content factors. On first consideration it seems irrational to unconfound paradigm and processing factor. That is, it makes sense that we must measure working memory, for example, with one kind of test and processing speed with a rather different kind. For example, working-memory capacity is probably best tested using paradigms that induce errors, whereas processing speed is best measured using paradigms that minimize errors.

However, there is one kind of unconfounding, part-whole, that does make sense over rows, and is employed to a limited extent in the CAM-4 battery. Part-whole unconfounding, under the labels of the subtraction method, the additive factors method, and the pure insertion assumption, among others, has been used extensively in the information-processing literature on individual differences (e.g., Kyllonen, Tirre, & Christal, 1991). The idea involves constructing two tasks, a part task and a whole task, to be identical save for the requirement for an additional amount of processing in the more complex task variant (i.e., the whole task). One factor may then be posited to account for performance on the part task, and that same factor along with an additional factor may then be posited to account for performance on the whole task (for discussion, see Donaldson, 1983; Kyllonen, et al., 1991).

In the CAM-4 battery, processing-speed tasks are part tasks and corresponding working-memory tasks are whole tasks, as shown in Fig. 7.3. An example may make the relationship clear. One processing-speed paradigm is called two-term ordering (adapted from Baddeley, 1968). Subjects are shown a sentence such as "Bird comes before cow" next to a display of the two terms, such as "bird cow"; their task is to indicate whether the display ordering is consistent with the order suggested by the sentence. This is a fairly simple task, and most high-school students should respond correctly most of the time, unless, of course they rush their response or do not attend to the task. Subjects do vary in how quickly they respond. This is the primary measure of their performance on the two-term ordering task, and hence serves as an indication of their processing speed. The working-memory version of the task, called four-term ordering, is similar except that subjects are required to order more terms: "Bird comes before cow, chair does not follow table, and the furniture does not come before the animals." This task is quite a bit more difficult than the two-term ordering task and, consequently, the probability of error rises quite dramatically. The two-term ordering task is a part task, and the four-term ordering task is a whole task. Similar part-whole relationships characterize the other three working-memory and processing-speed paradigms.

In all cases, given suitable models, the construction of these kinds of part-whole linkages allows one to estimate process factors (processing-speed and working-memory factors) that are less confounded by method (paradigm) variance than they would be if such a technique were not employed. This enables the researcher to more confidently implicate the particular process (or content) factor in validity studies of various kinds. As an example of where this might be useful, consider studies where one wants to compare the importance of say, processing-speed and working-memory capacity factors in their relationship to some third factor, Y, such as general ability or learning success. With part-whole links one can examine the relationship of processing speed with Y and the relationship between that part of working-memory task performance that is not associated with processing speed with Y.

The degree to which the sorts of distinctions and refinements in the CAM-4 battery discussed in this section make a notable empirical difference remains to be seen. Although we have collected data from more than 800 subjects on the complete 12-hour CAM-4 battery to date, we have not yet completed analyses of those data.

CAM Taxonomy: Extensions

Analysis of CAM-4 data already in hand should lead to adjustments to the CAM taxonomy and battery. In addition, further development of the CAM taxonomy will involve (a) the incorporation of new testing paradigms, (b) the imposition of additional part-whole linkages binding more taxonomy rows, (c) the inclusion of additional ability cells tapping real-time cognitive abilities such as temporal and motor abilities, and (d) the addition of a new orthogonal dimension to the taxonomy reflecting the differences between what sometimes is called cold (normal) versus hot (under stress) cognition.

Additional Paradigms

Paradigms (sometimes confused with factors) organize significant chunks of work in cognitive psychology. For example, extensive literatures exist on mental scanning tasks, categorical learning tasks, memory span tasks, implicit learning tasks, and so on.

From an individual-differences perspective, a taxonomic scheme, such as CAM, for organizing the paradigms themselves is useful in at least two ways. It forces attention at the right level, the level of the factor or construct, rather than the level of the paradigm, in thinking about what it is we really are interested in measuring in individuals. And it suggests a natural ordering of hypothesis tests to be conducted when new paradigms arrive. Many of the paradigms employed in cognitive psychology (and, we hope, many new paradigms still to come) can be placed a priori in a CAM taxonomy cell, from even a superficial task analysis. A natural initial individual-differences question is whether the new paradigm taps any ability beyond what is tapped by other cell paradigms. A simple way to address the question is by creating multiple paradigm variants, say one in each content domain, and then to determine the uniqueness of the new paradigm factor with respect to other cell paradigm factors. Once this is completed, a next step is to evaluate the uniqueness of the new paradigm factor with respect to other CAM rows.

The next generation of the CAM taxonomy (version 5) will include several additional new paradigms. Scott Chaiken is currently evaluating various inspection time paradigms for measuring processing speed. Our current processing speed tests present stimuli that stay on the screen until the subject responds. Processing speed is measured as the latency between stimulus onset and subject response. The problem with these paradigms is that a high proportion of the total response latency is devoted to motor responding when what we are most interested in is cognitive response time (e.g., speed of retrieval from long-term memory). In the inspection-time paradigm, stimuli are presented only briefly (on the order of milliseconds), and the test is whether the subject can process the stimuli before it disappears and is masked. Response latency does not enter into the score and therefore motor response time per se does not contaminate estimates of processing speed.

A second new paradigm we are evaluating is category learning as an indicator of declarative-learning ability. Our current declarative-learning paradigms include two standard study-test procedures (recall and recognition) and an implicit-like learning paradigm. Given the attention paid to category learning in the cognitive literature, and the sophistication of associated neural-network-based performance models (e.g., Gluck & Bower, 1988), we thought it would be interesting to compare associative-learning parameters yielded by performance models with the associative (declarative)-learning factor yielded by our existing declarative tests. Further details on these two new paradigms and others we are developing can be found elsewhere (Kyllonen, in press).

There is a question as to the ideal number of paradigms within a row. A minimum number of paradigms is three or four, which is necessary to identify a factor. Lloyd Humphreys (1984) has argued that the ideal number of paradigms is an even larger number, in that the greater the diversity of ways of measuring a particular factor, the better the measure of that factor ("systematic heterogeneity"). The Wonderlic intelligence test takes this idea to an extreme in that almost each item is a new paradigm. The argument is sound, but the problem is that unless one uses standard paradigms that subjects already understand, there is huge overhead for teaching instructions. The overhead increases the time it takes to collect test data from subjects to an impractical degree. Improvements in how test items are presented may mitigate this effect in the future.

Another question is what constitutes a good paradigm. The ideal paradigm factor is one with high "row" centrality, that is, one that correlates highly with other paradigm factors for that process but that does not correlate highly with other process factors or other process paradigm factors. If a paradigm factor does not correlate highly with other same-process paradigm factors and does not correlate highly with other process factors and other process paradigm factors (i.e., a paradigm factor with high uniqueness), that may indicate a new process row or simply a bad paradigm, depending on whether similar bad paradigms can be found and on whether a psychologically interesting argument can be made for incorporating a new process row.

Additional Part-Whole Links

The CAM-4 battery links only the processing-speed and working-memory tests via part-whole relationships. The remaining process rows confound test type with process. But there may be other natural candidates for linking in future CAM batteries. For example, declarative- and procedural-learning paradigms could be linked and general and specific knowledge tests could be linked as if they were related in part-whole fashion.

In previous studies examining the relationship between CAM-type factors and declarative- and procedural-learning factors (Kyllonen & Stephens, 1990; Shute & Kyllonen, 1990) we have linked the factors as follows. We assume that declarative learning is the general (associative) learning factor and that it influences performance on any learning task. We assume that procedural learning is a more specific learning factor and that it influences performance only on procedural learning tasks. In the prototypical study of cognitive skill acquisition (e.g., computer programming skill), the student is first presented the declarative knowledge relevant to the development of the cognitive skill (i.e., declarative-learning tasks), then is given problems to solve (i.e., procedural-learning tasks). Using the part-whole linking strategy, we assume that the declarative-learning task is the part task and the procedural-learning task is the whole task. Thus, performance on the initial declarative portion of a learning task is assumed to be governed by the declarative-learning factor and performance on the subsequent procedural part is assumed to be governed by both declarative- and procedural-learning factors.

We have not organized the CAM declarative- and procedural-learning tasks in this fashion, but we could. For example, one set of CAM-4 procedural-learning tasks follow what we call the "if-then" paradigm. Subjects are shown numbers on the screen and are to respond by pressing either the "L" or "D" keys on the keyboard. They do this after memorizing rules such as, "If the object on the screen is a number, then determine if it is odd or even; if it is odd then determine if it is above 10 or below 10; if it is above press L otherwise press D." Clearly, one could test declarative knowledge of the rules taught through the use of the standard declarative-learning paradigms (e.g., recall, recognition).

General and specific declarative-knowledge tests could also be linked in this fashion. One could assume that the general declarative-knowledge factor underlies performance on both general and specific knowledge tests (where the paradigm for probing that knowledge is held constant), but that an additional specific knowledge factor underlies performance on only the specific knowledge tests. That is, the assumption would be that one's specific knowledge in a particular domain (e.g., computer programming) is determined by the amount of general knowledge one possesses as well as the amount of domain-specific knowledge one possesses.

The advantage to this kind of linking is that it allows for a clearer interpretation of linked-factor relationships to other factors. If some interesting criterion variable is regressed on two correlated factors (e.g., declarative and procedural learning as measured in CAM-4), it is not clear how to interpret the resulting regression coefficients. If that same criterion variable is regressed on two factors that are uncorrelated (i.e., unconfounded) through the use of the linking procedure (linked factors are necessarily orthogonal), interpretation of the regression coefficients is straightforward. One can achieve orthogonality between two factors without linking (i.e., the variance of one factor can be partialled out of another no matter what the nature of the factors), but orthogonality is not the only issue involved. The linking concept necessarily involves in addition the idea of a part-whole (or something similar) relationship between two tasks or paradigms.

A New CAM Column: Temporal Abilities

We have recently begun work on temporal abilities, that is, those abilities associated with processing time and timing information. An example task would be one where a subject is shown a stopwatch-like digital-timer display that counts up from 0 to 100 at a constant rate. At some point, say 50, the display goes blank, and the subject's task is to estimate when the timer would have reached 100 if it had continued. A spatial analog would be one in which an object is shown moving across a display screen, which is 100 units across. At some point, say at the 50th unit, the object disappears, and the subject's task is to estimate when the object would have reached the end of the display (i.e., the 100th unit). Although this latter kind of task has sometimes appeared under the heading "dynamic spatial task" (Hunt, Pellegrino, Frick, & Alderton, 1988), data we have collected on these two tasks show them to be highly correlated. Thus, we believe the implicated underlying ability has more of a temporal processing flavor than a dynamic spatial flavor. Further, we and others have found that the temporal processing factor is not perfectly predicted by other cognitive factors, such as spatial ability, and thus we have begun considering how such a factor could be incorporated into the CAM taxonomy.

For both the empirical reasons just discussed and on rational grounds, we believe that temporal processing warrants greater status than paradigm, and so the question is whether it ought to be considered either an additional row, an additional column, or an additional dimension to the CAM taxonomy. A new dimension would be indicated if all current CAM taxonomy tasks could be constructed in both temporal-processing and nontemporal-processing flavors. This does not seem sensible, and so the question is whether to add a row or a column to the CAM matrix. For quite some time, I thought of temporal processing as a new row. The problem was that while it was easy enough to construct temporal processing tasks (such as those desribed above) in the quantitative (involving counting) and spatial (involving tracking) domains, a natural verbal (noncounting) variant did not seem possible. Scott Chaiken, from our research group, suggested incorporating temporal as a domain (see Fig. 7.4) and he has begun developing temporal domain tasks in the various process areas (temporal working memory, temporal processing speed, etc.). Although we are in the early stages of this work, we believe that temporal will fit more naturally as a domain than as a process factor.

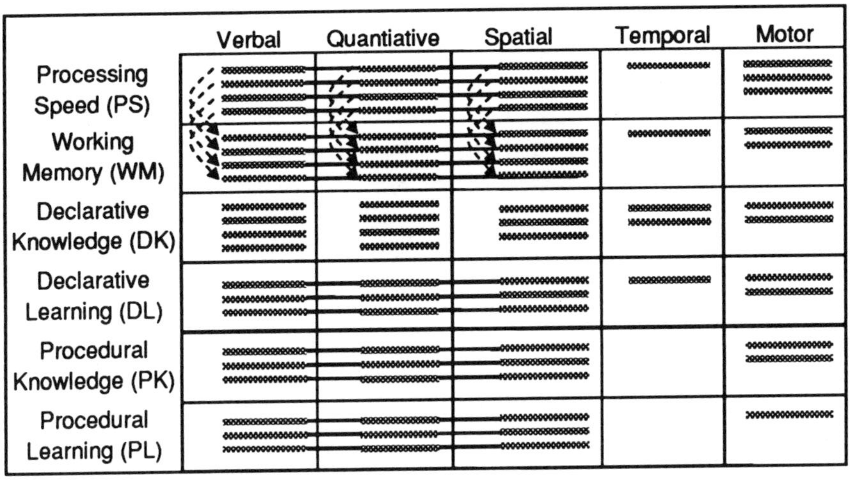

	Verbal	Quantiative	Spatial	Temporal	Motor
Processing Speed (PS)					
Working Memory (WM)					
Declarative Knowledge (DK)					
Declarative Learning (DL)					
Procedural Knowledge (PK)					
Procedural Learning (PL)					

FIG. 7.4. CAM taxonomy (version 5?). Grey bars represent tests. Lines connecting grey bars represent shared paradigms (across columns). Dotted arrows represent part-whole relationships between tests (across rows). This taxonomy is identical to the CAM taxonomy, version 4 (see Fig. 7.3) with the addition of two new domain columns, Temporal and Motor.

A New CAM Column (?): Motor Abilities. If the CAM taxonomy must be stretched a bit to accommodate temporal processing tasks, it probably will require a major expansion at a minimum to accommodate psychomotor tasks. Nevertheless, we intend over the next several years to conduct considerable research in the psychomotor area. There are extant taxonomies of psychomotor abilities (e.g., Fleishman & Quaintance, 1984) that should greatly assist our own research efforts. These extant taxonomies appear to be at a fairly early stage of development, however, probably at about the level of the ETS's Kit of Cognitive Reference Tests in the cognitive area.

As a rough initial guess, we intend to incorporate motor abilities into the CAM taxonomy as a domain column. As a thought exercise one can imagine motor working-memory tasks, motor processing-speed tasks, motor learning tasks (although motor declarative-learning tasks seem somewhat problematic), and perhaps even motor knowledge tests. Whether this accommodation of the motor domain into the CAM taxonomy in the end turns out to be stifling and restrictive or a stimulus to thinking about psychomotor abilities remains to be seen.

A New CAM Dimension: Cognition Under Stress ("Hot Cognition").
Normal or "cold" cognition has been an almost exclusive concern of abilities
researchers over the decades.   There have been the occasional studies of
cognitive task performance under stressors of various kinds, and of cognitive task
performance in unusual environments (e.g., the deep sea, space), but these have
been conducted primarily to evaluate the degree to which stressors impair
cognition in general. To my knowledge, with the possible exception of the test-
anxiety literature, there has been no systematic treatment of the interaction
between stressors and abilities.   The question certainly is one of applied
importance. If applicants for jobs performed in "hot" environments (e.g., pilot,
air traffic controller) are selected with ability tests given under cold
circumstances, there is a least a legitimate question as to how much validity
might improve with a better temperature match.

The CAM framework seems to be ideally suited for addressing important
theoretical questions concerning the interaction between temperature and
cognition.   Imagine an experiment in which a group (or two groups) of
examinees is given the full CAM battery under two conditions, normal and
stressed (e.g., with noise, time pressure, light fluctuations). With models derived
from the CAM taxonomy it is possible to address substantive hypotheses about
both mean changes in performance, factor by factor, and changes in covariance
structure, using structural equation modeling methods. For example, one can test
the hypothesis that working memory per se is the factor most susceptible to
stress, along with the hypothesis that some individuals are particularly susceptible
to working-memory loss under stress. The role played by the CAM taxonomy
in such studies would be not only to highlight the ability susceptible to stress, but
also to pinpoint the level at which a stressor had an effect—the test level, the
paradigm level, or the factor level.

HOW SHOULD THEY BE MEASURED? INTERFACE ISSUES

Interface issues (instructions, pacing, stimulus display, etc.) become important to
experimental psychologists when experiments fail. With the belief that one's
hypothesis could not be wrong, one instead goes back and tidies up the details,
such as the interface, that might have led to things going awry.   Because
correlational studies never really fail ("the correlation might really be zero"),
there is a danger that correlational psychologists might downplay the importance
of interface issues. Interface issues are important, particularly with computerized
tests. Poorly designed test interfaces can lead to inefficient data collection, or
even worse, a situation in which the test measures different abilities for different
examinees.   There are many interface issues (for additional discussion, see
Kyllonen, 1991), but two that warrant particular attention are those associated
with speed-accuracy trade-off and those associated with the adaptivity of a test.

Speed-Accuracy Trade-off

Differences between subjects in how they respond to the competing response goals of "maximize speed" and "maximize accuracy" can have a tremendous impact on their test scores. This is particularly true with the processing-speed tasks and the procedural-learning tasks in the CAM battery, which typically involve responses that take less than two seconds, but it is also true on virtually any cognitive task. The speed-accuracy problem has received considerable attention, both in the general cognitive literature and in the individual-differences literature, but the field does not seem close to solution. The speed-accuracy problem is critical in computer testing. There is a tremendous need in the field for a systematic evaluation of various approaches to dealing with speed-accuracy trade-off.

Instructions

Paper-and-pencil tests finesse the speed-accuracy trade-off problem by imposing standard time limits, which have the virtue of at least being understood by all examinees. Computer tests are more flexible than are group-administered paper-and-pencil tests, and latencies can be recorded rather than simply restricted. But this flexibility is accompanied by confusion induced in the examinee who now does not know how long he or she should take to respond. This is a problem perhaps most naturally addressed by instructing the examinee as to what is expected. Extensive pilot testing with CAM battery tests showed that examinees often were confused over whether they should emphasize speed or accuracy. The standard instruction appearing before each test, "Work as quickly as you can without making mistakes," was simply inadequate.

Currently in the CAM we now divide tests into three categories:

1. Those where only accuracy matters and there is a loose deadline (e.g., knowledge tests).
2. Those where only accuracy matters but there is a strict time deadline (e.g., some of the procedural-learning and working-memory tests).
3. Those without deadlines where speed is important (e.g., the processing-speed tests).

Each of these tests is associated with a speed-accuracy trade-off screen that explains which category of test it is.

Scoring

For fairness purposes, and as at least as a rough first swipe, scoring Category I and II tests is usually noncontroversial. One's score is simply the number correct. (However, even for these tests there is typically interesting variance associated with the latency measure.) Scoring Category III tests, on the other hand, is tricky. The ideal score would be a single score, rather than separate latency and accuracy scores, because examinees can be told, in the form of feedback, how the score behaves in response to their speed-accuracy trade-off shifts. Examinees can learn, through practice, how to optimize a single score by balancing the goals of working fast and being accurate. It is impossible to instruct subjects on how to optimize a weighted sum of two scores with unknown weights, which is what we essentially are doing when we ask them to "Work as quickly as you can without making errors."

We have found empirically that the single speed-accuracy product score (e.g., percentage correct divided by mean latency) is often psychometrically the well-behaving score for Category III tasks. For example, the data from the procedural-knowledge and processing-speed tasks presented earlier in this chapter used this score. David Wright from Plymouth University in Great Britain (personal communication, June 1992) has suggested displaying a variant on this score (number correct over cumulative response time) in the form of a graph to study changes in test performance over trials. We are currently experimenting with presenting such a graph to examinees immediately after each item response. The graph displays concretely to the examinee the costs of slow responses and errors.

Adaptivity

In almost any applied testing context, testing time is severely limited. The goal is always to gain as much information from an examinee in as little time as is possible. The problem of testing time constraints is certain to become even more severe if we are serious about increasing the number of paradigms administered to subjects to measure each CAM factor, as was discussed in a previous section of this chapter. The obvious solution to this problem is to make tests adaptive. We have initiated two projects concerned with adaptivity, one for most of the CAM tests (the "Smartests" project), and one for the knowledge tests (the "20-Questioner" project).

The Smartests Project

The goal of the Smartests project is to develop an algorithm to use with computerized tests that enables adaption to the capabilities of the test taker. The algorithm will generate harder items (not simply present prestored harder items) if the examinee is doing well on the test, easier items if the examinee is doing poorly. That is, the test self-adjusts its difficulty level in response to an examinee's performance. The Smartest has both adaptive and generative capabilities. With these, the Smartest will be capable of more precisely measuring ability at a wider range of abilities than current tests can measure.

Current tests accurately measure ability with maximum precision only if the test taker is at an average ability level. But if the test taker is considerably above average, the test cannot measure the test taker precisely because the test will contain very few items that are appropriate in difficulty (most items for such an examinee will be too easy). Similarly, the test will not be able to measure low-ability individuals precisely; most items will be missed by such an examinee.

Benefits of Adaptiveness. The Smartest capability of precisely measuring an ability over a very wide range has application potential in diverse areas. In aptitude testing (selection and classification), the same Smartest will be usable for both enlisted personnel and officers. This will result in substantial test item development costs as compared with the current system, in which enlisted and officer test development are independent activities. In aging research (e.g., to test age effects on pilot performance) the same Smartest will be usable across the age span. And in performance testing and evaluation research applications, the same Smartest will be usable pre-, during-, and post-treatment, even if the treatment greatly changes (interferes with or enhances) the ability the test is designed to measure. This solves a well-known psychometric problem with current tests used in such research: Tests fail to detect treatment (or concomitant variable) effects if the treatment (or concomitant variable) changes examinees' ability level to a point other than that the test was designed to measure.

Benefits of Generativeness. With a Smartest, not only will test development be unified, but there will be less of a necessity for it. Current tests are made up of "hard-coded" items that must undergo a continuous and costly development-evaluation cycle, and even then are vulnerable to compromise (e.g., being stolen). Smartests are made up of "soft-coded" (generative) items, where only the specifications rather than the items themselves have to be developed. The computer does the work of generating the items. Smartest items would be low cost, inexpensive to maintain, and invulnerable to compromise.

Details. The Smartest project combines two technologies from the psychometric and the cognitive psychological research literatures that have not yet been so combined. The psychometric technology is item response theory (IRT), which is a family of models for characterizing item difficulty, that is, an item's sensitivity for a particular examinee ability level. It includes with it the computer adaptive testing (CAT) capability of presenting items to match the examinee's ability level. However, IRT does not have item generation capabilities; that is the contribution of cognitive psychology. Item generative capability is made available through the use of faceted tests. These are tests that conform to a specification or information-processing model of how item features affect difficulty level. By altering these features, the test developer (or computer) can mechanically adjust item difficulty level.

IRT methodology provides the most exact specification of item difficulty. Faceting methodology provides a simplified specification of item difficulty. The research question addressed in the Smartest project is how much of IRT item difficulty can be accounted for by a test's facets. If facets account for much (say, r < .70) of the IRT item difficulty, then the test for which that is true is amenable to the Smartest approach, and therefore could be relatively easily made both generative and adaptive. If facets do not account for much (say r << .7) of the IRT item difficulty variance, then the test could be developed to be adaptive but not generative.

The research would involve estimating IRT item difficulties on the 45 faceted tests of LAMP's Cognitive Ability Measurement (CAM, version 4.0) battery. These difficulty parameters then would be regressed on the item facets. These regressions would indicate the degree to which the facets accounted for the item difficulties.

Knowledge Tests (The 20-Questioner Project)

The goal of the 20-Questioner project is to develop a technology capable of estimating an individual's knowledge level over a wide variety of topics. It does this using a sophisticated knowledge interrogation strategy similar to one employed by an expert player of the game "20 questions." That is, the 20-Questioner system will intelligently ask a set of questions designed to zero in on what an examinee knows about a particular topic, such as engines, automobiles, electricity, computers, math, logic, literature, and so on.

The assumption of the 20-Questioner is that there is a large but finite number of general facts relevant to some domain (e.g., the domain of Air Force enlisted jobs). Suppose there are 100,000 facts. Without any knowledge of an examinee, we can assume knowledge of these 100,000 facts at the average of the population's knowledge. That is, the default examinee is likely to know the easy facts (e.g., there is a 99.9% probability he or she will know "cars have four wheels") and unlikely to know the esoteric facts (there is a .01% probability he or she will know that "EGR is a kind of emission control"). But by asking just one question, the 20-Questioner can begin to fine tune those default probabilities in the 100,000 question database. Not only will the system know whether the examinee knows the answer to the particular question asked, but by knowing the correlations and dependency relations among questions, the system will also be in a position to guess whether the examinee knows the answer to questions not asked. For example, if the examinee does not know the difference between integers and real numbers, the system can safely conclude that the examinee does not know what an integral is, does not know what the square root of minus one is, probably does not know the formula for gravity, and more likely than not does not know who the third president of the United States was. Note that these latter assertions are not as closely related or dependent on the initial question as the former assertions are, but they are still plausible. The point of the 20-Questioner project is to quantify this kind of plausibility.

The 20-Questioner can be used in any situation where the goal is to assess what an examinee knows. The two primary applications would be in aptitude testing and adaptive training. Current enlisted aptitude testing systems measure knowledge in several areas, such as electronics, auto and shop, mechanical, mathematical, and general science. But they do so with a very small number of questions (about 100 altogether), and therefore can provide only ballpark assessment of what an examinee knows in broad domains. For adaptive-training applications, it is even more important to guess what an examinee knows on a whole range of topics for the purpose of being able to optimize instruction. For example, if an examinee does not know about hydraulics, water analogies are not likely to be of much use in explaining how electricity works.

The 20-Questioner can be viewed as the knowledge counterpart to the Smartest project. Both systems will require adaptiveness algorithms to zero in on what an examinee can do. The difference between the two is that ability tests can be generative (the computer can mechanically generate items), but knowledge tests cannot (knowledge items have to be prestored).

Details. The 20-Questioner project is a four-stage activity, involving (a) the generation of a domain taxonomy, (b) item generation based on the domain taxonomy, (c) the formation of an empirical database of item difficulties and dependencies, and (d) the development of interrogation algorithms. The first stage would involve listing the target-domain specialty areas (e.g., a subset of Air Force specialties), in preparation for sampling facts from those areas. One way to list specialty areas would be by Air Force job specialty codes, using the existing Air Force job classification system. Another would be to use knowledge or job taxonomies based on projects that have clustered jobs in various ways, such as those that have gathered "ease-of-movement" ratings, or those that have used the Comprehensive Occupational Data Analysis Programs (CODAP) system. In the second stage, after a specialty-area taxonomy was developed, the project would generate a pool of facts from each of the various specialty (content) areas using existing sources (e.g., achievement tests, test materials, textbook study questions). In the third stage, once the pool was assembled, these facts would be administered as test questions to a large group of Air Force enlisted examinees. More facts would be generated than any single examinee could be expected to respond to, and so a matrix-sampling design could be employed to obtain estimates of the population knowledge levels for each fact, and of the correlation and dependency relations among all the facts. This would result in a large asymmetric matrix of facts, where each x,y element in the matrix indicated the probability that an examinee knew x given that he or she knew y, or some other similar parameter.

In the fourth stage, an interrogation strategy, that is, a smart "20-questions" type strategy would be developed. This would include a means for updating the knowledge base following a response, and a strategy for what question to ask next to maximize the benefit of the response. It also would specify in some fashion what kind of confidence band to place around its assessments of what a particular individual knows at any particular time.

SUMMARY

Earl Hunt suggested several years ago in an editorial in the journal *Intelligence* (1992) that a concerted five-year effort to put together what we know about psychometrics, cognitive psychology, and computerized testing could pay off in the form of a quantum improvement in how we test aptitudes in personnel selection and classification environments. Although the CAM project is by no means of the scope Hunt may have had in mind, and does not pretend to be a realization of what he had intended, it is inspired by the belief that much of what is necessary is in place for real progress. Aptitude testing in the military services as well as elsewhere is not much different today in quality or in kind from what it was 30 or 40 years ago. At the same time, the supporting scientific and technological infrastructure has experienced dramatic growth. Computers enable the testing of abilities that paper-and-pencil tests simply could not measure, cognitive psychology informs us in a much more sophisticated manner about what it is that we are measuring, and new statistical and psychometric models allow us to refine both our abilities models and our tests in a manner never before possible. It behooves us to take advantage of these developments and to finish the job of developing the next-generation aptitude testing system.

REFERENCES

Baddeley, A. D. (1968). A 3 min reasoning test based on grammatical transformation. *Psychonomic Science, 10*, 341-342.

Carroll, J. B. (1992). Cognitive abilities: The state of the art. *Psychological Science, 3*, 266-271.

Daneman, M., & Carpenter, P. A. (1980). Individual differences in working memory and reading. *Journal of Verbal Learning and Verbal Behavior, 19*, 450-466.

Donaldson, G. (1983). Confirmatory factor analysis models of information processing stages: An alternative to difference scores. *Psychological Bulletin, 94*, 143-151.

Ekstrom, R. B., French, J. W., & Harman, H. H. (with Dermen, D.). (1976). *Manual for kit of factor-referenced cognitive tests*. Princeton, NJ: Educational Testing Service.

Fleishman, E. A., & Quaintance, M. K. (1984). *Taxonomies of human performance: The description of human tasks*. Orlando: Academic Press.

Gluck, M. A., & Bower, G. H. (1988). From conditioning to category learning: An adaptive network model. *Journal of Experimental Psychology: General, 117*, 227-247.

Guilford, J. P. (1967). *Nature of human intelligence*. New York: McGraw-Hill.

Gustafsson, J. E. (1989). Hierarchical models of abilities. In R. Kanfer, P. Ackerman, & R. Cudeck (Eds.), *Learning and individual differences: Abilities, motivation, and methodology*. Hillsdale, NJ: Lawrence Erlbaum Associates.

Humphreys, L. G. (1984). *Systematic heterogeneity of items in tests of meaningful and important psychological attributes: A rejection of unidimensionality.* Unpublished manuscript. Champagne: University of Illinois.

Hunt, E. (1982). Towards new ways of assessing intelligence. *Ingelligence, 6,* 231-240.

Hunt, E. B., Frost, N., & Lunneborg, C. (1973). Individual differences in cognition: A new approach to intelligence. In G. Bower (Ed.), *The psychology of learning and motivation* (Vol 7). New York: Academic Press.

Hunt, E., Pellegrino, J. W., Frick, R. W., & Alderton, D. L. (1988). The ability to reason about movement in the visual field. *Intelligence, 12,* 77-100.

Kyllonen, P. C. (1991). Principles for creating a computerized test battery. *Intelligence, 15,* 1-15.

Kyllonen, P. C. (1993). Aptitude testing inspired by information processing: A test of the four-sources model. *Journal of General Psychology, 120,* 375-405.

Kyllonen, P. C. (in press). CAM: A framework for cognitive ability measurement. In D. Detterman (Ed.), *Current topics in human intelligence: Theories of intelligence.* Norwood, NJ: Ablex.

Kyllonen, P. C., & Christal, R. E. (1989). Cognitive modeling of learning abilities: A status report of LAMP. In R. Dillon & J. W. Pellegrino (Eds.), *Testing: Theoretical and applied issues.* New York: Freeman. [Also (1989) Tech. Paper No. AFHRL-TP-87-66, Brooks AFB, TX: Manpower and Personnel Division, Air Force Human Resources Laboratory.]

Kyllonen, P. C., & Christal, R. E. (1990). Reasoning ability is (little more than) working memory capacity?! *Intelligence, 14,* 389-433.

Kyllonen, P. C., & Stephens, D. L. (1990). Cognitive abilities as determinants of success in acquiring logic skill. *Learning and Individual Differences, 2,* 129-160.

Kyllonen, P. C., Tirre, W. C., & Christal, R. E. (1991). Knowledge and processing speed as determinants of associative learning proficiency. *Journal of Experimental Psychology: General, 120,* 1-23. [Also (1989) Tech. Paper AFHRL-TP-87-68, Brooks AFB, TX: Manpower and Personnel Division, Air Force Human Resources Laboratory.]

Marshalek, B., Lohman, D. F., & Snow, R. E. (1977). *The complexity continuum in the radex and hierarchical models of ability organization.* Unpublished manuscript, Stanford University.

Shute, V. J., & Kyllonen, P. C. (1990). *Modeling individual differences in programming skill acquisition* (AFHRL-TP-90-76). Brooks AFB, TX: Manpower and Personnel Division, Air Force Human Resources Laboratory.

Snow, R. E., Kyllonen, P. C., & Marshalek, B. (1984). The topography of ability and learning correlations. In R. J. Sternberg (Ed.), *Advances in the psychology of human intelligence, Volume 2.* Hillsdale, NJ: Lawrence Erlbaum Associates.

Sternberg, R. J. (1977). *Intelligence, information processing, and analogical reasoning: The componential analysis of human abilities.* Hillsdale, NJ: Lawrence Erlbaum Associates.

Thurstone, L. L. (1938). Primary Mental Abilities. *Psychometric Monograph, No. 1.* Chicago: University of Chicago Press.

Turner, M. L., & Engle, R. W. (1989). Is working memory capacity task dependent? *Journal of Memory and Language, 28,* 127-154.

CHAPTER

8

THE UBIQUITOUS PREDICTIVENESS OF *g*

Malcolm James Ree
James A. Earles
Armstrong Laboratory

> What's in a name? That which we call a rose
> by any other name would smell as sweet.
>
> William Shakespeare

In our work we have studied human mental abilities on the basis of Spearman's *g* theory and Cattell's (1987) theory of experience modifying general ability to yield testable skills while retaining the general ability—*g* to be modified as situations required. Cattell has identified fluid *g* and crystallized *g* as the resource and the skill. Others have chosen to study verbal ability, working memory, or elemental cognitive components. We have chosen *g* because the research shows that it is almost always predictive of criteria and it is readily estimable in existing databases. It requires no special equipment such as computers and is very inexpensive to measure. That others find additional cognitive components of interest is no surprise. However, a long list of correlates of *g*, presented by Brand (1987) (also see Jensen, 1987), compels attention. The entire list is presented in the appendix to this chapter; Brand provided the original references for all the studies. Some correlates presented are expected, such as ability scores, reaction times, and memory. Others are not expected, such are altruism, practical knowledge, dietary preferences, and smoking. As Brand observed, "*g* is to psychology as carbon is to chemistry" (p. 257).

Before considering the study of *g*, it is necessary to offer cautions about rotated factors, censored samples, and unreliability. The first concern is rotated factors. When factors have been rotated, the variance of the first unrotated factor, typically *g* in tests and other cognitive measures, is distributed across the other factors. The first factor, therefore, appears to be absent, whereas in fact it usually becomes the dominant variance in each of the rotated factors. For example, the verbal factor, V, repeatedly found in tests such as the Armed

Services Vocational Aptitude Battery (ASVAB), is still mostly g as a consequence of the rotation. This accounts, in large part, for the correlation of the factors in multiple- aptitude tests and for the correlation of topographically dissimilar linear composites in ASVAB. To be accurate we should call verbal not V but

$$g + \text{v}.$$

As a topical example, a wide variety of cognitive tests were shown by Kranzler and Jensen (1991) to be mostly g. To avoid problems associated with rotation, either don't rotate or use residualized hierarchical factor techniques.

The second caution: Censored samples can likewise lead to erroneous conclusions about ability. As Brand (1987) observed, many studies seeking to factorially isolate components or to evaluate the efficacy of g and other variables have been conducted in samples that have been censored with respect to g. The variance of the censored variable is reduced, which artificially diminishes observed correlations. Military, college student, and most occupation samples have been selected to some (frequently large) degree on g. For instance, in Air Force samples it is usual to find ASVAB test variances reduced from 100 to 25 by prior selection. The resultant range restriction leads often to a false conclusion that g is not strongly related to other variables studied. Actually, what is being concluded is the consequence of statistical artifact. Meta-analysts (Hunter & Schmidt, 1990) have sounded the most recent warning on this problem, echoing McNemar's (1964) famous APA presidential address. To avoid range restriction problems due to censored samples, statistical corrections should be applied.

The third problem that leads to erroneous conclusions is to use tests (or cognitive tasks) which are so unreliable that they cannot correlate with any other tests, falsely giving the appearance of uniqueness. Such tests must be made more reliable; lengthen the test or remove ambiguity from the items. Failing these remedies, discard it. At the very least, all experimental tests and cognitive tasks should be administered twice to the same subjects to estimate reliability for use in the correction-for-attenuation formula. Although the appropriate time interval for retest is not agreed on, we believe that several days' separation is more desirable than same-day retesting.

To conduct studies it is often necessary to estimate the general ability of individuals. Using large samples of young adults we showed (Earles & Ree, 1991; Ree & Earles, 1991a) that with ordinary paper-and-pencil test batteries (multiple-aptitude tests) any positive weighting of the tests of the batteries will yield almost identical estimates of g. Common weighting schemes to estimate g are usually derived from the statistical procedures of component or factor analyses. Correlations among our g estimates never dropped below .93, and often exceeded .99! This was because all the tests, regardless of overt content, form, and title, measured *g* or general ability in large part. This accounts for the uniformly positive correlations among all tests first reported by Spearman (1904) and those reported ever since. We have yet to see cognitive tests that do not measure *g* to some large extent. Recently Kranzler and Jensen (1991) demonstrated the positive manifold of elementary cognitive tasks (ECT), which measure the cognitive components studied by some. They also showed the high *g* saturation of ECTs.

What remains after *g* is statistically removed from tests is non-*g*, that portion of the score due to intelligence but strongly enough influenced by experience to be factorially distinct (Cattell, 1987). Having determined ways to measure *g* and non-*g* portions for tests and for individuals, we then investigated the utility of *g* and non-*g* for predicting job performance criteria.

Job performance, especially in our service economy, has several components. One is possessing the skills, knowledge, and techniques of the job. Training and retraining for new positions or promotions, as well as learning to stay even with changing responsibilities of the "same" position, are significant aspects of most employment. The second component is the application of these skills, knowledge, and techniques to achieve organizational goals. Job performance determinants such as physical strength, individual motivation, personality, and other nonintellectual components will not be addressed; other chapters in this volume cover those topics.

A test's utility in predicting training success, the first component of job success, comes predominantly from that share of the test measuring *g*. The *g* loadings of the 10 ASVAB tests were correlated with their average validity for predicting training success for more than 24,000 enlisted subjects in 37 diverse jobs. The Spearman's rank order correlation was .75 (Jones, 1988); correcting the loadings for the unreliability of the tests, this figure becomes .98. This correlation was estimated in another sample of more than 78,000 subjects across 150 jobs and computed to be .96. When computed within the mechanical, administrative, general-technical, and electronic job groupings the Air Force uses, the correlations were much the same. The higher the *g* loading of a test, the more valid it was.

A study of the incremental validity of non-*g* to *g* was conducted (Ree & Earles, 1989) using the ASVAB. Performance in a sample of 78,049 airmen in 89 technical job training courses was predicted by both *g* and non-*g*. Psychometric *g* was uniformly found to be the most potent predictor for each technical training course and the contributions of the non-*g* portions were found to be small or nonexistent. The average correlation of *g* with the criterion was .76, when corrected for range restriction due to prior use of the test for selection. Adding the non-*g* portions to the 89 prediction equations increased the average correlation by .02. One job was found in which the non-*g* portion added .10, and for one third of the jobs the only significant predictor was *g*. No estimate was made of the expected variance of the additional predictive power of non-g. We cannot dismiss the hypothesis that the variance of the incremental validity of non-g was expected sampling variance. The predictive efficiency of g for training performance was high and was helped little by non-g.

A study to determine whether g predicted job training success in about the same way regardless of the kind of job or the difficulty of the job was conducted (Ree & Earles, 1991b), again using ASVAB. Linear models statistical analyses were used to determine whether the relationships of g to training performance were the same for 82 jobs. While we found statistical evidence that the relationships of g to the criteria differed by job, these differences were small and appeared to be of no practical predictive consequence. The relationship of g and performance was practically the same for all jobs. Aggregating the jobs in one predicting equation reduced the correlation less than one half of one percent.

The non-g portions of ASVAB have been found to add only a little beyond g in prediction of training success. For some Air Force jobs, special classification tests were specifically developed to augment the predictiveness of ASVAB. Two additional test measures, one for the selection of computer programmers and one for the selection of intelligence operatives, were investigated to determine whether they were other than measures of g (Besetsny, Earles, & Ree, 1993; Besetsny, Ree, & Earles, 1993). Linear models analyses showed incremental validity gains of .0001 and .0165, respectively, for the two jobs. These two tests, intended to add unique measure, contributed little beyond g for selection into these two jobs.

The second component of job success, the accomplishment of the job's primary tasks, has been much less studied—particularly the role played by g. This is primarily due to the difficulty and expense of obtaining criterion measures of job performance.

A study was conducted to investigate the incremental validity of non-g to g in prediction of job sample performance (Morales, 1991). A group of about 5,500 college-graduate first lieutenants, half in pilot training and half in navigator training, was studied to determine how well g and non-g predicted five flying and five navigation criteria. For the pilots, the criteria were actual samples of flying and academic performance. For the navigators, the criteria were samples of day and night navigation and academic performance. Very few students failed training for academic reasons; most failed for inability to control the aircraft (pilots) or to correctly use the navigation instruments (navigators) on check rides.

Results found for prediction of pilot and navigator academic and job sample performance were similar to those for technical training performance: g was the best predictor (average $r = .33$, range corrected to represent selected college graduates, not the general population, which makes the coefficient an underestimate of population values). However, the non-g portions provided a larger average increase in predictive accuracy, .05.

We also investigated the validity and incremental validity of *g* and non-*g* for several criteria across a variety of jobs (Ree, Earles, & Teachout, 1992). A sample of 1,545 airmen with about two years' job experience was used to determine whether *g* was the best predictor of on-the-job performance in eight jobs; two each from the mechanical, administrative, general-technical, and electrical job families as used by the Air Force. The criteria were work samples of hands-on job performance, technical interviews in which the incumbent explained how tasks were done step by step, and supervisory ratings. The use of multiple criteria had several purposes. Work samples were seen as having the highest fidelity with on-the-job performance. Interviews sampled a greater number of job tasks than did the hands-on work samples, particularly those that were expensive to test, removed machinery from service, or presented a danger. The supervisory ratings were administered as a possible surrogate for the very expensive hands-on work samples. As before, *g* and non-*g* were used to predict the criteria. Again *g* was the best predictor (range corrected average $r = .44$) of all the job performance measures. The mean increase by adding non-*g* was about .06, similar to the value found in the pilot-navigator study.

Many psychologists have searched for predictors of job performance other than *g* (see, for example, McHenry, Hough, Toquam, Hanson, & Ashworth, 1990). Among the most familiar are scores from psychomotor tests. These predictors look different from paper-and-pencil tests and, therefore, are believed to measure something different. This is an example of the topographical fallacy, the belief that appearances necessarily indicate what is being measured.

In a study in progress, preliminary results indicate that the psychomotor portions of a computer-administered pilot selection test, the Air Force BAT (Carretta, 1990), added .02 (uncorrected for range restriction) above *g* for predicting passing/failing in pilot training. The Air Force officer selection test (AFOQT) was used to estimate *g* for this sample of 678 trainees. This increment to the validity of *g* is similar to the increment reported by the Army in Project A (McHenry et al., 1990). In a sample of 4,039 Army enlisted troops, psychomotor tests added (corrected for range restriction) no more than .02 to any of their five criteria, with a mean of .014 across all the jobs considered.

Recently we studied the possibility that psychomotor tests were mostly measures of *g* (Ree & Carretta, in press), which would explain their relatively small incremental validity. A sample of 354 airmen were administered a battery of eight psychomotor tests and the ASVAB (as the measure of *g*). These psychomotor tests have a long history in the literature (Thorndike & Hagen, 1959) and are well known and well regarded (Fleishman & Quaintance, 1984). The observed correlations of *g* and the psychomotor tests averaged .30–.52 after correction for range restriction, and .73 when *g* and the psychomotor tests were corrected for both range restriction and unreliability.

A principal components analysis showed that all the psychomotor and paper-and-pencil tests loaded as expected on the first unrotated principal component. A congruence analysis showed that the paper-and-pencil loadings were identical, except for scale (congruence coefficient = .99), to the loadings found when paper-and-pencil tests were analyzed alone. This result demonstrates that the first unrotated principal component of the ASVAB and the psychomotor tests analyzed together was still g.

A confirmatory residualized hierarchical factor analysis disclosed a structure with each test contributing to the g factor, psychomotor as well as paper and pencil. The g factor accounted for 57% of the variance. Additionally, there was a higher-order psychomotor factor that accounted for 9% of the variance.

We have provided a body of evidence for the ubiquity and primacy of g in the prediction of several facets of job performance. Further, there is a hint that the predictiveness of some noncognitive measures comes, at least in part, from g. All research on predictors of job performance should include measures of g. The uniqueness of the predictors from g and, when appropriate, the incremental validity of the predictors beyond g should be investigated. Additionally, the utility of g and non-g predictors should be estimated in dollars, where applicable. Indeed, the increments to g reported could have large utility values under specific conditions.

None of what has been stated should be interpreted to imply that g is the only predictor worth considering. Clearly, McHenry et al. (1990) showed how personality and temperament measures can predict criteria such as "effort and leadership," "personal discipline," and "physical fitness and military bearing." However, for the prediction of training performance and job success, g is ubiquitous.

ACKNOWLEDGMENTS

The opinions expressed are those of the authors and not necessarily those of the Air Force or the United States Government. We thank our colleagues and co-workers: L. Besetsny, T. Carretta, G. Jones, P. Kyllonen, M. Miller, M. Morales, W. Tirre, L. Valentine, H. Wainer, and L. Walters for their many conversations, ideas, efforts, and help in the studies reported here. Special thanks are extended to A. Jensen and F. Schmidt.

APPENDIX

The following list of correlates of *g* by broad construct is derived from Table 2 of C. Brand (1987), "The Importance of General Intelligence," in S. Modgil and C. Modgil (Eds.), *Arthur Jensen: Consensus and Controversy*, New York: Falmer Press. We have subjectively grouped the correlates to show the diversity of constructs related to *g*. That some might argue with these groups or names is inconsequential to the understanding that the diversity of constructs is large. Those entries with a "(-)" show negative correlation with *g*; all others show positive correlation.

Abilities

Reaction time (-)
Reading ability
Analytic style
Aptitude
Educational attainment
Eminence, genius
Learning ability
Memory
Piaget-type abilities

Creativity/Artistic

Craftwork
Creativity
Artistic preferences and ability
Musical preferences and ability

Health and Fitness

Aging (-)
Infant mortality(-)
Dietary preference for low fat
Health, fitness, longevity
Smoking (-)
Height
Weight/height ratio, obesity (-)

Interests/Choices

Choice of marital partner
Sports participation at university
Media preferences
Extra-curricular attainment
Involvement in school activities
Breadth and depth of interests

Moral

Falsification (lie scores) (-)
Delinquency (-)
Crime (-)
Racial prejudice (-)
Moral reasoning and development
Values and attitudes

Occupational

Socio-economic status achieved
Socio-economic status of origin
Occupational success
Occupational status
Military rank
Voluntary migration
Income
Leadership

Perceptual

Perceptual ability for brief stimuli
Myopia
Field-independence

Personality

Achievement motivation
Acquiescence (-)
Alcoholism (-)
Altruism
Anorexia nervosa
Authoritarianism (-)
Dogmatism (-)
Emotional sensitivity
Impulsivity (-)
Hysteria vs other neuroses (-)

Psychoticism (-)
Response to psychotherapy
Sense of humor
Truancy (-)

Practical

Supermarket-shopping ability
Social skills
Practical knowledge

Other

Regional differences
Talking speed
Conservatism of social views (-)
Motor skills
Accident-proneness (-)

REFERENCES

Besetsny, L. K., Earles, J. A., & Ree, M. J. (1993). Little incremental validity for a special test for Air Force intelligence operatives. *Educational and Psychological Measurement, 53,* 993-997.

Besetsny, L. K., Ree, M. J., & Earles, J. A. (1993). Special tests for computer programmers? Not needed. *Educational and Psychological Measurement, 53,* 507-511.

Brand, C. (1987). The importance of general intelligence. In S. Modgil & C. Modgil (Eds.), *Arthur Jensen: Consensus and controversy.* New York: Falmer.

Carretta, T. R. (1990). Cross-validation of experimental USAF pilot training performance models. *Military Psychology, 2,* 257-264.

Cattell, R. (1987). *Intelligence: Its structure, growth and action.* The Netherlands: Elsevier.

Earles J. A., & Ree, M. J. (1991). *Air Force Officer Qualifying Test: Estimating the general ability component* (AL-TR-1991-0039). Brooks AFB, TX: Armstrong Laboratory.

Fleishman, E. A., & Quaintance, M. K. (1984). *Taxonomy of human performance: The description of human tasks.* Orlando: Academic Press.

Hunter, J. E., & Schmidt, F. L. (1990). *Methods of meta-analysis.* Newbury Park, CA: Sage.

Jensen, A. R. (1987). The g beyond factor analysis. In R. R. Ronning, J. A. Glover, J. C. Conoley, & J. C. Dewitt (Eds.). *The influence of cognitive psychology on testing and measurement.* Hillsdale, NJ: Lawrence Erlbaum Associates.

Jones, G. E. (1988). *Investigation of the efficacy of general ability versus specific abilities as predictors of occupational success.* Unpublished master's thesis, St. Mary's University, San Antonio, Texas.

Kranzler, J. H., & Jensen, A. R. (1991). The nature of psychometric g: Unitary process or a number of independent processes? *Intelligence, 15,* 397-422.

McHenry, J. J., Hough, L. M., Toquam, J. L., Hanson, M. A., and Ashworth, S. (1990). Project A validity results: The relationship between predictor and criterion domains. *Personnel Psychology*, *43*, 335-354.

McNemar, Q. (1964). Lost: Our intelligence? Why? *American Psychologist, 19*, 871-882.

Morales, M. (1991). *The function of general and specific abilities in the validity of the Air Force Officer Qualifying Test.* Unpublished master's thesis, St. Mary's University, San Antonio, Texas.

Ree, M. J., & Carretta, T. R. (in press). The correlation of cognitive and psychomotor tests, *International Journal of Selection and Classification.*

Ree M. J., & Earles, J. A. (1989). *The differential validity of a differential aptitude test* (AFHRL-TR-89-59). Brooks AFB, TX: Manpower and Personnel Division.

Ree, M. J., & Earles, J. A. (1991a). The stability of convergent estimates of g. *Intelligence, 15*, 271-278.

Ree, M. J., & Earles, J. A. (1991b). Predicting training success: Not much more than g. *Personnel Psychology, 44*, 321-332.

Ree, M. J., Earles, J. A., &, Teachout, M. (1992). *General cognitive ability predicts job performance* (AL-TR-1991-0100). Brooks AFB, TX: Human Resources Directorate.

Spearman, C. (1904). "General Intelligence," objectively determined and measured. *American Journal of Psychology, 15*, 201-293.

Thorndike, R. L., & Hagen, E. (1959). *Ten thousand careers.* New York: Wiley.

CHAPTER

9

DIMENSIONS OF ABILITY: DIMINISHING RETURNS?

David L. Alderton
Gerald E. Larson
Navy Personnel Research and Development Center

INTRODUCTION AND PURPOSE

Given that this is a session on testing, and that cognitive ability, general intelligence, personality, physical abilities, and measurement problems have all been discussed prior to this paper, it's quite a challenge to say something that's not redundant with earlier presentations. Therefore, our attempted contribution is to comment on the status of military testing research, and to suggest implications for the future.

We focus on the development of the Enhanced Computer Administered Test battery, or ECAT, and the current ECAT Joint-Service validity study. ECAT is the product of the last wave of military aptitude research. It is important to this conference because, given ECAT's broad sampling of abilities, one must question whether there are any unique dimensions left to exploit. We do not want to become "cryptopsychometricians," always searching for hidden abilities, because we believe that such an endeavor will provide diminishing returns. Hence the title of our paper.

HISTORY

We are nearing the culmination of a 10-year wave of research on military personnel testing. The impetus for this research began in 1973, following the end of the Vietnam War, when the draft was terminated and the Services reverted to an all-volunteer force. Over the next decade the quality of Service applicants declined severely (Eitelberg, Laurence, Waters, & Perelman, 1984), as did the quantity (Ramsberger & Means, 1987). Further complicating the grim personnel outlook was the military's tremendous technological modernization, a development placing even greater intellectual demands on the average enlistee.

137

Yet, even as the military's need for talented people grew more acute, our tools for identifying talent, that is, aptitude tests, came under growing attack from critics. In 1978, the *Uniform Guidelines on Employee Selection Procedures* (Equal Employment Opportunity Commission, 1978) were adopted by the federal government—an action that, in part, led to the 1981 Congressional directive requiring that the Services better document the relationship between education, test scores, and actual job performance. Collectively, these forces fostered a modern, resurgent interest in military personnel testing beginning in 1981.

To keep our discussion of the 1980s at a simple, manageable level, I'll just state that the Armed Services Vocational Aptitude Battery (ASVAB) was the military's primary test battery, and that there were two main "ASVAB improvement" themes during the decade. The first concerned efforts to reformat the ASVAB, whereas the second theme was to broaden the ASVAB by including new aptitude constructs. The main ASVAB reformatting project was an Item Response Theory-based, computerized, and adaptive version of the ASVAB. We call this CAT-ASVAB, and the bulk of the work was done by the Navy; we will have little more to say about this.

Attempts to broaden the ASVAB were extensive and ambitious and seemed to involve nearly everyone, with each of the Services conducting research. In 1981, the Army's Project A was conceived, and in September 1982, the contract was let initiating the project (Campbell, 1990). This project had a very broad charter with sweeping objectives: Identify the predictor domain for entry-level, skilled military jobs and obtain or develop representative tests; identify the criterion domain and develop measures for it; and determine the validity and utility of new measures against job performance criteria. There were others, but these are our focus.

In the same time frame, the Air Force's Learning Abilities Measurement Project (LAMP) began. This project focused on developing a better understanding of intellectual performance, particularly those aspects of performance that would predict learning in military technical schools. Smaller testing programs were also started in the Navy.

Several common contextual stimulants independently shaped the Services' attempts to broaden the ASVAB and produced some convergent effects. For example, the combination of the availability of relatively inexpensive microcomputers and the momentum behind the computerization of the ASVAB led the Services to develop new tests that were primarily computer based. Indeed, the Air Force and Navy test development was exclusively computer based and, in most cases, computer dependent. Moreover, the cognitive *zeitgeist* in American psychology during the mid-1970s and 1980s strongly influenced all of the programs. For example, all of the Services investigated the use of reaction time measures. The Air Force's LAMP was built around a cognitive information-processing model, and the Navy's research was driven by cognitive theories of aptitude, working memory, and mental imagery.

Unfortunately, although there were many common themes in these attempts to broaden the ASVAB, there was far too little collaboration. However, a Joint-Service transition began in the mid-1980s when the Military Accession Policy Working Group (MAPWG), under pressure to improve the ASVAB, took the opportunity to initiate Joint-Service collaboration on new tests. In 1985, the Joint-Service Future Testing Committee was formed to share and evaluate research on new tests; representatives from each of the Services were included. As work on CAT-ASVAB neared fruition, and the date of a national renorming of ASVAB was anticipated, additional impetus was provided to evaluate the possibility of adding new aptitude dimensions to the ASVAB. In a memorandum dated 14 December 1988, the Office of the Assistant Secretary of Defense (Force Management and Personnel) (OASD/FM&P) redirected the CAT-ASVAB program to "include a Joint-Service validation of the Services' new computerized cognitive and psychomotor tests."

In response to OASD's redirection of CAT-ASVAB, the Technical Advisory Selection Panel (TASP) was established, and first met in January 1989 to evaluate and select tests for the Joint-Service validation battery. The Services conducting new predictor research submitted hundreds of pages of documentation supporting the inclusion of various tests. The Panel's charter was to select the best tests in terms of their psychometric properties and theoretical justifications within the constraint that the battery could not exceed three hours.

In June 1989, the panel chose nine tests that were combined into a battery named ECAT. A research design was approved, the necessary software and hardware were developed and/or acquired, and in February 1990 the study began. Twenty-one months and 16,000 examinees later, testing finally ended. The sample included enlisted personnel in the Army, Navy, Air Force, and Marine Corps, representing 19 military occupational specialties (MOS). Criteria data collection will be complete in mid-summer 1992; analyses will be complete in the fall; and a full evaluation of the study will take place in March 1993. This undoubtedly represents the largest single validation of a computerized test battery.

ABILITY DIMENSIONS

Thus far we've described the process of broadening the ASVAB. Now let's focus on abilities, which, of course, is the real topic of this session and presentation.

The goal of ECAT was to broaden the ASVAB. Table 9.1 shows the 10 tests that comprise the ASVAB. These tests represent four factors: Verbal Ability, Mathematical Ability, Technical Knowledge, and Perceptual Speed. Across Services, the ASVAB's four-factor structure became the focal or starting point for new predictor research. Specifically, the assumption was made that the scope of human intellectual and nonintellectual skills was much greater than that represented by the ASVAB, and that capturing this breadth held the greatest promise for improving personnel selection and/or classification. That was the goal. Now let's look at the results of these extensive efforts to broaden the ASVAB. We say "extensive" because, for example, the staff of Project A alone reviewed more than 10,000 documents to identify important abilities.

TABLE 9.1
Tests in ASVAB Forms 8/9/10 to Present

Test	Description
Paragraph Comprehension (PC)	A 157-item reading-comprehension test: 13 min.
Word Knowledge (WK)	A 35-item vocabulary test using words embedded in sentences or synonyms: 11 min.
General Science (GS)	A 25-item knowledge test of physical and biological sciences: 11 min.
Arithmetic Reasoning (AR)	A 30-item arithmetic word-problem test: 36 min.
Math Knowledge (MK)	A 25-item test of algebra, geometry, fractions, decimals, and exponents: 24 min.
Mechanical Comprehension (MC)	A 25-item test of mechanical and physical principles: 19 min.
Auto and Shop Information (AS)	A 25-item knowledge test of automobiles, shop practices, tools, and tool use: 11 min.
Electronic Information (EI)	A 20-item test about electronics, radio, and electrical principles and information: 9 min.
Numerical Operations (NO)	A 50-item speeded addition, subtraction, multiplication, and division test using one- and two-digit numbers: 3 min.
Coding Speed (CS)	An 84-item speeded test requiring the recognition of number strings arbitrarily associated with words in a table: 7 min.

Table 9.2 shows the nine tests that comprise the ECAT battery, including a brief description of each of the tests. The battery requires a maximum of three hours, with most individuals finishing in just under two hours. Fig. 9.1 combines ASVAB tests/constructs and the supplemental ECAT tests/constructs. One interesting point is that, even though the Services independently chose new aptitude constructs for research, there was a large measure of agreement as to

which dimensions were the best candidates for improving the ASVAB. This consensus was clearly reflected in the proposals to the ECAT test selection panel.

TABLE 9.2
Tests in the Joint-Service ECAT Battery

Test	Description
Integrating Details	A 40-item spatial problem-solving test
Assembling Objects	A 32-item spatial and semi-mechanical test
Spatial Orientation	A 24-item spatial apperception/rotation test
Sequential Memory	A 35-item working-memory test using numerical content; a nonverbal reasoning test
Mental Counters	A 40-item working-memory test using figural content; a nonverbal reasoning test
Figural Reasoning	A 35-item series-extrapolation test using figural content; a nonverbal reasoning test
Target Identification	A 36-item RT-based figural perceptual speed test
One-Hand Tracking	An 18-item single-limb psychomotor tracking test
Two-Hand Tracking	An 18-item multi-limb psychomotor tracking test

For example, of the intellectual abilities identified in the Army's Project A review and not measured by the ASVAB, spatial ability is the most evident shortcoming, given that a spatial factor is the most frequently reported psychometric construct next to verbal ability. Independently, the Navy arrived at the same conclusion: The ASVAB should include spatial ability tests. Both Army and Navy spatial tests are now part of ECAT.

The Services also independently concluded that information-processing measures were good candidates for supplementing the ASVAB. Information-processing measures are broadly defined here to cover the whole array of test types that emerged from cognitive and experimental psychology beginning in the mid-1970s. The tests included simple and choice reaction-time tests, reaction-time-based reasoning tasks, divided and selective attention measures, and power-oriented working-memory tests. Hundreds of such tests have been developed and field tested.

If we look at the ASVAB and ECAT tests as two groups, one thing becomes immediately apparent: The military's collective efforts to broaden the dimensionality of the ASVAB have produced an almost classic verbal versus performance or crystallized versus fluid dichotomy, with the addition of a psychomotor dimension, which is indicated in Fig. 9.1.

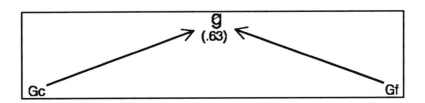

Gc—Crystallized	Gf—Fluid
Verbal Ability	**Spatial Ability**
Paragraph Comprehension	Integrating Details
Work Knowledge	Assembling Objects
General Science	Spatial Orientation
Mathematical Ability	**Nonverbal Reasoning**
Arithmetic Reasoning	Sequential Memory
Math Knowledge	Mental Counters
Technical Knowledge	Figural Reasoning
Mechanical	**Perceptual Speed**
Auto-Shop Information	Target Identification
Electronic Information	**Psychomotor**
Perceptual Speed	One-Hand Tracking
Numerical Operations	Two-Hand Tracking
Coding Speed	

FIG. 9.1. Relationship between ASVAB and ECAT: Tests, factors, and constructs.

This, then, is the ironic conclusion: Systematic attempts to broaden a general aptitude battery have merely fleshed out the classic hierarchical portrait of general intelligence, with correlated fluid and crystallized subfactors, where each subfactor is comprised of highly correlated tests. For example, our data indicate that the spatial, reasoning, and working memory tests in ECAT are all correlated in the .60s. Further, the ASVAB and ECAT general factors are also highly correlated; as shown in Fig. 9.1, the uncorrected raw correlation between the first principal components is .63 (in a sample of 500 Navy recruits).

This brings us to one additional point of agreement across the Services: the central importance of general intelligence (or g). The results from the concurrent validation study of Project A (McHenry, Hough, Toquam, Hanson, & Ashworth, 1990) certainly support the importance of g and the efficacy with which the ASVAB measures it, even though there is room to improve on it. Outside of LAMP, however, Ree and Earles (1991) also emphasized g over other measures, as has some of the Navy's research. Therefore, instead of broadening the ASVAB, we may have simply refined the measurement of its core general aptitude dimension.

CONCLUSIONS AND RECOMMENDATIONS

Let's review the implications of the entire ECAT process. First, each Service invested significant time, effort, and money to identify promising new ability dimensions. The fact that the independent conclusions agreed so strongly is evidence that few promising new aptitude constructs were described in the literature. Specifically, our conjecture is that if everything were begun again, with the goal of ending up with a Project A or ECAT-like battery designed to maximally predict military job performance, we would reproduce the current results; although the particular tests might differ, their emphasis and the distribution of tests by constructs would essentially be the same.

We believe this to be axiomatic given the stable picture of the major individual difference dimensions reported in the literature since the early 1980s (e.g., Gustafsson, 1984; Snow, Kyllonen, & Marshalek, 1984; Undheim, 1981), in conjunction with the overwhelming evidence for the dominance of general intelligence in predicting performance (e.g., Gottfredson, 1986; Hunter, 1983; Hunter & Hunter, 1984). This is not to say that additional theoretical work would be fruitless; indeed, our understanding of intelligence, particularly general intelligence, is woefully lacking. Rather, our point is that we are unlikely to discover new sets of intellectual abilities that will significantly improve the level of prediction afforded by a combination of the ASVAB, Project A, and ECAT tests.

While we thus see little room to improve our general aptitude battery, there may still be room for localized validity increments in specific jobs that require more than general intelligence. For example, the Project A tracking tests showed improved prediction in tank crew personnel. However, this is only one Service-specific job and it may not have a sufficiently large Service-wide payoff to warrant inclusion in a Department of Defense ASVAB-like battery.

The value of job-specific tests may soon change, however, since several Services are considering post-enlistment testing and the ASVAB Review Technical (ART) Committee is considering two-stage testing as an alternative operational concept for the future. Under two-stage testing, the first stage would be general selection or military qualification testing followed by more extensive classification testing. This scenario could make job-specific testing cost effective because it would be administered only to Service-qualified (or accessed) individuals, and not to all military applicants.

To summarize, we are nearing the end of a decade of important research in U.S. military personnel testing. We feel strongly that little would be gained from another round of similar work directed at unearthing new abilities for entry-level military personnel. This does not mean that there is no need for further research, including theoretical research, nor does it mean that no gains have been made. However, the nature and direction of future research efforts should be guided by the acceptance of agreed-on and available models of human ability, including the predominant role of general intelligence.

REFERENCES

Campbell, J. P. (1990). An overview of the Army Selection and Classification Project (Project A). *Personnel Psychology* (Special Issue), *41*(2), 231-239.

Eitelberg, M. J., Laurence, J. H., Waters, B. K., & Perelman, L. S. (1984, September). *Screening for Service: Aptitude and Education Criteria for Military Entry.* Washington, DC: Office of Assistant Secretary of Defense (Manpower, Installations, and Logistics).

Equal Employment Opportunity Commission, U.S. Civil Service Commission, U.S. Department of Labor, & U.S. Department of Justice (1978, August 25). *Uniform Guidelines on Employee Selection Procedures* (43 Fed. Reg. 166, 38290-38309).

Gottfredson, L. S. (Ed.) (1986). The *g* factor in employment. *Journal of Vocational Behavior* (Special Issue), *29*(3).

Gustafsson, J. E. (1984). A unifying model for the structure of intellectual abilities. *Intelligence*, *8*, 179-203.

Hunter, J. E. (1983). *Test validation for 12,000 jobs: An application of job classification and validity generalization analysis to the General Aptitude Test Battery* (Test Research Rep. No. 45). Washington, DC: U.S. Employment Service.

Hunter, J. E., & Hunter, R. F. (1984). Validity and utility of alternative predictors of job performance. *Psychological Bulletin, 96*, 72-98.

McHenry, J. J., Hough, L. M., Toquam, J. L., Hanson, M. A., & Ashworth, S. (1990). Project A validity results: The relationship between predictor and criterion domains. *Personnel Psychology, 43*, 335-354.

Ramsberger, P., & Means, B. (1987). *Military performance of low-aptitude recruits: A reexamination of data from Project 100,000 and the ASVAB misnorming period* (HumRRO Final Report 87-31). Alexandria, VA: Human Resources Research Organization.

Ree, M. J., & Earles, J. A. (1991). Predicting training success: not much more than *g. Personnel Psychology, 44*, 321-332.

Snow, R. E., Kyllonen, P. C., & Marshalek, B. (1984). The topography of ability and learning correlations. In R. J. Sternberg (Ed.), *Advances in the psychology of human intelligence* (Vol. 2, pp. 47-104). Hillsdale, NJ: Lawrence Erlbaum Associates.

Undheim, J. O. (1981). On intelligence IV: Toward restoration of general intelligence. *Scandinavian Journal of Psychology, 22*, 251-265.

IMPLICATIONS OF COGNITIVE PSYCHOLOGY FOR ABILITY TESTING: THREE CRITICAL ASSUMPTIONS

David F. Lohman
University of Iowa

The focus of this chapter is at once broader and narrower than the issue of speed and error scores that I was asked to address. I discuss speed and error later, but first I take a broader look at the more general issue of how information-processing psychology can contribute to the measurement of individual differences, and why its impact has been far less than many of us expected it would be. The reasons, I believe, are rooted in basic assumptions about how performance can be decomposed into component processes, and what effect this decomposition has on the estimation of individual differences.

I then suggest other ways in which information-processing analyses can contribute to the practical business of assessment. One of these contributions is through the application of speed-accuracy models. Another, even narrower, topic is through better measures of spatial abilities. Thus, the broad topic is cognitive-psychological approaches to measurement, the narrower topic is speed-accuracy models, and the particular example is spatial abilities. First the broad view.

THREE ASSUMPTIONS

Since 1975, I have been involved in the effort to apply cognitive psychology to measurement. This is not a long time, as careers go, but certainly long enough to give me some license to question what we have accomplished. Simply put, I do not think that cognitive psychology has had nearly the impact on measurement that a few brave souls prophesied it would have, and that an even larger audience of less daring but equally optimistic folk expected it would have. Indeed, many of the early enthusiasts have abandoned the effort and quietly moved on to other topics.

Those who were not involved from the beginning can little imagine the sense of excitement that pervaded the field in the early 1970s. Cognitive psychology promised to rescue differential psychology from psychometrics and return it to the mainstream of psychological research. But this has not happened. As I read the reports of Project A, I was struck by how little cognitive psychology had informed what was done here or how it was interpreted. This is not a criticism; indeed, I think the designers of this ambitious program were probably well advised not to have depended on such methods, at least as they have been most widely used.

Lest I wander too far afield, let me state and, as best I can in a brief time, defend my claims. I claim that much of the information-processing research on abilities has been guided by three key assumptions, two of which are false, and one of which is misleading.

Assumption 1: We can decompose overall individual differences in perform-ance on a task or ability factor into component scores that reflect individual differences in mental processes. It follows that we could account for all of the individual differences in performance on a task if we could identify all of the mental processes subjects use and estimate individual differences in each. Indeed, most research on abilities in the information-processing paradigm has sought to decompose individual differences on global constructs such as verbal ability or reasoning ability into smaller, process-based units.

I claim, however, that these component scores do not decompose and therefore cannot explain individual differences in overall performance on such tasks. Rather, component scores salvage systematic individual difference variance from the error term. This may be a useful activity, but it does not help explain the main source of individual differences on the task.

Assumption 2: Psychometric tests make good cognitive tasks, and, conversely, cognitive tasks make good psychometric tests. The most interesting information we can obtain from an information-processing analysis of a task concerns how subjects solved the task. However, the test-like tasks that are subjected to information-processing analyses are generally designed to reduce and, if possible, eliminate qualitative differences in strategy. Indeed, the presence of such strategy differences on conventional tests and laboratory tasks can usefully caution our interpretation of scores derived from such tests, although they do not go very far in telling us what the ability construct might be.

If the goal is to discover interesting information about individual differences in cognitive processes, then information-processing analyses would be more usefully applied to tasks explicitly designed to elicit qualitative differences in knowledge or strategy from examinees. Thus, the second assumption, while not patently false, is certainly misleading.

Assumption 3: Latency and error are essentially interchangeable aspects of performance. First, this means that task demands, convenience, or personal preference can determine which aspect of performance we choose to record. Second, it means that we can expect to explain individual differences in one aspect of performance by measuring the other. And third, it means that we can examine one aspect of performance while ignoring or attempting to hold constant the other aspect of performance.

On the contrary, I maintain that although response latency and response error are inextricably intertwined, they nevertheless reflect quite different aspects of performance, and there are excellent theoretical and practical reasons for estimating how they covary for each examinee.

Each of these assumptions is a large topic, and if the literature on altering beliefs is itself to be believed, then it is unlikely that I will effect much change in anyone's opinion by oral and written argument alone. But perhaps we are more rational than that literature suggests. Further, I hope it will be clear that I am not standing outside passing critical judgment on those who toil within, but have myself at one time or another been beguiled by each misconception I now disclaim. Further, my aim here is not to thwart efforts to apply cognitive psychology to measurement, but rather to suggest how we might redirect our efforts along more productive paths. First, then, the issue of component scores.

COMPONENT SCORES

The great promise of the information-processing approach to the study of abilities was that it provided a method to operationalize formerly vague notions of mental process and to test models that specified how these processes combined to produce responses. Several methods have been proposed to accomplish this task (see Sternberg, 1977; Sternberg & Detterman, 1979). When individual differences are the object of investigation, interest centers (a) on the nature of the model that best accounts for trial-to-trial variation in each subject's performance, and (b) on variation across individuals in scores that estimate the action of particular component processes. I focus on component scores here, but return to the issue of model or strategy later.

Estimating Component Scores

Component scores can be estimated by subtracting a subject's average perform-ance on one type of trial from that subject's average performance on another type of trial. For example, Hunt, Frost, and Lunneborg (1973) estimated component scores for a lexical access process by subtracting mean latency on physical identity trials from mean latency on name identity trials in a letter-matching task.

Sternberg (1977) showed how component scores could be estimated using a more sophisticated regression model. For example, consider the much-studied mental rotation task. In this task, subjects are shown two stimuli that differ in orientation. They must determine whether the two stimuli can be brought into congruence. Shepard and Metzler (1971) proposed that subjects confronted with such problems form mental images of the stimuli, rotate one of these images the required distance, compare the two images, and then respond. They tested their model by regressing angular separation between stimuli on response latency. The slope of this function estimates the rate at which stimuli are rotated, whereas the intercept estimates time for the encoding, comparison, and response processes. Sternberg (1977) showed how researchers interested in individual differences could fit models of this sort to each individual's data, use the b weight as a measure of the rotation component process, and then correlate this component score with other variables.

The expectation has been that the slope parameter would provide a relatively pure measure of spatial ability unsullied by encoding, comparison, and response processes. However, if anything, it is the intercept parameter that shows consistent correlations with other variables; correlations for the slope vary widely, from highly negative (Lansman, 1981) through zero (Egan, 1976) to moderately positive (Poltrock & Brown, 1984). Such results have dampened enthusiasm for using estimated rate of rotation as a measure of spatial ability, but have not seriously challenged the fundamental assumptions of the method.

Known Limitations of Component Scores

Reliability. Most observers attribute these inconsistent results to one or more of the many problems that attend this type of model fitting. For example, the slope is like a difference score. This is easy to see when the independent variable has only two levels, in which case the slope is equal to the difference between mean performance at the two levels of the independent variable. If the independent variable has several levels, then the slope is simply a combination of several difference scores in a weighted average.[1] Difference scores are known to be unreliable and to suffer from several other nasty statistical problems, such as ceiling and floor effects. Thus, according to this reasoning, the fundamental problem in the estimation of individual differences in component scores was to find methods to improve their reliability.

---

[1] Consider the case of a model in which the independent variable has four levels. We estimate the slope by multiplying the four cell means by -3, -1, 1, and 3 (and then normalizing the contrast by the sum of squared coefficients). This is simply the difference between two weighted means.

Speed-Error Confounds. Others—including myself—focused on the fact that subjects err when attempting to perform this task. Further, the number of errors committed is highly correlated with ability. Thus, the conventional practice of excluding latencies for incorrect responses excludes different portions of the data matrix for different subjects. Indeed, subjects can be responding randomly on a forced-choice task yet be credited with solving half of the trials correctly. Add to this the fact that subjects adopt different trade-offs between speed and accuracy, and one is left with the inescapable conclusion that we need better methods to index performance than can be had by modeling either latencies or errors alone. I still believe that this is a good idea, but do not think that it will in any way solve the problem of component scores.

Inadequate Process Models. Finally, it is always possible that something is wrong with the basic information-processing model itself. For example, we know that, at least on some rotation tasks, some subjects do not always rotate stimuli. Other subjects attempt to rotate stimuli several times, especially on trials requiring the most rotation. The slope parameter then also estimates the number of attempted rotations, not simply the rate of rotation (see Lohman, 1988, for examples).

Component Scores and the Residual Variance Component

Given all of these problems in estimating component scores on such a straight-forward task, it is little wonder that many of us were beguiled into thinking that component scores would someday be useful, but only if we could first solve these problems of reliability, error-latency confounds, and strategy shifting. I now realize that this is not the case. Indeed, even if we had subjects whose performance conformed to our model, who made no errors, who all adopted the same speed-accuracy trade-off, and whose component scores could be estimated reliably, we would still find that component scores did not help us explain individual differences in overall task performance. Here is why.

Imagine a simple person-by-item data matrix whose entries X_{pi} represent the scores of n_p persons on n_i items or trials. Fig. 10.1 shows how the variability in scores may be partitioned into three sources: the person source, the item source, and the residual. The person source represents variability in row means, that is, in the average performance of each person on the task. This would be the score ordinarily reported on a mental test. The item source represents variability in column means, that is, in average differences in item (or trial) difficulty. In the rotation example, a large fraction of this variability could be attributed to the amount of rotation required. The residual is composed of the person-by-item interaction and other disturbances. In the rotation example, individual differences in the slope of the function relating response latency to angular separation will account for the linear portion of the p by i interaction. Note that average affects

of angular separation will be captured
by the item source, and individual
differences that are consistent across
items will be captured by the person
source.

Individual differences are represented by sources of variance that lie
within the *p* circle in Fig. 10.1.
Indeed, we estimate the generalizability of individual differences in
overall task performance by the ratio
of the two variance components in
the *p* circle: *p* and *pi,e* (the latter,
of course, being divided by the
number of times it is sampled).
There are three claims here.

First, if the goal is to understand
individual differences on a task, then
we are most interested in the *p*

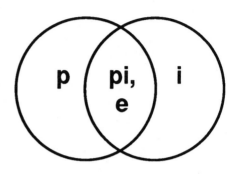

FIG. 10.1. Components of variance
for person-by-item (p x i)
score matrix.

variance component, which represents individual differences in mean performance on the task. Correlations between this score and other variables are
typically high and are what motivate our interest in the task in the first place.

Second, the *p* variance component is generally quite large on the sort of
homogeneous ability tests we can subject to componential analysis (and also on
the sort of information-processing task from which we can estimate meaningful
component scores). Estimates of internal consistency (such as Cronbach's alpha)
show this, usually being in the range of $\alpha = .85$ to .95.

Third, component scores help explain variance in the *i* and *pi* variance
components, not the *p* variance component. Adding additional terms to the
regression model that estimate the action of other mental processes further
subdivides the *i* and the *pi* variance components. In other words, the primary
contribution of component scores is to help explain average and individual
sources of task difficulty. Individual differences in component scores help
salvage variance from the *p* by *i* component that formerly was treated as error.
However, they do not decompose and, therefore, cannot help explain the typically
much larger *p* variance component.

In fact, mean scores for each person that are reflected in the p variance
component will generally show high correlations with the intercept of the
regression model. This is why the intercept often shows interesting and
significant correlations with reference abilities, whereas component scores show
inconsistent correlations with such measures.

The Intercept as an Individual Difference Measure

This is clear if we examine the model that is fitted to each subject's data. I treat the simple case of one independent variable. Extension to several independent variables is straightforward. For each subject, the model is simply:

$$\hat{Y}_{pi} = I_p + B_p X_i \qquad (1)$$

Where $\hat{Y}_{pi}$ is the predicted score for person p on item i, I_p is the intercept for person p, B_p is the slope for person p, and X_i is the angular separation between stimuli on item i. The relationship between the intercept for each person, I_p, and the person's mean score on the task, $\overline{Y}_{p.}$, is easy to see. Recall that the regression line for each person always passes through the mean $\overline{X}_.$, $\overline{Y}_{p.}$. Substituting these values into Equation 1 gives:

$$\overline{Y}_{p.} = I_p + B_p \overline{X}. \qquad (2)$$

Solving for I_p gives:

$$I_p = \overline{Y}_{p.} - B_p \overline{X}. \qquad (3)$$

Equation 3 tells us that the correlation between I_p and $\overline{Y}_{p.}$ will be moderated by the variability in B_p across persons. The upper limit for this variability is given by the size of the *pi* variance component. When this component is large relative to the *p* component, then there may be large variability in slopes across individuals. However, when the *pi* interaction is relatively small, then there is little variability to be explained.

Highly homogeneous tasks—such as the mental rotation task—typically show good internal consistency, that is, a large *p* component and a small *pi,e* component. Equation 3 shows that, when this is the case, mean scores for individuals will capture most of the systematic individual differences and will be highly correlated with intercepts, because slopes, whether large or small, will be relatively constant across persons. In the mental rotation example, the slope B_p is usually quite large, which indicates that angular separation between stimuli has a substantial effect on response latency. However, the variance in B_p is comparatively small, which indicates that subjects who are slowest on items requiring the least rotation are also slowest on items requiring the most rotation.

In other words, individual component scores can explain only that portion of the individual difference variance ordinarily relegated to the residual when a total (or mean) score is reported. They do not explain or decompose the typically much larger variance captured by the person component, that is, in individual variability that is consistent across items and that is captured by the intercept.

The assertion that component scores do constitute a decomposition of the individual differences on a task is explicit in Sternberg's (1977) work, and implicit in the work of Hunt et al. (1973), Jensen (1982), Snow, Marshalek, and Lohman (1976), and the vast majority of studies in this tradition (see Carroll, 1980, for a review). Sternberg (1977) discusses it as one of the main features of the external validation of a componential analysis. The expectation, shown here in Fig. 10.2, is that individual differences in factor scores can be reconstituted from component scores. I do not think that this is the case. Indeed, it is quite possible to have a good understanding of how each individual in a sample solved a task but still have no idea what generated individual differences on the task. More concretely, one can have a regression model with many large and significant coefficients, and model fits that are very high, yet still find that the intercept shows highest correlations with other measures.

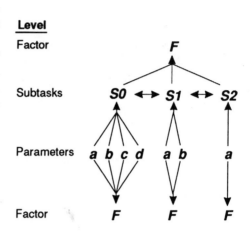

FIG. 10.2. Design of a structural regression model for external validation of a componential model. Parameters a, b, c, and d are component scores. After Sternberg (1977). Reprinted by permission.

Cronbach (1975) once observed that strange ironies abound in the history of mental testing. Surely this one should be added to the catalog. The intercept, which is the residual or wastebasket term in componential models, is actually the locus of individual difference variance that is consistent across trials, whereas component scores, which capture consistent variation in item difficulty, can only help explain residual individual difference variance.

The Importance of Model Fitting

I am not claiming that component scores are useless or that such scores do not sometimes show interesting correlations with other variables (see, e.g., Bethell-Fox, Lohman, & Snow, 1984; Sternberg & Gardner, 1983), although these correlations can be artifactual if cell variances are not homogeneous. If cell variances are not equal, then the rank order of individuals on the component score will be biased by the rank order of individuals in the cell with the greatest variance.

This frequently happens when latency is the dependent measure, because means and variances are usually correlated. In the mental rotation example, the slope may be better interpreted as time to solve problems requiring the most rotation rather than as an index of rate of rotation. In part, the increase in response latency on more difficult problems is due to the fact that subjects are unable to achieve the same error rate on difficult problems as on easy problems, and thus begin to trade substantial increases in latency for small decreases in error rate (see Lohman, 1986). Thus, even significant correlations between component scores and other variables must be interpreted with caution.

I am also not challenging the utility of fitting information-processing analyses models to individual data. On the contrary, such analyses provide one of the few systematic ways to test hypotheses about how subjects attempted to solve items on a task. Indeed, I argue that when possible, tests should be designed so that such models can be routinely fitted to each subject's data and some estimate of model fit reported along with the subject's total score on the test. Rather, the claim is that component scores do not decompose and therefore do not help explain individual differences in overall task performance.

When are component scores most useful? Generally, when the p component is small and the p by i component is large. In the extreme, this would be on a task on which everyone received the same total score ($\sigma_p^2 = 0$) and on which individual differences were entirely reflected in the pattern of scores obtained by each subject. This leads to the second assumption.

COGNITIVE TESTS AS COGNITIVE TASKS, AND VICE VERSA

Why has there been so much interest in estimating individual differences in particular component processes and so little interest in understanding strategy? Surely part of the reason is a misunderstanding of what individual differences in component scores represent. But I believe there is another, even more important reason. It was the assumption that psychometric tests would make good cognitive tasks (Carroll, 1976) or, conversely, that cognitive tasks would make good psychometric tests (Hunt et al., 1973).

Sternberg's (1977) early discussion of componential analysis placed considerable emphasis on possible strategy (or model) differences between subjects. However, he found that differences in strategy explained little of the variability in adult analogical reasoning on the test-like tasks he studied. The focus, therefore, naturally shifted from model to component processes as the main source of individual differences on the task. This was unfortunate, because the most important contribution of an information-processing analysis of individual performance on a task is information on how subjects solved that task. It follows that such analyses will be most useful when there are interesting differences in the way subjects solve a task that can be discovered by such analyses. In particular, differences in processing strategy are most interesting when they show systematic relationships with other variables, such as overall ability level.

Unfortunately, these are not the sort of individual differences we are likely to find in analyses of performance on test-like tasks modeled after homogeneous ability tests or laboratory tasks. For example, information-processing analyses of mental rotation tell us that a major source of individual differences on such tasks is the average speed or accuracy with which subjects can rotate stimuli. Did anyone seriously doubt this? What is news is when we find subjects who do not rotate stimuli or who persist in rotating stimuli in one direction when rotation in the other direction would be shorter (Ippel & Beem, 1987), or when we find that some subjects make several attempts to rotate a stimulus whereas others are successful on their first attempt (Lohman, 1988).

However, such differences are difficult to detect, primarily because the typical rotation task is not designed to reveal them. Further, such differences do not tell us much about the ability construct we hope to understand. Instead, they caution our interpretation of tests by showing that even homogeneous tasks may be solved in different ways by different subjects. But they do not go very far in telling us what those abilities might be.

My claim, then, is that ability tests often do not make informative cognitive tasks, especially if the goal is to develop process theories of ability constructs. Elsewhere (Lohman & Ippel, 1993), Ippel and I argued that tasks which everyone can solve but which admit a variety of solution methods offer greater promise. Such tasks have been studied for many years by developmental psychologists, among others.

Homogeneous tasks can tell us much about human information processing. However, if strategy differences are minimal or inconsistent, and if component scores do not decompose overall individual differences, then what has cognitive psychology to offer for the practical business of selection and classification? I discuss three contributions: first through what I call confidence indices, second through theory-based tests, and third through better methods to decompose overall task performance.

Confidence Indices

I have argued that tasks that elicit systematic differences in solution strategy can be most useful when the goal is to understand what abilities are, and how they develop. However, the aim of this conference is not how to develop psychological theories of ability constructs. Rather, it is how to improve the selection and classification of new recruits. For this task, information-processing analyses can help us determine when subjects are attempting to solve tests in ways that compromise the interpretation of their scores. This can be done in two ways: first, through learning and performance models that examine the effects of various sources of difficulty on each subject's performance and in changes in performance over trials, and second, through analyses of the type of errors the subject makes.

An example of the first approach would be to fit the Shepard-Metzler (1971) model to each subject's latency data on a computer-administered version of any standard mental rotation task. If this model does not fit the data well, then we are probably not justified in interpreting overall performance on the task as a measure of spatial ability. Model fits may also assist us in deciding whether to average scores on different tests, to reject some scores and accept others, or to test further. Note that the statistic of interest here is R^2 or some other index of model fit, not individual differences in the regression coefficient that estimates rate of rotation.

The second approach focuses on the nature of the errors subjects make rather than the duration of the response or its correctness. An example of this approach would be to classify examinees' errors on an analogical reasoning test with items of the form "$A:B::C:D_1D_2D_3D_4$." Less able and younger examinees sometimes choose the response alternative that is an associate of one of the terms in the problem stem, usually the "C" term. Scores for such examinees should not be interpreted as estimating reasoning ability. The work of Tatsuoka (e.g., Tatsuoka & Baillie, 1982) may be particularly useful here, even though behavior may not be as rule-bound as this analysis assumes. The idea is to construct foils so that choice among them may signal misunderstanding of the task or an attempt to circumvent it.

What I have in mind here is something like a confidence index that would be reported alongside each subject's scores on a test. Information-processing analyses provide two sources of evidence for such indices: first, through learning and performance models fitted to latency and error data; and second, through qualitative analyses of error choices. Such models may help explain inconsistencies in performance across presumably parallel parts of a test or between tests that sample similar abilities. Statistically, the problem is when to average and when to choose.

Figure 10.3 shows a simple example. The figure shows a scatterplot of scores for 242 subjects on two mental rotation tests: Thurstone's (1938) Cards and Figures tests. These tests are identical except for the stimuli that must be rotated. We certainly do not expect each subject to achieve the same score on both tests, but is it reasonable to assume that performance can differ by one, two, or even three standard deviation units from one test to the other? For example, slightly more than one half of the subjects in Fig. 10.3 show changes of more than .5 standard deviation unit from one test to the other. Of these 123 subjects, 69 had test scores that differed by .5 SD to 1.0 SD unit, 47 had test scores that differed by 1.0 to 2.0 SD units, and 7 had test scores that differed by more than 2 SD units. These are very large changes in performance to be found across such similar tests.

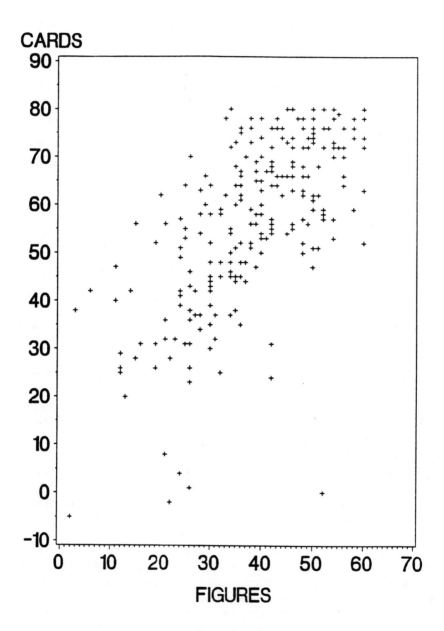

FIG. 10.3. Plot of scores on Card Rotations versus Figure
Rotations for 242 subjects. Scores on
both tests have been corrected for guessing.

Such patterns are commonly observed. Yet with equal commonality we average scores because we have no better explanation for the discrepancies than to attribute them to an undifferentiated error of measurement. But do changes of one or more SD units represent random fluctuations? It seems more likely that the subject misunderstood the directions on one task, or was not familiar with such tasks and did poorly on the first, or adopted quite different speed accuracy trade-offs for the two tests. Yet classical test theory assumes that both are equally good estimates of ability that should be averaged. In the absence of additional information, this may indeed be the best that we can do. My point, though, is that a more careful internal analysis of each examinee's performance might provide such additional information.

Thus, the first role proposed for cognitive psychology is not particularly glamorous. It is simply to make better use of information that is already being gathered in many cases (especially when tests are theory based and computer administered), to flag those individuals in need of further testing, and, in some cases, to help choose among discrepant scores for the same examinee.

Generating Tests and Test Items

Cognitive psychology has another, oft-overlooked contribution to make. Recall that the primary contribution of such analyses is to explain stimulus or item variance. Thus, such models can be used to generate test items with predictable difficulty values. This can be an enormous asset in computer-based testing, or in situations in which multiple forms of a test are needed. Of course, it is much easier to do this for process-rich tests such as reasoning, spatial, and perceptual speed tests than for knowledge-rich tests such as vocabulary or reading comprehension. Good examples of this approach are given by Butterfield, Nielsen, Tangen, and Richardson (1985), Irvine, Dann, and Anderson (1990), and Snow and Petersen (1985).

Psychological theory can also guide the construction of new tests, especially in those areas where existing tests are inadequate or poorly grounded in theory. As I see it, spatial tests certainly fit this description. In spite of hundreds of attempts to develop measures of spatial ability (Eliot & Smith, 1983, provide examples of 392), spatial tests have rarely attained the predictive utility their designers expected to achieve. Surely this is in part a criterion problem: Supervisor ratings or performance in training courses may reflect other sources of individual differences. But I believe it also reflects some basic inadequacies in the tests themselves and in the assumptions typically made about what spatial ability is and how it is used in everyday life.

Most spatial tests present figural stimuli that the examinee must bend, fold, punch holes in, rotate, combine, or otherwise transform. I claim, however, that we rarely use these sorts of figural problem-solving abilities in everyday life. Rather, spatial abilities are most commonly used as a mental scratch pad to construct mental models that help us understand what we hear or read, or to think about complex problems of all sorts. A test of such abilities is unlikely to be factorially pure, because integration and coordination of information from several sources is required. Thus, factorially (or componentially) pure measures are not the goal.

Accordingly, we devised a spatial test based explicitly on Baddeley's (1986) model of working memory in which examinees listened to verbally presented problems that required a verbal response, but which seemed to demand that they construct and use a mental image. Ackerman and Kanfer (1993) administered this test along with a large battery of other mental tests representing a wide range of general and specific ability constructs to two large samples. In the first study (N = 112 undergraduates), scores on this short test fell closest in a multi-dimensional scaling of all predictor variables to the criterion score (number planes successfully landed over three days on an air traffic control simulation). In the second study (N = 206 FAA trainees), it was the single best predictor of successful completion of training at the FAA school for air traffic controllers.

I mention this research because it illustrates that theory-based tests can be constructed that are practically useful, that such tests need not use expensive technology (although sometimes this helps), that careful matching of the information-processing demands of the task to information-processing demands of the job is more important than factorial purity (indeed, predictive utility of tests probably declines monotonically as their factorial purity increases), and, finally, that better measures of spatial abilities may indeed be possible.

Thus, cognitive psychology can contribute to the practical business of measurement in several ways: first, through indices that caution our interpretation of individual scores or signal the need for further testing; second, by using information about sources of difficulty to construct items of predictable difficulty levels; third, through tests that are explicitly designed to reflect the manner in which abilities are used in criterion tasks and field achievements; and fourth, through better methods to represent and interpret the limits of human performance on a task. It is to this last contribution I now turn. But first some background on why it is necessary.

ERRORS, LATENCIES, AND SPEED-ACCURACY MODELS

Speed-Accuracy Trade-off

The third assumption that has plagued research on individual differences in cognitive processes concerns the relationship between response latency and response error. There are really two problems here, both of which are magnified considerably when individual differences are the object of measurement rather than something relegated to the error term.

The first problem is that subjects trade increases in speed for decreases in accuracy, and vice versa. Fig. 10.4 shows the typical form of this relationship. The trade-off occurs within subjects, for example, as subjects gain confidence or become fatigued, and between subjects, such as when some subjects are, on average, more cautious or careless than others. In either case, comparisons of performance for the same subject across parts of one or more tasks, or comparisons of scores for different subjects on the same task, can be seriously distorted, especially when latency is the dependent measure. Small, statistically nonsignificant changes in response error can be associated with large changes in response latency, particularly when subjects are operating near the asymptote of the curve. Indeed, when performance has reached asymptote, response latency is independent of response accuracy.

Most investigators recognize this problem but assume that it is only a minor confound. Sometimes this view is based on the fact that they have computed the correlation between the average error rate and average response latency for each subject and found the correlation to be small. The reasoning is as follows.

If subjects differ on the speed or accuracy emphasis they adopt, then they will fall at different points along the speed-accuracy curve. For example, Subject A in Fig. 10.4 is slower and more accurate than is Subject B. The linear correlation between accuracy and latency will thus be positive if subjects differ in speed-accuracy trade-off. In addition to the obvious fact that a linear correlation may not be the best way to represent a nonlinear relationship, there is the troubling assumption here that the performance of all subjects can be described by a single speed-accuracy curve. This is simply not the case on tasks of nontrivial difficulty on which subjects differ in asymptotic level of performance. (A good approximation to the variability in asymptotes will be given by variability in error rates.)

Fig. 10.5 shows how this occurs. Here, the form of the speed-accuracy curve is the same for two subjects. However, the curve for Subject A reaches a higher asymptote than does the curve for Subject B. First consider what happens if Subject A is cautious whereas Subject B is hasty (open circles). This would lead to a positive correlation between accuracy and latency. However, the correlation will hold only if it is generally the case that less-able subjects are fast and inaccurate whereas more-able subjects are slow and accurate. This seems

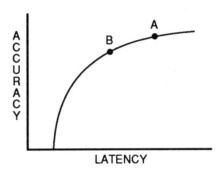

FIG. 10.4. Hypothetical accuracy-latency curve. Subject A is slower and more accurate than Subject B. The same accuracy-latency curve is assumed to apply to both subjects.

highly unlikely. In fact, the reverse situation (closed circles) seems only slightly less implausible. According to this scenario, more-able subjects achieve a high level of accuracy when responding quickly, whereas less-able subjects struggle, but still make more mistakes. Now the correlation between accuracy and latency would actually be negative. Once again, this correlation would hold only if the same patterns applied to other less- and more-able subjects.

Note that these patterns would be further complicated by individual differences in intercepts and curvatures of the accuracy-latency curves. Thus, if there is a speed-accuracy trade-off, then the correlation between accuracy and latency can be positive, negative, or zero. If there is no speed-accuracy trade-off, the correlation can also be positive, negative, or zero. In short, the presence or absence of a correlation between accuracy and latency is not a very good indicator of the presence or absence of a speed-accuracy trade-off.

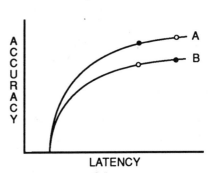

FIG. 10.5.   Hypothetical accuracy-latency curves for two subjects.   Subject A is considered more able. Open circles show a positive correlation between accuracy and latency; closed circles show a negative correlation.

Error-Response Latencies

The second problem, logically distinct from the first, stems from the fact that subjects frequently differ in ability to solve items on a test. We cannot use latencies from items subjects did not solve to make inferences about how they they solved items. The problem is exacerbated by the fact that the number of errors subjects make is systematically related to their ability in the domain. Thus, when latency is the dependent variable, the problem is what to do with error-response latencies, and, less commonly, when error is the dependent measure, it is how to compare response correctness when response latency differs.

Consider an example. In one experiment we administered a 60-item semantic matching task. On each item subjects saw a target word in the center of the computer display and two alternatives below. Their task was to indicate which of these alternatives was closest in meaning to the target word. Subjects were given the customary instructions to respond "as rapidly and as accurately as possible."

Items were grouped into four sets based on prior estimates of their difficulty. Average accuracy and latency were then computed for each subject on each set of items and correlated with reference measures of verbal ability and perceptual speed, separately at each of the four difficulty levels. The rather uninteresting results of this little exercise are shown in Table 10.1.

TABLE 10.1
Means, Standard Deviations, and Correlations of Response Latency and Response Accuracy With Perceptual Speed (Ps) and Verbal Composites for Each of Four Difficulty Levels in the Self-Paced Condition of the Meaning-Match Task ($N = 36$)

| | Mean | SD | Correlation With | |
			Ps	Verbal
Latency (msec)				
Difficulty 1	2160	670	-.26	-.42**
Difficulty 2	2194	718	-.16	-.30
Difficulty 3	2334	821	-.13	-.33*
Difficulty 4	2640	873	-.18	-.15
Accuracy				
Difficulty 1	.883	.075	-.14	.39*
Difficulty 2	.824	.138	.11	.29
Difficulty 3	.707	.121	-.16	.56**
Difficulty 4	.482	.158	-.06	.58**

* $p < .05$. ** $p < .01$.
Note. From Lohman (1989a). Reprinted by permission.

As commonly happens, correlations between latency and verbal ability declined as difficulty increased, whereas accuracy scores showed the reverse trend. But it is difficult to defend either set of correlations. For example, average error rate was 11.7% for the easiest trials (range 0 to 26.7%), and rose to an average of 52.8% for the most difficult trials. Even for the easiest trials, we cannot unambiguously compare latencies for the person who missed over one quarter of the trials with the person who missed none. Perhaps we should use latencies only for error-free trials. But then we base our correlations on different trials for different subjects: all of the trials for some subjects, but only the easier 75% of these trials for the subjects who were most error prone.

Combining error and latency in a multivariate analysis would certainly be better than performing separate univariate analyses, especially if one or both scores are first transformed so that the relationship between them is linear. But such techniques also have their drawbacks. First, some procedures, such as canonical analysis, will combine latency and error in completely arbitrary ways, the only concern being to maximize the relationship between dependent and independent variables. This makes it difficult to compare results across studies, because the composition of the dependent variable (i.e., the first and second

canonical variates) is constantly changing.   Second, the behavior of the
fast-inaccurate subject is not somehow made the same as that of the slow-
accurate subject by such analyses.

At best, then, standard multivariate analyses provide some compensation for
between- subjects variance in speed-accuracy trade-off, and may even remind us
that, in part, latency and error reflect quite different aspects of performance. But
they do not tell us what this uniqueness might be, nor do they tell us anything
about the nature of the within-subject speed-accuracy trade-off.   And this
information is actually much more informative. Unfortunately, the form of the
within-subject trade-off can be completely independent of the between-subject
trade-off (Wood & Jennings, 1976). The bottom line is this: We can get much
more information out of a speed-error response surface that describes the
within-subject trade-off than can ever be squeezed out of a single point in that
space, even if we have the good sense to analyze both coordinates of the point
instead of just one.

Can We Adjust for Speed-Accuracy Trade-off?

Scoring Formulae. The problem of individual differences in speed-accuracy
trade-off has been approached in several ways. Dennis and Evans (1990, 1991)
explored the utility of several alternative formulae that combine latency and error
in a single score so as to minimize the influence of speed-accuracy trade-off. It
is noteworthy that a score based on the conventional correction for guessing
behaved worst both in their computer simulations and in a subsequent empirical
study. However, their approach is feasible only if speed and accuracy are
interchangeable aspects of ability that may be traded off against each other. If,
instead, speed and accuracy reflect different aspects of ability, then there is no
one way to combine them to define ability in the domain.

Speed-Accuracy Plots. We have also attempted to correct for speed-
accuracy trade-off, but in a different way. We began by estimating a speed-
accuracy trade-off function for each subject, at each level of trial complexity.
For example, in one study (Lohman, 1986) we presented three- dimensional
rotation problems for various fixed exposures, and then plotted accuracy as a
function of stimulus exposure. However, it soon became apparent that, although
we could easily control for speed or for accuracy, controlling for speed-accuracy
trade-off was a bit more difficult. Fig. 10.6 shows why. The figure shows the
speed-accuracy curves that were fitted to data for low- and high-spatial subjects.
Solid lines are for low spatials, dotted lines are for high spatials. There are five
curves for each group, one for each of five levels of angular separation between
stimuli (30, 60, 90, 120, and 150 degrees).

We can fix accuracy by drawing a horizontal line and then recording the
latency coordinate of each point of intersection. However, for any given level

of accuracy, the point of intersection would be nearer (perhaps even beyond) asymptotic level of performance for easy trials and low-ability subjects than it would be for difficult trials and high-ability subjects. Fixing latency produces the opposite set of problems. We could in some sense fix speed-accuracy trade-off if each curve had a point of inflection. Unfortunately, exponential functions have no point of inflection.

Perhaps the closest we could come would be to define a point on each curve that is some constant percentage between random responding and asymptotic performance, say 90% of asymptote. But what value do we choose? Each arbitrary cutoff yields a set of accuracy and latency scores that

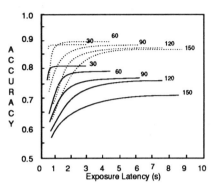

FIG. 10.6. Accuracy-latency curves for low-spatial subjects (solid lines) and high-spatial subjects (dotted lines) at each of the five levels of angular separation between figures. The length of each curve indicates the range of exposure latencies for trials requiring a given amount of rotation. From Lohman (1986). Reprinted by permission.

differ to the extent that curvatures and intercepts vary across curves. Further, we must first know the asymptote of each curve before we can apply the procedure. Thus, it would seem better simply to describe the performance function that relates response accuracy to response latency rather than trying to find the single point on this curve that can be compared across conditions and subjects. Indeed, by estimating the form of this function we also solve the problem of error-response latencies (or its converse).

Curve Fitting. Elsewhere, I have given more detailed justification for these claims and have reviewed various methods that have been used to generate speed-accuracy curves (Lohman, 1989a, 1989b). In most of our studies, we present stimuli for one of several predetermined exposures. Stimulus offset is the subject's cue to respond. Further, responses must be made within some brief window after stimulus offset. Probability of a correct response can thus be varied from chance to asymptote by increasing stimulus exposure.

Following Wickelgren (1977), we then fit the exponential function given in Equation 4 to each subject's data, separately at each level of task complexity.

$$P(C) = \lambda (1 - e^{-\beta (t - \delta)}), t > 0 \qquad (4)$$

If data for individual subjects are too noisy for curve fitting, data are first averaged over subjects grouped in some way (e.g., by sex or ability) and then curves are fitted to these means. Many details of these procedures for data collection and analysis need attention. For example, there is some controversy over whether to represent response accuracy by the probability of a correct response, d´, or some other measure. I will not attempt to discuss these issues here. Nevertheless, I do need to give a brief description of the three parameters in Equation 4 and how they might be interpreted.

Figure 10.7 shows the correspondence between the three parameters of Wickelgren's (1977) model and the typical speed-accuracy curve. The first parameter, λ, is the asymptote, or the level of accuracy achieved under liberal time allotment. The second parameter, δ, is the intercept. It approximates the point at which the curve rises above the level of random responding.

The third parameter, β, describes the curvature. Steep curvature signals a rapid increment in response accuracy for each additional unit of processing time. Note that this parameter seems better to describe a system in which information about the response to be made gradually accumulates over time, rather than being made available in an all or none fashion. Thus, the basic form of the speed-accuracy model is more in keeping with a system that operates in parallel or cascade than with a system that presumes strictly serial processing in independent stages.

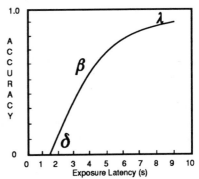

FIG. 10.7. Mapping the three parameters of Wickelgren's (1977) model on to an accuracy-latency curve. δ is the intercept, β is the curvature, and λ is the asymptote. Exposure latency is the sum of presentation latency and response latency.

Cascade Model. McClelland's (1979) cascade model is perhaps the best-known model of this sort. It is basically a model of how activation is accumulated at different levels in a hierarchically ordered system. The "information" in this information-processing system is activation. Using examples and derivations, McClelland has shown how variations in the parameters of the basic equation describing the cascade model are reflected in the form of the accuracy-latency performance curve.

The intercept of the curve reflects time taken by relatively fast processes in the system. Adding a new fast process to the system will simply shift the curve to the right, and will not alter either its curvature or its asymptote (see Fig. 10.8A). The curvature, on the other hand, is dominated by the slowest process in the system. Increasing the rate of execution of this process makes the curve rise more steeply; decreasing its rate flattens the curve (see Fig. 10.8B). Finally,

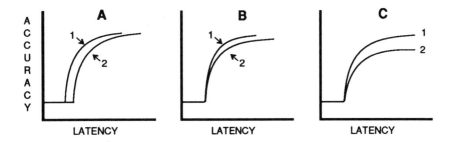

FIG. 10.8. Examples of McClelland's (1979) cascade model. Panel A shows an improvement in the rate of execution of one or more fast processes for Condition 1. Panel B shows
an improvement in the rate of execution of a slow process for Condition 1. Panel C shows
a stronger activation or trace strength for Condition 1.

the asymptote reflects the final activation level achieved. This will depend on
many factors (e.g., primed units should show higher activation), stimulus quality
(e.g., degraded units should show lower asymptotes), and stimulus identity (e.g.,
well-learned units should attain higher asymptotes) (see Fig. 10.8C). Thus, the
cascade model provides a set of plausible interpretations for the three parameters
we typically estimate in our speed-accuracy studies.

Does It Matter?

I have argued that if we are interested in performance on relatively homogeneous
tasks, then it is better to represent performance as a curve (or set of curves) that
define a response surface than as a single point in this space or, worse yet, as the
projection of this point on one of the axes that define the space. Further, I claim
that this simultaneously eliminates two messy problems in individual difference
studies: speed-accuracy trade-off and error-response latencies. Finally, I note
that each of the three parameters of the model typically fit to such data can be
readily linked to aspects of information processing. But does it matter? In other
words, is this a difference that makes a difference?

Time does not permit reviewing more than a small fraction of the research
conducted in an attempt to answer this question. Here are some of the tasks that
have been studied: mental rotation (Lohman, 1986), letter matching (or clerical
speed) (Lohman, 1989a), synonyms (Lohman, 1989a), numerical analogies (Ha,
1988), figural analogies (Nichols, 1990), repetition priming (Lohman, 1991), and
the training and transfer of spatial abilities (Lohman, 1993).

Spatial Ability. In the mental rotation study (Lohman, 1986), for example,
we found massive differences between high- and low-spatial subjects in
asymptotes, but only one marginally significant difference in curvature (see

Fig. 10.6). This clearly challenges the hypothesis that spatial ability consists in the rate at which spatial information can be processed and, instead, supports the hypothesis that spatial ability consists primarily in how much spatial information can be maintained in working memory or, alternatively, the level of activation that can be achieved for a given image. Other analyses showed that sex differences in rate of mental rotation were entirely a function of differences in asymptotes, not response latency, as others have reported.

Repetition Priming. How accuracy differences can masquerade in this way as latency differences was demonstrated in a study of repetition priming. Several investigators have reported large and persistent differences between response latencies on repeated and nonrepeated trials. This facilitation in processing an unannounced repetition of a trial is called repetition priming. Effects for semantic comparison tasks range from 300 to 400 milliseconds when trials are repeated immediately to 100 milliseconds when trials are repeated after an eight-day delay. Errors are also lower on repeated trials, although effects are small and often not significant. Because of this, repetition priming effects are usually measured by latency savings rather than by error savings (see, e.g., Woltz, 1990).

If my earlier critique of component scores has merit, then we should not expect individual differences in repetition priming to explain much of the variability in overall performance on semantic comparison tasks, and, indeed, this is the case. Nevertheless, the priming effect is itself robust, and there is some interesting variation between individuals that is worth examining.

Fig. 10.9 shows the general effects of repetition priming. Circles are for repeated trials, squares for nonrepeated trials. The two closed symbols at the far right show means for self-paced trials. These two points differ minimally in accuracy, but substantially in response latency. Thus, it would seem reasonable to measure priming effects by latency savings. However, data from the speed-accuracy study (open symbols) show that, as McClelland (1979) predicted, the curve for primed stimuli has the

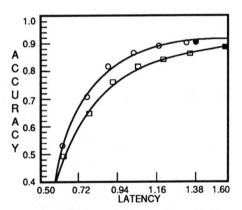

FIG. 10.9. Means and accuracy-latency curves for all subjects ($N = 168$). Circles are repeated trials; squares are nonrepeated trials. Adjusted means for self-paced trials are shown by the two filled symbols. Large difference in latency between these two points is clearly an artifact of speed-accuracy trade-off.

higher asymptote. Differences in latency occur only because subjects achieve similar levels of accuracy for all stimuli.

Figure 10.10 shows what happens when data for subjects high and low in verbal knowledge were analyzed separately. For lows, priming affected asymptotes, not curvatures, whereas for highs, effects were just the opposite. One interpretation of this result is that low verbal subjects attend to stimuli, whereas highs attend to the relationship between them. Woltz and I are investigating this and other possibilities in a recent study. However, the effect is small, and so it certainly does not explain much of the variability in verbal ability. That variance is better explained by a comparison of the overall performance of the two groups. Notice that—if we ignore the effects of priming—highs show much steeper curves than do lows. These are the main effect differences that disappear when we examine only differences or component scores within subjects (or, here, means for groups of subjects).

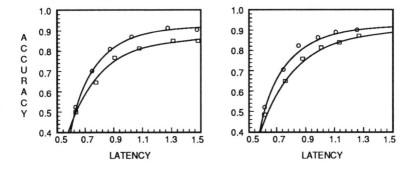

FIG. 10.10. Data and accuracy-latency curves for the lowest and highest quartiles on the Knowledge composite. $N = 41$ per group. Circles are repeated trials, squares are nonrepeated trials. Left panel (low-ability group) shows shallow curvatures and priming effect on asymptotes. Right panel (high-ability group) shows steep curvatures and priming effect on curvature.

This was shown clearly in the earlier study in which we also used a semantic comparison task. Recall that items were divided into four difficulty levels, with the easiest items most like those used in the semantic priming study. Items were administered in both a self-paced condition and a speed-accuracy condition. Results for the self-paced condition were shown in Table 10.1. Data from the speed-accuracy condition were more interesting. First, the three parameter exponential functions shown in Equation 4 were fitted to each subject's data, separately at each of the four levels of item difficulty. These parameters were then correlated with reference scores for verbal and perceptual speed abilities. The results are shown in Table 10.2.

TABLE 10.2

Correlations between the Curvature, Intercept, and Asymptote Parameters
and Reference Perceptual Speed (Ps) and Verbal (V) Composites for the
Meaning-Match Task ($N = 36$)

Difficulty Level	N[a]	Curvature (β)		Intercept (δ)		Asymptote (λ)	
		Ps	V	Ps	V	Ps	V
1	30	.16	.51**	-.10	.49**	.25	.36*
2	31	.41*	.27	.30	.49**-	.10	.56**
3	31	.03	.34	-.03	.50**	.17	.55**
4	15	-.17	.06	-.09	.28	-.10	.71**

[a] Subjects for whom R^2 was significant only.
* $p < .05$. ** $p < .01$.
Note. After Lohman (1989a). Reprinted by permission.

As in the semantic priming study, high-verbal subjects showed steeper speed-accuracy curves, but only for the easiest items ($r = .51$). Thus, the rate at which subjects could retrieve and compare meanings of relatively familiar words was significantly related to verbal ability. As difficulty increased, however, so did correlations between verbal ability and asymptotes. This was expected, because difficulty was defined by percentage of subjects in another sample who responded correctly to the item. Note that the intercept also showed significant correlations with verbal ability, and that the correlations were all positive. This means that high-verbal subjects were slower in accumulating initial information about the stimuli. Perhaps this slowness represents the fact that they must search a larger or more richly interconnected semantic network.

These are but a few of the many interesting relationships we have found between parameters of speed-accuracy curves and other variables, usually ability constructs. For example, in this same study, we found that correlations between the intercept parameter and a Reasoning composite were $r = -.44, +.47, -.06$, and $-.06$ for difficulty Levels 1 through 4, respectively. The negative correlation for easiest trials is reminiscent of the result Jensen (1982) obtained in his choice RT studies. By difficulty Level 2, however, the situation was completely reversed. Now subjects with high scores on the Reasoning factor were slower. This corresponds to Sternberg's (1985) conclusion that more-able subjects spend more time encoding terms on problems of nontrivial difficulty.

However, I do not want to suggest that this is simply a correlational free-for-all with three parameters of a curve instead of two coordinates of a point on that curve. Rather, the key idea is that we get a much clearer picture of performance by determining both its limits— that is, the minimum amount of time required before some information about the response is available, to the point at which the accuracy of responding has reached a limit—and the rate at which the transition is made between these two boundaries. There are many situations in which the individual is not in control of the rate at which stimuli are presented and yet must respond as quickly as possible. Other situations present the opposite demands, with liberal time allotments but the quality of the response crucial. Testing across the full range can help us better understand and predict performance in situations that present various mixtures of these extremes.

From the standpoint of training, a speed-accuracy performance curve provides a good way to index the effects of practice on skill acquisition and transfer. For example, as learners practice a skill, which aspects of their performance improve? Do different treatments produce qualitative differences in performance curves? After training, what aspects of performance transfer to other tasks? If a general, rate-limiting process has been improved, then we should see changes in curvature rather than in intercept or asymptote (see Fig. 10.8). Thus, the key contribution of these methods is not so much that they eliminate the annoyance of speed-accuracy trade-offs and error-response latencies (although these certainly do disappear). Rather, it is that they generate a more accurate picture of performance, one that is less subject to misinterpretation and one whose parameters can be immediately linked to theory.

Limitations

Finally, I hasten to add that I do not see the speed-accuracy study as a panacea. Rather, I merely offer it as a relatively unexplored alternative to the conventional practice of indexing one coordinate of one aspect of performance. One of the more important limitations of speed-accuracy studies is that they require many more observations than do conventional experiments, which means that they place even greater demands than usual on the assumption that behavior is in a relatively steady state.

For tasks that show large practice effects, subjects must first be practiced to the point at which their performance is not showing dramatic improvements. Practice effects can then be controlled statistically before speed-accuracy models are fitted. However, fitting nonlinear models to individuals is often difficult, and the parameters of the models themselves are sometimes not stable. As with component scores, one must worry about the reliability of the curvature parameter, which is also like a difference score. Recent developments in growth curve approach to the measurement of change offer some help here (Rogosa & Willett, 1985). However, my limited experience suggests that obtaining reliable parameters may be more of a problem of how data are collected than how they are analyzed.

SUMMARY AND CONCLUSIONS

In summary, cognitive psychology has not had the impact on measurement that many of us expected it would have. There are several reasons for this. First, much effort has been expended searching for measures of basic information-processing capabilities that would show strong, consistent correlations with traditional ability estimates. Instead, correlations have been generally weak and, when strong, inconsistently so. I believe that this is in large measure an inevitable consequence of the fact that component scores, while useful, essentially salvage systematic individual difference variance from the error term. Ironically, it is the intercept from such models that captures individual differences that are consistent across trials.

The fixation on component scores was in part the consequence of a second assumption, that is, that cognitive tests would make interesting cognitive tasks, and vice versa. On the contrary, I would argue that, from the perspective of an individual difference analysis, these are often the least interesting sorts of tasks to subject to such intensive scrutiny. Primarily, that is because such tasks minimize or obscure the very sort of differences in solution strategy that cognitive analyses can detect. It is like using a powerful microscope to determine the color of an object. Information about how subjects solved a task is more likely to be informative when tasks admit a variety of solution strategies, and these strategies can be systematically related to ability or some other construct we hope to understand.

When cognitive analysis is applied to conventional mental tests, one of its main contributions should be to detect when subjects are using solution strategies that compromise the interpretation of their scores. Thus, confidence indices should be developed and used more routinely. Cognitive psychology can also contribute to the construction of new tests, either through the generation of items with predictable difficulty values, or through tests designed to reflect a particular theory of cognition. Recent efforts to develop spatial ability in this way show some promise in this respect.

For homogeneous ability tests and cognitive tests, I suggest that we make better use of both latency and error data. One way to do this is through the speed-accuracy study. In many situations it would seem eminently worthwhile to test the limits of each subject's performance. Our preliminary efforts to use these methods produced many encouraging findings, but also revealed an equally large number of problems in how best to collect and analyze such data. Nevertheless, I am confident that such methods can make a useful contribution both to the practical problems of selection and classification, and to the larger problem of understanding what it is that we measure—or ought to measure.

REFERENCES

Ackerman, P. L., & Kanfer, R. (1993). Integrating laboratory and field study for improving selection: Development of a battery for predicting air traffic controller success. *Journal of Applied Psychology, 78*(3), 413-432.

Baddeley, A. (1986). *Working memory*. Oxford, England: Clarendon Press.

Bethell-Fox, C. E., Lohman, D. F., & Snow, R. E. (1984). Adaptive reasoning: Componential and eye movement analysis of geometric analogy performance. *Intelligence, 8*, 205-238.

Butterfield, E. C., Nielsen, D., Tangen, K. L., & Richardson, M. B. (1985). Theoretically based psychometric measures of inductive reasoning. In S. E. Embretson (Ed.), *Test design: Developments in psychology and psychometrics* (pp. 77-148). New York: Academic Press.
Carroll, J. B. (1976). Psychometric tests as cognitive tasks: A new "structure of intellect." In L. B. Resnick (Ed.), *The nature of intelligence* (pp. 27-56). Hillsdale, NJ: Lawrence Erlbaum Associates.
Carroll, J. B. (1980). *Individual differences in psychometric and experimental cognitive tasks* (NU 150-406 ONR Final Report). Chapel Hill, NC: L. L. Thurstone Psychometric Laboratory, University of North Carolina.
Cronbach, L. J. (1975). Five decades of public controversy over mental testing. *American Psychologist, 30*, 1-14.
Dennis, I., & Evans, J. (1990). *The consequences of speed-accuracy trade-offs for latency based testing* (HAL Tech. Rep. 5-1990). Plymouth, England: Polytechnic South West, Department of Psychology, Human Assessment Laboratory.
Dennis, I., & Evans, J. (1991). *Speed-accuracy tradeoff in testing: An empirical study* (HAL Tech. Rep. 1-1991). Plymouth, England: Polytechnic South West, Department of Psychology, Human Assessment Laboratory.
Egan, D. E. (1976). *Accuracy and latency scores as measures of spatial information-processing* (NAMRL Rep. No. 1224). Pensacola, FL: Naval Aerospace Medical Research Laboratory.
Eliot, J. C., & Smith, I. M. (1983). *An international directory of spatial tests*. Windsor, England: NFER-Nelson.
Ha, D. H. (1988). *Using a speed-accuracy model to describe individual differences in components of numerical analogy solution*. Unpublished doctoral dissertation, University of Iowa, Iowa City.
Hunt, E. B., Frost, N., & Lunneborg, C. (1973). Individual differences in cognition: A new approach to intelligence. In G. Bower (Ed.), *The psychology of learning and motivation* (Vol. 7, pp. 87-122). New York: Academic Press.
Ippel, M. J., & Beem, A. L. (1987). A theory of antagonistic strategies. In E. DeCorte, H. Lodewijks, R. Parmentier, & P. Span (Eds.), *Learning and instruction: European research in an international context* (Vol. 1, pp. 111-121). Oxford, England: Leuven University Press and Pergamon Press.
Irvine, S. H., Dann, P. L., & Anderson, J. D. (1990). Towards a theory of algorithm-determined cognitive test construction. *British Journal of Psychology, 81*, 173-195.
Jensen, A. R. (1982). The chronometry of intelligence. In R.J. Sternberg (Ed.), *Advances in the psychology of human intelligence* (Vol. 1, pp. 255-310). Hillsdale, NJ: Lawrence Erlbaum Associates.
Lansman, M. (1981). Ability factors and the speed of information-processing. In M. P. Friedman, J. P. Das, & N. O'Connor (Eds.). *Intelligence and learning* (pp. 441-458). New York: Plenum.
Lohman, D. F. (1986). The effect of speed-accuracy trade-off on sex differences in mental rotation. *Perception and Psychophysics, 39*, 427-436.
Lohman, D. F. (1988). Spatial abilities as traits, processes, and knowledge. In R. J. Sternberg (Ed.), *Advances in the psychology of human intelligence* (Vol. 4, pp. 181-248). Hillsdale, NJ: Lawrence Erlbaum Associates.
Lohman, D. F. (1989a). Estimating individual differences in information-processing using speed-accuracy models. In R. Kaufer, P. L. Ackerman, & R. Cudeck (Eds.), *Abilities, motivation, and methodology: The Minnesota symposium on learning and individual differences* (pp. 119-164). Hillsdale, NJ: Lawrence Erlbaum Associates.

Lohman, D. F. (1989b). Individual differences in errors and latencies on cognitive tasks. *Learning and Individual Differences, 1*, 179-202.

Lohman, D. F. (1991). *Estimating rate of decay of activation in semantic memory using a speed-accuracy methodology* (Tech. Rep. AFOSR-89-0385). Iowa City: University of Iowa, Lindquist Center for Measurement.

Lohman, D. F. (1993) *Effects of practice and training on the acquisition and transfer of spatial skills: Two speed-accuracy studies* (Tech. Rep. AFOSR-91-0367). Iowa City: University of Iowa, Lingquist Center for Measurement.

Lohman, D. F., & Ippel, M. J. (1993). Cognitive diagnosis: From statistically based assessment toward theory based assessment. In N. Frederiksen, R. Mislevy, & I. Bejar (Eds.), *Test theory for a new generation of tests* (pp. 44-71). Hillsdale, NJ: Lawrence Erlbaum Associates.

McClelland, J. L. (1979). On the time relations of mental processes: An examination of systems in cascade. *Psychological Review, 86*, 287-330.

Nichols, P. D. (1990). *Cognitive assessment of figural analogical reasoning: A theory-driven approach toward test development.* Unpublished doctoral dissertation, University of Iowa, Iowa City.

Poltrock, S. E., & Brown, P. (1984). Individual differences in visual imagery and spatial ability. *Intelligence, 8*, 93-138.

Rogosa, D. R., & Willett, J. B. (1985). Understanding correlates of change by modeling individual differences in growth. *Psychometrika, 50*, 203-228.

Shepard, R., & Metzler, J. (1971). Mental rotation of three-dimensional objects. *Science, 171*, 701-703.

Snow, R. E., Marshalek, B., & Lohman, D. F. (1976). *Correlation of selected cognitive abilities and cognitive processing parameters: An exploratory study* (Tech. Rep. No. 1). Stanford, CA: Stanford University, Aptitude Research Project, School of Education.

Snow, R. E., & Peterson, P. (1985). Cognitive analyses of tests: Implications for redesign. In S. E. Embretson (Ed.), *Test design: Developments in psychology and psychometrics* (pp. 149-166). Orlando: Academic Press.

Sternberg, R. J. (1977). *Intelligence, information-processing, and analogical reasoning: The componential analysis of human abilities.* Hillsdale, NJ: Lawrence Erlbaum Associates.

Sternberg, R. J. (1985). *Beyond IQ: A triarchic theory of human intelligence.* New York: Cambridge University Press.

Sternberg, R. J., & Detterman, D. K. (Eds.) (1979). *Human intelligence: Perspectives on its theory and measurement.* Norwood, NJ: Ablex.

Sternberg, R. J., & Gardner, M. K. (1983). Unities in inductive reasoning. *Journal of Experimental Psychology: General, 112*, 80-116.

Tatsuoka, K. K., & Baillie, R. (1982). *Rule space, the product space of two score components in signed-number subtraction: An approach to dealing with inconsistent use of erroneous rules* (Research Report 82-3-ONR). Urbana: University of Illinois, Computer-based Education Research Laboratory.

Thurstone, L. L. (1938). Primary mental abilities. *Psychometric Monographics, 1*.

Wickelgren, W. A. (1977). Speed-accuracy trade-off and information-processing dynamics. *Acta Psychologica, 41*, 67-85.

Woltz, D. J. (1990). Repetition of semantic comparisons: Temporary and persistent priming effects. *Journal of Experimental Psychology: Learning, Memory, and Cognition, 16*, 392-403.

Wood, C. C., & Jennings, J. R. (1976). Speed-accuracy trade-off functions in choice reaction time: Experimental designs and computational procedures. *Perception & Psychophysics, 19*, 92-101.

CHAPTER

11

ENVIRONMENTS FOR PRESENTING
AND AUTOMATICALLY SCORING COMPLEX
CONSTRUCTED-RESPONSE ITEMS

Randy Elliot Bennett
Educational Testing Service

The term *constructed response* refers to a wide array of tasks ranging from simple modifications of multiple-choice items to complex performances (Bennett, 1993a). The major characteristic that distinguishes these tasks from multiple choice is that they require a response to be generated instead of selected from a small set of presented options. Such items may be preferred over multiple-choice questions because they generally reflect the tasks examinees encounter in academic and work settings more faithfully, contain more information about cognitive structure (Birenbaum & Tatsuoka, 1987), and, in some instances, reduce adverse impact for population groups, particularly females (Bolger & Kellaghan, 1990; Mazzeo, Schmidt, & Bleistein, 1993).

Our work has centered on a class of complex constructed-response tasks for which the answers contain multiple elements, have correct solutions that take many forms, and, although they require judgment to evaluate, are machine scorable (Bennett, 1993b). These tasks are computer delivered.

Computer delivery provides several capabilities not easily available in paper-and-pencil form. First, responses can be collected in ready condition for machine scoring; no transcription is required, eliminating considerable cost and potential error. Second, responses can be analyzed in real time, which permits adaptive testing as well as instantaneous score reporting. Third, new information can be obtained, including response latency and measurement of improvement associated with dynamically presented machine-generated hints. Finally, some of the difficulties associated with using human judges can be reduced. For example, scoring can be conducted continuously without any degradation in accuracy.

In this chapter we explore the use of computer-delivered constructed-response tasks in three areas: computer science, algebra, and verbal reasoning. In each area, we have built experimental, interactive assessment systems.

We developed these systems as research tools for educational contexts: selection, course placement, and instructional assessment. Although the systems were not built to test skills or serve populations of direct interest to the Army, each system has characteristics that the Army might wish to emulate in its predictor and criterion measures for selection and classification.

We describe three such systems, one in each of the content areas just denoted. For each system, we briefly discuss the computer presentation interface, the task formats, the scoring method, and the relevant research.

THREE SYSTEMS FOR CONSTRUCTED-RESPONSE TESTING

Computer Science

Our work in automated constructed-response testing began in computer science. We chose this content area for two reasons. First, considerable related research had centered on understanding how students learn to program and on improving programming instruction. This research, done in the field of intelligent tutoring, produced several laboratory systems for analyzing students' programming productions on which we could build (e.g., Johnson, 1986; Johnson & Soloway, 1985). Second, computer science classes represent one of the few instances in which a ready infrastructure for computer-based testing exists: Machines are readily available and teachers and students are technologically sophisticated, requiring a minimal degree of support.

Our explorations began with the Advanced Placement Computer Science (APCS) examination, a program of the College Board offered in many high schools for advanced placement or credit toward college coursework. The examination is given at the culmination of the year-long APCS course and includes multiple-choice and free-response sections. The free-response section consists of several problems that require the examinee to write or design a short procedure or data structure, and at times to analyze the efficiency of certain operations involved in the solution.

The program we originally used to score and qualitatively analyze solutions to these free-response problems was MicroPROUST. MicroPROUST is a demonstration version of PROUST (Johnson, 1986; Johnson & Soloway, 1985), a batch-processing laboratory tool. Three studies have been conducted with MicroPROUST focusing on automatic analysis. For these studies, data were gathered using paper-and-pencil tests and transcribed to machine-readable form.

The first study examined agreement between the program and human readers in analyzing solutions to two APCS free-response problems (Bennett, Gong, et al., 1990). Results showed MicroPROUST produced an analysis for approximately 70% of the 88 solutions given it. For this subset, it generated scores and qualitative diagnoses that agreed well with human readers for one problem and that were not dramatically different from reader judgments for the second (the correlations with reader scores were .96 and .75, respectively). In a cross-validation sample, however, the program was able to analyze only 42% of the responses; for this subset, agreement with the scores awarded by a human judge remained high.

The second study assessed the impact of limiting the constructed-response task by requiring the student to debug a wrong solution instead of writing a procedure anew (Braun, Bennett, Frye, & Soloway, 1990). A sample of 737 students was given this "faulty solution" task (which was adapted from one of the problems used in the previous study). MicroPROUST was able to analyze substantially more of these solutions (83%), while maintaining a reasonable level of scoring agreement (the correlation with a human rater was .86). Concurrence on error diagnosis was more moderate, with agreement on the exact nature and location of individual bugs achieved in 56% of cases.

The last study dealt with the relationship of MicroPROUST's faulty solution scores to the APCS examination (Bennett, Rock et al., 1990). Faulty solution scores were factor analyzed along with scores from APCS multiple-choice items and manually graded APCS free-response tasks. Data were analyzed for two examinee samples, differing in the number of bugs placed in the faulty solution items administered to them. In the sample with a single seeded bug, the three item types measured the same factor, supporting the validity of MicroPROUST's scores as indicators of the computer science proficiency underlying the APCS examination. The second sample was administered a solution having three bugs. Here, the item type appeared to measure a factor distinct from APCS, the nature of which could not be discerned from the analysis.

The results of these studies were intriguing enough to cause us to pursue further research on automatic scoring. We felt this research could be most productively done if responses could be gathered by computer and if a more powerful analysis program could be written.

The Advanced Placement Computer Science (APCS) Practice System was developed to answer this need (Bennett, Sack, & Soloway, 1992). The APCS System is a prototype interactive environment for presenting and analyzing answers to free-response problems similar to those presented on the APCS examination. The system might have both diagnostic and summative uses. It could conceivably be placed in the classroom as a tool for practicing programming skills and getting immediate feedback, or used as a standardized testing device for summative decision making. The latter use could be as a single end-of-year assessment or as repeated performance samplings taken over the school year.

The APCS System is built around a programming editor that presents free-response problems. The student can construct an answer in the form of a short Pascal program; compile, run, and modify that program; and automatically analyze the result to produce a partial-credit score and qualitative analysis.

The qualitative analysis describes errors in the solution and gives hints as to how they might be corrected. Scores and analyses are produced at the item level only; no aggregation of responses has yet been implemented. Fig. 11.1 shows the APCS editor and part of an example problem. Fig. 11.2 shows part of an example solution.

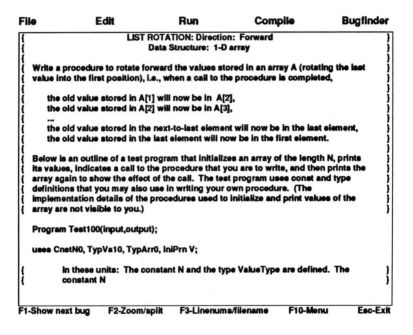

FIG. 11.1. The APCS Practice System editor and an example problem. Given program
declarations are partially shown. Editing and system function commands
are shown as items above and below the window. From the Advanced
Placement Computer Science Practice System, copyright (c) ETS, 1991.
Reprinted by permission of Educational Testing Service.

Students' solutions are processed by an analyzer that calls on a knowledge base composed of patterns representing correct and incorrect pieces of the problem solution. These patterns can be combined in many ways to capture much of the variability that characterizes examinee solutions to such problems. Knowledge bases are developed through cognitive analysis, that is, by examining a large corpus of solutions to identify how a problem is typically decomposed and what errors are commonly made.

Because knowledge bases are costly to develop and specific to a narrow class of problems, the latest version of the system contains a small number of

File	Edit	Run	Compile	Bugfinder

```
Procedure Rotate(var A: ArrayType);
{ Pre:  A = (a1, a2, ..., a(N-1), a(N))                         }
{ Post: A = (a(N), a1, ..., a(N-2), a(N-1))                     }


    var
       Temp : ValueType;
       I : 1..N;
    begin
       for I : = 1 to n do
       begin
          A[1] : = A[I];
       end;
    end;
```

F1-Show next bug	F2-Zoom/split	F3-Linenums/filename	F10-Menu	Esc-Exit

FIG. 11.2. A procedure written in response to the programming problem shown
in Fig. 11.1.   From the Advanced Placement Computer Science
Practice System, copyright (c) ETS, 1991. Reprinted by permission
of Educational Testing Service.

problem classes. Problems in a class call for the examinee to perform some manipulation on a list of data elements (e.g., counting the elements, eliminating elements that meet a given criterion). The classes themselves differ in the data structure that must be used to solve the problem (e.g., array, record, linked list). Responses to problems in the same class are analyzed by a single knowledge base.

The APCS System provides an interesting problem-solving environment within which to study assessment approaches relevant to Army selection and classification. One of its most potentially valuable features is that it allows the examinee to solve problems iteratively by writing program code, testing it, viewing the output, making modifications, and so on. This feature makes it possible to assess how effectively the examinee uses feedback. Two types of feedback, both obtainable at the examinee's option, are available (i.e., in addition to the low-level, syntactic information given by a Pascal compiler). Feedback on program functioning is produced by running the compiled code and examining the result, whereas information on program structure can be obtained from the system's analyzer.

Several potentially valuable proficiency measures might be derived. One is the type of feedback required—functional or structural: The more proficient programmer should be able to infer how to fix the program by examining its output, as opposed to being told what component is misspecified. (At the same time, we should expect the better programmer to seek structural feedback—as he or she would from a colleague—if repeated attempts to complete the program using functional information fail.) A second measure might be the frequency of feedback requests, for example, how many times the examinee needs structural hints before arriving at a correct solution. Finally, overall time to solution, as well as time to solution after receiving feedback, might prove useful—the latter another possible indicator of the ability to benefit from hints.

A second relevant problem-solving feature of the APCS System is the capability to evaluate transfer. Transfer can be assessed by presenting the examinee with a problem from the same class that uses the same data structure but that varies some relatively isolated component. For example, in a problem calling for the rotation of an array, the direction of rotation might be reversed. A more distant transfer task might be produced by changing the data structure to be manipulated.

The ability to benefit from feedback and to transfer learning to the performance of related tasks is important in many problem-solving contexts, including those of Army jobs. The APCS model should be useful for measuring these qualities for any system that produces an observable output and must be adjusted when functioning is not as desired. Electrical, cooling, hydraulic, and mechanical systems are examples.

Interestingly, there is relatively little research on how useful this model might be. Several investigators have developed intelligent tutors for training individuals to service such systems (e.g., J. R. Frederiksen & White, 1988; Lesgold, Lajoie, Bunzo, & Eggan, 1992; Towne & Munro, 1988). Among other things, these tutors use response to feedback and transfer to make real-time adjustments in instruction. In the academic context, Feuerstein (1979)—under the rubric "dynamic assessment"—has long employed similar indicators for clinically assessing the intellectual skills of retarded students. Also in that context, Campione and Brown (1987) provided preliminary evidence of the value of these measures for predicting scholastic achievement. Finally, Embretson (1987) illustrated approaches for addressing the psychometric problems raised, including issues associated with the measurement of change.

Algebra Problem Solving

The APCS environment permits a system—in the form of a computer program—to be constructed and run. This construction can then be analyzed to produce a score and qualitative feedback. The process of constructing the program also can be captured as the series of intermediate productions, compilations, executions, and structural feedback requests that eventually leads to the final program.

Algebra word problems, the second domain in which we have been working, have in common with programs the fact that solutions can be structurally analyzed. However, they also differ from programs in important ways. Unlike programs, word-problem solutions are not normally written in electronic environments, posing a problem for capturing data in machine-readable form; duplicating in an electronic environment the naturalistic aspects of problem solving in paper and pencil is a challenging task. Word-problem solutions also are not automatically executable, so externally provided functional feedback is not available. Third, word-problem solutions differ from computer programs in that the solution often recapitulates important elements of the problem-solving process by showing the sequence of steps leading to the end result. Fourth, this sequence of steps is often hierarchical in that subsequent steps depend on previous ones. Finally, steps may be present by implication: Students often leave out components they have computed mentally.

The Algebra Assessment System (Sebrechts, Bennett, & Katz, 1993) is an interactive prototype for presenting algebra word problems of the type found on postsecondary admissions and course placement tests. The system permits the examinee to enter the problem solution as a series of equations and intermediate calculations. Four problem formats are being used: open ended (giving only the problem stem), goal specification (presenting the problem stem and identifying the givens and unknowns), equation setup (presenting the problem stem and general equations leading to a solution), and faulty solution (giving the problem stem and a wrong response).

Fig. 11.3 shows the Algebra Assessment System interface. The problem stem appears in the top left window accompanied by format information on the right. In the center of the screen is a scrollable work space in which the examinee can enter any equation consisting of whole numbers, decimals, and fractions together with alphanumeric labels. Equations are entered either by typing on the keyboard or by clicking the mouse on-screen "buttons" located below the work space. The screen buttons are arranged to reflect the layout of the computer keyboard and include the numerals 0-9, letters for use as variable and constant names, the four primary mathematical operators, and parentheses.

Several constraints are imposed on solution entry to facilitate automatic analysis. First, solutions must be expressed alpha-numerically. As a consequence, answers tend to be expressed linearly and sequentially, making the solution process easier to trace. How this restriction affects problem solving needs to be studied, as does the possibility of incorporating mechanisms for entering and scoring diagrammatic solutions. Second, as in a programming environment, certain syntax errors are detected and appropriate messages displayed. For example, when an equation is entered it is checked for unbalanced parentheses, thus forcing the examinee to clarify the precedence of operations.

On the far right of the display is a five-function calculator used at the examinee's option. Entries are made by clicking on the operand and operator

keys with the mouse or by using the keyboard. These actions produce a
scrollable "tape," which comprises a recallable record of all entries and results.

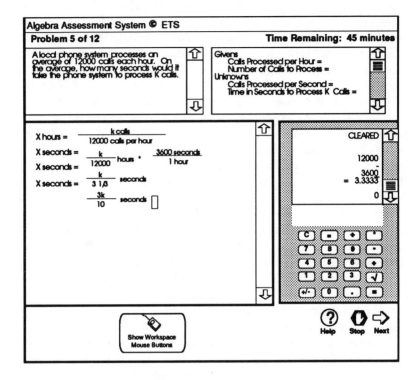

FIG. 11.3. The Algebra Assessment System interface with an example problem and solution.
From the Algebra Assessment System, copyright (c) ETS, 1992.
Reprinted by permission of Educational Testing Service.

Responses are analyzed offline by GIDE, a knowledge-based program that
produces a series of comments about errors present in the equations that compose
the solution (Sebrechts, LaClaire, Schooler, & Soloway, 1986; Sebrechts &
Schooler, 1987; Sebrechts, Schooler, LaClaire, & Soloway, 1987). Based on
these errors, GIDE awards a partial-credit score.

As with the APCS System, GIDE analyzes responses by consulting
problem-specific knowledge bases developed through cognitive analysis. In
general, GIDE functions much like the APCS System's analyzer. GIDE builds
an understanding of the examinee's response in terms of a "goal-plan" structure,
in which goals are the objectives to be achieved in solving a problem (e.g., the
result of an intermediate step) and plans are stereotypical means (i.e., procedures)
for achieving those goals.

In determining whether a goal is satisfied, GIDE attempts to match one of the several plans it has for each goal to a portion of the examinee's solution, working in this manner until matches have been attempted for all goals. The hierarchical nature of algebra solutions plays an important role here: GIDE uses it to determine if unmatched goals are present by implication (e.g., omitted because they were computed mentally) or unintentionally left out.

The accuracy of GIDE's partial-credit scores has been analyzed by determining its agreement with human raters (Sebrechts, Bennett, & Rock, 1991). In this study, 30 examinees who had recently taken the GRE General Test completed three items in each of the four constructed-response formats denoted previously. (Conducted prior to developing the Algebra Assessment System interface, these responses were collected in paper-and-pencil form.) Five raters then independently scored each item response. The rater mean scores were next correlated with the scores awarded by GIDE and the distribution of discrepancies computed for each item. Correlations between GIDE and the raters' mean scores for the 12 problems ranged from .74 to .97, with a median of .88; the largest mean absolute discrepancy between GIDE and the raters was 1.2 points for questions graded on a 16-point scale. No obvious differences in scoring agreement among the four constructed-response formats emerged.

A second study factor analyzed the responses of 249 examinees to ascertain the degree to which scores from the four constructed-response formats related to the General Test's quantitative section, an established measure of quantitative reasoning skill (Bennett, Sebrechts, & Rock, 1991). Two highly correlated dimensions—GRE-quantitative and constructed response (the latter comprised of the four question formats)—emerged from this analysis. Along with the agreement analysis, these results suggest that GIDE can duplicate the judgments of content experts reasonably well in numerically scoring solutions to constructed-response algebra items, and that these scores are consistent with those from a well-established quantitative ability measure.

GIDE's qualitative analyses also have been evaluated (Bennett & Sebrechts, 1994). Problems were presented to three examinee samples, one taking the questions in paper-and-pencil form and the other two on computer. Responses were then diagnostically analyzed by GIDE and by four ETS mathematics test developers using the same fine-grained categorization of error types that GIDE uses. Results were highly consistent across the samples, showing human judges to agree among themselves almost perfectly in describing responses as right or wrong, but at much lower levels in categorizing the specific nature of bugs they detected in incorrect solutions. (For the three samples, respectively, the majority of judges agreed on 64%, 37%, and 46% of the total bugs detected by the judges individually.) GIDE agreed highly with the judges' right/wrong decisions (95% to 97% concurrence) and somewhat less closely (71% to 74%) with the bug categorizations on which the judges themselves agreed. Seven principal causes of machine-rater disagreement were detected, most of which could be remedied by making adjustments to GIDE, modifying the Algebra Assessment System interface to constrain the form of examinee solutions, and working with test developers to specify rules for automatically dealing with special cases.

The contrast between the relatively high accuracy found for GIDE's partial-credit scoring and the more limited accuracy of its qualitative analyses deserves comment. Accurate qualitative analyses may be more difficult to render because these characterizations often take more forms and require finer distinctions. GIDE computes an item score by summing the points awarded for each goal or intermediate result. A goal is scored, in turn, by detecting errors and subtracting points depending on number and type. For scoring a goal, GIDE need only distinguish three error types: missing problem components, structural flaws, and computational mistakes. For qualitative purposes, GIDE breaks the latter two types into several dozen specific bugs, some of which are only subtly different. Thus, the greater number of qualitative categories forces a many-to-one mapping that makes it possible for GIDE to misdiagnose errors (within types) without diminishing its scoring accuracy.

Like the APCS System, the Algebra Assessment System has potential as a dynamic testing environment. Although it cannot execute problem solutions, once integrated with GIDE it will provide structural feedback keyed to the examinee's response. Because it is clear that even human experts disagree in their specific interpretations of erroneous responses, GIDE's feedback might be modified to give more general guidance (e.g., identifying conceptual versus computational errors). In addition, or as an alternative, it should be possible to combine elements of the different constructed-response formats to produce a series of progressively specific hints. In this conception, a problem in open-ended format would be presented. Clicking the mouse on the format window would identify the problem givens and solution goals. A menu might permit the examinee to opt next for information on particular goals. Choosing a goal might first reveal a set of general expressions and then the specific equations for solving that goal. Here again, the amount of assistance required and the degree to which that assistance is successfully used might be valuable measures for selection and classification.

Before the Algebra Assessment System was developed, we conducted a paper-and-pencil study to determine whether providing progressively specific information aided problem solving (Bennett, Sebrechts, & Yamamoto, 1991). This study provided little support for the notion, possibly because the paper-and-pencil arrangement was functionally quite distant from the above conception. With relatively little effort, the Algebra Assessment System could be modified to deliver these progressive hints, thereby allowing a more definitive investigation to be carried out.

Ill-Structured Verbal Problems

Both the Algebra Assessment System and the APCS System present problems for which it can be determined with reasonable certainty when a solution is achieved. In contrast, our most recent effort utilizes ill-structured problems. Ill-structured problems (a) have more complex and less definite criteria for knowing when a solution is reached; (b) do not include in the instructions all the information needed to solve the problem, and offer only a vague sense as to what information is relevant; and (c) have no simple "legal move generator" for finding all of the alternative possibilities at each solution step (Simon, 1978). Many of the more important problems encountered in academic disciplines, in job settings (including some Army jobs), and in everyday life are of this kind (N. Frederiksen, 1984).

The particular problem type we are using is called, "Formulating- Hypotheses" (F-H) (N. Frederiksen, 1959). The F-H item presents a situation and asks the examinee to generate plausible causes for it. The situations are constructed to be sufficiently ambiguous to elicit divergent responses.

The ability to generate divergent responses is relevant to performance in many domains. One class of domains encompasses tasks that have no correct answer. Design tasks are typical (e.g., for a building, machine, or even a battlefield operation). Here, many qualitatively different solutions might respond to the same functional specification. A range of alternatives needs to be generated and the implications of each evaluated before pursuing a particular course.

A second class of domains includes tasks that do have correct answers, as in equipment troubleshooting and medical diagnosis. For these domains, the divergent thinking ability tapped by F-H is arguably relevant when the diagnostician is pitted against a puzzling set of symptoms, for example, when several conditions interact. In such cases, the diagnostician must construct an array of possibilities, evaluating each for fit with the observable data.

The history of the F-H item type is quite interesting. Work on it began over 30 years ago in an attempt to measure skills similar to those used by scholars in interpreting research findings (N. Frederiksen, 1959). Subsequent studies, which applied the task to graduate admissions testing, proved quite successful. Construct validity analyses suggested that the item type reliably measured important proficiencies—including divergent thinking and cognitive flexibility—and further, that the measure overlapped only minimally with the constructs captured by the GRE General Test (N. Frederiksen & Ward, 1978; Ward, N. Frederiksen & Carlson, 1980). Perhaps even more interesting, the F-H items improved the prediction of certain criteria; they were more effective than General Test scores in forecasting subsequent self-appraisals of some professional skills and accomplishments.

The major drawback of the F-H item was its operational cost. Because of its open-ended format and the divergent nature of the task, scoring required considerable human time and judgment. Attempts to optimize the F-H item by recasting it in a machine-scorable, multiple-choice format failed as the adapted item no longer measured the same proficiency as its constructed-response counterpart (Ward, Carlson, & Woisetschlaeger, 1983; Ward et al., 1980).

Chances for realizing the promise of the F-H item improved with the growing availability of personal computers and with advances in natural language processing. Reviewing the status of F-H, Carlson and Ward (1988) advised that the task be computer delivered and that an automated scoring system be developed based on semantic processing.

Figure 11.4 shows the F-H interface. The problem situation is presented in the scrollable window on the upper left. Directions that explain the task are given below this window. At the lower right is the Edit window; the examinee enters a hypothesis by typing it here. Clicking on the "Save" button moves the hypothesis to the numbered list in the upper-right window. To edit a saved hypothesis, the examinee highlights it by selecting it with the mouse and then presses the "Edit" button, moving the hypothesis back to the lower-right box.

Creditable responses must explain the situation and must not duplicate the meaning of any other response on the list. In their earlier research, N. Frederiksen and Ward (1978) studied the effectiveness of various indices, including the number of unduplicated hypotheses, the number of unusual hypotheses, the number that were both unusual and of high quality, the average quality of an examinee's ideas, the quality of the idea the examinee thought was best, and the highest-quality idea offered by the examinee. Validity analyses showed the number of unduplicated hypotheses to be the most powerful measure, and it is this index that we use in our current work.

To study the efficacy of the computer-delivered F-H task, we administered an 8-item test to 192 graduate students (Bennett & Rock, in press). Half of the items restricted examinees to 7 words per explanation, and half allowed up to 15 words. Generalizability results showed high interrater agreement, with tests of between two and four items scored by one judge achieving coefficients in the .80s. As in studies of paper-and-pencil versions, validity analyses found that although F-H was highly reliable, it was only weakly related to GRE General Test scores, differing from that test primarily in relating more strongly to a measure of ideational fluency (the ability to generate ideas within relatively broad constraints). Versions of F-H based on different response limits tapped somewhat different abilities, with items employing the 15-word constraint appearing more useful for graduate assessment. These items added to conventional measures like the GRE in explaining school performance and creative accomplishment. Finally, although the overwhelming majority of examinees found the F-H interface easy to use, some experienced difficulty, suggesting the possibility that computer familiarity constitutes a source of irrelevant variance in F-H scores.

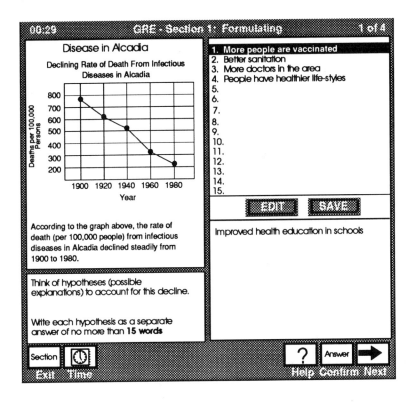

FIG. 11.4. The Formulating-Hypotheses interface showing a problem and response.
From the Formulating-Hypotheses Test, copyright (c) ETS, 1993.
Reprinted by permission of the Educational Testing Service.

The validity results reported previously were based on a count of the number of hypotheses posed by the examinee. For a subsample of 30 examinees from the larger dataset, this count correlated almost perfectly with the number found acceptable by human judges. In a research setting, a simple count of the number of hypotheses offered is a reasonable proxy for a more refined evaluation of responses. However, this approach would not be workable in a "high-stakes" testing situation. Consequently, we are exploring the feasibility of using machine analysis to assist judges in scoring responses.

The program we are using is the Free-Response Scoring Tool (FRST) (Kaplan, 1992), an extension of pattern-matching approaches to natural language processing. The FRST is based on sublanguage analysis. In sublanguage analysis, a grammar is formally specified for a small subset of natural language. This grammar can then be used to recognize productions that do and do not belong to the sublanguage. With human assistance, FRST can form such a grammar for a test item from a sample of responses. The grammar is a canonicalization of the responses such that many varied responses can be captured with a small number of abstract language strings. The canonicalization is an arbitrary one based on the semantics of the particular test item.

In the case of F-H, human judges use a pretest sample to categorize the vocabulary for each item response into semantic classes. These classes are next used to form abstract strings representing each correct answer. Once duplicate strings are removed, this list becomes the item's scoring key. The program can then score new responses by transforming each one to a classification string and comparing it against the key, placing those that cannot be recognized as correct into a class of unscored responses. FRST does not produce diagnostic analyses nor does it depend on the same level of knowledge-based analysis that character-izes GIDE or the APCS System. This latter characteristic permits FRST to score answers to new items with far less preparation than these other systems require.

One study has explored FRST's accuracy in scoring F-H items (Kaplan & Bennett, 1994). In this study, scores were generated by FRST and, independ-ently, by five human raters for 30 examinees' responses to each of eight items. Accuracy was analyzed for item scores (i.e., the number of creditable hypotheses given for an item) and for individual hypotheses, which were scored as right or wrong. On its initial scoring run, FRST agreed highly with the raters' item scores for some questions. As modifications to the automatic scoring were made, FRST improved its concurrence substantially for the other items. By the final run, correlations between the program and the raters on item scores ranged from .89 to .97, depending on the item, and mean human-machine discrepancies ran from .6 to 1.1 on a 16-point scale. At the individual-hypothesis level, the proportion agreement between FRST and the raters ranged from .80 to .94 for the final run. However, because the overwhelming majority of responses in the sample were, in fact, correct, this performance level was at or just beyond chance (kappa values ranged from .00 to .26). Further, a tendency on the part of the program to erroneously classify wrong responses as correct was detected. These results suggest the need to enhance FRST so that it can more assuredly recognize which responses it can and cannnot accurately grade. With this capability, the program could become part of a semiautomatic system in which questionable responses were routed to human judges for resolution.

CONCLUSION

This paper described three computer-based systems for presenting and automatic-ally scoring complex constructed-response items. These systems use tasks closer to the problem-solving situations that examinees encounter in academic disciplines and work settings. They employ partial-credit scoring, enable rapid reporting, and generate performance information not easily gathered from conventional tests. This latter information potentially includes response latency, qualitative and quantitative analysis of the process used to arrive at a solution, and the degree of improvement associated with dynamically presented hints.

These systems raise several important issues. One issue concerns the two major threats to validity, construct underrepresentation and construct-irrelevant variance (Messick, 1989). With respect to construct underrepresentation, computer-based testing suits some tasks better than others. The Algebra Assessment System, for example, cannot now analyze responses to ill-structured problems or to well-structured items that tend to be solved using linguistic simulations or diagrams. These system characteristics are problematic to the extent that such tasks uniquely measure important aspects of the construct we wish to assess.

We can obtain coverage of ill-structured problems by supplementing performance estimates with results from paper-and-pencil tests scored by human judges. To handle simulations and diagrams, we might add linguistic processing capabilities similar to FRST's, and graphical analysis techniques drawn from the development of complex constructed-response testing systems for architectural certification (Bejar, 1991; Braun, in press). The general concern, however, is that we take care not to underrepresent the focal construct by choosing a particular delivery mechanism or scoring technology that excludes critical tasks.

Construct-irrelevant variance, the second threat to validity, can be a factor in computer-based tests because examinees may be differentially adept at using the computer or differentially comfortable with it. Such is probably not the case for the APCS System, which was intended for students proficient with computers and standard programming editors. As suggested by Bennett and Rock (in press), the F-H System is potentially more problematic, for the examinee must not only type, but know how to enter, save, and edit hypotheses. We are addressing this validity threat by giving all examinees a tutorial prior to taking the test, allowing extremely liberal time limits (about 10 minutes per item) to reduce the impact of typing skill, and working with a computer-literate population, applicants to graduate school. Even so, the effect of familiarity—especially, typing skill—requires careful study if it is to be ruled out as a plausible competing hypothesis for the meaning of F-H scores.

Generalizability is a second principal issue. The scores and qualitative analyses rendered by these systems should be generalizable across various conditions. These conditions will depend on the assessment purpose, but will most often include generalizability to other tasks sampled from the same domain and to other raters. That is, the performance estimate should remain essentially the same regardless of the sample of tasks administered and no matter who renders the score, expert human judge or machine.

Task generalizability is a salient issue for lengthy problems, such as those contained in the APCS System. Because each task takes considerable time to solve, relatively few can be presented in the time period conventionally allowed for standardized tests. Large-scale testing programs, like Advanced Placement, often address the problem by combining performance on a few such items with a highly correlated multiple-choice test. The resulting score gains some breadth of coverage from the multiple-choice section and depth from the more involved constructed-response tasks. The APCS System allows an additional option that may be appropriate in some contexts: repeated testing at different points in time and thus, the opportunity to administer more tasks.

Our research on the generalizability of item scores across raters in algebra and in computer science has been very positive. At this time, the greater need may be to improve the accuracy of qualitative analyses. The success of any dynamic assessment strategy keyed to knowledge-based structural hints obviously depends on the accuracy of these analyses: Wrong analyses might confuse the examinee, adding to response latency and underestimating the ability to benefit from hints. (Note, however, that dynamic assessment strategies based on functional feedback produced by executing the program or on a fixed set of progressively specific structural hints sidestep this problem by not requiring knowledge-based analysis.) Qualitative analyses also explain item performance. A summary of these analyses may be important for justifying scores in selection and classification situations when judgments are based on automatically processed constructed-response items.

Given the state of our capabilities, we are still at least a few years from the accuracy levels needed to automatically process responses of this complexity in operational testing programs. These accuracy levels may always require human verification, extensive in the early stages and dropping off as the technology becomes more dependable and accepted.

Some test sponsors, such as the National Council of Architectural Registration Boards, have already committed to examinations that incorporate complex automatically scored responses (Braun, in press). Initially, these responses probably will be machine scored subsequent to the test administration, and in a central location where accuracy can be ensured. Eventually, the analysis mechanism will be merged with the delivery system so that scores can be issued immediately at the conclusion of the testing session.

A third issue concerns the knowledge-based analytical approach used in the APCS and Algebra Assessment Systems. This approach is extremely labor inten- sive because a new, finely detailed knowledge base is required for each narrow class of problems. This high cost is, in substantial part, a function of the immaturity of the endeavor. Efficiency requires a specialized infrastructure similar to the one built for multiple-choice tests over the past 60 years. The corresponding infrastructure for automatic scoring will require new components, including knowledge-base development tools, modules that can be shared across knowledge bases, and, eventually, large knowledge-base libraries.

As this infrastructure evolves, the costs of incorporating new item classes will become more reasonable. Given the time and investment to develop this infrastructure, however, it is likely that for the near term most testing programs will opt for constructed-response tasks requiring simpler responses scorable by less demanding mechanisms (e.g., Bridgeman, 1992; Bridgeman & Rock, 1993; Manning, 1987; Martinez, Ferris, Kraft, & Manning, 1990), or for incrementally integrating small numbers of complex tasks with more conventional formats.

Finally, our work has centered on scoring at the item level. We have completed one preliminary investigation that aggregated information across problems, using both qualitative measurement models and item response theory (Bennett, Sebrechts, & Yamamoto, 1991). Far more work needs to be conducted, first to resolve what information to extract from item responses (e.g., latency, correctness, improvement), and second, to connect those extractions to desired inferences in a manner that accounts for the uncertainty associated with real data.

The experimental systems described in this chapter represent a first generation of interactive performance assessment tools that illustrates exciting possibilities for improving assessment, particularly by presenting problems more similar to criterion tasks and by providing new kinds of performance information. At the same time, it is clear that significant challenges must be solved to achieve these improvements. Issues to be resolved include questions related to construct underrepresentation and irrelevant variance, generalizability, efficiency, and response aggregation. We believe that these issues can be effectively addressed, permitting interactive performance systems to eventually become a common means for cognitive assessment.

ACKNOWLEDGMENTS

The systems described in this chapter were developed in collaboration with several individuals and funded by several sources. Warren Sack, Elliot Soloway, and Jeff Wadkins were principal collaborators on the APCS Practice System, which was funded by the College Board, the Richard Lounsbery Foundation, and Educational Testing Service. Marc Sebrechts and Irvin Katz were primary developers of the Algebra Assessment System, supported by the GRE Board. Randy Kaplan and Harriet Trenholm were the principal designers of the F-H System, which also was supported by the GRE Board. Portions of this chapter were adapted from Martinez and Bennett (1992).

REFERENCES

Bejar, I. I. (1991). A methodology for scoring open-ended architectural design problems. *Journal of Applied Psychology, 76*, 522-532.

Bennett, R. E. (1993a). On the meanings of constructed response. In R. E. Bennett & W. C. Ward (Eds.), *Construction versus choice in cognitive measurement: Issues in constructed response, performance testing, and portfolio assessment* (pp. 1-27). Hillsdale, NJ: Lawrence Erlbaum Associates.

Bennett, R. E. (1993b). Toward intelligent assessment: An integration of constructed response testing, artificial intelligence, and model-based measurement. In N. Frederiksen, R. J. Mislevy, and I. Bejar (Eds.), *Test theory for a new generation of tests* (pp. 99-123). Hillsdale, NJ: Lawrence Erlbaum Associates.

Bennett, R. E., Gong, B., Kershaw, R. C., Rock, D. A., Soloway, E., & Macalalad, A. (1990). Assessment of an expert system's ability to grade and diagnose automatically student's constructed responses to computer science problems. In R. O. Freedle (Ed.), *Artificial intelligence and the future of testing* (pp. 293-320). Hillsdale, NJ: Lawrence Erlbaum Associates.

Bennett, R. E., & Rock, D. A. (in press). Generalizability, validity, and examinee perceptions of a computer-delivered Formulating-Hypotheses test. *Journal of Educational Measurement.*

Bennett, R. E., Rock, D. A., Braun, H. I., Frye, D., Spohrer, J. C., & Soloway, E. (1990). The relationship of expert-system scored constrained free-response items to multiple-choice and open-ended items. *Applied Psychological Measurement, 14,* 151-162.

Bennett, R. E., Sack, W., & Soloway, E. (1992). *A practice and feedback system for Advanced Placement Computer Science* (RM-92-9). Princeton, NJ: Educational Testing Service.

Bennett, R. E., & Sebrechts, M. M. (1994). *The accuracy of automatic qualitative analyses of constructed-response solutions to algebra word problems* (RR-94-4). Princeton, NJ: Educational Testing Service.

Bennett, R. E., Sebrechts, M. M., & Rock, D. A. (1991). Expert system scores for complex constructed-response quantitative items: A study of convergent validity. *Applied Psychological Measurement, 15,* 227-239.

Bennett, R. E., Sebrechts, M. M., & Yamamoto, K. (1991). *Fitting new measurement models to GRE General Test constructed-response item data* (RR-91-60). Princeton, NJ: Educational Testing Service.

Birenbaum, M., & Tatsuoka, K. K. (1987). Open-ended versus multiple-choice response formats—it does make a difference for diagnostic purposes. *Applied Psychological Measurement, 11,* 385-395.

Bolger, N., & Kellaghan, T. (1990). Method of measurement and gender differences in scholastic achievement. *Journal of Educational Measurement, 27,* 165-174.

Braun, H. I. (in press). Assessing technology in assessment. In E. L. Baker & H. F. O'Neil, Jr. (Ed.), *Technology assessment: Vol. 1—education and training.* Hillsdale, NJ: Lawrence Erlbaum Associates.

Braun, H. I., Bennett, R. E., Frye, D., & Soloway, E. (1990). Scoring constructed responses using expert systems. *Journal of Educational Measurement, 27,* 93-108.

Bridgeman, B. (1992). A comparison of quantitative questions in open-ended and multiple-choice formats. *Journal of Educational Measurement, 29,* 253-271.

Bridgeman, B., & Rock, D. A. (1993). Relationships among multiple-choice and open-ended analytical questions. *Journal of Educational Measurement, 30,* 313-329.

Campione, J. C., & Brown, A. L. (1987). Linking dynamic assessment with school achievement. In C. S. Lidz (Ed.), *Dynamic assessment: An interactional approach to evaluating learning potential* (pp. 82-115). New York: Guilford.

Carlson, S. B., & Ward, W. C. (1988). *A new look at formulating hypotheses items* (RR-88-12). Princeton, NJ: Educational Testing Service.

Embretson, S. E. (1987). Toward development of a psychometric approach. In C. S. Lidz (Ed.), *Dynamic assessment: An interactional approach to evaluating learning potential* (pp. 141-170). New York: Guilford.

Feuerstein, R. (1979). *The dynamic assessment of retarded performers: The Learning Potential Assessment Device, theory instruments, and techniques.* Baltimore: University Park Press.

Frederiksen, J. R., & White, B. Y. (1988). Implicit testing within an intelligent tutoring system. *Machine-Mediated Learning, 2,* 351-372.

Frederiksen, N. (1959). *Development of the test "Formulating Hypotheses": A progress report* [Office of Naval Research Technical Report, Contract Nonr-2338(00)]. Princeton, NJ: Educational Testing Service.

Frederiksen, N. (1984). The real test bias: Influences of testing on teaching and learning. *American Psychologist, 39,* 193-202.

Frederiksen, N., & Ward, W. C. (1978). Measures for the study of creativity in scientific problem-solving. *Applied Psychological Measurement, 2,* 1-24.

Johnson, W. L. (1986). *Intention-based diagnosis of novice programming errors.* Los Altos, CA: Morgan Kaufmann.

Johnson, W. L., & Soloway, E. (1985). PROUST: An automatic debugger for Pascal programs. *Byte, 10*(4), 179-190.

Kaplan, R. (1992). *Using a trainable pattern-directed computer program to score natural language item responses* (RR-91-31). Princeton, NJ: Educational Testing Service.

Kaplan, R. M., & Bennett, R. E. (1994). *Using the Free-Response Scoring Tool to automatically score the Formulating-Hypotheses item* (RR-94-8). Princeton, NJ: Educational Testing Service.

Lesgold, A., Lajoie, S., Bunzo, M., & Eggan, G. (1992). SHERLOCK: A coached practice environment for an electronics troubleshooting job. In J. H. Larkin & R. W. Chabay (Eds.), *Computer assisted instruction and intelligent tutoring systems: Shared goals and complementary approaches* (pp. 201-238). Hillsdale, NJ: Lawrence Erlbaum Associates.

Manning, W. H. (1987). *Development of cloze-elide tests of English as a second language* (RR-87-18). Princeton, NJ: Educational Testing Service.

Martinez, M. E., & Bennett, R. E. (1992). A review of automatically scorable constructed-response item types for large-scale assessment. *Applied Measurement in Education, 5,* 151-169.

Martinez, M. E., Ferris, J. J., Kraft, W., & Manning, W. H. (1990). *Automatic scoring of paper-and-pencil figural responses* (RR-90-23). Princeton, NJ: Educational Testing Service.

Mazzeo, J., Schmidt, A. P., & Bleistein, C. A. (1993). *Sex-related performance differences on constructed-response and multiple-choice sections of Advanced Placement examinations* (College Board Report 92-7). New York: College Board.

Messick, S. (1989). Validity. In R. L. Linn (Ed.), *Educational measurement* (3rd ed., pp. 13-103). New York: MacMillan.

Sebrechts, M. M., Bennett, R. E., & Katz, I. R. (1993). *A research platform for interactive performance assessment in graduate education.* Princeton, NJ: Educational Testing Service.

Sebrechts, M. M., Bennett, R. E., & Rock, D. A. (1991). Agreement between expert system and human raters' scores on complex constructed-response quantitative items. *Journal of Applied Psychology, 76,* 856-862.

Sebrechts, M. M., LaClaire, L., Schooler, L. J., & Soloway, E. (1986). Toward generalized intention-based diagnosis: GIDE. In W. C. Ryan (Ed.), *Proceedings of the 7th National Educational Computing Conference* (pp. 237-242). Eugene, OR: International Council on Computers in Education.

Sebrechts, M. M., & Schooler, L. J. (1987). Diagnosing errors in statistical problem solving: Associative problem recognition and plan-based error detection. In E. Hunt (Ed.), *Proceedings of the Ninth Annual Cognitive Science Meeting* (pp. 691-703). Hillsdale, NJ: Lawrence Erlbaum Associates.

Sebrechts, M. M., Schooler, L. J., LaClaire, L., & Soloway, E. (1987). Computer-based interpretation of students' statistical errors: A preliminary empirical analysis of GIDE. In W. C. Ryan (Ed.), *Proceedings of the 8th National Educational Computing Conference* (pp. 143-148). Eugene, OR: International Council on Computers in Education.

Simon, H. A. (1978). Information-processing theory of human problem solving. In W. K. Estes (Ed.), *Handbook of learning and cognitive processes: Human information processing* (Vol. 5, pp. 271-295). Hillsdale, NJ: Lawrence Erlbaum Associates.

Towne, D. M., & Munro, A. (1988). The intelligent maintenance training system. In J. Psotka, L. D. Massey, & S. A. Mutter (Eds.), *Intelligent tutoring systems: Lessons learned* (pp. 479-530). Hillsdale, NJ: Lawrence Erlbaum Associates.

Ward, W. C., Carlson, S. B., & Woisetschlaeger, E. (1983). *Ill-structured problems as multiple-choice items* (RR-83-6). Princeton, NJ: Educational Testing Service.

Ward, W. C., Frederiksen, N., & Carlson, S. B. (1980). Construct validity of free-response and machine-scorable forms of a test. *Journal of Educational Measurement, 17,* 11-29.

CHAPTER

12

MULTIMEDIA TESTING

Jeffrey J. McHenry
Microsoft Corporation

Neal Schmitt
Michigan State University

Since the 1970s, there has been considerable research on computer-based testing. Most of this research has been undertaken on paper-and-pencil tests that have been adapted for computer use from their original paper-and-pencil format (e.g., Henly, Klebe, McBride, & Cudeck, 1989), or for purposes of developing computer adaptive tests (Moreno, Wetzel, McBride, & Weiss, 1984; Wise, McHenry, Chia, Szenas, & McBride, 1989). Although these advances in computer testing are important, they fail to take advantage of the computer's potential to assess new skills and abilities that have been difficult or extremely expensive to measure via traditional testing formats. In some respects, using a computer only to administer traditional types of test items is akin to owning a Ferrari but driving it only on trips to the corner grocery. The Ferrari will certainly get you to and from the grocery, but round trips to the grocery store hardly begin to take advantage of the Ferrari's capabilities. Consequently, many selection experts have called for test developers to identify creative uses of "computer capabilities to tap new human functions not measurable by printed tests" (Fleishman, 1988, p. 685).

During the past 5 years, many test developers have heeded Fleishman's advice. Some have used the computer to measure perceptual/psychomotor abilities that have proven difficult to assess using paper-and-pencil tests. For example, McHenry, Hough, Toquam, Hanson, and Ashworth (1990) reported that the mean validity of a battery of six computer-administered perceptual/psychomotor tests for predicting general soldiering proficiency in nine Army enlisted specialties was .57.

Other test developers have focused their attention on using the computer to develop work sample tests based on real-life job situations. Work sample tests require examinees to perform the same behaviors that they would be required to perform on the job. The rationale underlying work sample tests is that examinees who perform the behaviors effectively on the test also will be able to perform the behaviors effectively on the job, whereas those who perform ineffectively on the test will not be able to perform the required behaviors on the job (Schmitt & Ostroff, 1986; Wernimont & Campbell, 1968). In their reviews, Campion (1972) and Hunter and Hunter (1984) demonstrated that work sample tests can be highly valid predictors of job performance. However, many organizations have shied away from using work sample selection tests because ongoing testing costs are often very high. Typically, work sample tests are administered one on one by a test administrator, who subsequently must score test results by hand. To ensure reliable, consistent scoring across administrators, test administrators must be trained extensively (Wigdor & Green, 1991). For many organizations, the costs of administrator training and test administration outweigh the benefits of valid prediction that work sample tests provide.

One of the first organizations to struggle with the costs of work sample testing was the Army Air Forces (AAF), which, during World War II, was faced with the challenge of selecting and classifying almost 300,000 aircrew personnel (i.e., pilots, navigators, and bombardiers) (Flanagan, 1947). The results of job analyses and validation studies using paper-and-pencil perceptual ability tests (Guilford & Lacey, 1947) had convinced the AAF that perceptual abilities were critical to pilot success. However, AAF psychologists believed that work sample tests that presented realistic aerial combat situations would measure perceptual ability better than would paper-and-pencil tests, and also keep test administration costs under control. During the course of World War II, AAF psychologists developed and analyzed 15 "motion picture" work sample tests that measured the ability to estimate velocity and distance, the ability to maintain one's orientation in an airplane, and the ability to quickly perceive and identify objects (Gibson, 1947). Even though the internal consistency reliabilities of most of these tests were only in the .50s and .60s, several of the tests that measured the ability to perceive and identify objects proved to be valid predictors of pilot success in training (median $r = .18$).

Since World War II, many organizations have used video work sample tests to present job situations to examinees, who then answer multiple-choice questions about each situation. This approach has enabled a single test administrator to administer the test to a group of examinees, greatly reducing test administration costs. However, there are still limits to video testing technology. Tests must be scored by hand. The complexity of situations and response options is limited to those that could be shown in a relatively short video clip.

In the past five years, however, significant advances in computer, video, and CD-ROM technology have greatly expanded assessment possibilities. The computer can be used to present realistic video work samples under highly standardized conditions in multiple testing locations, capture examinees' responses to test items, and generate test scores. Because these tests rely on integrated audio, video, and computer graphic technology, they have come to be called *multimedia tests*.

Although more and more selection researchers and practitioners are expressing interest in multimedia testing, there is little guidance available to test developers. There are few published research studies (cf. Schmitt, Gilliland, Landis, & Devine, 1993) and only a handful of papers that offer helpful hints to test developers. The purpose of this chapter is to summarize what we currently know about multimedia tests. The following three sections of the chapter describe how to develop multimedia tests, measurement issues that must be considered during test development, and several unique ongoing administrative challenges that multimedia tests present. Throughout these sections, we describe our own experiences and the experiences of others who have developed multimedia tests, and we offer several suggestions for avoiding the pitfalls that have caused some of us to stumble during test development and implementation. These three sections are followed by examples of four multimedia tests that have been developed during the past few years. These example tests further illustrate testing challenges and opportunities with multimedia. The section after that summarizes the costs and benefits of multimedia testing in an effort to help practitioners consider whether multimedia testing is right for their organization. Finally, we conclude with a list of issues for future multimedia test researchers to consider.

DEVELOPING MULTIMEDIA TESTS

Test development for multimedia tests typically proceeds through the following six interrelated steps:

1. Conduct a job analysis to identify the tasks that will be incorporated into the test.
2. Decide on the format of the test (linear versus interactive).
3. Decide on the job scenario for testing (i.e., whether the test will be based directly on job situations or on comparable situations in another job).
4. Develop work sample items.
5. Develop scoring rules and procedures for ensuring reliable scoring.
6. Produce the test (i.e., program the computer; produce the video, audio, and graphics; etc.).

Each of these steps is discussed in turn.

Selection of Tasks

The identification of the tasks and work situations used in a multimedia work sample test must be based on a thorough job analysis. There are three job analysis approaches that test developers have used successfully for this purpose.

Task Analysis. The purpose of a task analysis is to create a complete listing of the tasks that incumbents perform on the job. Test developers often gather judgments about each task to help them better understand the job (e.g., time spent on each task, task importance, task difficulty, how long it takes to learn how to perform the task) (Gatewood & Feild, 1990). The results from the task analysis are used to select a representative sample of tasks/situations for inclusion in the work sample test. If the task sample is not representative, there is no guarantee that it will measure all of the behaviors that are critical to success on the job.

One of the critical questions facing test developers is how to select a representative sample of tasks. Test developers must resist the temptation to select or omit tasks for work sample testing based solely on how easy or difficult it will be to develop a test for the task. The cost of developing work samples is significant and may be a factor in test developers' decisions about how to sample tasks so as to measure as many critical job behaviors as possible. In addition, some tasks may be physically dangerous to the untrained and unfit examinee, and therefore must be omitted from testing. However, tasks should not be omitted from work sample testing simply because they pose difficult testing challenges. On that issue, virtually all selection experts are in agreement.

However, there are differences of opinion about the best way to sample representative tasks following a task analysis. Some contend that only a truly random sampling (or a stratified random sampling based on task dimensions) is scientifically defensible. Others hold that random sampling is not necessary, nor is it an efficient use of typically limited assessment time. They contend that a purposive sampling of job tasks that results in a limited number of critical, difficult, and/or high-frequency tasks that encompass the range of task content areas is superior. This controversy was a point of debate among researchers working on the U.S. military's Joint Service Job Performance Measurement/ Enlistment Standards Project (JPM). A comparison of a random sampling approach to the selection of tasks for the job of radio operator in the Navy to the purposive sampling that was actually carried out revealed that the purposive sampling approach yielded tasks that were performed more frequently and were less complicated to perform than the universe of tasks performed by Navy radio operators (Wigdor & Green, 1991). However, this does not necessarily mean that random sampling will yield a more valid measure of an examinee's behavioral competency than will a purposive sampling. Further, as a practical matter, even in the JPM project where the four U.S. military services provided between 4 and 12 hours of time per examinee for work sample testing, time constraints required a purposive sampling of job tasks. As in other attempts to use work sample measures, the time required to administer work samples dictated that only a relatively few could be used.

In fact, cost and time constraints are in evidence in every attempt to develop work samples of which we are aware. Because of these constraints, we believe it is important to carefully and purposively choose test tasks so as to represent as broadly as possible the domain of job behaviors that the test developer is interested in measuring.

Critical Incident Analysis. For a critical incident analysis (Flanagan, 1954), job experts (usually incumbents and/or supervisors) provide examples of effective and ineffective job performance. Included in these examples are descriptions of the situation or task facing the incumbent, the actions taken by the incumbent, and the results of the incumbent's actions. To ensure that the critical incidents adequately capture the range of challenging situations incumbents encounter on the job, Latham and Wexley (1982) recommended that test developers gather at least 300 incidents from at least 30 job experts (i.e., 10 incidents per job expert). These numbers represent absolute minimums, and some test development experts would recommend gathering many more incidents from many more job experts. For example, Motowidlo, Dunnette, and Carter (1990) gathered 1,200 critical incidents from 139 job experts to develop work sample tests for telecommunications industry managers.

After all critical incidents have been gathered, test developers group together incidents that are based on a common task or situation. These are the tasks and situations that differentiate effective from ineffective job incumbents—that is, some incumbents perform tasks effectively in these situations and others perform poorly, as evidenced by the critical incidents. Thus, it makes sense to use these tasks to evaluate how effectively or ineffectively examinees are likely to perform on the job.

From this point forward, task selection for work sample testing works much the same way as it did for task analysis. Our recommendation is that test developers carefully and purposively choose test tasks so as to represent as broadly as possible the domain of task situations. If time constraints will require test developers to choose only a relatively small number of tasks for testing, we strongly recommend gathering input from job experts as to which tasks are most critical to job success.

KSAO Analysis. A third approach to task selection is based on a KSAO analysis (Goldstein, Zedeck, & Schneider, 1993). This approach has been used by a number of multimedia testing researchers, including Ashworth and McHenry (1992), Dalessio (1992), and Schmitt et al. (1993).

As a starting point for the KSAO analysis, test developers complete a task analysis. Tasks are then grouped into task dimensions on the basis of common job function (a factor analysis of task-importance or time-spent ratings can be used to help identify dimensions). Test developers also interview and conduct workshops with job experts to identify the KSAO requirements of the job. Next, at least 15 to 20 job experts are asked to rate the overall importance of each KSAO to job success and the KSAO requirements of each task dimension. The overall KSAO ratings are used to decide which KSAOs need to be measured in the work sample assessment. The ratings of KSAO requirements for each task dimension are used to help select a small, efficient number of task dimensions that provide coverage of all critical KSAOs. Critical tasks within each task dimension are then selected for work sample testing.

Although a KSAO analysis requires more steps than does a task or critical incident analysis, there are at least two potential advantages. First, it helps ensure that the tasks selected for work sample testing cover all of the KSAOs critical to effective job performance. Second, in the event that test developers decide to base tests on another job (i.e., other than the job or job family that examinees will be applying for), the KSAO analysis can help test developers choose an appropriate job scenario, as described previously (Ashworth & McHenry, 1992). This is discussed in more detail later in this section.

Test Format

After the job analysis has been completed and tasks have been selected for testing, the test developer must choose between linear and interactive test formats (Frank, 1993). In a linear test, a video vignette is prepared for each task and examinees answer one or more questions about the best way of performing the task. Usually all of the vignettes are set in a single organization and there are a small number of characters who reappear in many vignettes. Each examinee sees all of the vignettes in the same order; an examinee's responses have no effect on the vignettes, questions, or response options that are presented. Linear video tests are based on the principle of behavior consistency, which holds that the best predictor of future performance is past performance in similar situations. In the case of linear video tests, examinees are presented with situations similar to those they will encounter on the job to predict how they are likely to perform in job situations.

Of course, there are several differences between the situations presented in the video vignettes and actual job situations. One obvious difference is that the situations shown in the video vignettes are on video rather than live. Another is that examinees typically respond to a linear video test by filling out information on an answer sheet or entering information into a computer, whereas they typically respond to comparable job situations by talking to others, writing memos, and so forth. A third difference, which we have noted previously, is that the situations presented in the video test may be set in a job or organization that is different from the job and organization for which examinees are applying. Because of these differences, the "fidelity" between a linear video test and the job is low (Motowidlo et al., 1990). Although this may sound like a threat to the validity and usefulness of the test, there is a great deal of evidence that low-fidelity work sample tests can be valid predictors of job performance (Latham, Saari, Purcell, & Campion, 1980; Motowidlo et al., 1990; Tenopyr, 1969).

In an interactive test, the examinee is typically presented with several tasks that must be completed. The examinee then chooses how and in what order to complete the tasks. Video vignettes provide background information that the examinee must use to prioritize and/or perform each task. However, it is often up to the examinee to request or review the background information he or she needs to prioritize or complete tasks efficiently. For example, one interactive video test allows examinees to retrieve information from a file cabinet or by placing phone calls to those in the know, much as they would on the job (Ashworth & McHenry, 1992, 1993). The computer branches from one video to another, depending on the information the examinee requests and the actions the examinee takes. Generally speaking, because interactive video tests allow examinees to gather information, set priorities, and branch from one situation to another, interactive tests have higher fidelity than do linear video tests.

Frank (1993) noted that linear tests are much less costly to develop because they typically require less-sophisticated equipment and are much simpler to program on a computer. For that reason, linear testing is far and away the more common multimedia test format. However, if the KSAO requirements of the job include the ability to deal with frequent interruptions and the ability to manage multiple priorities, it may be difficult to assess these with a linear test. An interactive test may measure these KSAOs much more accurately because it will provide data about how the examinee actually behaves when interrupted or when faced with conflicting demands and competing priorities (Ashworth & McHenry, 1992; Schmitt et al., 1993).

Job Scenario

As we have noted, work sample tests may be based directly on job situations (Latham et al., 1980), or they may be based on comparable situations in another, similar job (Motowidlo et al., 1992; Schmitt & Ostroff, 1986).

Basing work sample tests directly on job situations is the most straightforward approach, because it yields an unquestionably clear linkage between test behaviors and job requirements. However, there are at least two reasons why it may be more prudent to base the work sample test on another job. First, basing the test on another job provides applicants having no prior job experience with an opportunity to score as well on the test as applicants who have job experience (Motowidlo et al., 1992; Schmitt & Ostroff, 1986). If the test is based directly on the job, applicants with job experience may have specialized knowledge of job demands and requirements, which enables them to outperform inexperienced applicants on the test. If this specialized knowledge can be imparted easily to new hires during training, then basing the test on another job will help ensure that the test measures only those knowledges, skills, abilities, and other personal characteristics (KSAOs) required for long-term success on the job. Second, the organization may be interested in using the test for several jobs that all require the same KSAOs. Some departments may not be willing to use the test if it is based on a job in another department. However, it may be acceptable to all departments if the job is based on a well-known job with similar KSAO requirements found outside the company.

As an example, Ashworth and McHenry (1992) described how they developed a multimedia in-basket for claim adjusters at Allstate Insurance Company. A job analysis showed that problem solving, decision making, managing multiple priorities, and planning and prioritizing were critical to success in this job; hence these were the four KSAOs that Ashworth and McHenry attempted to measure with the test. However, the claim department did not want applicants who were familiar with the claim adjuster job to have an advantage in testing, because the company was committed to providing complete training on claim policies and procedures. In addition, there were several other jobs with similar KSAO requirements at Allstate, and senior management in these departments had expressed an interest in using the in-basket test if it did not "look like a claim adjuster test." Test developers for Allstate reviewed the *Dictionary of Occupational Titles* (Department of Labor, 1977) and identified 16 jobs that required the four targeted KSAOs. They examined job descriptions for these jobs and concluded that the job of airline customer service representative presented situational challenges very similar to those for the claim adjuster job. On this basis, they selected airline customer service representative for their job scenario.

Work Sample Items

The next step in test development is converting the tasks into work sample items. Typically, test developers create a fictional organization and employees. This organization is used as the setting for all work sample items. At the start of the test, the instructions provide examinees with a few facts about the organization that help examinees understand and respond to the vignettes. Using a single organization for all vignettes also increases examinee interest in the test—they enjoy learning about the organization and getting to know the characters. This motivates examinees to do their best on the test.

Vignettes. Then test developers must prepare and script a vignette for each task. The vignette includes a description of the situation leading up to the task and a script of all the action and dialog that occurs. For example, if the task is "calms angry customers," the vignette would include a detailed script describing why the customer was angry, how the customer would show anger, what the customer would say to the employee, what was happening in the background while the customer approached the employee, and so forth. The situation and script need to be faithful to what actually happens on the job. Critical incidents are particularly useful for developing vignettes, because they contain rich information about job situations. We have found that it is extremely useful to review vignettes with job experts during script development to ensure that the situation and dialog are true to the job.

Response Options. Multimedia tests may use either of two response formats. Some multimedia tests require that examinees use a fixed-choice response format and select from a set of predetermined options, as in a traditional multiple-choice test. Other multimedia tests use a free-response format, which results in an infinite number of possible examinee responses.

If a fixed-choice format is used, the test developer must generate the response options that will be presented to examinees. The best way to generate response options is to show the vignettes to job experts and ask them to write how they would respond to each task situation. Usually, 15 to 20 experts will generate a reasonable range of feasible alternative responses to the work sample situations. These responses are then edited by the test developer with the goal of producing a set of five to seven nonredundant and feasible response options. The response options should include alternatives that reflect good performance as well as reasonable alternatives that reflect poorer performance but nonetheless will be attractive to less-competent examinees.

If a free response format is selected, the test developer does not need to develop specific response options to present to the examinee. However, the test developer must be aware of the range of possible examinee responses so that scoring standards can be developed. We say more about this in our discussion of scoring rules.

Scoring Rules

Most researchers employing psychological tests assume that observed differences among individuals represent true differences on the ability of interest. To ensure that this basic notion is reasonable, various steps are taken to standardize the testing conditions. For example, when paper-and-pencil tests are administered, scoring directions are read from a prepared script by trained administrators, and extraneous variables such as heat and noise disturbances are kept to a minimum. Scoring is often done by optical scanners and, assuming that examinees follows directions in marking their answer sheets, it is relatively error free. In multimedia testing, test directions and the test items themselves are typically administered by video or computer; hence the administration of the test is usually highly standardized. The major source of standardization problems in multimedia testing is the scoring of the test.

In setting the scoring rules for work sample tests, it is necessary to consider the response format of the test. The fixed-choice and free-response formats pose quite different problems for the test developer and user/scorer. The fixed-choice format means that special care must be taken in developing test items and alternatives such that a defensible answer is present and the alternatives represent feasible wrong responses. Once this developmental work is completed satisfactorily, scoring is mechanical and should be error free. The free-response format requires effort in delineating all the possible responses that the examinee group might make and in developing a scoring key that can accommodate or account for the myriad possible answers. If the test is to be scored by hand, as is usually the case, scoring instructions must be developed. Instructions and scorer training must be adequate to ensure interscorer agreement and/or reliability. If free-response items are to be scored by computer, scoring instructions must be developed in sufficient detail so they can be programmed to yield an accurate score for each examinee—which is not as easy as it sounds. Next, we describe the means with which we and others have attempted to resolve these basic scoring problems for each response format.

Fixed-Choice Response Scoring. As indicated previously, test developers must draft a vignette and five to seven response options that reflect a range of performance for each task that is tested. For scoring purposes, test developers must then determine how to score each response option.

Multimedia test developers have used two different strategies for assigning scores to response options, one based on expert judgment and the other on empirical keying. The development of a scoring key based on expert judgment typically includes the following steps:

1. The proposed response options are evaluated by a panel of job experts (usually around 30 to 35 incumbents and supervisors) who are asked to indicate the best and the worst alternative solutions to each problem and rate the relative effectiveness of each solution.

2. The expert ratings are analyzed to see if the experts agree about the best and worst response options and rate the vignettes reliably. If there is poor agreement or reliability, test developers may need to edit the vignette and response options or drop the vignette from the test.

3. Test developers produce a video enactment of each of the "surviving" vignettes and response options (more about video production later).

4. This set of video items is then evaluated by another panel of experts (usually around 30 to 35 people) who are asked to indicate the best and the worst alternative solutions to each item and rate the relative effectiveness of each response option.

5. A scoring key is then developed. There have been several different procedures used to develop scoring keys for paper-and-pencil work sample tests, and all of these would appear applicable to video tests. For example, Motowidlo et al. (1990) asked a panel of job experts to rate the most and least effective

alternative responses to a number of work situations. Examinees then were asked to identify the best and worst alternatives. Examinees received a +1 for selecting the highest-rated alternative as the best alternative, +1 for selecting the lowest-rated alternative as the worst alternative, -1 for selecting the lowest-rated alternative as the best alternative, and -1 for selecting the highest-rated alternative as the worst alternative. Thus, examinee scores on each item can range from -2 to +2. To a large extent, the validity of the scoring key depends on high interrater agreement and reliability for the job experts' judgments of the most and least effective response alternatives. There is ample evidence that expert judgments of response alternatives for paper-and-pencil work sample tests can meet professional standards for agreement and reliability (e.g., Motowidlo et al., 1990). However, to our knowledge, there are no research reports available that report reliability or agreement indices for video presentations of response alternatives.

The alternative scoring strategy, empirical keying, is commonly used to score biodata items (Mitchell & Klimoski, 1982). For example, Dalessio (1992) used empirical keying to develop a scoring key for a multimedia selection test for insurance agents. Developing an empirical scoring key involves the following steps:

1. The video is produced and the multimedia test is then administered to a sample of at least 500 new hires. Each new hire rates the best and worst alternative for each item.

2. The new hires are observed over a period of time (often a year), and then divided into "successful" and "unsuccessful" groups on the basis of some performance outcome (e.g., survival versus attrition, sales volume, acceptable versus unacceptable performance rating).

3. Positive or negative weights are assigned to a response option if there are significant differences in the percentages of successful and unsuccessful new hires selecting that option. A variety of empirical keying techniques are available for assigning weights (see Telenson, Alexander, & Barrett, 1983).

The problem with the empirical keying approach is that it often results in a scoring key that is difficult to defend rationally. On many occasions, the response option that seems worst to job experts will receive a positive weight, while the response option that seems best will receive a negative weight. On the other hand, the expert judgment scoring procedure often is very tedious to implement because it can be difficult to gain agreement among experts concerning the best and worst response alternatives (Desmarais et al., 1992).

Clearly, the development of alternative response options and an objective scoring scheme will add tremendously to the time and expense of test development. However, once developed, the application of this scoring scheme should be error free and provide for rapid feedback of results. Using video-based assessments with fixed-choice response options, Frank (1993) reported that he was able to provide feedback reports within a matter of minutes.

Free-Response Scoring. If an examinee is presented with a work situation and asked to describe (in his or her own words) what action is appropriate, or if the examinee is presented with a task and asked to complete a work product, there are an infinite number of response possibilities. In such a case, there must be a clear statement of scoring rules that takes into account all possible responses that examinees may provide. These rules then can be used as the basis for scorer training (if the tests are to be scored by hand) or for programming scoring rules on a computer.

If tests are to be scored by hand, there must be satisfactory interscorer agreement and reliability. The key to achieving satisfactory interscorer agreement and reliability is to develop a clear notion of the response one wants to a particular item. Test developers must keep this response in mind as they prepare scoring materials and scorer training.

Schmitt et al. (1993) achieved high scorer agreement for a number of computer-administered clerical work samples (e.g., mail log, telephone messages) that were part of a multimedia test battery used to select secretaries. To develop their scoring key, Schmitt et al. asked several people whose skill level was similar to job applicants' to respond to each work sample. They then examined the work sample stimulus material in light of the responses and developed a checklist of items that they believed should be present in a good response. The checklist items were specific and concrete in nature and represented actions that some (but not all) examinees had performed correctly. Fig. 12.1 contains an example of the checklist that they used to score two electronic messages that secretarial applicants were asked to send.

Schmitt et al. used the checklists to score a set of responses from another sample of respondents. This effort at scoring and the results of item and reliability analyses were used to identify checklist items that all respondents got correct, or all got wrong, or about which scorers could not agree as to the presence or absence. Appropriate checklist modifications were made to correct these problems. All tests were then rescored using the modified checklist, with the total score set equal to the simple sum of the number of checklist items that the examinee performed correctly. The variance and reliability of the total score were calculated. If the reliability or variance was not adequate, Schmitt et al. attempted to determine whether the problem was in the checklist, in which case it was again modified, or in the work sample itself. In several instances, they concluded that the work sample was not sufficiently "rich" or complex to provide any variation in performance. In those instances, they either revised the work sample stimulus material if the job analysis information indicated that this would be appropriate, or they developed a new work sample to measure the task. By developing their scoring materials in this manner, Schmitt et al. were able to train scorers to score examinees with a very high degree of reliability (well over .90).

Candidate Social Security Number: _____

Place a check next to each item indicating that it was completed in a satisfactory manner. Acceptable answers are in parentheses following each item. Responses other than these should be considered incorrect.

Maximum Number of Checks: 8   Checkmarks Earned:

1. ( )   S sent message to correct individuals (Dana Landis & Sam Gilliland) (First initials are also acceptable).
2. ( )   S entered the correct titles (Marketing & Finance) (If Director is added to either title it should also be considered correct).
3. ( )   S entered the boss's name in the space provided (Pat Gully) (Spelling must be correct) (First initial is also acceptable).
4. ( )   S indicated subject of meeting (budget projections meeting or budget summary meeting).
5. ( )   S had the right date (7/16).
6. ( )   S indicated where meeting was to occur (in Gully's office).
7. ( )   S indicated what day the meeting was for (7/18).
8. ( )   S indicated what time the meeting was (9:30 a.m.).

FIG. 12.1. Checklist for First E-Mail Message

In addition to the checklist scoring format, Schmitt et al. also found that it was useful to ask scorers to provide an overall evaluation of each product produced by the examinee. For example, one of the tasks that they tested was letter writing. The scoring key was useful for measuring the degree to which the details in that communication were correct, but Schmitt et al. were also interested in the overall persuasiveness of the letter. They developed behaviorally anchored rating scales for use in evaluating persuasiveness. In developing these scales, they used expert judgments concerning what constitutes highly persuasive and unpersuasive elements of a written communication. Although interrater reliabilities for these overall judgments were not as high as for the checklist rating scales, the reliabilities still met normally acceptable standards (above .80).

Scorer training is absolutely essential to achieving satisfactory reliability and agreement. Scorers must be knowledgeable about the tasks being tested (hence the training should include taking the test). They also must have a common understanding of the behavior that constitutes correct performance at each step of the task and how these behaviors are to be rated. It is often useful to develop training videos in which good and bad performance is depicted, to provide the scorers with the same set of materials to score, and then to discuss disagreements in light of the standards that should be applied in scoring the examinees' work product. Wigdor and Green (1991) reported that there are many ways to provide effective training, but a considerable amount of such training is always necessary to ensure standardization of scoring.

Computerized scoring of free-response answers has also been attempted. Ashworth and McHenry (1992) described how they developed computerized scoring procedures for a very complex multimedia in-basket used to select insurance claim adjusters. Because examinees were presented with a number of different tasks, and the response options available for one task were often contingent on what was done in response to other tasks, there were thousands of possible response combinations. Ashworth and McHenry were interested in developing a scoring algorithm for planning and prioritizing and for managing multiple priorities that took into account how well examinees prioritized their work and the number of high-priority tasks that examinees completed. They held workshops with job experts, who were asked to identify the highest-priority tasks in the in-basket (planning and prioritizing) and assign scores for completing different combinations of tasks (managing multiple priorities). The expert judgments were then used to develop scoring algorithms that took into account all possible response combinations. Some of the computer-administered secretarial tasks developed by Schmitt et al. (1993) also were scored by computer, but those that required scanning a text to find a particular response (or one of several responses that might be equally adequate) were scored by trained scorers.

Clearly, the capacity to mechanically score interactive tests is limited by the test developer's ability to specify the range of correct responses, even when test responses are collected by computer. A great deal of developmental effort and research will be needed before we can specify with any degree of confidence the capacities and limitations of computerized scoring of interactive tests. What should be clear is this: Just as it is true that we do not allow technology to dictate the selection of the tasks that we test, we should not let the capacities or limitations of the technology dictate the content or scoring of the exam.

Summary. This discussion of scoring rules has illustrated some of the unique challenges posed by fixed-choice and free-response test formats. Test developers who choose a fixed-response format must identify and develop scoring rules for plausible response options. Although this process may be costly, it usually results in scoring rules that are easy to program, which means that there will be relatively low operating costs for the tests. On the other hand, test developers who choose a free-response format must develop scoring rules that consider all possible responses that examinees may provide. These rules may be extremely expensive to program, leaving the test developer with a Hobson's choice: paying an exorbitant amount to program the scoring rules so tests can be scored by computer versus paying an exorbitant amount to train and monitor scorers who must score each test by hand.

Despite the differences, there are also at least two key similarities in the development of scoring rules for fixed-choice and free-response test formats. First, both formats are heavily dependent on expert judgment for development of scoring rules. Second, the complexity of developing scoring rules often creates difficult scoring problems for the test developer. The test developer must resist the temptation to remove or include items or test content simply because of the difficulty or ease with which these scoring problems can be resolved.

Test Production

In addition to making decisions about test content and scoring, those who develop multimedia tests also face a number of difficult decisions about producing the test. Unfortunately, few test developers have much training or background in video and audio production, computer electronics, or software engineering. Consequently, they must assemble and depend on a team of diverse professionals in order to make proper decisions about the testing platform, video and audio production and engineering, and pilot testing.

Pulling Together a Team of Diverse Professionals. One of the first things someone interested in developing a multimedia test should do is assemble a team of technical advisors. The team should include at least one person who understands video and audio production and at least one who understands computer technology. Eventually, this team may expand to include script writers, graphic artists, directors, camera operators, lighting and make-up professionals, set designers, prop artists, actors and actresses, video editors, programmers, videodisc and/or videotape specialists, hardware experts, human-computer interface specialists, and a legion of other technicians and professionals. Unfortunately, as Ashworth and McHenry (1993) noted, many of these people do not understand and are not particularly concerned about the psychometrics or legal and professional standards for selection testing! And it will not be possible to educate them all. Therefore, it is critical from the start for test developers to identify and educate a small number of technical advisors who can help make decisions about hardware, software, and audiovisual production. We will say more about this in our discussion of video and audio production and engineering.

Testing Platform. One of the first decisions the test development team will have to make is the testing platform. What combination of hardware, software, and peripherals should be used to present the test? This decision is critical because the hardware, software, and peripherals selected may limit options for presenting vignettes (e.g., by limiting the number of "windows" that can be open on the screen at one time to present test stimuli, instructions, and help) and capturing examinee responses (e.g., by limiting the number of "response buttons" available on a touch screen).

What factors should be considered in choosing a platform? According to Midkiff, Dyer, Desmarais, Rogg, and McCusker (1992), here are a few questions the test development team should ask:

1. Will the test require the computer to communicate with several peripheral devices, jump quickly from audio to video to programming code, write large data files, make complex calculations, and perform several other complicated tasks? If so, the computer will need a fast central processing unit (CPU).

2. Will the examinee use a keyboard to enter responses? If so, will special modifications be needed to avoid input errors (e.g., placing a shield over the keyboard that blacks out the keys that will not be used during the test)? If not, what type of input device will be used (e.g., mouse, joystick, touch screen)? The computer must be capable of communicating with this device and appropriate communications software has to be purchased.

3. What types of graphics and motion will be displayed on the monitor? The monitor, video technology, and software must support this motion and graphics.

4. Will there be freeze frames? Will the video be shown hundreds and hundreds of times? If the answer to either of these questions is yes, videotapes may not be adequate for presenting video; laser discs may be required.

5. Is high-quality audio important? If so, speakers will be needed.

6. Will examinees be tested in a private room? If not, then they may need headphones to hear the audio and to prevent the test from disturbing others.

7. Who will program the test? Who will maintain the program? If all programming and maintenance will be completed by software professionals, then it may be OK to use an authoring language that is well known to software engineers, even if the language is inscrutable to testing professionals. However, if testing professionals will program some parts of the test or be partially responsible for test maintenance, it will be important to use an authoring language that is relatively easy to learn.

Unfortunately, there are no easy answers to any of these questions. Multimedia testing is in its infancy; hence our knowledge base for testing platforms is extremely limited. Further, the technology is changing very rapidly. Any hardware or software recommendations we might make today surely would be outdated by the time this book is in print. Two things are clearly true, however. First, if you wait for the technology to stabilize before choosing a platform, you will never choose a platform. Technology will never stabilize, at least not in our lifetimes. Second, as Midkiff et al. (1992) noted, even if you dislike or are not particularly interested in technology, "you *will* have to concern yourself with these 'technical' issues, because they will haunt your development and validation work" (p. 2). Choosing good technical advisors will help you make much better hardware and software decisions, but you cannot allow your technical advisor to make these decisions for you. Your ability to present test stimuli will be totally dependent on your technology—plan to stay involved in every technology decision.

Video and Audio Production and Engineering. Video and audio production and engineering is the process of turning work sample vignettes and response options into an integrated multimedia test, complete with audio, video, graphics, and computer-controlled administration and scoring. There are abundant opportunities for problems during production and engineering—problems that are often compounded by test developers' ignorance of video production and computer technology. As Dyer, Desmarais, Midkiff, Colihan, and Olson (1992) noted in the midst of their multimedia test development project, "EVERYTHING turned out to be much more difficult than anticipated." The experiences of those who have developed multimedia tests suggest that there are three areas that deserve special concern during production and engineering.

First, test instructions must be clear and concise. Test instructions must serve two purposes. They must explain how the examinee will use the computer and any peripherals (e.g., joysticks, special keys on the keyboard, touch screen) to control presentation of test items and to make responses. This includes instructions for obtaining help, scrolling backward and forward during the test, repeating items and response options, and so forth. The instructions will have to provide enough detail and allow sufficient practice time such that examinees are comfortable with the equipment and understand how to take the test before beginning the test. Test instructions also must establish the job scenario for the test. Typically, multimedia tests use video to introduce the job scenario, including the organization where the vignettes take place and the characters involved in the vignettes. As part of this introduction, a narrator usually describes how the test is related to the job that the examinee is applying for. This introduction to the job scenario increases the face validity of the test and elevates examinee motivation to do well on the test. A potential problem with test instructions is length. It may take 10 to 15 minutes to train examinees on the equipment and introduce them to the job. This leaves 10 to 15 fewer minutes for assessing examinee skills. If the test developer can save even two or three minutes on instructions, it may provide time for four or five additional questions that improve the reliability and validity of the test. Therefore, it is essential for test developers to be as concise as possible in the test instructions.

Second, test developers need to be prepared to keep the reins on creative talent (e.g., script writers, actors) during test production. We should say at the outset that we strongly recommend hiring professional talent to write scripts and produce and act in the videos. In the videos we have seen, it is always clear whether production was in the hands of amateurs or professionals. We have no data, but we suspect that the face validity of the test and examinee motivation suffer when the video is amateurish. Good script writers will turn the work sample vignettes into high-quality scripts that are ready for video and audio production. However, the script writers may be tempted to enhance the drama of the vignettes to make them more interesting for examinees; or actors and actresses may decide that what their character would really do in a particular situation is somewhat different from the way it is scripted. Subtle changes (e.g., a nod, a grimace, a brief ad lib) may wreak havoc on the content validity of a test item. The test developer must make sure that all audio, video, and graphics are faithful to the tasks and situations that were identified in the job analysis.

Third, the test developer must pay attention to human-computer interface issues. Many things can be done to make the test more user friendly. Icons can be used to draw examinees' attention to key points and to convey information quickly. For example, Desmarais et al. (1992) used a finger with a string tied around it to point examinees to information to remember, and Ashworth and McHenry (1992) used telephone and file cabinet icons on a touch screen so examinees could quickly find these items when they needed to use them. Consistent use of color combinations and graphics is important. It can help an examinee navigate between test items and instructions, and can aid him or her in remembering how to respond to items or obtain information. The choice of colors and font sizes also can make a big difference in the legibility of text and graphics. In addition, there are test fairness issues that must be considered in designing the human-computer interface. Two issues mentioned by Desmarais et al. (1992) were handedness and colorblindness. For example, if the <ENTER> key is used to record responses on a speeded test, left handers may be at a disadvantage because they cannot hit the <ENTER> key as quickly as can right handers. And certain color combinations may make it extremely difficult for colorblind people to complete the test. Graphic artists and human factors engineers who specialize in human-computer interface can be a big help in choosing colors, designing graphics and computer screens, and deciding on input devices. Finally, yet another word of caution about creative types. The test developer must beware of the software engineer who gets a new color palette or a new graphics program during test production. Screens that were simple and legible one day may be fancy and uninterpretable the next. Insist on knowing about all proposed software and hardware changes!

Pilot Testing. Pilot testing is extremely important with multimedia tests to help clarify instructions, vignettes, and response options and to help ensure that test items are reliable and show adequate variance. However, pilot testing presents special challenges to multimedia test developers because of the expense of video production. With paper-and-pencil tests, if pilot testing reveals the need for minor wording changes, these are relatively easy to make. But it is virtually impossible to modify video vignettes after they have been shot. Because most multimedia tests are based on a story line involving a cast of characters, any revised or new vignettes would need to feature the same group of actors and actresses. The costs of reassembling this same group of actors and actresses on the same set for a one- or two-minute video would be prohibitive.

Because it is impractical to pilot test and subsequently modify video vignettes, most multimedia test developers have pilot tested their tests using other media. For example, prior to video production, Wilson Learning (1990) conducted a pilot test of an audio version of its Customer Service Skills Assessment. They used item analysis results from the pilot test results to eliminate two-thirds of the vignettes that they had developed. Ashworth and McHenry (1992) pilot tested first a paper-and-pencil version and then a computer graphic (no video) version of the Allstate Multimedia In-Basket prior to video production. The Allstate pilot tests were used to adjust the difficulty level of items, clarify instructions, and evaluate the scoring key.

Summary

In many respects, the development of multimedia tests parallels the development of paper-and-pencil work sample tests. The choice of a job scenario, the selection of tasks, and the development of items and scoring rules may be very similar. However, there are many features of multimedia test development that make it quite different from developing paper-and-pencil tests. The development of items and scoring rules for multimedia tests may be much more complex if an interactive test format is selected. In addition, working with computer and video technology requires test developers to work with professionals from other disciplines who may not be sensitive to the legal and technical requirements of selection testing or the needs of examinees. To develop an effective multimedia test, the test developer must learn about technology, educate others about testing, and protect against changes in vignettes or poorly designed instructions that would threaten the validity of the test.

MEASUREMENT ISSUES IN MULTIMEDIA TESTING

We now turn to a description of the particular set of measurement problems confronted by users of multimedia testing. Even after test development has been completed, the developer still must demonstrate the test's reliability and validity and examine subgroup performance differences. Those who develop other forms of tests face similar challenges, but we believe it is particularly important that the potential test developer or user be aware of the unique measurement issues that must receive attention with multimedia testing.

Reliability

Traditionally, observed score variance on a test is presumed to be a function of true variability on the construct of interest plus error variance. Test-retest estimates of reliability assess the degree to which differences associated with the timing of test administration contribute to error variance; correlations between alternate forms of a test allow assessment of the error associated with content specific to one form or the other; and correlations of alternate forms of a test with a time interval between their administration allow the assessment of both content and time sources of error. Homogeneity of test item content also can be assessed by measures of internal consistency.

Assessment of the reliability of work samples, of which the multimedia test is usually an example, is almost always more complicated, because the number of potential sources of error are greater. This has led some researchers to assess the reliability of these tests using generalizability theory (Cronbach, Gleser, Nanda, & Rajaratnam, 1972). Because scoring these tests often involves scorers or raters, raters as a source of unreliability must be considered. Often different tasks are included as parts of a work sample; thus, task differences must be considered. If the test is also administered by different people or at different locations, these differences might contribute to error in the estimation of examinees' true standing on a variable. In addition, these various sources of error may interact with each other and with examinees to produce yet other sources of potential error.

Use of traditional reliability formulations has two limitations that are addressed when generalizability theory approaches are used. The first limitation is that any single version of reliability involves "averaging over" or ignoring many other sources of error. The second limitation is that we have multiple estimates of reliability and must choose which is the right one. Generalizability theory allows the estimation of each individual source of error in measurement. This, in turn, provides for the possibility that steps can be taken to assess the magnitude of these problems and develop procedures by which they can be minimized.

An example of the use of generalizability theory was provided by Shavelson (1991) and Kraiger and Teachout (1990) in work done on the military's JPM project. A hypothetical example of the use of generalizability theory in the assessment of various "reliabilities" for a work sample test is presented in Table 12.1. In this example, 30 examinees were assessed in four different tasks and scored by three raters. For ease of presentation, all three factors were crossed; that is, each examinee was assessed in each task by each scorer. In this case, reliability was .611 when both scorers and tasks were considered random factors (i.e., we selected them randomly from some pool of available scorers and tasks), and .904 when both scorers and tasks remained the same (i.e., they were fixed).

TABLE 12.1
Example of Generalizability Analysis of Work Sample Performance
of 30 Examinees in Four Tasks Scored by Three Scorers

Source	df	MS	Variance Component
Examinee (E)	29	2.742	.140
Scorer (S)	2	1.420	.005
Tasks (T)	3	2.319	.009
Examinee by scorer (ES)	58	.348	.022
Examinee by task (ET)	87	.975	.239
Scorer by task (ST)	6	.754	.017
Examinee by scorer by task (EST)	174	.259	.259

Computation of Variance Components

Effect	Formula	Computation
E	$(MS_E - MS_{ES} - MS_{ET} + MS_{EST})/N_S N_T$	$(2.742 - .348 - .975 + .259)/12 = .140$
S	$(MS_S - MS_{ST} - MS_{ES} + MS_{EST})/N_E N_T$	$(1.420 - .754 - .348 + .259)/120 = .005$
T	$(MS_T - MS_{ST} - MS_{ET} + MS_{EST})/N_E N_S$	$(2.319 - .754 - .975 + .259)/90 = .009$
ES	$(MS_{ES} - MS_{EST})/N_T$	$(.348 - .259)/4 = .022$
ET	$(MS_{ET} - MS_{EST})/N_S$	$(.975 - .259)/3 = .239$
ST	$(MS_{ST} - MS_{EST})/N_E$	$(.754 - .259)/30 = .017$
EST	(MS_{EST})	$.259$

To generalize to a similar situation in which three randomly selected scores and four randomly selected tasks are used to supply scores for a group of examinees, reliability would be computed as follows:

$$r^2 = VC_E/(VC_E + VC_{ES}/N_S + VC_{ET}/N_T + VC_{EST}/N_S N_T)$$

$$= .140/(.140 + .022/3 + .239/4 + .259/12) = .611$$

If we want to generalize to a new situation in which both scorers and tasks are fixed; that is, they are the same, then reliability is computed as follows:

$$r^2 = (VC_E + VC_{ES}/N_S + VC_{ET}/N_T)/(VC_E + VC_{ES}/N_S + VC_{ET}/N_T + VC_{EST}/N_S N_T)$$

$$= (.140 + .022/3 + .239/4)/(.140 + .022/3 + .239/4 + .259/12) = .904$$

The variance components and computations also tell us that tasks are a much
more important source of error than are scorers. This may or may not be
desirable given the manner in which performance is conceptualized. If it is seen
as a unidimensional phenomenon, then this would be of concern. If it is
recognized that performance is multidimensional, then this may confirm the
investigators' a priori notions about the dimensionality of the performance
construct. In any event, the data from the generalizability analysis indicates that
examinees' performance is likely to be dependent on the task they are asked to
accomplish.

Our point in presenting this material here is to emphasize that multimedia
work sample tests usually involve an examination situation in which multiple
sources of unreliability are possible. Generalizability analysis would, therefore,
seem to be especially appropriate for linear multimedia tests, where all
examinees complete all test items (or, at the least, all test items on the form they
are assigned). For linear tests, generalizability analysis will allow the test
developer to evaluate the relative and absolute importance of these various
factors and to be better informed in taking action to ensure the quality of
measurement.

Assessing reliability becomes significantly more complex for interactive
multimedia tests. Assessing the variance due to sources such as test form,
scorers, or time presents no special challenges, but assessing the variance due to
items (i.e., the internal consistency reliability) does. For example, Drasgow,
Olson, Keenan, Moberg, and Mead (1993) developed a multimedia test to assess
managers' skills at resolving conflict. Examinees view a conflict vignette, then
answer two questions about how they would behave in that situation before
moving on to the next vignette. The second question posed for each vignette
depends upon how the examinee answers the first question. Thus, each examinee
responds to only a fraction of the full set of test items. F. Drasgow (personal
communication, August 20, 1993) reported that they plan to use item response
theory to calibrate test items and estimate the standard error of estimate for each
examinee.

There is one more issue that should be noted in connection with the reliability
of multimedia work sample tests. Often, these tests take a relatively (e.g., as
compared to a paper-and-pencil multiple choice test) large amount of time to
produce scorable data. For example, a 40-item paper-and-pencil work sample
test may take only 20 minutes to administer, but a 40-item multimedia work
sample may require 45 minutes or more (Dyer, Desmarais, & Midkiff, 1993).
Because only a few items or aspects of the task are scored, the variance of scores
may be small. This obviously has implications for the level of reliability we can
expect. In these circumstances, it is very important that raters be well trained as
to the standards by which task performance should be rated.

Finally, with respect to reliability assessment, it should be noted that often
raters are only asked to indicate the presence or absence of some behavior or

some aspect of the product produced as a result of performing a work sample task. In these instances, it is important to assess interrater agreement rather than reliability (see Tinsley & Weiss, 1975).

Doubtless the reader is now wondering whether multimedia tests are reliable, and how their reliability compares to paper-and-pencil and traditional work sample tests. The answer is, we don't know. So far as we know, no one has ever completed a generalizability analysis of multimedia work sample tests. In fact, we found virtually no information about the reliability of multimedia test scores.

Validity

Three aspects of the validity of work samples are important. The first is the degree to which the work sample is representative of the domain of job performance tasks. This is essentially a content validity question. As we stated previously, we believe that the best way to ensure that a work sample test adequately represents the task domain is to purposively sample tasks based on task dimension, criticality, KSAOs required, and testing time and cost considerations (cf. Wigdor & Green, 1991).

A second aspect of the validity of work samples concerns the degree to which the work sample relates to other measures of job performance. Vance, Coovert, MacCallum, and Hedge (1989) reported data regarding supervisory-, peer-, and self-ratings and a work sample test evaluating the performance of Air Force jet engine mechanics. They found evidence supporting the convergence of evaluations of mechanics' ability to perform in three dimensions of their job across all four sources of information. However, there remained significant method factor loadings indicating that all four methods represented unique aspects of performance.

Wigdor and Green (1991) presented representative data from the JPM project that show modest (between .39 and .61) correlations between job knowledge and work sample performance for 15 different military specialties, somewhat lower (.09 to .45) correlations between ratings and work sample performance across 15 jobs, and correlations between .14 and .58 between job knowledge assessed during training and the work sample test for 9 different specialties. These correlations certainly don't indicate a perfect correspondence between these alternate measures, but one would not expect (nor necessarily want) these correlations to be perfect as they likely represent different aspects of the examinee's potential contribution to the organization. For example, the work sample is most likely a measure of whether a job candidate or incumbent (if the measure is used as a job performance measure as was true of the military studies) can perform a job task, whereas ratings are likely some combination of an assessment of the candidate's willingness and ability to perform well (Campbell, McHenry, & Wise, 1990).

More work directed to understanding the nature of the constructs measured by work samples is certainly needed. Issues related to the necessary physical and psychological fidelity of these measures, their representativeness of the job as a whole, and their motivational and performance correlates all need to be addressed.

The third aspect of validity that is important is, of course, the criterion-related validity: Do multimedia tests predict subsequent job performance? To date, there are no published criterion-related validity studies for multimedia tests in refereed journals. Validity coefficients presented in technical reports (Wilson Learning, 1989a, 1989b, 1990, 1992) and in conference papers (Frank, 1993) range from the .30s to the .60s.

There are many published validity studies for "conventional" (i.e., non-multimedia) work sample selection tests. If we can generalize from the validity of conventional work sample tests to the validity of multimedia work sample tests, we should find that the criterion-related validity of multimedia tests is equal to or higher than that of other predictors (Hunter & Hunter, 1984; Robertson & Kandola, 1982; Schmitt, Gooding, Noe, & Kirsch, 1984). We have little evidence of the degree to which work sample tests correlate with more traditional paper-and-pencil cognitive ability tests, but Campion (1972) found that such correlations ranged from .10 to .62, with most correlations below .30. This also suggests that including a work sample as one component of a test battery should result in significant incremental validity.

Adverse Impact

Mean differences between minority and majority groups in performance on work sample tests appear to be appreciably smaller than are comparable mean differences for cognitive ability tests. Data reported by Wigdor and Green (1991) for 21 studies showed that mean differences between African-American and nonminority personnel averaged .85 standard deviation for the Armed Forces Qualification Test (AFQT), .78 standard deviation for a job knowledge test, and .36 standard deviation for a hands-on work sample test. In all cases, minority scores were lower, but the mean differences for the work sample were considerably less.

Results from these large sample studies confirm research results involving smaller samples that were previously published. For example, Schmidt, Greenthal, Berner, Hunter, and Seaton (1977) found no significant minority-majority differences between two work sample tests, but the usual large differences (around one standard deviation) for a set of paper-and-pencil measures of job knowledge in a group of 87 metal trades apprentices. Similar positive results were reported by Brugnoli, Campion, and Basen (1979) and Cascio and Phillips (1979). These positive results also seem to apply to work sample measures of ability that are more interpersonal in nature (e.g., see Moses

& Boehm's, 1975, comparison of the performance of men and women in assessment centers).

Although these results certainly should encourage the use of work sample predictors whenever the issue of subgroup differences is important, additional research should be conducted to determine why subgroup differences are relatively less or nonexistent for work sample measures when relatively large differences exist for other valid measures of ability. Certainly one would surmise that the need to write and read rather than do may be one explanation, but there are also potential motivational explanations when one is confronted with different types of selection procedures (Schmitt & Gilliland, 1992).

ONGOING TEST ADMINISTRATION ISSUES IN MULTIMEDIA TESTING

One of the advantages of multimedia testing over traditional paper-and-pencil testing is that, in theory, multimedia tests are self-administering; that is, the computer handles most of the responsibilities of a test administrator. In practice, however, multimedia tests pose a number of ongoing test administration challenges, for which the test user needs to be prepared.

Mechanical Glitches

Sooner or later, hardware will break down and software will fail to perform as expected. The test use must have policies in place for handling such glitches, which invariably seem to occur in the middle of testing. For example, there should be policies about whether the test should be halted, restarted at the point where the system crashed, or restarted from the beginning of the test. If the policy is to halt the test, the policy must specify whether partial test scores based on items completed by the examinee should be considered in selection decisions. Data from pilot tests and validation studies (e.g., reliability estimates, item validities) may help with these policy decisions.

In addition, test users must have procedures for restoring the test platform to working order. If testing is conducted at far-flung sites around the country, the user must train a test coordinator at each site how to troubleshoot equipment problems and how to handle examinees when equipment breaks down. The user may need to identify a technician or engineer who can provide ongoing hotline support to test coordinators.

Test Updates and Data Transmission

Test users need some way of updating tests (e.g., changing the scoring key, updating instructions, eliminating or adding vignettes). They also need a system for capturing examinee data for ongoing evaluation of the test. If the test is administered via a mainframe or via personal computers connected to a mainframe, program and data transfer can be handled from a central location. This simplifies matters considerably. Otherwise, the test coordinator at each site must be trained how to perform updates and transmit data. If there are a large number of test sites, training can pose a tremendous challenge, and it is virtually certain that there will be sites where updates and data transfers are not completed in a timely manner.

Retesting

The test user must develop policies that specify how long examinees who are not hired must wait before retesting. Unfortunately, there is little research to guide users. We know little about what effects general knowledge of the test procedure or practice has on examinees' performance on multimedia tests. For example, if examinees taking a test know that they will have to send and receive E-mail messages; that databases will have to be completed, manipulated, and used; that they will have to play the role of an insurance claims adjuster or a middle manager; or that new software commands will need to be mastered, will they do better than will examinees who do not have that knowledge? We do routinely give samples of GREs and SATs and many other exams to prospective examinees. What effect such preparation and practice has on paper-and-pencil test performance is known to some extent, but there is no available information on the effect of such preparation on work sample tests to our knowledge. Until more research is conducted, users must exercise their best judgment in formulating retesting policies, and then must make certain that all examinees are treated equitably.

Accommodating Applicants With Disabilities

Since the passage of the Americans With Disabilities Act (ADA) in 1990, much has been made of the need to develop testing accommodations for applicants whose disabilities make it impossible to assess their qualifications accurately using conventional testing procedures. With paper-and-pencil tests, this may require reading test items to blind or sight-impaired examinees, recording test answers for examinees who cannot mark their answer sheet, and/or relaxing test time limits. Slowly but surely, organizations are developing policies for administering paper-and-pencil tests to disabled examinees (Lohss, 1993).

Alas, with multimedia testing, accommodation issues are far more complex. What accommodations are appropriate for blind examinees, who can hear audio but are unable to see the video that often provides contextual information (e.g., the ethnic background of the characters) that is critical to understanding and responding correctly to test items? Are any accommodations needed for colorblind examinees, who may have trouble perceiving some video or computer graphic images presented using certain color combinations? Is closed captioning an appropriate accommodation for examinees who are deaf? How should examinees be accommodated if they have physical disabilities that make it impossible for them to operate keyboards, mouses, touch screens, or other devices used to capture examinee responses? What adjustments should be made to test time limits for different types of disabilities? Clearly, multimedia test users must have policies for dealing with situations such as these. At this point, however, they may be able to do little more than develop policies based on their own best judgment, with guidance from services such as the National Federation for the Blind, which assist employers interested in making appropriate workplace accommodations for disabled workers.

EXAMPLES OF MULTIMEDIA TESTS

Throughout our discussion of multimedia test development and measurement and test administration issues, we have talked about a variety of efforts to develop, evaluate, and validate multimedia tests. We thought it might be useful to provide more detailed examples of several multimedia tests that are currently in use or under development to further illustrate some of the points we have been making. For this purpose, we have selected four multimedia tests to serve as examples of tests based directly on the job and tests based on a closely related job (job scenario), as well as linear and interactive tests (test format) (see Table 12.2).

TABLE 12.2
Example Multimedia Tests

| | Test Format | |
Job Scenario	Linear	Interactive
Same job (job that examinees are applying for)	IBM Workplace Situations Test (Dyer et al., 1993)	Ford Secretary Selection Test Battery (Schmitt et al., 1993)
Different job (job similar to the job examinees are applying for)	Customer Service Skills Assessment (Wilson Learning, 1990)	Allstate Multimedia In-Basket (Ashworth & McHenry, 1992, 1993)

Test Based Directly on the Job, Linear Format: IBM Workplace Situations Test. The IBM Workplace Situations Test (Dyer et al., 1993) is part of a multimedia test battery that WFS Workforce Solutions, an IBM company, is developing to help select entry-level manufacturing production employees. The Workplace Situations Test is designed to measure an examinee's ability to deal with the interpersonal challenges and problems that arise on the manufacturing job. The test was based on a comprehensive job analysis of manufacturing jobs conducted by the WFS staff (Dyer et al., 1992).

The test is set in a fictional company called Quintronics, a high-tech manufacturing firm. During the test, examinees see 30 vignettes depicting employees interacting on the job. Each vignette poses an interpersonal challenge or work-related dilemma for one of the employees. At the end of each vignette, examinees are asked what the employee should do. Five response options are presented in writing (the response options are not acted out on video). Examinees must choose the best option and enter their response on a computer. For example, in one vignette an employee is chatting amiably with a second employee who is spilling water on the floor, creating an unsafe work environment. What should the first employee say in this situation? Should the first employee tell the second employee to clean up her area? The possible answers range from aggressive warnings about going to the manager to oblique questions about whether a rag might be available. The 30 vignettes are independent; that is, examinees are told not to base their answer to one question on the answers they provided to previous questions, and examinees are not permitted to return to earlier questions to change their answers. However, to create continuity and maintain examinee interest—and also to reduce test development costs—the same characters reappear in many of the vignettes.

WFS has completed a series of pilot tests with IBM job incumbents (Dyer et al., 1993). Incumbents' reactions have been extremely positive. However, WFS researchers have two significant concerns about the test. First, they note that administration time is long. On average it takes about 30 seconds to present each vignette, plus another 45 seconds for examinees to review the response options and record their response. In addition, there are about six minutes of instructions at the beginning of the test. This means that it can take 50 minutes or more to obtain 30 items of data from examinees—far more time than a paper-and-pencil low-fidelity work sample test (Motowidlo et al., 1990) would require. Dyer et al. hoped that the reliability, validity, and applicant and management appeal of the test would justify the administration time. Second, developing scoring rules for the test has proven complex. Dyer et al. reported that they had some difficulty getting employees and managers to agree on the best response option and on four plausible (but less correct) distracters. They are exploring scoring schemes based on expert judgment as well as schemes based on empirical keying and hybrid approaches.

Test Based on Another Job, Linear Format: Wilson Learning Customer Service Skills Assessment. Wilson Learning has developed a wide variety of multimedia tests to assess applicants for sales (Wilson Learning, 1989a), banking (Wilson Learning, 1989b), supervisory (Wilson Learning, 1992), customer service (Wilson Learning, 1990), and other positions. The Customer Service Skills

Assessment is particularly interesting because it was designed to be used for many different customer service jobs.

Test developers began with a KSAO analysis of 50 customer service jobs, including cashiers, receptionists, rental car clerks, auto parts counterpersons, and body shop advisors (Wilson Learning, 1990). Six skill areas were identified as essential for all jobs: developing positive customer relations, discovering customer needs, responding to customer wants, anticipating customer needs, working together to meet customer needs, and ensuring customer loyalty. The KSAO analysis was used to link these skills to customer service tasks. Job experts were consulted to clarify the customer service situations that would prompt employees to perform these tasks.

One of the biggest challenges facing test developers was selecting a job scenario. Three criteria guided their selection. First, the scenario had to be acceptable to the employers who would be using the test. The test developers knew that an employer probably would not accept the test unless it featured one or more vignettes based on jobs in the employer's organization. Second, the scenario needed to be acceptable to examinees. Examinees seem to accept a multimedia test better when they have an opportunity to follow and become familiar with the characters through a variety of vignettes. This gives continuity to the test and maintains examinees' interest. Third, the scenario had to be rich enough so that test developers could test all of the critical KSAOs they had identified. The "job scenario" finally selected by the test developers was to show a day in the life of a couple preparing for their wedding. During the course of the day, this couple must deal with customer service representatives in a wide variety of jobs—a clerk at a dry cleaner, a retail sales associate, rental car and airline reservations agents, an employee in a fast-food restaurant, a customer service representative in an auto repair shop, and so forth. This allowed the test developers to include vignettes featuring jobs from many industries (first criterion), created an interesting story line for examinees (second criterion), and provided test developers with tremendous flexibility to assess the target KSAOs (third criterion).

Using the situations they identified with job experts, the test developers created 50 vignettes showing the engaged couple's interactions with customer service employees. In most cases, test developers were able to develop two or three questions about each vignette. Each question had four response options. Job experts provided input about the clarity and realism of vignettes and response options and rated the effectiveness of each option. Their input was used to refine the test prior to pilot testing. The pilot test version of the test included 135 multiple-choice questions.

Because of the expense of video production, Wilson Learning pilot tested an audio version of the test. Ninety-four incumbents in a variety of customer service jobs completed the test. Performance ratings for these 94 examinees were gathered from supervisors. Item analyses (item difficulty, item-criterion correlations) were used to reduce the test to 16 vignettes and 46 multiple-choice questions.

A video version of the test was produced. Each vignette was shown on video. Following the vignette, the examinee was asked which of the four response options was the best way of dealing with the customer service situation portrayed in the vignette. These response options were acted out and shown on the video. If the examinee's response matched the response option that was identified as best by job experts, the examinee received a score of +1 for the item; otherwise, the examinee received 0. A concurrent validation study was conducted. Test data and performance ratings were gathered for a sample of 186 incumbents in a variety of customer service jobs. Test scores correlated .40 with performance ratings for the 126 Canadian employees in the sample and .34 for the 60 American employees.

Test Based Directly on Job, Interactive Format: Ford Secretary Selection Test Battery. The purpose of the Ford Secretary Selection Test Battery is to assess the ability of applicants to learn and use word processing, database, and electronic message software (Schmitt et al., 1993). Several operational testing objectives drove the test developers toward multimedia testing: face and content valid selection, minimal role for the test administrator, easy transportability of the test to other test sites, quick feedback to examinees, a testing procedure that was equally fair to examinees who had training and experience with a variety of other software and hardware, and immediate entry of test data into a centralized organizational computer network.

Based on job analysis data just described, Schmitt et al. decided to develop a battery of eight tests: word processing, correction (correcting errors in a letter), mail log, database, letter (composing and typing a letter from handwritten instructions), travel expense form, telephone message, and electronic mail. To ensure that prior experience with a particular software package would not provide any examinees with an advantage, Schmitt et al. created their own word processing, database, and e-mail software. Video instructions and practice exercises were provided prior to each test to ensure that examinees understood their task and to familiarize them with the software. Examinees then proceeded at their own pace to complete the tests. All but the telephone message test and the mail log test were completed directly on the computer. The telephone test was administered in the midst of the mail log test, when examinees were twice interrupted by a ringing telephone in the video. The telephone message was recorded on a special phone message form that was provided to all examinees.

The most complex part of test development was creation of scoring keys and scorer training. Because the number of possible responses to some subtests was very large, it was not practical to program a computer to do the scoring for these subtests. Schmitt et al. therefore decided that these subtests should be scored by hand. The process used to develop scoring procedures (i.e., development and refinement of scoring checklists) was described previously. These procedures resulted in very high levels of interscorer agreement and reliability.

Schmitt et al. were not able to conduct a concurrent validation. However, they were able to administer the tests to groups of secretaries and university students. The tests are not highly intercorrelated and show considerable variance, suggesting the potential for favorable validity results. Examinee reaction to the tests also was very positive.

Test Based on Another Job, Interactive Format: Allstate Multimedia In-Basket. As we described previously, the purpose of the Allstate Multimedia In-Basket was to assess applicants' ability to solve problems, make good decisions, establish plans and priorities, and manage multiple priorities (Ashworth & McHenry, 1992). These KSAOs originally were identified in a KSAO analysis of the claim adjuster job. However, test developers did not want to give an advantage to examinees with prior job experience. Also, test developers hoped they might be able to use the in-basket to help select applicants for other Allstate jobs with similar KSAO requirements. Therefore, they chose to use airline customer service representative, which also requires the four target KSAOs, as the job scenario for the test.

At the outset of the test, examinees receive video instructions from their "boss" welcoming them to their first day on the job. The boss explains that he will be gone for the next 45 minutes, so the examinee should get started working on his or her in-basket. The boss instructs the examinee to complete as many items in the in-basket as possible, paying special attention to the high-priority items. The boss also reminds the examinee about the company's philosophy of putting customers first.

The in-basket contains 10 phone messages. These messages were chosen to present problems similar to those that a claim adjuster encounters on the job. Job experts helped develop the messages and provided ratings that documented that the problems described in the messages vary from high to low priority. The experts also helped develop an exhaustive list of all possible effective and ineffective ways of responding to each message. A brief description of each message is provided on a touch screen monitor. Examinees press the touch screen to obtain more information about each message.

After all messages have been reviewed, the test begins. Examinees must establish priorities and complete as many high-priority tasks as possible in the allotted time. A telephone is available on the touch screen so examinees can call co-workers and customers to obtain any information they need and respond to the messages. There is also a file cabinet available via the touch screen that contains flight schedules and information about airline policies and regulations. During the test examinees are interrupted by the phone on several occasions. In effect, these phone calls add to their in-basket, and examinees must determine how to prioritize and solve the problems introduced by the phone calls along with their other in-basket messages.

Two of the most difficult challenges in creating the Allstate Multimedia In-Basket were pilot testing and developing a scoring key. The test developers' approach to these challenges was described previously. Briefly, the Allstate Multimedia In-Basket was pilot tested using first a paper-and-pencil version of the in-basket, then a version presented via computer graphics (with no audio or video), and finally a video version. The first two pilot tests allowed developers to refine the vignettes and response options before videotaping, which saved a great deal of money in video and audio production costs. All scoring was done by computer. To obtain scores for each of the four KSAOs, job experts provided ratings that were used to develop scoring formulas based on number of high-priority tasks completed (planning and prioritizing), total number of tasks completed (managing multiple priorities), the efficiency of the information-gathering strategies used to research the problems presented in the phone messages (problem solving), and the quality of responses (decision making). The interrater reliability of these ratings ranged from .81 for managing multiple priorities to .95 for decision making.

To date, there are no data on the test's reliability or criterion-related validity. However, 30 recent college graduates (which is the recruiting pool for claim adjusters and many other Allstate jobs) who took the Allstate Multimedia In-Basket reported that the test is very engaging and left them with a favorable impression of Allstate. Also, claim adjusters who have completed the test reported that it does an excellent job of mimicking the requirements and work demands of their job.

BENEFITS AND COSTS

By now it should be clear that the decision to employ some form of multimedia testing should be preceded by careful consideration of benefits and costs. Although this consideration will certainly involve unique organizational circumstances (i.e., alternative selection procedures, the number and job level of applicants to be evaluated, need for greater standardization), our experience with multimedia testing suggests that test developers should almost always take into account the following potential benefits and costs.

Benefits

The face validity of multimedia tests is usually high; hence, applicants will perceive that they have been evaluated fairly and on job-relevant bases. When developed well, such tests can also provide a realistic preview of the job itself, which may improve subsequent worker commitment and satisfaction (Premack & Wanous, 1985).

Most multimedia tests involve the collection and correction of tests by computer, so that the possibility of immediate feedback with respect to test performance is possible. This immediate feedback, the obvious care with respect to evaluation of human resources that is evident with multimedia testing, and the usual face validity of these techniques should all serve to enhance the examinees' perception of the company.

If the scoring and administration of the test are computerized, the user will surely reap the benefits of increased standardization of the test, low or non-existent costs for program operation, and immediate availability of data on which to make decisions.

The data described previously regarding adverse impact on minority groups is encouraging with respect to potential legal liabilities resulting from use of work samples.

As we noted earlier, we have reason to believe that the criterion-related validity of multimedia tests will be equal to or higher than that of other predictors. There is also some evidence that multimedia tests will significantly increment the validity of a battery of paper-and-pencil cognitive ability tests.

Finally, many multimedia tests require that applicants actually be trained or learn to take certain test components. For example, the testing procedure described by Schmitt et al. (1993) required that candidates learn the simple commands that operated the word processing, database, and electronic mail components of their software. This necessity to learn is common to most jobs in which computers (and perhaps any modern technology) are used, because computer hardware and software are continually changing. The willingness and capacity to learn, then, are being assessed indirectly by the multimedia test; hence test scores should generalize to later occasions when the hired applicant confronts the need to develop his or her skills.

Costs

Although the potential benefits from multimedia testing are great, test developers need to be aware that the potential costs and problems are great as well. We'd like to highlight several of the (often unexpected) costs and problems we have encountered.

The first we have already touched on. Anyone who is going to use the computerized technology in the administration or scoring of tests must be prepared to learn about the technology. This is necessary because computer engineers do not share our jargon and we do not understand their language. Schmitt et al. (1993) reported that they gave their computer experts an outline of the screens that needed to be developed and the tasks that the job applicants would be required to perform, and they expected that the computer experts then would supply them with a product that they could proof and test. Schmitt et al. found that was naive in the extreme. They ended up writing the screens, and the computer experts then transferred the screens directly into the program. Learning the technology also is important because it enables test developers to fully exploit the technology's capabilities. One must also know the technology because it is almost indispensable in the debugging or revision phase. Knowing a little about programming and how a programmer thinks and works will go a long way when one is getting rid of the last troublesome, fatal crashes.

A second problem that can occur with the use of performance assessment of the type we described is that it may result in a measure of a relatively narrow or incomplete part of the job domain. Part of the problem is related to the developmental costs associated with developing multiple tests of different aspects of a job, but it is also test-taking time. Part of test administration time will inevitably be spent familiarizing candidates with equipment and instructions. Instructions for most paper-and-pencil tests will take only a minute or two, whereas for some of the multimedia tests described in this chapter the instructional component may take 10 to 15 minutes or more.

A third potential problem is that the technology may become obsolete very quickly. At the beginning of one project we started in 1990, the organizational personnel said with confidence that software developed for an IBM 286 computer would be as sophisticated as they ever wanted to become. Three years later, the 286 computer has virtually disappeared. Software has also evolved, to take advantage of ever more powerful personal computers. Each passing month seems to bring new standards for state-of-the-art audio and video. As a result, we suspect that video produced for multimedia tests this year will look "old" and unsophisticated within five years. Test developers need to give serious thought as to the likelihood that aspects of multimedia tests will become obsolete—and how they will deal with that obsolescence—before they begin development of these tests.

A fourth problem is that out-of-pocket test development costs are likely to exceed initial estimates. Dyer et al. (1992) said it best: "Double your time estimates, and then expect not to make schedules; double your budget; and, most importantly, invest in lots of aspirin" (p. 14). We also have found that the cost of computer consultation may be double or more than the amount that consultants first estimate. This is not because the computer consultants are dishonest or incompetent; instead, there always seem to be new items that appear absolutely essential and that cost just a little more. This, we think, is another reason why one should be familiar with the technology involved. You can be more certain of exactly what you will want and more capable in judging final cost estimates.

Fifth, the cost of development is only the beginning. If you are going to use computers or other sophisticated equipment, you must be prepared to purchase and maintain sufficient work stations to handle the applicant flow. Some of this problem can be handled by increasing the number of times the test is administered, but this "solution" has two implications: (a) You will probably need additional personnel to administer the testing program, and (b) you may need alternate forms of the test material.

This brings us to a sixth potential problem, test security. With paper-and-pencil tests security is certainly a problem, but it is relatively inexpensive to develop alternate forms of a paper-and-pencil test. These alternate forms promote test security because (a) examinees can never be sure which form they will receive, (b) examinees are unlikely to be able to memorize the correct answer to every item on every form of the test if there are several alternate forms, and (c) there is little likelihood that examinees will have access to all the alternate forms of a test, especially if there are several. Moreover, even if the security of one alternate form is compromised, testing can continue using the alternate forms. Unfortunately, development of alternate forms of some of the multimedia selection procedures described in this chapter would be extremely difficult and costly. It would seem virtually impossible to develop and equate alternate forms of complex, interactive multimedia work samples.

Another potential problem with the use of performance testing is that giving feedback to examinees may be more difficult. Performance tests are often scored in terms of the particular work products involved. We can tell examinees their scores on each of these work products, but we can't be very helpful with respect to diagnostic feedback. For example, is the examinee's poor performance due to an inability to take oral instruction, inadequate attention to detail, poor typing skills, inability to read and learn from written instruction, or something else? Perhaps this problem is not inherent in technologically sophisticated testing systems (in fact, we suspect they can be developed to diagnose various types of difficulties), but we do believe the problem is inherent in performance-based testing in which output rather than process is scored. Again, some a priori planning may be very useful in ensuring that the final feedback will include useful diagnostic information, if indeed that is important.

In conclusion, we would like to note that we have focused on the costs and problems associated with the development and use of multimedia tests not because we believe they should not be used, but rather because we think attention to these issues will maximize their practicality and advantages. These advantages include greater examinee and consumer acceptability, provision of a realistic job preview, perhaps lessened impact on disadvantaged groups and therefore lessened legal liability, and the potential opportunity to measure constructs that may not be accessible using other selection procedures. Many of these constructs, such as the ability and willingness to learn, would seem to be of increasing importance as technology and jobs change at an increasing speed.

RESEARCH ISSUES

Throughout this chapter, we have described a number of multimedia testing research issues that need attention. With so many possible questions to choose from, the interested researcher may be unsure where to begin! Here are our top three priorities.

Construct Validity

Evidence from low-fidelity and hands-on work sample tests strongly suggests that multimedia tests will measure the KSAOs required to perform critical job tasks. In addition, because multimedia tests often require an examinee to follow complex instructions and learn new computer systems, they may provide indirect measures of the ability and willingness to learn. Ability and willingness to learn are likely to become ever more critical to career success as the pace of technological change (and associated changes in job content) accelerates. Ability and willingness to learn certainly should receive more attention from selection researchers, and we believe multimedia work sample tests may be one vehicle whereby these constructs can be further studied.

Incremental Criterion-Related Validity

As we have noted, evidence from paper-and-pencil and hands-on work sample tests suggests that multimedia tests may contribute unique variance to the prediction of job performance (i.e., above and beyond the prediction provided by traditional paper-and-pencil cognitive ability and personality tests). Indeed, if multimedia tests capture ability and willingness to learn as well as other critical job-related KSAOs, their incremental validity may be quite large. We need well-designed validity studies for multimedia tests that incorporate a wide range of predictors (e.g., paper-and-pencil ability and personality tests, low-fidelity work samples, situational and behavioral interviews), as well as a full array of job performance criteria (e.g., performance ratings, job knowledge tests, archival measures of productivity and citizenship). Not only will these validity studies establish the incremental validity of multimedia tests for different performance criteria, they also will help us better understand what multimedia tests measure.

Impact on Examinees

Results from pilot tests at Allstate and IBM suggest that applicants will have a high regard for multimedia tests (Ashworth & McHenry, 1992; Dyer et al., 1993). One of the indirect benefits of multimedia testing may be that it creates a favorable impression of the organization among applicants, making it easier for the organization to hire the applicants it most desires. This favorable impression also may increase applicants' motivation to work hard after they are hired. In addition, the multimedia test may provide applicants with a realistic job preview that helps them determine whether they are well suited to the job and the organization. In turn, the job preview may facilitate subsequent socialization into the organization for those who are hired. Many organizations are concerned about their reputation in a given labor market and community. If so, they may be concerned about the impact of multimedia tests (as well as other selection procedures) on candidates who are not hired by the organization. Research is needed to determine which, if any, of these benefits actually accrue from multimedia testing. If these benefits can be established empirically, it certainly would greatly increase the utility of multimedia testing.

SUMMARY

In summary, multimedia tests present a number of test development, measurement, and ongoing test administration challenges to test developers and users. These challenges make multimedia tests costly to develop relative to paper-and-pencil tests. However, based on research with other types of work sample tests, there is reason to believe that multimedia tests will significantly increment the criterion-related validity of traditional cognitive ability and personality tests. In addition, multimedia tests may create a favorable impression of the organization that enhances the work motivation of new hires and helps facilitate their entry into the organization. Research is needed to help overcome test development challenges and to establish the benefits of multimedia testing. We are optimistic that multimedia tests will prove to have high utility for personnel selection, and we are certain that research on multimedia tests will lead to an improved understanding of human abilities, job performance, and organizational socialization.

REFERENCES

Ashworth, S. D., & McHenry, J. J. (1992, September). *Development of a computerized in-basket to measure critical job skills.* Paper presented at the fall meeting of the Personnel Testing Council of Southern California, Newport Beach.

Ashworth, S. D., & McHenry, J. J. (1993, April). *Developing a multimedia in-basket: Lessons learned.* Paper presented at the conference of the Society for Industrial/Organizational Psychology, San Francisco.

Brugnoli, G. A., Campion, J. E., & Basen, J. A. (1979). Racial bias in the use of work samples for personnel selection. *Journal of Applied Psychology, 64,* 119-123.

Campbell, J. P., McHenry, J. J., & Wise, L. L. (1990). Modeling job performance in a population of jobs. *Personnel Psychology, 43,* 313-333.

Campion, J. E. (1972). Work sampling for personnel selection. *Journal of Applied Psychology, 56,* 40-44.

Cascio, W. F., & Phillips, N. F. (1979). Performance testing: A rose among thorns? *Personnel Psychology, 32*, 751-766.

Cronbach, L., Gleser, G., Nanda, A., & Rajaratnam, N. (1972). *Dependability of behavioral measurements: Theory of generalizability for scores and profiles.* New York: Wiley.

Dalessio, A. (1992, May). *Predicting insurance agent turnover using a video-based situational judgment test.* Paper presented at the conference of the Society for Industrial/Organizational Psychology, Montreal.

Department of Labor (1977). *Dictionary of Occupational Titles.* Washington, DC: U.S. Government Printing Office.

Desmarais, L. B., Dyer, P. J., Midkiff, K. R., Barbera, K. M., Curtis, J. R., Esrig, F. H., & Masi, D. L. (1992, May). *Scientific uncertainties in the development of a multimedia test: Trade-offs and decisions.* Paper presented at the conference of the Society for Industrial/Organizational Psychology, Montreal.

Drasgow, F., Olson, J. B., Keenan, P. A., Moberg, P., & Mead A. D. (1993). Computerized assessment. *Personnel and Human Resources Management, 11*, 163-206.

Dyer, P. J., Desmarais, L. B., & Midkiff, K. R. (1993, April). *Multimedia employment testing in IBM: Preliminary results from employees.* Paper presented at the conference of the Society for Industrial/Organizational Psychology, San Francisco.

Dyer, P. J., Desmarais, L. B., Midkiff, K. R., Colihan, J. P., & Olson, J. B. (1992, May). *Designing a multimedia test: Understanding the organizational charge, building the team, and making the basic research commitments.* Paper presented at the conference of the Society for Industrial/Organizational Psychology, Montreal.

Flanagan, J. C. (Ed.) (1947). *The Aviation Psychology Program in the Army Air Forces* (Army Air Forces Aviation Psychology Program Research Rep. No. 1). Washington, DC: U.S. Government Printing Office.

Flanagan, J. C. (1954). The critical incident technique. *Psychological Bulletin, 50*, 327-358.

Fleishman, E. A. (1988). Some new frontiers in personnel selection research. *Personnel Psychology, 41*, 679-699.

Frank, F. D. (1993, April). *Video-based assessment.* Paper presented at the conference of the Society for Industrial/Organizational Psychology, San Francisco.

Gatewood, R. D., & Feild, H. S. (1990). *Human resource selection* (2nd ed.). Orlando: Dryden Press.

Gibson, J. J. (Ed.) (1947). *Motion picture testing* (Army Air Forces Aviation Psychology Program Research Rep. No. 7). Washington, DC: U.S. Government Printing Office.

Goldstein, I. L., Zedeck, S., & Schneider, B. (1993). An exploration of the job analysis-content validity process. In N. Schmitt & W. C. Borman (Eds.), *Personnel selection in organizations.* San Francisco: Jossey-Bass.

Guilford, J. P., & Lacey, J. E. (Eds.) (1947). *Printed classification tests, Parts I and II* (Army Air Forces Aviation Psychology Program Research Rep. No. 5). Washington, DC: U.S. Government Printing Office.

Henly, S. J., Klebe, K. J., McBride, J. R., & Cudeck, R. (1989). Adaptive and conventional versions of the DAT: The first complete test battery comparison. *Applied Psychological Measurement, 13*, 363-371.

Hunter, J. E., & Hunter, R. F. (1984). Validity and utility of alternative predictors of job performance. *Psychological Bulletin, 96*, 72-98.

Kraiger, K., & Teachout, M. S. (1990). Generalizability theory as construct-related evidence of the validity of job performance ratings. *Human Performance, 3*, 19-36.

Latham, G. P., Saari, L. M., Purcell, E. D., & Campion, M. A. (1980). The situational interview. *Journal of Applied Psychology, 65*, 422-427.

Latham, G. P., & Wexley, K. N. (1982). *Increasing productivity through performance appraisal.* Reading, MA: Addison-Wesley.

Lohss, W. E. (1993, August). *Employment testing of blind and visually impaired job applicants.* Paper presented at the annual conference of the American Psychological Association, Toronto.

McHenry, J. J., Hough, L. M., Toquam, J. L., Hanson, M. A., & Ashworth, S. D. (1990). Project A validity results: Relationship between predictor and criterion domains. *Personnel Psychology, 43,* 335-354.

Midkiff, K. R., Dyer, P. J., Desmarais, L. B., Rogg, K., & McCusker, C. (1992, May). *The multimedia test: Friend or foe?* Paper presented at the conference of the Society for Industrial/Organizational Psychology, Montreal.

Mitchell, T. W., & Klimoski, R. J. (1982). Is it rational to be empirical? A test of methods for scoring biographical data. *Journal of Applied Psychology, 67,* 411-418.

Moreno, K. E., Wetzel, C. D., McBride, J. R., & Weiss, D. J. (1984). Relationship between corresponding Armed Services Vocational Aptitude Battery (ASVAB) and computerized adaptive testing (CAT) subtests. *Applied Psychological Measurement, 8,* 155-164.

Moses, J. L., & Boehm, V. R. (1975). Relationship of assessment center performance to management progress of women. *Journal of Applied Psychology, 60,* 527-529.

Motowidlo, S. J., Carter, G. W., Dunnette, M. D., Tippins, N., Werner, S., Burnett, J. R., & Vaughan, M. J. (1992). Studies of the behavioral interview. *Journal of Applied Psychology, 77,* 571-587.

Motowidlo, S. J., Dunnette, M. D., & Carter, G. W. (1990). An alternative selection procedure: The low-fidelity simulation. *Journal of Applied Psychology, 75,* 640-647.

Premack, S. L., & Wanous, J. P. (1985). A meta-analysis of realistic job preview experiments. *Journal of Applied Psychology, 70,* 706-719.

Robertson, I. T., & Kandola, R. S. (1982). Work sample tests: Validity, adverse impact, and applicant reaction. *Journal of Occupational Psychology, 55,* 171-183.

Schmidt, F. L., Greenthal, A. L., Berner, J. G., Hunter, J. E., & Seaton, F. W. (1977). Job sample vs. paper-and-pencil trades and technical tests: Adverse impact and examinee attitudes. *Personnel Psychology, 30,* 187-198.

Schmitt, N., & Gilliland, S. W. (1992). Beyond differential prediction: Fairness in selection. In D. M. Saunders (Ed.), *New approaches to employee management.* Greenwich, CT: JAI Press.

Schmitt, N., Gilliland, S. W., Landis, R. S., & Devine, D. (1993). Computer-based testing applied to selection of secretarial applicants. *Personnel Psychology, 46,* 149-165.

Schmitt, N., Gooding, R. Z., Noe, R. A., & Kirsch, M. P. (1984). Meta-analyses of validity studies published between 1964 and 1982 and the investigation of study characteristics. *Personnel Psychology, 37,* 407-422.

Schmitt, N., & Ostroff, C. (1986). Operationalizing the "behavioral consistency" approach: Selection test development based on a content-oriented approach. *Personnel Psychology, 39,* 91-108.

Shavelson, R. J. (1991). Generalizability of military performance measurements. In A. K. Wigdor and B. F. Green, Jr. (Eds.), *Performance assessment for the workplace: Vol II.* Washington, DC: National Academy Press.

Telenson, P. A., Alexander, R. A., & Barrett, G. V. (1983). Scoring the biographical information blank: A comparison of three weighting techniques. *Applied Psychological Measurement, 7,* 73-80.

Tenopyr, M. L. (1969). The comparative validity of selected leadership scales relative to success in production management. *Personnel Psychology, 22,* 77-85.

Tinsley, H. A., & Weiss, D. J. (1975). Interrater reliability and agreement of subjective judgments. *Journal of Counseling Psychology, 22,* 358-376.

Vance, R. J., Coovert, M. D., MacCallum, R. C., & Hedge, J. W. (1989). Construct models of task performance. *Journal of Applied Psychology, 74,* 447-455.

Wernimont, P. F., & Campbell, J. P. (1968). Signs, samples, and criteria. *Journal of Applied Psychology, 52,* 372-376.

Wigdor, A. K., & Green, B. F., Jr. (1991). *Performance assessment for the workplace.* Washington, DC: National Academy Press.

Wilson Learning (1989a). *Validation report for the Financial Sales Assessment Program.* Longwood, FL: Wilson Learning.

Wilson Learning (1989b). *Validation report for the Customer Service Skills Assessment Program.* Longwood, FL: Wilson Learning.

Wilson Learning (1990). *Validation report for the Teller Assessment Program (TAP).* Longwood, FL: Wilson Learning.

Wilson Learning (1992). *Electronic assessment of first-line supervisors: A criterion-related validation report.* Longwood, FL: Wilson Learning.

Wise, L. L., McHenry, J. J., Chia, W. C., Szenas, P. L., & McBride, J. R. (1989). *Refinement of the Computerized Adaptive Screening Test (CAST).* Alexandria, VA: U.S. Army Research Institute.

13

THEORETICAL AND APPLIED DEVELOPMENTS IN MODELS OF INDIVIDUAL DIFFERENCES: PHYSICAL ABILITIES

Joyce Hogan
University of Tulsa

The predictor domain of the Army's Project A contains no physical ability tests. This is surprising because some of the jobs that were studied are physically demanding, and one of the five job-performance factors identified in the criterion domain is "physical fitness and military bearing." Moreover, correlations between predictor and criterion domain variables show that the variables studied only weakly predict the "physical fitness and military bearing" criterion. Additionally, most of the prediction is accounted for by self-reports of "physical condition" from the subscales in the Assessment of Background and Life Experiences (ABLE).

We now know more about human physical abilities and their role in occupational performance than we knew at the start of Project A. The assessment of individual differences in physical abilities may be an area of future interest for Army research. This chapter summarizes some recent developments.

Since the late 1970s, people have studied individual differences in physical abilities almost exclusively in the context of personnel selection. This is likely to continue over the next 10 years in both military and civilian settings because, for the military, there are issues of maximizing human capability in an all-volunteer force, and, for civilian employment decisions, civil rights have been extended to include disabled Americans (cf. Americans With Disabilities Act of 1990—ADA). The ADA will have a greater impact on employment in physically demanding work than does Title VII of the Civil Rights Act.

The fundamental problem in studying physical performance is a lack of an adequate taxonomy of (a) work requirements and (b) individual differences associated with those requirements. The source of the problem is at least twofold. First, relative to the study of cognitive abilities, only a small amount of research has been done on physical abilities in the workplace. Historically, considerations other than performance tests were used to make hiring decisions.

Such considerations, which included gender, physical characteristics, and manual labor restrictions, were prohibited under Title VII of the Civil Rights Act of 1964. The use of physical ability tests to select people for physically demanding jobs is relatively recent. Note that the first physical-abilities-test validation research published in an American Psychological Association journal appeared in 1979 (Reilly, Zedeck, & Tenopyr, 1979). Second, research in physical performance is interdisciplinary and draws on knowledge from physiology, biomechanics, and ergonomics. Although an interdisciplinary approach will produce new insights, it is also divisive in that it is difficult to generate a consensus about a framework for taxonomic representation.

PHYSICAL REQUIREMENTS OF WORK

The characteristics necessary for successful performance depend on what a job requires. This is as true for military specialties as it is for civilian jobs. What should we study to understand the physical requirements of jobs, and how should the analysis proceed? For the purposes of personnel selection and placement, a comprehensive job analysis will identify what is done and what it takes to do it. Any number of job analysis procedures allow the analyst to describe what is done; the outcome of a typical job analysis is task-oriented information that describes the behavior that is necessary to produce a product or service (Ash, 1988, p. 4).

For physically demanding jobs, perhaps the most commonly used procedure is the task inventory questionnaire, where task statements are developed by the job analyst and are subsequently evaluated by respondents on indices of importance (Christal, 1974; Gael, 1983). However, structured questionnaires also provide categories of task-oriented job content where the categories have been developed rationally. Perhaps the two most widely used standardized procedures that cover physical task requirements are the *Revised Handbook for Analyzing Jobs* (Department of Labor, 1991) and the Position Analysis Questionnaire (McCormick, Jeanneret, & Mecham, 1972). These questionnaires contain a relatively small number of rationally derived task categories, examples of which appear in Figs. 13.1 and 13.2. The foregoing methods are known as task-oriented procedures.

Another approach is to focus on what it takes to accomplish the job tasks. Job analysts refer to this as the person-oriented approach (Ash, 1988, p. 4), and it is used to identify the knowledge, skill, and ability resources needed for task performance. Like task-oriented information, ability requirements can be developed by subject matter experts on their own (e.g., Landy, 1988), or by using standardized procedures such as the Threshold Traits Analysis system (Lopez, 1988) or Ability Requirements Scales (Fleishman & Mumford, 1988).

Things: Inanimate objects as distinguished from human beings; substances or materials machines, tools, equipment, and products. A thing is tangible and has shape, form, and other physical characteristics.

Things Functions

Precision Working: Using body members and/or tools or work aids to work, move, guide, or place objects or materials in situations where ultimate responsibility for the attainment of standards occurs and selection of appropriate tools, objects, or materials, and the adjustment of the tool to the task require exercise of considerable judgment.

Setting Up: Adjusting machines or equipment by replacing or altering tools, jigs, fixtures, and attachments to prepare them to perform their functions, change their performance, or restore their proper functioning if they break down.

Operating-Controlling: Starting, stopping, controlling, and adjusting the progress of a machine or equipment.

Driving-Controlling: Starting, stopping, and controlling the actions of machines or equipment for which a course must be steered, or which must be guided, in order to fabricate, process, and/or move things or people.

Tending: Starting, stopping, and observing the functioning of machines and equipment. Involves adjusting materials or controls of the machine.

Feeding-Offbearing: Inserting, throwing, dumping, or placing materials in or removing them from machines or equipment which are automatic or tended or operated by other workers.

Handling: Using body members, hand tools, and/or special devices to work, move, or carry objects or materials.

Note: Excerpt from Department of Labor (1991), *Handbook for Analyzing Jobs (Rev.),* pp. 3-10 - 3-15.

FIG. 13.1. Physical task requirements of Department of Labor things functions.

The Threshold Traits Analysis system uses supervisors or incumbents to determine the relevancy, level, and practicality of 33 traits, including five physical traits, for job performance. Similarly, the Ability Requirements Scales contain 50 abilities, including 18 physical ability scales, which subject matter experts evaluate in terms of criticality for job or task performance. The traits used in the Threshold Traits Analysis system were developed rationally, whereas the abilities included in the Ability Requirements Scales were developed by both factor analytic and rational techniques. Examples of these person-oriented job descriptors appear in Fig. 13.3. The Ability Requirements Scales evaluate abilities for their relevance for either job or task performance; respondents are asked to rate and to nominate a task that requires the ability listed.

Division 3: Work Output[a]

No.	Technical Title	Operational Title
9.	Using machine/tools/equipment	Using machine/tools/equipment
10.	General body versus sedentary activities	Performing activities requiring general body movements
11.	Control and related physical coordination	Controlling machines/processes
12.	Skilled/technical activities	Performing skilled/technical activities
13.	Controlled manual/related activities	Performing controlled manual/related activities
14.	Use of miscellaneous equipment/devices	Using miscellaneous equipment/devices
15.	Handling/manipulating/related activities	Performing handling/related manual activities
16.	Physical coordination	General physical coordination

---

[a] Excerpt from McCormick & Jeanneret (1988, p. 829).

FIG. 13.2. Position Analysis Questionnaire physical task requirements dimensions.

In order to avoid developing arbitrary conceptions of work requirements, we need to combine the strengths of both job analysis approaches, apply them to a range of physically demanding jobs, and then analyze the mathematical structure of the results. However, Landy (1988) correctly pointed out that the typical method of linking task statements with corresponding abilities needs to be standardized. The strategy he recommended begins with Fleishman's taxonomy of human abilities (viz., Fleishman, 1982; Fleishman & Mumford, 1988, pp. 920-921) and assumes that a finite set of categories is needed to describe the range of human task performance. For the most part, these abilities were identified through factor analysis of test scores; for job analysis, they provide a comprehensive starting point for describing and organizing task requirements.

Starting with Fleishman's Ability Requirements Scales (Hogan, Jennings, Ogden, & Fleishman, 1980; Hogan, Ogden, & Fleishman, 1979), we adapted and revised his physical ability dimensions. We defined dimensions so as to reflect physiological functioning, and we omitted some dimensions because they were not useful for evaluating work performance. We identified seven physical performance dimensions that are consistent with industrial task content as well as human physiology; they appear in Fig. 13.4. We used these constructs to evaluate the structure of physically demanding tasks.

Threshold Traits Analysis[a]

Job Functions	Trait	Description—can:
Physical Extension	Strength	Lift, pull, or push physical objects
	Stamina	Expend physical energy for long periods
Bodily Activity	Agility	React quickly; has dexterity, coordination
Sensory Inputs	Vision	See details and color of objects
	Hearing	Recognize sound, tone, and pitch

Ability Requirements Scales[b]

Ability	Definition

Static Strength: This is the ability to use muscle force in order to lift, push, pull, or carry objects. It is the maximum force that one can exert for a brief period of time.

Explosive Strength: This is the ability to use short bursts of muscle force to propel oneself or an object. It requires gathering energy for bursts of muscle effort over a very short time period.

Dynamic Strength: This is the ability of the muscles to exert force repeatedly or continuously, over a long time period. This is the ability to support, hold up, or move the body's own weight and/or objects repeatedly over time. It represents muscular endurance and emphasizes the resistance of the muscles to fatigue.

Truck Strength: This ability involves the degree to which one's stomach and lower back muscles can support part of the body repeatedly or continuously over time. The ability involves the degree to which these trunk muscles do not "give out," or fatigue, when they are put under such repeated or continuous strain.

Extent Flexibility: This is the ability to bend, stretch, twist, or reach out with the body, arms, or legs.

Dynamic Flexibility: This is the ability to bend stretch, twist, or reach out with the body, arms, and/or legs, both quickly and repeatedly.

Gross Body Coordination: This is the ability to coordinate the movement of the arms, legs, and torso together in activities where the whole body is in motion.

Gross Body Equilibrium: This is the ability to keep or regain one's body balance, or to stay upright when in an unstable position. This ability includes being able to maintain one's balance when changing direction while moving or when standing motionless.

Stamina: This is the ability of the lungs and circulatory (blood) systems of the body to perform efficiently over long time periods. This is the ability to exert oneself physically without getting out of breath.

[a] Excerpt from Lopez (1988, p. 882).
[b] Excerpt from Fleishman & Mumford (1988, p. 921).

FIG. 13.3. Person-oriented physical requirements.

Muscular Strength	
Muscular tension:	Requires exerting muscular force against objects. It is used to push, pull, lift, lower, and carry objects or materials.
Muscular power:	Requires exerting muscular force quickly.
Muscular endurance:	Requires exerting muscular force continuously over time while resisting fatigue.
Cardiovascular Endurance	
Cardiovascular endurance:	Requires sustaining physical activity that results in increased heart rate.
Movement Quality	
Flexibility:	Requires flexing or extending the body limbs to work in awkward or contorted positions.
Balance:	Requires maintaining the body in a stable position, including resisting forces that cause loss of stability.
Coordination:	Requires sequencing movements of the arms, legs, and/or body to result in skilled action.

Balance: Requires maintaining the body in a stable position, including resisting forces that cause loss of stability.

Low			Average			High
1	2	3	4	5	6	7
Requires No Effort to Remain Stable						Requires Extreme Effort to Remain Stable

From Hogan, J. (1991b). Adapted by permission.

FIG. 13.4. Physical performance construct definitions and sample rating scale.

One study of metal- and chemical-processing occupations is illustrative. Hogan, Pederson, and Zonderman (1981) analyzed the physical requirements of 597 tasks across 63 jobs. Incumbents rated those tasks that were identified as physically demanding, using questionnaire methods. Trained subject matter experts, who observed every task and rated each one using seven physical ability dimension scales, generated links between the critical tasks and the physical abilities needed to perform them. The rating data were analyzed in a discriminant analysis, which produced weighted optimal linear combinations of dimensions to maximize the discriminability of jobs with respect to physical requirements. Five statistically significant canonical variates were found and the canonical weight matrix was transformed for interpretability. The transformed or rotated loadings and the correlations among the rotated components are presented in Table 13.1.

We hypothesized that the seven physical performance constructs would load in a specific way on the five canonical dimensions, and we found this hypothesized structure after rotation. These components were (a) muscular strength, (b) endurance, (c) movement quality, and (d) residuals. As seen in Table 13.1, the components are moderately intercorrelated, with the residual components showing the highest correlations with other factors.

Using principal components analysis, we evaluated the physical requirements of more than 150 jobs, and the results are consistent with the foregoing (Hogan, 1991b). Physical requirements of work can be described with as few as two components—muscular strength and endurance, and movement quality. This simple structure is independent of job or task, it is consistent across different types of trained raters, and it is independent of rating method. This structure appears to be the core of our seven physical performance constructs (Fig. 13.4) as well as Fleishman's physical ability taxonomy (Fig. 13.3). With these results regarding the physical requirements of work, we can make recommendations about what to study and how to study it.

PREDICTING PERFORMANCE OF PHYSICALLY DEMANDING WORK

Over the last 15 years, the goals of physical abilities research have been remarkably similar to some of those identified for Project A (Peterson et al., 1990). Researchers are primarily concerned with developing a set of predictors that are maximally related to criteria of importance. For the predictor domain, we need to identify individual difference dimensions that correspond to job analysis results, we need to select or develop tests that will maximize incremental prediction of the criterion space, and we need to construct measures that are psychometrically sound and administratively feasible. For the criteria domain, we need to develop a model of performance based on job analysis results, we need to construct measures that correspond to job components in the model, and we need to design methods to evaluate the accuracy of data collected using the measures. When Project A began in 1983, the state of the art in physical abilities research was not well advanced. However, I can summarize subsequent research in three points.

First, physical ability tests are valid predictors of job performance when the critical tasks are physically demanding. At least three reviews of empirical validation studies support this assertion. Lewis (1989) computed a meta-analysis of 24 physical ability selection samples, where he classified the predictors as muscular strength tests, anthropometric measures, muscular power tests, and muscular endurance tests, and the criterion measures as work sample measures,

TABLE 13.1

Canonical Variates and Correlations Between Physical Performance Ratings

Canonical Variate Weights for Physical Performance Ratings[a]

Rating Scale	Factor 1	Factor 2	Factor 3	Factor 4	Factor 5
	Unstandardized canonical variables				
Muscular tension	.33	-.35	-.43	-.69	-.27
Muscular power	-.17	.67	.83	.04	.24
Muscular endurance	.13	-.47	.25	-.56	-.67
Cardiovascular endurance	-.11	.83	-.81	.41	-.03
Flexbility	-.13	-.11	.30	-.26	.02
Balance	.15	-.28	.33	.97	-.52
Coordination	.79	.15	-.30	-.11	.88
Eigenvalue	.88**	.51**	.29**	.27**	.16*
Canonical correlation	.68	.58	.48	.46	.37
Percentage of variance	36	22	12	11	7
	Rotated factor loadings				
Muscular tension	.61	.09	.00	-.61	-.04
Muscular power	.32	.02	.01	.04	.12
Muscular endurance	.51	.39	.01	-.61	.10
Cardiovascular endurance	.06	.86	.01	-.03	-.09
Flexbility	.13	-.06	.31	-.07	.-.15
Balance	-.12	.10	.63	.07	-.36
Coordination	.02	-.03	.59	.01	.86

* $p < .05$.   ** $p < .01$.

Correlations Between Rotated Physical Performance Factors[a]

Factor	1	2	3	4	5
1	--				
2	.40	--			
3	.35	.46	--		
4	.90	.28	.20	--	
5	-.07	.21	.63	-.06	--

supervisor ratings, and training performance. Table 13.2 presents his results and, as can be seen, the highest mean validity (rho = .82) is between muscular strength tests and work sample measures. Also, note that, in general, the work sample criterion yields higher validities than do rating or training criteria. The overall average validity across muscular tests and criteria is .39.

TABLE 13.2
Summary Validities of Physical Ability Tests

Lewis (1989) Meta-Analysis of Physical Tests

	Criterion								
	Work Sample			Supervisor Rating			Training Criteria		
Predictor	rho	N	K	rho	N	K	rho	N	K
Muscular strength	.816	2064	10	—	—	—	.23	396	3
Anthropometric	.49	2176	12	.255	1426	6	.23	396	3
Muscular endurance	.367	1740	6	.23	2022	9	.30	750	5
Muscular power	—	—	—	.26	1699	5	—	—	—

Note: rho = corrected mean validity; N = number of subjects; K = number of samples.

Hogan (1991a) Mean Validity Coefficients of Physical Tests

	Criterion		
Predictor	Objective	Subjective	Work Sample
Muscular strength	.36	.30	.79
Endurance	.21	.13	.49
Movement quality	.38	.11	.44

Blakely, Quinones, & Jago (1992) Strength Test Mean Validity Coefficients

	Criterion	
Job	Supervisor Ratings	Work Sample
Police officer	.36	.33
GAS service	.33	.75
Construction	.29	.72
Pipefitter	.24	.69
Maintenance	.29	.50
Utility	.17	.48
Average validity	**.34**	**.68**

Hogan (1991a) reviewed 14 empirical physical ability test validation studies that were conducted between 1979 and 1988. The predictors were classified according to the physical performance dimensions listed in Fig. 13.4, and the criteria were labeled as objective (e.g., training time, injuries sustained), subjective (i.e., supervisor ratings), or work sample scores. The strength tests yielded the highest average validities regardless of criterion measure used, and those correlations ranged from .30 to .79. Lower validities also were obtained for the endurance measures; the average correlations were .21 and .49 for the objective and work sample criteria, respectively. The average validities for the movement quality tests, as a group, were .38 and .44, respectively, with the objective and work sample criteria. Mean validities were lowest for tests correlated with supervisor ratings and, consistent with Lewis' analysis, were highest with the work sample measures. These results appear in Table 13.2.

Blakely, Quinones, and Jago (1992) summarized studies of the jobs of police officer, customer gas service technician, construction worker, pipefitter, pipeline construction and maintenance worker, and utility worker. The predictors were four isometric muscular strength tests, and the criterion measures were supervisors' ratings of physical performance and work sample scores. Across the jobs in the total sample (N = 1276), the average validities for the summed strength test scores with supervisors' ratings and work sample simulations were .34 and .68, respectively.

My second point regarding progress since 1983 is that, based on the validity results, we now understand the structure of predictor batteries derived from job analysis data. Hogan (1991b) analyzed the structure of seven physical performance test batteries used in empirical validation studies across a wide range of jobs and concluded that test performance can be described in terms of three dimensions—muscular strength, endurance, and movement quality.

Perhaps the most comprehensive study available is Denning's (1984) study of physical requirements of 112 production jobs and 17 maintenance jobs in chemical, plastics, synthetics, and paint processing manufacturing. Based on a thorough job analysis, she identified nine physical tests for the experimental battery in a concurrent validation strategy. She tested 853 male and 203 female employees across 10 plant locations. The test battery consisted of body fat skinfold (a proxy for cardiovascular endurance), static strength (push, pull, upper-extremity cable pull), medicine ball throw (muscular power), sit and reach (flexibility), arm cranking (muscular endurance), balance, and eye-hand coordination tests. The results of varimax rotated principal components analysis of the test correlation matrix appear in Table 13.3. The first factor was defined by the muscular strength tests, with the muscular tension and power tests loading highest. Factor two was defined by the coordination, flexibility, and balance tests, and factor three was defined exclusively by the skinfold measure. Body fat, which is what skinfold measures indicate, is inversely related to cardiovascular fitness (McArdle, Katch, F., & Katch, V., 1991).

TABLE 13.3
Principal Components Analysis of Physical Performance Tests
(Chemical, plastics, synthetics, and paint processing maintenance and production technicians)[a]

Test	Factor 1	Factor 2	Factor 3
Skinfold	-.20	.08	-.87
Balance	.10	.42	.38
Static push	.88	-.15	.06
Static pull	.89	.00	-.17
Cable pull	.79	.08	.25
Coordination	-.08	-.77	.26
Sit and reach	-.05	.68	.11
Medicine ball throw	.82	.07	.29
Cranking (arm)	.63	.24	.26
Percentage of variance	40	19	12

[a] Based on data compiled by Denning (1984).
Note. From Hogan, J. (1991b). Adapted by permission.

The remaining studies analyzed by Hogan (1991b) also reveal these dimensions. The structure of test performance appears to be uninfluenced by test type, as long as the predictor battery is sufficiently complex. Also, results appear not to be a function of statistical method; nearly identical results were obtained after both orthogonal and oblique rotations.

My third point regarding progress is that because muscular strength, endurance, and movement skill tests are valid predictors of job performance, and because these measures are statistically independent, we would expect incremental validity when each of these measures is added to a regression equation. There is support for this proposition when complex experimental test batteries are evaluated. Denning (1984) reported a multiple R of .45 with the medicine ball (muscular strength), skinfold (endurance), and coordination (movement quality) as independent variables and overall supervisors' ratings as the dependent variable. She did not report the variance accounted for by each variable; however, the zero-order correlations for the variables listed above were .26, -.17, and -.13, respectively. Similarly, Reilly et al. (1979) combined experimental predictors using stepwise regression to predict time-to-complete training in pole climbing school. They reported a multiple R of .45 with measures of body density (endurance), balance (movement quality), and static strength defining the equation.

These studies suggest that tests from the three performance domains made significant independent contributions to the prediction of the criterion space. In terms of the relation between physical performance tests and other domains, we

HOGAN

speculate that physical ability is unrelated to cognitive ability and modestly related to some factors in the psychomotor and personality domains.

IMPLICATIONS FOR ARMY RESEARCH

I would like to summarize my observations in terms of three points. First, the purpose of a military organization is to project force at a distance. The process of projecting force will involve physical actions—pushing and shoving. Under conventional conditions, combat is not a push-button activity, at least not for certain specialties. When pushing and shoving are involved, as in the case of the infantry, physical abilities are needed. Although physical abilities are an important part of the military job, and although physical abilities are about 20% of the Project A criterion space, they were not well represented in the predictor battery.

Second, a fair amount is known in a reliable way about the structure of physically demanding jobs, but this information was not available at the outset of Project A. The most recent example of this research is a study of physical ability tests and their relation to latent structure of strength and endurance involved in police officer performance (Arvey, Landon, Nutting, & Maxwell, 1992). This paper, which exemplifies construct validation, will be a model for future research. To enhance construct validation, we must pay greater attention to the structure of the performance domain in order to maximize our predictor resources.

Third, I disagree with the conclusion of Campbell, McHenry, and Wise (1990, p. 332) that one cannot generalize from civilian to military jobs when talking about the structure of physical abilities. In a study of Navy explosive ordnance divers—one of the most physically demanding specialties in the military—I found that the structure of physically demanding work in bomb disposal is identical to the structure of such work in the civilian workplace (cf. Hogan, 1985). When we consider how well Project A predicted the criterion space occupied by "core technical proficiency" and "general proficiency," we see an opportunity to improve the prediction of the "physical fitness and military bearing" dimension. Consequently, it seems prudent for the military to reevaluate their position regarding the importance of physical abilities in military performance and our ability to assess them.

REFERENCES

Arvey, R. D., Landon, T. E., Nutting, S. M., & Maxwell, S. E. (1992). The development of physical ability tests for police officers: A construct validation approach. *Journal of Applied Psychology, 77*, 996-1009.

Ash, R. A. (1988). Job analysis in the world of work. In S. Gael (Ed.), *Job analysis handbook for business, industry, and government* (Vol. 1, pp. 3-13). New York: Wiley.

Blakely, B. R., Quinones, M. A., & Jago, I. A. (1992, May). *The validity of isometric strength tests: Results of five validity studies.* Paper presented at the conference of the Society for Industrial and Organizational Psychology, Montreal.

Campbell, J. P., McHenry, J. J., & Wise, L. L. (1990). Modeling job performance in a population of jobs. *Personnel Psychology, 43,* 313-333.

Christal, R. E. (1974). The United States Air Force occupational research project. *JSAS Catalog of Selected Documents, 4,* no. 61 (Ms, No. 651).

Denning, D. L. (1984, August). *Applying the Hogan model of physical performance of occupational tasks.* Paper presented at the convention of the American Psychological Association, Toronto.

Department of Labor, Employment and Training Administration (1991). *Handbook for analyzing jobs (Rev.).* Washington, DC: U.S. Government Printing Office.

Fleishman, E. A. (1982). Systems for describing human tasks. *American Psychologist, 37,* 821-834.

Fleishman, E. A., & Mumford, M. D. (1988). Ability requirements scales. In S. Gael (Ed.), *Job analysis handbook for business, industry, and government* (Vol. 2, pp. 917-935). New York: Wiley.

Gael, S. (1983). *Job analysis: A guide to assessing work activities.* San Francisco: Jossey-Bass.

Hogan, J. (1985). Test for success in diver training. *Journal of Applied Psychology, 70,* 219-224.

Hogan, J. (1991a). Physical abilities. In M. D. Dunnette and L. M. Hough (Eds.), *Handbook of industrial and organizational psychology* (Vol. 2, pp. 751-831). Palo Alto, CA: Consulting Psychologists Press.

Hogan, J. (1991b). Structure of physical performance in occupational tasks. *Journal of Applied Psychology, 76,* 495-507.

Hogan, J., Jennings, M. C., Ogden, G. P., & Fleishman, E. A. (1980). *Determining the physical requirements of Exxon apprentice jobs: Job analyses and test development.* Bethesda, MD: Advanced Research Resources Organization.

Hogan, J., Ogden, G. P., & Fleishman, E. A. (1979). *The development and validation of tests for the order selector job at Certified Grocers of California, Ltd.* Bethesda, MD: Advanced Research Resources Organization.

Hogan, J., Pederson, K. R., & Zonderman, A. B. (1981). *Job analysis and test development for physically demanding Dow Chemical jobs.* Baltimore: Johns Hopkins University Press.

Landy, F. J. (1988). Selection procedure development and usage. In S. Gael (Ed.), *Job analysis handbook for business, industry, and government* (Vol. 1, pp. 271-287). New York: Wiley.

Lewis, R. E. (1989). *Physical ability tests as predictors of job-related criteria: A meta-analysis.* Unpublished manuscript.

Lopez, F. M. (1988). Threshold traits analysis system. In S. Gael (Ed.), *Job analysis handbook for business, industry, and government* (Vol. 2, pp. 880-901). New York: Wiley.

McArdle, W. D., Katch, F. I., & Katch, V. L. (1991). *Exercise physiology.* Philadelphia: Lea & Febiger.

McCormick, E. J., & Jeanneret, P. R. (1988). Position Analysis Questionnaire (PAQ). In S. Gael (Ed.), *Job analysis handbook for business, industry, and government* (Vol. 2, pp. 825-842). New York: Wiley.

McCormick, E. J., Jeanneret, P. R., & Mecham, R. C. (1972). A study of job characteristics and job dimensions as based on the position analysis questionnaire (PAQ). *Journal of Applied Psychology, 56,* 347-368.

Peterson, N. G., Hough, L. M., Dunnette, M. D., Rosse, R. L., Houston, J. S., Toquam, J. I., & Wing, H. (1990). Project A: Specification of the predictor domain and development of new selection/classification tests. *Personnel Psychology, 43,* 247-276.

Reilly, R. R., Zedeck, S., & Tenopyr, M. L. (1979). Validity and fairness of physical ability tests for predicting craft jobs. *Journal of Applied Psychology, 64,* 262-274.

CHAPTER

14

BASIC RESEARCH ON PERSONALITY STRUCTURE: IMPLICATIONS OF THE EMERGING CONSENSUS FOR APPLICATIONS TO SELECTION AND CLASSIFICATION

Lewis R. Goldberg
University of Oregon and Oregon Research Institute

The past decade has witnessed an electrifying burst of interest in one of the most fundamental problems in the scientific study of human personality, namely, the development of a taxonomy of personality traits. Of more importance, the beginning of a consensus is emerging about the general framework of such a taxonomic structure. As a consequence, the scientific study of personality dispositions, which had been cast into the doldrums in the 1970s (Goldberg, in press), is again an intellectually vigorous enterprise poised on the brink of a solution to a scientific problem whose roots extend back at least to Aristotle. In the words of Moses, "More than two decades after personality assessment fell out of the mainstream of industrial-organizational psychology and nearly disappeared, it is back" (1991, p. 9).

THE LEXICAL HYPOTHESIS

The variety of individual differences is nearly boundless, yet most of these differences are not of sufficient importance in our daily interactions with each other to have become codified in our language. Sir Francis Galton may have been among the first scientists to recognize explicitly the fundamental "lexical hypothesis"—namely, that the most important individual differences in human transactions will come to be encoded as single terms in some or all of the world's languages. Moreover, Galton (1884) was certainly one of the first scientists to consult a dictionary as a means of estimating the number of personality-descriptive terms in the lexicon, and to appreciate the extent to which trait terms share aspects of their meanings. Galton's estimate of the number of personality-related terms in English was later sharpened empirically, first by Allport and Odbert (1936), who culled such terms from the second edition of

Webster's Unabridged Dictionary, and later by Norman (1967), who supplemented the earlier list with terms from the third edition. Galton's insight concerning the relations among personality terms has been mirrored in efforts by later investigators to discover the nature of those relations, so as to construct a structural representation of personality descriptors.

THE BIG FIVE

One of the first scientists to apply empirical procedures to the task of constructing a personality taxonomy was Raymond B. Cattell, who began with a perusal of the approximately 4,500 trait-descriptive terms included in the Allport and Odbert (1936) compendium. Cattell (1943) used this trait list as a starting point, eventually developing a set of 35 highly complex bipolar variables; these were then employed in various studies, in each of which the correlations among the variables were factored using oblique rotational procedures (e.g., Cattell, 1947). Cattell has repeatedly claimed to have identified at least a dozen oblique factors.

However, when Cattell's variables were later analyzed by others, only five factors were proven to be replicable (e.g., Digman & Takemoto-Chock, 1981; Fiske, 1949; Norman, 1963; Tupes & Christal, 1961). Similar five-factor structures based on other sets of variables have been reported by a number of other investigators (e.g., Borgatta, 1964; Digman & Inouye, 1986; Goldberg, 1990, 1992; McCrae & Costa, 1985, 1987), and these studies have now been reviewed extensively (e.g., Digman, 1990; John, 1990; McCrae & John, 1992; Wiggins & Pincus, 1992).

The "Big-Five" factors are now typically numbered and labeled: (**I**) *Surgency* (or Extraversion), (**II**) *Agreeableness*, (**III**) *Conscientiousness*, (**IV**) *Emotional Stability* (vs. Neuroticism), and (**V**) *Intellect* (e.g., Digman & Takemoto-Chock, 1981; Peabody & Goldberg, 1989) or *Openness to Experience* (e.g., McCrae & Costa, 1987). Although there is some disagreement about the precise nature of these five broad domains, there is widespread agreement that some aspects of the language of personality description can be organized hierarchically (e.g., Cantor & Mischel, 1979; Hampson, John, & Goldberg, 1986). In such a representation, the Big-Five factors are located at the highest level that is still descriptive of behavior, with only general evaluation located at a higher and more abstract level (John, Hampson, & Goldberg, 1991). When thus viewed hierarchically, it should be clear that proponents of the five-factor model have never intended to *reduce* the rich tapestry of personality to a mere five traits. Rather, they seek to provide a scientifically compelling framework in which to organize the myriad individual differences that characterize humankind.

Indeed, these broad domains incorporate hundreds, if not thousands, of bipolar traits: *Factor I (Surgency or Extraversion)* contrasts such traits as Talkativeness, Assertiveness, and Activity Level with traits such as Silence, Passivity, and

Reserve; *Factor II (Agreeableness or Pleasantness)* contrasts traits such as Kindness, Trust, and Warmth with such traits as Hostility, Selfishness, and Distrust; *Factor III (Conscientiousness or Dependability)* contrasts such traits as Organization, Thoroughness, and Reliability with traits such as Carelessness, Negligence, and Unreliability; *Factor IV (Emotional Stability vs. Neuroticism)* contrasts traits such as Stability and Imperturbability with such traits as Nervousness, Moodiness, and Temperamentality; and *Factor V (whether labeled as Intellect or Openness to Experience)* contrasts such traits as Imagination, Intelligence, and Creativity with traits such as Shallowness and Imperceptiveness.

Any complete taxonomy of personality traits must include both the vertical and the horizontal features of their meanings. The vertical aspect refers to the hierarchical relations among traits (e.g., Reliability is a more abstract and general concept than Punctuality), whereas the horizontal aspect refers to the degree of similarity among traits at the same hierarchical level (e.g., Wit involves aspects of both Intelligence and Humor). Scientists who emphasize the vertical aspect of trait structure could employ multivariate techniques such as hierarchical cluster analysis, or they could employ oblique rotations in factor analysis, and then factor the correlations among the primary dimensions, thus constructing a hierarchical structure. Scientists who emphasize the horizontal aspect of trait structure could employ discrete cluster solutions or orthogonal factor rotations. In fact, however, there has been no one-to-one relation between the emphasis of investigators and their methodological preferences.

For example, both Eysenck (1970) and Cattell (1947) developed explicitly hierarchical representations, Eysenck's leading to three highest-level factors, Cattell's to eight or nine. However, whereas Cattell has always advocated and used oblique factor procedures, Eysenck has typically used orthogonal methods. Historically, the five-factor model grew out of exploratory factor analyses by investigators using orthogonal rotations (e.g., Goldberg, 1990; McCrae & Costa, 1985, 1987; Norman, 1963; Tupes & Christal, 1961). Yet some of these same investigators construe the model in an expressly hierarchical fashion (e.g., Costa, McCrae, & Dye, 1991; McCrae & Costa, 1992), whereas others emphasize its horizontal aspects (e.g., Hofstee, de Raad, & Goldberg, 1992; Peabody & Goldberg, 1989).

HORIZONTAL APPROACHES TO TRAIT STRUCTURE

The defining feature of horizontal models is that the relations among the variables are specified by the variables' locations in multidimensional space. When that space is limited to only two dimensions, and the locations of the variables are projected to some uniform distance from the origin, the resulting structures are referred to as "circumplex" representations. The most famous example of such models is the Interpersonal Circle (e.g., Kiesler, 1983; Wiggins, 1979, 1980), which is based on Factors I (Surgency) and II (Agreeableness) in the five-factor model. Other examples of circumplex models include those that incorporate Big-Five Factors I, II, and III (Peabody & Goldberg, 1989; Stern, 1970), and Factors I, II, and IV (Saucier, 1992).

A more comprehensive circumplex representation has recently been proposed by Hofstee et al. (1992). Dubbed the "AB5C" model, for Abridged Big Five-Dimensional Circumplex, this representation includes the ten bivariate planes formed from all pairs of the Big-Five factors. In the AB5C model, each trait is assigned to the plane formed by the two factors with which it is most highly associated (e.g., its two highest factor loadings). As evidence for the reasonableness of this limitation to two of the five dimensions, a mere 3% of the varimax-rotated factor loadings from a representative pool of 540 English trait adjectives were .20 or higher on three or more factors; indeed, less than 1% of the factor loadings were .25 or higher, and none of the loadings were .30 or higher, on three or more factors.

The article by Hofstee et al. (1992) provided the AB5C locations of these 540 traits, based upon analyses of 636 self (N = 320) and peer (N = 316) ratings. The Big-Five factor loadings were derived from varimax rotations of the 100 unipolar factor markers from Goldberg (1992), and the resulting five orthogonal factor scores were used to calculate the loadings of the remaining 440 traits. Of the ten AB5C planes, the most densely populated were those associated with Factors I and II (the Interpersonal Circle) and Factors II and IV; the most sparsely populated planes were those associated with Factor V, especially II/V and IV/V. The distributions of traits around the circles varied substantially across the ten planes. Factors I and II (the Interpersonal Circle) formed a near-perfect circumplex. In contrast, in five planes (II/III, III/V, I/IV, II/IV, and III/IV) more terms were located in the evaluatively congruent quadrants (e.g., II+/III+) than in the evaluatively incongruent ones (e.g., II+/III-), which results in a distinct northeast by southwest orientation of the traits in those planes. Finally, four planes (I/III, I/V, II/V, and IV/V) were relatively devoid of interstitial variables (i.e., factor blends) and thus appeared more simple-structured.

The three panels in Fig. 14.1 provide examples of the ten bivariate planes: Factor I and Factor II (a nearly perfect circumplex), Factor I and Factor III (a configuration relatively close to simple structure), and Factor II and Factor IV (a configuration that shows the distinct northeast by southwest orientation that results when there are more terms of the same evaluative valence than of different ones). The location of each trait in each plane is provided twice, once as defined by its angular position and its distance from the origin within the circle, and again when it is projected onto the circumference of the circle. The triangles in Fig. 14.1 indicate the locations of the factor-univocal traits, which by definition have very low secondary loadings, in each of the four planes other than the one containing their actual secondary loadings.

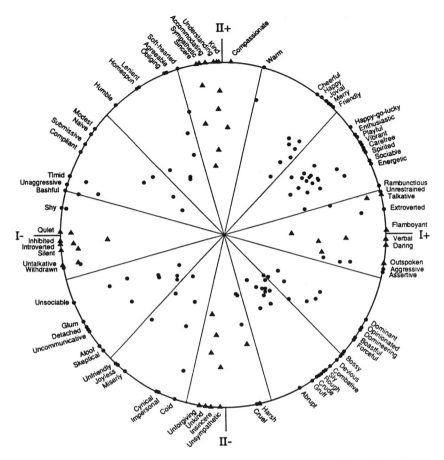

FIG. 14.1A. Three of the Ten Planes in the AB5C Model: (A) Factors I and II.

In Fig. 14.1, solid lines are used to divide each circle into 12 regions, each of 30°, which form the facets of the AB5C model. These facets can be conceptualized as blends of two factors in a matrix in which the columns represent the primary loadings and the rows represent the secondary ones; however, the ten cells representing combinations of the positive and negative poles of the same factor in this 10 by 10 matrix are necessarily empty. If the remaining 90 facets elicited equal frequencies of the 540 traits, each facet would contain six traits. Instead, the number of traits ranged from zero in six cells to 24 in the II+/IV+ cell. A table providing the traits within each of the AB5C facets is given in Hofstee et al. (1992).

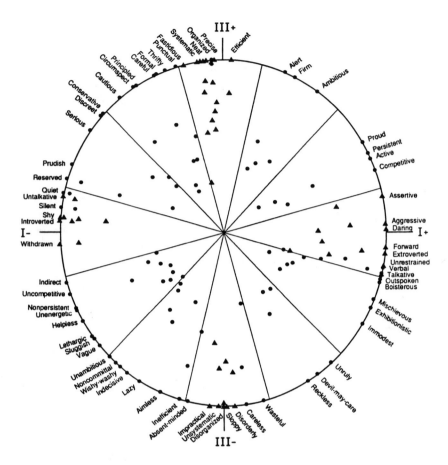

FIG. 14.1B. Three of the Ten Planes in the AB5C Model: (B) Factors I and III.

Every gap in a circular structure is a challenge. Circumplex models are tantalizing, in part, because they provoke conjectures about the nature of their missing segments. To discover traits associated with the empty facets in our analyses of the 540 traits, I recently carried out an AB5C analysis of 1,710 trait adjectives (Goldberg, 1982), which had been used by a sample of 187 college students to provide self descriptions. In this much larger pool of trait descriptors, the average facet would include 19 terms. In fact, the number of traits in each facet varied from 3 in facet I-/V+ to 50 in II-/I+; other facets that included many traits were II-/IV+ (49) and II-/IV- (40). Table 14.1 provides a representative trait from each of the 90 facets.

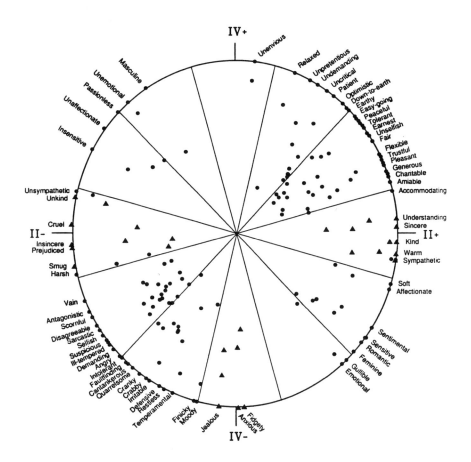

FIG. 14.1C. Three of the Ten Planes in the AB5C Model: (C) Factors II and IV.

VERTICAL APPROACHES TO TRAIT STRUCTURE

The defining feature of hierarchical models of personality traits is that they emphasize the vertical relations among variables (e.g., from the most specific to the most abstract), to the exclusion of the relations among variables at the same level. All structural representations based on factor-analytic methodology can be viewed from either vertical or horizontal perspectives. Factor analysis can be used to construct hierarchical models *explicitly* with oblique rotational procedures and *implicitly* even with orthogonal solutions, since any factor can be viewed as being located at a level above that of the variables being factored; that is, even orthogonal factors separate the common variance (the factors) from the total (common plus specific) variance of the measures. One could therefore

TABLE 14.1
Illustrative Traits in Each of the 90 Facets,
Based on AB5C Analyses of 1,710 Trait Terms

	I+	II+	III+	IV+	V+
I+	Extraverted	Warm	Ambitious	Self-Confident	Expressive
II+	Conversational	Kind	Tidy	Relaxed	Creative
III+	Assertive	Courteous	Organized	Steady	Intellectual
IV+	Confident	Pleasant	Practical	Worriless	Innovative
V+	Witty	Tender	Thorough	Fearless	Philosophical
I-	--	Soft-hearted	Careful	Calm	Complex
II-	Aggressive	--	Stern	Unemotional	Rebellious
III-	Unreserved	Acceptant	--	Easygoing	Abstract
IV-	Loud	Feelingful	Particular	--	Complicated
V-	Chitchatty	Tenderminded	Prompt	Unromantic	--

	I-	II-	III-	IV-	V-
I+	--	Rude	Impulsive	Overexcitable	Thick-witted
II+	Unaggressive	--	Inefficient	Emotional	Simple
III+	Taciturn	Uncharitable	--	Tense	Unartistic
IV+	Quiet-spoken	Cold-hearted	Untidy	--	Unreflective
V+	Secretive	Cynical	Undisciplined	Temperamental	--
I-	Quiet	Cold	Imprecise	Fretful	Uningenious
II-	Unsociable	Cruel	Haphazard	Irritable	Narrow
III-	Unassured	Impolite	Disorganized	Confused	Unintellectual
IV-	Inhibited	Spiteful	Inconsistent	High-strung	Unoriginal
V-	Nonvocal	Coarse	Unthorough	Fearful	Unphilosophical

AB5C = Abridged Big-Five-Dimensional Circumplex

emphasize the vertical aspect by grouping the variables by the factor with which they are most highly associated, thereby disregarding information about factorial blends. Alternatively, one could concentrate on the horizontal features of the representation, as in the AB5C model.

McCrae and Costa (1992) argued that hierarchical structures are to be preferred to the extent to which the variances of the traits are specific, as compared to the extent that they are related to the five broad factors. These investigators demonstrated that, after the five-factor common variance was partialed out from both self and other ratings on the facet scales from the revised NEO Personality Inventory (NEO-PI-R), the residual variance in these scales was still substantial enough to elicit significant correlations among self-ratings, spouse ratings, and peer ratings of the same trait. From this finding, they argued in favor of hierarchical representations, in which relatively small amounts of common variance produce the higher-level factors, with ample amounts of specific variance still available for predictive purposes.

This assumption has powerful implications for the role of trait measures when used in multiple regression analyses in applied contexts, such as personnel selection and classification. Because one always loses specific variance as one amalgamates measures, the optimal level of prediction is a function of statistical power, and thus of sample size. In the population (i.e., samples of unlimited size), optimal prediction will always be at the level of individual items; that is, for huge samples it would be silly even to amalgamate the items into scales, since one would inevitably lose some specific variance at the item level that could serve to increase predictive accuracy. Indeed, it is only the problem of capitalization on chance that justifies the use of scales as compared to items, and analogously of factor scores as compared to scale scores, when making predictions by regression analyses in applied contexts.

Although military samples are typically larger than their civilian counterparts, they are never of unlimited size, and rarely "huge." In addition, there are limits on the amount of testing time that can be required from applicants in any setting. As a consequence, even investigators in military settings must compromise between bandwidth and fidelity in their selection of predictor measures. Other things being equal, as one's sample size increases one will profit by including more predictors; in terms of a hierarchical representation, that means reaching down lower in the hierarchy to select one's initial predictor variables. For small samples, one must stay with only the highest level factor scores to avoid capitalizing on the chance vagaries of one's derivation sample. (For example, the analyses of Goldberg [1972] suggest that for sample sizes around 75, the optimal number of predictors is 5 ± 2.) For large samples, one should employ all of the individual facet scales, because each contains some additional variance beyond the highest level factors.

The availability of a general taxonomic structure for personality traits now permits a more rational selection of measures both at the highest level and at the level of the specific facets. For example, at the highest level Big-Five factor markers are available in the form of questionnaire statements (e.g., Costa & McCrae, 1993) as well as trait-descriptive adjectives (Goldberg, 1992; Trapnell & Wiggins, 1990). At an intermediate level are the 30 facet scales (six marking each of the Big-Five factors) in the recently revised NEO Personality Inventory (Costa & McCrae, 1993). And, finally, at the level of even more specific facets, there are the 100 clusters developed by Goldberg (1990) and the 90 facets in the AB5C model of Hofstee et al. (1992). Indeed, these 90 AB5C facets can now be used as the specifications for the future development of a comprehensive set of questionnaire scales.

IMPLICATIONS FOR SELECTION AND CLASSIFICATION

Over the past decade, evidence has been accruing about the utility of personality measures as predictors of diverse criteria (e.g., Hough, Eaton, Dunnette, Kamp, & McCloy, 1990). Recently, both qualitative (e.g., Hogan, 1991; Schmidt & Ones, 1992) and quantitative (e.g., Barrick & Mount, 1991; Tett, Jackson & Rothstein, 1991) reviews of the literature have concluded that personality measures, when classified within the Big-Five domains, are systematically related to a variety of criteria of job performance. For example, Barrick and Mount concluded that: "The results of the present study have implications for both research and practice in personnel selection. From a practitioner's standpoint, the results suggest that if the purpose is to predict job performance based on an individual's personality, then those measures associated with Conscientiousness [Factor III in the five-factor model] are most likely to be valid predictors for all jobs. *In fact, it is difficult to conceive of a job in which the traits associated with the Conscientiousness dimension would not contribute to job success*" (pp. 21-22, emphasis added).

The meta-analytic review of Tett et al. (1991) clearly confirmed the fact that "personality measures have a place in personnel selection research" (p. 732), and concluded that: "Our optimism [about the promise of personality measures in personnel selection] derives not only from the overall positive findings obtained in the present study, but also from perceived correctable weaknesses in current validation practices. In particular, we believe the full potential of personality traits in personnel selection will be realized only when confirmatory research strategies employing personality-oriented job analysis become the standard practice for determining which traits are relevant to predicting performance on a given job, and when greater attention is directed to the selection of psychometrically sound [and] construct valid personality measures." (p. 732)

Research on personality-performance relations is now of absolutely crucial importance for the optimal deployment of human resources. First of all, the findings from McHenry, Hough, Toquam, Hanson, & Ashworth (1990) demonstrate quite clearly that some personality measures can provide *substantial* incremental validities over cognitive measures for the prediction of a variety of job-related criteria. In their words: " . . . potentially the largest gains in validity can be obtained by using the temperament- personality scales . . . to improve the prediction of [such criteria as] Effort and Leadership, Personal Discipline, and Physical Fitness and Military Bearing. These are critical components of overall performance and should not be overlooked by a personnel selection and classification system. Performance is more than being able to perform critical tasks under standardized conditions. It is not one thing," (McHenry et al., 1990, p. 353)

In addition, unlike most cognitive measures, personality scales tend to have little if any differential impact on protected groups, and thus they are less prone to raise discriminatory concerns (Hogan, 1991). Moreover, although there is no doubt that most personality measures <u>can</u> be distorted when subjects are instructed to fake their responses, the admittedly scanty available evidence suggests that the vast majority of genuine job applications appear to refrain from such response distortion (e.g., Hough et al., 1990); for a review of this literature in a more specific context, see Goldberg, Grenier, Guion, Sechrest, and Wing (1991).

The development of more valid and precise predictors of job performance will require a major investment in personality-related research. There is widespread agreement that noncognitive factors are heavily implicated in many, if not most, aspects of job-related activities. Intellectually able individuals falter on the job when their personality traits are not congruent with task requirements. During the decade of the 1990s, research must focus on the development of (a) personality-oriented job analyses, (b) reliable measures of job-related personality traits, and (c) optimal procedures for linking applicants' personality profiles with job requirements. The Big-Five model of personality traits should prove useful as a framework for each of these three problems. In the words of Barrick and Mount (1991), ". . . in order for any field of science to advance, it is necessary to have an accepted classification scheme for accumulating and categorizing empirical findings. We believe that the robustness of the 5-factor model provides a meaningful framework for formulating and testing hypotheses relating individual differences in personality to a wide range of criteria in personnel psychology, especially in the subfields of personnel selection, performance appraisal, and training and development." (p. 23)

ACKNOWLEDGMENTS

Portions of this chapter have been adapted from Goldberg (1993a) and Goldberg (1993b), and readers who desire a more detailed discussion of these issues should consult those sources. The writing of the chapter was supported by Grant MH-49227 from the National Institute of Mental Health.

REFERENCES

Allport, G. W., & Odbert, H. S. (1936). Trait-names: A psycho-lexical study. *Psychological Monographs, 47*(1, Whole No. 211).

Barrick, M. R., & Mount, M. K. (1991). The Big Five personality dimensions and job performance: A meta-analysis. *Personnel Psychology, 44,* 1-26.

Borgatta, E. F. (1964). The structure of personality characteristics. *Behavioral Science, 9,* 8-17.

Cantor, N., & Mischel, W. (1979). Prototypes in person perception. In L. Berkowitz (Ed.), *Advances in experimental social psychology* (Vol. 12, pp. 2-52). New York: Academic Press.

Cattell, R. B. (1943). The description of personality: Basic traits resolved into clusters. *Journal of Abnormal and Social Psychology, 38,* 476-506.

Cattell, R. B. (1947). Confirmation and clarification of primary personality factors. *Psychometrika, 12,* 197-220.

Costa, P. T., Jr., & McCrae, R. R. (in press). *Revised NEO Personality Inventory (NEO-PI-R) and NEO Five-Factor Inventory (NEO-FFI) manual.* Odessa, FL: Psychological Assessment Resources.

Costa, P. T., Jr., McCrae, R. R., & Dye, D. A. (1991). Facet scales for Agreeableness and Conscientiousness: A revision of the NEO Personality Inventory. *Personality and Individual Differences, 12,* 887-898.

Digman, J. M. (1990). Personality structure: Emergence of the five-factor model. In M. R. Rosenzweig & L. W. Porter (Eds.), *Annual Review of Psychology* (Vol. 41, pp. 417-440). Palo Alto, CA: Annual Reviews.

Digman, J. M., & Inouye, J. (1986). Further specification of the five robust factors of personality. *Journal of Personality and Social Psychology, 50,* 116-123.

Digman, J. M., & Takemoto-Chock, N. K. (1981). Factors in the natural language of personality: Re-analysis, comparison, and interpretation of six major studies. *Multivariate Behavioral Research, 16,* 149-170.

Eysenck, H. J. (1970). *The structure of human personality* (3rd ed.). London: Methuen.

Fiske, D. W. (1949). Consistency of the factorial structures of personality ratings from different sources. *Journal of Abnormal and Social Psychology, 44,* 329-344.

Galton, F. (1884). Measurement of character. *Fortnightly Review, 36,* 179-185.

Goldberg, L. R. (1972). Parameters of personality inventory construction and utilization: A comparison of prediction strategies and tactics. *Multivariate Behavioral Research Monograph (7,* Whole No. 72-2).

Goldberg, L. R. (1982). From Ace to Zombie: Some explorations in the language of personality. In C. D. Spielberger & J. N. Butcher (Eds.), *Advances in Personality Assessment* (Vol. 1, pp. 203-234). Hillsdale, NJ: Lawrence Erlbaum Associates.

Goldberg, L. R. (1990). An alternative "Description of Personality": The Big-Five factor structure. *Journal of Personality and Social Psychology, 59,* 1216-1229.

Goldberg, L. R. (1992). The development of markers of the Big-Five factor structure. *Psychological Assessment, 4,* 26-42.

Goldberg, L. R. (1993a). The structure of phenotypic personality traits. *American Psychologist, 48,* 26-34.

Goldberg, L. R. (1993b). The structure of personality traits: Vertical and horizontal aspects. In D. C. Funder, R. D. Parke, C. Tomlinson-Keasey, & K. Widaman (Eds.), *Studying lives through time: Personality and development* (pp. 169-188). Washington, DC: American Psychological Association.

Goldberg, L. R. (in press). What the hell took so long? Donald Fiske and the Big-Five factor structure. In P. E. Shrout & S. T. Fiske (Eds.), *Advances in personality research, methods, and theory: A Festschrift honoring Donald W. Fiske.* Hillsdale, NJ: Lawrence Erlbaum Associates.

Goldberg, L. R., Grenier, J. R., Guion, R. M., Sechrest, L. B., & Wing, H. (1991). *Questionnaires used in the prediction of trustworthiness in pre-employment selection decisions: An A.P.A. Task Force report.* Washington, DC: American Psychological Association.

Hampson, S. E., John, O. P., & Goldberg, L. R. (1986). Category breadth and hierarchical structure in personality: Studies of asymmetries in judgments of trait implications. *Journal of Personality and Social Psychology, 51,* 37-54.

Hofstee, W. K. B., de Raad, B., & Goldberg, L. R. (in press). Integration of the Big Five and circumplex taxonomies of traits. *Journal of Personality and Social Psychology.*

Hogan, R. (1991). Personality and personality measurement. In M. D. Dunnette & L. M. Hough (Eds.), *Handbook of Industrial and Organizational Psychology* (2nd ed., Vol. 2, pp. 873-919). Palo Alto, CA: Consulting Psychologists Press.

Hough, L. M., Eaton, N. K., Dunnette, M. D., Kamp, J. D., & McCloy, R. A. (1990). Criterion-related validities of personality constructs and the effect of response distortion on those validities. *Journal of Applied Psychology, 75,* 581-595.

John, O. P. (1990). The "Big-Five" factor taxonomy: Dimensions of personality in the natural language and in questionnaires. In L. A. Pervin (Ed.), *Handbook of personality theory and research* (pp. 66-100). New York: Guilford.

John, O. P., Hampson, S. E., & Goldberg, L. R. (1991). The basic level in personality-trait hierarchies: Studies of trait use and accessibility in different contexts. *Journal of Personality and Social Psychology, 60,* 348-361.

Kiesler, D. J. (1983). The 1982 interpersonal circle: A taxonomy for complementarity in human transactions. *Psychological Review, 90,* 185-214.

McCrae, R. R., & Costa, P. T., Jr. (1985). Updating Norman's "adequate taxonomy": Intelligence and personality dimensions in natural language and in questionnaires. *Journal of Personality and Social Psychology, 49,* 710-721.

McCrae, R. R., & Costa, P. T., Jr. (1987). Validation of the five-factor model of personality across instruments and observers. *Journal of Personality and Social Psychology, 52,* 81-90.

McCrae, R. R., & Costa, P. T., Jr. (1992). Discriminant validity of NEO-PI-R facet scales. *Educational and Psychological Measurement, 52,* 81-90,

McCrae, R. R., & John, O. P. (1992). An introduction to the five-factor model and its applications. *Journal of Personality, 60,* 175-215.

McHenry, J. J., Hough, L. M., Toquam, J. L., Hanson, M. A., & Ashworth, S. (1990). Project A validity results: The relationship between predictor and criterion domains. *Personnel Psychology, 43,* 335-354.

Moses, S. (1991, November). Personality tests come back in I/O. *A.P.A. Monitor,* p. 9.

Norman, W. T. (1963). Toward an adequate taxonomy of personality attributes: Replicated factor structure in peer nomination personality ratings. *Journal of Abnormal and Social Psychology, 66,* 574-583.

Norman, W. T. (1967). *2800 personality trait descriptors: Normative operating characteristics for a university population.* Ann Arbor: University of Michigan, Department of Psychology.

Peabody, D., & Goldberg, L. R. (1989). Some determinants of factor structures from personality-trait descriptors. *Journal of Personality and Social Psychology, 57,* 552-567.

Saucier, G. (1992). Benchmarks: Integrating affective and interpersonal circles with the Big-Five personality factors. *Journal of Personality and Social Psychology, 62,* 1025-1035.

Schmidt, F. L., & Ones, D. S. (1992). Personnel selection. In M. R. Rosenzweig & L. W. Porter (Eds.), *Annual Review of Psychology* (Vol. 43, pp. 627-670). Palo Alto, CA: Annual Reviews.

Stern, G. G. (1970). *People in context: Measuring person-environment congruence in education and industry.* New York: Wiley.

Tett, R. P., Jackson, D. N., & Rothstein, M. (1991). Personality measures as predictors of job performance: A meta-analytic review. *Personnel Psychology, 44,* 703-742.

Trapnell, P. D., & Wiggins, J. S. (1990). Extension of the Interpersonal Adjective Scales to include the Big Five dimensions of personality. *Journal of Personality and Social Psychology, 59,* 781-790.

Tupes, E. C., & Christal, R. E. (1961). *Recurrent personality factors based on trait ratings* (ASD-TR-61-97). Lackland Air Force Base, TX: U.S. Air Force.

Wiggins, J. S. (1979). A psychological taxonomy of trait-descriptive terms: The interpersonal domain. *Journal of Personality and Social Psychology, 37,* 395-412.

Wiggins, J. S. (1980). Circumplex models of interpersonal behavior. In L. Wheeler (Ed.), *Review of personality and social psychology* (Vol. 1, pp. 265-294). Beverly Hills, CA: Sage.

Wiggins, J. S., & Pincus, A. L. (1992). Personality: Structure and assessment. In M. R. Rosenzweig & L. W. Porter (Eds.), *Annual Review of Psychology* (Vol. 43, pp. 473-504). Palo Alto, CA: Annual Reviews.

CHAPTER

15

REGULATIVE FUNCTION
OF PERCEIVED SELF-EFFICACY

Albert Bandura
Stanford University

Recent years have witnessed major changes in the conception of human ability. Ability is not a fixed attribute in a behavioral repertoire. Rather, it is a generative capability in which cognitive, social, motivational, emotional, and behavioral skills must be organized and effectively orchestrated to serve innumerable purposes. There is a marked difference between possessing knowledge and skills and being able to use them proficiently under diverse circumstances, many of which contain ambiguous, unpredictable, and stressful elements.

Self-referent thought plays a prominent role in the translation of knowledge and ability into proficient performance. Among the different forms of self-referent thought, none is more central or pervasive than people's beliefs in their capability to exercise control over their own functioning and over environmental demands (Bandura, 1986). Such self-beliefs affect how people think, feel, motivate themselves, and behave. Thus, with the same set of skills people may perform poorly, adequately, or extraordinarily depending on their self-beliefs of efficacy.

EFFICACY-ACTIVATED PROCESSES

Self-efficacy beliefs regulate human functioning through four major types of processes: cognitive, motivational, emotional, and selection.

Cognitive Processes

The effects of self-efficacy beliefs on cognitive processes take a number of different forms. Much human behavior, being purposive, is regulated by forethought embodying cognized goals. Personal goal setting is influenced by judgments of personal capabilities. The stronger the perceived self-efficacy, the higher the goal challenges people set for themselves and the firmer their commitment to them.

Most courses of behavior are initially shaped in thought. People's beliefs about their efficacy influence the types of anticipatory scenarios they construct and rehearse. Those who have a high sense of efficacy visualize success scenarios that provide positive guides for performance. Those who judge themselves as inefficacious tend to visualize failure scenarios that undermine performance by dwelling on personal deficiencies and on how things will go wrong. A major function of thought is to enable people to predict the occurrence of events and to create the means for exercising control over those that affect their lives. Discovery of such predictive rules for the relations between environmental happenings and between actions and outcomes requires effective cognitive processing of multidimensional information that contains ambiguities and uncertainties.

In ferreting out predictive rules, people must draw on their preexisting knowledge to construct options, to weigh and integrate predictive factors into composite rules, to test and revise their judgments against the immediate and distal results of their actions, and to remember which factors they had tested and how well they had worked. It requires a strong sense of efficacy to remain task oriented in the face of pressing situational demands and judgment failures that can have important social repercussions.

The powerful influence of self-efficacy beliefs on cognitive processes is revealed in a program of research on complex organizational decision making (Wood & Bandura, 1989a). Managers direct a computer-simulated organization in which they have to match their supervisees to subfunctions based on the supervisees' talents, and to learn and implement managerial rules to achieve organizational levels of performance that are difficult to fulfill. Certain organizational properties are varied and belief systems are instilled that can enhance or undermine the managers' beliefs in their organizational capabilities (Bandura & Jourden, 1991; Bandura & Wood, 1989; Jourden, 1991; Wood & Bandura, 1989a).

For example, otherwise talented individuals who are led to believe that complex decision making is an inherent aptitude, that organizations are not easily controllable, and that other managers perform better than they do, and who receive feedback highlighting shortfalls in their performance, exhibit progressive deterioration of their managerial functioning. They are beset by increasing self-doubts about their managerial efficacy as they encounter problems; they become more and more erratic in their analytic thinking; they lower their organizational aspirations; and they achieve progressively less with the organization they are managing. In contrast, belief that complex decision making is an acquirable skill and that organizations are controllable, and feedback that highlights their comparative capabilities and the gains they are making, enhance organizational functioning. Managers operating under the latter conditions display a resilient sense of efficacy, set themselves increasingly challenging organizational goals, and use good analytic thinking for discovering managerial rules. Such a self-efficacious orientation pays off in rising organizational attainments.

Path analyses confirm the postulated causal ordering of self-regulatory determinants. When initially faced with managing a complex unfamiliar environment, people rely heavily on their past performance in judging their efficacy and setting their personal goals. But as they began to form a self-schema concerning their efficacy through further experience, the performance system is powered more strongly and intricately by self-perceptions of efficacy (Fig. 15.1). Perceived self-efficacy influences performance both directly and through its strong effects on personal goal setting and proficient analytic thinking. Personal goals, in turn, enhance performance attainments through the mediation of analytic strategies.

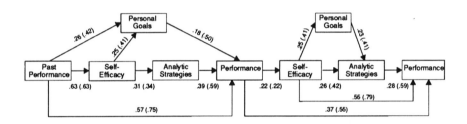

FIG. 15.1. Path analysis of causal structures. The initial numbers on the paths of influence are the significant standardized path coefficients; the numbers in parentheses are the first-order correlations. The network of relations on the left half of the figure is for the initial managerial efforts, and that on the right half is for later managerial efforts (Wood & Bandura, 1989b, Fig. 5. Reprinted by permission).

Motivational Processes

Self-beliefs of efficacy play a central role in the self-regulation of motivation. Most human motivation is cognitively generated. In cognitive motivation, people motivate themselves and guide their actions anticipatorily through the exercise of forethought. They form beliefs abut what they can do, they anticipate likely outcomes of prospective actions, they judge the causes of their performances, they set goals for themselves, and they plan courses of action designed to realize valued futures. Different theories—attribution theory, expectancy-value theory, and goal theory—have been built around these various forms of cognitive motivators (Fig. 15.2).

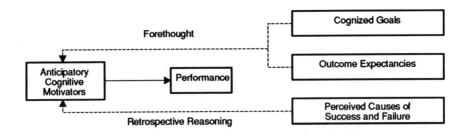

FIG. 15.2. Schematic representation of conceptions of cognitive motivation based on cognized goals, outcome expectancies, and causal attributions.

Perceived self-efficacy operates as a central factor in each of these variant forms of cognitive motivation (Bandura, 1991b). Self-beliefs of efficacy bias the attributing of causes for successes and failures. People who regard themselves as highly efficacious tend to ascribe their failures to insufficient effort, whereas those who regard themselves as inefficacious view the cause of their failures as stemming from low ability (Alden, 1986; Collins, 1982; Silver, Mitchell, & Gist, 1989). Causal attributions affect motivation and performance mainly through the mediating influence of self-efficacy beliefs (Bandura, 1991b).

People act on their beliefs about what they can do, as well as their beliefs about the likely outcomes of various courses of actions. The effects of outcome expectancies on performance motivation are, therefore, partly governed by self-beliefs of efficacy. There are many activities that, if done well, guarantee valued outcomes, but they are not pursued by people who doubt they can do what it takes to succeed (Beck & Lund, 1981; Betz & Hackett, 1986; Dzewaltowski, Noble, & Shaw, 1990; Wheeler, 1983). A low sense of efficacy can thus nullify the motivating potential of alluring outcome expectations. Recent efforts to increase the predictiveness of expectancy-value models have added an efficacy-like factor to the usual set of predictors. It explains a significant amount of variance in performances (Madden, Ellen, & Ajzen, 1992).

The capacity to exercise self-influence by personal challenge and evaluative reaction to one's own attainments provides the third cognitive mechanism of motivation and self-directedness. Innumerable studies have shown that challenging goals enhance motivation across heterogeneous activities, settings, populations, social levels, and time spans (Locke & Latham, 1990). Goals operate largely through self-referent processes rather than regulate motivation and behavior directly. The major self-influences include affective self-evaluation, perceived self-efficacy for goal attainment, and ongoing readjustment of personal standards. Goals motivate by enlisting self-evaluative involvement in the activity. When people make self-satisfaction conditional on certain accomplishments, they seek self-satisfactions from fulfilling valued standards and are prompted to intensify their efforts by discontent with substandard performances.

Perceived self-efficacy contributes in several ways to motivation through goal systems (Bandura, 1991b; Locke & Latham, 1990). It is partly on the basis of self-beliefs of efficacy that people choose what challenges to undertake, how much effort to expend in the endeavor, how long to persevere in the face of obstacles and failures—that is, their resilience in the face of adversity. A growing body of evidence indicates that human attainments and positive well-being require an optimistic sense of personal efficacy (Bandura, 1986). This is because ordinary social realities are strewn with difficulties. They are full of impediments, failures, adversities, setbacks, frustrations, and inequities. People must have a robust sense of personal efficacy to sustain the perseverant effort needed to succeed. The goals people set for themselves at the outset of an endeavor are likely to change, depending on how they construe the pattern and level of progress they are making and readjust their aspirations accordingly (Campion & Lord, 1982). They may maintain their original goal, lower their sights, or adopt an even more challenging goal. Thus, the third constituent self-influence is the ongoing regulation of motivation concerns readjusting personal goals in light of one's attainments.

When attainments fall short of a goal being pursued, people who are discontented with a substandard performance and have a high sense of efficacy intensify their efforts and persist until they succeed (Bandura & Cervone, 1983). Those who judge themselves inefficacious to reach the goal and are satisfied with a substandard performance slacken their efforts and display a substantial decline in motivation as they continue the activity (Fig. 15.3).

Studies in which discrepancy levels are varied systematically shed further light on how the three self-reactive influences operate in concert in the regulation of motivation through goal systems (Bandura & Cervone, 1986). The more self-influences that are operating—high perceived self-efficacy, challenging goals, and discontent with substandard performance—the higher and more persistent is the motivation (Fig. 15.4).

Most theories of motivation are founded on a negative feedback system. In this view, discrepancy between one's perceived performance and an adopted standard motivates action to reduce the disparity. However, motivation by negative discrepancy tells only half the story, and not necessarily the more interesting half. In fact, people are proactive, aspiring organisms. Human motivation relies on discrepancy production as well as discrepancy reduction. As already shown, people motivate and guide their actions by setting themselves challenging goals and then mobilizing their skills and effort to reach them. After people attain the goal they have been pursuing, those with a strong sense of efficacy set higher goals for themselves. Adopting further challenges creates new motivating discrepancies to be mastered.

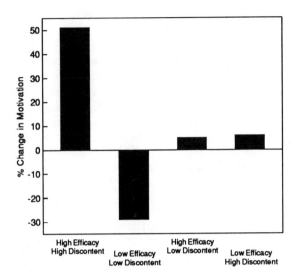

FIG. 15.3. Percentage changes over time in motivational level under conditions combining goals and performance feedback as a function of different combinations of levels of self-dissatisfaction and perceived self-efficacy for goal attainment. Adapted from Bandura & Cervone, 1983. Reprinted from *Nebraska symposium on motivation*, Vol. 38, by permission of the University of Nebraska Press. Copyright © 1991 by the University of Nebraska Press.

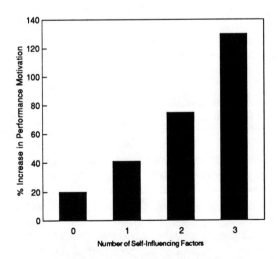

FIG. 15.4. Mean percentage change in motivational level as a function of the number of self-reactive influences operating in given individuals. The three self-reactive factors included strong perceived self-efficacy for goal attainment, self-dissatisfaction with substandard performance, and adoption of challenging goals. Plotted from data of Bandura and Cervone, 1986. From Bandura (1991c), reprinted by permission.

Affective Processes

People's beliefs in their capabilities affect how much stress and depression they experience in threatening or taxing situations, as well as their level of motivation. There are three principal ways in which self-efficacy beliefs affect the nature and intensity of emotional experiences (Bandura, 1992). Such beliefs create attentional biases and influence how potentially aversive life events are construed the cognitively represented; they operate in the exercise of control over perturbing thought patterns; and they sponsor courses of action that transform distressing environments into more benign ones. These alternative paths of affective influence are amply documented in human anxiety and depression.

People who believe they can exercise control over threats do not conjure up apprehensive cognitions and, hence, are not perturbed by them. However, those who believe they cannot manage potential threats experience high levels of anxiety arousal. They dwell on their coping deficiencies, view many aspects of their environment as fraught with danger, magnify the severity of possible threats, and worry about perils that rarely, if ever, happen. Through such inefficacious thought they distress themselves and constrain and impair their level of functioning. It is not the sheer frequency of perturbing cognitions, but the perceived inefficacy to turn them off, that is the major source of distress (Kent & Gibbons, 1987). People base their actions on self-beliefs of efficacy rather than on anxiety arousal in situations they regard as risky (Williams, 1992). The weaker the perceived coping self-efficacy, the more avoidant the behavior.

A low sense of efficacy to exercise control produces depression as well as anxiety. Self-beliefs of efficacy contribute to depression in at least three different ways. One route to depression is through unfulfilled aspiration. People who impose on themselves standards of self-worth they judge they cannot attain drive themselves to bouts of depression. A second efficacy route to depression is through a low sense of social efficacy to develop social relationships that bring satisfaction to one's life and cushion the adverse effects of chronic stressors. A low sense of social efficacy contributes to depression both directly and by curtailing development of socially supportive relationships (Holahan & Holahan, 1987). The third route to depression is through thought control efficacy. Much human depression is cognitively generated by dejecting ruminative thought. A low sense of efficacy to exercise control over ruminative thought contributes to the occurrence, duration, and recurrence of depressive episodes (Kavanagh & Wilson, 1989).

Other efficacy-activated processes in the affective domain concern the impact of perceived coping efficacy on physiological reactions to environmental stressors. Exposure to stressors with perceived efficacy to control them has no adverse physiological effects. But exposure to the same stressors without perceived self-efficacy to control them activates autonomic, catecholamine, and opioid systems and suppresses various components of the immune system

(Bandura, 1991a). However, stress aroused in the process of coping efficacy over chronic stressors can enhance immunocompetence (Wiedenfeld et al., 1990).

Selection Processes

The discussion so far has centered on efficacy-activated processes that enable people to create beneficial environments and to exercise some measure of control over them. People are partly the product of their environment. Hence, beliefs of personal efficacy can shape the course lives take by influencing choices of activities and environments. People tend to avoid activities and situations they believe exceed their coping capabilities, but they readily undertake challenging activities and pick social environments they judge themselves capable of handling. Any factor that influences choice behavior can profoundly affect the direction of personal development. This is because the social influences operating in selected environments continue to promote certain competencies, values, and interests long after the efficacy decisional determinant has rendered its inaugurating effect. Career choice and development is but one example of the power of self-efficacy beliefs to affect the course of life paths through choice-related processes (Betz & Hackett, 1986; Lent & Hackett, 1987).

Collective Efficacy

The preceding analyses document the diverse ways in which perceived self-efficacy affects the quality of human functioning at the individual level. People often operate collectively within interactive social systems rather than as isolates. The strength of groups and organizations rests partly in members' sense of collective efficacy that they can manage the problems and challenges they face. People's beliefs in their collective efficacy influence what they choose to do as a group, how much effort they put into it, how well they use their talents and resources, and their endurance when collective efforts fail to produce quick results.

The role of perceived collective efficacy in group functioning is revealed in research on the collective beliefs of school staffs to promote academic attainments. Collective efficacy was assessed by aggregating teachers' beliefs in the instructional efficacy of their school as a whole, as well as their own instructional capabilities. A number of characteristics of the composition of student bodies and teachers' instructional experiences were also assessed.

Figure 15.5 shows the causal structure of the factors measured at the beginning of the academic year and school-level achievement in reading and mathematics at the end of the academic year. Adverse characteristics of student body populations reflecting largely socioeconomic disadvantage erode schools' sense of instructional efficacy. Thus, the higher the proportion of students from low socioeconomic levels and the higher the student turnover and absenteeism,

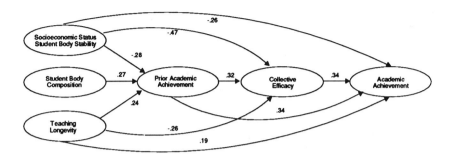

FIG. 15.5. Path analysis showing the role of perceived collective efficacy in the causal structure of school-level academic achievement. From Bandura (1993), reprinted by permission.

the weaker the faculties' beliefs in their efficacy to achieve academic progress and the poorer the schools fare academically. Student body characteristics reflecting low racial composition and ethnic diversity are weakly linked to schools prior achievements but have no direct influence on schools' collective sense of efficacy or on subsequent school achievement.

Longevity in teaching has a small positive effect on school achievement but, interestingly, it also seems to create in teachers a jaundiced view of their schools' collective instructional efficacy. Staffs' collective sense of efficacy that they can promote high levels of academic progress contributes significantly to their schools' level of academic achievement. Indeed, perceived collective efficacy contributes independently to variance in achievement between schools after controlling for the effects of the characteristics of student bodies, teachers' characteristics, and prior school level achievement. With staffs who firmly believe that, by their determined efforts, students are motivatable and teachable whatever their background, schools heavily populated with minority students of low socioeconomic status achieve at the highest percentile ranks based on national norms of language and mathematical competencies.

SUMMARY

The substantial body of research on the diverse effects of perceived personal efficacy can be summarized as follows: People who have a low sense of efficacy in a given domain of functioning shy away from difficult tasks, which they tend to perceive as personal threats; have low aspirations and weak commitment to the goals they choose; maintain a self-diagnostic focus rather than concentrate on how to perform successfully; dwell on personal deficiencies, obstacles, and adverse outcomes; attribute failures to deficient capability; slacken their efforts or give up quickly in the face of difficulties; are slow to recover their sense of efficacy after failures or setbacks; and are prone to stress and depression.

In contrast, people who have a strong sense of efficacy approach difficult tasks as challenges to be mastered rather than as threats to be avoided; set challenging goals and sustain strong commitment to their goals; maintain a task-diagnostic focus that guides effective performance; attribute failures to insufficient effort or deficient knowledge or skills that are acquirable; heighten and sustain effort in the face of difficulties; quickly recover their sense of efficacy after failures or setbacks; and display low vulnerability to stress and depression.

The multiple benefits of a sense of personal efficacy do not arise simply from the incantation of capability. Saying something should not be confused with believing it to be so. Simply saying that one is capable is not necessarily self-convincing. Self-efficacy beliefs are the product of a complex process of self-persuasion that relies on cognitive processing of diverse sources of efficacy information conveyed enactively, vicariously, socially, and physiologically (Bandura, 1986). Once formed, self-efficacy beliefs contribute significantly to the level and quality of human functioning.

REFERENCES

Alden, L. (1986). Self-efficacy and causal attributions for social feedback. *Journal of Research in Personality, 20,* 460-473.

Bandura, A. (1986). *Social foundations of thought and action: A social cognitive theory.* Englewood Cliffs, NJ: Prentice-Hall.

Bandura, A. (1991a). Self-efficacy mechanism in physiological activation and health-promoting behavior. In J. Madden, IV (Ed.), *Neurobiology of learning, emotion and affect* (pp. 229-270). New York: Raven.

Bandura, A. (1991b). Self-regulation of motivation through anticipatory and self-regulatory mechanisms. In R. A. Dienstbier (Ed.), *Perspectives on motivation: Nebraska symposium on motivation* (Vol. 38, pp. 69-164). Lincoln, University of Nebraska Press.

Bandura, A. (1991c). Social cognitive theory of self-regulation. *Organizational Behavior and Human Decision Processes, 50,* 212-247.

Bandura, A. (1992). Exercise of personal agency through the self-efficacy mechanism. In R. Schwarzer (Ed.), *Self-efficacy: Thought control of action* (pp. 3-38). Washington, DC: Hemisphere.

Bandura, A. (1993). Perceived self-efficacy in cognitive development and functioning. *Educational Psychologist, 28,* 117-148.

Bandura, A., & Cervone, D. (1983). Self-evaluative and self-efficacy mechanisms governing the motivational effects of goal systems. *Journal of Personality and Social Psychology, 45,* 1017-1028.

Bandura, A., & Cervone, D. (1986). Differential engagement of self-reactive influences in cognitive motivation. *Organizational Behavior and Human Decision Processes, 38,* 92-113.

Bandura, A., & Jourden, F. J. (1991). Self-regulatory mechanisms governing the impact of social comparison on complex decision making. *Journal of Personality and Social Psychology, 60,* 941-951.

Bandura, A., & Wood, R. E. (1989). Effect of perceived controllability and performance standards on self-regulation of complex decision making. *Journal of Personality and Social Psychology, 56,* 805-814.

Beck, K. H., & Lund, A. K. (1981). The effects of health threat seriousness and personal efficacy upon intentions and behavior. *Journal of Applied Social Psychology, 11,* 401-415.

Betz, N. E., & Hackett, G. (1986). Applications of self-efficacy theory to understanding career choice behavior. *Journal of Social and Clinical Psychology, 4,* 279-289.

Campion, M. A., & Lord, R. G. (1982). A control systems conceptualization of the goal-setting and changing process. *Organizational Behavior and Human Performance, 30,* 265-287.

Collins, J. L. (1982, March). *Self-efficacy and ability in achievement behavior.* Paper presented at the annual meeting of the American Educational Research Association, New York.

Dzewaltowski, D. A., Noble, J. M., & Shaw, J. M. (1990). Physical activity participating: Social cognitive theory versus the theories of reasoned action and planned behavior. *Journal of Sport and Exercise Psychology, 12,* 388-405.

Holahan, C. K., & Holahan, C. J. (1987). Self-efficacy, social support, and depression in aging: A longitudinal analysis. *Journal of Gerontology, 42,* 65-68.

Jourden, F. (1991). *The influence of feedback framing on the self-regulatory mechanisms governing complex decision making.* Manuscript submitted for publication.

Kavanagh, D. J., & Wilson, P. H. (1989). Prediction of outcome with a group version of cognitive therapy for depression. *Behavior Research and Therapy, 27,* 333-347.

Kent, G., & Gibbons, R. (1987). Self-efficacy and the control of anxious cognitions. *Journal of Behavior Therapy & Experimental Psychiatry, 18,* 33-40.

Lent, R. W., & Hackett, G. (1987). Career self-efficacy: Empirical status and future directions. *Journal of Vocational Behavior, 30,* 347-382.

Locke, E. A., & Latham, G. P. (1990). *A theory of goal setting and task performance.* Englewood Cliffs, NJ: Prentice-Hall.

Madden, T. J., Ellen, P. S., & Ajzen, I. (1992). A comparison of the theory of planned behavior and the theory of reasoned action. *Personality and Social Psychology Bulletin, 18,* 3-9.

Silver, W. S., Mitchell, T. R., & Gist, M. E. (1989). *The impact of self-efficacy on causal attributions for successful and unsuccessful performance.* Unpublished manuscript, University of Washington, Seattle.

Wheeler, K. G. (1983). Comparisons of self-efficacy and expectancy models of occupational preferences for college males and females. *Journal of Occupational Psychology, 56,* 73-78.

Wiedenfeld, S. A., O'Leary, A., Bandura, A., Brown, S., Levine, S., & Raska, K. (1990). Impact of perceived self-efficacy in coping with stressors on components of the immune system. *Journal of Personality and Social Psychology, 59,* 1082-1094.

Williams, S. L. (1992). Perceived self-efficacy and phobic disability. In R. Schwarzer (Ed.), *Self-efficacy: Thought control of action* (pp. 149-176). Washington, DC: Hemisphere.

Wood, R. E., & Bandura, A. (1989a). Impact of conceptions of ability on self-regulatory mechanisms and complex decision making. *Journal of Personality and Social Psychology, 56,* 407-415.

Wood, R. E., & Bandura, A. (1989b). Social cognitive theory of organizational management. *Academy of Management Review, 14,* 361-384.

16

IF PAST BEHAVIOR REALLY PREDICTS FUTURE, SO SHOULD BIODATA'S

Fred A. Mael
U.S. Army Research Institute

Most parents would assert that their children exhibit propensities and characteristics that distinguish them from their siblings and their peers. These may be tendencies to traits and dispositions, as well as an idiosyncratic blend of cognitive and physical strengths and weaknesses.

These parents would also assert, however, that their offspring are not totally bound or limited by their innate dispositions or abilities. Parents go to great lengths to expose their children to situations that they believe will enhance their minds, "toughen them up," increase their compassion, improve their figures, or provide them with the elusive qualities of maturity and well-roundedness. Similarly, adults embrace firmly held, though sometimes questionable, beliefs that young people are enriched by experiences such as part-time work (Stephens, 1979; Wildavsky, 1989); organized, competitive sports (Gould, Horn, & Spreemann, 1983); extracurricular clubs and hobbies (Holland & Andre, 1987; Marsh, 1992); and military service (Elig, 1984). Conversely, it is axiomatic that negative and traumatic experiences, such as sexual or parental abuse, drug use, or incarceration, can blunt even an exceptional person's potential for adaptation and successful employment and relationships.

Both of these realms—individual differences in abilities and dispositions, and differences in previous behaviors and experiences—have interested researchers and practitioners involved in personnel selection and placement. The former has generally been captured by the use of temperament or ability tests. The latter has traditionally been the domain of biographical data (biodata), and is also captured more superficially in application blanks and resumés.

In the former realm, ability tests, notably those measuring cognitive ability, have been most widely used in selection, whereas temperament tests have generally been viewed as ineffective. Recently, however, literature reviews by Kamp and Hough (1988) and meta-analyses by Barrick and Mount (1991) have demonstrated that stable and significant prediction with dispositional measures is possible with conceptually relevant job criteria. Moreover, temperament dimensions tend to be relatively independent of cognitive ability measures (McRae & Costa, 1987). Other work has demonstrated that some temperament dimensions, especially positive and negative affectivity, strongly influence job satisfaction and attitudes, regardless of job and organizational characteristics (Arvey, Bouchard, Segal, & Abraham, 1989; Rafaeli & Sutton, 1989; Staw, Bell, & Clausen, 1986). Even in prediction of leadership, meta-analysis of previous studies has spurred reconsideration of temperament variables as useful predictors of performance (Lord, De Vader, & Alliger, 1986).

Unlike temperament, biodata has been used successfully in personnel selection since the beginning of this century (Ferguson, 1962; Goldsmith, 1922). Biodata measures have fared well in meta-analytic reviews of selection instruments (Asher & Sciarrino, 1974; Ghiselli, 1973; Reilly & Chao, 1982). In spite of their long record of success, however, biodata instruments have been subjected to criticism. With the traditional method of utilizing biodata—empirical keying—weights are typically assigned to each item alternative based on its mean score on the criterion of interest, so that the continuum of values within the item is rearranged to reflect scores on the criterion. While purely empirical keying can lead to optimal correlations with criteria, it is sensitive to sample characteristics, so that on cross-validation of the key the prediction regression is vulnerable to excessive shrinkage. The method has also been derided as "dustbowl empiricism" for being atheoretical and failing to advance under-standing of antecedents of successful performance (Dunnette, 1962; Pace & Schoenfeldt, 1977).

The Rational Keying Alternative

Some researchers instead champion a rational approach in which item alternatives are assigned a priori values, based on their theorized relationships to specific constructs (cf. Mitchell & Klimoski, 1982; Stricker, 1988). Advocates of rational biodata also claim that their method will result in less shrinkage, an assertion that has received some support (Clifton, Kilcullen, Reiter-Palmon, & Mumford, 1992; Schoenfeldt, 1989), but has also been challenged (Mitchell & Klimoski, 1982). Because the rational approach is typically used to measure unitary constructs, items that can be clearly related to a single construct and then combined into homogeneous scales are preferred. In turn, this approach should generally lead to a preference for subjective, temperament-like items that can be focused on one, and only one, construct. By contrast, performance of heterogeneous, objective behaviors often draws on multiple individual characteristics, and responses to items about these behaviors are difficult to assign to the influence of a single construct.

Temperament/Biodata Confusion

The rational approach receives additional support from those who argue that distinctions between temperament and biodata are illusory (Hough, 1989). In fact, many items termed "biodata" by some researchers are indistinguishable from the types of self-report items found in temperament and attitude measures (Ashworth, 1989; Crosby, 1990). It is not uncommon to find items about internal states, opinions, and reactions to hypothetical situations in some biodata measures. Other researchers have addressed the apparent similarity between temperament and biodata items and acknowledge some degree of overlap between the domains (Anastasi, 1982; Mumford & Stokes, 1991). In some ways, the argument is tautological: When those who see no difference write biodata instruments that include temperament items, others, if not the same researchers, then proclaim that these hybrid instruments "prove" the lack of any distinguishing features. Occasionally, a test is mislabeled. For example, the Army's Assessment of Background and Life Experiences (ABLE) was originally developed from a number of temperament and biodata scales, is referred to in Project A literature as a temperament and biodata measure (Peterson et al., 1990), and bears an appropriate name for a biodata scale. However, the resultant measure is indistinguishable from other temperament scales, and is currently described only as a personality or temperament instrument (Hough, Eaton, Dunnette, Kamp, & McCloy, 1990; White, Nord, Mael, & Young, 1993).

The confusion between the two types of measures is especially problematic, however, in light of claimed advantages of biodata. For example, biodata items are presumed to achieve higher validities and be more resistant to socially desirable responding and faking than are temperament items (Asher, 1972; Asher & Sciarrino, 1974; Mumford & Owens, 1987; Telenson, Alexander, & Barrett, 1983). However, this may be true only of certain types of biodata, such as objective and verifiable items, which are most dissimilar to temperament items. Conversely, the claimed cross-cultural stability of biodata (Brown, Corrigan, Stout, & Dalessio, 1987; Laurent, 1970) is less likely with items measuring objective background behaviors that are likely to be rewarded and reinforced differentially in different societies.

Hybrid Approaches to Rational Biodata

In order to avoid this problem, some researchers have tried to be more selective in the types of items they include in their biodata inventories, while still trying to comprehend the items in terms of a priori constructs. Two ongoing research programs of this type are being conducted at the U.S. Army Research Institute.

In one (Kilcullen, White, Mumford, & Mack, 1993; White & Kilcullen, 1992), both subjective and objective items are written to capture existing temperament constructs. While the approach is predominantly rational, in that virtually all items are written with a priori values, discretion is used to favor items that relate to overt behaviors, and minimize the use of items purporting to measure internal states or attitudes.

The other is more a quasi-rational approach (Mael & Hirsch, 1993; Mael & Schwartz, 1991; Mael & White, 1994), designed to be used with so-called "hard" items, items that are historical, objective, and in many cases verifiable, as defined in a review of biodata item attributes by Mael (1991). Recent empirical research confirms that adhering to these attributes can result in significantly less socially desirable responding (Becker & Colquitt, 1992; Mael & Hirsch, 1993; McManus & Masztal, 1993). With this approach, items are empirically keyed directly to temperament scales. Those items that are related to the temperament scale measuring a specific construct form a biodata analog to that scale. From that point on, the biodata analog is used as a rational scale with a priori values. This approach is rational in the sense that items are not keyed directly to the criterion, and are focused on measurement of a priori constructs, yet empirical in the sense that item values were generated, at least initially, by their empirical relationship to an external referent, in this case temperament scales. Hence, the term *quasi-rational*.

The goal of both of these approaches has been to determine if biodata scales could parallel individual temperament scales in their relationships to criteria. Both approaches have proved successful, in terms of both parallel validities and lower correlations with a measure of social desirability (Kilcullen et al., 1993; Mael & Hirsch, 1993). What is hopefully gained over temperament items is greater response accuracy, whereas interpretability is improved relative to empirically keyed biodata.

One may argue, however, that these approaches achieve gains in the measurement of temperament or other constructs, and are primarily a more foolproof way of getting at dispositional constructs. All "understanding" is in terms of pre-ordained psychological concepts. What is not enhanced is the understanding of biodata, in the sense of the significance of the wide range of behaviors and experiences reflected in biodata. As argued by T. Mitchell, to use biodata only to measure personality traits is to "take advantage of only a small part of the predictive power of biodata technology, as it has been used for the past 80 years" (1990, p. 3).

Behaviors and Experiences Matter

The argument of this paper is that the effects of previous behaviors and experiences matter. They matter to the people who try to avail themselves and their loved ones of positive experiences. They matter to the people who try to prevent traumatic events, and to those who try to counsel or rehabilitate the victims of those events. They matter to the people who decide whether to fund training programs, recreational facilities, and other sources of potentially beneficial experiences. They matter to judges and juries who assess financial penalties for harming others, based on perceived damage to future functioning. Finally, they most certainly matter to those who select others for jobs. Should a high school diploma or college degree be a prerequisite for a job? Should a recruit or applicant have to be a certain age, gender, or height? Should adultery, a prison record, acts of sexual harassment, or membership in a racist organization be sufficient basis to reject someone for an important position? Answers to all these questions demand knowledge derived from the traditional realm of biodata. Biodata research and practice has always started from the premise that a person's experiences matter, that they are capable of imprinting on the future, and can thereby predict future behavior. The rational approach, although providing useful information about temperament constructs, homogenizes behaviors, so that one remains unaware of how specific behaviors or experiences are linked to desired outcomes, and to what extent. One only knows that it is good to *be* a certain way, not the paths by which one could become that sort of person.

Undoubtedly, it is possible for the same item to be utilized with either a rational (construct-oriented) or a behavior-oriented approach. However, interpretation of the item will differ drastically. Even when an actual behavior is sampled in a rational scale or a temperament measure, the behavior is viewed as a tangible manifestation of a preexisting disposition. According to the currently ascendant interactionist perspective in personality theory, temperament items presume temporal, if not cross-situational, consistency (Kenrick & Funder, 1988; Pervin, 1985). A relatively fixed dispositional orientation is presumed to influence the behaviors sampled.

From the traditional, behavioral biodata perspective, however, behaviors and experiences are not only indications of underlying dispositions in some cases but, more important, shapers of subsequent behavior and potential modifiers of future dispositional responses (Mael, 1991). Use of biodata items in their own right, rather than intermediate criteria of temperament, is based on the assumption that behaviors and experiences are capable of shaping or even overriding initial dispositions.

BIODATA: INTERPRETABILITY AND SHRINKAGE

What needs to be resolved, however, are the two most consistent arguments against the empirical, behavior-oriented approaches: lack of interpretability and instability, as reflected in shrinkage. Regarding interpretability, two possible solutions have been proposed in recent years: subgrouping and rainforest empiricism.

Subgrouping

One example of a technique that retains the behavioral flavor of biodata information while imparting meaning to the data is subgrouping (Mumford & Owens, 1987; Owens, 1976), an approach Fleishman (1988) labeled a novel and important trend in personnel selection research. The subgrouping method draws on Toops' (1959) observation that "the most profound remark a psychologist can make is to say, 'A kind of people acts alike, thinks alike, even tends to emote alike'" (1959, p. 191). The subgrouping method, analogous to lifestyle segmentation in market research (Mitchell, 1983; Plummer, 1974), is used to identify clusters of intact variables that together form a subgrouping of individuals. Each subgroup is comprised of members with specific characteristics and likely developmental patterns (Fleishman, 1988). The defining characteristics may be educational level, religious preference, or other complex variables, as well as dispositions. The subgrouping method enables one to acknowledge that variables such as occupation, sports team membership, or preferred hobbies are themselves multifaceted syndromes, not easily captured by a single explanatory construct. Rather than forcing these types of variables to measure only one construct (i.e. aggressiveness, dependability, dominance), the full range of tendencies associated with that aspect of social identity is retained. Thus, subgrouping is a more naturalistic attempt to combine behaviors and events, which better reflects the conceptual view of biodata as a description of experiences that may have shaped subsequent behavior.

Rainforest Empiricism

Mael (1991; Mael & Hirsch, 1993) has advocated an alternative to the so-called "dustbowl empiricism," which is meant to evoke a dry, sterile image. Instead, he has proposed a "rainforest empiricism" approach, which has short- and long-term components. In the short term, it represents a variation of empirical keying, in which theoretical discretion is used in the choice and keying of the items, leading to a more conservative but hopefully more meaningful derivation key. In the long term, empirically keyed items would be tracked over many iterations, until stable patterns of relationships could be ascertained. This tracking would be done in tandem with a review of the relevant literature for each item, which may reside in other psychological specialties and in other disciplines.

Moreover, he has proposed a clearinghouse for documentation of objective biodata items, complete with previous results and optimal keyings of items measuring behaviors. The clearinghouse would also be the repository of meta-analyses of consistently used items from previous biodata studies, as well as reviews of pertinent literature from other domains. At each step, an attempt would be made to follow Pace and Schoenfeldt's advice to "insure that the 'hand of reason' has been injected into the process" (1977, p. 165). The idea behind this approach is not new; it was advocated in essence by researchers such as Cureton, Owens, and Otis, at a 1965 biodata conference (Henry, 1965, p. 5). Moreover, the short-term component of the approach is implicitly endorsed in practice by numerous experienced biodata researchers.

The rainforest approach, especially through the vehicle of the proposed clearinghouse, could provide the following benefits (Mael, 1991). First, empirical keys shown to be stable across numerous studies could be used, so that new users of the items could avoid idiosyncratic empirical keying of their data. This tracking would reduce the chance of shrinkage upon cross-validation. Second, documentation of item validity and directionality could provide support for the legal job-relatedness of these types of items. Third, documentation, together with theoretical rationales, could also help demonstrate to skeptical managers the logic behind the validity and job-relatedness of subtle items. Fourth, documentation of objective experiences could allow psychologists to provide research-based information to career counselors, educators, and parents regarding what types of developmental activities or environmental conditions could prove most beneficial to those considering specific careers.

Perhaps the most important gain would be to reestablish the respectability of the empirical approach to biodata. The notion of a dry and sterile "dustbowl" empiricism could be replaced with an enlightened "rainforest" empiricism. Rainforest empiricism would use the cumulative efforts of multiple iterations of empirical keying; theory development based on the full richness of a behavior or experience, rather than a single a priori construct; and the findings of other disciplines, to develop a solid foundation of knowledge.

Shrinkage

The other consistent criticism of traditional, empirically keyed biodata has been that it yields unstable scoring keys that are prone to shrinkage. However, a few points should be made. First, in the previous reviews of biodata in which biodata compared favorably to other predictors, it was the cross-validities of empirically keyed instruments that were utilized (Asher & Sciarrino, 1974; Ghiselli, 1973; Reilly & Chao, 1982). Rothstein, Schmidt, Erwin, Owens, and Sparks (1990) also demonstrated that stability may be even higher than previously thought.

Second, shrinkage problems can be minimized by using large samples and relatively long scales (Devlin, Abrahams, & Edwards, 1992). In fact, some of the significant threats to stable cross-validities, such as small sample sizes, range restriction, and poorly chosen item pools (Schwab & Oliver, 1974), are "equally if not more troublesome for the rational approach" (Mitchell & Klimoski, 1982, p. 417). Third, split-sample cross-validation involves a loss of information that may mask the true stability of the instrument (Picard & Cook, 1984). In fact, Mary Tenopyr, in an unpublished manuscript (1993), has advocated adapting the single-sample cross-validation techniques of Browne and Cudeck (1989) to biodata in order to ameliorate this problem.

Finally, one must differentiate between short-term and long-term shrinkage. In the former, cross-validities may be found to be unstable even when using a split-sample technique, or two concurrent samples. In the latter, keys may retain their stability for a few years, only to decay at a later date.

These threats to stability are in no way alike. Evidence of short-term instability indicates that the relationship of the behavior to the criterion may in fact be spurious, and the obtained validities dependent on chance. If common artifactual errors have been ruled out (Schmidt & Hunter, 1977), and other variables in the same setting retain their stability across the samples or subsamples, one would be concerned that the underlying behavior does not, and did not, have a consistent relationship with the criterion. There is no basis, however, to dismiss all objective biodata items as being inherently unstable. Some objective biodata items have provided excellent, stable prediction, such as the relationship between educational attainment and military attrition (LaRocco, Pugh, & Gunderson, 1977; White, Nord, Mael, & Young, 1993). The type of clearinghouse mentioned previously could provide a mechanism for differentiating between stable and nonstable behaviors and items.

Studies of long-term stability in biodata have also pointed out the possibility of decaying validity over time and the need for rekeying (Thayer, 1977; Wernimont, 1962), although some studies have shown that biodata structures do retain much of their validity at a later date (Brown, 1978; Lautenschlager & Shaffer, 1987). Long-term instability, however, is not necessarily indicative of poor items. Rather, it is often indicative of changes in cultural values, lifestyles, and job or organizational requirements (Cascio, 1991). As long as society, jobs, and the work force continue to change (Johnston & Packer, 1987; Kalleberg & Loscosco, 1983), relationships between items and criteria will also change. As psychological and biodata research acknowledges that concurrent cultures and societies differ from each other (Hinrichs, Haanpera, & Sonkin, 1976; Hofstede, 1993; Maurice & Sellier, 1979), it would also acknowledge that a culture and its work subcultures could change across eras. Thus, even the type of clearinghouse proposed previously would not put an end to the need for periodic rekeying and updating.

Another threat to long-term stability is the possibility of response key compromise (Brown, 1978), in which the "correct" answers become known to test-takers or their advisors, such as recruiters. It has been argued elsewhere (Mael, 1991) that the proposed clearinghouse would not in itself lead to this type of compromise. Moreover, Clinton Walker (personal communication) suggested that a very large pool of items, such as proposed with the clearinghouse concept, would facilitate development of equivalent forms that could be generated on-line, and would prevent items from being overexposed.

Finally, research on subgrouping stability has shown that over time, the members of homogeneous subgroups may take divergent paths (Davis, 1984), and that subgroupings need periodic updating (Owens & Schoenfeldt, 1979). In other words, the constellation of behaviors and experiences that defines similarity of profiles at one stage of life does not inhibit the influence of experiences at later stages, nor does it prevent cultural or economic shifts from making other aspects of a person's behavior more salient in defining their similarity with others. Anyone who ever outgrew old friends or jobs, changed political or religious affiliation, or otherwise reconsidered the path of his or her life will attest to the verity of this idea. Although these changes may be individualistic and idiosyncratic, some may be better understood in the context of life-cycle development trajectories.

UNIQUE CONCERNS OF A BEHAVIOR-ORIENTED APPROACH

In the realm of personnel selection, certain philosophical assumptions or practices that are suitable for or applicable to the use of both abilities and temperaments as predictors may be questionable when applied to behavior-oriented biodata. Some of these assumptions, and their implications for use of biodata, are discussed next.

Abilities and Temperaments Are Job Necessities

Optimally, what is sought from measures of abilities and traits are defining necessities of the job, in which insufficiencies on that skill, ability, or trait will make performance difficult, if not impossible. One tries to identify abilities that are essential precursors to any motivation to succeed, and stable dispositions that would be more enduring than any situational imperative to expend effort. For example, no matter how motivated, a slow or overweight person will be presumed incapable of performing well as a professional basketball or hockey player, and a person with an IQ of 75 will not be accepted into training as a nuclear physicist. Similarly, for those who endorse use of temperaments in selection, a person who scores low on certain desirable traits, or high on certain pathological ones, is considered to have a difficult time of overcoming his or her predispositions, regardless of whether they were innate or learned. If ability or temperament items are allowed to compensate for each other, it is usually because they are considered to be measures of the same construct.

When thinking about the experiences and behaviors that underlie good biodata items, however, this tenet is not so readily apparent. A positive earlier experience that predicts future behavior is generally not the only way to achieve success. This is for two reasons. First, biodata allows for the principle of equipollence (T. Mitchell, 1990), meaning that there is more than one way to reach a desired outcome. For example, it may become known that either experience or additional training could prepare a person for a job, or that a degree in either of two disciplines would be equally suitable preparation for an occupation.

Second, a researcher who uses biodata need not embrace a deterministic or fatalistic world view. Rather, people may be presumed to have a degree of free will to compensate for previous misfortunes, or to squander the gains they accrued through previous experiences. People from broken homes, poor schools, and victims of various abuses sometimes rise above their surroundings. Conversely, sometimes even highly credentialed scholars, decorated soldiers, and members of renowned families manage to spend their lives in mediocrity or disgrace. Thus, much of what is termed "error variance" in biodata, although inefficient for personnel selection, should be a source of comfort for all people. In a society not dominated by rigid caste systems, one in which people are sometimes given a second chance, and in which people cannot rest on their laurels indefinitely, none need be bound to the path set by their earlier circumstances and actions. Obviously, though, most people do show behavioral consistency, as demonstrated by the predictive validity of biodata. When we take pleasure in reading of those who have triumphed against all odds, it is precisely because those odds—the predictability of their biodata, so to speak—are usually correct.

Necessary Abilities and Dispositions Can Be Seen on the Job. Because incumbents often demonstrate their abilities while involved in their jobs, those conducting job analysis seek to elicit job descriptions and critical incidents that reflect the knowledge, skills, and abilities needed for the job. Job incumbents are also asked by job analysts to identify and venture opinions, based on on-the-job observations, as to which temperaments and dispositions are exhibited by and required from those who succeed at that job.

This is often not true about objective biodata. If incumbents are now successful because of previous experiences with sports, hobbies, friends, or anything not directly job relevant, these sources of success will not be visible on the job, and may not even be the common knowledge of peers and subject matter experts. Thus, when attempting a job analysis as a prelude to developing criterion measures or predictors, great care needs to be taken to avoid completely ignoring the role of objective behavioral biodata. New methods for eliciting such information, which would not capitalize on egocentric or self-serving recollections of job incumbents, need to be developed. A more restricted group of subject matter experts, those familiar with the backgrounds of large numbers of successful incumbents, may need to be consulted. In lieu of novel approaches, when developing objective biodata predictors, the first round of efforts will almost always have to fall back on some degree of accumulated knowledge and educated guesswork.

Ability and Temperament Differences Are Fair

It is not considered unfair by most people that brighter people get better academic placements, that only attractive people get modeling jobs, and that people with more musical talent get greater opportunities to enhance their skills, even if they did not "earn" their talents. Job applicants are penalized for deficient cognitive aptitude and education, even if these result from conditions beyond their control.   Similarly, people are held responsible for their dispositional failings, even if these can be traced to genetics or poor upbringing, rather than their own desire to be lazy or obnoxious.

In the realm of biodata, however, some researchers are convinced that all behaviors to be sampled must be controllable, and the results of the person's life choices, thus excluding anything that happened to the person (Stricker, 1988). As the biodata instruments of numerous researchers include both controllable and noncontrollable items (England, 1971; Glennon, Albright, & Owens, 1966; Mumford & Stokes, 1991; Richardson, Bellows, Henry, & Co., 1985; Russell, Mattson, Devlin, & Atwater, 1990), this view is hardly unanimous. From the perspective that all life events have the potential to shape and affect later behavior, there is no difference between consciously undertaken experiences and those that have been components of the person's environment. Just as a decision to join ROTC or study chemistry may lead a person in a behavioral direction, the climate in a person's home and community could also affect subsequent behavior. Moreover, even seemingly optional behaviors, such as the decision to smoke or the amount of time spent studying, are partially shaped by noncontrollable influences.

Stricker (1988) also considered items dealing with skills and experiences not equally accessible to all applicants, such as tractor-driving ability or playing varsity football, as unfair. Some advocate muting the advantages of nonequal access through a strategy of matching items, such as pairing softball (for women) with football (for men). Unfortunately, the gain is often illusory, for although one subgroup (female athletes) is compensated, others (short males, students in schools without varsity teams) are not.

The dispute over the appropriateness of including nonequally accessible behaviors would appear to stem from differing perspectives on biodata. Stricker, who favored a rational, temperament-based approach (1988), treated biodata items as indices of previously existing characteristics. Thus, if some persons are excluded from an activity, it would be unfair to infer from their nonparticipation that they lack a certain quality that is utilized in the activity. However, from the behavioral perspective advanced previously, participation in an activity is itself a potential source of future behavior, in that the participant begins to identify with role requirements, adopt prototypical behavioral patterns, and possibly gain expertise in fulfilling the role. Thus, it is irrelevant if Person A had unfair access to a role, and Person B did not; what matters is that the former has been enriched (or harmed) by exposure to a specific experience or referent group, whereas the latter has not.

The two perspectives can be illustrated by Stricker's own example of football team captaincy. Stricker argued that because some cannot even be on the team, (because of size, gender, or size of school), they could certainly not compete for the role of captain. If one is to take being football team captain as merely an expression of some existing quality (e.g., dominance, leadership potential, charisma), then Stricker would be correct. The person who could not be on the team and was thereby assessed as lacking in the underlying construct would be unfairly penalized. However, the real intent of the item may be that the captain experienced a leadership role and took on characteristics of football team captains and of persons who must motivate or dominate. If so, the captain had enriched his social identity or expertise in this realm in a way that the noncaptain or nonplayer had not.

While the goal of fairness expressed by Stricker (1988) is admirable, definitions of "fairness" and "ethical" vary widely with one's philosophical bent (Hunter & Schmidt, 1976). In addition, there are organizational and sector (public versus private) differences in the relative value placed on efficiency versus fairness (Wilson, 1989). However, given that ability and temperament predictors are not limited to wholly controllable attributes, it is valid to ask why biodata items are held to a different and subjectively higher standard. Were one to dissect a person's resumé and account for how they managed to attend prestigious schools, attain certain employment, or even be a co-author on the work of senior researchers, similar issues of unfairness would also need to be raised. These issues of fairness and inconsistent application of fairness guidelines are discussed in detail next.

Misfortunes, Failings, and Biodata. In psychological disciplines other than personnel psychology, behaviors and life experiences that impair short- or long-term adaptive functioning are accorded much attention. Extensive research has looked at a host of these behaviors and experiences, such as alcoholism (Cotton, 1979; Kurtz, Googins, & Howard, 1984), adolescent pregnancy (Caldas, 1993), and postpartum depression (Albright, 1993). Often, numerous deleterious effects, including anxiety, mood swings, lack of motivation, and inability to concentrate on and perform the types of tasks required by jobs, are noted. In some cases, explicit connections are made between the maladaptive experience or experiential pattern and the inability to work competently or retain a steady job. Other misfortunes, such as drug addiction, rape, physical or sexual harassment, miscarriage, getting robbed or mugged, death of parents or spouse, divorce, or spousal abuse, are presumed to hamper a person's ability to work, and case studies will often note the loss of a job or series of jobs as part of the person's travails. When these misfortunes result from criminal acts, the victim's lawyer will often invoke work-related disruptions as part of the injury inflicted by the accused perpetrator, in order to gain a larger financial settlement for his or her client.

Yet, in the realm of biodata, these experiences and their implications for personnel selection are treated with silence. Use of such items is considered unethical, as if one is blaming victims for their misfortunes. Thus, no matter how statistically likely, it is implicitly forbidden to anticipate the above-average probability of work failure by these persons, and make personnel decisions based on this knowledge. That an employer is proscribed from using this type of item as a go/no go hurdle is eminently reasonable; after all, no misfortune of this type, unless resulting in physical or cognitive damage that makes work impossible, can be said to absolutely prevent appropriate work behavior. However, the same objection is even lodged against using this type of item as part of a questionnaire, in which other items can compensate and demonstrate the person's overall likelihood of success. The question is why.

Another question is why this stance is not inconsistent with accepted usage of other predictors. When we use temperament scales, we ask job candidates to provide self-incriminating evidence about their personalities. We encourage them to admit that they lack drive, are often anxious, do not wish to be dominant, and so forth—and we will refuse them employment based on this information. If they try to "fake good," in order to give themselves the opportunity to overcome their dispositional limitations, we go to great lengths to combat this strategy with warnings, faking detectors, and the like. Similarly, we will refuse people employment based on substandard scores on aptitude, dexterity, and other tests, even though we don't know what misfortunes led to their status. We are disinterested about whether we are actually punishing them yet again for prenatal or postnatal malnutrition, parental substance abuse, an impoverished school district, or the effects of local environmental toxins. Yet, we refuse even to consider the explicit effects of behavioral or experiential misfortunes from a biodata perspective. One may conclude that although using explicit negative experiences is in bad taste, focusing on lowered abilities or poor dispositions that result from those behaviors allows the tester to cover his or her tracks and retain the veneer of compassion.

One might respond that the issue is simply invasion of privacy. This, however, does not resolve the issue. Definitions of privacy from a legal perspective are in flux, and also have situationally dependent parameters (Arnold, 1990; Van Rijn, 1980). Conceptually, the concept of "privacy" still remains murky in a selection context (Mael, 1991), and requires additional clarification.

It would be facile simply to advocate use of such items. There is an understandable desire to avoid doing what would be perceived as punishing victims even more, by denying them employment on top of the other pain they have endured. Many (though not all) would argue that organizations should forego some degree of predictive validity in order to spare applicants additional pain. The question then becomes whether a "false positive," hiring a person unlikely to succeed, is bad for the employee as well as the organization. Perhaps being fair to someone by ignoring the problems he or she brings to the job is cruel in the sense that the employee and his or her leader, co-workers, and subordinates must all "make do" with a potentially intolerable situation. For example, if the selection system ignores the stressors that may have made a worker prone to depression and hysteria, the problem will be placed in the laps of co-workers, who may not have the time, leeway, or resources to be sympathetic or cover for this employee.

Clearly, the answer is not to advocate that all such experiences be used in testing, and no doubt such a stance would be pilloried in the media. Rather, the point is that ultimately, consistent values and policies need to be explicated. Consistent principles need to guide when compassion is to be extended, in order to make employment fair and when, conversely, all pertinent information will be used, to save both employee and employer from the aggravation of a failed work relationship. Perhaps a person identified as potentially unable to work regularly needs to enter the job with external sources of counseling or social support in place. These issues go to the heart of what a society as a whole is willing to make employers do to compensate for the shortcomings of potential employees.

All three aforementioned subjects—using biodata items not controlled by the person (e.g., birth order, size of hometown), using items that capture misfortunes and failings, and invasion of privacy—merit further collaborative deliberation by respected members of the profession, as well as by public policy specialists. In the interim, perhaps one could make the following initial distinctions regarding the inappropriateness of items. These guidelines make no pretense of reflecting current legal opinion, but are simply a starting point for classifying what might be termed "unfair" or "unethical"!

1. Some item topics may conjure up such negative feelings, or may be so personal, that no one, save for purposes of national security, should ever be required to reveal them, no matter how well the answers were to be safeguarded. Examples may be rape and sexual and spousal abuse.

2. Some items may not inherently draw the same resistance, but may be objected to under the following two conditions: One, if the item could possibly be used as a stand-alone hurdle. Even if not intended as such, if an interviewer or decision maker with relevant prejudices or preconceived notions could disqualify the applicant solely on the basis of his or her response, then the item should be treated as invasive and self-incriminating. Two, if the item's response could become known to anyone in the organization who was in a position to disseminate the information to co-workers. Thus, if the item-level responses were to be seen only by a personnel researcher, who would forward the information to decision makers in the form of a total scale score, concerns could be alleviated, and the items could conceivably be used. Items in this category

may include: number of dependents, religious participation (not religious beliefs), marriage and divorce history, and familial substance abuse. Logically, temperament scales dealing with personal failings at either the item or scale level should be treated with the same stringency.

3. Those items that are inoffensive, even though their responses were not under the control of the applicant, should not have to be excluded from use. They are not excluded from use in nonbiodata measures, nor from many biodata instruments, as discussed previously. Examples would be birth order, number of siblings, and size of hometown. The burden of argument lies upon those who call these items unfair and/or unethical.

SUMMARY

A number of researchers have heralded the arrival of rational keying as the salvation of biodata, rescuing it from the status of dustbowl empiricism. This exclusive perspective unfortunately repudiates much of what biodata has had to offer for most of this century. Whether rationally keyed construct measures, utilizing primarily subjective items, should be called biodata (McManus & Masztal, 1993), is not the issue; the term *biodata* is neither copyrighted nor a concept that requires ideological purity. What is also acknowledged is that rational keys are a methodologically sounder way of measuring temperament or other constructs, and as such make a significant and valued contribution. However, those who advocate using only rational keys, and decry the use of objective items in their own right, minimize the significance of biodata's traditional focus: the importance of life experiences and behavior on future actions. By homogenizing all behaviors as mere manifestations of pre-existing attributes, true understanding is obscured rather than gained. The message of traditional biodata is that actions, in their own right, matter.

Unavoidably, taking behaviors seriously raises disturbing questions about personnel selection, highlighting conflicts among valued principles such as free will, fairness, equality in a society of haves and have-nots, compassion, and productivity. Optimally, these are issues that the field as a whole would be emboldened to discuss, rather than hiding behind safe and familiar constructs. Corporations, special interest groups, and the courts all operate from value systems; what are the values driving the practice of personnel selection?

In conclusion, there is much to be done in understanding if the activities that people undertake, for themselves and their offspring, really effect changes in subsequent work performance. If we really believe that the past predicts the future, then we should look to biodata's previous accomplishments and enhance them. Biodata's future can best be built on its illustrious past.

REFERENCES

Albright, A. (1993). Postpartum depression: An overview. *Journal of Counseling and Development, 71*, 316-320.

Anastasi, A. (1982). *Psychological Testing* (5th ed.). New York: Macmillan.

Arnold, D. W. (1990). Invasion of privacy: A rising concern for personnel psychologists. *The Industrial/Organizational Psychologist, 28*, 37-39.

Arvey, R. D., Bouchard, T. J., Jr., Segal, N. L., & Abraham, L. M. (1989). Job satisfaction: Environmental and genetic components. *Journal of Applied Psychology, 74*, 187-192.

Asher, J. J. (1972). The biographical item: Can it be improved? *Personnel Psychology, 25*, 251-269.

Asher, J. J., & Sciarrino, J. A. (1974). Realistic work sample tests: A review. *Personnel Psychology, 27*, 519-533.

Ashworth, S. D. (1989). The distinctions that I/O psychologists have made between biodata and personality measurement are no longer meaningful. In T. W. Mitchell (Chair), *Biodata vs. personality: The same or different classes of individual differences?* Symposium presented at the annual meeting of the Society for Industrial and Organizational Psychology, Boston.

Barrick, M. R., & Mount, M. K. (1991). The big five personality dimensions and job performance: A meta-analysis. *Personnel Psychology, 44*, 1-26.

Becker, T., & Colquitt, A. (1992). Potential versus actual faking of a biodata form: An analysis along several dimensions of item type. *Personnel Psychology, 45*, 389-406.

Brown, S. H. (1978). Long-term validity of a personal history item scoring procedure. *Journal of Applied Psychology, 63*, 673-676.

Brown, S. H., Corrigan, J. E., Stout, J. D., & Dalessio, A. T. (1987). In S. D. Ashworth (Chair), *The use of biodata in the 80s and beyond.* Symposium presented at the 95th Annual Convention of the American Psychological Association, New York.

Browne, M. W., & Cudeck, R. (1989). Single sample cross-validation indices for covariation structures. *Multivariate Behavioral Research, 24*, 445-455.

Caldas, S. J. (1993). Current theoretical perspectives on adolescent pregnancy and childbearing in the U.S. *Journal of Adolescent Research, 8*, 4-20.

Cascio, W. F. (1991). *Applied psychology in personnel management* (4th ed.). Englewood Cliffs, NJ: Prentice-Hall.

Clifton, T. C., Kilcullen, R. N., Reiter-Palmon, R., & Mumford, M. D. (1992, August). *Comparing different background data scaling procedures using triple cross-validation.* Paper presented at the annual meeting of the American Psychological Association, Washington, DC.

Cotton, N. S. (1979). The familial incidence of alcoholism. *Journal of Studies on Alcohol, 40*, 89-116.

Crosby, M. M. (1990). *Social desirability and biodata: Predicting sales success.* Paper presented at the annual conference of the Society for Industrial and Organizational Psychology, Miami Beach.

Davis, K. R. (1984). A longitudinal analysis of biographical subgroups using Owens' developmental-integrative model. *Personnel Psychology, 37*, 1-14.

Devlin, S. E., Abrahams, N. M., & Edwards, J. E. (1992). Empirical keying of biographical data: Cross-validity as a function of scaling procedure and sample size. *Military Psychology, 4*, 119-136.

Dunnette, M. D. (1962). Personnel management. *Annual Review of Psychology, 13*, 285-314.

Elig, T. W. (1984). *The 1982 Department of the Army survey of personnel entering the Army* (Research Product 84-02). Alexandria, VA: U.S. Army Research Institute.

England, G. W. (1971). *Development and use of weighted application blanks* (rev. ed.). Minneapolis: University of Minnesota, Industrial Relations Center.

Ferguson, L. W. (1962). *The heritage of industrial psychology.* Hartford, CT: Author.

Fleishman, E. A. (1988). Some new frontiers in personnel selection research. *Personnel Psychology, 41*, 679-702.

Ghiselli, E. E. (1973). The validity of aptitude tests in personnel selection. *Personnel Psychology, 26*, 461-477.

Glennon, J. R., Albright, L. E., & Owens, W. A. (1966). *A catalog of life history items.* Greensboro, NC: Creativity Research Institute of the Richardson Foundation.

Goldsmith, D. B. (1922). The use of the personal history blank as a salesmanship test. *Journal of Applied Psychology, 6*, 149-155.

Gould, D., Horn, T., & Spreemann, J. (1983). Competitive anxiety in junior elite wrestlers. *Journal of Sport Psychology, 5*, 58-78.

Henry, E. R. (1965). *Research conference on the use of autobiographical data as psychological predictors.* Greensboro, NC: The Richardson Foundation.

Hinrichs, E. E., Haanpera, S., & Sonkin, L. (1976). Validity of a biographical information blank across national boundaries. *Personnel Psychology, 29*, 417-421.

Hofstede, G. (1993). Cultural constraints in management theories. *Academy of Management Executive, 7*, 81-94.

Holland, A., & Andre, T. (1987). Participation in extracurricular activities in secondary school. What is known, what needs to be known? *Review of Educational Research, 57*, 437-466.

Hough, L. M. (1989). Biodata and the measurement of individual differences. In T. W. Mitchell (Chair), *Biodata vs. personality: The same or different classes of individual differences?* Symposium presented at the annual meeting of the Society for Industrial and Organizational Psychology, Boston.

Hough, L. M., Eaton, N. K., Dunnette, M. D., Kamp, J. D. & McCloy, R. A. (1990). Criterion-related validities of personality constructs and the effect of response distortion on those validities. *Journal of Applied Psychology, 75*, 581-595.

Hunter, J. E., & Schmidt, F. L. (1976). Critical analysis of the statistical and ethical implications of various definitions of test bias. *Psychological Bulletin, 83*, 1053-1059.

Johnston, W. B., & Packer, A. E. (1987). *Workforce 2000: Work and workers for the 21st century.* Indianapolis: Hudson Institute.

Kalleberg, A., & Loscosco, K. A. (1983). Aging values and rewards: Explaining age differences in job satisfaction. *American Sociological Review, 48*, 78-90.

Kamp, J. D. & Hough, L. M. (1988). Utility of temperament for predicting job performance. In L.M. Hough (Ed.), *Literature review: Utility of temperament, biodata, and interest assessment for predicting job performance* (Research Note 88-02). Alexandria, VA: U.S. Army Research Institute.

Kenrick, D. T. & Funder, D. C. (1988). Profiting from controversy: Lessons from the person-situation debate. *American Psychologist, 43*, 23-34.

Kilcullen, R. N., White, L. A., Mumford, M. D., & Mack, H. (1993). *Assessing the construct validity of rational biodata scales.* Unpublished manuscript.

Kurtz, N. R., Googins, B., & Howard, W. C. (1984). Measuring the success of occupational alcoholism programs. *Journal of Studies on Alcohol, 45*, 33-45.

LaRocco, J. M., Pugh, W. M., & Gunderson, E. K. (1977). Identifying determinants of retention decisions. *Personnel Psychology, 30*, 841-852.

Laurent, H. (1970). Cross-cultural cross-validation of empirically validated tests. *Journal of Applied Psychology, 54*, 417-423.

Lautenschlager, G. J., & Shaffer, G. S. (1987). Reexamining the component stability of Owens's biographical questionnaire. *Journal of Applied Psychology, 72*, 149-152.

Lord, R. G., De Vader, C. L., & Alliger, G. M. (1986). A meta-analysis of the relation between personality traits and leadership perceptions: An application of validity generalization procedures. *Journal of Applied Psychology, 71*, 402-410.

Mael, F. A. (1991). A conceptual rationale for the domain and attributes of biodata items. *Personnel Psychology, 44,* 763-792.

Mael, F. A., & Hirsch, A. C. (1993). Rainforest empiricism and quasi-rationality: Two approaches to objective biodata. *Personnel Psychology, 46,* 719-738.

Mael, F. A., & Schwartz, A. C. (1991). *Capturing adaptability constructs with objective biodata* (Technical Report 939). Alexandria, VA: U.S. Army Research Institute.

Mael, F. A., & White, L. A. (1994). Motivated to lead: Dispositional and biographical antecedents of leadership performance. In H. O'Neil & M. Drillings (Eds.), *Motivation: Research and theory.* Hillsdale, NJ: Lawrence Erlbaum Associates.

Marsh, H. W. (1992). Extracurricular activities: Beneficial extension of the traditional curriculum or subversion of academic goals? *Journal of Educational Psychology, 84,* 533-562.

Maurice, M., & Sellier, F. (1979). Societal analysis of industrial relations: A comparison between France and West Germany. *British Journal of Industrial Relations, 17,* 322-336.

McCrae, R. R., & Costa, P. T., Jr. (1987). Validation of the five-factor model of personality across instruments and observers. *Journal of Personality and Social Psychology, 49,* 710-721.

McManus, M. A., & Masztal, J. J. (1993). *Attributes of biodata: Relationships to validity and socially desirable responding.* Paper presented at the annual meeting of the Society for Industrial and Organizational Psychology, San Francisco.

Mitchell, A. (1983). *Nine American lifestyles: Who we are and where are we going.* New York: Macmillan.

Mitchell, T. W. (1990). Can biodata predict personality? In M. G. Aamodt (Chair), *What does biodata predict?* Paper presented at the annual meeting of the International Personnel Management Association Assessment Council, San Diego.

Mitchell, T.W., & Klimoski, R.J. (1982). Is it rational to be empirical? A test of methods for scoring biographical data. *Journal of Applied Psychology, 67,* 411-418.

Mumford, M. D., & Owens, W. A. (1987). Methodology review: Principles, procedures, and findings in the application of background data measures. *Applied Psychological Measurement, 11,* 1-31.

Mumford, M. D., & Stokes, G. S. (1991). Developmental determinants of individual action: Theory and practice in the application of background data. In M.D. Dunnette (Ed.), *The handbook of industrial and organizational psychology* (2nd ed.). Orlando: Consulting Psychologists Press.

Owens, W. A. (1976). Background data. In M. D. Dunnette (Ed.), *Handbook of industrial psychology.* New York: Rand McNally.

Owens, W. A., & Schoenfeldt, L. F. (1979). Toward a classification of persons. *Journal of Applied Psychology, 65,* 569-607.

Pace, L. A., & Schoenfeldt, L. F. (1977). Legal concerns in the use of weighted application blanks. *Personnel Psychology, 30,* 159-166.

Pervin, L. A. (1985). Personality: Current controversies, issues, and directions. *Annual Review of Psychology, 36,* 83-114.

Peterson, N. G., Hough, L. M., Dunnette, M. D., Rosse, R. L., Houston, J. S., Toquam, J. L., & Wing, H. (1990). Project A: Specification of the predictor domain and development of the new selection/classification tests. *Personnel Psychology, 43,* 247-276.

Picard, R. R., & Cook, R. D. (1984). Cross-validation of regression models. *Journal of the American Statistical Association, 79,* 575-583.

Plummer, J. T. (1974). The concept and application of life style segmentation. *Journal of Marketing, 38,* 34.

Rafaeli, A., & Sutton, R. I. (1989). The expression of emotion in organizational life. In L. L. Cummings & B. M. Staw (Eds.), *Research in Organizational Behavior, 11,* 1-42.

Reilly, R. R., & Chao, G. T. (1982). Validity and fairness of some alternative employee selection procedures. *Personnel Psychology, 35,* 1-62.

Richardson, Bellows, Henry, & Co. (1985). *Supervisory profile record.* Washington, DC: Author.

Rothstein, H. R., Schmidt, F. L., Erwin, F. W., Owens, W. A., & Sparks, C. P. (1990). Biographical data in employment selection? Can validities be made generalizable? *Journal of Applied Psychology, 75,* 175-184.

Russell, C. J., Mattson, J., Devlin, S. E., & Atwater, D. (1990). Predictive validity of biodata items generated from retrospective life experience essays. *Journal of Applied Psychology, 75,* 569-580.

Schmidt, F. L., & Hunter, J. E. (1977). Development of a general solution to the problem of validity generalization. *Journal of Applied Psychology, 62,* 529-540.

Schoenfeldt, L. F. (1989). *Biographical data as the new frontier in employee selection research.* Address presented at the annual meeting of the Division of Evaluation, Measurement and Statistics of the American Psychological Association, New Orleans.

Schwab, D. P. & Oliver, R. L. (1974). Predicting tenure with biographical data: Exhuming buried evidence. *Personnel Psychology, 27,* 125-128.

Staw, B. M., Bell, N. E., & Clausen, J. A. (1986). The dispositional approach to job attitudes: A lifetime longitudinal test. *Administrative Science Quarterly, 31,* 56-77.

Stephens, W. (1979). *Our children should be working.* Springfield, IL: Charles C. Thomas.

Stricker, L. J. (1988). *Assessing leadership potential at the Naval Academy with a biographical measure.* Paper presented at the Annual Meeting of the Military Testing Association, San Antonio, TX.

Telenson, P. A., Alexander, R. A., & Barrett, G. V. (1983). Scoring the biographical information blank: A comparison of three weighting techniques. *Applied Psychological Measurement, 7,* 73-80.

Tenopyr, M. L. (1993). *Implications of new concepts in measurement on life history research and development.* Unpublished manuscript.

Thayer, P. (1977). Somethings old, somethings new. *Personnel Psychology, 30,* 513-524.

Toops, H. A. (1959). A research utopia in industrial psychology. *Personnel Psychology, 12,* 189-225.

Van Rijn, P. (1980). *Biographical questionnaires and scored application blanks in personnel selection.* Washington, DC: U.S. Office of Personnel Management, Personnel Research and Development Center.

Wernimont, P. F. (1962). Re-evaluation of a weighted application blank for office personnel. *Journal of Applied Psychology, 52,* 372-376.

White, L. A., & Kilcullen, R. N. (1992, August). *The validity of rational biodata scales.* Paper presented at the annual meeting of the American Psychological Association, Washington, DC.

White, L. A., Nord, R. D., Mael, F. A., & Young, M. (1993). The Assessment of Background and Life Experiences (ABLE). In T. Trent & J. Lawrence (Eds.), *Adaptability screening for the Services.* Washington, DC: Office of the Assistant Secretary for Defense, Force Management and Personnel.

Wildavsky, B. (1989). McJobs: Inside America's largest youth training program. *Policy Review, 49,* 30-37.

Wilson, J. Q. (1989). *Bureaucracy: What government agencies do and why they do it.* New York: Basic Books.

CHAPTER

17

THE MEASUREMENT OF
VOCATIONAL INTERESTS

Jo-Ida C. Hansen
University of Minnesota

E. K. Strong, Jr., in his classic book *Vocational Interests of Men and Women* (1943), said:

> some people in various walks of life, including psychologists, have considered the study of interests as of "no scientific value," "extremely silly and pernicious stuff," "a sheer waste of time," "useless and inane." (p. x)

Yet, 50 years later, hundreds of thousands of interest inventories are taken each year by vocational counseling clients.

Educators were the first to recognize that consideration of a person's interests might lead to improved quality of life (Parsons, 1909). In the 1920s, industry also recognized the financial worth of having a person interested in her or his job. Thus, early research in interest measurement was conducted by psychologists such as Moore (1921), who tried to understand differences between sales and design engineers; Miner (1922), who attempted to help students analyze their work interests; and Ream (1924), who explored the interests of successful and unsuccessful salesmen.

As psychologists began to explore the possibility of interest measurement, they were attempting to supplement existing measures of special and general abilities. For example, E. K. Strong, Jr., suggested that:

> It is not the ability but interest in the work that the test is designed to measure. Such a test is badly needed since many [people] can do the work at which [they are] now employed, but will resign very soon because [they are] not interested in it. (Strong, 1927, p. 297)

An early study by Darley (1941b), whose participants were followed up by Berdie (1955), supported Strong's contention that the assessment of interests could add valuable predictive information to the data used in making career choice. In a large study involving more than 1,000 students, Darley administered a battery of ability (Thurstone Primary Mental Abilities Test; Thurstone, 1939), achievement (Cooperative Social Studies, English, National Science, & Mathematics Tests; Cooperative Test Service, 1940), interest (Strong Vocational Interest Blank; Strong, 1933), and personality (Minnesota Personality Inventory; Darley, 1937) instruments; he also obtained high school scholastic ranks, and freshman grade-point averages. He found that scores on the personality scales were slightly more related to interests than were scores on the abilities tests.

Berdie (1955) completed a follow-up on Darley's freshmen who obtained degrees within the following 10-year period. He was interested in determining the extent to which freshman tests differentiated among the various curricular groups. Although achievement tests and verbal and reasoning ability tests significantly differentiated among the curricular groups, vocational interest scores were even more effective in differentiating among the curricular groups. The personality inventory scales, however, did not differentiate among the groups. Berdie concluded that, at the college level, differential interests were more important than differential abilities in determining educational and vocational choices.

What began, then, as an attempt to improve on validity of using only ability measures in vocational and educational guidance has grown into a field with its own separate and viable identity. The study and measurement of interests currently are viewed as more than "silly and pernicious stuff."

Although the importance of interests as a psychological trait has been established (Parsons, 1909; Strong, 1927; 1943), the need for the measurement of interests, in addition to or in place of self-reports of interests, occasionally is questioned. Predictive validity studies do indicate that expressed and inventoried interests probably are equally predictive of occupational entry (Borgen & Seling, 1979; Enright & Pinneau, 1955; Holland & Gottfredson, 1975; McArthur & Stevens, 1955). However, the large number of 18- and 19-year-olds who are "undecided" in their career goals, and, therefore, have no "expressed" interests, suggests that interest assessment can make an important contribution to any placement or selection procedure (Hansen & Swanson, 1983).

REVIEW OF THE LITERATURE IMPORTANT TO THE USE OF INTEREST INVENTORIES FOR SELECTION AND CLASSIFICATION

Theories, Origin, and Development of Interests

Most major interest theorists (Berdie, 1944; Darley, 1941a; Darley & Hagenah, 1955; Strong, 1943; Super, 1949) have included five major determinants or components, or some combination of the five, in their definitions of interests. One major variable to which interests frequently is linked is personality (Berdie, 1944; Darley, 1941a; Holland, 1966). A second major variable in various definitions of interests is motivation or drive (Berdie, 1944; Darley & Hagenah, 1955; Strong, 1955). A third recurring variable is one labeled by some psychologists as an expression of "self-concept" (Bordin, 1943) and by other psychologists as "identification" (Kitson, 1925) or "role" (Tyler, 1960).

Two additional components or determinants of interests may be classified as *dynamic* factors or *static* factors. The dynamic point of view describes vocational interests as the product of a wide range of psychological and environmental influences and emphasizes the effect of socialization and learning on the development of interests. The static point of view regards interests as genetically predetermined.

The importance of the five components or determinants of interests to each theory varies and depends more on how the theorist describes the choice or career development process than on how she or he hypothesizes that interests develop. Although most theorists include environmental influences and learning theories in their explanations of the development of interests, the appearance of interest choices at a young age in the behavior of a child, and the subsequent stability of interests, make explanations based strictly on nurture unsatisfying. Therefore, most theorists, some with more qualifications than others, acknowledge an heritability component to interests.

A recent study, in fact, determined familial correlations among eight kinships and estimated the proportion of observed variance in vocational interests that could be explained by genetic influences and environmental influences. Model-fitting analyses were run to estimate additive genetic, nonadditive genetic, shared environmental, and nonshared environmental effects. On average, the results suggest that the variance of vocational interests can be attributed to 55% non-shared environmental effects and measurement error, to 9% shared environmental effects, and to 24% nonadditive genetic and 12% additive genetic effects for a total of 36% genetic variance (Betsworth et al., in press)

Structural Analyses of Interests

Structural analyses of interests (e.g., Guilford, Christenson, Bond, & Sutton, 1954) have been acknowledged by theorists as having a potent influence on their thinking (Holland, 1959; Roe, 1957). Thurstone (1931a), for example, first used data acquired from E. K. Strong, Jr., to demonstrate techniques of factor analysis. The result of Thurstone's factor analysis of 18 of Strong's Occupational Scales (Thurstone, 1931b) was four factors that he labeled: Science, Language, People, and Business. As more Occupational Scales were developed for the Strong Vocational Interest Blank (SVIB), additional factor analyses were computed (Strong, 1943). Strong reported that four identical factors emerged in each of his four analyses and that his factors indicated the same classification of occupations as Thurstone had found working with fewer Occupational Scales. Eventually, Strong even organized the SVIB into categories identified by factor analyses.

Table 17.1 presents the results of a wide range of factor analyses dating back to Thurstone in the 1930s. Generally, an analysis of the structure of interests at the item level produces between 14 and 18 factors or clusters, and an analysis using scale scores produces 4 to 11 factors.

TABLE 17.1

Factors Emerging in Factor Analysis of Interests

Author	Thurstone, 1931b	Crissy & Daniel, 1939	Strong, 1943	Guilford, et al., 1954
Subjects	Male adults	Female adults	Male adults	Male adults
Inventory/ Variables Analyzed	18 SVIB-M Occupational Scales	18 SVIB-W Occupational Scales	25,30,32 & 36 SVIB-M Occupational Scales	98 short scales constructed for the study
Resulting Factors	▸Science ▸Language ▸People ▸Business	▸Science ▸Language ▸People ▸Detail	▸Science ▸Language ▸People ▸Business	▸Outdoor ▸Mechanical ▸Science ▸Aesthetic ▸Social Welfare ▸Business ▸Clerical
Author	Schutz & Baker, 1962	King & Norrel, 1964	Zytowski, 1976a	Zytowski, 1976a
Subjects	Male college students	Male college students	Female adults	Male adults
Inventory/ Variables Analyzed	Kuder-Occupational Scales	Kuder-Occupational Scales	Kuder-DD Women's Scales	Kuder-DD Men's Scales
Resulting Factors	▸Outdoor ▸Engineering-Phys. science Health scientist ▸Verbal-directive ▸Aesthetic-business ▸Interpersonal-directive ▸Business-detail	▸Outdoor technical ▸Engineering-Phys. science ▸Health scientist ▸Verbal ▸Artistic-business ▸Social service	▸Mathematic-numeric ▸Psychology ▸Socio-political ▸Science ▸Language ▸Art ▸Homemaking ▸Medical serv. ▸Helping ▸Lower level, easy	▸Agriculture ▸Skilled trades ▸Phys. science ▸Mathematic-numeric ▸Psychology ▸Political science ▸Language ▸Art ▸Medical services ▸Helping

(Continued)

TABLE 17.1 (Continued)
Factors Emerging in Factor Analysis of Interests

Author	Farnsworth, 1969	Rounds & Dawis, 1977	Rounds & Dawis, 1977	Droege & Padgett, 1979
Subjects	Female adults	Female adults	Male adults	Female and male adults
Inventory/ Variables Analyzed	Items on the SVIB for Women	Items of the SVIB for Women	Items on the SVIB for Men	307 activity items
Resulting Factors	▸Mechanical ▸Agrarian ▸Law enforcement ▸Research ▸Quantitative ▸Social sci. ▸Humanities ▸Dramatics ▸Literary ▸Artistic ▸Children and teaching ▸Culinary ▸Sewing ▸Religious ▸Political ▸Sales and Business ▸Secretarial	▸Mechanical and athletic ▸Medical sci. ▸Mathematics ▸Aesthetics ▸Teaching ▸Religion ▸Domestic arts ▸Fashionable appearance ▸Meeting and directing people ▸Business ▸Clerical	▸Mechanical activities ▸Athletics ▸Nature ▸Military activities ▸Adventure ▸Scientific activity ▸Mathematics ▸Aesthetics ▸Nonconformity ▸Social service ▸Religion ▸Public Service ▸Meeting and Directing People ▸Business	▸Mechanical ▸Industrial ▸Plants and animals ▸Protective ▸Scientific ▸Artistic ▸Accommodating ▸Humanitarian ▸Leading-influencing ▸Selling ▸Business ▸Detail

The factor analysis study most frequently acknowledged as affecting the thinking of interest theorists was conducted by Guilford and his colleagues (1954). Using new tests and samples they developed and collected themselves, they verified earlier factor analyses of the Strong Vocational Interest Blank. They found seven interest factors: outdoor work, mechanical, scientific, aesthetic expression, social welfare, business, and clerical. Their data also provided information on the relationship of vocational and nonvocational interest factors as well as the relationship of interest factors to one another. They concluded, based on their data, that vocational factors were genuine psychological entities.

Holland's Theory

John Holland's theory of vocational choice, which has had more impact than any other on interest measurement, grew out of a series of empirical and theoretical reports that began with development of the Vocational Preference Inventory (Holland, 1958, 1959, 1966, 1973, 1985). Subsequent vocational psychology literature is replete with research that was stimulated by Holland's theory as it applies to everything from vocational satisfaction (Walsh, Spokane, & Mitchell, 1973), to vocational choice (Williams, 1972), to vocational stability (Villwock, Shnitzen, & Carbonari, 1976; Walsh & Lacy, 1969). His typology has been used to describe interests as they relate to people, jobs, and environments; to organize occupational materials; and to provide an integration of variables relevant to career choice—interests, abilities, values, needs, and personalities—under one system.

Holland's theory states that (a) people can be divided into six personality types or some combination of the six types; (b) environments also can be described according to the six types; and (c) choices are made as people seek the type of environment that matches, or is congruent with, their personality type. Holland's six types are Realistic, Investigative, Artistic, Social, Enterprising, and Conventional; he suggested that the six types can be arranged around a hexagon in an R-I-A-S-E-C order, as illustrated in Fig. 17.1, and that types adjacent to one another are more related (more highly correlated) than are types diametrically opposed to one another on the hexagon.

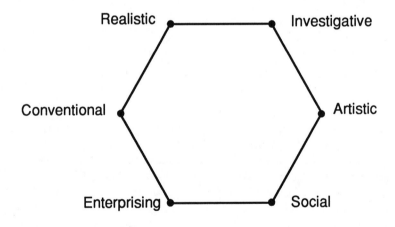

FIG.17.1. Holland's six types
arranged in R-I-A-S-E-C hexagonal order.

Many analyses have sought to verify the accuracy of Holland's hexagonal representation of the structure of interests for women and men. Results from studies with White males generally indicate that the world of work does organize itself in approximation to Holland's hypothesized hexagon (Cole & Hanson, 1971; Edwards & Whitney, 1972; Hansen & Campbell, 1985; Hansen, Collins,

Swanson & Fouad, 1993; Prediger, 1982; Rounds, Davison, & Dawis, 1979). Studies with White females typically show the hexagon order that Holland hypothesized (i.e., R-I-A-S-E-C), however, the hexagon shape varies across populations. Results from studies with cross-cultural and ethnic minority participants have had mixed results; typically the hexagon order, but not shape, is invariant (Dawis, 1992; Hansen, 1992; Swanson, 1992). Generally speaking, controversy still exists on how best to develop and use vocational theories and interest inventories fairly with women and culturally diverse populations.

Racial Differences in Interests

A number of studies have explored the validity of Holland's theory specifically, and interest measurement generally, for African-American (Bingham & Walsh, 1978; Doughtie, Chang, Alston, Wakefield, & Yom, 1976; Lamb 1978; O'Brien & Walsh, 1976; Wakefield, Yom, Doughtie, Chang, & Alston, 1975), Native American (Lamb, 1978; Scott & Anadon, 1980), and Hispanic subjects (Fouad, Cudeck, & Hansen, 1984; Fouad, Hansen, & Arias, 1989; Harrington & O'Shea, 1980; Lamb, 1978) using college students, non-college-degreed subjects, college-degreed subjects, and high school students. The general conclusion is that interests correspond to Holland's model almost as well for African Americans, Native Americans, and Hispanics as they do for Whites.

Research on the use of interest inventories with ethnic minorities, as opposed to research on the structure of interests, has received less attention. Some studies suggest that norms composed primarily of White U.S. subjects are useful with U.S. minority groups. Barnette and McCall (1964), for example, used the Minnesota Vocation Interest Inventory (MVII; Clark, 1961) with vocational/technical high school students and found no differences between African Americans and Whites. Haviland and Hansen (1987) found that the Strong Interest Inventory (SII) (Hansen & Campbell, 1985) predicted college majors for Native American students. However, a study by Hines (1983) showed poor predictive validity of the SII for African Americans who were predominantly lower-income students at an urban college. In another study, a comparison of the interests of Hispanic and White college students using the SII, found no significant differences, and the authors concluded that Hispanics are combining their values with mainstream culture (Montoya & DeBlassie, 1985).

Two reviews on the validity of the use of the Strong Interest Inventory (Hansen & Campbell, 1985) within ethnic minorities came to different conclusions. Carter and Swanson (1990) concluded that "little evidence exists for the psychometric validity of the Strong with Blacks." However, Arbona (1990) concluded, after a thorough review of research based on the SII as well as other interest inventories, that "Hispanic students' view of the world of work is similar to the view held by the majority culture."

Gender Differences in Interests

Gender differences in vocational interests have concerned test developers throughout the history of interest measurement. Early attempts by Gaw (1928-29), Hogg (1927), and Manson (1931) to measure interests of women, using techniques similar to those employed by E. K. Strong, Jr., with men, were disappointing. A few broad occupational groups were identified, but the scales for women did not differentiate occupations as well as did the scales developed for men.

In 1933, Strong developed the first interest inventory for women that was widely used. He later attempted to develop combined-gender scales to measure the interests of women and men in the same occupation but found, as did Hansen (1976) and Kuder (1977) over 40 years later, that for many occupations separate-gender scales were more valid (Strong, 1943). Kuder (1977) reported that, for 13 matched-gender occupations, only one occupation (interior decorator) had interests for the two genders that were closer to each other than either was to the interests of some other occupational group of the same gender. He concluded that failure to use separate gender norms for the two genders would reduce the effectiveness of counseling. Data from several attempts to develop combined-gender scales for the Strong Interest Inventory (Campbell & Hansen, 1981; Hansen 1976) led to the same conclusion. Occupational differences in the interests of women and men also contribute to the need for separate-gender norming for homogeneous interest scales.

The reason for the findings by Strong, Kuder, and Hansen is that women and men report different interests; the differences appear early and persist into adulthood (Campbell & Hansen, 1981; Riley, 1981). Interest differences are obvious when women and men in general are compared but, perhaps even more important, the same differences between women and men in general also are found between women and men in the same occupation (Hansen, 1978).

Data on the interests of women and men (Hansen, 1978; 1982b) suggest that gender differences between females and males may be classified into two categories: cultural differences, which are predictable and almost invariably appear in the Realistic area (with men scoring higher) and in the Artistic area (with women scoring higher), and occupationally related differences, which are not as predictable and vary from occupation to occupation (Hansen, 1984).

Structural analyses of the interests of women in general have found a convergence of Holland's Realistic and Investigative types, suggesting that women discriminate less between these two categories than do men. Another example of a deviation for women from the hexagonal model of Holland is the positioning of the Social type toward the center of the polygon. The centrality of the Social type for women compared to men suggests a salience for social service in the interests of women. This may be a function of the traditional socialization of women to develop characteristics such as nurturance, sensitivity, warmth, and emotional expressiveness (Hansen et al., 1993).

Some have argued that the gender differences in vocational interests found by early researchers, may be diminishing in response to growing awareness that many aspects of traditional gender roles are arbitrary (Diamond, 1975). Hansen (1981, 1988) studied that possibility, as well as the possibility that dramatic changes in women's interests would result from entering more diverse occupations, progressing up career ladders, and entering occupations previously closed to them. She examined, at both the item and scale score level, female-male similarities and differences in interests over time by comparing occupational samples collected over a period of 50 years. Her data illustrate the stability of gender differences in vocational interests. Societal changes seem not to have had a dramatic effect on the interests of women, and the differences in the 1920s and 1930s between women and men in general, as well as women and men in the same occupation, still occurred in the 1980s.

Studies documenting cultural and occupational gender differences in interests have led to retention of empirically developed scales that are based on separate-gender criterion samples and to development of separate-gender norm groups for homogeneous scales. However, separate-gender scales have the potential to create knotty problems depending on the final interpretation of the 1991 Civil Rights Act (Adler, 1993).

Stability of Interests

The degree to which interests are stable is important to the predictive power of inventories. If interests are fickle and unstable, interest inventory scores will not explain any of the prediction variance. As a consequence, stability of interests was one of the earliest concerns of researchers in interest measurement (Strong, 1943). Cross-sectional and longitudinal methods have been used in a plethora of studies to document that interests are stable even at relatively young ages of 15 or 16 years. By age 20, the stability of interests is obvious even over test-retest intervals of 5 to 10 years, and by age 25, interests are very stable (Johansson & Campbell, 1971). In fact, perhaps the best-documented knowledge in the entire field of interest measurement is the remarkable stability of interests of individuals (Hansen & Stocco, 1980; Strong, 1955), occupational groups (Campbell, 1966a, 1966b; Hansen, 1988), and society in general (Hansen, 1988; Johansson, 1975).

One large project made use of 50 years of data on interests of working adults collected on the Strong Interest Inventory in the 1930s, 1960s, 1970s, and 1980s (Hansen, 1981, 1988). More than 30 occupations, as well as women in general and men in general (large samples of women and men from a variety of occupations), were tested at least three times during that period. Interests of the in general samples tested over five decades were virtually identical for women, whereas there were a few small changes for men (higher scores in the 1980s in Enterprising areas of interest and on Adventure); the same trend of stability existed within specific occupations. As Fig. 17.2 illustrates (using male lawyers

Basic Interest Scales			
Scale	30s	60s	70s	Percentage
Nature	44	46	48	
Adventure	48	52	54	
Mechanical Activities	47	47	48	
Science	50	49	48	
Mathematics	51	50	48	
Medical Service	46	48	50	
Music/Dramatics	47	50	52	
Art	44	45	48	
Writing	50	52	53	
Teaching	45	50	49	
Social Service	47	49	46	
Athletics	50	52	50	
Public Speaking	54	59	58	
Law/Politics	57	59	58	
Merchandising	44	49	49	
Sales	45	49	49	
Business Management	46	51	5°	
Office Practices	46	47	46	
General Occupational Themes			
Theme	30s	60s	70s	Percentage
R-Theme	46	47	50	
I-Theme	48	50	50	
A-Theme	46	49	50	
S-Theme	46	51	49	
E-Theme	46	52	52	
C-Theme	48	47	45	

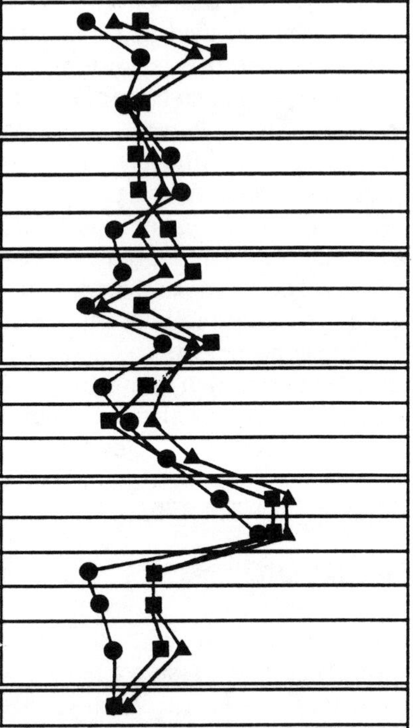

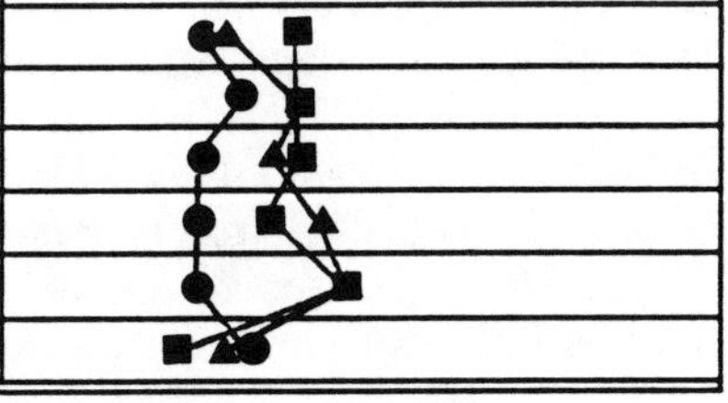

FIG.17.2. Mean interest profile for male lawyers tested in the 1930s
(●----●), the 1960s (▲------▲), and the 1970s (■-------■).

as an example), even when the scale scores had shifted to some small extent, the general configuration of the profile for a particular occupation remained the same, and the relative importance of various interests for a particular occupation had not changed.

Another cross-sectional method for analyzing stability of interests is to compare several age groups, all of whom are tested at roughly the same time (e.g., comparing interest patterns of adolescents and adults). Using this approach, Strong (1943) reported correlations of .82 between the interests of 15- and 25-year-old men; .73 between 15- and 55-year-old men, and .88 between 25- and 55-year-old men. These high correlations suggest more similarities than differences among interests of 15- to 55-year-olds. Strong concluded that by age 25 a person's interests have stabilized, that age does not affect the composition or configuration of interests to any great degree, and that experience as an adult will change a person's interests very little.

An additional consideration in evaluating the usefulness of interest inventories for career exploration, selection, and classification is the stability of the configuration of an individual's interest profile over time. By examining test-retest profile similarity indices, it is possible to determine the distribution of interest consistency of a sample of subjects. Using this method, Hansen and Stocco (1980) examined the stability of individual SII Occupational Scale profiles for high school and college students tested and retested over a period of three and a half years. The median correlation between test and retest profiles was .80 for the college students and .72 for the high school students, indicating that a large percentage of the students had reasonably stable interests patterns throughout their educational careers. However, the range of correlations for the adolescent sample (-.31 to .96) and young adult sample (.17 to .97) was large, suggesting that the stability of measured interests is not universal.

Using a similar design with older participants (college freshman at Time 1) and a test-retest interval of 12 years, Swanson and Hansen (1988) found mean SII profile stability coefficients of .78 (range .14 to .96) and .77 (range .04 to .92) for females ($n = 242$) and males ($n = 167$) respectively. The range of correlations in this study also suggests that stability of interests is not universal. However, little is known at this time about variables that may distinguish people with stable interest—nonchangers—from people with unstable interests—changers.

USE OF MEASURED INTERESTS FOR ENLIGHTENMENT, SELECTION, AND CLASSIFICATION

Interest measurement has been employed to help individuals make enlightened choices and for selection with the goal of maximizing predictions of success, satisfaction, and persistence in training as well as on the job. Interest measurement, however, has been used infrequently for classification.

Enlightened Choice

The major use of assessed interests, usually reported as interest inventory scores, is in career counseling that leads to decisions such as choosing a major, selecting an occupation, making a mid-career change, or preparing for retirement. One of the most popular designs for demonstrating criterion validity of interest inventories is to show that the inventories can predict future decisions such as choice of a major or an occupation. Numerous studies have been done that show hit rates of about 60% to 75% (Bartling & Hood, 1980; Gade & Soliah, 1975; Hansen, 1986; Hansen & Swanson, 1983; Hansen & Tan, 1992; Lau & Abrahams, 1971). The variability in hit rates reflects the Schmidt (1974) caveat that validity will vary as a function of base rate and the relative values of true and false positives and negatives.

Counselors use interest inventory profiles to develop hypotheses about clients that may be discussed, confirmed, or discarded during career exploration. The interest scores and profile provide a framework for interest exploration and a mechanism for helping the client to integrate his or her his past history with current interests. Inventory results can encourage some individuals to broaden their perspectives. Others, however, find interest inventory scores useful for narrowing the range of possible choices; a final group of people find that their interest scores merely confirm a previously expressed interest. Typically, interest inventory scores are used in conjunction with other data (e.g., abilities, life histories, values, and personality scores) to gain a clearer picture of the person prior to making a decision (Hansen, 1993).

Selection

Interest inventories also are used to assess interests during employment selection evaluations. Among qualified candidates, interest inventories can help to identify those most likely to be successful, those most likely to complete the training program and stay in the profession, and those most likely to be satisfied (Berdie & Campbell, 1968; Reeves & Booth, 1979). Even after initial selection, interest inventories may be used to help an employee find the right job within the company (Dunnette & Kirchner, 1965). Generally, measured interests predict tenure and satisfaction better than they predict performance and success. However, the relationships of interests with success, persistence, and satisfaction are not simple, and the quest continues for moderator and mediator variables that affect the relationships.

Interests and Success. A major problem in studying the relationship between interests and success is determining the criterion to represent success. Criteria that have been used include receipt of organizational rewards over years of employment, such as increases in income level or in job responsibilities; the number and types of promotions; honors, awards, and special assignments; persistence in the discipline or organization; the individual's perceived success in reaching career goals (Howes, 1981); and academic success such as grades or completion of training.

Studies that have used innovative techniques for identifying the criteria of success, for constructing scales, and for considering the effect of moderator and mediator variables have found a relationship between interests and success. For example, studies with a variety of experimental designs suggest that interests in combination with ability may determine success or failure. Clark (1961) used ability as a mediator variable and found interest scores more predictive of success at some ability levels than others. For example, he studied a sample of electronic technicians and found that the highest correlation (.47) between interests and achievement was for the subgroup whose intelligence scores were just below the mean for the entire sample. Gordon and Alf (1962) found that scales on the Navy Activities Preference Blank (NAPB) had statistically significant predictive validity against a naval training grade for 41 out of 51 schools.

Reeves and Booth (1979) found that adding the hospital corpsman (HM) interest scores from the Navy Vocational Interest Inventory (NVII) to verbal and arithmetic aptitude measures in a multiple regression equation increased the validity for predicting HM effectiveness significantly. At a cost of 15% of the effective HMs, they found that the percentage of ineffective HMs identified by the aptitude test alone was 39%, but that 47% were identified by using interest and ability scores. Effectiveness was defined as those individuals who completed paramedical training, who remained on the job for two years, and who advanced in their position. Other research (Barak & Rabbi, 1982; Wiley & Magoon, 1982) has used Holland's construct of "consistency" (i.e., similarity between primary and secondary interests as defined by their proximity to each other on Holland's hexagon) as a mediator variable in studies of the relationship between interests and academic success. Generally, results indicated that students with consistent interests had a higher level of persistence in college and a higher level of achievement, as measured by cumulative grade point average, than did students with inconsistent interests.

The various studies suggest that combining assessments of, at the very least, interests and abilities or aptitudes will improve prediction of achievement or success in academic or work settings. As a rule, persons with interests in, and the necessary ability for, an occupation will do well in it; persons with the necessary ability but not the interest can do well but may not.

Interests and Satisfaction.   Many studies, examining the relationship between interest scores and ratings of job satisfaction, have found low correlations (Carp, 1958; Schletzer, 1966; Schweiker, 1959; Zytowski, 1976b). One factor contributing to the difficulty in establishing the relationship between interests and satisfaction is that variance in satisfaction among groups with homogeneous interests is very small. In fact, a six-year study of job satisfaction in the 1970s (Weaver, 1980) showed that, between 1972 and 1978, 88% of American workers said that they were somewhat satisfied or very satisfied with their job. In addition, numerous variables other than interests may influence job satisfaction. For example, Doré and Meacham (1973) found a positive correlation (.38) between the Manager Scale of the SVIB and job satisfaction for managers in a medium-sized insurance company. However, the best validity coefficient that they obtained was a multiple correlation of .44 that resulted from a combination of the SVIB Manager Scale score and difference scores between measures of Self-Concept (how a person perceives self) and Required-Self-Concept (how a person perceives role requirements of the job).

Yet, a review of 21 studies, including six with military personnel, conducted for Project A reported median correlations of about .30, suggesting that an expectation of correspondence between interests and job satisfaction is reasonable (Hough, 1988). For example, Alley and Matthews (1982) showed that 18 subscales from the Air Force Vocational Interest-Career Examination (VOICE) predicted job satisfaction within a majority of the 20 Department of Defense occupational clusters. Their data also indicated that satisfaction in a given job cluster may involve interests in more than one domain. Nearly 100% of the participants who were predicted to have job satisfaction for their assigned job were actually satisfied. However, only 30% of those assigned to jobs in which they were predicted to be dissatisfied were actually satisfied. Lau and Abrahams (1971), using the NVII, found that (a) the probability of predicting occupational membership improved when an individual's entire profile of scores was used rather then one or two scores. They also found that (b) those who reported dislike for their jobs and (c) lower than average job performance, and (d) those who did not reenlist, had lower test and retest scores on the scale relevant to that job.

Multifactor measures of satisfaction seem to provide the best mechanism for capturing the relationship of interests to satisfaction. Wiener and Klein (1978), for example, found that subjects in jobs congruent with their interests had correlations of .37 and .42, respectively, with measures of "satisfaction with pay, promotion, and co-workers." They also found that subjects with less than two years' experience on the job had negative correlations between interests and satisfaction with work (-.12) and with supervision (-.09), suggesting that elapsed time may be a critical factor in planning satisfaction follow-up studies.

Holland's concept of congruence (degree of match between job and vocational interests), in conjunction with ratings of job satisfaction, has shown reasonable correlations between job-interest congruence and satisfaction in some studies ($r = .45$ for engineers; $r = .44$ for registered nurses) (Hener & Meir, 1981; Meir & Erez, 1981). However, a recent meta-analysis of 22 studies found an overall mean congruence-satisfaction correlation ($r = .17$) that was not significant. Type of congruence measure, Holland type, academic versus job setting, and gender did not moderate the satisfaction-congruence relation (Tranberg, Slane, & Ekeberg, 1993). An examination of the satisfaction-congruence relation by type was strongest for Social types (mean $r = .33$) and weakest for Realistic types (mean $r = .05$). Another study suggested that the capacity for satisfaction in spite of an interest-job mismatch, may vary by types. Investigative types, for example, are most satisfied when they are in investigative jobs, but Artistic types can be equally satisfied in nonartistic jobs (Tranberg, Slane, & Ekeberg, 1992).

Other factors found to contribute to job satisfaction that might serve as useful mediator or moderator variables in studying the relationship of interests and satisfaction are gender; occupational level (Lee, Mueller, & Miller, 1981), career stage and role perception (Stumpf & Rabinowitz, 1981), flexible working hours (Orpen, 1981), and religious affiliation (Vecchio, 1980). Clearly, research that is conceptually complex is needed. Simply correlating measures of satisfaction with interest-job congruence will not contribute appreciably to knowledge in this area.

Classification

The contribution of measured interests to the prediction of occupational satisfaction, persistence, and success suggests that measured interests can contribute to classification procedures just as they contribute to selection. To date, however, interest inventories typically have not been included in classification batteries.

Measured interests do satisfy several parameters of classification decision-making models. First, the relationship of interests to satisfaction suggests that incorporating measured interests in classification models will help to minimize attrition across jobs and will help to minimize the number of problem employees by enhancing satisfaction. Second, although data certainly indicate that measures of ability should be used heavily in selection, subsequent classification that incorporates measured interests may improve on performance. And third, classification gains are greater if jobs differ on the variable of "interest"; a plethora of validity studies have shown that interest inventory scales do have the power to differentiate among occupations and jobs.

A fourth parameter, that classification gains are greater when the number of distinct jobs or job families is larger, is met at least partially. Although the *Dictionary of Occupational Titles* lists thousands of jobs, the correlations between interests of many jobs are large. Even an instrument like the Strong Interest Inventory, with scales representing only about 100 occupations, suffers from redundancy. In other words, many scales for jobs with distinct occupational titles are in fact highly correlated (e.g., the *f Computer Programmer Scale* correlates .94 with the *f Systems Analyst Scale*). The question, then, is whether the power of interest inventories to differentiate related occupations is sufficient to make a contribution to classification batteries that would improve job assignment decisions. The usefulness of measured interests in classification may be limited to fairly discrete scales, such as those in the VOICE or AVOICE, that have been shown to have the capacity to differentiate among occupations, including specialties within the military (Alley & Matthews, 1982; Alley, Wilbourn, & Berberich, 1976; Clark, 1961; Echternacht, Reilly, & McCaffrey, 1973; Hahn & Williams, 1945; Reilly & Echternacht, 1979; Rosenberg & Izard, 1954).

One project, which used the item pool of the Strong Interest Inventory to construct Occupational Scales for nine Marine Corps MOS, found that the empirical method of contrast groups did produce scales that differentiated seven of the nine MOS. The MOS scales with the most promise for future research were engineer, tank, amphibian vehicle, communication, ground supply, aviation supply, and data systems. The scales showed good concurrent validity for MOS for Marine Corps officers who were Naval Academy graduates and for students from The Basic School (TBS). Also, each of the seven acceptable scales differentiated that scale's MOS criterion sample from the other MOS by at least ½ standard deviation (Hansen, 1982a). The results from this study suggest that occupational scales, constructed using the empirical methods of contrast groups, could be developed for many (but not all) military MOS, and that the scales would be discrete enough to contribute to classification batteries.

IMPLICATIONS FOR ARMY SELECTION AND CLASSIFICATION

The prospect of developing a program of research to systematically research the use of interest measures in selection and classification is exciting from the perspective of both basic and applied research. The questions to be answered are many and, to some extent elementary, including:

- What level of specificity of interest measurement is discrete enough to contribute to classification batteries?

  1. General scales, such as those found on the Strong Interest Inventory or the Vocational Preferences Inventory, which measure Holland's six types.
  2. More specific scales, such as the basic interest scales found on the VOICE, AVOICE, or Strong.
  3. Empirically constructed occupational scales using the item pools of inventories, such as the VOICE, AVOICE, or Strong.

- Conversely, what level of specificity of job titles is discrete enough to contribute to classification batteries?

  1. Individual MOS titles.
  2. Job clusters [e.g., existing clusters such as those reported by Campbell & Zook (1990), and Wise, Peterson, Hoffman, Campbell and Arabian

(1991), and those enlisted and officer clusters included in *Military Careers*, a Department of Defense publication referenced in Appendix D of the *Counselor Manual for the Armed Services Vocation Aptitude Battery Forms 18/19* (1992)].
3. General-level scales or categories based on Holland's six types (e.g., the ASVAB Occu-find).

- What combination of interest scores contributes the most to classification strategies?

   1. Single-scale prediction (e.g., one general theme à la Holland, one basic interest scale, or one occupational scale).
   2. Some configuration of scales selected through MDA, or multiple regression analysis, or a combination of the two.
   3. Profile comparisons that use all available information.

- Does interest measurement contribute anything—for all, some, or none of the job clusters or MOS—to classification efforts to maximize the utility of performance or to minimize attrition and problem employees versus jobs?

- Can moderator and mediator variables that affect the relationship between interests and satisfaction, persistence, and success be systematically identified?

- Do gender differences in interests have an impact on classification strategies?

- Do racial differences in interests have an impact on classification strategies?

- Does counseling that incorporates interest assessment prior to a recruit's opportunity to choose an MOS improve the validity of the recruit's expressed choice?

CONCLUSION

Vocational psychologists know in their hearts that a person x environment match increases satisfaction, success, and persistence. Enough data support this hypothesis to fuel a continued interest in teasing apart the complex relationships that determine how long, how well, and how happily people do their jobs. To begin with basic research designed to isolate moderator and mediator variables, then move on to applied research to systematically answer selection- and classification-problem questions, will require a systematic program of research that rarely, if ever, has been conducted in the field of interest measurement. This research could be a classic, providing the ultimate integration of basic and applied research and major contributions to the scientific literature on interest.

REFERENCES

Adler, T. (1993, January). Separate gender norms on tests raise questions. *APA Monitor, 3.*

Alley, W. E., & Matthews, M. D. (1982). The vocational interest career examination: A description of the instrument and possible applications. *The Journal of Psychology, 112,* 169-193.

Alley, W. E., Wilbourn, J. M., & Berberich, G. L. (1976). *Relationships between performance on the Vocational Interest Career Examination and reported job satisfaction* (AFHRL-TR-76-89). Lackland AFB, TX: Personnel Research Division, Air Force Human Resources Laboratory.

Arbona, C. (1990). Career counseling research on Hispanics: A review of the literature. *The Counseling Psychologist, 18,* 300-323.

Barak, A., & Rabbi, B. (1982). Predicting persistence, stability, and achievement in college by major choice consistency: A test of Holland's consistency hypothesis. *Journal of Vocational Behavior, 20,* 235-243.

Barnette, W. L., Jr., & McCall, J. N. (1964). Validation of the Minnesota Vocational Interest Inventory for vocational high school boys. *Journal of Applied Psychology, 48,* 378-382.

Bartling, H. C., & Hood, A. B. (1980). *Validity of measured interests for decided and undecided students.* Paper presented at the conference of the American Psychological Association, Washington, DC.

Berdie, R. F. (1944). Factors related to vocational interests. *Psychological Bulletin, 41,* 137-157.

Berdie, R. F. (1955). Aptitude, achievement, interest, and personality tests: A longitudinal comparison. *Journal of Applied Psychology, 39,* 103-114.

Berdie, R. F., & Campbell, D. P. (1968). Measurement of interest. In D. K. Whitla (Ed.). *Handbook of measurement and assessment in behavioral sciences.* Reading, MA: Addison-Wesley.

Betsworth, D. G., Bouchard, T. J., Jr., Cooper, C. R., Grotevant, H. D., Hansen, J. C., Scarr, S., & Weinberg, R. A. (in press). Genetic and environmental influences on vocational interests assessed using adoptive and biological families and twins reared apart and together. *Journal of Vocational Behavior.*

Bingham, R. O., & Walsh, W. B. (1978). Concurrent validity of Holland's theory for college-degreed Black working women. *Journal of Vocational Behavior, 13,* 242-250.

Bordin, E. S. (1943). Theory of vocational interests as dynamic phenomena. *Educational and Psychological Measurement, 3,* 49-65.

Borgen, F. M., & Seling, M. F. (1979). Expressed and inventoried interests revisited: Perspicacity in the person. *Journal of Counseling Psychology, 25,* 536-543.

Campbell, D. P. (1966a). Stability of interests within an occupation over thirty years. *Journal of Applied Psychology, 50,* 51-56.

Campbell, D. P. (1966b, June). The stability of vocational interests within occupations over long time spans. *Personnel and Guidance Journal,* 1012-1019.

Campbell, D. P., & Hansen, J. C. (1981). *Manual for the SVIB-SCII* (3rd ed.). Palo Alto, CA: Stanford University Press.

Campbell, J. P, & Zook, L. M. (Eds.). (1990). *Improving the selection, classification, and utilization of Army enlisted personnel: Final report on Project A.* Alexandria, VA: U.S. Army Research Institute.

Carp, F. M. (1958). *Relationships between airmen interests and career satisfaction* (WAOC-TR-58-90, AD-151 038). Lackland AFB, TX: Personnel Laboratory, Wright Air Development Center.

Carter, R. T., & Swanson, J. L. (1990). The validity of the Strong Interest Inventory with Black Americans: A review of the literature. *Journal of Vocational Behavior, 36,* 195-199.

Clark, K. E. (1961). *The vocational interests of non-professional men.* Minneapolis: University of Minnesota Press.

Cole, N. S., & Hanson, G. (1971). An analysis of the structure of vocational interests. (ACT Research Report No. 40). Iowa City: American College Testing Program.

Cooperative Test Service (1940). *The Cooperative General Achievement Tests: Information concerning their construction, interpretation and use.* New York: Cooperative Test Service.

Crissy, W. J. E., & Daniel, W. J. (1939). Vocational interest factors in women. *Journal of Applied Psychology, 23,* 488-494.

Darley, J. G. (1937). *An analysis of attitude and adjustment tests: With special reference to conditions of change in attitudes and adjustments.* Unpublished doctoral dissertation, University of Minnesota.

Darley, J. G. (1941a). *Clinical aspects and interpretation of the Strong Vocational Interest Blank.* New York: The Psychological Corporation.

Darley, J. G. (1941b). *A study of the relationships among the Primary Mental Abilities Test, selected achievement measures, personality tests, and tests of vocational interests,* (studies in higher education, Biennial report of the Committee on Education Research, 1938-40). Minneapolis: University of Minnesota Press.

Darley, J. G., & Hagenah, T. (1955). *Vocational interest measurement.* Minneapolis: University of Minnesota Press.

Dawis, R. V. (1992). The structure(s) of occupations: Beyond RIASEC. *Journal of Vocational Behavior, 40,* 171-178.

Department of Defense (1992). *Counselor Manual for the Armed Services Vocational Aptitude Battery Forms 18/19.* Monterey, CA: Defense Manpower Data Center, DoD Testing Center.

Diamond, E. E. (Ed.). (1975). *Issues of sex bias and sex fairness in career interest inventories.* Washington, DC: National Institute of Education.

Doré, R., & Meacham, M. (1973). Self-concept and interests related to job satisfaction of managers. *Personnel Psychology, 26,* 49-59.

Doughtie, E. B., Chang, W. C., Alston, H. L., Wakefield, J. A., Jr., & Yom, B. L. (1976). Black-White differences on the Vocational Preference Inventory. *Journal of Vocational Behavior, 8,* 41-44.

Droege, R. C., & Padgett, A. (1979). Development of an interest-oriented occupational classification system. *The Vocational Guidance Quarterly, 27,* 302-310.

Dunnette, M. D., & Kirchner, W. K. (1965). *Psychology applied to industry.* New York: Appleton-Century-Crofts.

Echternacht, G. J., Reilly, R. R., & McCaffrey, P. J. (1973). *Development and validity of a vocational and occupational interest inventory* (AFHRL-TR-73-38). Lackland AFB, TX: Personnel Research Division, Air Force Human Resources Laboratory.

Edwards, K. J., & Whitney, D. R. (1972). A structural analysis of Holland's personality types using factor and configural analysis. *Journal of Counseling Psychology, 19,* 136-145.

Enright, J. B., & Pinneau, S. R. (1955). Predictive value of subjective choice of occupation and the Strong Vocational Interest Blank over fifteen years. *American Psychologist, 10,* 424-425.

Farnsworth, K. E. (1969). Vocational interests of women: A factor analysis of the women's form of the SVIB. *Journal of Applied Psychology, 53,* 353-358.

Fouad, N. A., Cudeck, R., & Hansen, J. C. (1984). Convergent validity of the Spanish and English forms of the SCII for bilingual Hispanic high school students. *Journal of Counseling Psychology, 31*, 339-348.

Fouad, N. A., Hansen, J. C., & Arias, F. C. (1989). Cross-cultural similarity of vocational interests of professional engineers. *Journal of Vocational Behavior, 34*, 88-89.

Gade, E. M., & Soliah, D. (1975). Vocational preference inventory high point codes versus expressed choices as predictors of college major and career entry. *Journal of Counseling Psychology, 22*, 117-121.

Gaw, E. A. (1928-29). Occupational interests of college women. *Personnel Journal, 7*, 111-114.

Gordon, L. V., & Alf, E. F. (1962). The predictive validity of measured interest for Navy vocational training. *Journal of Applied Psychology, 46*, 212-219.

Guilford, J. P., Christenson, P. R., Bond, N. A., Jr., & Sutton, M. A. (1954). A factor analysis study of human interests. *Psychological Monographs, 68* (Whole No. 375), 1-38.

Hahn, M. E., & Williams, C. T. (1945). The measured interest of Marine Corps women reservists. *Journal of Applied Psychology, 29*, 198-211.

Hansen, J. C. (1976). Exploring new directions for Strong-Campbell Interest Inventory occupational scale construction. *Journal of Vocational Behavior, 9*, 147-160.

Hansen, J. C. (1978). Sex differences in vocational interests: Three levels of exploration. In C. K. Tittle & D. G. Zytowski (Eds.), *Sex-fair interest measurement: Research and implications*, Washington, DC: U. S. Government Printing Office.

Hansen, J. C. (1981). *The effect of history on the vocational interest of women.* Paper presented at the conference of the American Psychological Association, Los Angeles.

Hansen, J. C. (1982a). *Development and evaluation of Strong-Campbell Interest Inventory Scales to measure interests of Military Occupational Specialties of the Marine Corps* (NPRDC TR 82-60). San Diego: Office of Naval Research.

Hansen, J. C. (1982b). Sex differences in interests and interpreting opposite sex scores on the Strong-Campbell Interest Inventory. *Illinois Guidance and Personnel Quarterly, 84*, 5-12.

Hansen, J. C. (1984). The measurement of vocational interests: Issues and future directions. S. D. Brown & R. L. Lent (Eds.), *Handbook of counseling psychology* (pp. 99-136). New York: Wiley.

Hansen, J. C. (1986). *12-year longitudinal study of the predictive validity of the SVIB-SCII.* Paper presented at the conference of the American Psychological Association, Washington, DC.

Hansen, J. C. (1988). Changing interests: Myth or reality? *Applied Psychology: An International Review, 37*, 133-150.

Hansen, J. C. (1992). Does enough evidence exist to modify Holland's theory to accommodate individual differences of diverse populations? *Journal of Vocational Behavior, 40*, 188-193.

Hansen, J. C. (1993). *User's guide for the Strong Interest Inventory* (2nd ed.). Palo Alto, CA: Consulting Psychologists Press.

Hansen, J. C., & Campbell, D. P. (1985). *Manual for the SVIB-SCII* (4th ed.). Stanford, CA: Stanford University Press.

Hansen, J. C., Collins, R. C. Swanson, J. L., & Fouad, N. A. (1993). Gender differences in the structures of interests. *Journal of Vocational Behavior, 42*, 200-211.

Hansen, J. C., & Stocco, J. L. (1980). Stability of vocational interests of adolescents and young adults. *Measurement and Evaluation in Guidance, 13*, 173-178.

Hansen, J. C., & Swanson, J. L. (1983). Stability of vocational interest and the predictive and concurrent validity of the 1981 Strong-Campbell Interest Inventory for college majors. *Journal of Counseling Psychology, 30*, 194-201.

Hansen, J. C., & Tan, R. N. (1992). Concurrent validity of the 1985 Strong Interest Inventory for college major selection. *Measurement and Evaluation in Counseling and Development, 15,* 53-57.

Harrington, T. F., & O'Shea, A. J. (1980). Applicability of the Holland (1973) model of vocational development with Spanish-speaking clients. *Journal of Counseling Psychology, 27,* 246-251.

Haviland, M. L., & Hansen, J. C. (1987). Criterion validity of the Strong-Campbell Interest Inventory for American Indian college students. *Measurement and Evaluation in Counseling and Development, 19,* 196-201.

Hener, T., & Meir, E. I. (1981). Congruency, consistency, and differentiation as predictors of job satisfaction within the nursing occupation. *Journal of Vocational Behavior, 18,* 304-309.

Hines, H. (1983). The Strong-Campbell Interest Inventory: A study of its validity with a sample of Black college students (University Microfilms No. 84-19, 502). *Dissertation Abstracts International, 45*(06), 1901B.

Hogg, M. I. (1927-28). Occupational interests of women. *Personnel Journal, 6,* 331-337.

Holland, J. L. (1958). A personality inventory employing occupational titles. *Journal of Applied Psychology, 42,* 336-342.

Holland, J. L. (1959). A theory of vocational choice. *Journal of Counseling Psychology, 6,* 35-45.

Holland, J. L. (1966). *The psychology of vocational choice.* Waltham, MA: Blaisdell.

Holland, J. L. (1973). *Making vocational choices: A theory of careers.* Englewood Cliffs, NJ: Prentice-Hall.

Holland, J. L. (1985). *Making vocational choices* (2nd ed.). Englewood Cliffs, NJ: Prentice-Hall.

Holland, J. L., & Gottfredson, G. D. (1975). Predictive value on psychological meaning of vocational aspirations. *Journal of Vocational Behavior, 6,* 349-363.

Hough, L. M. (Ed.). (1988). *Literature review: Utility of temperament, biodata, and interest assessment for predicting job performance* (ARI Research Note 88-02). Alexandria, VA: U.S. Army Research Institute.

Howes, N. J. (1981). Characteristics of career success: An additional input to selecting candidates for professional programs? *Journal of Vocational Behavior, 18,* 277-288.

Johansson, C. B. (1975). Strong Vocational Interest Blank in-general samples. *Journal of Counseling Psychology, 22,* 113-116.

Johansson, C. B., & Campbell, D. P. (1971). Stability of the Strong Vocational Interest Blank for Men. *Journal of Applied Psychology, 55,* 34-36.

King, D. P., & Norrel, G. (1964). A factorial study of the Kuder Preference Record-Occupational, Form D. *Educational and Psychological Measurement, 24,* 57-64.

Kitson, H. D. (1925). *The psychology of vocational adjustment.* Philadelphia: Lippincott.

Kuder, G. F. (1977). *Activity interests and occupational choice.* Chicago: Science Research Associates.

Lamb, R. R. (1978). Validity of the ACT Interest Inventory for minority group members. In C. K. Tittle & D. G. Zytowski (Eds.) *Sex-fair interest measurement: Research and implications.* Washington DC: U.S. Government Printing Office.

Lau, A. W., & Abrahams, N. M. (1971). *Reliability and predictive validity of The Navy Vocational Interest Inventory* (TR-71-16). San Diego: Naval Personnel and Training Research Laboratory.

Lee, R., Mueller, L. B., & Miller, K. J. (1981). Sex, wage-earner status, occupational level, and job satisfaction. *Journal of Vocational Behavior, 18,* 362-373.

Manson, G. E. (1931). Occupational interests and personality requirements of women in business and the professions. *Michigan Business Studies, 3,* 281-409.

McArthur, C., & Stevens, L. B. (1955). The validation of expressed interests as compared with inventoried interests: A fourteen year follow-up. *Journal of Applied Psychology, 39,* 184-189.

Meir, E. I., & Erez, M. (1981). Fostering a career in engineering. *Journal of Vocational Behavior, 18,* 115-120.

Miner, J. B. (1922). An aid to the analysis of vocational interests. *Journal of Educational Research, 5,* 311-323.

Montoya, H., & DeBlassie, R. R. (1985). SCII comparisons between Hispanic and Anglo college students: A research note. *Hispanic Journal of Behavioral Science, 7,* 285-289.

Moore, B. V. (1921). Personnel selection of graduate engineers. *Psychological Monograph, 30,* 1-85.

O'Brien, W. F., & Walsh, W. B. (1976). Concurrent validity of Holland's theory for non-college degreed Black working men. *Journal of Vocational Behavior, 8,* 239-246.

Orpen, C. (1981). Effect of flexible working hours on employee satisfaction and performance: A field experiment. *Journal of Applied Psychology, 66,* 113-115.

Parsons, F. (1909). *Choosing a vocation.* Boston: Houghton Mifflin.

Prediger, D. J. (1982). Dimensions underlying Holland's hexagon: Missing link between interests and occupations? *Journal of Vocational Behavior, 21,* 259-287.

Ream, M. J. (1924). *Ability to sell: Its relations to certain aspects of personality and experience.* Baltimore: Williams and Wilkens.

Reeves, D. J., & Booth, R. F. (1979). Expressed versus inventoried interests as predictors of paramedical effectiveness. *Journal of Vocational Behavior, 15,* 155-163.

Reilly, R. R., & Echternacht, G. J. (1979). Some problems with the criterion-keying approach to occupational interest scale development. *Educational and Psychological Measurement, 39,* 85-94.

Riley, P. J. (1981). The influence of gender on occupational aspirations of kindergarten children. *Journal of Vocational Behavior, 19,* 244-250.

Roe, A. (1957). Early determinants of vocational choice. *Journal of Counseling Psychology, 4,* 212-217.

Rosenberg, N., & Izard, C. E. (1954). Vocational interests of naval aviation cadets. *Journal of Applied Psychology,* 38, 354-358.

Rounds, J. B., Jr., Davison, M. L., & Dawis, R. V. (1979). The fit between Strong-Campbell Interest Inventory General Occupational Themes and Holland's hexagonal model. *Journal of Vocational Behavior, 15,* 303-315.

Rounds, J. B., Jr., & Dawis, R. V. (1977). *Factor analysis of SVIB items.* Paper presented at the conference of the American Psychological Association, San Francisco.

Schletzer, V. A. (1966). SVIB as a predictor of job satisfaction. *Journal of Applied Psychology, 50,* 5-8.

Schmidt, F. L. (1974). Probability and utility assumptions underlying use of the Strong Vocational Interest Blank. *Journal of Applied Psychology, 59,* 456-464.

Schutz, R. E., & Baker, R. L. (1962). A factor analysis of the Kuder Preference Record-occupational, Form D. *Educational and Psychological Measurement, 22,* 97-194.

Schweiker, R. F. (1959). Stability of interest measures and their validation for selection and classification. *USAF WADC Tech. Rep,* No. 59-36.

Scott, T. B., & Anadon, M. (1980). A comparison of the vocational interest profile of Native American and Caucasian college-bound students. *Measurement and Evaluation in Guidance, 13,* 35-42.

Strong, E. K., Jr. (1927). Vocational guidance of engineers. *Industrial Psychology Monthly, 11,* 291-298.

Strong, E. K., Jr. (1933). *Vocational Interest Blank for Women.* Palo Alto, CA: Stanford University Press.

Strong, E. K., Jr. (1938). *Vocational Interest Blank for Men.* (revised). Palo Alto, CA: Stanford University Press.

Strong, E. K., Jr. (1943). *Vocational Interests of Men and Women.* Palo Alto, CA: Stanford University Press.

Strong, E. K., Jr. (1955). *Vocational interests eighteen years after college.* Minneapolis: University of Minnesota Press.

Stumpf, S. A., & Rabinowitz, S. (1981). Career stage as a moderator of performance relationships with facets of job satisfaction and role perceptions. *Journal of Vocational Behavior, 18,* 202-218.

Super, D. E. (1949). *Appraising vocational fitness.* New York: Harper & Row.

Swanson, J. L. (1992). The structure of vocational interests for African-American college students. *Journal of Vocational Behavior, 40,* 144-157.

Swanson, J. L., & Hansen, J. C. (1988). Stability of vocational interests over 4-year, 8-year, and 12-year intervals. *Journal of Vocational Behavior, 33,* 185-202.

Thurstone, L. L. (1931a). Multiple factor analysis. *Psychological Review, 38,* 406-427.

Thurstone, L. L. (1931b). A multiple factor study of vocational interests. *Personnel Journal, 3,* 198-205.

Thurstone, L. L. (1939). *Manual of instructions for the Primary Mental Abilities Tests.* Washington, DC: American Counsel on Education.

Tranberg, M. D., Slane, S. D., & Ekeberg, S. E. (1992). *Job satisfaction as a function of congruence and personality types.* Unpublished manuscript, Cleveland State University.

Tranberg, M. D., Slane, S. D., & Ekeberg, S. E. (1993). The relation between interest congruence and satisfaction: A meta-analysis. *Journal of Vocational Behavior, 42,* 253-264.

Tyler, L. E. (1960). The development of interests. In W. L. Layton (Ed.), *The Strong Vocational Interest Blank: Research and uses.* Minneapolis: University of Minnesota Press.

Vecchio, R. P. (1980). A test of a moderator of job satisfaction-job quality relationship: The case for religious affiliation. *Journal of Applied Psychology, 65,* 195-201.

Villwock, J. D., Shnitzen, J. P., & Carbonari, J. P. (1976). Holland's personality constructs as predictors of stability of choice. *Journal of Vocational Behavior, 9,* 77-85.

Wakefield, J. A., Jr., Yom, B. L., Doughtie, E. B., Chang, W. C., & Alston, H. L. (1975). The geometric relationship between Holland's personality typology and the Vocational Preference Inventory for Blacks. *Journal of Counseling Psychology, 22,* 58-60.

Walsh, W. B., & Lacey, D. W. (1969). Perceived change in Holland's theory. *Journal of Counseling Psychology, 16,* 348-352.

Walsh, W. B., Spokane, A. R., & Mitchell, E. (1973). Consistent occupational preferences and satisfaction, self-concept, self-acceptance, and vocational maturity. *Journal of Vocational Behavior, 3,* 453-464.

Weaver, C. N. (1980). Job satisfaction in the United States in the 1970's. *Journal of Applied Psychology, 65,* 364-367.

Wiener, Y., & Klein, K. L. (1978). The relationship between vocational interests and job satisfaction: Reconciliation of divergent results. *Journal of Vocational Behavior, 13,* 298-304.

Wiley, M. O., & Magoon, T. M. (1982). Holland high point social types: Is consistency related to persistence and achievement? *Journal of Vocational Behavior, 20,* 14-21.

Williams, C. M. (1972). Occupational choices of male graduate students as related to values and personality: A test of Holland's theory. *Journal of Vocational Behavior, 2,* 39-46.

Wise, L. L., Peterson, N. G., Hoffman, R. G., Campbell, J. P., & Arabian, J. M. (1991). *The Army synthetic validity project: Report of Phase III results, Vol I.* (ARI Technical Report 922). Alexandria, VA: U.S. Army Research Institute.

Zytowski, D. G. (1976a). Factor analysis of the Kuder Occupational Interest Survey. *Educational and Psychological Measurement, 9,* 120-123.

Zytowski, D. G. (1976b). Predicting validity of the Kuder Occupational Interest Survey: A 12- to 19-year follow-up. *Journal of Counseling Psychology, 23,* 221-233.

CHAPTER

18

THE PRSVL MODEL OF
PERSON-CONTEXT INTERACTION
IN THE STUDY OF HUMAN POTENTIAL

Robert J. Sternberg[1]
Yale University

Upon entering the HumRRO Building in Alexandria, Virginia, I encountered a challenging problem. I entered at the ground level, walked into an elevator, and pressed the button marked "4" in order to get to the fourth floor. The button didn't light, but the door closed. Instead of ascending, the elevator descended, and took me to the parking level. I reentered the elevator, and again pressed the button marked "4". The button didn't light, but the door closed. I pressed the "Door Open" button. The door opened, and I walked out. I tried to summon another elevator, but none of the others would come because one was already here. Clearly there was something wrong with this elevator.

I walked to the stairwell and entered it, trying the doorknob from the inside to make sure that I would later be able to get out of the stairwell. I walked up to the fourth floor. The door from the staircase to the office was locked, so I walked down to the ground floor and into the lobby. I pressed the button to summon an elevator. A new elevator arrived. I entered the elevator and pressed the button for the fourth floor. The button did not light. The door closed and the elevator once again descended to the parking level. I then concluded that something was wrong with all of the elevators.

As I walked up a flight of steps to the lobby, I pondered if something was wrong with me. In the lobby, a woman approached me and asked if I wanted to go to the HumRRO suite. I nodded. We entered the elevator and she inserted a card into a slot in the wall. The elevator rose to the fourth floor. I had finally reached my destination.

It is always humbling to be confronted with an intelligence test shortly before one starts to speak about intelligence testing. But this particular

---

[1] The author served as the discussant for Session Two, "Conceptualizing and Measuring Individual Differences," at the S&C Conference.

intelligence test raised four points that I believe are critical to our understanding of human intelligence in particular, and of human potentials more generally. First, defining problems narrowly (in this case, in terms of problems with the elevators or with myself) renders the problem insoluble: I could have gone on pressing buttons in various elevators forever without solving the problem.

Second, in understanding and assessing human potentials, we need to take into account the context in which people live and function. In the elevator example, the context was affected by a set of security measures ensuring that unauthorized people don't come up to the HumRRO floor outside of regular hours. In general, real-world problems cannot be widely understood outside the context in which they occur. We need to take into account the interaction of the person with the overall context, not merely the specific person or the specific task the person faces.

Third, if we define our universe of assessment narrowly (as have Kyllonen, Ree, Lohman, and Alderton, in this volume), we will always come back to g: Mental abilities of the kind measured by intelligence tests, whether psychometrically or cognitively analyzed, are simply not enough. They will always yield a g, but a limited one.

Fourth, it's not enough even to look at other abilities, such as physical ones (Hogan, in this volume), or personality (Goldberg, in this volume). We need to look at the person-context interaction that goes beyond abilities as well as personality.

If our only goal is to obtain a rough-and-ready assessment of abilities for entry-level recruits in the Army or some other organization, we may not want to be bothered by testing beyond that which gives us a measure of the traditional psychometric g. But if we're interested in broader questions, and perhaps more important ones, we need to expand our horizons. For example, why do so many CEOs drive their companies to ruin? Is it simply a lack of general intelligence? What is the difference between a good person and a good leader? What makes one person a natural lawyer, another a pilot, and another a scientist? Why do so many people with high IQs and GRE scores amount to so little? Why do people who do well in one organization not do as well in another? What's Donald Trump's problem? To answer questions such as these, we need to go well beyond the traditional universe of testing.

In this chapter, I describe the PRSVL (pronounced the same way as the name of the knight, Parsifal) model of person-context interaction in the study of human potentials. This model considers the person from a broad perspective, and also considers the many facets of context in which the person functions. Most important, though, it looks at the interaction between the person and his or her context. It considers jointly five variables: the person, the roles the person can take, the situations in which a person can find himself or herself, the person's values, and the luck that impinges on the person's life. Table 18.1 sketches the model as a whole.

TABLE 18.1
The PRSVL Model of PERSON X CONTEXT Interactions

1 PERSON (who)	3 SITUATIONS (where, when)

Abilities
  Mental
    Memory-analytic
    Synthetic-creative
    Practical-contextual
  Physical
	High stress vs. low stress
	Close supervision vs. far supervision
	Short-term goals vs. long-term goals
	Physical comfort vs. physical discomfort

Knowledge
  Declarative
  Procedural
	4
	VALUES
	(why)

Styles
  Legislative-executive-judicial
  Monarchic-hierarchic-
    oligarchic-anarchic
  Local-global
  Internal-external
	People vs. productivity
	Process vs. product
	Conformity vs. independence
	Individualism vs. group orientation
	Altruism vs. self-interest
	Innovation vs. stability
	Appearance vs. reality

Personality
  Tolerance of ambiguity
  Persistence in overcoming obstacles
  Willingness to grow
  Willingness to take sensible risks
	5
	LUCK
	(whoops!)

Motivation
  Intrinsic
  Task-focused
	Status variables
	  SES of family of origin
	  Race
	  Gender
	  Handicaps

2 ROLES (what)	Nationality

Leader vs. follower
Entrepreneur vs. manager
Thinking vs. doing
Staff vs. line
	Event variables
	  Hazards
	  Opportunities

In trying to learn about people in their contexts, we often ask the question of who, what, where, when, why, and how? The PRSVL taxonomy deals with all of these questions, precisely because it considers the person in his or her total context. The question of who is addressed by the person category. The question of what is addressed by the roles category. The questions of where and when are addressed by the situations category. The questions of why and how are addressed by the values category. Finally, the luck category addresses an additional factor, which might be labeled the whoops! factor—the background variables and events in one's life over which one has no control.

THE PERSON

In order to consider fully the potentials of a person, we need to go beyond just looking at abilities. In particular, we need to look at five qualities: abilities, knowledge, thinking and learning styles, personality, and motivation. In considering abilities, I consider only mental ones, although the physical abilities discussed by Hogan are important as well. Let's now consider each of these five aspects of the person in turn.

Abilities

I distinguish between three broad categories of mental abilities: memory-analytic, synthetic-creative, and practical-contextual. Each of these types of ability is important to success in a variety of endeavors.

Memory-Analytic Abilities. In my triarchic theory of intelligence (Sternberg, 1985, 1988c), I described three kinds of information-processing components in memory-analytic abilities: metacomponents, which are higher-order thought processes involved in planning what one is going to do, monitoring it while one is doing it, and evaluating it after it is done; performance components, which are involved in executing the instructions of the metacomponents; and knowledge-acquisition components, which are involved in learning how to do something in the first place.

I have written extensively about the functioning of these kinds of components, and won't repeat much of it here. It will suffice to give a few examples of each kind of component. Examples of metacomponents are recognizing that one has a problem in the first place, defining what the problem is, setting up a strategy to solve that problem, monitoring one's strategy as one is implementing it, and evaluating the success of the strategy after implementing it. Examples of performance components are inferring relations between two concepts, and applying what one has learned to a new context. Examples of knowledge-acquisition components are selectively encoding information so as to screen out what is relevant from what is irrelevant in a stream of input, and selective comparison, which involves bringing old information to bear on the solution of new problems.

Memory-analytic abilities are obviously important in intellectual functioning, and they are the focus of the chapters by Kyllonen, Ree, Lohman, and Alderton in this volume. Equally, they are the focus of the large majority of research projects undertaken by both psychometrically oriented and cognitively oriented psychologists. But in the PRSVL framework, they are only a small portion of the factors that need to be taken into account in understanding and assessing human potential. From the present point of view, *g* is a very small *g* indeed. It may be general, but only within a narrow universe of discourse.

I am not arguing against the importance of *g* in many tasks and in many situations. The very fact that it keeps recurring in a variety of different kinds of assessments attests to its importance. But one has only to go to a scientific convention or read a scientific journal in order to understand just how limited *g* can be: It is marvelous how well so many people can solve problems of little or no consequence as they pursue their scientific work. To me, the problem in science, as well in so many other fields, is not that the professional practitioners are unable to solve problems (i.e., lack sufficient levels of *g*), but rather that the problems they choose to solve are often of such narrow scope or consequence in the first place.

I believe it unfortunate that the short-term rewards of many fields are with high-*g* people who are good problem solvers but not necessarily discriminating about the problems they solve. For example, in order to have journal articles accepted or grant proposals funded, one needs to demonstrate convincingly the "tightness" of one's approach. But any research, including tightly conceived research, can be sterile, and much of what we read and hear about is just that. Fortunately, the long-term rewards of the field are won with more boldness, and with the imagination and creativity that is often not rewarded in the short term.

Synthetic-Creative Abilities. Although they are little represented by the research in this conference, synthetic-creative abilities are of great importance in many occupations. With the world changing at an unprecedented pace, the need to be flexible and to see old problems in new ways has never been greater. The military, for example, is now in a period of retrenchment and downsizing, making new perspectives all the more important.

The ability to think in a synthetic manner has been measured in a variety of ways (see, e.g., essays in Sternberg, 1988b). In our own research, we have used both convergent and divergent measures. For example, among the convergent measures are nonentrenched-reasoning problems and conceptional-projection problems. Nonentrenched-reasoning problems (Sternberg & Gastel, 1989) involve seeing analogies, classification, series, and the like, but with contrary-to-fact premises. For example, what would appear to be an ordinary analogy might be preceded by a statement such as, "Sparrows play hopscotch," or "Villains are lovable." The examinee then has to solve the analogy as though the premise were true. Conceptual-projection problems require examinees to reason with unfamiliar concepts that are novel in kind, such as *grue*, meaning, "green until the year 2000 and blue thereafter" (see Sternberg, 1982). The people who do well on these measures of novel ways of thinking are not necessarily the ones who do well on more conventional kinds of assessments.

We have also assessed synthetic abilities through the use of divergent measures (Sternberg & Lubart, 1991). For example, we have asked our examinees to write short stories, draw, generate advertising campaigns, and solve unusual scientific problems for which there are no single correct answers. In this research, we have found the quality of the creative product to be moderately domain-specific: Although there is some correlation across domains, it is only moderate (about .4). Our research is based on our "investment theory of creativity" (Sternberg & Lubart, 1991, 1992), according to which creative people are those who "buy low and sell high" in the world of ideas. In others words, they generate ideas that are not very popular, such as stocks with low price-earning ratios. The ideas are often not well received, and may even be rejected outright. But creative people persist with these ideas, trying to persuade other people of their value. When they finally do, they "sell high" and move on to the next idea, again championing an unpopular cause.

This research has yielded some interesting findings. For example, our data support the notion that creative people do indeed buy low and sell high. Moreover, we have found relations between creativity and other aspects of our investment theory, including intelligence, knowledge, styles of thinking, personality, and motivation.

We have also found "cohort-matching." When we plotted the rated creativity of the works we received against the ages of our subjects, we found, as had many before us, that degree of creativity tends to decrease as people age. Generally, the decrease begins around the age of 40. But we also plotted the ages of our subjects against the ages of our raters, and found that raters tend to rate as more creative, at least in some domains (such as advertising and science), the works of subjects in their own age cohort. In other words, at least some of the decline observed in older people may be due to cohort-matching. As most raters are in the middle of the age distribution (in our case, roughly 20 to 70), one would expect rated creativity first to rise with subject age, as the ages of the subjects match more closely the ages of the raters, and then to fall as the ages become more discrepant. Thus, the often-observed decline in creativity after the age of 40 or so may be due to rater effects rather than to loss of creativity itself.

Practical-Contextual Abilities. Although practical-contextual abilities involve more than adaption to the environment, our research focus has been on adaptation, especially for managers in business. We have also examined adaptation in salespeople, professors, and students. The qualitative patterns of data are similar across domains.

Our focus has been on the measurement of tacit knowledge, that is, knowledge that is not explicitly taught and often isn't even verbalized, but that is necessary for adapting successfully to an environment. We measured tacit knowledge via scenarios that simulate the kinds of problems that people encounter in their jobs on an everyday basis (Sternberg, Wagner, & Okagaki, 1993; Wagner & Sternberg, 1986). For example, in one exercise we might familiarize a business executive with a hypothetical business context and then provide a list of things he or she needs to get done in the next two months. The executive does not, however, have enough time to do them all. Given the list of activities, the executive indicates the priorities for getting each of them done. Or, in another exercise, the business executive might be asked to rate the quality of pieces of advice that a senior executive might give to a junior executive.

What have we found in such investigation? First, tacit knowledge increases, on the average, with experience. But experience is not sufficient for an increase in tacit knowledge. Rather, what seems to matter is how effectively one exploits one's experience. In other words, the critical variable is not experience, per se, but learning from experience.

Second, level of tacit knowledge does not correlate with g, at least not within the range of people who actually go into the occupations we have studied. In other words, with a sufficient range of IQs, tacit knowledge would probably correlate with IQ, as would almost anything else. But the natural range to use is that for people who actually enter the occupation. People who are mentally retarded, or geniuses for that matter, rarely become business executives. Thus, including the normal distribution of IQs in the population as a whole would be spurious in validating a test for business executives.

Third, scores on the Inventory of Tacit Knowledge do not correlate with scores on the Armed Services Vocational Aptitude Battery, with measures of styles (such as the Myers-Briggs), or with personality variables. Thus, tacit knowledge is not just another name for a variable that is already measured by commonly used tests.

Fourth, tacit knowledge predicts various measures of job success at about the .4 level of correlation, uncorrected for restriction of range, attenuation, or anything else.

Fifth, when one computes subscores for tacit knowledge, such as tacit knowledge for managing oneself, managing others, and managing tasks, the scores are correlated. Thus, there is "little g" for tacit knowledge. This little g is not the same as psychometric g.

Sixth, tacit knowledge correlates moderately across occupations (at about the .4 level). Seventh, the content of tacit knowledge differs across levels within an occupation; for instance, the tacit knowledge one needs to be a successful higher-level executive is different from the tacit knowledge one needs to be a lower-level executive. Finally, tacit knowledge is teachable, although it is best taught through role modeling and through mediated learning.

Our research with tacit knowledge suggests that there is more to success on the job than psychometric g. Other abilities, such as the ability to acquire tacit knowledge, matter as well. However, we are not claiming that tacit knowledge is all that is necessary for job success, or even that tacit knowledge is all of practical intelligence. Clearly, it is only part of what leads to success on the job. And with respect to practical intelligence, the abilities to select and shape environments are important as well, but are not measured by tests of tacit knowledge (Sternberg, 1985). Thus, tacit knowledge is just one element of many that leads to success on the job.

Knowledge

Knowledge is important for success on the job and in life. Knowledge can be either declarative or procedural, and each kind of knowledge is used separately as well as in interaction. Obviously, expertise in any area requires a vast store of knowledge. It is for this reason that we teach adults as well as children, and have on-the-job training in order to perfect skills of people in various jobs. Oddly enough, though, it is possible to have too much of a good thing.

I suspected for some time that too much knowledge could lead to an entrenched perspective on problems. In other words, one becomes so used to seeing things in a certain way that it becomes difficult to see them in any other way. Thus, with increased crystallization can come a loss of flexibility. Peter Frensch and I conducted a study that illustrated this point (Frensch & Sternberg, 1989). We had expert and novice bridge players play bridge against a computer. As would be expected, the experts did better than did the novices. When we made superficial structural changes in the game, the performance of both experts and novices was hurt slightly. Both groups, however, quickly recovered. When we made deep structural changes in the game, however, the experts were affected more than were the novices. This finding makes sense, because novices, by definition, don't have a deeply structured approach to accomplishing a task. Thus, our results confirmed the notion that with desirable knowledge can come undesirable entrenchment, and so as people become experts, they need to find ways to maintain their flexibility in their domain of expertise.

Thinking and Learning Styles

Styles of thinking and learning can also influence performance, both in training and on the job. My own work on styles is motivated by my theory of mental self-government (Sternberg, 1988a). The basic idea is that real-world forms of government are not coincidental or arbitrary, but are external reflections of ways in which we organize our minds. Just as countries or states or cities need to be governed, so do people.

A style is not a level or even a kind of ability, but rather a way of utilizing an ability or set of abilities. In other words, it is a proclivity, not a talent. Consider just a few examples of the styles in the theory of mental self-government.

Just as governments have three different functions—legislative, executive, and judicial—so do the minds of people. These three governmental functions correspond to three different thinking styles. A legislative person is someone who likes to come up with new ideas, new ways of doing things, and who basically has his or her own agenda and goals. An executive person may be just as intelligent, but prefers to be told what to do. Given directions, executive stylists can do a very good job in an intellectual task, but they prefer to work within the framework that is provided for them. Judicial people tend to be analytical and critical, evaluating and judging most things and people.

Different styles are ideally suited to different occupations. For example, as I tend to be a legislative stylist, my job as a university professor is probably well suited to me. I am paid to generate ideas and experiments, and within broad restrictions, can do whatever I want. At the same time, a contract lawyer I know is clearly an executive stylist. He draws up contracts between investment bankers. The perfect contract, he says, is one that is so airtight the bankers can't get out of it without paying him additional legal fees. Another friend with a judicial style has found an ideal job as a psychotherapist. He spends his days evaluating the problems of other people and deciding how to treat them.

Do styles matter in learning? Data collected by Elena Grigorenko and me suggest that they do (Grigorenko & Sternberg, 1992). We measured styles of both students and teachers, testing the hypothesis that, independent of student ability, the match between a student's and a teacher's profile of styles would be a predictor of the student's performance in the teacher's course. Put more bluntly, the hypothesis was that teachers prefer students whose styles match their own. Our hypothesis was confirmed.

Styles also matter on the job. Consider, for example, what styles one might seek in a lower-level business executive. One would probably want an individual who has an executive style—one who will do well whatever he or she is told to do. One would probably also look for someone who is rather local in the kinds of problems that he or she prefers to deal with, as the problems confronted by lower-level executives tend to be more local than global. Finally, one might seek an individual who is "monarchic," meaning that the individual focuses his or her sights on a particular problem and then pursues that problem until a solution is reached, not allowing other things to interfere with the problem solving. Monarchic people are strongly oriented toward the attainment of a single goal, to the exclusion of all else.

But if you ask yourself what you want in an upper-level executive, it would probably be quite different. You would probably want someone who is legislative or possibly judicial rather than executive, someone who is global rather than local in orientation, and someone who is hierarchical rather than monarchic. Styles sought at the lower levels of management may be quite different from the styles sought at the upper levels of management. The problem is that when one promotes successful lower-level managers, one may be promoting precisely those people whose styles do not match the needs of higher-level management. At the same time, one is derailing those people whose styles would be more appropriate for the upper reaches of management. Thus, the system of promotion may promote exactly the wrong people!

This problem is not limited to management. If one asks what stylistic characteristics lead to success in science as it is taught in most schools, one would probably come to the conclusion that it pays off for a scientist to be executive and local. For example, in order to get good grades in school science, one needs to be able to memorize textbooks and solve problems at the back of chapters. But if one asks how many times professional scientists actually do these things, the answer probably is never. Rather, scientists need to be legislative and global in their work, trying to formulate large questions of scientific and practical significance. Once again, some of the students who potentially may make the best scientists may be derailed during their school careers. I am particularly sensitive to this fact because I received a grade of C in introductory psychology, a course that essentially involved memorizing a book. At that point, I decided to seek out another major, mathematics. After doing worse in mathematics than I did in psychology, I returned, fortunately, to psychology. But the point is that we may derail from a given scientific pursuit those who later would actually thrive in it, and we may encourage others to pursue one career when they might be ideally suited to something else.

Personality

The work of Goldberg (this volume) and others in the "Big Five" of personality provides a useful basis for understanding the personality bases that may lead to success or failure on the job as well as in training. The evidence of Goldberg and others on these personality attributes is now so strong that we scarcely need to look further for understanding, at least at the top level of the hierarchy of personality attributes. Other personality attributes can be important to success on the job, however. For example, in our investment theory of creativity, Todd Lubart and I (Sternberg & Lubart, 1991) emphasized attributes that seem to be key to creative endeavors: tolerance of ambiguity, persistence in overcoming obstacles, willingness to grow, willingness to take risks, and courage. One could have all the cognitive attributes of creativity, but not the personal ones. Such a person might never do any creative work because of a fear of taking the risks necessary to buy low and sell high, or because of a lack of the courage needed to go against the grain. In general, then, one needs to match personality traits to the demands of the job, and select people who are a good fit.

Motivation

Perhaps no single personal attribute is more important to success or learning on the job than is motivation. It is interesting to note that the Japanese, who have been so successful both in the outcomes of their schooling and in the competitiveness in the world marketplace, have little interest in or tolerance of our theories of intelligence. They believe that the difference between levels of success is dependent on how hard people work—in other words, their motivation (Stevenson & Stigler, 1992). I believe their approach is wrong, but at the same time, I also believe it probably leads to more beneficial outcomes than does our own implicit theory of success. According to the Japanese, success can be attained if one just tries hard enough. Such a theory motivates people to work harder. On the other hand, the American theory—that some people can do the job and others can't, or that some people can learn and others can't—leads many people into discouragement, frustration, and ultimately, failure to make the effort necessary for success. Thus, an implicit theory of success that emphasizes motivation may be more likely to lead to success than one that emphasizes immutable abilities.

There is a great deal of work that suggests people do their most creative work when they are highly intrinsically motivated for that work (Amabile, Hennessey, & Grossman, 1986). In other words, creative people almost always love what they do. In steering children toward careers, therefore, and in steering employees toward lines of work, we should take their interests into account at least as much as their abilities. Although there may be a correlation between what people like to do and how well they do it, it is far from perfect. Many people who lack the talent want to be professional athletes, for example, just as some people with great athletic ability would prefer to do something other than sports. In assigning people to jobs, we sometimes forget that one of the best predictors of how well they will do is how much they really want to do the job.

We need also to remember the now well-replicated finding that emphasizing extrinsic rewards can undermine intrinsic motivation (Lepper & Green, 1978). In the United States, for example, we tend to place a great deal of emphasis on extrinsic motivators—grades, money, tokens, trophies, and the like. The problem with this emphasis is that it leads those people who are intrinsically motivated to come to believe that they're working for the extrinsic rewards, rather than for intrinsic satisfactions. As we undermine intrinsic motivation, we undermine the creativity that accompanies it. Thus, we need to redirect our emphases in order to help people do their best on the job, and maximize their creativity.

ROLES

In considering how to optimize human potentials, one aspect of the Person X Context interaction is to look at the kinds of roles in which a person feels comfortable. Some people prefer to be leaders; others, followers. Some people enjoy entrepreneurial roles; others, managerial roles. Some people would rather be thinkers; others, doers. Some people prefer staff jobs; others, line jobs. We can expect far greater productivity and creativity in work when the kind of role a person plays matches the kind of role the person feels comfortable taking.

Consider, for example, the scientist. One could give a set of ability tests, and even interest tests as well, and conclude that a person would make a good scientist. Some people would be happy to say that all they need is a high level of g (Hunter & Schmidt, 1990). But such analyses are superficial. Different scientific jobs emphasize different roles. For instance, the demands on a person who enters a university setting as a scientist are quite different from those on a person who chooses to work in industry. Even within such jobs, there are different roles. Some scientists prefer the role of researcher to that of teacher, whereas others prefer the reverse; still others prefer a balance. Some scientists are comfortable in the role of adaptors to existing scientific paradigms, whereas others prefer to shape such paradigms. Some scientists are intellectual entrepreneurs, whereas others prefer to be team players. Some scientists enjoy performing research, whereas others prefer to be research managers, rarely involving themselves except at the level of orchestrating and coordinating research. Thus, even within a single occupation, there are many role possibilities, some of which will work better for a given person than will others.

The same is true in other jobs. Consider, for example, the lawyer. Some lawyers might prefer the role of prosecutor; others, that of defense attorney. Some lawyers prefer corporate law; others, trial law. Some prefer a specialty such as tax; others, criminal law. Some prefer public interest law; others, the private sector. Once again, satisfaction and productivity on the job are more likely to be related to the specific roles within the job than to the name of the job itself. We need to take into account what a person actually does, not what he or she is called.

SITUATIONS

People's satisfaction with and adjustment to jobs will depend not only on their personal attributes and the roles they play, but also on the kinds of situations in which they find themselves. For example, some jobs involve high stress and others involve low stress. Some jobs involve close supervision; others, less supervision. Jobs differ as well in terms of whether the goals that need to be met are short term or long term. Further, an employee may work in a situation that is physically comfortable, or one that is physically uncomfortable. A person's fit to a job, I would argue, depends largely on how the situation in which the job is carried out fits that person's needs. For example, I had a secretary who might well have been perfect except for her tendency to crumble under conditions of high stress. Because there were always times that were in fact stressful—for example, right before the submission date for a grant proposal—she did not adjust well to the job. She had the abilities, and was comfortable with the role, but one particular situation in which she occasionally found herself was a poor fit to her needs.

The same issues apply to other jobs, such as the scientific and legal jobs considered previously. For example, some scientists may find themselves happy only when they're working in an area of endeavor that is very competitive, and in which individual scientists or teams of scientists are competing to make the same discovery first. Other scientists may prefer to work out of the mainstream, or in paradigms that are not as "hot," precisely so that they may avoid competition. Similarly, the kinds of stresses involved on the job are different for university scientists than for industrial scientists. Tenured professors who have very productive careers with job security might find that they are unable to function effectively without it.

Similarly, the situations are quite different for a lawyer in the courtroom versus one in the law office, as a partner versus as an associate, or defending minor criminals versus defending federal felons. How well the lawyer adapts to his or her job may depend as much on the kinds of situations faced as on any abilities or roles that are relevant to the legal profession.

VALUES

The match between the values of a person and the organization for which he or she works is another variable that I believe tends to be neglected. I have personally known any number of people who have had far more than the requisite amount of ability to succeed in their job, yet they either did not succeed, or decided to leave the job despite their success, because of a mismatch between their own values and those of the organization for which they worked.

A number of different kinds of values enter into play in the world of work, as well as in the world of the school. For example, some organizations emphasize productivity at the expense of people, whereas others focus on the people that work for them. Some care only about the products, others about the process by which the products are achieved. In some organizations individualists thrive, whereas in others the values lean toward a group orientation. In some organizations, the only key to advancement is the valuing of one's own self-interest, whereas in other organizations one can succeed and still be altruistic.

Once again, we can see the effects of values on specific occupations. Consider once again the scientist. Some organizations, such as university departments, highly value theory, and are less concerned with the particular empirical operations used to validate theories. My own university department values theory highly, and atheoretical presentations do not tend to be well received, regardless of how clever the experimental work may be. Other organizations and departments value empirical work much more highly, whether or not it is backed by a well-elaborated theory. Similarly, organizations differ with regard to valuing quality versus quantity in research. Our own department, for example, is more concerned with quality and with the impact the work has on the field. Other departments count publications when decisions are made about hiring or promotion. Similarly, departments differ in their relative valuing of teaching versus research. The professor, especially the nontenured professor, who puts a great deal of time into teaching may find, to his or her frustration, that he or she is not valued by a research-oriented department. The same is true of the scientist who values research in a teaching-oriented department.

The same kinds of issues arise in business. For example, organizations vary in terms of the extent to which they value the quality of the products they make versus simply how the products sell, regardless of the quality that backs them. If someone who values quality works for a firm in which quality is only a back-burner issue, he or she is bound to be frustrated. Organizations also differ in the extent to which they value stability versus innovation. An innovator in a firm that discourages invention will once again be frustrated. Thus, the fit of values between the individual and the organization influences the extent to which the person succeeds in the organizational setting.

I have proposed a theory of contextual modifiability (Sternberg, 1992) that considers different organizational climates that result from different value systems within an organization. Two of the key variables in this theory are the desire for change on the part of the organization and the desire for the appearance of change. The two variables are not the same: Some organizations genuinely desire to change, whereas others may desire only the appearance of change without any real modification at all. If employees who value growth and change find themselves in an organization that doesn't, they are likely to feel very frustrated.

LUCK

We may not like to talk about it, but luck plays a role in whether a person is able to get a job and how well the person does in a job. Status variables such as the socioeconomic status of the family of origin, gender, ethnic group, nationality, and handicaps all play a role in whether one can be considered for or is likely to obtain a job. For example, a Catholic woman cannot be a Roman Catholic priest, no matter how much she may want to be. A woman is also at a disadvantage if her goal is to become a professional boxer. Any resident of Bosnia is at a distinct disadvantage these days in being able to pursue a satisfying career, given that the country has become a war zone. And as much as a given person might want to become Prince of Monaco, he is not a likely candidate unless he happens to have been born into the right family at the right time.

Event variables also enter into one's ability to adapt to a job. For example, various kinds of hazards can affect one's degree of success. These hazards can be earthquakes, fires, wars, prejudice, and the like. Lucky breaks in opportunities also affect one's ability to take a job. For example, in many European countries, there is just one professor per department. Other members of the faculty can wait years until the current professor dies in the hope that they will be chosen to replace him or her. Or, to take another example, Prince Charles is still waiting to be King of England, and is likely to wait a bit longer until his mother either dies or decides to abdicate.

CONCLUSION

In conclusion, several variables—person, roles, situations, values, and luck—need to be taken into account in considering what it is that determines a person's ability to interact successfully with his or her context. A view that takes into account only abilities or, worse, only general ability, is inadequate. We once thought that the earth was at the center of the universe. It's not: The geocentric theory was wrong. Some now think that g is at the center of the universe. It's not: The new g-centric theory is wrong as well.

REFERENCES

Amabile, T. M., Hennessey, B. A., & Grossman, B. S. (1986). Social influences on creativity: The effects of contracted-for reward. *Journal of Personality and Social Psychology, 50*, 14-23.

Frensch, P. A., & Sternberg, R. J. (1989). Expertise and intelligent thinking: When is it worse to know better? In R. J. Sternberg (Ed.), *Advances in the psychology of human intelligence* (Vol. 5, pp. 157-188). Hillsdale, NJ: Lawrence Erlbaum Associates.

Grigorenko, E., & Sternberg, R. J. (1992). *Thinking styles in schools.* Manuscript submitted for publication.

Hunter, J. E., & Schmidt, F. L. (1990). *Methods of meta-analysis: Correcting error and bias in research findings.* Newbury Park, CA: Sage.

Lepper, M. R., & Green, D. (1978). Turning play into work: Effects of adult surveillance and extrinsic reward on children's intrinsic motivation. In M. R. Lepper & D. Green (Eds.), *The hidden costs of reward* (pp. 109-148). Hillsdale, NJ: Lawrence Erlbaum Associates.

Sternberg, R. J. (1982). Nonentrenchment in the assessment of intellectual giftedness. *Gifted Child Quarterly, 26*, 63-67.

Sternberg, R. J. (1985). *Beyond IQ: A triarchic theory of human intelligence.* New York: Cambridge University Press.

Sternberg, R. J. (1988a). Mental self-government: A theory of intellectual styles and their development. *Human Development, 31*, 197-224.

Sternberg, R. J. (1988b). *The nature of creativity: Contemporary psychological perspectives.* New York: Cambridge University Press.

Sternberg, R. J. (1988c). *The triarchic mind: A new theory of human intelligence.* New York: Viking.

Sternberg, R. J. (1992). *Reforming school reform.* Unpublished manuscript.

Sternberg, R. J., & Gastel, J. (1989). If dancers ate their shoes: Inductive reasoning with factual and counterfactual premises. *Memory and Cognition, 17*, 1-10.

Sternberg, R. J., & Lubart, T. I. (1991). An investment theory of creativity and its development. *Human Development, 34*, 1-31.

Sternberg, R. J., & Lubart, T. I. (1992). Buy low and sell high: An investment approach to creativity. *Current Directions in Psychological Science, 1*(1), 1-5.

Sternberg, R. J., Wagner, R. K., & Okagaki, L. (1993). Practical intelligence: The nature and role of tacit knowledge in work and at school. In H. Reese & J. Puckett (Eds.), *Advances in lifespan development* (pp. 195-227). Hillsdale, NJ: Lawrence Erlbaum Associates.

Stevenson, H. W., & Stigler, J. W. (1992). *The learning gap.* New York: Summit Books.

Wagner, R. K., & Sternberg, R. J. (1986). Tacit knowledge and intelligence in the everyday world. In R. J. Sternberg & R. K. Wagner (Eds.), *Practical intelligence: Nature and origins of competence in the everyday world* (pp. 52-83). New York: Cambridge University Press.

CHAPTER

19

THE FUTURE OF PERSONNEL SELECTION IN THE U.S. ARMY

Frank L. Schmidt
University of Iowa

The clusters of papers dealing with conceptualizing and measuring individual differences are intended to suggest future directions for military selection and classification—in both research and practice. Do these papers succeed in providing information useful for that purpose? I believe they do. At the very least, these papers stimulate thought about basic issues in personnel assessment and selection. The ideas these contributions stimulated for me are discussed in this chapter. I attempt to present them in a manner that I hope will be helpful for determining future research and practice.

COGNITIVE ABILITIES

The military services, like other employers, have used mental ability tests for selection (and classification) since the early part of this century. The major reason for this long history of use is the evidence showing that they work: Predictive validity studies have long shown that ability measures predict subsequent performance in training and on the job. A key research question is therefore, "How can we improve the validity of ability tests, so as to maximize prediction and its associated practical value (utility)?" Since the 1920s there have been two answers to this question, based on competing theories of ability. It is in the context of these two theories that we can understand the four chapters devoted to mental abilities in this volume (Alderton & Larson; Kyllonen; Lohman; and Ree & Earles).

The first theory, the g factor theory, holds that what is important in prediction of real-life performances from mental ability is the general mental ability factor that is always found in analysis of test intercorrelations. In the investment theory of general ability (Cattell, 1971, pp. 117-129), each individual is hypothesized to have a certain amount of mental ability that he or she uses to learn skills and knowledge as directed by the individual's interests and values.

For example, someone with strong mechanical interests will invest more mental ability in the development of mechanical skills than will someone with low interests in that area. This process produces the specific aptitudes that show up in factor analysis: spatial ability, quantitative ability, verbal ability, and others. It also explains why these specific aptitudes are highly correlated with g, and it explains why these factors (aptitudes) do not disappear when general ability is partialled out.

According to this theory, when an individual learns a new job, the same process takes place: The individual uses his or her general intelligence to learn the job in the same way that he or she has used g to acquire (learn) specific aptitudes. Thus this theory predicts that the components of specific aptitudes that are uncorrelated with g are not used in learning or performing jobs or other real-life tasks (Hunter, 1986). It, therefore, predicts that specific aptitudes will contribute nothing to prediction over and above the predictive power of a reliable measure of g. The g factor theory, therefore, states that the route to maximization of validity for mental ability is to produce better measures of general mental ability. This means measures that are more reliable. It also means measures that have broader coverage (i.e., that sample more of the skill domains in which people are likely to have "invested" their g). The use of more vehicles for assessing g increases the validity of the measure of g by helping to ensure that important manifestations of g, indicated by particular mental skills people could have employed their g in developing, are not omitted (Humphreys, 1979, 1986).

The other major theory is specific aptitude theory. This theory holds that specific aptitudes have predictive and causal status independent of general mental ability. That is, it holds that the components of specific aptitudes that are independent of g are used in learning and performing jobs and other real-world nontest tasks. This theory therefore holds that prediction of job performance is maximized by using the optimal battery of measures of specific aptitudes and weighting these aptitudes optimally (usually using regression weights).

During the 1980s, well-conducted large sample studies appeared that successfully pitted these two theories against each other. These studies indicate that for all but a small percentage of jobs, specific aptitudes contribute little or nothing to prediction over and above the effect of general mental ability. In their chapters in this volume, Ree and Earles and Alderton and Larson described some of this evidence, but there is much more (see, for example, Hunter, 1986; Jensen, 1980, 1986; Thorndike, 1986).

Alderton and Larson described a 10-year research program conducted simultaneously in different military services to increase the validity of the Armed Services Vocational Aptitude Battery (ASVAB) by adding measures of new specific aptitudes. That is, they described an extended and thorough research project based on the assumptions of specific aptitude theory; a major test of that theory against g factor theory. This project failed to find new abilities that enhanced ASVAB validity. Specific aptitude theory was disconfirmed and g factor theory was supported.

Ree and Earles (1992) described a series of independent studies conducted with Air Force data that pitted these two theories against each other using principal components analysis and regression methods. They found that the specific aptitudes in the batteries they studied contributed little to prediction beyond the effect of g. I would add that there are good statistical reasons to believe that even these small increments to validity are overestimates (see Schmidt, Ones, & Hunter, 1992, p. 646). In addition, they found that the average validity of the 10 ASVAB subtests across 37 jobs correlated .98 with the g loadings of the tests; this finding is very strong evidence for g factor theory and against specific aptitude theory.

The Lohman chapter is related to the foregoing papers. Lohman described the research program in cognitive analysis that is now nearly 20 years old. This research program, sometimes called "information processing psychology" and sometimes called "componential analysis," was based on the assumption (among others) that human mental performance on typical test items could be decomposed into independent components. It was believed that the study and understanding of these components would lead to development of new and more valid measures of specific abilities (aptitudes), which would, in turn, enhance prediction of job and training performance. As Lohman related, this promise was not fulfilled. As a result, he now sees a rather modest role for this research program: providing methods for determining when examinees are using inappropriate strategies on a test, and as an aid in test construction.

The major reason for the failure of this research program is probably the fact that those pursuing it systematically ignored the ubiquity of the g factor in mental ability data, including their own data. Before launching this program, these researchers did not first refute the findings related to g. In fact, they did not, in general, even attempt to critique them in any meaningful way. They simply ignored these findings and, without providing justification, implicitly assumed that specific aptitude theory provided a veridical (but incomplete) description of mental reality.

This is essentially the approach taken in this volume by Kyllonen. However, Kyllonen did not completely ignore the crucial question of whether specific aptitude theory can lead to measures that increase validity over that available from g alone. On the other hand, he skimmed over this question very quickly, merely stating, "CAM battery performance predicts learning success more accurately than does ASVAB battery performance." He presents no discussion of methodology used and presents no numerical results. After this assertion in the second paragraph of the chapter, he never returns to the question of incremental validity; he spends the rest of the paper discussing (a) what (specific) abilities should be measured, and (b) how they should be measured.

In addition, his statement on validity is ambiguous. He stated that his CAM battery increments validity over that produced by the ASVAB, but he did not state whether this difference is large or small. A small or even moderate apparent difference could easily be created by differential capitalization on chance if there are more subtests in the CAM battery than the 10 in the ASVAB. Kyllonen did not state the number of subtests in the CAM battery. Thus it is difficult to evaluate his validity claim. However, in light of the evidence discussed previously, one would have to be skeptical about the existence of any substantial amount of incremental validity. If substantial incremental validity over *g* is possible, why did it not turn up in the extended and extensive multi-Service research program described by Alderton and Larson?

In my own case, there is another reason to be skeptical. Kyllonen described work done in the LAMP (Learning Abilities Measurement Program) at the Air Force laboratories. A few years ago, when I was chair of the Defense Advisory Committee on Military Enlisted Testing (DAC), our committee asked the LAMP group to present their research to us, with particular emphasis on evidence that their measures could increment validity over that obtained from the paper-and-pencil ASVAB. We found that there was no convincing evidence available for incremental validity.

One thing that the Kyllonen chapter did do is show that specific ability factors can be identified that correspond to process and content. Factors can be identified that correspond to content: verbal, quantitative, and spatial content. Factors can be identified that correspond to processes: working memory, processing speed, declarative knowledge, and so forth. More important, factors can be found in the data that correspond to each combination of content and process—for example, a verbal speed factor, a quantitative working-memory factor, and so forth.

However, what is not shown is that these factors make any difference in any real-world task performance. What is not shown is that they increment validity in any way. And this is what is critical. There may be an implicit assumption here that if such specific factors can be identified, they will have predictive value. If so, such an assumption is not scientifically justified. Scientific standards require evidence; assumptions are not enough. If there is such an assumption (and there may not be), then this situation is analogous to one encountered in research on nature versus nurture. Researchers with an environmentalist orientation often show, for example, that certain kinds of people are treated differently and then assume that this different treatment has an effect on mental or emotional development of the individual. For example, it has been found that parents treat first-born children differently than later-born children. It has been shown that parents and others treat physically attractive children differently. It is then assumed, without further evidence, that this difference has an effect on the personality or development of the child. However, research conducted by behavior geneticists—a different group of researchers—has found that such effects apparently do not exist. No evidence of any effect shows up in the data (Bouchard, 1993).

One might argue that even if these specific factors do not increment validity and do not have any real-world, nontest correlates, they are nevertheless of psychological interest and importance. That is, one might argue that they provide important information on the organization of abilities. But even this is not necessarily true. Interpreted in light of the investment theory of mental ability (Cattell, 1971), these factors would be seen as reflecting only idiosyncratic individual decisions about the investment of one's *g* resources in particular content areas or processes. Because these decisions are driven by interests and values rather than by abilities, the resulting factors may not be relevant to the question of the organization of basic ability. Instead, they may be (indirectly) relevant to the study of interests and values (Goff & Ackerman, 1992).

Sternberg's chapter is also relevant to the question of the role of cognitive abilities in military selection. Sternberg argued that no complete selection and assignment system can be based on only the measurement of general mental ability. He argued that one must also consider personality, interests, values, knowledge, motivation, roles, and situations. It is hard to dispute this proposition; obviously, there are many noncognitive characteristics and many situational variables that affect work performance. However, his chapter appears to imply that one cannot study or use any predictor of performance unless one studies and uses all predictors of performance. Those challenging tests often make this argument. They state, for example, that it is inappropriate to use a mental ability test in hiring because the test does not measure motivation, and motivation is important in job performance. Is this reasonable? Certainly, we would all like to measure every valid trait and take into account every situational contingency. The question is how. How can we identify all the noncognitive traits that are valid? How many that appear to be valid (i.e., are plausible) are really valid? Could we get enough resources to research them all? How can we measure them if we could identify them? Do we have enough testing time for them all? It is doubtful whether it will be possible any time soon to measure all relevant traits in any selection system. And we may never be able to anticipate all relevant situational variables.

Further, some of the variables that Sternberg contended are valid predictors are of questionable status as constructs. For example, he contended that "tacit knowledge" and "practical intelligence" are two important predictors of job performance that have heretofore been overlooked or ignored by selection researchers. However, it is doubtful if these are really new contructs. There is considerable reason to believe that these two variables are really just job knowledge, with tacit knowledge corresponding closely with the traditional concept of job knowledge and practical intelligence being a broader form of job knowledge (Schmidt & Hunter, 1993; see also Ree & Earles, 1993).

NONCOGNITIVE TRAITS

The foregoing discussion indicates that if we want to increment validity over what is already being measured by the ASVAB, we must look outside the cognitive domain for additional predictors. This means looking at physical abilities (discussed by Hogan), personality traits (discussed by Goldberg), biographical data (explored by Mael), and vocational interests (treated by Hansen). We should also evaluate the self-efficacy constructs as suggested by Bandura.

Hogan described the considerable progress that has been made recently in the study of physical abilities. We now know that there are three major factors of physical ability: muscular strength, endurance, and movement quality (balance, coordination, etc.). These three factors show up in factor analyses of tests derived from job analysis of physically demanding jobs, provided only that the initial battery of measures is sufficiently complex. Further, for physically demanding jobs, these three abilities have substantial criterion-related validity, particularly for job sample criterion measures of performance. Finally, there is evidence that the physical abilities required and the validities of physical abilities are probably the same or similar for similar military and civilian jobs.

Because these research findings were not available at the time Project A began, Project A did not include physical abilities measures. (However, Project A did include some psychomotor measures, which Hogan should probably have mentioned.) Hogan felt that this is unfortunate and suggested that the Army examine the possibility of adding physical abilities measures for selection and classification purposes.

If only a minority of recruits are to be assigned to physically demanding jobs, use of physical abilities tests for job assignment (classification) could well have substantial utility. It is somewhat less likely that such measures would have high utility for initial selection into the Army. Most recruits are young, healthy, and male. Thus, even without use of physical ability tests in selection, there will likely be a sufficient number of soldiers with high physical ability (on all three factors) for assignment to combat and other specialties requiring high levels of physical ability. Thus, use of physical abilities measures in classification but not in selection avoids the possibility that potential recruits high on other desirable traits—cognitive ability in particular—would be screened out at selection because of mediocre physical ability.

Another promising noncognitive domain for incremental validity is personality. As in the case of physical abilities, there has been much recent research progress in this domain, and Goldberg summarized many of these advances. As he noted, much of this progress stems from the recent emergence of the Big Five theoretical scheme as the dominant model for conceptualizing personality. Unlike physical abilities, personality measures were included in Project A, and the relevant findings were heartening. The personality dimensions of dependability and achievement orientation, both components of the Big Five trait of Conscientiousness, were found to be correlated with several criteria (Effort and Leadership, Personal Discipline, and Physical Fitness and Military Bearing). These findings are consistent with civilian studies, such as the meta-analysis of Barrick and Mount (1991), which found that Conscientiousness correlated with ratings of job performance in all job families studied. More recently, Ones, Viswesvaran, and Schmidt (1993), in a meta-analysis of over 600 validity coefficients, found that integrity tests predicted supervisory ratings of job performance and composites of "counterproductive behaviors" on the job (e.g., excessive absenteeism, disciplinary problems, violence on the job, alcohol and drug use on the job). A subsequent study (Ones, 1993) showed that most of the variance in the integrity tests was accounted for by the personality trait of Conscientiousness. The validities in Project A and in Barrick and Mount (1991) were concurrent, but Ones et al. (1993) were able to perform separate analyses for predictive validities computed using applicants to jobs. They found that, despite any response distortion that might have occurred, the validities held up and were substantial (around .40).

Goldberg described the hierarchical structure of the personality domain and posed a very important question: From what level in this hierarchy should we draw the scales to be used to predict job performance? Should we measure at the level of the Big Five traits? Each of these five traits can be broken down into component personality facets. Should we measure at the level of these facets, with each scale measuring a separate facet? Should we go to an even lower level? The answer to this question depends on whether or not specific factor variance contributes to incremental validity. This question should sound very familiar: It is the same question encountered earlier in connection with the cognitive domain. As discussed previously, in that domain research has shown that specific factors (specific aptitudes) contribute little or nothing to incremental validity, over and above the predictive power of the general mental ability factor. In the personality domain, there is no single general factor; instead, there are five factors at the top of the hierarchy (but see later discussion). However, the question is otherwise the same, and in the personality domain, we do not yet know the answer. The answer may not be the same as in the mental abilities domain; in the personality domain, specific factors may have incremental validity over the Big Five. On the other hand, they may not.

This question is critical to the future of personality research in selection. In discussing it, Goldberg took a purely empirical approach. His position was that if one had infinitely large sample sizes (and thus did not have to worry about sampling error and capitalization on chance), it would be optimal to examine prediction treating each item as a separate scale, so as to maximize the opportunity of specific factors to contribute to incremental validity (if they are indeed capable of so contributing). This multiple correlation could then be compared to that produced when the items are aggregated into facet scales and when the items are aggregated into Big Five scales, and so forth. This approach is not practical, as he acknowledged, because not even the Army has sample sizes large enough to make it technically feasible. However, even beyond this, there is another problem—sampling error is not the only type of error to be taken into account; there is also measurement error. Individual items are highly unreliable, and, as a result, regression weights for individual items—already small at the parameter level—would be tiny at the observed level.

Most discussions of the question of the optimal levels of analysis and scale construction implicitly assume that specific factors in the personality domain probably have at least some level of incremental validity and that, therefore, the optimal level of analysis is apt to be some level lower than the Big Five. However, this may not be the case. As stated previously, Ones (1993) found that most of the variance of integrity tests is accounted for by Conscientiousness. However, some of it is accounted for by Agreeableness and some by Emotional Stability, two other Big Five personality traits. Now, along with that, consider this finding: The evidence to date indicates that integrity tests have higher validity for predicting job performance than do measures of Conscientiousness—in fact, over 50% higher (Ones, 1993). Further, in a large sample of examinees, these three traits—Conscientiousness, Agreeableness, and Emotional Stability—were found to be substantially correlated and to define a higher-order factor. (The other two Big Five traits—Extraversion and Openness to Experience—did not load on this factor.) Thus, the optimal level of aggregation may be higher than the Big Five level. If this finding holds up, the situation with respect to specific factors in the personality domain will turn out to be similar to that in the cognitive abilities domain, a very interesting turn of events indeed.

In any event, Goldberg was correct, in my judgment, in his conclusion that the personality domain is a promising one for military selection research. This area is worth a considerable investment of research effort. The resulting increments to validity could be substantial. Based on the analyses presented in Ones et al. (1993), the average increase in validity could be from about .50 to approximately .65, a 30 percent increase. The practical value of such an increase would be immense.

At first glance, the variable of self-efficacy discussed by Bandura would appear to belong in the personality domain and, therefore, to be potentially relevant to selection. But to determine whether this is correct, we need to know where the individual's perception of his or her self-efficacy comes from. What causes self-efficacy? Bandura's chapter is almost entirely devoted to examination of the "effects" of self-efficacy—its correlations with motivation and performance. Little attention is devoted to the question of the origins of self-efficacy. However, there is one relevant statement early in the paper: ". . .people rely heavily on their past performance in judging their efficacy." By the time they are adults, people have had considerable opportunity over the years to observe their performance. Performance depends to a great extent on ability and personality traits. If individuals' evaluations of their past performance are accurate, then self-efficacy is a veridical belief based in large part on the person's abilities and personality traits as these have affected past performance. If so, one could question the relevance of self-efficacy for selection; selecting on perceptions of self-efficacy would to a considerable extent amount to selecting on ability and various personality traits.

It is not clear that Bandura advocated use of self-efficacy in selection. His chapter focused mostly on laboratory research showing that certain *treatment conditions* can increase or decrease perceptions of self-efficacy, which, in turn, can affect self-confidence, persistence, motivation, and ultimately, performance. That is, his approach appears to be more oriented to the question of how people should be *managed* (and motivated) than to how they should be *selected*. However, even this takes us back to questions of the origins and accuracy of initial perceptions of self-efficacy in applicants for jobs. If people's beliefs about self-efficacy are based on years of repeated observations of their capabilities and performances and are accurate, we have to ask whether induced increases in perceived self-efficacy can be permanent and permanently effective in increasing performance. In short-term laboratory studies there is an effect, as shown by the research reviewed by Bandura, but what about long-term, real-life performance? This is an important unanswered question.

On the other hand, perhaps treatments (e.g., embedded in training programs) that increase perceptions of self-efficacy could have lasting effects. The treatments described by Bandura that increase self-efficacy are essentially confidence builders. People are led to believe that they can perform at a high level, if they try hard. An important question, then, becomes whether or not such confidence builders are or are not already built into military training programs. Based on my limited experience, I would say that to some extent, perhaps to a great extent, they are. The importance of self-confidence and morale have long been recognized by the military services. In any event, this is a question that deserves close examination. The contribution of Bandura's chapter is that it underlines the importance of this question.

Another noncognitive domain with the potential to increment validity in military selection is that of biographical data, discussed by Mael. Mael described current research efforts at the U.S. Army Research Institute aimed at developing biodata scales that measure personality traits previously measured only by personality inventories. Biodata items are selected for inclusion in each scale based on their correlations with scores on the relevant personality measure. In addition, those items that "relate to overt behaviors" are favored for retention, and those "purporting to measure internal states or attitudes" are disfavored. The goal is to create measures of personality traits that are less susceptible to response distortion (including faking and social desirability response biases) than typical personality tests. Mael reported that this approach (and variations thereof) have proven successful in that they have produced criterion-related validities similar to those of personality tests, and also lower correlations with measures of social desirability. However, one important question is left unanswered: How highly do these biodata "personality" scales correlate with the original personality scales? If they are indeed measuring the same personality traits, these correlations should be close to 1.00 after correcting for measurement error in both scales. Is this the case? We are not told.

Biodata scales have a history of established validity that goes back several decades. A key question is: What is the explanation for this record of validity? One possibility, of course, is that biodata measures some combination of traits that conduces to high criterion performance. Mael rejected this theory in favor of a passive theory of experience. That is, he adopted the theory that experiences that happen to people change them in ways that affect later performances of all types. He stated, "Biodata research and practice has always started from the premise that a person's experiences matter, that they are capable of imprinting on the future, and can thereby predict behavior."

This theory is contrary to, and is undermined by, recent research findings in behavior genetics. For example, studies of identical and fraternal twins (reared both apart and together) indicate that experiences do not just happen to people; instead, people actively select experiences and activities of all kinds based on their abilities, interests, and values—which, in turn, are strongly genetically influenced. Thus, the experiences people have tend to be determined by their pre-existing traits (Lykken, Bouchard, McGue, & Tellegen, 1993). Experiences do not happen to people randomly or accidentally. As an example of how an experience can affect an individual's development, Mael discussed the experience of being captain of a high school football team. He stated that the intent of an item assessing this experience is that "the captain experienced a leadership role and *took on characteristics of football team captains and of persons who must motivate or dominate*" (emphasis added). But according to findings in behavior genetics research, this is precisely the kind of experience that would be determined by preexisting characteristics of the individual; individuals with certain traits would seek out this role, and others would not. Behavior genetics research suggests that this item's validity is probably due to the fact that it is an indicant of these preexisting characteristics—and is probably not due to any developmental effects of the experience per se.

Another example cited by Mael is the well-verified negative relationship between educational attainment (having a high school diploma) and military attrition. Again, the experience per se of staying in high school to graduation is probably not the source of this relationship. Rather, people with certain traits (rebelliousness, lack of conscientiousness, etc.) cannot adjust to the demands of high school—and, likewise, cannot meet the demands of military life. Thus, preexisting traits are probably responsible for the relationship (validity).

One might argue that this is purely an academic question. Who cares why biodata works, as long as it works? In fact, there are very important practical implications. First, the theory from which one operates determines the type of items selected and the character of the resulting biodata scales—and may well ultimately affect the level of validity attained. Second, the answer affects the critical question of whether biodata items are "fair"—the question to which Mael devoted one third of his chapter. If biodata measures experiences that just "happened to happen" to people, then people who had less opportunity to have these experiences can claim that biodata is unfair to them. But, as Mael noted, selection instruments that measure individual traits are usually viewed as fair—whether or not individuals have control over their development of traits. Further, if experiences are viewed as reflections of traits, then a much wider variety of experiences (activities) that would be manifestations of that trait is likely to be sampled in constructing the biodata scale. Thus, examinees would have more opportunities to indicate that they had demonstrated the trait, and would have less basis for feelings of unfairness.

Mael was correct in maintaining that there appears to be a double standard in judgments of fairness: Biodata items are often considered to be unfair because it often appears that respondents have no control over the past events measured by biodata, but the fact that respondents have little if any control over their levels of traits, such as intelligence or extroversion, is rarely viewed as unfair. However, the resolution of the fairness issue is going to depend on resolution of the question of what it is that biodata measures—that is, the question of the source of the validity of biodata.

Thus, the broad theoretical question of what it is that biodata measures is very important. And in attempting to answer this question, biodata researchers cannot isolate themselves from relevant research in other areas. They must take into account relevant findings. In this case, the findings from behavior genetics research are very pertinent.

Mael argued that the basic conceptual rationale for using abilities and personality traits in selection is different from the rationale for using biodata. He maintained that "what is sought from measures of abilities and traits are *defining necessities of the job*, in which insufficiencies on that skill, ability, or trait will make performance difficult, if not impossible" (emphasis added). That is, he stated that in the ability and personality domains, the attempt in selection is to predict failure, not to predict degree of success. He argued that biodata, in contrast, is based on the "principle of equipollence (T. Mitchell, 1990), meaning that there is more than one way to reach a desired outcome." This is a false distinction. Both types of measures yield scores that encode probabilities of performance at different levels on a continuous criterion of success. For both types of measures, relationships with criterion measures have been found to be predominantly linear. Higher scores indicate higher performance, and the relation is best described by a straight line. Further, the relation between measures of skills, ability, personality traits, and biodata scales is compensatory; that is, higher levels on one dimension can compensate for lower levels on another (Schmidt, Ones, & Hunter, 1992). For example, higher levels of job knowledge can compensate for a lower level of ability; a higher level of Conscientiousness can compensate for a lower level of ability. Thus, in both cases, "there is more than one way to reach a desired outcome." There is no essential difference in the underlying conceptual model of selection for biodata versus abilities and personality traits.

Finally, a minor point: Mael stated that the term "dustbowl empiricism" in biodata "is *meant* to evoke a dry, sterile image" (emphasis added). It may indeed evoke such an image, but it was not meant to. The atheoretical empirical approach evolved during the 1930s in a number of universities that happened to be located in or near the great drought of that decade; hence, the term "dustbowl empiricism." Were this approach to evolve today in the same universities, it would probably be called "floodplain empiricism"!

Although I take issue with specific positions taken by Mael, I am in agreement with his fundamental thesis: Biodata is a promising avenue for incrementing validity over that attainable from general mental ability. Research by Rothstein, Schmidt, Erwin, Owens, and Sparks (1990) has shown that biodata scales constructed by methods similar to those advocated by Mael can yield substantial validities that are generalizable over organizations and that hold up over several decades. Further, this biodata scale increments the validity of general mental ability (Schmidt, 1988). Thus, it is appropriate for the U.S. Army Research Institute to be devoting resources to research on biodata.

As indicated previously, the evidence suggests that biodata is probably measuring traits or proclivities of some sort. A key question, then, is whether biodata can measure traits different from those measured by personality or interest tests—or can measure them more validly (e.g., with less response distortion). The fact, noted previously, that biodata increments the validity of general ability rules out the possibility that biodata is measuring only g. (The correlation between the biodata scale in Rothstein et al., 1990, and general mental ability was approximately .50, a value small enough to allow for incremental validity.)

A final potential area in the noncognitive realm that could contribute incremental validity is the measurement of vocational interests. During the 1950s and 1960s, the measurement of vocational interests was an important area of research for military selection researchers, at least in the Navy. Under Navy contract, Kenneth Clark and his associates (Clark, 1961) developed the Navy Vocational Interest Inventory (NVII), which has separate interests scales for the various skilled trades. As indicated in the chapter by Hansen, this instrument was quite successful. It was also widely recognized as an excellent research and development achievement in interest measurement, and was widely discussed and taught in graduate programs in I/O psychology. In addition to research on the NVII, Hansen summarized other studies that suggest that the measurement of vocational interests could be a promising route to incremental validity. In light of these facts, one is left wondering why so little emphasis was placed on this area of research by the military services after the 1960s. Her suggestion that perhaps military researchers might want to take another look at this area is a good one.

Hansen's chapter provided an excellent overview and summary of research findings on vocational interests since the 1920s. The interesting and admirable thing about much of this research is that the early findings have held up so well. Research findings from the 1930s showing that interests are quite stable after late adolescence continued to be confirmed in the 1980s. Early research findings on gender differences in interests are replicated today. Despite major changes in social roles, majors, and occupations entered, women's interests are found to have changed little, if at all, over the last 50 years. The stable and cumulative nature of these findings contrasts sharply with some other areas of psychology, in which no conclusion is regarded as valid for more than a few years.

However, in one critical area—the research evidence for the validity of interest measures for predicting job performance—the situation is different, unfortunately. Hansen's review of this validity evidence was similar to most I have seen in this area. First, studies were discussed one by one; evidence was not combined across studies using meta-analysis, as we have come to expect in the abilities domain and, more recently, in the personality domain. The findings in individual studies were susceptible to sampling error and other distorting artifacts. Second, each study typically reported a number of validity coefficients and other relationships; often only certain of these were selected for emphasis and extended discussion, resulting in potentially serious capitalization on chance configurations in the results. In fairness to Hansen, there may not be enough studies of the validity of interests for predicting job performance to allow a meta-analysis to be conducted. But this is precisely why more resources need to be devoted to studying the validity of vocational interests.

NONTRADITIONAL TESTING METHODS

I have classified the remaining two chapters in this group under the heading "nontraditional testing methods" because they are explorations of particular methods of measurement rather than discussions of substantive questions, and because the methods are nontraditional and infrequently used. These chapters are by McHenry and Schmitt on multimedia testing and by Bennett on constructed response items.

The McHenry and Schmitt chapters focused only on job sample tests. However, these are not traditional job sample tests but rather job sample tests that employ "integrated audio, video, and computer graphic technology"—in other words, hi-tech job sample tests. The overall thrust of this chapter is quite puzzling. The authors first asserted that, although traditional job sample tests have proven to be quite valid, they have a number of practical disadvantages that have caused some employers to conclude that the costs outweigh the benefits. The authors next stated that recent advances in computer, video, and CD technology have now made multimedia job sample tests possible and that these tests have potential for overcoming the problems associated with traditional job sample tests, thus leading to expanded use of job sample tests. Most of the remainder of the chapter is a (very good) discussion of methods and pitfalls in constructing, scoring, and using multimedia job sample tests. The strange thing, however, is that this discussion makes it clear that the costs and difficulties in constructing and using these tests are worse than those for traditional job sample tests! The net effect is to discourage the reader from considering the use of multimedia job sample tests. Further, the authors concluded that the available criterion-related validity evidence indicates that multimedia job sample tests are about as valid as—but no more valid than—traditional job sample tests. Although this means that they are indeed quite valid, it also means there is no gain in validity to be had as the payoff for the added trouble and expense of developing and using multimedia job sample tests.

Examples of disincentives for multimedia tests include the following. One may need several different panels of job experts—each of which must meet several times. In producing and filming the video, hundreds of unexpected problems can arise, many stemming from difficulties of communication between video production specialists and personnel psychologists. Programming the response modes for the computer can cause innumerable difficulties. The authors quoted one team of personnel psychologists as follows: "*Everything* turned out to be much more difficult than anticipated" (emphasis in original). And: "Double your time estimates, and then expect not to make schedules; double your budget; and, most importantly, invest in lots of aspirin." In contrast to the litany of difficulties, the limited advantages the authors cited for multimedia job sample tests over traditional job sample tests appear meager indeed!

The authors presented a useful discussion of how Cronbach's Generalizability Theory can be used to assess different sources of unreliability in multimedia (or, for that matter, traditional) job sample tests. However, they omitted one important source of measurement error: instability of examinees' responses over time, known as "transient error" (Hunter & Schmidt, 1990, p. 123). The generalizability model they presented involved administration of the test at only one point in time. It did not address the question of whether examinees would respond in the same manner two days or two weeks later; that is, it did not address the potentially important question of transient response error. In all fairness, most other studies of the reliability of job sample tests have also omitted examination of this source of measurement error.

I first became acquainted with the transient error problem years ago, when I found that the two-month stability of scores on the job sample test described in Schmidt, Greenthal, Berner, Hunter, and Seaton (1977) was quite low. We know this source of error is not a serious problem for written tests of ability or job knowledge: Test-retest reliability coefficients (whether with the same or parallel test forms) are quite high for such measures. But this may not be true for measures that are more in the nature of overt performances.

Performance in the employment interview appears to be one such example. When two different interviewers interview the same applicants at the same time (i.e., both interviewers are present at the same interview), the average level of agreement between the interviewers is quite high—.86; average of 216 values. However, when each interviewer interviews the applicants on different occasions, the average correlation between interviewers is much lower—.52; average of 41 values (McDaniel, Whetzel, Schmidt, & Maurer, in press). This is true even though the occasions may be only a day or two apart—or even on the same day. This difference can only be due to instability of responses (performance instability) on the part of interviewees. This difference of .34 indicates that, on average, 34% of the variance of interview scores is due to response instability (transient error). Thus transient error is not a minor source of error.

I suspect that the situation is similar for many job sample tests, whether traditional or multimedia. For both job sample tests and interviews, this (typically undetected) unreliability may be the explanation for the finding of smaller score differences by race: Group differences are always smaller for less-reliable measures. This hypothesis becomes more plausible when one considers that there is no credible theoretical reason why group differences should be smaller for job sample tests than for measures of job knowledge. Thus for both these reasons, transient error is a question that deserves more research attention.

It is interesting to note that the mean inter-interviewer correlation of .52 is virtually identical to the mean inter-rater correlation of .50 found by Rothstein (1990) for supervisory ratings of job performance. The fact that supervisors have the seeming advantage of longer observational periods does not appear to make a difference.

Response formats for the multimedia tests discussed by McHenry and Schmitt can be either multiple choice or free-response. If they are multiple choice, the examinee chooses from a (usually short) list of possible responses, and scoring is relatively simple and can be automated. If a free-response format is used, then human judges must score the responses. This means that rules for the scoring process must be carefully delineated and scorers must be thoroughly trained. It also means that the scoring process will be somewhat expensive. All these things are just as true for traditional job sample tests as for multimedia tests. The key contribution by Bennett is the discussion of methods for automating the scoring of free responses (which he calls "constructed responses"). This automated scoring is to be accomplished by complex computer programs, some of which are capable of improvement through learning as they are used. Bennett also discussed computer-based presentation (administration) of problems to examinees, but these methods are really not new or unusual. It is the possibility of automated computer-based scoring of free-response answers that is the real meat of this chapter.

Bennett was very explicit in stating that attempts to develop these automated scoring programs are quite new and that many problems remain to be solved.

This is not a finished technology ready for use; it is a research program for the next decade. Nevertheless, the beginnings that have been made are promising enough to encourage further research investment.

It is not clear that the most promising payoffs from this technology will be in the areas of selection or classification. The major payoffs may occur in the area of measurement of training success in military technical training schools. This would tend particularly to be true for those training schools that result in some degree of computer literacy—because this may be a prerequisite for efficient use of this measurement technology. Conceivably, such automatically scored constructed response tests could be used to certify training mastery at the end of technical training school.

Bennett cited some research that he interpreted as showing that the problem-type "formulating hypotheses" can contribute to prediction of some criteria over and above predictability from general mental ability. If this does indeed turn out to be true (and it would be surprising if it did), the reason might be that such free-response problems to some extent measure personality traits (such as flexibility or risk taking), as well as skills and abilities. This possibility should be given some research attention. We need to know what the constructs are that are being measured by the "formulating hypotheses" problems.

Finally, it is important to remember that the discussion of transient errors of measurement presented previously in connection with multimedia job sample tests applies equally to the kinds of tests discussed by Bennett. It is not enough the know whether the automated scoring programs yield scores that agree with those from human scorers. We must also know whether both types of scores are stable from occasion to occasion or are substantially affected by transient factors in mood, feeling, fluctuations in performance, and so on. To the extent that they are so affected, measurement may have to be extended to include several occasions, which would considerably increase costs.

CONCLUSIONS

The various chapters in this group present many useful suggestions for future research aimed at improving selection and classification measures in the Army. However, not all the suggestions are equally tenable when considered in light of cumulative research findings in the literature. As I hope this chapter has made clear, I believe the evidence indicates that the most promising research directions are in the various noncognitive areas. After over 50 years of research, including some very major research efforts during the 1980s, it is now evident that refinements in the measurement of abilities and aptitudes are unlikely to contribute nontrivial increments to validity beyond that which is produced by good measures of general mental ability. The areas of personality, biographical data, physical abilities, and perhaps interests are considerably more promising in that respect. It is in those directions that the major research efforts should be pointed.

REFERENCES

Barrick, M. R., & Mount, M. K. (1991). The big five personality dimensions and job performance: A meta-analysis. *Personnel Psychology, 44*, 1-26.

Bouchard, T. J. (1993). Genetic and environmental influences on adult personality: Evaluating the evidence. In J. Hettema and I. J. Deary (Eds.), *Foundations of personality* (pp. 15-44). The Netherlands: Kluwer Academic Publishers.

Cattell, R. B. (1971). *Abilities: Their structure, growth, and action.* Boston: Houghton Mifflin.

Clark, K. E. (1961). *The vocational interests of non-professional men.* Minneapolis: University of Minnesota Press.

Goff, M., & Ackerman, P. L. (1992). Personality-intelligence relations: Assessment of typical intellectual engagement. *Journal of Educational Psychology, 84*, 537-552.

Humphreys, L. G. (1979). The construct of general intelligence. *Intelligence, 3*, 105-120.

Humphreys, L. G. (1986). Commentary. *Journal of Vocational Behavior, 29*, 421-437.

Hunter, J. E. (1986). Cognitive ability, cognitive aptitudes, job knowledge, and job performance. *Journal of Vocational Behavior, 29*, 340-362.

Hunter, J. E., & Schmidt, F. L. (1990). *Methods of meta-analysis: Correcting error and bias in research findings.* Newbury Park, CA: Sage.

Jensen, A. R. (1980). *Bias in mental testing.* New York: The Free Press.

Jensen, A. R. (1986). g: Artifact or reality? *Journal of Vocational Behavior, 29*, 301-331.

Lykken, D. T., Bouchard, T. J., McGue, M., & Tellegen, A. (1993). Heritability of interests: A twin study. *Journal of Applied Psychology, 78*, 649-661.

McDaniel, M. A., Whetzel, D. L., Schmidt, F. L., & Maurer, S. (in press). The validity of employment interviews: A review and meta-analysis. *Journal of Applied Psychology.*

Mitchell, T. (1990). Can biodata predict personality? In M. G. Aamodt (Chair), *What does biodata predict?* Paper presented at the annual meeting of the International Personnel Management Association Assessment Council, San Diego.

Ones, D. S. (1993). *The construct validity of integrity tests.* Unpublished doctoral dissertation, University of Iowa, Iowa City.

Ones, D. S., Viswesvaran, C., & Schmidt, F. L. (1993). Comprehensive meta-analysis of integrity test validities: Findings and implications for personnel selection and theories of job performance. *Journal of Applied Psychology Monograph, 78*, 679-703.

Ree, M. J., & Earles, J. A. (1992). g is the best predictor of job performance. *Current Directions in Psychological Science, 1*, 86-89.

Ree, M. J., & Earles, J.A. (1993). g is to psychology what carbon is to chemistry: A reply to Sternberg and Wagner, McClelland, and Calfee. *Current Directions in Psychological Science, 2*, 11-12.

Rothstein, H. R. (1990). Interrater reliability of job performance ratings: Growth to asymptote level with increasing opportunity to observe. *Journal of Applied Psychology, 75*, 322-327.

Rothstein, H. R., Schmidt, F. L., Erwin, F. W., Owens, W. A., & Sparks, C. P. (1990). Biographical data in employment selection: Can validities be made generalizable? *Journal of Applied Psychology, 75*, 175-184.

Schmidt, F. L. (1988). The problem of group differences in ability test scores in employment selection. *Journal of Vocational Behavior, 33*, 272-292.

Schmidt, F. L., Greenthal, A. L., Berner, J. G., Hunter, J. E., & Seaton, F. W. (1977). Job sample vs. paper-and-pencil trades and technical tests: Adverse impact and examinee attitudes. *Personnel Psychology, 30,* 187-198.

Schmidt, F. L., & Hunter, J. E. (1993). Tacit knowledge, practical intelligence, general mental ability, and job knowledge. *Current Directions in Psychological Science, 2,* 8-9.

Schmidt, F. L., Ones, D. S., & Hunter, J. E. (1992). Personnel selection. *Annual Review of Psychology, 43,* 627-670.

Thorndike, R. L. (1986). The role of general ability in prediction. *Journal of Vocational Behavior, 29,* 332-339.

Part III

Operational Models for

Selection and Classification Decisions:

Making Use of Predictor and Criterion Information

CHAPTER

20

GOALS OF THE SELECTION AND CLASSIFICATION DECISION

Lauress L. Wise[1]
Defense Manpower Data Center

The first step in evaluating any program or system is to identify the goals that the program or system was designed to achieve. The process of selecting and classifying enlisted personnel is complex and costly. Across all of the Services, more than 200,000 youth were enlisted last year and were assigned to fill positions in well over 500 jobs. Defense remains a very significant area of investment for our federal resources and the return on the investment is a function of the quality of our Armed Forces. Selection and classification (S&C) decisions are the first step in determining that quality. The purpose of this chapter is to discuss specific goals of S&C classification decisions for military enlistees, in order to provide a starting point for evaluating our current system and alternatives.

The issues raised here are a variation on the "criterion problem." The development of criteria for evaluation or validation analyses involves specifying goals for the process being evaluated or validated, and then developing measures of the degree to which those goals are achieved. In this chapter the concepts of the "goals of" and "criteria for" S&C decisions are used more or less interchangeably.

Linda Gottfredson (1991) discussed the criterion problem as it relates to alternative job performance measures, in conjunction with the National Academy of Sciences' review of the Job Performance Measurement (JPM) project. This chapter, however, is not very much about measurement. It is primarily directed at the more general questions, such as "What do we mean by job performance?" and "Is maximizing job performance the sole objective of the S&C decision?"

The chapter is organized into four main sections. The first section addresses the issue of judging the quality of different answers to the question of goals for

---

[1] The views expressed in this chapter are those of the author and do not necessarily reflect the position of Defense Manpower Data Center or other agencies within the Department of Defense.

S&C decisions. Are some specifications of goals "better" than others? Why? The second section of the chapter describes alternative answers to the question of goals. The approach taken is inductive. Alternative answers that come to mind or have been previously proposed are explored in order to develop an approach to describing dimensions of the domain of possible answers. The third section is an attempt to apply the criteria from the first section to the alternatives described in the second section. The final section suggests areas where further research and development might be most fruitful.

CRITERIA CRITERIA

How will we know a good answer to the question of S&C goals when we find one? This is, in effect, a "meta-question," seeking criteria for evaluating the adequacy of our criteria. Gottfredson (1991) listed five criteria for evaluating criterion measures: validity, reliability, susceptibility to compromise, cost, and acceptability to interested parties. The present problem, evaluating the criterion constructs rather than the measures, is similar but not identical. Five criteria criteria are presented here for assessing the usefulness of a goal or set of goals in evaluating the quality of S&C decisions. These are: relatedness, completeness, measurability, relationship to costs, and acceptability to policy makers.

Relatedness. S&C goals are more valid to the extent that there is a clear relationship between the S&C decision and the goal. It would not be plausible, for example, to suggest that a goal of the S&C decision is to increase the gross national product (GNP). It might be possible to describe a causal model that linked the quality of S&C decisions to the GNP through, say, the security of foreign markets that was influenced, albeit weakly, by the readiness of our Armed Forces, which, in turn, depended on the quality of S&C decisions. The problem is that the relationship, even if it exists, would be too weak and there would be too many other causal factors that would have to be held constant in analyzing the hypothesized relationship. Even an economist would have trouble with the analyses. A better example would be training success, which is much more directly related to the quality of the match of individual attributes to job requirements. This is not to say that we must be limited to very proximal goals, only that the relationship between the S&C decision and the goal must be significant. Needless to say, there also should be an explicit model of the path linking the S&C decision to the goal.

Completeness. A second criteria criterion is that the goal should cover as much of the total impact of the S&C decision as possible. For example, one concern with training success as a criterion is that it does not also include the impact of S&C decisions on subsequent performance, thus leading us to underestimate the cost of poor decisions or the benefit from good ones. Other things being equal, a more complete specification of goals for S&C decisions will lead to a more accurate assessment of the impact of S&C decisions.

Measurability. A third criteria criterion is that it should be possible to measure the degree to which the goal is achieved. It would be plausible to suggest that the goal of S&C decisions is to maximize force readiness, but unless we have an operational measure of readiness, it will not be possible to determine the degree of difference in readiness associated with different decisions. The feasibility of measurement also must be considered. It might be reasonable to say that the goal of S&C decisions is to maximize future job proficiency as measured by hands-on performance tests. Because it will clearly not be feasible to develop and administer hands-on tests for all jobs, this type of goal would require us to use surrogates or models of predictive relationships developed from available data.

Relationship to Costs. Other things being equal, a goal that is related to cost savings will have advantages over one that is not. Ultimately, decision makers may be asked to invest in changes to the S&C process. If the proposed changes are related to specific cost savings, the decision will be much easier than if they are not. Training success is an appealing criterion because it is relatively easy to develop estimates of the cost of training failures. The value of improved job performance is generally harder to quantify to decision makers.

Acceptability to Policy Makers. In the final analysis, the goals of S&C decisions are whatever policy makers say they are. The question posed, however, is not what the goals are but what they should be. The four factors just described would seem to be useful in deciding among alternative specifications of S&C goals. It would be foolish, however, to begin any evaluation of the S&C process without being certain that policy makers will accept the specification of goals to be used in the evaluation.

DESCRIPTION OF THE GOAL SPACE

Now that some criteria have been suggested for evaluating the adequacy of different goal specifications, it is time to describe a set of plausible goals. This allows us to apply the above criteria to different goals and identify the best ones.

Alternative Goals

A review of prior evaluation efforts makes it clear that a very long list would be necessary to specify a set of plausible goals completely. Wise (1992) described a wide range of criteria that might be used in validating selection tests. When the entire S&C decision is considered, the range of criteria will doubtless be even broader. The approach taken here is to review examples and then try to specify the dimensions along which alternative goals vary. The term *goal space* is used to describe the range of alternative goals, and our immediate task is to determine some major dimensions for this space. The approach taken is inductive. A number of specific goals will be described first and then dimensions will be inferred from key differences among these goals. Following are some suggested goal alternatives.

Seat Fill. One goal of S&C decisions is to fill all available training seats with applicants who meet minimum qualifications for the position. This is, in fact, the exact goal of S&C decisions as viewed by recruiters. While this goal is very high on relatedness and measurability, it does lack something in terms of completeness, relationship to cost, and probably acceptability to most policy makers. For the most part, we will be seeking to evaluate alternative specifications of "qualification" for different jobs. Holding the conception of qualification to current minimums would not serve us well in this regard.

Training Success. Initial attempts to validate the Armed Services Vocational Aptitude Battery (ASVAB) used training success as the primary criterion. Success was sometimes defined as pass or fail or, more commonly, measured by final school grades. Here, too, relatedness and measurability are high, but completeness is still limited. The fact that policy makers funded the JPM project indicates some concern with the acceptability of training success as a complete specification of the goals of S&C decisions. Training success is related to cost but not really to benefit, and the goal of S&C decisions should probably be more than cost avoidance.

Reduced Attrition. The concept of success in training might be extended to the entire first tour, with success in the first tour being defined as nonattrition. Attrition is readily measurable and can reasonably be converted to costs. However, it is a somewhat incomplete criterion, because soldiers who do complete their first tour do not all contribute equally. Optimal predictors of attrition are typically different from predictors of performance in training and on the job, so the use of an attrition criterion may lead to a different evaluation of S&C decisions.

Job Proficiency. Soldiers are hired to perform various jobs. It is reasonable to suggest that the goal of S&C decisions should be to place applicants in jobs at which they will be proficient. This was largely the view of the JPM project as described by the NAS Committee (Wigdor & Green, 1991), where a measure of the percentage of the job that the recruit could perform successfully was developed as the primary criterion for validation of selection composites.

Job Performance. A multidimensional model of job performance that was derived from Project A data was described by Campbell, McHenry, and Wise (1990). The five dimensions identified divided into two "can do" measures of proficiency (job specific and general), two "will do" measures (effort and discipline), and physical fitness. In Project A, a soldier's total contribution was modeled as a function (weighted linear composite) of all five dimensions. In comparison to a job proficiency criterion, the use of this type job performance criterion would lead to much more emphasis on noncognitive factors (e.g., dependability and achievement orientation) in S&C decisions.

Qualified Months of Service. A model for S&C criteria that combined attrition with proficiency levels to define "qualified" months of service was developed by Armor, Fernandez, Bers, and Schwarzbach (1982). The overall model included separate predictions of the likelihood of attrition and the likelihood that the recruit would attain a satisfactory level of job proficiency (as measured by Skill Qualification Test scores) for each month of service. One typical reaction to this model is that a dichotomous measure of proficiency (or performance) is incomplete. However, it should be noted that under common assumptions (multivariate normality), a logistic regression model using a dichotomized criterion will yield the same prediction equations as would be obtained through ordinary regression analyses using the original criterion.

Total Career Performance. Models that extend only through the first tour necessarily ignore the contribution made by soldiers who choose to, and are invited to, reenlist and make a career of military service. It seems likely that leadership and higher-level technical abilities are much more important for career soldiers in comparison to first-tour soldiers. If career-force requirements are ignored in the criteria for evaluating S&C decisions, it is possible that leadership and higher-level technical aptitudes may be undervalued.

Performance Utility. Matching applicants to jobs necessarily involves trade-offs between different levels of expected performance in different jobs. Measures such as attrition or percentage of job proficiency provide a common scale across jobs, but the scale alone does not reflect the relative cost of attrition or value of job performance in the different jobs. A utility scaling of performance in different jobs, such as that reported by Sadacca, Campbell, DiFazio, Schultz, and White (1990), might provide a more comprehensive criterion for S&C decisions.

Total MOS Performance. S&C decisions are made for individuals, but there may be some reasons for considering larger units of analyses for evaluating the outcomes of these decisions. When individual performance is used as the criterion, "optimal" assignment algorithms usually lead to layering solutions where the most capable applicants are assigned to one job, the next most capable assigned to another, and so on. Common sense indicates that the some highly capable recruits are needed in each job, so these "optimal" assignment algorithms must be wrong. Why? One reason is that most jobs consist of a number of different duty areas and not all incumbents perform all duty areas. This allows for optimality by assigning the most capable to be assigned to the most difficult areas and the least capable to the least difficult areas. Further, individuals frequently work in teams where one highly capable individual can lead the work of the entire team.

A total-MOS criterion would assign utility levels to variability in expected performance as well as mean levels. For jobs where everyone worked independently at the same tasks, greater variability would lead to lower overall utility. For other jobs, an optimum level of variability in expected performance would depend on the variability in difficulty across duty positions and, where recruits work in teams, variability in task difficulty.

Unit Performance/Readiness. Another step beyond individual outcomes as criteria is to consider units consisting of recruits from different jobs. The ability to work in teams is frequently cited as an essential employment skill. Such skills do not play a significant role in current S&C decision procedures, perhaps in large part because we evaluate S&C decisions in terms of individual outcomes. Group outcome criteria could lead to more complete evaluations of S&C decisions, but very significant measurement problems would have to be resolved first.

Social Benefit/Problem Avoidance. The fairness of S&C procedures for all applicant groups is of current high interest. It would be highly desirable to reduce the degree of adverse impact inherent in current cognitive screening procedures so that all segments of society would have access to military training and job experience. Military service has frequently been viewed as an essential path to upward mobility and full participation in our society for groups whose past opportunities, including particularly educational and training opportunities, have been less than equal.

Accommodating Recruit Preferences. The applicant is an integral part of the S&C decision and it may be appropriate to consider his or her goals in addition to the Army's goals in making a selection and classification decision. It also may be appropriate to consider the benefits to the recruit that extend beyond the period of military service. A successful job match may ensure viable employment opportunities after military service as well as productivity during service. Benefits that extend beyond military service may have societal as well as individual consequences.

Goal Dimensions

The previous list is long enough to illustrate the diversity of possible answers to the question of reasonable goals for S&C decisions. Inspection of this list suggests at least three dimensions by which the goals vary. These are:

- **Period covered**—Ranging from time of accession through training, first tour, and the entire military career.

- **Type of metric**—Ranging from simple counts (number of qualified months of service) through individual difference measures (proficiency or performance) to utility units.

- **Unit of analysis**—Including individuals, jobs, units, and, perhaps, society as a whole.

Figure 20.1 depicts a goal-space cube that arrays alternative criteria along these three dimensions.

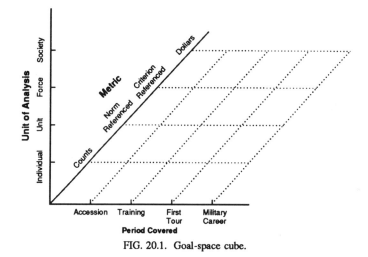

FIG. 20.1. Goal-space cube.

EVALUATION OF ALTERNATIVE GOALS

At the outset, it should be stated that the correct answer to the question of appropriate goals for S&C decisions is "all of the above." A complete evaluation of S&C procedures requires attention to the whole array of outcomes, ranging from filling available training seats to societal benefits at large. The real question is more one of emphasis. How much weight should be given to near-term versus longer-term outcomes, to different types of measures of these outcomes, and to individual versus group criteria? The discussion that follows applies the five criteria criteria to each of the three dimensions of the goal space to suggest areas for appropriate emphasis.

Period Covered. Several criteria suggest greater emphasis on earlier periods of service in comparison to later periods. Early success is more directly related to S&C decisions than in later success. Later success (posttraining, particularly after the first tour) depends on organizational policies and climate as much as on factors involved in the S&C decision. Good measures of early success tend to be more readily available, and it is easier to relate enlistment and training success to specific costs. The completeness criterion suggests, however, that some attention be given to the entire range of outcome periods so that characteristics essential to later success are not ignored. It is difficult to determine, without asking, the acceptability to policy makers of criteria from different career periods. It seems likely that acceptance will reflect a trade-off between completeness and confidence in the measures that are used.

Type of Metric. The type of metric is generally independent of the relatedness criteria. There is probably a trade-off between simpler measures (counting or dollars) that are more meaningful to policy makers and more readily related to costs, and more complex measures (proficiency, performance, utility) that may give a more complete assessment of the full impact of the S&C decision.

Unit of Analysis. Individual outcomes are more directly related to the S&C decision, easier to measure, and more readily related to costs than are more highly aggregated outcomes. Outcomes at the unit and force level may be of greater interest to policy makers. One important reason for consideration of higher units of analysis is that it may allow a more complete assessment of the range of critical skills that should be considered in S&C decisions. There may be some doubt whether policy makers are very concerned about societal outcomes but, in the current environment, altogether ignoring adverse impact is probably not acceptable.

Overall, the evaluation criteria suggest that it is appropriate to place greatest emphasis on early outcomes measured as simply and convincingly as possible. Such an approach should yield estimates of benefits from alternative S&C procedures that are clear and compelling to policy makers, albeit perhaps understated. Some attention to longer-term and more complex criteria is still needed, however, in order to appropriately value more complex skills such as leadership, higher-order thinking, and team skills.

The Rand qualified person-months model (Armor et al., 1982) represents a start at integrating multiple outcomes into an overall model. Further work is needed to include reenlistment and career outcomes, to begin to recognize leadership and team skills, and to incorporate more precise metrics of the value of performance in different jobs. The most satisfactory system for evaluating S&C decisions should involve reasonably sophisticated simulations of the whole range of outcomes associated with S&C decisions. It is likely to require collaborative efforts by personnel psychologists, labor economists, and team members with other areas of expertise.

AREAS FOR FURTHER RESEARCH

Satisfactory outcome measures are not currently available for several of the outcome types discussed previously. Further research might increase the feasibility of more comprehensive models of S&C outcomes. A brief discussion of some of the more substantial areas for further research is given here as an epilogue to the discussion of goals for S&C decisions.

Operational Performance Assessment. Data for the routine evaluation of S&C decisions are not routinely available. Training success measures are not accessible to researchers, and the Army SQT program is no longer being administered. Current administrative records do provide a limited basis for evaluating S&C outcomes, but a more comprehensive system is needed. A system of readiness checks for individuals, and perhaps for units as well, would be extremely useful for evaluating initial training programs and assessing the need for continuing training, as well as for measuring outcomes of S&C decisions.

Performance Utility. The work of Sadacca et al. (1990) provided a good beginning for specifying the functional relationship between performance measures and a common utility metric. The approach taken in that effort was essentially normative, with a two-stage process required to map levels on specific performance measures onto a percentile metric and then onto a utility metric. One important next step would be to develop a model specifying the form of the utility function for each job as a function of known characteristics of the job. Additional work on empirical bases for the utility functions to complement the current judgmental bases would also be desirable.

Marginal Utility. Nord and White (1988) have pointed out that the utility of different levels of expected performance for a new enlistee will depend on the current distribution of performance levels for the job into which the enlistee is classified. The concept is that performance utility is always "at the margin" with current performance levels held constant. Given current dramatic changes in force structure, it is clear that we will be at much different margins than in the past. Research on the relationship of job characteristics to the utility of different distributions of performance levels would provide some basis for predicting the impact of changes in force structure and recruit quality on performance utility functions.

Unit Effectiveness. Although considerable research has been, and is being, conducted on unit effectiveness, we still do not know very much about how individual characteristics that might be used in S&C decisions contribute to unit effectiveness. This would be another area for fruitful research.

Societal Benefit. We should know a great deal more about how to ensure fairness in selection and classification processes and how to minimize adverse impact for all applicant groups. We also need to know more about how to value improvements in this area. It is unlikely that new tests could both maintain current validity levels and significantly reduce adverse impact. Policy guidance will drive decisions about trade-offs between adverse impact (or equal participation in military service by all population groups), recruiting costs, training costs, and job performance levels. Methods are needed for collecting policy judgments and converting them to operational weights for different types of outcomes.

A Composite Model. Finally, a most important area for further research is the integration of all of the different types of outcomes into a composite model. As the model evolves, procedures for simulating composite outcomes as a function of changes in S&C procedures will be needed. The ultimate outcome of this area of research could be an ongoing system for identifying and implementing improved S&C procedures.

REFERENCES

Armor, D. J., Fernandez, R. L., Bers, K., & Schwarzbach, D. (1982). *Recruit aptitudes and Army job performance: Setting enlistment standards for infantrymen* (R-2874-MRAL). Santa Monica, CA: Rand Corporation.

Campbell, J. P., McHenry, J. J., & Wise, L. L. (1990). Modeling job performance in a population of jobs. *Personnel Psychology, 43*, 313-333.

Gottfredson, L. S. (1991). The evaluation of alternative measures of job performance. In A. K. Wigdor & B. F. Green (Eds.), *Performance assessment for the workplace.* Washington, DC: National Academy Press.

Nord, R., & White, L. A. (1988). The measurement and application of performance utility: Some key issues. In B. F. Green, H. Wing, & A. K. Wigdor (Eds.), *Linking military enlistment standards to job performance: Report of a workshop.* Washington, DC: National Academy Press.

Sadacca, R., Campbell, J. P., DiFazio, A. S., Schultz, S. R., & White, L. A. (1990). Scaling performance utility to enhance selection/classification decisions. *Personnel Psychology, 43,* 367-378.

Wigdor, A. K., & Green, B. F. (Eds.).(1991). *Performance assessment for the workplace.* Washington, DC: National Academy Press.

Wise, L. L. (1992). The validity of test scores for selecting and classifying enlisted recruits. In B. R. Gifford & L. C. Wing (Eds.), *Test policy in defense: Lessons from the military for education, training, and employment.* Boston: Kluwer.

CHAPTER

21

FAIR TEST USE: RESEARCH AND POLICY

Robert L. Linn
University of Colorado at Boulder

During the last three decades, the U.S. military services in general, and the Army in particular, have substantially outpaced the private sector in providing opportunities for American minorities. The participation of African Americans in the Army has been at rates higher than their percentage of the general population throughout the enlisted ranks during the past 20 years. In 1986, for example, 29.6% of the Army enlisted personnel were African American. The percentages by rank went from a low of 22.2% for privates to a high of 36% for sergeants. Percentages for officers were lower than for enlisted personnel, but the percentages increased substantially during the 1970s and 1980s. In 1986, 10.4% of Army officers were African American, compared to 3.9% in 1972. The percentage of generals who were African American increased from 0.7% to 7.0% during that same period (Wigdor & Green, 1991, p. 39).

Participation by other minorities has not been at as high a rate as that of African Americans, but is still substantial when compared to the civilian sector. In 1989, 62% of Army active-duty enlisted personnel were White, 31% were African American, and 7% were other minorities, whereas the corresponding percentages of civilians between 18 and 44 years were 85%, 12%, and 3%, respectively (Wigdor & Green, 1991). The other military Services have also had relatively high minority participation rates, but not as high as those achieved by the Army. The military is clearly seen as a source of opportunities for many minority group members. In addition to opportunities provided in the form of military careers, the military has provided "an important route to upward mobility for American minority group members" (Wigdor & Green, 1991, p. 38).

The achievement of this record can be attributed to many factors. Certainly the relative lack of opportunities for minorities in many civilian sectors has enhanced the attractiveness of the military. Although acknowledging that many other factors may make the military attractive to African-American youths, Binkin and Eitelberg (1986) argued that "the common factor that influences its overall attractiveness, particularly to young black males, is the dismal civilian labor market that confronts them" (p. 77). But the contrast in opportunities in the civilian labor market and the military is itself the result of explicit military policy to provide equal opportunity by fully integrating the Services.

The goal of racial balance across specialties within the Services has been more difficult to achieve than has the distribution across the enlisted ranks. Percentage distributions of enlisted personnel for large clusters of jobs across Services changed substantially for African Americans between fiscal years 1973 and 1989 and moved closer to distribution for all personnel in fiscal year 1989. Between 1973 and 1989, there was a decrease in the percentage of African Americans in the two clusters of jobs that include infantry and functional and service support services. There was a corresponding increase in the percentages in the two more technical clusters of jobs that include medical and allied specialties and electronic and mechanical repair specialties. There has been considerable progress in moving the percentages of African Americans who are in these broad clusters of specialties to be more in line with the overall distribution. However, there is still a tendency for African Americans to be more heavily concentrated in the occupational specialties requiring less technical skill.

There are both general enlistment standards on the Armed Forces Qualification Test (AFQT) and job-specific standards on composite scores derived from the Armed Services Vocational Aptitude Battery (ASVAB). For the population of enlistment-age youth as a whole, a smaller percentage of African Americans and Hispanics are qualified for enlistment because, on the average, they have lower scores on these cognitive tests than do Whites. These differences were graphically documented by Eitelberg (1988). Eitelberg used the data from the *Profile of American Youth* (Department of Defense, 1982) to estimate the percentages of White, African-American, and Hispanic youth, subdivided by gender, who were qualified for enlistment in the Army. He also estimated the percentages for the least and most selective occupations. The percentages qualified for the least selective jobs were 35%, 50%, and 83% for African Americans, Hispanics, and Whites, respectively. The corresponding percentages for the most selective jobs were 3%, 9%, and 30%. The progress in African-American representation in more technical jobs appears particularly impressive in the context of the large discrepancies in estimated qualification rates shown by Eitelberg.

In addition to general enlistment qualifications based on mental, physical, and moral tests, candidates must qualify for a particular job specialty. Performance on aptitude area composites is taken into consideration, but the decision to offer a candidate a particular slot is influenced by a variety of other factors, including job popularity, availability of spaces in the relevant training schools, and the projected fill of slots earmarked for a particular job. Minority and gender balance by specialty are also considered.

DIFFERENTIAL PREDICTION

This brief overview of participation and qualification rates of minorities provides some context for considering issues of prediction bias and fair test use. The narrower technical issue of prediction bias for members of particular groups defined by race or gender will be considered first. Although studies of prediction bias are confronted with a number of technical problems, they are less complicated and less controversial than are questions of fairness, which necessarily involve questions of social values.

Although the issue of predictive bias had been addressed to a limited extent prior to that time, concern about this potential problem came to the forefront in the mid-1960s. As noted by Cole and Moss (1989), the dominance of bias as "a testing issue began during the civil rights movement of the 1960s and gained fuel from the women's rights movement that followed" (p. 201). Work in the late 1960s was motivated by concerns of fairness, but was limited to a particular perspective. Specifically, the work was stimulated by a hypothesis that tests were unfair to minorities in the sense that they underestimated performance in nontest situations. That is, it was expected by many that total-group predictions based on test scores would underpredict the criterion performance of minority group members.

More global and only partially articulated concerns about test bias and whether it was fair to interpret test scores of minority candidates in the same way as scores of their majority group counterparts got translated into a technical issue of predictive bias or differential prediction by group. If the criterion performance of one group is systematically higher or lower than predicted from their test scores, the prediction is biased in favor of or against members of that group. The commonly expected finding of underprediction for minorities (most often African American and somewhat less frequently Hispanic) was generally not found. Rather, in educational, industrial, and military settings, either there were no significant differences in prediction equations for minority and majority groups or there was some degree of overprediction for the minority group (Hunter, Schmidt, & Hunter, 1979; Linn, 1982; Valentine, 1977).

According to the original conception of predictive bias, the most common finding of overprediction for African Americans or Hispanics when differences were found is consistent with a conclusion that predictive bias is either nonexistent or actually in favor of the minority group. There are, however, artifacts that could produce the overprediction. In particular, less than perfect reliability of the predictor, specification error (e.g., the exclusion of an important predictor from the equation), and differential selectivity for the two groups being compared can yield an artifactual overprediction for the group with lower scores on the test (Linn, 1983; Linn & Hastings, 1984; Linn & Werts, 1971; and Reilly, 1973).

The 1987 *Principles for Validation and Use of Personnel Selection Procedures* published by the Society for Industrial and Organizational Psychology (SIOP) essentially dismissed the idea of differential prediction for major ethnic groups:

> There is little evidence to suggest that there is differential prediction for the sexes, and the literature indicates that differential prediction on the basis of cognitive tests is not supported for the major ethnic groups (Schmidt, Pearlman, & Hunter, 1980; Hunter, Schmidt, & Rauschenberger, 1984). There is no compelling research literature or theory to suggest that cognitive tests should be used differently for different groups (National Academy of Sciences, 1982; SIOP, 1987, p. 18 [note that the National Academy of Sciences reference is shown here as Wigdor & Garner, 1982]).

Two studies involving military data, one published the same year as the *Principles* and one the following year (Dunbar & Novick, 1988; Houston & Novick, 1987), reported results that are inconsistent with the general dismissal of the issue. Houston and Novick reported results comparing the prediction equations for African-American and White enlisted personnel in nine Air Force mechanical specialties. Within specialty, sample sizes ranged from 101 to 361 for African Americans and from 399 to 2,699 for Whites. Final training course grades were used as the criterion and the ASVAB Mechanical Composite was used at the primary predictor. The Johnson-Neyman procedure was used to define regions where the two regression lines were significantly different. In eight of the nine specialties, there were regions of significant difference for the two predictors. Across those eight specialties, between 29% and 76% of the African-American airmen had predictor scores in the regions where the predictions were significantly different. In all cases, the slope was flatter for the African-American airmen than for the White airmen, and the lines intersected within the range of observed scores.

Fig. 21.1 displays the regression lines for the two groups for the Bombardment Aircraft Maintenance specialty, which is the specialty with the largest sample of African Americans (361) and the second largest sample of Whites (2,695). The minimum Mechanical Composite score required for that specialty is 35. The regions of significant difference include Mechanical Composite scores less than 61 or greater than 70. Thus, there is significant overprediction of course grades for African Americans with Mechanical Composite scores greater than 70, but there is significant underprediction for African Americans with scores less than 61. The mean and standard deviation for African Americans were 64.4 and 11.4, respectively. Clearly, grades are underpredicted for a substantial fraction of African Americans in the region. More importantly, it is in this region between the minimum composite score of 35 and 61 where decisions about placement in the specialty are most likely to occur.

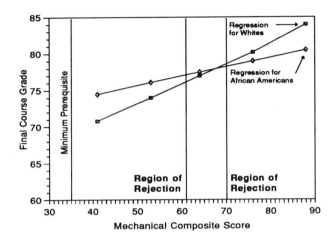

FIG. 21.1. Predictions of bombardment aircraft maintenance course grades by group and regions of significant difference (Ns = 361 African Americans and 2,695 Whites). The squares and diamonds on the regression lines are at predictor scores equal to the mean for African Americans, the mean plus and minus one standard deviation, and the mean plus and minus two standard deviations. Figure based on numerical results presented in Houston and Novick (1987, Tables 2, 3, & 4).

One Air Force specialty is not enough to reject the conclusion expressed in the *Principles*. However, the findings for the specialty shown in Fig. 21.1 are similar to those in five of the other eight specialties analyzed by Houston and Novick (1987). Fig. 21.2 displays the differences between the criterion predictions obtained from the race-differentiated regression lines expressed in standard deviation units for the African-American sample. The prediction from the equation for African Americans is subtracted from the one for Whites. Thus, a negative number implies underprediction and a positive number implies overprediction. The differences are shown for three points on the predictor scale: the mean for African Americans minus one standard deviation, the mean, and the mean plus one standard deviation. Job number nine in Fig. 21.2 is the Bombardment Aircraft Maintenance specialty that was shown in Fig. 21.1. The solid African Americans bars, representing differences in prediction for predictor scores one standard deviation below the mean for African Americans are all negative. Thus, there is a tendency for the White equation to underpredict the criterion performance of African Americans with low Mechanical Composite scores. For six of the nine jobs, the underprediction is three tenths of a standard deviation or greater. The overprediction that was observed was for high predictor scores, which reflects the flatter regression slope for African Americans than for Whites in all nine jobs.

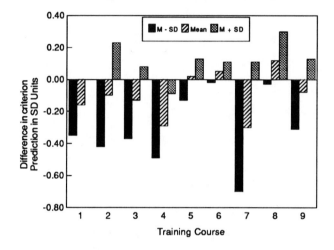

FIG. 21.2. Differences in criterion predictions (White-African American) expressed in standard deviation units for African Americans predictor values at the African-American mean minus 1 SD, the African-American mean, and the African-American mean plus 1 SD. Based on Houston and Novick (1987, Table 5).

The Houston and Novick (1987) results lead me to question the conclusion in the *Principles* regarding differential prediction for major ethnic groups. Results from a study by Dunbar and Novick (1988), as well as findings in educational contexts (Linn, 1982), provide reasons to question the conclusion about little differential prediction by gender. Dunbar and Novick compared the prediction for men and women in nine clerical specialties in the U.S. Marine Corps. The equation for men underpredicted the course grades of women in all nine specialties. At the mean score on the clerical composite, the amount of underprediction ranged from a low of .17 standard deviation to a high of .62 standard deviation and had a weighted mean of .33 (see Fig. 21.3). The amount of underprediction was reduced when comparison was made for high school graduates only. The weighted mean underprediction for the latter comparison was .18 standard deviation. Nonetheless, there is more than a "little evidence to suggest that there is differential prediction for the sexes" (SIOP, 1987).

The Joint Services Measurement/Enlistment Standards project provides additional data that are worth considering. A summary of the differential prediction results can be found in Wigdor and Green (1991, pp. 173-178). The focus of those analyses is on the use of hands-on performance measures as the criterion. However, it is useful to briefly contrast the results for studies where job knowledge measures were used with the overall results for the studies with hands-on performance measures. The average correlation of the predictors with the job knowledge criterion measures is noticeably lower for African Americans than for Whites (.26 versus .43 using the selection composite as the predictor, and .20 versus .38 using the AFQT as the predictor). This tendency for the correlation to be lower for African Americans than Whites is consistent with the Houston and Novick (1987) finding that the regression slope for African Americans is lower than that for Whites.

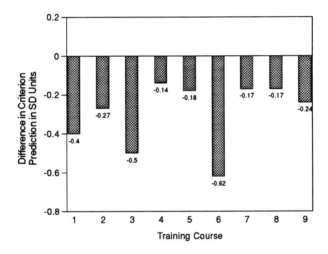

FIG. 21.3. Differences in criterion predictions (men-women) expressed in standard deviation units for women for clerical scores equal to the mean for women. Based on Dunbar and Novick (1988, Table 3).

When hands-on performance measures are used as the criterion, however, the correlations for the two groups are more similar, albeit lower for both groups. The slopes for the regression equations based on White and African-American personnel were not significantly different for any of the 21 specialties when hands-on performance was regressed on the selection composite for the specialty. Although the differences in intercepts were small, intercepts tended to be higher for Whites than for African Americans, a finding that is consistent with earlier research showing some small amount of overprediction.

Figure 21.4 displays the standardized differences between predicted hands-on scores for African Americans at selection composite values at the African-American mean minus one standard deviation, at the African-American mean, and at the African-American mean plus one standard deviation. The three values plotted for each predictor value are the averages across studies with different size samples of African Americans. As can be seen, for all three sample sizes there is a small amount of overprediction at all three score levels. It should be noted, however, that the largest average overprediction occurs for the seven studies with the smallest samples of African Americans (fewer than 25 per study). For the six studies that each had 75 or more African Americans, the amount of overprediction averages only about a tenth of a standard deviation.

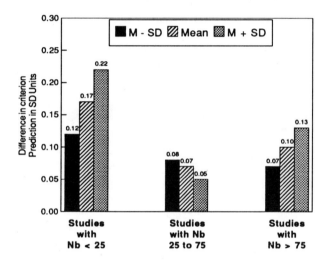

Note. The weighted average differences are for seven studies where the number of African Americans (Nb) was less than 25 per study, eight studies with Nb between 25 and 75, and six studies with Nb greeater than 75. Differences in predictions are shown for selection composite scores for African Americans at the mean minus one standard deviation, the mean, and the mean plus one standard deviation. Based on Wigdor and Green (1991, Table 8-17).

FIG. 21.4. Weighted average difference in predicted hands-on scores (White-African American) from selection composites for African-American and pooled equations.

Unlike the Houston and Novick (1987) results where final course grades served as the criterion measure, the regression lines generally did not cross within the region of observed scores. It is tempting to speculate that the difference in results may be due to the difference in the nature of the criterion measures. The larger difference in correlations for the job knowledge criterion, which is presumably more like the course grade criterion, than for the hands-on measure provides some modest degree of support for this notion.

Although, with the exception of Houston and Novick results, differential prediction rarely shows a predictive bias that leads to underprediction of minority group performance, it does not seem wise to adopt the view expressed in the SIOP *Principles* that implies that prediction bias can safely be ignored. Thus, I would recommend that differential prediction continue to be a topic on the validation research agenda.

FAIR TEST USE

But what about the larger question of fair test use? The existence or absence of predictive bias does not, by itself, indicate whether a particular use of a test is fair. What is considered fair test use depends not only on technical findings of predictive bias but on social values. The SIOP *Principles* make the distinction as follows:

> Fairness is a social rather than a psychometric concept. Its definition depends on what one considers to be fair. Fairness has no single meaning, and therefore, no single statistical or psychometric definition. Fairness or lack of fairness is not a property of a selection procedure, but rather a joint function of the procedure, the job, the population, and how the scores derived from it are used. (SIOP, 1987, p. 18)

Following this statement, the *Principles* move immediately into a discussion of predictive bias. The clear implication seems to be that the technical concept of predictive bias fits within the domain of validation of selection tests, but analyses of different definitions of and perspectives regarding fairness fall outside of that domain. Even differential prediction is essentially dismissed, as was seen in the section of the *Principles* that was quoted previously. I believe that this position represents too narrow a conception of the validation process.

Justification of test use in selection based only on the demonstration of a predictive relationship between a test and a criterion valued by the institution and the absence of differential prediction is consistent with the goal of enhancing productivity. As is evident from the effort made to achieve better proportional representation of minorities in technical specialties, however, there are other goals. Conceptions of validity, such as the one articulated by Messick (1989), would include a consideration of multiple goals and consequences of test use. He emphasized the need to develop not only an evidential basis of test use and interpretation but a consequential basis as well. Following is his argument for the consideration of multiple value perspectives in the process of validation.

By giving primacy to productivity and efficiency, a selection procedure downplays the significance of other important goals in education and the workplace. Coordinately, by highlighting the polarity of individual equity and group parity and by calling for flexible decision rules to effect a tolerable compromise between the two (Wigdor & Garner, 1982), the resulting selection procedures de-emphasize other basis of fairness and leave other value conflicts unattended. Nor is it that some other value, such as equality or need, should be given primacy or equal status, although this too seems appropriate on many occasions. Rather no single value principle should systematically color our thinking about the functions of selection or of test use more generally, especially in education. Instead, we should evaluate test use in the context of multiple value perspectives to assure that a broad range of potential social consequences of testing are addressed in the validation process. (Messick, 1989, p. 87)

In the civilian sector, the initial question in evaluating the fairness of an employee selection process concerns adverse impact. Although professional standards require evidence of validity whether or not there is adverse impact, legal demands for validity evidence and evidence that a selection test does not have predictive bias are triggered by a demonstration of adverse impact as defined in the *Uniform Guidelines* (Equal Employment Opportunity Commission et al., 1978).

Although the requirements of *Uniform Guidelines* do not apply to the military services, it is clear from the percentages described above that the Army as a whole would not have any difficulty demonstrating a lack of adverse impact for African Americans, and probably not for other minorities as well. For highly skilled specialties with high-aptitude composite requirements, however, representation is more of an issue. As stated by Wigdor and Green (1991), "The problem of military planners ... is to figure out what can be done to smooth out the distribution of minority populations across the career spectrum while still fulfilling the primary organizational mission" (p. 43). The current mechanism for dealing with this potential issue is through the use of minority fill-rate information as part of the computer-based system that provides lists of suggested jobs to Service classifiers at Military Entrance Processing Stations.

Clearly, the introduction of a mechanism that encourages the assignment to technical specialties of a minority candidate rather than an equally qualified White candidate involves a policy decision rather than a technical one. However, technical analyses can inform the policy decisions. Such technical analyses are a reasonable part of a broadly conceived validation process.

Alternative models of fair selection, such as those introduced two decades ago by Thorndike (1971) and Cole (1973), served an important function by showing that a procedure which was considered fair according to one model would not be fair according to another model. Each model "accords a different important or social value to the various subsets of selected versus rejected and successful versus unsuccessful individuals in the different population groups" (Messick, 1989, p. 81). As Hunter and Schmidt (1976) argued, they represent different ethical positions.

Peterson and Novick (1976) demonstrated that, with the exception of the standard approach to predictive bias based on the regression model, a converse model with a contradictory definition of fairness existed for each of the proposed alternative models of selection fairness. This demonstration was influential in creating a consensus around the regression model. This is evident in the following comment from the *Principles*: "Although other definitions of bias have been introduced, only those based upon the regression model, as the definition given here is, have been found to be internally consistent (Peterson & Novick, 1976)." (SIOP, 1987, p. 18)

In my view, it is not the existence of converse models with contradictory definitions of fairness that limits the value of the various models. It is the lack of explicit statements of values that correspond to the different models that is a greater concern. Making values explicit through applications of models based on utility theory is more appealing conceptually, but limited in practicality because of the difficulty in converting value positions to quantifiable utilities. Nonetheless, analytical results such as those by Hunter and Hunter (1984) comparing outcome for alternative selection rules (e.g., top-down, random above a low cut score, or top-down within-group), and analyses based on the different models such as those presented in National Research Council report on the use of the General Aptitude Test Battery by the U.S. Employment Service (Hartigan & Wigdor, 1989) can provide valuable information for policy makers who must take conflicting values into account.

Messick (1989) summarized the complications of multiple perspective on fairness well:

> At this point, it appears difficult if not impossible to be fair to individuals in terms of equity, to groups in terms of parity or avoidance of adverse impact, to institutions in terms of efficiency, and to society in terms of benefits and risks--all at the same time. In principle, a workable balancing of the needs of each of the parties is likely to require successive approximations over time, with iterative modifications of utility matrices based on experience and the consequences of decision processes to date (Darlington, 1971). In practice, however, such balancing of needs and values almost always comes down to a political resolution." (Messick, 1989, p. 81)

I would only add that comprehensive validation that includes analyses showing the consequences of different actions, such as the impact on the number of minorities classified to particular jobs and the impact on the distribution of criterion performance, should at least provide information about the consequences of various possible resolutions.

REFERENCES

Binkin, M., & Eitelberg, M. J. (1986). Women and minorities in the all volunteer force. In W. Bowman, R. Little, & G. T. Sicilia (Eds.), *The all-volunteer force after a decade: Retrospect and prospect* (pp. 73-102). Washington, DC: Pergamon-Brassey.

Cole, N. S. (1973). Bias in selection. *Journal of Educational Measurement, 10,* 237-255.

Cole, N. S., & Moss, P. A. (1989). Bias in test use. In R. L. Linn (Ed.), *Educational measurement* (3rd ed., pp. 201-219). New York: Macmillan.

Darlington, R. B. (1971). Another look at "cultural fairness." *Journal of Educational Measurement, 8,* 71-82.

Department of Defense. (1982). *Profile of American youth: 1980 nationwide administration of the Armed Services Vocational Aptitude Battery.* Washington, DC: Office of the Assistant Secretary of Defense (Manpower, Reserve Affairs, and Logistics).

Dunbar, S. B., & Novick, M. R. (1988). On predicting success in training for men and women: Examples from Marine Corps clerical specialties. *Journal of Applied Psychology, 73,* 545-550.

Eitelberg, M. J. (1988). *Manpower for military occupations.* Washington, DC: Office of the Assistant Secretary of Defense (Force Management and Personnel).

Equal Employment Opportunity Commission, Civil Service Commission, Department of Labor, and Department of Justice (1978). Adoption by four agencies of uniform guidelines of employee selection. *Federal Register, 43*(166), 38290-38315.

Hartigan, J. A., & Wigdor, A. K. (1989). *Fairness in employment testing: Validity generalization minority issues and the General Aptitude Test Battery.* Washington, DC: National Academy Press.

Houston, W. M., & Novick, M. R. (1987). Race-based differential prediction in Air Force technical training programs. *Journal of Educational Measurement, 24,* 309-320.

Hunter, J. E., & Hunter, R. F. (1984). Validity and utility of alternative predictors of job performance. *Psychological Bulletin, 96,* 72-98.

Hunter, J. E., & Schmidt, F. L. (1976). Critical analysis of the statistical and ethical implications of various definitions of test bias. *Psychological Bulletin, 86,* 721-735.

Hunter, J. E., Schmidt, F. L., & Hunter, R. F. (1979). Differential validity of employment tests by race: A comprehensive review and analysis. *Psychological Bulletin, 86,* 721-735.

Hunter, J. E., Schmidt, F. L., & Rauschenberger, J. (1984). Methodological and statistical issues in the study of bias in mental testing. In C. R. Reynolds & R. T. Brown (Eds.), *Perspectives on bias in mental testing.* New York: Plenum.

Linn, R. L. (1982). *Ability testing: Uses, consequences, and controversies: Part II* (pp. 335-388). Washington, DC: National Academy Press.

Linn, R. L. (1983). Predictive bias as an artifact of selection procedures. In H. Wainer & S. Messick (Eds.), *Principles of modern psychological measurement: A Festschrift for Frederic M. Lord* (pp. 27-40). Hillsdale, NJ: Lawrence Erlbaum Associates.

Linn, R. L., & Hastings, C. N. (1984). Group differentiated prediction. *Applied Psychological Measurement, 8,* 165-172.

Linn, R. L., & Werts, C. E. (1971). Considerations in studies of test bias. *Journal of Educational Measurement, 8,* 1-4.

Messick, S. (1989). Validity. In R. L. Linn (Ed.), *Educational measurement* (3rd ed., pp. 13-103). New York: Macmillan.

Petersen, N. S., & Novick, M. R. (1976). An evaluation of some models for culture-fair selection. *Journal of Educational Measurement, 13,* 3-39.

Reilly, R. R. (1973). A note on minority group prediction studies. *Psychological Bulletin, 80,* 130-133.

Schmidt, F. L., Pearlman, K. & Hunter, J. E. (1980). The validity and fairness of employment and educational tests for Hispanic Americans: A review and analysis. *Personnel Psychology, 33,* 705-724.

Society for Industrial and Organizational Psychology (SIOP). (1987). *Principles for the validation and use of personnel selection procedures* (3rd ed.). College Park, MD: American Psychological Association.

Thorndike, R. L. (1971). Concepts of culture-fairness. *Journal of Educational Measurement, 8,* 63-70.

Valentine, L. D. (1977). *Prediction of Air Force technical training success from ASVAB and educational background* (AFHRL-TR-77-18). Lackland AFB, TX: Air Force Human Resources Laboratory, Personnel Research Division.

Wigdor, A. K., & Garner, W. R. (Eds.). (1982). *Ability testing: Uses, consequences, and controversies: Part I.* Washington, DC: National Academy Press.

Wigdor, A. K., & Green, B. F., Jr. (Eds.). (1991). *Performance assessment in the workplace* (Vol. I). Washington, DC: National Academy Press.

IS PERSONNEL CLASSIFICATION A CONCEPT WHOSE TIME HAS PASSED?

Joseph Zeidner
Cecil D. Johnson
The George Washington University

The objectives of this chapter are to describe a new theory of personnel classification, differential assignment theory (DAT); to outline several theoretical and practical controversies involving classification efficiency; to provide research findings of model sampling experiments and of empirical studies on classification efficiency; and to detail the operational implications of findings. This chapter is intended for researchers concerned with selection and assignment of individuals from a common applicant pool to multiple jobs in the employment testing context, and for those professionals interested in work-force productivity and vocational counseling.

A critical first step in developing a classification-efficient job matching technology is the adoption of a theoretical framework. Three competing theories have emerged to explain the value of predicted performance in the context of multiple jobs. Two theories are directed principally at explaining the value of selection in terms of predictive validity. In the third, focus is directed at the effect of differential validity in the joint predictor-criterion space as measured by mean predicted performance.

General cognitive ability theory suggests that one general ability factor underlies all specific cognitive abilities. Proponents of the theory believe that the underlying variable, g, causes specific aptitudes to have validity in predicting job performance. If it is true that a single factor (g) underlies specific aptitudes, and specific aptitudes do not provide any greater prediction than g alone, then the efficient classification of individuals to jobs based on specific aptitudes, or group aptitudes, is not a pertinent issue. However, if there are several factors that differentially predict performance in various jobs, then classification efficiency is a relevant issue.

Specific aptitude theory, on the other hand, suggests that job performance is best predicted by one or more specific aptitudes required by the job, rather than by general cognitive ability. For example, performance as an editor would be better predicted by verbal and perceptual speed abilities than by g alone. According to this theory, g has only an indirect relation to job performance, because it is mediated by specific aptitudes (i.e., g results from the correlations among specific aptitudes). It is rare that specific aptitude theory is mentioned in the literature except in critical terms by proponents of the validity generalization movement or by those extolling the sufficiency of a single g factor. Defined primarily by its detractors, this theory is described in terms of predictive validity in a way that precludes its acceptance by competent psychometricians. This theory strongly contributes to the concept of situational specificity to explain subtle differences in job requirements in different settings.

We propose a third theory, differential assignment theory (DAT), postulating that several factors differentially predict performance in various jobs. We believe DAT provides a more coherent framework for job classification, although recognizing g as the dominant predictor of performance. DAT stresses the difference between predicted performance measures across jobs and explains classification efficiency as a function of mean predictive validity, mean intercorrelation among predicted performance measures, the number of jobs to which individuals are assigned, and the selection ratio. DAT states that the joint predictor-criterion space is multidimensional with useful factors contributing a nontrivial amount of classification efficiency in addition to the unidimensional space defined by the g factor.

In recent years, most measurement specialists have emphasized predictive validity in multiple job situations rather than using an index of classification efficiency. A number of these specialists, many in the forefront of the validity generalization movement, have concluded that because a single general cognitive ability measure dominates most personnel test batteries, the mean predicted performance (MPP) obtainable from the use of differential test composites in an independent sample can only trivially exceed the MPP obtainable from a single efficient measure of g. Those advocating the stability of the g factor across different collections of diverse mental ability tests, and the central role of g in the predicting of job performance, were instrumental in the general, and appropriate, rejection of the earlier theory of situational specificity; that theory required a tailored selection composite for predicting performance in each separate job situation (Zeidner, 1987).

Although DAT accepts many of the tenets of the validity generalization movement, it avoids the pessimism of many of its proponents regarding the utility of personnel classification; DAT also emphasizes the importance of measuring classification efficiency by means of MPP (Johnson & Zeidner, 1991). It is consistent with a National Academy of Sciences conclusion that, although the technical challenge of developing job area aptitude composites that provide differential prediction is great, the continued pursuit of more sophisticated occupational classification systems (including the use of classification-efficient tests and job families) is still worthwhile (Hartigan & Wigdor, 1989, p. 147).

CLASSIFICATION CONCEPTS

Prediction and Classification

Traditionally, only a single job is involved in simple selection and placement, and selection can be accomplished with one or more predictors. The outcome is determined by an individual's position along a single predicted performance continuum. Classification or multidimensional selection decisions provide the basis for assigning a single pool of individuals to more than one job. As in simple selection, these assignments can be made on the basis of a single predictor continuum adjusted to predict the value of each individual's performance by reflecting job validities, criterion variances, and/or job values.

When the predicted performance scores of individuals and the predictability (or value) of jobs are placed in the same rank order on two parallel continua, layering of individuals and jobs occupying the same interval on these two continua provides a means of classifying personnel. The matching of individuals and jobs within the same intervals, or layers, on these two continua maximizes the MPP obtainable from the use of a single predictor continuum. We refer to this person-job matching procedure as *hierarchical layering*, and the result is called *hierarchical classification* (Johnson & Zeidner, 1991). The result is clearly one type of personnel classification. The use of a predicted performance based on a single predictor to optimally assign individuals to jobs in a linear programming algorithm (maximizing either mean predicted performance or mean performance value as the objective function) will provide the same set of assignments to jobs as hierarchical layering provides.

Classification accomplished in the absence of a hierarchical layering effect is referred to as *allocation* (Johnson & Zeidner, 1991). Although hierarchical classification can be unidimensional (i.e., based entirely on a single predictor), allocation requires multiple predictors measuring more than one dimension in the joint predictor-criterion space. Validity is determined individually against each job's performance criterion; the set of job criteria should also be multidimensional. Thus, a classification battery requires a separate assignment variable for each criterion (i.e., criterion-specific composites) if allocation is to be accomplished.

Brogden (1959) directly linked measurement of classification efficiency (CE) to mean predicted performance and, thus, to utility. His allocation equation expresses MPP as a function of predictive validity, intercorrelations among the least-square estimates (LSEs) of job performance, and the number of job families. The model makes it clear that predictive validity is only one term in the equation and, thus, classification efficiency cannot be described adequately by predictive validity alone.

Often Brogden's equation is misunderstood. For example, a National Academy of Sciences report stated that "Under some simplifying assumptions,

Brogden (1959) showed that the gain from *optimal assignment was proportional to (1-c), where* c *is the correlation between the predictors used in the different jobs"* (Hartigan & Wigdor, 1989, p. 243, italics added). Rather, c pertains to the full LSEs of job performance, and gain is a function of $(1 - c)^{1/2}$. The mean intercorrelation *(r)* among job performance estimates can be quite large and still allow for large potential CE, contrary to the Murphy and Davidshofer (1991) text: "The Armed Services Vocational Aptitude Battery (ASVAB) composites do *not* provide information about different sets of aptitudes, and that, in fact, any one of the composites could be substituted for another with little loss of information. For most of its major goals, the military would do just as well with a short test of general intelligence" (p. 247).

Hunter (1986) and Thorndike (1986) both argued similarly in a special issue of the *Journal of Vocational Behavior* concerned with the contribution of *g* in predicting job performance. They asserted that practical predictive validity of aptitude tests is largely dependent on *g* in the multiple job context. Jensen (1986) made the same argument concerning the contribution of psychometric *g* in tests, and in an earlier article (1985) also noted that "the rather uniform high *g* loadings of all the subtests [of the ASVAB] leave too little non-*g* variance to obtain sufficiently reliable or predictively valid differential patterns of the subtest scores for individuals" (p. 216).

In accordance with Brogden (1959), we define the classification efficiency (CE) index as the MPP standard score computed after personnel have been assigned to the job. The potential classification efficiency (PCE) index is the same as CE except that assignment to the job must make use of an optimal assignment procedure in which MPP is maximized in a back sample and each predicted performance score is expressed as a least-squares estimate of the performance criteria for each job. Each predicted performance score is computed using a full least squares (FLS) composite, that is, using the full classification battery. When we undertake research relating to the classification efficiency of instruments, test batteries, assignment (test) composites, or sets of job families, we usually prefer using PCE, the optimal assignment value, as the basis for making comparisons across alternative approaches (conditions).

The validity coefficient is proportional to MPP. It can be substituted for MPP as the measure of systems benefits only in the context of selection research focused on single jobs. Obtaining MPP as a measure of classification efficiency also requires simulating the classification process as part of the process of computing the best possible measure of performance resulting from classification—that is, predicted performance of assigned personnel. The only exception to the need to simulate the assignment of entities to jobs is the case where a simple measure weighted by job value, and/or predictive validity, is used to make assignments to all jobs. MPP can be directly computed in such a hierarchical classification model using an hierarchical layering algorithm; such an algorithm would yield results equal to those obtainable from the use of an optimal linear programming algorithm. Because simulation is central to the measurement of MPP and the design of experiments, the simulation process is explained next.

Research Paradigm

The first step in simulating the classification system is designating a population. It can be represented either by a database or, in the case of model sampling, by variance/covariance and validity matrices. These two matrices may be obtained from a single credible study or be constructed as a composite of several studies. The entities drawn, or generated, from the designated population are used to compute the assignment and evaluation variables. The latter variables are used to compute MPP at the conclusion of each simulation.

The use of scores from a database to provide entities for selection and assignment under prescribed experimental conditions provides realism while limiting the size and number of independent samples. A number of simulation studies have been conducted in which data from Project A were used to define the designated population for one or more model sampling experiments. In these studies, the designated population is used to generate vectors of synthetic scores to form the entities in each required sample. Model sampling permits the generation of as many independent samples as desired from the population from which recruiting and selection are accomplished, and thus allows the use of a research design that controls or measures the effects of different sources of sampling error bias.

From Fig. 22.1 we can graphically follow the flow of information in a typical research paradigm for differential assignment theory. A set of large empirical validation samples are corrected for restriction in range and criterion unreliability to provide an estimate of the validities and predictor covariances for the desired population—usually a youth or applicant population. We typically define the designated population in terms of an n (number of tests) by n intercorrelation matrix among the predictors, R_t, and an m (number of jobs or job families) by n validity matrix, V.

This designated population is the basis for generating the entities within each of the samples required for the conduct of the experiment. One of these samples is the analysis sample used to compute various decision variables including , for example, regression weights for assignment variables, selection of tests and test composites, clustering of jobs into job families, and determination of cut scores for selection and assignment. As many cross-validation samples as desired, typically 20 to 30 in our studies, can be generated for transformation into various experimental conditions prior to the simulation of selection and assignment policies and the evaluation of these conditions and policies by the computation of MPP. The weights for computing evaluation variables can be obtained either from the designated population or from separately generated evaluation samples.

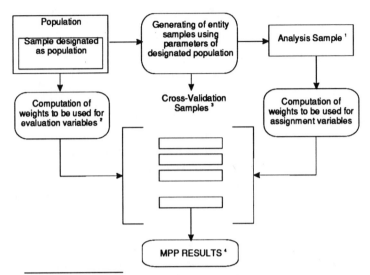

FIG. 22.1.   Typical model sampling research paradigm.

Note that analysis samples and evaluation samples are both "back" samples whereas the more numerous samples from which MPP scores are computed are all "cross" samples.

DIFFERENTIAL ASSIGNMENT THEORY

Differential assignment theory (DAT) was first proposed by Johnson and Zeidner (1990, 1991) as the conceptual basis for initiating and interpreting research intended to improve classification efficiency when measured in terms of mean predicted performance. The concept of DAT is derived from an integrative review of personnel classification literature, especially the contributions of Brogden (1951, 1959) and Horst (1954, 1955), combined with the systematic development of methodologies for improving classification efficiency.

The DAT Concepts

Several fundamental concepts form the basic assumptions for DAT. The first is that there is a nontrivial degree of multidimensionality in the joint predictor-criterion space—despite the inevitable presence of a strong general cognitive ability factor, g, and the usual finding that the first principal component explains 70% to 85% of the total variance in the joint predictor-criterion space. It should be emphasized that, apart from the multidimensionality issue, there is no inconsistency between DAT and validity generalization theory as originated by Mosier (1951) and the more recent literature on validity generalization, or g, as it pertains to the unidimensional model for both selection efficiency and utility. We avoid assuming that concepts true for traditional selection are necessarily applicable to classification efficiency or multidimensional selection and placement.

The second concept of DAT is one of optimism regarding the possibility of designing, developing, and implementing personnel classification and assignment systems far superior to the existing operational systems—as a result of a deliberate application of DAT. For example, we believe that the potential classification efficiency of both counseling and selection-classification test batteries can be greatly improved through a determined effort to select or construct measures in accordance with DAT. We believe that most operational classification systems developed or modified over the last two decades were designed and/or evolved from the pessimistic belief that a number of prevalent misconceptions about classification efficiency (described later in this section) were true.

The third concept holds that, in the general case, a complex set of principles define separate approaches or methods for optimizing selection or classification procedures. There is an exception to this general case where full least-squares composites containing all the tests in the battery are optimal for use as both selection and assignment variables for each job, each job family consists of a single job, and an optimal algorithm is used to select and assign entities to jobs in either one or two stages. All deviations from this special situation require that a decision be made as to whether it is desired to maximize the effectiveness of selection or classification.

The fourth concept of DAT maintains that utility models, where the object is to maximize the benefits over the costs, provide the best approach for evaluating alternative policies and procedures for selection, classification or placement, and assignment of personnel to jobs.

The fifth concept argues that computer technology has reached the state where it is practical to implement any selection/classification algorithm that can be shown to provide a useful gain in MPP.

Additional basic concepts of DAT can be derived from an examination of the examples of some 10 DAT principles provided by Johnson and Zeidner (1990, 1991). A number of these principles are supported by the results of our research.

The principles confirmed include: It is effective to use FLS composites as assignment variables in place of unit-weighted composites designed to maximize predictive validity; MPP increases as the number of job families is increased; MPP increases further as improved job family structure raises FLS composite validities and reduces FLS composites intercorrelations; and the joint predictor-criteria space, as commonly encountered, provides a nontrivial degree of multidimensionality and can be rotated into a classification-efficient simple structure of sufficient quality to provide a practical amount of CE.

The heritage of DAT includes the evolution of g factor-based concepts of the structure of the intellect provided by a succession of theorists, from Spearman's (1904, 1927) general mental ability factor to Jensen in his 1991 review of the predictive power of general ability. It has drawn also from the introduction of measurement technology based on multiple factors such as Thurstone's primary factors (1938, 1947). The development of DAT also incorporates the personnel selection and classification models of Brogden (1959) and Horst (1954), and the elaboration of validity generalization concepts from Mosier (1951) to Schmidt and Hunter (1981), especially their conclusions relating to traditional selection efficiency for individual jobs rather than the multiple job context. Each contributed concepts and findings useful in building an integrated understanding of simple selection and of multidimensional selection and classification of personnel embraced by DAT.

The late 1940s and the 1950s was the period of greatest popularity for traditional multiple factor analysis. The factoring of correlation matrices, with communalities in the diagonals to obtain primary factors by rotation to simple structure, was common (Cattell, 1953; Guilford, 1956). This period overlapped with the first wave of popularity for personnel classification (Brogden, 1946, 1954). The idea of creating factor-pure tests for use in counseling and personnel classification appeared to some to be an attractive solution to the difficult task of developing new predictors that could provide meaningful classification efficiency. Proponents of such an approach assumed, much too optimistically, that correlations between aptitude factors were quite low, that relatively pure factor tests could be constructed, and that factor-pure tests would retain their low intercorrelations in cross samples; then these tests could be used with great effectiveness in vocational counseling and personnel classification.

Simple structure also played an important conceptual role in the personnel classification model. Most investigators viewed simple structure as a method for determining the psychological meaningfulness of factors. It could also be used to simultaneously identify ideal sets of variables corresponding to job clusters for use in classification, provided that simple structure in the joint predictor-criterion space (the common or overlapping space of predictor and criterion measures) was also found in independent (cross) samples. Eventually it was found that neither factor-pure tests nor their rotation to simple structure in the joint space seemed to occur in real, unbiased situations.

Many of those who shared in the mistaken euphoria of the era, in which classification efficiency was perceived to be a relatively easy goal to achieve, may have been counting on the realization of "primary," factor-pure tests. Others may have been assuming that the commonly believed requirement of low inter-correlations of predictors could readily be achieved. We believe that much of the pessimism that later followed may be attributable to a number of insupportable beliefs or assumptions that arose during this initial hopeful period, namely that:

- Tests approximating Thurstone's primary factor abilities could be developed, and such tests would have high correlations with performance in a few jobs and low or, better yet, negative correlations with most others.

- Test composites tailored to jobs or job families would readily provide a substantial improvement in predictive validity compared to that of a single predictor composite that approximates the psychometric general factor.

- Addition of more predictor domains (e.g., self-description tests without special consideration of differential validity) would provide increased dimensionality relevant to classification efficiency.

- "Best" test composites selected by traditional test selection methods would provide composites with low or no more than moderately high intercorrelations.

- Simple structure in test space, rather than in the joint predictor-criterion space, is directly relevant to classification efficiency.

- Adjusting test composites to reduce the overlap in the total set of test composites would increase classification efficiency in the back sample.

- Deletion of tests loaded highly on g, in order to further reduce the intercorrelations among composites, would improve the classification efficiency of the set of test composites in the back sample.

- Changing the least-squares estimates that are optimal for simple selection (e.g., to reduce intercorrelations) can also improve classification efficiency in the back sample.

Such beliefs or assumptions were found to be overly optimistic and, as data accumulated, were generally recognized as erroneous. If these implied phenomena were true, they would facilitate achieving classification efficiency, but none are vital to the realization of classification efficiency. In the process of rejecting these insupportable beliefs, some investigators have allowed the pendulum to swing too far in the other direction, leading to a new set of more recent erroneous beliefs that, if true, would completely discredit the viability of multidimensional selection and classification methods. Several of these recent misconceptions, including truly erroneous beliefs or myths, are:

- The joint predictor-criterion space (JP-C) is virtually unidimensional; one test composite measuring g can provide all but a trivial portion of the predicted criterion variance associated with multiple jobs. The criterion variance explained by tests tailored to specific jobs is almost entirely due to the presence of g in the composites.

- Failure of job-specific composites to provide an increase in validity, as compared to a composite measuring psychometric g, is incontrovertible evidence that nothing can be gained from the use of tailored (job- or job-family-specific) composites.

- When test composites, including those that are LSEs or have overlapping tests, have very high intercorrelation coefficients, no practical amount of classification efficiency is obtainable.

- The size of the standard errors of regression weights, particularly when there are 10 to 15 (or even more) independent variables, and/or when there are independent variables having high intercorrelations (possibly due to a common high loading on g), virtually precludes a useful level of classification efficiency in independent samples from the use of LSEs as assignment variables.

- The well-known fact that FLS composites provide the highest MPP (in the back sample) for either a selection or a classification process means that most psychometric methods best for selection are also best for classification. This includes test selection for either experimental or operational batteries, selection of tests for inclusion in composites, or job clustering.

These erroneous beliefs are discussed, in order, next.

The Myth of Unidimensionality of the Joint Predictor-Criterion Space

The first of these misconceptions is a general statement representative of those claiming the superiority of composites measuring g as compared to composites tailored to the prediction of separate job families in the multiple job context. Jensen (1984), for example, provided an unmistakable message of the relative efficiency of g compared to other measures: "For most jobs, g accounts for all of the significantly predicted variance; other testable ability factors, independent of g, add practically nothing to the predictive validity" (p. 101). Schmidt, Hunter, and Larson (1988) also believed that only the g component in the ASVAB makes a nontrivial contribution to validity:

> Recent research by Hunter (1983, 1984, 1985) based on very large military samples appears to indicate that general cognitive ability is as good or better a predictor of performance in training in most military job families as ability composites derived specifically to predict success in particular job families . . . the model that fits the data best is one in which the only ability causing performance is general cognitive ability and in which aptitudes are themselves caused by general cognitive ability. . . . This theory of the underlying processes causing performance predicts that for military job families, general cognitive ability would predict performance at least as well as regression-based composites of specific aptitude derived to predict performance in the particular job family. (1988, pp. 1-2)

The authors again made a similar point, citing path analysis:

> Hunter's path analytic studies were conducted using average validities across all jobs for which validity data were available; these studies led to the prediction that general cognitive ability should have higher validity than regression-based composites of specific aptitudes for every job. (p. 4)

Ree and Earles (1991) used a different basis for concluding that weighted composites drawn from the ASVAB are unlikely to provide reliable measures of anything other than g. The authors interpreted Wilks (1938) as providing:

> a mathematical proof that the correlation of two linear composites of variables will tend toward 1.0 under commonly found conditions . . . g may be found . . . by unrotated principal components, unrotated principal factors, or any one of a large number of possible hierarchical factor analogies, but also (up to scale) by any other reasonable set of positive weights. (pp. 276-277)

The authors concluded that the Wilks theorem makes these results predictable and generalizable to all measures of human cognitive aptitude that display positive manifold. It is only a small extension of this logic to assume that composites, with weights tailored to a specific job family, and containing tests drawn from a set of tests displaying a positive manifold, would also be just another measure of g.

Hunter, Crossen, and Friedman (1985), referring to a situation in which predictors are all indications of the same underlying general factor, a situation that they appear to believe to be highly prevalent, concluded that:

Optimal prediction is achieved . . . when the individual predictors are weighted according to the degree to which they correlate with the general factor . . . . (p. 37)

In addition, they stated:

What may be surprising to some is the finding that General Cognitive Ability is the best predictor for all jobs. For all military data sets considered, the path models were basically the same. The relationship between specific aptitudes and performance is causally mediated by General Cognitive Ability. (p. 143)

There are many ways to argue against the myth of unidimensionality in the joint predictor-criterion (JP-C) space. For example, in terms of predictive validity the "best" three out of 29 predictor variables in Project A would be considered by many to be an excellent, virtually comprehensive, measure of g. However, we find a both practical and statistically significant increase in MPP obtained from the use of the best 10 variables selected to optimize predictive validity as contrasted with the best five variables, used as LSEs assignment variables in an optimal assignment model.

For another example, if the JP-C was unidimensional, the best five predictor variables selected to maximize classification efficiency should not provide more than a trivial increase in MPP, after optimal assignment to jobs, as compared to the best five predictor variables selected to maximize predictive validity. However, findings indicate that five classification-efficient variables provide a statistical and practical increase over five variables selected to increase predictive validity. Research results bearing on both examples provide strong support of the multidimensionality of the JP-C space (Johnson & Zeidner, 1991; Johnson, Zeidner, & Scholarios, 1990).

The omnificence of g also would preclude an increase in MPP from the use of tailored tests over that provided by the use of g scores weighted by the validity coefficient. Such an increase in MPP from the use of a multi-dimensional model over that provided by a unidimensional g model was reported by Whetzel (1991). The unidimensional g model is also refuted by the gain in MPP provided by the use of larger numbers of job families than are currently employed by the Services (Johnson, Zeidner, & Leaman, 1992).

The rejection of any one of the four additional myths described next would also constitute a basis for rejecting unidimensionality of the JP-C space.

The Myth of "Nothing Much More Than *g*"

The second erroneous belief was reflected in the Hunter et al. (1985) statement that:

> the role of the Technical Aptitude Factor in the prediction of performance in all jobs is rooted in its *important incremental contributions* to the measurement of the General Cognitive Ability composite. (p. 92; italics added)

The evaluation of the contribution of the technical aptitude factor in terms of its contribution to incremental validity was further discussed as follows:

> Hunter's (1985) reanalysis of the Thorndike data suggested a fourth aptitude, Perceptual Aptitude, when added to the general Cognitive Ability composite increased the average validity from .59 to .61, an increase of about 3 percent. *Since the increase in work productivity is proportional to validity*, this would mean an increase of 3 percent gain in productivity. (p. 145, italics added)

Hunter and others have presented evidence pointing to a lack of incremental validity over that provided by *g* as evidence of a total lack of usefulness of tailored test composites whenever a good measure of *g* is available. However, it appears that these investigators, in evaluating tailored composites in a multiple job context, are measuring the value of these composites entirely in terms of incremental validity, as in a simple selection model for individual jobs or job families, with each job selection being considered separately and independently of the other job selections.

We, on the other hand, contend that the purpose of a battery such as the ASVAB is either multiple job selection or selection and classification, and that the usefulness of tailored tests, even in the presence of a dominating *g*, should be assessed in terms of both these purposes rather than for single job selection. We also recognize that some operational systems used by the military during the past decade focused primarily on selection. Thus, we need to explore the usefulness of comparing *g* with tailored composites using predictive validity as the figure of merit in the context of selection from a single applicant stream in a multiple job situation.

Consider an operational situation in which the individuals of a single stream of recruits are allowed to apply for any job openings, and, if rejected, subsequently apply for a different available job, with no classification or counseling from the employment (or recruiting) staff. In this situation, both predictive validities and the various cutting scores for jobs are the primary determiners of MPP for the total set of jobs. However, the intercorrelations among tailored test composites also affect MPP. When a single measure of g is utilized, this intercorrelation is obviously equal to 1.0.

When, by means of either counseling or assignment procedures, an optimal assignment is specified for each individual using only a measure of g, it is very easy to compute the resulting total mean predicted performance, a measure we denote as $(MPP)_t$. An algorithm for such a process (hierarchical classification) is described by Johnson and Zeidner (1990, 1991).

Assuming the use of a measure of g and different cutting scores for each job, the aggregated effect of the separate selection ratios for each job on the single stream of applicants can be readily calculated by the more general algorithm. The selection of applicants for any one job reduces the number of applicants available for all other jobs, particularly for jobs having lower cutting scores. There is relatively little effect on the availability of applicants for jobs having higher cutting scores in our simplified model. This competition for individuals in a single applicant stream affects the cost of recruiting and/or the viability of cutting scores. Cutting scores may have to be reduced to meet job quotas, with a consequent reduction in MPP.

If separate tailored composites with intercorrelations less than 1.0 are used as the selection instruments for each job, there is less competition among jobs for the eligible applicants, as compared to use of a single measure of g for all jobs. Consequently, a larger expected value of $(MPP)_t$ results even if the validities for g and each of the tailored tests are equal. The computation of $(MPP)_t$ is more complex when selection is accomplished using tailored composites in a simplified model as compared to the case when g is used.

We find it difficult to visualize an operational situation involving the use of tailored composites for multiple jobs in which predictive validity is an appropriate index for reflecting the operational value of composites. Only in the unlikely operational situation in which there is a separate and independent stream of applicants for each job would predictive validity be an appropriate index of operational value of the selection measures, and an appropriate index for comparing tailored tests with g. If the rejected applicants for any job sometimes become applicants for a different job, the applicant streams are intertwined (if not completely merged) and the model of independent applicant streams does not apply.

Thus, in consideration of operational goals and psychometric accuracy, the effect of selecting individuals for one job in the applicant pool makes them unavailable for other jobs. These considerations clearly point to the unsuitability of predictive validity as an index for determining the relative value of g and tailored test composites drawn from an operational battery. We assert that MPP computed in a realistic context (of a common applicant stream for multiple jobs) is a much more suitable index for determining operational value. Although MPP can be computed analytically when only g is used for selection and/or classification, or a set of tailored tests are used in a simplified model of selection from a single stream of applicants, a simulation is required to compute the MPP obtainable from composites in an optimal assignment process.

Such a simulation should ideally reflect the operational process, including the recruitment, selection, and classification stream and the use of cutting scores and/or operational assignment algorithms. In a preliminary research stage, such as we are in today with respect to differential assignment theory, we believe it is defensible to measure potential selection and classification efficiency in a simulation that does not reflect all of the constraints imposed on the applicant stream and operational system. However, this does not justify simplifying the selection model to the degree that is required to make predictive validity a credible index of value in a multiple job situation.

The Myth of Unreliability of Difference Between Composites

The third myth is nourished by the high correlation coefficients commonly found among assignment variables that provide some investigators with an intuitive basis for doubting that the ASVAB or the General Aptitude Test Battery (GATB) could provide a sound basis for classifying personnel for multiple jobs. Hunter (1986), noting the correlations among the ASVAB composites, stated that:

> The only way to keep these correlations in the .80's or .90's is to restrict the number of tests in each composite and to artificially make the composites as close to non-overlapping as possible. Confirmatory factor analysis shows that these "reduced" correlations are only artifactually lower than .95 because of error of measurement. If the correlations were corrected for attenuation, only the clerical composites would differ from the others... A meta-analysis across hundreds of studies shows that the speeded tests make no contributions to the prediction of success in any occupational area except clerical and even there the contribution is minor. (Hunter, 1985, p. 356)

It is particularly disturbing to many that the average intercorrelations of either aptitude area composites or FLS composites almost equal or even exceed the average reliability of these composites. Most will agree that the reliability of the difference between a pair of assignment variables (AV) must be nonzero for a useful amount of CE to exist.

Gulliksen (1950) derived a well-known formula for the reliability of a difference, making the assumption that measurement error for two composites, x and y, is uncorrelated, simplifying the estimate $r_{(x-y)(x-y)} = r_d$, where:

$$r_d = \{ [(r_{xx} + r_{yy})/2] - r_{xy} \} / [1 - r_{xy}].$$

This formula for r_d clearly indicates that the reliability of the difference between two experimentally independent variables is zero if the average reliability of the two variables does not exceed their intercorrelation coefficient. Worse yet, in the event that $r_{xy} > (r_{xx} + r_{yy})/2$, the reliability of the difference is alleged to be negative.

The ASVAB FLS composites used to predict performance on Army jobs were found to have intercorrelations ranging from .90 to .95 (Nord & Schmitz, 1991). Although the reliabilities of these composites were not computed in their study, if the above formula for r_d were to be applied, the results would be close to zero. The intercorrelations between pairs of aptitude area composites also approach or exceed the average reliabilities of the composites.

If it were legitimate to apply the above formula for r_d to composites with overlapping tests, we would readily conclude that there is no reliable basis, using composites drawn from the ASVAB, to make assignment decisions between many, if not most, pairs of Army jobs. However, the application of this reliability formula to determine the reliability of either Aptitude Area (AA) or FLS composite differences is clearly inappropriate. Rather, the correct approach for computing the reliability of a difference between two composites containing overlapping tests, or for computing the correction for attenuation of the intercorrelation between two such composites, involves computing the correlation of a weighted composite of true scores with either a composite of raw scores having the same weights (to compare a validity coefficient) or with true scores having different weights (to compute a correlation coefficient corrected for attenuation).

The Myth of Instability of Standard Errors of Regression Weights

The often-noted large magnitudes of standard errors (SEs) of regression weights have convinced some researchers that FLS composites have little practical usefulness in making personnel assignment decisions. A number of investigators believe that test composites utilizing beta weights computed on moderately large analysis samples (e.g., $N = 300$) are patently useless for operational use. For example, Hunter et al. (1985) claimed:

> Since different aptitudes are highly correlated, very large samples are required for multiple regression. For good estimates of the population beta weights, *samples of 5,000 or more are needed* .... Consequently, the estimated beta weights tend to be far from their true values. (p. 18, italics added)

Speaking of the ASVAB, Hunter (1986) said:

> Ironically multiple regression on large samples leads to composites that differ only trivially from the composite that best estimates general cognitive ability

[for an early statement of this fact see Humphreys (1962, 1979); for a recent meta-analysis, see Thorndike (1985)]. Meta-analysis has shown that nearly all of *the increase in multiple correlation due to using tailored composites has been due to sampling error*." (pp. 356-357, italics added)

If the weights for tailored composites differ from the weights for *g* composites by no more than sampling error, there would be no point in using tailored tests in the personnel classification process. The best means of evaluating the value of tailored composites while considering the effects of sampling error is provided by the model sampling approach described in the next section. While we know that a composite using least-squares weights (i.e., an LSE) provides the best assignment variable for use in a "back sample," the possibility remains that some other composite would be better in an independent or cross sample. The magnitude of SEs for regression weights may well bear on this possibility.

The formula for the SE of a regression weight can be separated into a component, Q, that is constant across all independent variables for a particular LSE, and into a separate component, U, that varies across the m independent variables.

The removal of a pure measure of g from tailored predictor equations (LSEs) does not adversely affect the classification efficiency obtainable in the back sample. Because PCE is invariant to the presence or absence of *g* and the presence of *g* reduces the SE of regression weights, it would appear that the presence of *g* in a classification battery is at best extraneous and probably harmful to obtaining PCE in cross samples.

Brogden (1959, 1964) referred to a hypothetical *g*-type measure that has equal regression weights for all jobs to be predicted in a classification situation. Brogden used his 1964 model to demonstrate that this *g*-type variable can be deleted from all LSEs used as assignment variables in an optimal assignment model without causing a reduction in the resulting MPP. We use Brogden's better-known 1959 model to arrive at the same conclusion.

In the context of this model, MPP is invariant to changes in the value of *g*; the negative effect on MPP of the smaller R resulting from a reduction in the value of *g* is exactly offset by the positive effect of the smaller r. Brogden's 1964 and 1959 models are, in this respect, consistent. We conclude that the magnitude of MPP in the back sample remains the same whether or not a *g*-type variable is included as an independent variable in the FLS assignment composites in classification.

The evidence regarding the effect of regression weight standard errors on MPP in cross samples, far from leading to the rejection of the use of LSEs in optimal assignment procedures, suggests that the removal of a pure *g* variable from LSEs would reduce the average standard error of the regression weights. To the extent that these SEs are relevant to classification efficiency, one can surmise that eliminating such a pure measure of *g* should increase the magnitude of MPP in cross samples. This examination also leads us to believe that a weight stabilization goal for a classification model may be better met by reducing in *g* content rather than by increasing in *g* content. Unfortunately, most weight stabilization methods that are seriously proposed in the literature would result in an increased *g* content for the weighted composite as compared with the use of unadjusted regression weights.

Some of the methods for stabilizing weights that were found to improve predictive validity in small independent samples are clearly inappropriate for the classification model, for example, the use of the principal component factor as the basis for computing weights. Other methods that adjust weights in the direction of equalizing weights for all variables (e.g., ridge analysis) may also be ineffective in a classification situation.

The Myth That Psychometric Methods Best for Selection Are Also Best for Classification

The fifth erroneous belief, that procedures best for selection are also best for classification, is true only for one specific set of circumstances, but becomes more and more fallacious as aspects of these ideal circumstances are altered. An LSE of performance based on all tests in the operational battery is not only an optimal test composite for selection, but is also the optimal assignment composite for use in classification. The optimal job family for both selection and classification is provided by designating each job as a selection/assignment target (i.e., a job family).

Welsh, Kucinkas, and Curran (1990), in their review of the ASVAB literature, mistakenly attributed to Brogden the originating of a theory of "differential classification," which asserts that the validity, rather than the classification efficiency, of tailored composites will be maximized for their corresponding clusters of jobs. The authors stated that such a maximization of selection efficiency will maximize classification efficiency:

> According to the theory of differential classification, if each aptitude composite's validity is maximized in terms of its absolute validity, then there will be a maximization of the predicted performance of individuals within a cluster of specialties using the given composite. *The maximized predicted performance of jobs will in turn lead to maximized differences between job clusters in predicted performance, thus maximizing the differences in validities between clusters of jobs with differing composites (differential validity).* (p. 20, italics added)

The procedures for forming test composites that do not include all tests in the battery and the procedures for forming job families through the clustering of jobs produce different results when the goal is optimizing classification efficiency as contrasted with the goal of optimizing selection efficiency. In general, optimal procedures and strategies are not the same for achieving these alternative strategies. Fortunately, it is generally not difficult to achieve near optimal selection efficiency with very little effort if initial focus is on achieving classification efficiency.

RESTRUCTURING ARMY JOB FAMILIES

In this section, we focus on one model sampling experiment concerned with improving classification efficiency in the context of differential assignment theory by restructuring Army job families (Johnson, Zeidner, & Leaman, 1992). The experiment examines the gains in mean predicted performance (MPP) obtainable from a reconstitution of Army jobs into more numerous and more classification-efficient sets of job families for use in the classification process. Study findings enable us to refine and extend DAT and to specify immediate operational implications for the Army classification system.

Research Objectives

For more than a decade, a number of advocates have been calling for the reduction of the number of job families used by the Army in its classification system. These advocates steadfastly point out that there are no more than four strong content clusters (i.e., group factors) in the test content of the ASVAB and that four job families corresponding to the Air Force's four job groupings would adequately reflect ASVAB content. Such an argument, of course, requires the equating of predictor dimensionality with the number of job families to which these predictors can be used to make reliable assignments. Proving this argument to be fallacious is a major objective of this experiment.

A second major objective of this experiment is to compare an empirical classification-efficient (CE) method of job clustering with the Army's operational Career Management Field (CMF), a job family taxonomy based on decades of expert judgment and use of empirical validity data information.

The classification-efficient job-clustering algorithm designed for this study starts with the number of job families equal to the number of jobs. At each successive step, the number of job families (m_j) is then reduced by one by selecting two job families to be merged that will minimize the reduction in Horst's (1954) differential index (H_d)—until the desired number of job families is reached. When Brogden's 1959 assumptions are met and everyone is optimally assigned to a job family, MPP (i.e., classification efficiency) is proportional to H_d. Thus this method, one that retains the maximum amount of H_d at each step as m_j is reduced by one, can be expected to provide classification-efficient job clusters.

Other objectives include examining the effect of using a more economical and available criterion measure, the Skill Qualification Test (SQT), for use in determining job family structure and in computing "best" weights for assignment variables (AVs), and in examining the effect of the size and heterogeneity of the test battery from which AVs are formed.

Research Description

Johnson, Zeidner, and Leaman (1992) conducted the present study by generating sets (vectors) of synthetic scores separately based on the data from multiple samples of jobs, 18 and 60 respectively, provided by two major Project A empirical studies. The research design permits effects of both dimensionality and instability of regression weights to appropriately influence measures of classification efficiency. The results remain entirely free of the effect of all sample error and biases in one experiment (Design A) and are essentially free of all biases that might affect the comparisons of the primary conditions in the second experiment (Design B). A cross-validation design is used in both.

Each empirical data set is corrected for restriction in range due to selection effects; the criterion variables are corrected for unreliability. The corrected predictor covariances and validities are then used to represent the two separate designated populations from which synthetic scores are drawn. The Design A experiment used Project A concurrent study data which include the covariances of 29 predictors and validities for the core technical proficiency criterion for 18 Military Occupational Specialties (MOS). These 18 empirical samples provide the parameters to define the designated population for Design A.

Covariances among ASVAB tests and validities of these tests against SQT scores for 60 MOS were selected from a Project A databank, corrected for restriction in range and attenuation of the criterion, and used to compute the parameters to define the designated population for Design B. Both designated populations were obtained by correcting empirical samples to make them representative of the same youth population.

In Design A, the designated population is used to generate an analysis sample with the same number of entities in each MOS subsample as is present in the empirical data set used to define the designated population, and 20 independent cross samples of synthetic tests scores for use in the simulations. Each cross sample is used separately for each condition in a repeated measures design. The analysis sample is used in applying the empirical job-clustering method to form job families. It is also used in computing the "best" weights to be applied to cross-sample scores to form predicted performance measures (FLS composites) for use as AVs in the simulations. Weights from the designated population are applied to cross-sample synthetic test scores at the completion of each simulation to obtain the MPP standard scores used as measures of classification efficiency. (See Fig. 22.1 for a representation of the research paradigm.)

The designated population of Design B serves as the source of weights for both assignment and evaluation variables. Each assignment variable represents predicted performance for an entire job family, whereas the evaluation variables are the predicted performance measures computed separately for each job. After optimal assignment to a job family, each entity is randomly assigned to a job within that family and the entity's predicted performance score for that job is computed.

Although scores for all evaluation variables are computed using weights based on independent samples, avoiding traditional back sample inflation, the less well-known effect of correlated error across assignment and evaluation variables was not eliminated in Design B as it was in Design A. Since psychometricians lack experience in interpreting the effects of this kind of bias, the investigators avoid making the kind of experimental comparisons in Design B that would be most affected by its presence. They do, for example, contrast the classification efficiency of a priori and empirically determined weights for the test composites making up the assignment variables of Design B.

Major Findings

Although Design A uses the best criterion variables, it contains only 18 jobs. This severely limits what can be determined about the effect a sizable increase in the number of job families can have on MPP; this was the reason for including Design B, which allows 60 jobs to be utilized. Some of the most important conclusions of this study, however, are drawn from Design A, which incorporates both the more credible criterion variables and a more complete control of correlated error and bias.

In each cross-sample of synthetic test scores in Design A and Design B, 25% of the entities of each sample were rejected on the basis of their Armed Forces Qualification Test (AFQT) scores. The remaining entities were then optimally assigned to job families under differing experimental conditions. All MPP standard scores provided in the tables give adjusted MPP standard scores after the expected results of selection are subtracted from the total MPP standard score obtained as a result of simulating both selection and optimal assignment. Differences in MPP scores for all conditions were statistically significant at the .0001 level. For the baseline condition in Design A, 18 jobs are distributed into the current nine operational Army job families and the existing aptitude area (AA) composites from the ASVAB used as the assignment variables.

Making selection and assignment decisions by chance yields an MPP standard score equal to zero. Selecting the 75% of the entities having the highest AFQT scores provides an expected MPP of .225 for Design A under the hypothetical condition of random assignment to jobs. Using the operational AAs and job families in conjunction with an optimal assignment algorithm results in an MPP standard score of -.097, a value considerably lower than random assignment.

Nord and Schmitz (1991) found a low but positive MPP of .047 in a large Army data set different from Project A data. The finding of the present study again confirms that the current system designates highly inappropriate assignment composites for job families. It is worth noting that Nord and Schmitz (1991) and Zeidner and Johnson (1992) reported, on the basis of a comprehensive utility study, that an increase or decrease of .1 of a standard deviation unit in MPP results in a potential productivity gain or loss worth $130 million per year to the Army.

As noted previously, the investigators use this condition in Design A as the baseline against which to examine the gains obtainable from adding improvements by stages (see Table 22.1).

TABLE 22.1
Comparison of Gains in Mean Predicted Performance (MPP)
By Stages in Design A

Comparisons of Stages With Baseline	Mean MPP
Stage 1 (plus) FLS-ASVAB 9 family composites	.214
Stage 2 (plus) 9 classification- efficient families	.245
Stage 3 (plus) 12 classification- efficient families	.277
Stage 4 (plus) 20 Project A tests	.367

Note: Baseline of nine operational job families and AA composites mean is -.097. Use of six job families, rather than nine families, results in a reduction of MPP to .191, or 22% for FLS-ASVAB composites. Effects are due only to classification.

In Stage 1, the researchers substitute nine least-square weighted composites based on the full ASVAB (FLS-ASVAB composites) for the nine operational aptitude area composites. This yields an MPP attributable to classification effects of .214 compared to a baseline MPP of -.097.

In Stage 2, the researchers substitute the nine classification-efficient job families for the nine operational job families while using the corresponding FLS-ASVAB composites as assignment variables. This provides an MPP, adjusted for the contribution of selection, of .245, a gain over Stage 1 of 14.5%.

For Stage 3, job families are increased from 9 to 12 and classification-efficient clustering while still using corresponding FLS-ASVAB composites as assignment variables. This change provides an MPP due to classification of .277, an increase of 13% over Stage 2.

Stage 4 involves substituting the 29 Project A concurrent validation experimental variables for the nine ASVAB tests in computing the corresponding FLS composites. This provides a measure of the upper limit of the gain in MPP obtainable from the optimal use of the Project A experimental predictors to expand the dimensionality of the operational classification battery. The use of these FLS-experimental composites for making optimal assignments to the 12 classification-efficient job families provides an MPP due to classification of .367, an increase of 29% over Stage 3.

The reduction in the number of job families from nine to six provides a reduction in MPP to .191 when the FLS-ASVAB composites are used as AVs—a 22% reduction when compared to the stage two results. A reduction of 24% results if FLS-experimental composites are used instead of FLS-ASVAB composites in a parallel comparison of assignment to six classification-efficient job families as compared to the use of nine classification-efficient job families for this purpose.

In Design B, the 60 MOS for which Skill Qualification Test scores were available permitted the clustering of jobs into three sets of a priori job families as follows: the 9 operational job families used by the Army for initial classification and assignment; 23 of the Army's 35 Career Management Fields (CMFs); and an intermediate set of 16 families based on a compromise between the two sets of a priori clustering concepts. An empirical classification-efficient clustering algorithm was used to provide parallel sets of 9, 16, and 23 job families. MPP was computed after all of the entities were optimally assigned to a job family within one of the six sets of job families. The FLS-ASVAB composites were used as assignment variables for making optimal assignments to job families within each of the six sets.

The Design B baseline is provided by FLS-ASVAB composites using the 60 jobs formed into the nine operational job families. This results in an MPP standard score of .135. Table 22.2 compares MPP standard scores and percentage improvements in stages. The substitution of the empirically determined job families, for the a priori job families as shown in Table 22.2, increases MPP by 97% when there are 9 job families, 28% when there are 16 job families, and 26% when there are 23 job families. The total gain in MPP achieved from changing the structure of the 60 MOS from 9 operational job families to a classification-efficient set of 23 job families provides a gain of 177%, of which 120% is immediately obtainable from the increase in number of job families. The additional 57% can then be obtained also from using the improved method of structuring jobs. If the first change is in the method of forming job families, the first gain is 97% and the second gain, also from increasing job families from 9 to 23, is 80%.

TABLE 22.2
Comparison of Percentage Gains in Mean Predicted Performance (MPP)
By Stages in Design B

Comparisons of Stages With Baseline	Mean MPP	Percent Gain Over Baseline
Stage 1 (plus) 16 job families	.258	91
Stage 2 (plus) 23 job families	.297	120
Stage 3 (plus) 23 classification- efficient families	.374	177

Note. Baseline of nine FLS-ASVAB job family composites is .135. Effects due only to classification.

Conclusions and Recommendations

The findings of the Johnson, Zeidner, and Leaman (1992) study provide support for a number of DAT principles including:

1. The adoption of full least-squares (FLS) composites as replacements for aptitude area composites can provide a large immediate improvement for any presently existing personnel classification system.

2. The optimal number of job families for inclusion in an FLS composite-based personnel classification system is as many families as can be coupled with adequately valid assignment variables. The factor currently limiting the number of job families is availability of validity data.

3. Whenever it is not feasible to provide separate FLS composites for each job, it is essential that jobs be clustered into job families in a manner that maximizes classification efficiency.

4. The expansion of the dimensionality of the classification battery by including more predictors with greater heterogeneity also can be expected

to greatly increase potential classification efficiency if predictor measures are developed or selected with differential validity in mind.

As noted earlier, some investigators have suggested contradictory classification system guidelines based on erroneously equating classification efficiency to predictive validity. But when measurement of classification efficiency is made in terms of MPP, computed after entities have been optimally assigned to jobs, as in this study, DAT principles have been consistently validated.

A number of general conclusions can be drawn by examining these results. First, we see a higher classification efficiency inherent in the ASVAB than is usually posited. Second, the failure to obtain even higher differential gains from the addition of new experimental variables to the ASVAB probably reflects the general lack of emphasis given to classification efficiency by test development researchers over the past two decades. Third, the total gain of 299 percent achieved by implementing all of our proposed changes in the operational system, including the additional differential validity provided by Project A experimental tests, reflects a potential that cannot presently be fully realizable in an operational system. However, it definitely points to a route that should eventually lead to very substantial gains in MPP.

Although the procedures used to form the existing operational job families are clearly not optimal, they are much more effective than are the corresponding AA composites. Even the Career Management Field (CMF) clusters provide considerable improvement in classification efficiency when used to expand the number of job families to which assignment is accomplished. It would appear that job families that meet other administrative and training requirements apart from personnel classification, such as CMF, can be effectively utilized in a personnel classification system.

The authors of a significant technical report on Project A (McLaughlin, Rossmeissl, Wise, Brandt, & Wang, 1984) concluded that an empirical job-clustering process was inherently ineffective because of its dependence on presumed unstable regression weights used to form assignment variables (AVs). Our findings, however, show that even when sampling error is allowed to take its full toll, the MPP obtainable in independent samples is greatly improved by the use of empirical clustering of jobs into families and the representation of these families by FLS composites.

A major reconstitution of the job families in the Army's classification system should be based on all available validity data, as well as on information available from job analyses. We do not wish to suggest that the decisions on job family structure should be based on the limited data utilized in our methodological studies. However, we are confident that our major conclusions will be confirmed as additional data are collected and analyzed using simulations to obtain MPP values.

POLICY IMPLICATIONS OF DAT FOR MILITARY SELECTION AND CLASSIFICATION SYSTEMS

The findings reported here and from recently completed earlier studies point to very high potential benefits obtainable from a major overhaul of the selection and classification systems of the military Services, all of which have comparable selection and assignment policies and procedures. An effective redesign of these systems should start with the acceptance of the maximization of mean predicted performance (MPP) as an overarching objective.

The design of an effective selection and classification system requires the consideration of many practical issues outside the scope of DAT. Tradition and perceived necessity provide a number of entrenched solutions to operational problems concerned with matching job preferences of recruits; distributing personnel across MOS to meet quality standards; providing vocational opportunities for females, minorities, and underprivileged recruits; and using unit (or at least positive) weights for the tests in assignment variables. We believe DAT should be allowed to impact substantially on a reconsideration of many policy issues.

Zeidner and Johnson (1989, 1991a, 1991b) predicted that use of FLS composites instead of AAs could increase the potential MPP from a classification system by 100%. The results of a number of studies now confirm this prediction by showing that the gain from optimizing assignment variables is at least 100% and most probably much greater—if initial assignments could be accomplished using a linear programming algorithm without consideration of individual preferences. There still is a lack of information as to the effect that a concerted effort to persuade recruits to accept suitable assignments would have on recruiting costs (i.e., assignments to jobs in which their predicted performance is relatively high). Until recently, many thought that very little utility was lost through permitting preferences (often based on no information or, worse, serious misinformation about Army jobs) to be the primary determinant of initial assignments. These studies show that a great deal of utility is lost through failure to make more use of optimal assignment information.

Several policy issues pertaining to personnel classification and assignment must be resolved before a new system incorporating DAT concepts and principles can be implemented. A number of these issues are noted:

- The *g* controversy. Does the poor classification efficiency available from the existing operational AAs indicate that the Army should, as some validity generalization proponents contend, change to a system that uses a single measure of cognitive ability, plus measures of psychomotor ability and clerical speed?
- The feasibility of implementing linear programming algorithms. Can optimal assignment algorithms be implemented in the current recruiting

market? If not, can cut scores be differentially raised in such a way as to provide a similar level of MPP?

- Using FLS composites as assignment variables. Can FLS composites with both positive and negative weights be implemented? If not, can a comparably effective two-tiered strategy, in which the second tier uses composites with all positive weights, be implemented?
- The substitution of psychometric *g* for AFQT. Can a general composite optimized in the joint predictor-criterion space be substituted for AFQT as the selection instrument?
- Quality distribution. Can quality distribution policies be altered to use predicted performance instead of AFQT as the measure of personnel quality?
- Optimal simultaneous selection and assignment. Must the Army continue to use a two-stage selection and classification system in which selection and classification are accomplished in separate successive stages, instead of the more effective and equitable single-stage system in which selection and classification are accomplished simultaneously? Such a single-stage algorithm was described by Johnson and Zeidner (1990, 1991). It is called the *multidimensional screening* (MDS) *algorithm.* Future plans to make use of MDS should affect the choice of a job-clustering algorithm for the design of a new system.
- Assessing future requirements. Can the quality requirements of future weapon systems be assessed in terms of FLS composites or factor composites used in the second tier instead of through the use of AFQT?

Underlying all of our studies is the belief that classification efficiency can be greatly improved. The validity generalization movement has pointed out the great difficulty of the task, but it is inappropriate to suggest that personnel classification research is of limited practical value, given recent research findings and until DAT and related concepts receive the same attention and concern that has been expended on selection efficiency.

POSTSCRIPT[1]

Situational Specificity. We did not intend to suggest that there is sufficient situational specificity across jobs so that classification algorithms based on these

---

[1] Editors' note: The following postscript by Zeidner and Johnson amplifies on several points that are raised in Bobko's discussion (chapter 25), as well as during discussion sessions at the conference. Owing to the complexity of their original paper, we invited them to contribute this postscript. Eight issues are addressed in the reverse order of their discussion in chapter 25.

differences can increase the overall operating efficiency of an organization. Nor have we intended to suggest a relationship between DAT and either specific aptitude theory or situational specificity theory (SST). ALthough DAT has a critical dependence on the credibility of validity generalization theory (VGT), there is no such relationship between DAT and SST.

The importance of SST lies in its role as a fictitious *bête noir* pictured as the inevitable alternative to the acceptance of the *g* theorist's version of VGT. Because the nontrivial presence of situational specificity equally precludes both classification efficiency and validity generalization, the classification effects we report in our chapter cannot be logically ascribed to situational specificity.

We believe that Brogden (1959) was correct in claiming that classification efficiency is an approximate function of mean predictive validity, mean intercorrelation of predicted performance measures, the number of jobs to which individuals are assigned, and the selection ratio. The correlation among predicted performance composites corresponding to each job family can be very high, indicating low situational specificity, without precluding a substantial level of classification efficiency.

The presence of classification efficiency suggests the presence of validity generalization. In reference to validity generalization (VG), Wise (1992) stated, "as the term is now used, it refers to properties of a distribution of criterion-related validity coefficients generated by using one or more measures of the same construct to predict general job performance within broad families of jobs". (p. 139). It is clear that this kind of VG must exist in nontrivial amounts for classification efficiency to be found in an operational system. Our findings indicate that job families are preferably narrower and more numerous than implied by Wise, and certainly more so than generally thought to be practical based on the validity generalization literature. By taking proper account of the differential validity inherent in the ASVAB, using DAT technology we can obtain much greater classification efficiency than is now realized by the operational personnel systems. This could not occur if situational specificity played a major role in the relationship between ASVAB test scores and job performance.

Utility Analysis. The reviewer was concerned that in the military, utility is not a linear function of performance. Although it can be argued that there are at least as many research findings supporting the linearity of utility, we recognize the complexity of estimating utility associated with selection and classification. This is an issue that is difficult to address in a few words, and the resolution of the important side issue of criterion linearity lies outside the scope of our chapter.

We are aware that a substantial gain in MPP may erroneously appear to be trivial unless interpreted in meaningful terms. Thus, we cannot avoid addressing the meaning of gains in MPP (addressed in standard score form) due to either selection or classification. Elsewhere, we have expressed the relatively unfamiliar concept of MPP in terms of a better understood measure (i.e., dollars). The work of Nord and Schmitz (1991) permitted such a clarification; they were able to say that an increase in MPP of .1 in standard score form is worth at least $100 million a year—a statement supported by their comprehensive empirical analyses.

Nord and Schmitz showed consistency of utility estimates based on the "40 percent rule" estimate of SD_y and estimates based on an economic model of "opportunity costs." In the use of opportunity costs, one assumes that a given performance level for an organization is required. Comparisons then can be made of how much it would cost to achieve the given performance level by such procedures as recruiting a higher-ability-level input, training more intensively, and so forth. If one method is shown to be $100 million cheaper than any other method, then indeed the method is worth $100 million to that organization.

Gains in Mean Predicted Performance (MPP). The reviewer stated that although the gains in MPP found in this study are impressive, the effects may be a bit overstated and that it might be more realistic to take an average selection and classification view of the results. We maintain that our tables do not overstate the effects of the proposed changes because we clearly address methods of improving classification. We give both MPP and percentage values in the tables, and both the text and tables separate the constant effect due to selection from the effects of classification.

All of the classification studies reported in our chapter are conducted in the context of a two-stage model in which selection precedes classification. That is, selection and classification are not part of a single process. Each experimental condition relates to the classification stage without having any effect on the selection stage. Thus, we do not examine the experimental outcomes in terms of the combined effects of selection and classification.

However, the two most interesting findings of our tables are that classification effects can be much greater than selection effects, and that classification efficiency gains achieved by applying DAT principles are very great and can be obtained with little cost and risk.

Social Programs. The reviewer, in a comment related to the use of optimal assignment algorithms addressed later, stated that the military often seeks to adopt a social responsibility criterion as part of their system and asked if classification algorithms will continue this socially desirable trend. We have not yet investigated this possibility in a specific operational situation, but we do know, in general, that the social program of the Army is least well addressed when a single measure of cognitive aptitude is used in a hierarchical classification model to make assignments. At the other end, the most equitable distribution of minorities is obtained in exactly the conditions that yield the highest MPP, that is, through the use of optimal assignment using best full least squares composites as assignment variables and as many job families as the data will support with stable validity data.

Anastasi has reported this fact for more than two decades in her various editions of *Psychological Testing*. Using data supplied by Uhlaner (1974), Anastasi (1988) showed that 80 percent of applicants score above the average on their best aptitude area whereas only 56 percent are above average on a general measure, AFQT. "This apparent impossibility in which nearly everyone could be above average, can be attained by capitalizing on the fact that nearly everyone excels in *some* aptitude". (p. 193). In contrast to the use of a single general measure in a hierarchical layering approach, the allocation approach can usually succeed in meeting quotas while assigning most applicants to a job where they rank in the upper half of the applicant population with respect to predicted performance.

Optimal Assignment Algorithms. The reviewer was concerned that optimal assignment algorithms usually lead to layering solutions where the most capable applicants are assigned to one job, the next most capable to another, and so on. He was also concerned that "corner solutions" are probably not acceptable to the Armed Forces. The reviewer appeared to assume that the primary source of gains in MPP resulting from optimal assignment to multiple job families comes from placing the highest-scoring individuals in those jobs that have the highest validities or have the greatest worth, that is, from a hierarchical classification process, rather than from the placing of individuals in jobs associated with their strongest abilities (i.e., allocation). This layering effect would provide the entire explanation of the classification effects if the assignment variables used for classification were obtained by multiplying a single test composite (e.g., a measure of g) by the respective validities for each corresponding job family. However, this outcome would certainly not be true for any of the examples reported here, that is, where predicted performance measures based on best weighted tests, using all tests in the battery, are used as assignment variables.

We once thought that hierarchical layering might make a substantial contribution to MPP, even when tailored tests are used, if validities varied across job families and the tailored test composites were allowed to have variances proportional to their validities. We now know that this hierarchical layering effect verges on the trivial for tailored tests possessing the allocation efficiency of our examples. See Johnson and Zeidner (1991, Chapter 1, Appendix) and Whetzel (1991).

Explanation of Results in Terms of Psychological Theory. The reviewer asked why differential classification simulations provide increased efficiency. We suggest looking to psychometric theory first. DAT directly incorporates the psychometric theory utilized in the selection and classification models of

Brogden (1959) and Horst (1954). In contrast, the theory associated with *g* is useful only with respect to selection, providing little help for the classification (or counseling) process. DAT is no less theoretical than is general mental ability theory, although less attention has been devoted thus far to content characteristics of this newly introduced theory. One study in this area, based on Project A data, found at least seven useful dimensions, in addition to *g*, in the joint predictor-criterion space. The interpretation of factors in the context of simple structure and knowledge of test and job loadings, permits addressing psychological content (Statman, 1992).

The Use of Tailored Composites to Improve Predictive Validity. The reviewer seemed to be saying that evidence of an increase in classification efficiency of tailored tests, over that provided by *g*, is proof that the potential to provide a similar increase in predictive validity is also present. We address a number of insupportable beliefs in our chapter, including the belief that test composites tailored to jobs or job families will readily provide substantial improvement in predictive validity, as compared to that provided by *g*. The reviewer challenged this as "an allegedly insupportable belief" that he contends is in fact supported by the "improved power" obtained from our classification algorithms.

It is important not to confuse the presence of "improved power" from classification algorithms with effectiveness of selection composites as evidenced by predictive validity. We contend, with considerable evidence, that classification efficiency can be improved with the use of tailored tests, as compared with the use of a unitary measure of *g*, despite the small improvement in predictive validity commonly provided by tailored tests.

It is a major principle of DAT that predictive validity must not be used as an index of classification efficiency. It is also an important principle of DAT that the inclusion of a unitary cognitive ability measure in one or more tailored tests does not harm, but contributes nothing to, classification efficiency. However, such a measure of *g* will usually contribute a worthwhile increase in selection efficiency over that provided by the tailored tests. Conversely, the tailored tests are not expected to provide a practical increase in selection efficiency over that provided by *g*. This latter statement is the basis of one of our "insupportable beliefs or assumptions."

Predictive Validity as an Indicator of Classification Efficiency. The reviewer stated that differential prediction still has merit, even in light of a large body of research that notes that cognitive abilities generally predict a substantial proportion of performance in most jobs. We agree that cognitive abilities contribute substantial validity in selection for a single job and substantial differential validity in the multiple job context. We also contend that the joint predictor-criterion space is multidimensional with a useful number of factors, beyond *g*, contributing a nontrivial amount of classification efficiency—in addition to the contribution of the unidimensional space as defined by the *g* factor.

It is important to note that the value of differential validity in the context employed in this study can only be shown (or disproved) by a simulation study. This value cannot be determined by examining predictive validity alone. Thus, there is no scientific basis for surprise at finding substantial differential validity because a few cognitive tests can explain most of the predictive validity. As emphasized above, predictive validity should never be used as an index of classification efficiency.

REFERENCES

Anastasi, A. (1988). *Psychological Testing* (6th ed.). New York: Macmillan.

Brogden, H. E. (1946). An approach to the problem of differential prediction. *Psychometrika, 11*, 139-54.

Brogden, H. E. (1951). Increased efficiency of selection resulting from replacement of a single predictor with several differential predictors. *Educational and Psychological Measurement, 11*, 173-96.

Brogden, H. E. (1954). A simple proof of a personnel classification theorem. *Psychometrika, 19*, 205-208.

Brogden, H. E. (1959). Efficiency of classification as a function of number of jobs, percent rejected, and the validity and intercorrelation of job performance estimates. *Educational and Psychological Measurement, 19*, 181-90.

Brogden, H. E. (1964). Simplified regression patterns for classification. *Psychometrica, 29*, 393-396.

Cattell, R. B. (1953). *A universal index for psychological factors*. Urbana: Laboratory of Personnel Assessment and Group Behavior, University of Illinois.

Guilford, J. P. (1956). The structure of intellect. *Psychology Bulletin, 53*, 267-293.

Gulliksen, H. (1950). *Theory of mental tests*. New York: Wiley.

Hartigan, J. A., & Wigdor, A. K. (Eds.) (1989). *Fairness in employment testing: Validity generalization, minority issues, and the general aptitude battery*. Washington, DC: National Academy Press.

Horst, P. (1954). A technique for the development of differential prediction battery. *Psychological Monographs, 68* (9, Whole No. 380).

Horst, P. (1955). A technique for the development of a multiple absolute prediction battery. *Psychological Monographs, 69* (9, Whole No. 380), 1-22.

Humphreys, L. G. (1962). The organization of human abilities. *American Psychologist, 17*, 475-483.

Humphreys, L. G. (1979). The construct of general intelligence. *Intelligence, 3*, 105-120.

Hunter, J. E. (1983). *The prediction of job performance in the military using ability composites: The dominance of general cognitive ability over specific aptitudes*. Rockville, MD: Research Applications.

Hunter, J. E. (1984). *The prediction of job performance in the civilian sector using the ASVAB*. Rockville, MD: Research Applications.

Hunter, J. E. (1985). *Differential validity across jobs in the military*. Rockville, MD: Research Applications.

Hunter, J. E. (1986). Cognitive ability, cognitive aptitudes, job knowledge, and job performance. *Journal of Vocational Behavior, 29*, 340-362.

Hunter, J. E., Crossen, J. J., & Friedman, D. H. (1985). *The validity of the Armed Services Vocational Aptitude Battery for civilian and military job performance*. Rockville, MD: Research Applications.

Jensen, A. R. (1984). Test validity: *g* versus the specificity doctrine. *Journal of Social and Biological Structures, 7*, 93-118.

Jensen, A. R. (1985). The nature of black-white differences on various psychometric tests. *The Behavioral and Brain Sciences, 8*, 193-263.

Jensen, A. R. (1986). *g*: Artifact or Reality? *Journal of Vocational Behavior, 29*, 301-331.

Jensen, A. R. (1991). Spearman's *g* and the problem of educational equality. *Oxford Review of Education, 17*, 169-187.

Johnson, C. D., & Zeidner, J. (1990, April). *Classification utility: Measuring and improving benefits in matching personnel to jobs* (IDA Paper P-2240). Alexandria, VA: Institute for Defense Analyses.

Johnson, C. D., & Zeidner, J. (1991). *The economic benefits of predicting job performance: Vol. 2. Classification efficiency.* New York: Praeger.

Johnson, C. D., Zeidner, J., & Leaman, J. A. (1992). *Improving classification efficiency by restructuring army job families* (Tech. Rep. No. 947). Alexandria, VA: U.S. Army Research Institute.

Johnson, C. D., Zeidner, J., & Scholarios, D. (1990). *Improving the classification efficiency of the Armed Services Vocational Aptitude Battery through the use of alternative test selection indicies* (IDA Paper P-2427). Alexandria, VA: Institute for Defense Analyses.

McLaughlin, D. H., Rossmeissl, P. G., Wise, L. L., Brandt, D. A., & Wang, M. M. (1984, October). *Validation of current and alternative ASVAB area composites, based on training and SQT information of FY81 and FY82 enlisted accessions* (Tech. Rep. No. 651). Alexandria, VA: U.S. Army Research Institute.

Mosier, C. I. (1951). Problems and design of cross validation. *Educational and Psychological Measurement, 11*, 5-11.

Murphy, K. R., & Davidshofer, C. O. (1991). *Psychological testing, principles and applications.* Englewood Cliffs, NJ: Prentice-Hall.

Nord, R., & Schmitz, E. (1991). Estimating performance and utility effects of alternative selection and classification policies. In J. Zeidner and C. D. Johnson. *The economic benefits of predicting job performance: Vol. 3. The gains of alternative policies.* New York: Praeger.

Ree, M. J., & Earles, J. A. (1991). The stability of *g* across different methods of estimation. *Intelligence, 15*, 271-278.

Schmidt, F. L., & Hunter, J. E. (1981). Employment testing: Old theories and new research findings. *American Psychologist, 36*, 1128-37.

Schmidt, F. L., Hunter, J. E., & Larson, M. (1988, August). *General cognitive ability vs. general and specific aptitudes in the prediction of training performance. Some preliminary findings* (Contract No. Delivery Order 0053). San Diego: U.S. Navy Personnel Research and Development Center.

Spearman, C. (1904). "General Intelligence," objectively determined and measured. *American Journal of Psychology, 15*, 201-293.

Spearman, C. (1927). *The abilities of man.* New York: Macmillan.

Statman, M. A. (1992). *Developing optimal predictor equations for differential job assignment and vocational counseling.* Paper presented at the annual conference of the American Psychological Association, Washington, DC.

Thorndike, R. L. (1985). The central role of general ability in prediction. *Multivariate Behavioral Research, 20*, 241-254.

Thorndike, R. L. (1986). The role of general ability in prediction. *Journal of Vocational Behavior, 29*, 332-339.

Thurstone, L. L. (1938). Primary mental abilities. *Psychometric Monographs*, No. 1.

Thurstone, L. L. (1947). *Multiple factor analysis.* Chicago: University of Chicago Press.

Uhlaner, J. E. (1974). *Evaluation of a new ACB and aptitude area system.*

Welsh, J. R., Jr., Kucinkas, S. K., & Curran, L. T. (1990, July). *Armed Services Vocational Battery (ASVAB): Integrative review of validity studies* (AFHRL-TR-90-22). Brooks AFB, TX: Air Force Human Resources Laboratory, Air Force Systems Command.

Whetzel, D. L. (1991). *Multidimensional screening: Comparison of a single-stage personnel selection/classification process with alternative strategies.* Unpublished doctoral dissertation, George Washington University, Washington, DC.

Wilks, S. S. (1938). Weighting systems for linear functions of correlated variables when there is no dependent variable. *Psychometrica, 3,* 23-40.

Wise, L. L. (1992). The validity of test scores for selecting and classifying enlisted recruits. In B. R. Gifford and L. C. Wing (Eds), *Test policy in defense: Lessons from the military for education, training and employment.* Boston: Kluwer.

Zeidner, J. (1987, April). *The validity of selection and classification procedures for predicting job performance* (IDA Paper P-1977). Alexandria, VA: Institute for Defense Analyses.

Zeidner, J., & Johnson, C. D. (1989, July). *The utility of selection for military and civilian jobs* (IDA Paper P-1977). Alexandria, VA: Institute for Defense Analyses.

Zeidner, J., & Johnson, C. D. (1991a). *The economic benefits of predicting job performance: Vol. 1. Selection Utility.* New York: Praeger.

Zeidner, J., & Johnson, C. D. (1991b). *The economic benefits of predicting job performance, Vol. 3.* Estimating the gains of alternative policies. New York: Praeger.

Zeidner, J., & Johnson, C. D. (1991c). Classification efficiency and systems design. *Journal of the Washington Academy of Sciences, 81,* 110-128.

CHAPTER

23

SETTING RECRUIT QUALITY GOALS: A COST-PERFORMANCE TRADE-OFF MODEL[1]

Matthew Black
D. Alton Smith
Systems Research and Applications Corporation

Each year the Department of Defense (DOD) recruits more than 200,000 men and women into the enlisted ranks of the Army, Navy, Air Force, and Marine Corps. Probably the single most important issue in enlistment policy is determining the goals for recruit "quality," where quality is commonly measured by two characteristics: an individual's score on the Armed Forces Qualification Test (AFQT), part of a written test administered to all potential enlistees; and high school graduation status.

The average quality of an enlistment cohort directly affects both military capability and the personnel costs associated with recruiting and training cohort members. A large number of scientific studies have shown that "high"-quality recruits—those with above average AFQT scores and a high school diploma—perform better in the military, whether performance is measured by training outcomes, job performance tests, speed of promotion, or first-term attrition. But high-quality individuals also cost more to recruit in the all-volunteer force environment, where the military must compete with other employers for the services of talented individuals. The appropriate recruit quality goal represents a trade-off between increased military capability and increased personnel costs.

Although the conceptual issue is simple to state, policy decisions require information on the quantities involved in the trade-off: How much will it cost to recruit the quality needed to increase military performance by a given amount for a particular Service? Some estimate of the cost-performance trade-off curve, shown notionally in Fig. 23.1, is needed.

---

[1] The views, opinions, and findings contained in this paper are those of the authors and should not be construed as an official Department of Defense position, policy, or decision unless so designated by other official documentation.

Plotting values on this curve is not an easy task. Any given value of military performance can be obtained by different combinations of the number and average quality of an enlistment cohort. What is relevant for policy decisions, however, is the combination that produces the specified performance at minimum cost. Three analytical ingredients are necessary to solve for the cost-effective recruit quality level: an equation specifying the relationship between recruit quality and performance, equations representing the relationship between recruit quality and the elements of personnel costs, and an algorithm for finding the minimum-cost solution.

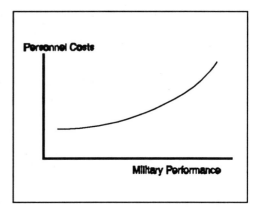

FIG.23.1. Cost-performance trade-off curve.

This chapter describes a model that defines the quantitative linkages between recruit quality, military performance, and personnel costs and uses that information to determine the cost-performance trade-off options available to DOD. The model was jointly developed by Systems Research and Applications (SRA) Corporation and the Human Resources Research Organization (HumRRO) for the Office of the Assistant Secretary of Defense (Force Management and Personnel).[2]

We are not the first to develop such a model. The essential structure of a cost-performance trade-off model for accession quality was described by Steadman (1981). Cost-performance trade-off models for a small number of Army occupations were implemented and tested by Armor, Fernandez, Bers, and Schwarzbach (1982) and Fernandez (1985). Accession quality models are also currently under development in several of the Services.

We will focus our discussion on the role of job performance measures in this type of policy analysis model. Our objectives are twofold. First, we want to show how the results of job performance measurement efforts can be used, in combination with cost and other data, to inform important resource management decisions. Results generated by the model show the significant contribution of job performance measures in determining recruit quality goals. When

---

[2] Paul Hogan of Lewin-ICF and D. Alton Smith of SRA designed the analytical model, collected the cost data, and built the computer model that implements the analytical framework. Dickie Harris and Rod McCloy of HumRRO estimated the statistical models linking recruit quality and job performance.

"performance" is defined only by expected person-years, the cost-effective quality level is only 50% of what it is when job performance test scores are included in the performance metric.

Second, we examine what the modeling effort has to say about the way job performance data are collected. Choices in test development and sample design affect the usefulness of the data for models such as ours.

ACCESSION QUALITY COST-PERFORMANCE TRADE-OFF MODEL

The Accession Quality Cost-Performance Trade-off (CPT) Model selects, for a set of occupation groups, the number of enlistments by recruit quality category that minimizes the sum of recruiting, training, and compensation costs while meeting first-term performance and optional personnel strength goals. Because of the significant variation in the quality-performance and quality-cost relationships across the Services, separate models are being developed by Service.

The model can answer two general types of policy questions:

- How should changes in the recruiting mission and environment affect both recruit quality goals and personnel costs? This is a direct application of the model under different scenarios defined by occupation-specific performance goals; strength goals, such as the required number of accessions; factors affecting recruiting costs, such as the unemployment rate; and the level of training and compensation costs.

- What is the performance impact of changes in personnel budgets? Used iteratively with different performance goals, the model traces out the cost-performance trade-off curve shown in Fig. 23.1. Because this curve shows the minimum costs of achieving various performance levels, it also plots the best-case performance effects of budget changes.

It is important to note that the CPT model does not choose the best overall recruit quality level, only the cost-minimizing level for a given amount of performance. Selecting the best overall level—the optimal point on the cost-performance trade-off curve—requires information on the dollar value of performance. In a market setting, where profit-maximizing firms compete for the services of employees, one can argue that the compensation paid to workers represents the value of their performance. It is much more difficult to make the same claim for public sector organizations that do not compete. Without using what must be arbitrary performance valuations, the CPT model can be used to define the efficient cost and performance options, an improvement in the information currently available to policy makers.[3]

In mathematical terms, the CPT model is a constrained minimization problem with three elements: enlistments by recruit quality category and occupation, which are the variables for which we solve; performance and personnel strength goals, which define the constraints on the problem; and personnel costs, which comprise the objective function. We describe the model in terms of these three elements. A formal statement of the model is presented in the appendix to this chapter.

Variables: Enlistments by Recruit Category and Occupation Group

There are 360 variables in the model for each Service—enlistment in 10 recruit categories for each of 36 occupation groups.

Recruit Categories. Although there are many ways to categorize recruit quality, our choice must be driven by the policy applications of the model. Therefore, we use AFQT score and high school graduation status, the two characteristics used to establish enlistment goals and measure recruiting performance for DOD. In particular, 10 recruit quality categories are defined by the interaction of five standard AFQT score groups (Category I, II, IIIA, IIIB, and IV) and two high school graduation groups (those with high school diplomas and those without).

Occupation Groups. Both the quality-performance and quality-cost relationships vary with military occupation, which means that the minimum-cost level of recruit quality will also vary by occupation. As an example, consider two occupations with different training costs but the same overall performance goal. The least-cost solution for staffing these occupations will have fewer recruits, of a higher average quality, in the occupation with high training costs. Because of their lower turnover, fewer high-quality recruits have to be trained to generate the same amount of performance, conserving training resources. Given these differences, it is important to understand how high-quality recruits should be allocated across occupations.

Ideally, the aggregate quality requirement for a Service would be determined as the sum of the levels of quality needed in each enlisted occupation in that Service. This would yield not only aggregate recruit quality goals but also targets for the process of classifying recruits into occupations as well. We use

---

[3] For a good example of a recruit quality model that employs a performance valuation function, see Nord and Kearl (1990).

grouped, rather than individual, occupations in the model for two practical reasons. First, as described later, there is not sufficient information in our performance data to establish a reliable relationship between performance and entry characteristics for every enlisted occupation in DOD. And second, increasing the number of occupations also increases the number of variables in the model. With up to 350 occupations in each Service, finding a solution to the constrained optimization problem becomes difficult enough to detract from the model's usefulness as a policy analysis tool.

There are 36 occupation groups in the model, which are defined hierarchically. At the top, occupations are divided into nine groups based on one-digit DOD Occupation Codes.[4] These codes provide a common classification of occupations across Services, facilitating the definition of performance and strength goals. Each of these nine groups is further divided into four subgroups based on training costs and an index of occupation characteristics.[5] These subgroups were chosen to increase the within-group homogeneity of the occupation groups on variables that are central to the cost-minimization problem, such as training costs. The more homogeneous the groups are, the less error is introduced into the recruit quality solution by the aggregation of individual occupations.

Constraints: Performance Goals by Occupation

In the CPT model, performance for an occupation group is the sum of expected hands-on performance test scores over the first term of service for recruits assigned to that group. Specifically, P_i, the performance value for occupation i, is defined as

$$P_i = \Sigma_j A_{ij} \left(\Sigma^t s_{ij}^t Z_{ij}^t \right) \tag{1}$$

where A_{ij} is the number of accessions (i.e., enlistments entering active duty) from recruit category j into occupation i; s_{ij}^t is the survival rate to year of service (YOS)t for a category j recruit in occupation i; and Z_{ij}^t is the predicted YOSt hands-on performance test score for a recruit from category j entering occupation i. The term in parentheses is the survival-weighted sum of performance test scores over the first term for an individual from a particular

---

[4] The one-digit DOD Occupation Codes are: infantry, gun crews, and seamen; electrical equipment repairers; communications and intelligence; medical and dental; other technical specialists; support and administration; mechanical equipment repairers; craftsmen; and service/supply handlers.

[5] Specifically, a performance index based only on occupation characteristics is constructed from the performance-recruit quality equations described in this chapter. This index indicates how a given individual's performance would vary if assigned to different occupations.

recruit category enlisting in a particular occupation.   Occupation group performance is the weighted sum across recruit categories of these expected scores, with weights equal to the number of accessions from each category.

As currently structured, the CPT model requires cohort performance goals for all occupations. For policy-making purposes, it would be preferable to set a series of annual performance goals, that include the contribution of all Service members in the occupation, and have the model derive the series of cohort performance values required to meet the annual goals. Two problems make this model more difficult to develop. First, the job performance test data available from the Job Performance Measurement (JPM) project, which we use to implement Equation (1), only include tests of first-term service members within a limited range of years of service. These data are not sufficient to develop the quality-performance relationships that would be required for members of the career force. Second, there are serious conceptual problems in defining the cost-minimization problem for multiple cohorts of recruits.[6]

Occupation group performance is a function of the number and quality distribution of recruits into that group, with quality affecting performance both through the hands-on performance test score and the probability of attrition. Although the use of hands-on tests represents an improvement over performance metrics based on training outcomes or job knowledge tests, this measure of occupation performance has four limitations:

- First, it reflects only the ability to perform selected tasks for each job, ignoring other dimensions of military job performance, such as leadership ability.

- Second, the same amount of performance for an occupation can be obtained with different combinations of the size and average quality of an accession cohort. As a practical matter, staffing requirements restrict the flexibility for trade-off between the number of recruits and their average quality. For example, each tank requires a crew of four to operate efficiently, regardless of the ability of individual crew members.

- Third, Equation (1) assumes that the first and last high-quality individuals added to an occupation yield the same gain in performance. In fact, the benefit to group performance of that first

---

[6] In particular, the solution depends arbitrarily on the number of years included in the problem. For a discussion of these issues see Hogan, Smith, Clifton, and Harris (1990).

high-quality recruit is probably greater than the marginal benefit of those that follow.[7]

- Fourth, military performance is, in most cases, a function of both personnel and equipment performance. Ignoring the effects of person-equipment trade-offs on both cost and performance can lead to incorrect estimates of the appropriate level of recruit quality.[8]

Fortunately, we can work around some of these limitations by using strength constraints in the model, as described later. The other issues represent areas where additional research is needed to improve the performance metric.

Constructing performance values in the CPT model would be straightforward if observations on hands-on performance test scores were available for all occupations, by recruit category and time in service. However, the cost of developing and administering hands-on performance tests limited the data available from the JPM project. Counting all four Services, we could use results from just 24 occupations to estimate the relationship between recruit quality and job performance for the CPT model.[9]

To generalize from this sample to a set of performance scores for the occupation groups in Equation (1), HumRRO estimated a multivariate model linking performance scores with characteristics of the test taker and the job. In this model, Z_n, the performance score for the nth individual in the sample is given by

$$Z_n = \alpha_m + \beta_m I_n + \varepsilon_n$$

where
$$\alpha_m = \alpha^o + \alpha^1 O_m + \eta_m \qquad (2)$$

$$\beta_m = \beta^o + \beta^1 O_m + \eta_m$$

and I_n is a set of individual characteristics, including AFQT score, high school graduation status, and time in service; O_m is a set of characteristics for the mth

---

[7] This issue is discussed in Black (1988).

[8] For example, see Daula and Smith (1992a). This study estimates the minimum-cost level of recruit quality needed to meet a given level of tank force performance, where performance is measured by scores on a firing range. Recognizing the role of equipment leads to a higher recruit quality requirement because increasing the quality of tank gunners and commanders allows the same performance requirement to be met with fewer tanks, at a considerable cost savings.

[9] The results from tests administered in seven additional occupations will be incorporated into the analysis in the near future.

occupation in the sample; the αs and βs are parameters to be estimated; and ε, η, and μ are random variables. The occupation characteristics included in the model are four factor scores, representing the extent to which a job deals with "things," the cognitive complexity of the job, the degree of unpleasant working conditions, and the fine motor control required. The factor scores were derived from a factor analysis of data on 44 job characteristics for the complete set of military occupations.[10]

This type of model is called a *multilevel model* in the psychology literature and a *random coefficients model* in econometrics. For the purposes of the CPT model, the essential advantage of this specification is that the hands-on performance test scores required for Equation (1) can be predicted for any occupation group. By substituting the average factor scores for an occupation group into Equation (2), we obtain a set of β_ms specific to the group that can be used to generate the necessary performance values.

The parameters of the linkage equation were estimated using a sample of approximately 8,400 test scores obtained for the 24 JPM occupations. While there are many ways to evaluate the estimation results, we will focus on two general findings about the AFQT-performance relationship, which is central to the functioning of the CPT model.[11] First, on average, there is a positive, statistically significant correlation between AFQT and job performance. More importantly, the size of the correlation is roughly consistent with that estimated in other studies using different performance metrics.[12] Second, our ability to measure the differences in the recruit-quality relationship across occupations is clearly restricted by the small sample of occupations. Many of the coefficients that capture these differences—the $\alpha's$ and $\beta's$—are not statistically significant and vary substantially with small changes in the functional form of the statistical model. Later we return to the issue of measuring the occupation-specific linkage between AFQT and job performance.

In contrast to the hands-on performance test scores, obtaining survival rates for the performance equation is relatively simple. Longitudinal personnel

---

[10] The military job characteristics are *Dictionary of Occupational Titles* (Department of Labor, 1977) characteristics for civilian jobs, which have been assigned to military jobs through a crosswalk of civilian and military occupations.

[11] Estimation results for various forms of the linkage equation are detailed in a report for OSD Accession Policy (McCloy et al., 1992).

[12] This statement is based on comparisons with selected studies familiar to us. For example, the correlation between AFQT and hands-on performance is similar to the correlation between AFQT and tank firing scores in Daula and Smith (1992a), and the correlation between AFQT and Army promotion times in Daula and Smith (1990). A formal review of the results in the literature should be conducted to validate this point.

records, sorted by occupation group and recruit category, can be used to estimate the probability of survival to various time-in-service points.

Constraints: Strength Goals

As noted above, we need strength constraints in the CPT model primarily to adjust for the limitations of the performance metric. Two types of strength constraints are included. First, a total accession constraint ensures that the number of recruits selected by the model fills the number of enlisted vacancies anticipated by a Service. Thus, the model can be prevented from generating solutions that are inconsistent with personnel requirements. Second, minimum high-quality percentage constraints (where high quality is specifically defined as AFQT Category I to IIIA, high school diploma graduates) can be placed on the solution by occupation. One adds these constraints to force a solution that recognizes the need for some high-quality recruits as leaders in every occupation, based either on their potential as future managers in the occupation or their role in increasing group performance.

Objective Function: Recruiting, Training, and Compensation Costs

The CPT model minimizes the sum of costs required to recruit, train, and pay an enlistment cohort over the first term of service. Although smallest of the three cost categories, recruiting costs have the biggest impact on the structure of the model. In particular, because of the nature of recruiting costs, one must jointly solve for the cost-minimizing level of recruit quality in all occupations; an occupation-by-occupation approach will not work. The requirement to find a simultaneous solution to recruit quality goals increases the number of variables in the cost-minimization problem and makes it necessary to estimate the quality-performance linkage across all occupations, a problem already discussed.

Recruiting is characterized by average costs that increase with the total number of high-quality individuals recruited. To attract more high-quality individuals into military service, either the monetary incentives for enlisting or the "sales" effort must increase, causing total costs to rise faster than the number of recruits. With increasing average costs, the cost-performance trade-off in occupation A depends not only on the number of high-quality individuals recruited for that occupation, but also on the number recruited for the other occupations. For example, an increase in the number of high-quality individuals recruited for occupation B increases the cost of quality to occupation A, reducing the attractiveness of high-quality individuals in that occupation relative to other quality categories. The increase in quality for occupation B, therefore, leads to a reduction in the cost-effective quality level for occupation A.[13]

In the CPT model, the costs to recruit a particular mix of individuals by quality level are predicted by a cost function. In economics, a cost function describes the minimum costs of producing a particular quantity of output. It is derived from a production function, which shows the relationship between the level of inputs and the output produced, and the prices of those inputs. For recruiting, our "production" function is based on historical estimates of the effect of recruiting resources, such as advertising or the number of recruiters, and the effect of the characteristics of the recruiting market on the number of high-quality enlistments. The prices of recruiting resources are calculated from recruiting budgets in a base year.

The advantages of determining recruiting costs from the underlying production function are threefold. First, the cost function estimates minimum recruiting costs for a particular mix of enlistments costs, a necessary input in determining the minimum personnel costs for a given set of performance goals.[14] Second, the cost function correctly captures the increasing marginal cost nature of recruiting costs.[15] This is particularly important given today's recruiting policy issues. Assuming constant marginal costs would overstate the costs of recruit quality for the smaller enlistment cohorts anticipated in the near future, resulting, as we demonstrate later, in recruit quality goals that are too low. Third, cost function estimates of recruiting costs vary with changes in the recruiting market, such as the level of unemployment. This provides the analytical link needed to estimate recruit quality goals for different recruiting environments.

The derivation of training and compensation costs in the CPT model is much simpler. The average cost of training an individual from a particular recruit category in a given occupation group is determined from two factors. First, we calculate the average training cost per graduate in the occupation group, using the costs of both basic training and initial skill training courses. Then, these costs are adjusted by training survival rates for the recruit category to obtain the

---

[13] To understand this point, consider the analytical process of finding the minimum cost level of recruit quality in a single occupation with just two recruit quality categories—high and low. Among the mixes of high- and low-quality recruits that satisfy the performance goal, the model will select that mix for which the cost per unit of performance is the same for high- and low- quality recruits. If these costs are not equal, it is possible to substitute from the high to low cost-per-unit category, providing the same level of occupation performance at a lower cost. Thus, anything that disturbs the balance in per unit costs across recruit quality categories affects the cost-minimizing solution.

[14] A useful by-product of this optimization within the larger optimization problem is the mix of recruiting resources that produces the minimum-cost solution.

[15] This makes the objective function a nonlinear function of accessions by recruit category, requiring the use of quadratic programming methods to find the minimum-cost solution.

per accession cost of training. Thus, the average training costs within an occupation group are lower for high-quality individuals, who have greater survival rates.

Expected compensation costs over the first term of service are calculated from survival rates and average compensation (basic pay, allowances, and retirement accrual) by year of service.

Results From the CPT Model

To facilitate its use in policy evaluation, the algorithms for the CPT model have been implemented in a microcomputer program featuring a menu-driven user interface.[16] Fure 23.2 summarizes the elements that define a run scenario and the results generated by each optimization run.

To date, CPT models have been developed for the Army and Navy. An initial evaluation of the models shows promising results on two scores. First, when run with FY90 performance goals and cost inputs, the models for both Services come close to predicting the actual recruit quality levels accessed in that year. For example, the cost-minimizing percentage of high-quality recruits required to achieve the Army's FY90 performance goals as determined by the model is 59%; the actual percentage in the accession cohort was 62%. For the Navy, the high-quality percentage from the model is 53%; the percentage in the FY90 accession cohort was 55%. These results are comforting, of course, only to the extent you believe that the current process for setting quality goals, like the model, attempts to find the cost-effective solution.

The models were less successful in replicating the actual quality levels by occupation group. For both the Army and Navy models, only four out of nine high-level occupation groups had high-quality percentages within 15 percentage points of the actual accession results. Assuming that the Service allocations of recruit quality across occupations are cost effective, one potential cause of the mismatch is the relatively inaccurate estimates of the AFQT-performance relationship at the occupation level.

A less ambiguous test of the model is whether the quality levels and associated personnel costs respond as expected to changes in individual elements of the run scenario, such as performance goals. The following examples illustrate two of the more interesting results from these sensitivity tests.

Scenario 1: A Higher Unemployment Rate. An increase in unemployment reduces the costs of recruiting high quality individuals. If performance goals remain unchanged, the optimal percentage of high-quality enlistments should

---

[16] The CPT model is written in FORTRAN and uses routines from the Numerical Algorithm Group (NAG) for the optimization process.

increase, because these individuals are now more attractive on a performance-to-cost basis. As expected, the cost-minimizing percentage of high-quality enlistments for the Navy increases from 56% to 62% when the unemployment rate increases from the FY90 level of 5.3% to 7.0%. Similar results were obtained for the Army. In other words, the model suggests that the Services should take advantage of the recruiting cost savings available in a slack labor market by recruiting more high-quality individuals.

Scenario Elements
- Performance goals, by occupation.
- Total accession or person years constraint.
- Minimum high-quality percentages, by occupation.
- Parameters of the recruit "production" function.
- Inflation factors for recruiting resources, training costs, and military compensation.

Optimization Results
- Number of recruits, by category and occupation group.
- Total performance, by occupation.
- Person years, by occupation and fiscal year.
- Recruiting, training, and compensation costs.
- Minimum-cost mix of recruiting resources.

FIG. 23.2. CPT scenario and results.

Scenario 2: No Effect of Quality of Performance Scores. Suppose that performance scores were not available, so that "performance" could be measured only by the expected person-years contributed by individuals in different recruit quality categories. Under this definition, the additional performance obtained by recruiting a high-quality individual is less than that when performance includes variation in test scores. As a result, the cost-effective level of quality should fall. To test the contribution of the performance test scores to the determination of recruit quality goals, we ran the CPT model with all performance test scores, the Zs in Equation (1), set equal to 1. For both the Army and the Navy, we found that the cost-minimizing level of quality falls by half, to about 30%. Clearly, being able to measure the additional job performance generated by high-quality individuals is important in establishing the correct recruit quality goals.

A timely question for recruiting policy is how quality goals should change as enlistments fall in response to the downsizing of military forces. Table 23.1 displays, for both Army and Navy, strength and cost results from the CPT model obtained at various percentages of FY90 performance levels. For example, to meet Army FY90 performance goals (the 100% column), the model recommends recruiting 85,400 individuals, of whom 50% should be high quality.[17]

---

[17] This result differs from the 59% high-quality goal described earlier, because of different accession strength constraints. In testing the model against FY90 results, we constrained the model to access only 84,400 individuals, the limit on Army accessions in FY90. In the downsizing

The costs to recruit, train, and compensate this cohort over the first four years of service would total $6,489 million, of which $391 million would be recruiting costs.[18]

The number of accessions and the total personnel costs associated with the enlistment cohorts fall at roughly the same percentages as performance. For example, at 75% performance, Army accessions are 73.5% of the FY90 level, and total personnel costs are 74.6%. In contrast, the optimal percentage of high-quality recruits and the proportion of recruiting costs in total costs rises. For the Army, the minimum-cost high-quality percentage increases from 50% to 67.5% and recruiting costs increase from 6% of total costs to about 7%. The Navy results in the lower panel of Table 23.1 show analogous patterns. The explanation for these results is straightforward. As the size of enlistment cohorts declines, the relative cost of recruiting high-quality individuals falls, making it cost effective to set higher-quality goals.

This section described the structure of a cost-performance trade-off model for setting recruiting goals, outlined some of the challenges faced in implementing the model, and presented results from an initial evaluation. In the next section, we turn to some lessons for performance measurement learned in the process of building and testing the CPT model.

LESSONS FOR PERFORMANCE MEASUREMENT

The CPT model offers a number of potential advantages as a policy analysis tool for setting and defending recruiting goals. There are, however, several research issues to resolve before relying on this prototype for policy or management decisions. The fundamental question concerns the accuracy of the model's estimates of the low-cost mix of recruit quality for each Service. From our experience in building and using the CPT model, we believe this question hinges largely on the performance-quality linkages. Next we discuss several ideas that may help in developing an agenda for future job performance research.

---

example, we want the model to determine the minimum-cost level of accessions and, therefore, do not include a constraint.

[18] Actual recruiting costs for Army enlisted personnel in FY90 were approximately $550 million. The difference between this number and the recruiting costs in Table 23.1 is due primarily to a difference in the recruiting mission, not inefficiencies in the recruiting effort. In FY90, the Army actually recruited (in contrast to accessed) 89,300 individuals, of whom 71% were high quality.

TABLE 23.1. CPT Strength and Cost Results
For the Downsizing Example

Army				
	Percentage of FY90 Performance			
Outcome	**100**	**85**	**80**	**75**
Accessions	85,400	71,800	67,300	62,800
Percentage high quality	50.0	59.2	63.0	67.5
Cost ($M) — Recruiting	391	349	335	321
Cost ($M) — Training	1,543	1,301	1,220	1,140
Cost ($M) — Compensation	4,555	3,850	3,615	3,380
Cost ($M) — Total	6,489	5,500	5,170	4,841

Navy				
	Percentage of FY90 Performance			
Outcome	**100**	**85**	**80**	**75**
Accessions	69,800	58,843	55,203	51,556
Percentage high quality	56.0	65.7	69.4	73.5
Cost ($M) — Recruiting	264	233	222	210
Cost ($M) — Training	1,244	1,502	989	925
Cost ($M) — Compensation	4,160	3,514	3,300	3,086
Cost ($M) — Total	5,668	4,799	4,509.9	4,220.7

Population of Inference

All Military Occupations. In the CPT model, occupational performance goals are the constraints that must be met by the least-cost quality mix of recruits over their initial term of service.   Hence, performance measures and performance-quality links in all occupations are germane for setting optimal entry standards.   The current model is based on only 24 military occupations for which we have job performance data.   Performance equations, estimated from these data, are used to impute performance goals to all military occupations, and compute the performance contribution of classifying recruits into each occupation.   From a sampling perspective, how well do these 24 observations represent the population of roughly 1,000 occupations across the four Services? Are the sampling errors tolerable?   For example, not all of the nine DOD one-digit occupational clusters are represented by the 24 JPM occupations.

Results from the CPT model suggest there is substantial sensitivity to the underlying linkage equations.   The coefficients in the linkage equations appear sensitive to alternate specifications, probably because of the small number of occupations and relatively large number of interactions in the estimating equations.   Therefore, there are really two reasons to expand the number of tested occupations: first, to provide additional degrees of freedom and greater statistical variation for estimating the linkage equations; and second, to obtain a more representative sample of military occupations.

The 24 JPM occupations were intended to support performance measurement research rather than constitute a database on which to run a CPT policy analysis model.   Looking ahead to potentially important policy applications, we believe that job performance measures are needed for additional occupations.   This, in turn, will require a carefully developed, stratified sampling plan to ensure adequate representation and acceptable confidence intervals.

First-Term Versus All Enlisted Personnel.   The CPT model focuses on minimizing costs for a given set of occupational performance goals only over the first four years of service—the period in which JPM performance measures are available.   To the extent that quality has a positive effect on job performance beyond the first enlistment term (and personnel costs do not vary by quality), the current CPT model will tend to underestimate the least-cost proportion of high-quality accessions.   This possibility remains moot, however, until performance tests are administered and analyzed for more experienced military personnel.

Occupation Versus Task Performance Measurement Orientation

Tasks performed within an occupation are not homogeneous on dimensions such as cognitive difficulty, number of procedural steps, and eye-hand coordination. In research performed for the Air Force, we have found much greater variation within occupations (individual task performance as well as task characteristics) than between occupations.[19] We have also found overlap across occupations in that some tasks are similar in terms of their job characteristics.

Focusing on task performance offers several potential advantages. First, performance-quality equations estimated at the task level may be more insightful and robust than those estimated with occupation-level data. Second, greater accuracy may be gained by constructing a weighted average of task performance scores and performance-quality linkages to obtain overall occupation measures and relationships.[20] This focus may allow for greater variation in the performance-quality linkages across occupations. Looking ahead, an interesting question is whether a task- or occupation-level focus would yield better results, assuming the same number of new tests were developed. A task-level approach is not without its costs. Preliminary analysis would be necessary to create a taxonomy (sampling frame) of extant tasks across occupations from which to draw a sample for test development and administration. At issue is how many tasks would be required versus the number of occupations, their respective costs, and the expected payoff in terms of better linkage equations.

Nonlinear Performance-Quality Linkage

Individual Perspective. The CPT model uses a linear performance-quality relationship. Each unit increase in quality yields the same increase in individual job performance in that occupation, other things equal. This assumption runs counter to classification standards that set minimum test scores for entry into many occupations. It is also likely that beyond some high level of quality, individual job performance will cease to increase. These possibilities suggest upper and lower bounds for the performance-quality relationship. The CPT model could be recalibrated to test the practical implications of these constraints.

Group Perspective. The current model assumes that the performance contribution of each additional recruit remains constant, for each occupation, regardless of the number of high-quality personnel assigned. There is no

---

[19] HumRRO developed written job knowledge tests for enlisted members in the Air Force Individual Ready Reserve. The data were analyzed by SRA to estimate task-level models of job performance as a function of individual and task characteristics [a fixed-effects model similar to Equation (2)]. For details, see Black, Davis, and Campbell (1989).

[20] This is what we do in the Air Force skill degradation model. Tasks within an occupation are rated by subject matter experts across a number of different dimensions or characteristics. Weights are also assigned to each task to represent the importance of each to overall job performance in that occupation. Based on these measures, and the estimated coefficients on task characteristics in the performance equation, the model computes a predicted occupational performance score for a given combination of individual attributes.

diminishing marginal productivity with respect to quality—the first high quality soldier classified into the infantry is predicted to have the same performance effect as the last comparably qualified infantry-bound recruit. A richer model would recognize that when occupations offering relatively high performance payoffs to quality become saturated with high-quality recruits, there are greater performance gains by classifying additional high-quality personnel to other occupations because of a declining value added in the former specialties.

Implicit in this assumption of "constant returns to quality" is that individual job performance is independent of other personnel, which is at odds with many military work situations. In fact, measurement of individual job performance is often complicated by the teamwork required for military tasks. Unfortunately, the dynamics of group performance are not well known and rarely measured. Currently, the CPT model permits the user to specify a minimum number of high-quality recruits per occupation to account for this nonlinearity. A useful next step would be to conduct sensitivity tests with the model to predict how alternate assumptions of declining marginal productivity to quality for each occupation (i.e., the interactions at the work group level) affect the least-cost quality mix of recruits and the distribution of high quality recruits across occupations.[21]

Trade-Offs Between Quality and Numbers of Recruits

Another feature of the model is the substitution of fewer high-quality recruits for lower-quality personnel, and vice versa—their respective costs, of course, would determine the optimal accession mix. For example, two individuals with AFQT scores of 75 are assumed to contribute the same to overall performance in an occupation as three recruits scoring 50. In principle, substitution is desirable. But there are operating constraints not quantified or reflected in the CPT model. Specifically, many weapon systems and equipment require fixed numbers of personnel to perform a mission or task.[22] Such personnel constraints, which vary across occupations and by task within an occupation, limit the degree of substitution. However, there is little empirical evidence to provide guidance. A first step would be to work with subject matter experts to compile a list of jobs for which "quality-numbers" substitutions would be possible. Rules of thumb

---

[21] The "constant returns to quality" assumption may partly explain why the model's predictions by occupation do not match up as well with actual distributions as do the aggregate predictions.

[22] Another type of substitution is the personnel-hardware tradeoff. For example, "smarter" weapons or equipment may reduce the number of required operators or maintainers but increase the requirements for high-quality personnel. In an era of force drawdowns, this type of substitution may take on greater importance, but little evidence exists for modeling purposes.

could be incorporated into the CPT model to bound the degree of permissible substitution.

Other Dimensions of Job Performance

Job performance in the CPT model is set by the JPM measures as reflected in the linkage equations. There are, of course, other aspects of performance, such as time to perform, leadership, initiative, and ability to perform in a hostile environment. To the extent that these performance measures are highly correlated with the JPM measure, there is little practical loss in excluding them from the model. However, if these performance measures are orthogonal to one another, and quality is positively linked to each, the model will underestimate the "true" least-cost percentage of high-quality accessions. The Air Force is examining time to perform as a complementary measure. For example, maintenance and warfighting tasks place a premium on performance time as well as performance quality—mean time to repair is crucial for aircraft availability and sortie generation rates, especially in combat. The ability to load, aim, and fire quickly is as crucial as is the ability to do it right—hit the target. Further research on the interplay between these two facets of performance seems warranted.

In summary, the CPT model points to a number of research paths that could add additional prediction accuracy and modeling capability to support decision makers. In a sense, the model provides an excellent platform to test the potential value of alternative research ideas. The model's ability to demonstrate the power of better information to senior DOD managers also contributes to the demand for future research and helps to target scarce resources to the most promising areas of job performance, selection, and classification.

APPENDIX: FORMAL STATEMENT OF THE CPT MODEL

We choose the number of accessions, A_{ij}, by occupation group i and recruit category j to minimize the first-term recruiting, training, and compensation costs, given by

$$R \left(\Sigma_i \Sigma_{j \in H} A_{ij}, \ \Sigma_i \Sigma_{j \in M} A_{ij}, \ \Sigma_i \Sigma_{j \in L} A_{ij}, \ R_p, \ R_F \right)$$

$$+ \ \{ T^B \Sigma_i \Sigma_j (s_{ij}^B A_{ij}) + \Sigma_i \left[T_i^I \Sigma_j (s_{ij}^I A_{ij}) \right] \}$$

$$+ \ \Sigma_i \Sigma_j \left[A_{ij} \Sigma^t (s_{ij}^t C_i) \right]$$

where

- R is the recruiting cost function, with arguments including the number of high (AFQT I-IIIA, diploma graduates), medium (AFQT I-IIIA, nongraduates), and low (all other recruit categories) quality accessions; the prices of recruiting resources, R_p; and recruiting market factors, R_F.

- T^B and T^I are the per-graduate variable costs associated with basic and initial skill training, respectively.[1]

- s_{ij} is the survival rate from accession to the completion of basic training (superscript B), initial skill training (superscript I), and year of service (YOS)t.

- C^t is the discounted present value of compensation costs in YOSt, including basic pay, allowances, and the retirement accrual charge.

These costs are minimized subject to the following set of constraints:

1. Minimum performance by occupation, specified as

$$\Sigma_j \left[A_{ij} \Sigma^t \left(s_{ij}^t \, Z_{ij}^t \right) \right] \geq Z_i^* \qquad \text{for all } i$$

where P_{ij}^t is the expected year t performance of a recruit from category j in occupation i and P^* is the performance goal.

2. Recruit category distribution constraints, which allocate the number of high-, medium-, and low-quality accessions to the 10 underlying recruit categories in proportion to the applicant population. These constraints are required because recruiting costs cannot be specified at the detailed recruit category level.

3. Total strength constraints, specified as

$$\text{Accession:} \quad \Sigma_i \Sigma_j A_{ij} \leq \text{ or } \geq A^*$$

$$\text{First-term Person-years:} \quad \Sigma_i \Sigma_j A_{ij} \left(\Sigma^t s_{ij}^t \right) \leq \text{ or } \geq MY^*$$

---

[1] Training costs are defined to include student compensation, which is excluded in the compensation cost element.

Accessions and person-years can be constrained to be greater than or less than the goals, A^* and MY^*.

4. High-quality accession constraints, which require a minimum proportion of these accessions in each occupation group.

Only the first two sets of constraints are necessary for the problem; the others are optional.

REFERENCES

Armor, D. J., Fernandez, R. L., Bers, K., & Schwarzbach, D. (1982). *Recruits aptitudes and Army job performance: Setting enlistment standards for infantrymen* (R-2874-MRAL). Santa Monica, CA: Rand Corporation.

Black, M. (1988). Job performance and military enlistment standards. In B. F. Green, Jr., H. Wing, & A. K. Wigdor (Eds)., *Linking military enlistment standards to job performance.* Washington, DC: National Academy Press.

Black, M., Davis, S, & Campbell, R. (1989). *Air Force skill degradation study.* Arlington, VA: Systems Research and Applications Corporation.

Daula, T., & Smith, D. A. (1990). Inequality in the military: Fact or fiction? *American Sociological Review, 55,* 714-718.

Daula, T., & Smith, D. A. (1992a). Are high quality personnel cost-effective? The role of equipment costs. *Social Science Quarterly, 73*(2), 266-275.

Department of Labor. (1977). *Dictionary of Occupational Titles* (4th ed.). Washington, DC: U.S. Department of Labor.

Fernandez, R. L. (1985). *Setting enlistment standards and matching recruits to jobs using job performance criteria* (R-3067-MIL). Santa Monica, CA: Rand Corporation.

Hogan, P. F., Smith, D. A., Clifton, D., & Harris, D. A. (1990, October). *Entry standards for military service: A cost-performance tradeoff model.* Working paper presented at the meeting of the Operations Research Society of America/The Institute for Management Science, Philadelphia.

McCloy, R. A., Harris, D. A., Barnes, J. D., Hogan, P. F., Smith, D. A., Clifton, D., & Sola, M. (1992). *Accession quality, job performance, and cost: A cost-performance tradeoff model* (HumRRO FR-PRD-92-11). Alexandria, VA: Human Resources Research Organization.

Nord, R. D., & Kearl, C. E. (1990). *Estimating cost-effective recruiting missions: A profit maximizing approach.* Alexandria, VA: U.S. Army Research Institute.

Steadman, E. (1981). *Relationship of enlistment standards to job performance.* Working paper, Office of the Secretary of Defense.

U.S. Department of Labor (1977). *Dictionary of occupational titles* (4th ed.). Washington, DC: Author.

RECENT ADVANCES IN CLASSIFICATION THEORY AND PRACTICE

William E. Alley
Armstrong Laboratory

In reviewing the historical antecedents of personnel selection and classification (S&C) technology, one could argue that the selection domain would have advanced (but perhaps not as quickly) whether or not military psychologists had taken an interest in it. The same could probably not be said for classification—the process of allocating applicants to jobs based on differences in the utility of alternative assignments (Zedeck & Cascio, 1984). From very early on, the U.S. military has sponsored research on the topic because it offered a means to improve the quality of initial assignments and there was sufficient opportunity to collect data to implement a credible system. Without the efforts of some early pioneers—Brogden, Horst, Ward, Votaw, Cronbach, Thorndike, and more recently Nord, Sorensen, Schmidt, Hunter, Ziedner, and Johnson—the area would not be nearly so advanced as we find it today.

The purpose of this chapter is to highlight some of the more recent advances in military classification R&D and to put them in a context that practitioners might find useful. It should be noted that the present-day concept of classification is broadly enough defined to include selection as a special case. Given a number of different positions to fill and a number of applicants to assign, how can the best use be made of available talent? If there are multiple vacancies for only one job and the number of applicants is greater than the number of job vacancies, then that is selection. Classification usually implies multiple job categories and may or may not involve having some number of nonselectees.

To provide some structure for the discussion that follows, topics are organized within the analytic framework used by the Air Force, as shown in Fig. 24.1. Five stages can be described with a potential feedback loop. In Stage I, data are assembled on a common set of predictors and corresponding performance criteria for entrants into two or more alternative job categories. Predictors are typically chosen on the basis of their potential to account for meaningful variation in the criterion of interest. Stage II involves deriving functional relationships between the predictors and the criteria independently for each job category. In Stage III, the estimating equations produced in the preceding step are applied to all candidates across all job categories to generate expectations of how well each person would perform in each of the alternative assignments. This produces an n x m payoff matrix, where n is the number of persons (rows) and m is the number of jobs (columns).

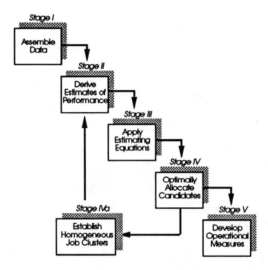

FIG. 24.1. Selection and Classification analytic framework.

In Stage IV, linear programming (or equivalent) techniques are used to assign each candidate a unique job that maximizes the overall expected performance, subject to appropriate constraints. Based on the optimal allocation, comparisons can be made to determine whether there is appreciable gain in expected payoff over other possible allocation strategies. If the number of potential composites exceeds some practical limitation, the process recycles through Stage IVa to reduce the number of alternative job categories (and composites). Here the jobs are grouped into homogeneous clusters based on similarities of the expected values and new estimates obtained for the clusters defined (Stage II). If the number of composites is within practical limitations, then the process moves to Stage V, where standardized prediction composites are developed to guide subsequent classification decisions.

In the remainder of the chapter, the five stages are discussed in turn, with particular focus on issues that have been resolved and those that remain problematic.

STAGE I—ASSEMBLE THE DATA

By far the most critical decisions that must be made at this stage concern the choice of an appropriate criterion measure. Comparatively speaking, the amount of thought and resources devoted to this issue is typically only a fraction of that devoted to the predictors, but it is not clear why this should be so. It is probably much more consequential to account for an important dependent variable with only moderate success than to have great success accounting for an unimportant variable. We typically resort to training outcomes as the dependent variable because they are inexpensive to measure and readily obtainable on large samples of people. The real question is whether the kind of improvements that can be anticipated are really going to make a practical difference.

Military psychologists have made considerable headway on this critical issue by exploring new performance measures beyond the formal training context. Recent work by the Services in the job performance measurement (JPM) domain has extended our concepts of criterion measurement from initial training through job performance during the first enlistment term and even into the second term. From our present perspective, there are at least two ways to view individual performance metrics: (a) measures of task or job proficiency at fixed performance times, and (b) measures of task or job performance times at fixed proficiency levels (see Fig. 24.2). Each would be expected to show characteristic skill acquisition curves as a function of increasing experience. Task pro-

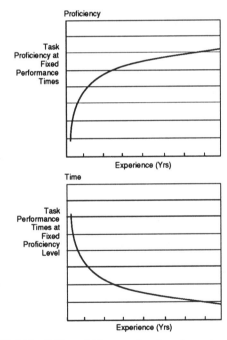

FIG. 24.2. Skill acquisition as a function of experience.

ficiency (at fixed performance times) would be expected to increase with repetition, and task performance times (at fixed proficiency levels) would be expected to decrease.

Personnel researchers typically take the task/job proficiency orientation, as was the case with the work done in the job performance measurement effort (Wigdor & Green, 1991). Here it was shown that task and job proficiency as measured within a fixed period of time increased with experience and aptitude as measured by the Armed Services Vocational Aptitude Battery (ASVAB). The difficulty comes with trying to specify how much proficiency is enough. Do people need to be able to perform 90% of the steps in a task correctly, or is 80% sufficient?

Military manpower planners, on the other hand, usually adopt the task performance-time orientation. Their concern is with the number of people needed to perform a certain amount of work—under the presumption that they do it proficiently. If the task needs to be performed eight times a day and it takes a competent technician two hours to perform it, then it would require at least two people to get the work done. The Air Force has experimented with this alternative orientation in its "productive capacity" work (Leighton, et al., 1992) and has found some promise to this approach—especially in communicating with functional managers who are more accustomed to thinking about how many and what type of people are needed to meet mission readiness requirements.

Whatever orientation one takes, most would agree that direct measurements of hands-on performance are extraordinarily expensive and difficult to collect. Lower-cost alternatives that would suffice for some purposes include walk-through performance measures (Gould & Hedge, 1987), supervisory ratings of proficiency (Wigdor & Green, 1991) and performance times (Carpenter, Monaco, O'Mara, & Teachout, 1989), and job knowledge tests (Wigdor & Green, 1991).

STAGE II—DERIVE ESTIMATES OF PERFORMANCE

In Stage II, the objective is to account for meaningful variation in the dependent variable with the common set of predictors. Alternative approaches used by the Air Force include linear regression, multiple linear regression, nonlinear regression, logit and probit analysis (if the criterion is binary), and neural nets (Wiggins, Engquist, & Looper, 1991).

Also during this stage, it's common to define various restricted models that can be used to test hypotheses about relationships among the expected values. Specifically, baseline measures such as those found in the ASVAB might be a useful restricted model to determine whether new predictors account for unique variation over and above the baseline. It might also be appropriate to constrain the weights on the predictors to some theoretical structure. For example, the occurrence of negative weights in an operational S&C system could have undesirable practical consequences if and when the composites are used with applicants. It is generally advisable to retain something equivalent to the full-least-squares composites as a reference point for judging how much is given up when the constrained models are applied.

STAGE III—APPLY THE ESTIMATING EQUATIONS

The purpose of Stage III processing is to generate expectations of performance (or payoffs) for all candidates across all jobs. The characteristics of the resulting n x m matrix determine whether an optimal allocation of recruits (Stage IV) will result in a net increase in expected benefits or not.

Brogden (1959) proposed a theoretical approach to estimating benefits based on the number of applicants who can be rejected (the selection ratio), the number of possible job assignments, and the validity and intercorrelation of the composites. He showed that potential benefits of simultaneous selection and classification increase as a function of the selection ratio, the average validity of the composites, and the number of jobs, where jobs ranged from 1 to 10. Benefits were inversely related to the level of intercorrelation among the composites.

Because some applications of S&C technology in the military involve more than 10 potential job categories, we have extended the table from 10 to 500 jobs, using a numerical simulation approach (Alley & Darby, in press). The effect size shown in the first 10 jobs (0.0 to 1.54 standard deviation units with zero rejection rate) increased to 1.87 for the second 10 jobs and to 2.04 SD units when there were 30 jobs (see Fig. 24.3). A 3.0 standard deviation unit increase was reached at job 439, and with 500 jobs, the value was 3.03 SD units. As the rejection rate increased from 0% to 90%, the benefits accumulated in the first 10 jobs (2.68 - 1.75 = .93) were doubled at the 264th job. The extended tables show promise for guiding manpower resource interventions that would produce the most gain at the least cost.

STAGE IV—OPTIMALLY ALLOCATE CANDIDATES

Linear programming techniques (Charnes, Cooper, & Henderson, 1953) are used to allocate candidates to jobs. The objective in this stage is to maximize the overall sum of the payoffs for assigned personnel, subject to whatever practical constraints need to be imposed. An operating version of this approach can be found in a number of software packages. The Air Force has had experience using LINDO (Schrage, 1984) for purposes of assigning pilots and navigators (Alley, Skinner, & Siem, 1993), enlisted personnel to the eight specialties used in the JPM project (Alley & Teachout, 1992), and pilots to different training tracks (Siem & Alley, 1992). Each of these applications has used a simple objective function as a payoff value (i.e., probability of completing training, expected job performance, expert rankings, etc.). More complex functions have also been developed. RAND has used qualified man-months (QMM) combining performance and expected tenure (Fernandez & Garfinkel, 1985), and the Air Force has used productive capacity (Carpenter et al., 1989) and future expected value (Stone, Rettenmair, Saving, & Looper, 1989). Finally, the Air Force and

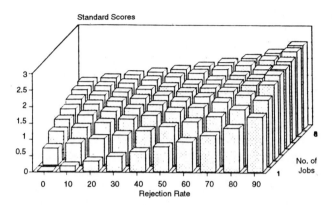

FIG. 24.3A. Allocation average as a function of number of jobs
and percent rejected.

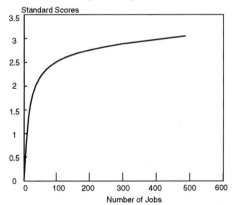

FIG. 24.3B. Allocation average as a function of number of jobs
when reduction ratio is zero.

the other Services have used even more complex policy functions that blend fit-
and-fill considerations into the payoff values (Kroeker, 1983; Schmitz, 1987;
Ward, Haney, Hendrix, & Pina, 1978). Here *fit* is defined as the effectiveness
of a particular person-job match (P-J-M), and *fill* addresses the issue of having
critical vacancies filled expeditiously.

Reviewing the results of an optimal allocation is usually done by comparing
the optimal solution with other nonoptimal reference solutions (Nord & Schmitz,
1987). The optimized objective function can be compared with a solution that
minimizes the function to establish an upper and lower boundary. Solutions that
might be expected to fall in intermediate positions on the scale would include a
random solution or the actual values obtained by current or baseline procedures
(see Fig. 24.4).

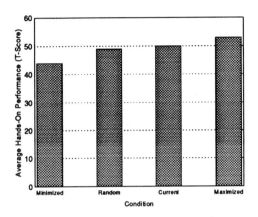

FIG. 24.4. Assignment outcomes under four different conditions
(*N* = 1250; 8 jobs).

It is important to note that the present discussion has centered mainly on batch solutions, although sequential assignments are probably much more common in applied contexts. J. H. Ward, Jr., who has done as much as anyone to further the Air Force work on classification R&D, described the use of a decision index (DI) for sequential applications (Ward, 1959). The matrix of DI values is computed for each element in the payoff matrix according to the formula:

$$DI_{pq} = \frac{1}{m(n-1)}[nc_{pq} - c_{p.} - c_{.q} + c_{..}]$$

Where n = number of persons to be assigned,
    m = number of jobs to be filled.
    C_{pq} = payoff of the pth person on the jth job.
    $C_{p.}$ = sum of the corresponding *m* row values in the payoff matrix.
    $C_{.q}$ = sum of the corresponding *n* column values in the payoff matrix.
    $C_{..}$ = grand sum of the row/column values in the payoff matrix.

The DI value represents the value a particular assignment would contribute to improving the overall sum of the payoffs, given the other candidates and job assignments in the matrix. A higher DI value for a candidate in any row reflects an assignment that would contribute more to the overall sum than would a lower DI value. In later work, Ward (1979) described the relationships between DI values, interaction variance in the matrix, and Horst's index of differential assignment (Horst, 1954).

STAGE IVa—ESTABLISH HOMOGENEOUS JOB CLUSTERS

It is sometimes the case that the number of original job categories and corresponding prediction composites exceeds the number that would be desirable for operational purposes. There may also be a need to reduce the number of job categories by eliminating potential redundancies among the columns of the payoff matrix. In this stage, the goal is to cluster the jobs based on the overall similarity of the payoff values.

A modified hierarchical grouping procedure was developed for this purpose (Ward, Treat, & Albert, 1985). In traditional grouping, clusters of jobs are formed based on the homogeneity of the regression weights for each job—including the weight on the unit vector or constant. Occasionally, clusters would be formed because they were characteristically high or low on the dependent variable, irrespective of the coefficients on the test measures. The modified technique clusters only on the test coefficients and, thus, minimizes the loss of interaction variance in the payoff matrix. An application of the procedure for homogeneous clustering of Air Force jobs was described in Alley, Treat, and Black (1988).

Once a desirable clustering solution is obtained, the process recycles back through Stage II to reestimate the equations in the new job clusters.

STAGE V—DEVELOP OPERATIONAL MEASURES

The final stage in the analysis process is to develop operational measures for use in assigning subsequent applicants. An example might be the unique set of test composites used by each Service to qualify recruits for specific jobs. In the Air Force, there are four such measures: the Administrative, Mechanical, General, and Electronics composites. What are we looking for in a good set of composites? From an allocation standpoint, it is desirable to have composites that are high if it would be good to assign an applicant to a particular job category, and low if it would be a poor assignment. Recall that these are also the characteristics of the DI values described earlier.

For pure classification purposes, standardized test composites can be formed to predict the DI values directly. Another alternative is to form them on the basis of the binary job assignment matrices that are also a product of Stage IV processing. Elements of the assignment matrix are coded 1 if the applicant has been assigned to a particular job category, 0 otherwise. For the two-group case, the binary assignments for Job 1 are perfectly negatively correlated with those in Job 2. In the pilot versus navigator problem mentioned earlier, a high value on the "pilot" composite was always associated with a low value on the "navigator" composite. In fact, in this limited case one of the composites carries completely redundant information.

If the intent is to select and classify with the same composites, the situation is a bit more complicated. The composites in this case need to retain information about the absolute level of expected achievement in addition to the information about where the candidate would best be assigned. Here, it might be desirable to develop standardized test measures to mimic the payoff matrix. The differential assignment component will be embedded in the measures that give the appearance of having higher intercorrelations than would pure classification composites based on the DI matrix or the binary assignment matrix. But this is the trade-off for having the composites serve both purposes.

One procedure that still causes enormous confusion has to do with making short predictive composites from full-least-squares equations. To illustrate, suppose that two composites were developed—one each for mechanical specialties and electronics specialties. If the composites have been developed from the payoff matrix, then they will probably correlate in the moderate to high range. We might also observe that they both share a significant weight on a common subtest. Because conventional wisdom says that classification composites should not correlate very highly, one might be inclined to delete the common subtest to make the resulting composites look more "differential." This would defeat the purposes of both selection and classification. The common subtests are needed if the composites are to retain an absolute indication of a candidate's expected performance.

If, on the other hand, the composites are to be used exclusively for classification, then there are more direct ways of constructing them—that is, use the DI matrix or the binary assignment matrix as the final criteria. Then decisions can be made about which subtests don't contribute sufficiently, and the equations can be shortened accordingly.

A final set of issues in the development of operational composites concerns possible adverse effects and bias due to gender or ethnicity. There are fairly standard paradigms for addressing these issues (Welch, Kucinkas, & Curran, 1990) and they are relatively independent of the processes described here—except that they involve the same predictor and criterion database. These issues have been problematic historically but are beyond the scope of the present paper.

FUTURE PROSPECTS AND CHALLENGES

While the state of the art in S&C has advanced steadily, and in some cases dramatically, over the past few years, the current level of practical utilization of this technology is high in selection but low in classification. Recent studies relating to the classification potential of the ASVAB to military performance criteria (Hunter, 1985; Johnson & Ziedner, 1990; Johnson, Ziedner, & Scholarios, 1990; Ree & Earles, 1991a, 1991b; Schmidt, Hunter, & Larson, 1988) have shown equivocal results. Hunter (1985), Schmidt et al. (1988), and Ree and Earles (1990, 1991a, 1991b) found that specific abilities added marginally to a general ability factor in predicting technical training and job performance criteria but did not document any practical benefits associated with the gain. Johnson and Ziedner (1990) and Johnson et al. (1990) found that noncognitive measures (interests and psychomotor performance) could add to the classification utility of the ASVAB if they were selected to enhance the differential content of the test battery. Finally, Alley and Teachout (1992) documented upper bound gains of approximately one-third standard deviation if the ASVAB composites were reconfigured to differentially assign entrants based on expected job performance. The major import line of these studies is that we are starting from a relatively modest baseline of practical utilization and have nowhere to go but up.

For the future, at least five critical areas would benefit from increased R&D attention:

1. Expand the predictor space to capitalize on recent advances in the theory of cognitive functioning, personality/temperament measurement, and interests and knowledge assessment. Much of this work is already under way in the Service laboratories and will not be discussed further.

2. Sharpen the criteria, especially linkages with military readiness and cost savings, to provide military planners with a more cogent basis for judging the merits of S&C technology. Both training and job performance criteria need to be defined to increase their relevance and reduce the cost of routine data collection.

3. Develop defensible generalization procedures to permit extrapolating current findings to jobs for which there are no data and jobs for which there can never be any data (i.e., newly defined jobs). Burke and Pearlman (1988) have provided an excellent summary of research needs in this area.

4. Extend cost-performance trade-off models to show the consequences of varying major parameters of the S&C system, including recruiting level (selection ratio), reconfiguring the test composites (validity and intercorrelation of the composites), defining new job structures (number/homogeneity of jobs), and adding new tests and/or assessment procedures (validity and intercorrelation of the composites).

5. Broaden S&C P-J-M concepts to provide the basis for improved personnel decision making beyond initial job assignment. Both the Navy and the Air Force have systems that address the problem of geographic assignment during the first and subsequent tours (Hillary et al., in press) and the issue of how to classify personnel for retraining at the end of the first enlistment (Pina, 1989). Also needed are lateral linkages to the manpower and training communities and to the operational Air Force. Can efficiencies introduced by better selection and classification technology lead to reduced personnel requirements? Reduced training requirements? More operational readiness? If the answer is yes, then future R&D investments in this area are likely to increase rather than decrease.

REFERENCES

Alley, W. E., & Darby, M. (in press). *Estimating the benefits of personnel selection and classification: An extension of the Brogden tables* (AL-TP-1994-XXXX). Brooks AFB, TX: Human Resources Directorate, Armstrong Laboratory.

Alley, W. E., Skinner, M. J., & Siem, F. M. (1993). *Differential assignment of pilots and navigators.* Unpublished manuscript.

Alley, W. E., & Teachout, M. S. (August, 1992). *Differential assignment potential in the ASVAB.* Paper presented at the annual convention of the American Psychological Association, Washington, DC.

Alley, W. E., Treat, B. R., & Black, D. E. (1988). *Classification of Air Force jobs into aptitude clusters* (AFHRL-TR-88-14). Brooks AFB, TX: Manpower and Personnel Division, Air Force Human Resources Laboratory.

Brogden, H. E. (1959). Efficiency of classification as a function of number of jobs, percent rejected and the validity and intercorrelation of job performance estimates. *Educational and Psychological Measurement, 19,* 181-190.

Burke, M. J., & Pearlman, K. (1988). Recruiting, selecting and matching people with jobs. In J. P. Campbell & R. J. Campbell (Eds.), *Frontiers in industrial/organizational psychology* (pp. 97-142). San Francisco: Jossey-Bass.

Carpenter, M. A., Monaco, S. J., O'Mara, F. E., & Teachout, M. S. (1989). *Time to job proficiency: A preliminary investigation of the effects of aptitude and experience on productive capacity* (AFHRL-TP-88-17). Brooks AFB, TX: Training Systems Division, Air Force Human Resources Laboratory.

Charnes, A., Cooper, W., & Henderson, S. (1953). *An introduction to linear programming.* New York: Wiley.

Fernandez, R., & Garfinkel, J. (1985). *Setting enlistment standards and matching recruits jobs using job performance criteria* (R-3067-MIL). Santa Monica, CA: RAND Corporation.

Gould, R. B., & Hedge, J. W. (1987). History, background and theoretical basis of walk-through performance testing. In J. W. Hedge and M. S. Lipscomb (Eds.), *Walk-through performance testing: An innovative approach to work sample testing* (AFHRL-TP-87-8). Brooks AFB, TX: Training Systems Division, Air Force Human Resources Laboratory.

Hillary, R. C., Buelatim, B. B., Krass, I. A., Liang, T. T., & Yau, M. C. (in press). Computerizing personnel assignment decision support. *Interfaces.*

Horst, P. A. (1954). A technique for the development of a differential prediction battery. *Psychological Monographs, 69,* 1-31.

Hunter, J. E. (1985). *Differential validity across jobs in the military.* Report for Research Applications, in partial fulfillment of DoD Contract No. F41689-83-C-0025.

Johnson, C. D., & Zeidner, J. (1990). *Classification utility: Measuring and improving benefits in matching personnel to jobs* (IDA Paper P-2240). Alexandria, VA: Institute for Defense Analyses.

Johnson, C. D., Zeidner, J., & Scholarios, D. (1990). *Improving the classification efficiency of the Armed Services Vocational Aptitude Battery through the use of alternative test selection indices* (IDA Paper P-2427). Alexandria, VA: Institute for Defense Analyses.

Kroeker, L. P. (1983). *CLASP: A recruit assignment model* (NPRDC TR 84-9). San Diego: Navy Personnel Research and Development Center.

Leighton, D. L., Kageff, L. L., Mosher, G. P., Gribben, M. A., Faneuff, R. S., Demetriades, E. T., & Skinner, M. J. (1992). *Measurement of productive capacity: A methodology for Air Force enlisted specialties* (AL-TP-1992-0029). Brooks AFB, TX: Human Resources Directorate, Armstrong Laboratory.

Nord, R. D., & Schmitz, E. J. (November, 1987). *Estimating the benefits and costs of classification and assignment systems.* Proceedings of the Tri-Service Topical Review on Personnel Classification/Assignment. San Diego.

Pina, M., Jr. (1989). *Development of a retraining person-job-match system.* Unpublished manuscript.

Ree, M. J., & Earles, J. A. (1990). *Relationships of general ability, specific ability, and job category for predicting training performance* (AFHRL-TR-90-46). Brooks AFB, TX: Manpower and Personnel Division, Air Force Human Resources Laboratory.

Ree, M. J., & Earles, J. A. (1991a). Predicting training success: Not much more than g. *Personnel Psychology, 44,* 321-332.

Ree, M. J., & Earles, J. A. (1991b). *General cognitive ability predicts job performance* (AL-TR-1991-0100). Brooks AFB, TX: Human Resources Directorate, Armstrong Laboratory.

Schmidt, F. L., Hunter, J. E., & Larson, M. (August, 1988). *General cognitive ability vs general and specific aptitudes in the prediction of training performance: Some preliminary findings.* Paper presented at the annual convention of the American Psychological Association, Atlanta.

Schmitz, E. J. (November, 1987). *Improving the Army's classification policy: The design of the Enlisted Personnel Allocation System.* Proceedings of the Tri-Service Topical Review on Personnel Classification/Assignment, San Diego.

Schrage, L. (1984). *Linear, integer and quadratic programming with LINDO.* Palo Alto, CA: Scientific Press.

Siem, F. M., & Alley, W. E. (April, 1992). *Optimal personnel assignment: An application to Air Force pilots.* Paper presented at the Conference of the Society for Industrial and Organizational Psychology, Toronto.

Stone, B. M., Rettenmair, A. J., Saving, T. R., & Looper, L. T. (1989). *Cost-based value models of Air Force experience* (AFHRL-TR-89-20). Brooks AFB, TX: Manpower and Personnel Division, Air Force Human Resources Laboratory.

Ward, J. H., Jr. (1959). *Use of a decision index in assigning Air Force personnel* (WADC-TN-59-38). Lackland AFB, TX: Personnel Research Laboratory, Wright Air Development Genter.

Ward, J. H., Jr. (November, 1979). *Interaction among people characteristics and job properties in differential classification.* Paper presented at the Military Testing Association meeting, San Diego.

Ward, J. H., Jr., Haney, D. L., Hendrix, W. H., & Pina, M., Jr. (1978). *Assignment procedures in the Air Force Procurement Management Information System* (AFHRL-TR-78-30). Brooks AFB, TX: Occupations and Manpower Research Division, Air Force Human Resources Laboratory.

Ward, J. H., Jr., Treat, B. R., & Albert, W. G. (1985). *General applications of hierarchical grouping using the HIER-GRP computer program* (AFHRL-TP-84-42). Brooks AFB, TX: Personnel Research Division, Air Force Human Resources Laboratory.

Welch, J. R., Jr., Kucinkas, S. K., & Curran, L. T. (1990). *Armed Services Vocational Aptitude Battery (ASVAB): Integrative review of validity studies* (AFHRL-TR-90-22). Brooks AFB, TX: Manpower and Personnel Division, Air Force Human Resources Laboratory.

Wigdor, A. K., & Green, B. F. (Eds.) (1991). *Performance assessment for the workplace.* Washington, DC: National Academy Press.

Wiggins, V. L., Engquist, S. K., & Looper, L. T. (1991). *Applying neural networks to Air Force personnel analysis* (AL-TR-1991-0118). Brooks AFB, TX: Human Resources Directorate, Armstrong Laboratory.

Zedeck, S., & Cascio, W. R. (1984). Psychological issues in personnel decisions. *Annual Review of Psychology, 35,* 461-518.

CHAPTER

25

ISSUES IN OPERATIONAL SELECTION AND CLASSIFICATION SYSTEMS: COMMENTS AND COMMONALITIES

Philip Bobko
Rutgers University

It was a pleasure to have the opportunity to read and attempt to integrate the five papers on selection and classification issues. I first comment on each of the papers individually. Then, I try to draw commonalities among them and link these commonalities to basic themes for future research in selection and classification.

LINN'S CHAPTER

In my opinion, the major point to be made in Linn's chapter (21) was about "test fairness." Linn suggested that there is no simple answer to whether or not a particular use of a test is fair, and the multitude of answers can only be considered/resolved (if they can be resolved at all) by an appeal to the underlying value structures of the various constituencies involved.

This appeal to values has been stated before (Bobko, 1985; Darlington, 1971; Keeley, 1983; Messick, 1989), but bears repeating. Further, Linn was concerned by "the lack of explicit statements of values that correspond to the different models." I agree and, for me, this is one of the primary functions that can be exploited within what our field labels "utility analysis." Certainly, utility analysis has its faults (including difficulties in obtaining accurate parameter estimates and a lack of acceptance of results by organizational decision makers). However, the "fun" part of utility analysis is the requirement that organizations state precisely what outcomes are possible in the selection process, the relationships among these outcomes, which outcomes are important, and the trade-offs among those important outcomes. Although the measurement properties of these utility decisions may not be the best in the world, thinking about utility in this systematic way should improve our selection and classification decisions.

BOBKO

Other, specific comments about the Linn chapter are:

First, Linn's chapter gave a good overview of the rates at which minorities hold military jobs. Linn noted that minorities hold jobs in the military in a higher proportion than the percentage of minorities in the population at large. He attributed this difference to explicit military policy and the relative lack of opportunities for minorities in the civilian sector (although this explanation may not completely hold in the future, where branches of the military are looking to significantly reduce force strength by 25% in the next several years).

Although the relative numbers of minorities in military jobs are high, Linn noted that a disproportionate number of minority personnel hold jobs in occupational specialties requiring relatively less technical skill (however, this disparity has been reduced in the last decade). With this fact as contextual backdrop, Linn questioned the commonly held assumption that cognitive tests typically do not underpredict performance for minority groups. In support of his concern, Linn cited a study by Houston and Novick (1987) comparing African-American and White regression lines in nine Air Force mechanic specialties. He also cited a study (Dunbar & Novick, 1988) that demonstrates underprediction for females, as compared to males, in nine Marine clerical specialties.

On the other hand, the literature that concludes that there is little, if any, underprediction of minority performance is based on a summation of a variety of studies across a variety of occupational groupings. Thus, these two studies can only be considered illustrative of the fact that, in any particular organizational setting, a generality may not hold. This is the contribution of these two studies to the differential prediction literature.

Perhaps the largest selection project ever funded in the military or private sector was the U.S. Army's Project A. My recollection of the Project A results is that differential prediction did exist in the same pattern as just discussed (flatter slope for the minority group). However, in almost all cases, the minority and majority regression lines intersected very near to the minimum predictor cutoffs (the so-called area aptitude cutoffs) for entry into the particular military occupational specialty (MOS). This finding is in contrast to the placement of the cutoff in Fig. 21.1, which is well below the point where the regression lines intersect. Thus, the practical effect of any differential regression was almost completely attenuated in the large-scale Project A research. It might be useful to investigate why the results of these large-scale studies lead to differing practical conclusions and implications.

Second, because the two studies cited by Linn used grades (course and training) as criteria, Linn also summarized validity evidence for military studies that used hands-on performance measures as criteria. The evidence points to the possibility that differential validity is less for hands-on tests than for job knowledge tests (see Table 21.1). Although these differences are in terms of correlations and not regression weights, the implication is that there will be less underprediction for minority groups if hands-on tests are adopted as criteria.

Several comments come to mind here. First, as noted by Linn, differential validity has only weak links to differential prediction. That is, the regression slope also depends on standard deviations of the two variables in the two groups. Second, comparing validity coefficients for hands-on and job knowledge criteria may be inappropriate unless there is some evidence that the two criterion measures are equally reliable. Perhaps corrections for unreliability will reduce any differences in Table 21.1. Third, the military must be careful not to unilaterally assume that hands-on measures are therefore better. (I'm overstating Linn's case: he only suggested that differential prediction remain a topic of research; he did not make such specific conclusions.) As noted by Campbell (1990), hands-on measures are themselves deficient, in the sense that they are probably better measures of maximal than typical performance. And, organizations probably value both kinds of measures (i.e., both can-do and will-do).

In sum, the chapter by Linn was very well thought through and very thought provoking. As noted befire, it exhorted us to reflect on what we mean by fairness and explicate the value systems that we hold. In terms of classification, Linn reminded us once again that classification algorithms must be more complex than originally conceived if they are to meet societal requirements. Further, the notion of differential prediction lines may not be a thing of the past and, if not, we need to incorporate this aspect of explicit social policy into our selection and classification systems.

WISE'S CHAPTER

In the chapter by Wise (20), he proposed two taxonomies to consider in developing and evaluating selection and classification (S&C) systems. One taxonomy lists a set of "plausible goals" that S&C systems might have. The other taxonomy is a list of criteria by which to evaluate those goals (the so-called "criteria criteria").

The set of plausible goals is fairly comprehensive and includes things like training success, job proficiency, seat fill, and so forth. Most of the goals are at the individual level. However, some goals are provided that are at higher levels of analysis (e.g., total MOS performance, unit performance, social benefits).

Wise's second taxonomy considered the questions, "How does one know which of these goals to adopt?" or "What are the criteria by which we evaluate the worthiness of these goals?" Wise's criteria included the relatedness of the S&C system to the goal, completeness, measurability, minimization of costs (all other things equal), and acceptability to policymakers. The set of plausible goals was evaluated in terms of these criteria, although the crossing of the two taxonomies was not complete and some goals were not evaluated on some criteria. It could prove useful to provide this more complete analysis in the future.

Nonetheless, Wise gave a very lucid and useful set of guidelines in helping us think about selection and classification systems. As in the Linn chapter, the value here is in getting our field to reflect on and explicate what we mean by selection and classification, and in assisting organizations in delineating what their goals are and what they ought to be. For example, in the training literature, the importance of conducting job analyses and needs assessments is routinely noted (cf. Goldstein, 1991). One of the components of a needs assessment, an organizational analysis, is assumed to be fundamentally critical, yet is not often systematically done. The organizational analysis is, in part, a statement of the goals and philosophies of the organization. I can think of no better way of obtaining this aspect of a needs assessment than by asking policy makers to consider why they might select and classify people in the first place. The Wise chapter provided two excellent taxonomies for systematizing this series of questions and documenting the answers to them.

Other, specific comments about the Wise chapter are:

First, one of the criteria for evaluating the efficacy of an S&C system is its relationship to cost savings. Wise stated "training success is an appealing criterion because it is relatively easy to develop estimates of the cost of training failures. The value of improved job performance is generally harder to describe." Although it is later noted that "training success is related to cost but not really to benefit," there may be even more optimistic ways of embracing a "cost" perspective. That is, it may be that a selection and classification system can improve a judgmental belief about performance improvement (e.g., we have a better chance of winning a war) at no extra cost to the way things are currently done. In this case, there is no cost saving, yet a judged increase in organizational effectiveness and efficiency. So, the lack of increased cost is also a positive factor when it is paired with the more subjective "performance improvement."

Second, Wise also reminded us of the potential for macro-level goals in S&C systems: increased total MOS performance, unit performance (or readiness), and social benefits (or problem avoidance). These are in addition to the individual-level goals of an S&C system. However, note that S&C systems are, by definition, organizational systems. As such, the list of individual goals may not be at the correct level of analysis. These individual goals are only appropriate only if one considers aggregating them across all individuals in the organization. This, of course, assumes additivity of performance across individuals—an assumption that is usually questioned where organizational performance is concerned (cf. Nord & White, 1987). Thus, it may be that the only appropriate goals are the organizational ones listed by Wise. The individual ones deserve listing only insofar as they are used to form a composite index for a specific macro level of analysis.

Third, Wise made yet another contribution by reminding us that the "period covered" (short vs. long term) certainly affects how we think about the efficacy of any S&C decision. However, it is stated that, "Early success is more directly related to S&C decisions than later success." I'm not sure this is always the case. For example, there may be jobs where the required training is extensive and particularly long and difficult. In these particular jobs, it may be many years before any initial individual differences become manifest in an important way. For example, in our work with air traffic controllers, it is common for training to take place across several years. After training, the value of performance is greatest and, in turn, the potential for error is greatest (in utility terms, the highest standard deviation of performance value comes after a substantial period of time).

On the same topic, Wise also said, "The evaluation criteria suggest that it is appropriate to place greater emphasis on early outcomes measured as simply as possible." Again, I'm not so sure about this. In the unfortunate case where war breaks out, isn't "winning a war" the criterion by which to judge any military S&C system? Short-term goals are useful only insofar as they can be related to long-term goals. Long-term goals should always be considered. They help sort out useful short-term goals from nonuseful ones.

Overall, the Wise chapter was an excellent start at taxonomizing both what S&C goals can be and what the goals ought to be. As with the Linn chapter, these thoughts help us reflect about our S&C decisions and explicitly delineate why we are making them and what their consequences are. In terms of overall utility, the implication was that the field should "develop a model specifying the form of the utility function for each job as a function of known characteristics of the job." I agree. Preliminary work has started, but not completed, such a modeling procedure: Bobko and Donnelly (1988) did this for understanding the mean utility across 19 Army MOS, whereas Sadacca, Campbell, DiFazio, Schultz, and White (1990) modeled the entire utility curve for Army MOS, but did not use characteristics of the job.

ZEIDNER AND JOHNSON'S CHAPTER

The chapter by Zeidner and Johnson (22) was a provocative summary of several of their valuable technical reports and book chapters, which demonstrated that attention to classification efficiency has the potential to increase organizational performance (defined as mean predicted performance, MPP).[1] The authors indicated that the power of differential assignment theory (DAT) and its algorithms comes from the fact that several factors differentially predict performance across several distinct sets of jobs.

---

[1] Thinking back to the chapter by Wise, note that the choice of criterion measure in the Zeidner and Johnson paper was an aggregated, individual-level measure of performance.

In a series of tables based on empirical analyses of the Army's Project A, the authors provided convincing evidence that classification-efficient algorithms can lead to increased MPP. These algorithms make use of two dimensions: (a) different combinations of predictor tests, and (b) different ways of creating job families. After accounting for shrinkage, Zeidner and Johnson demonstrated substantial increases in MPP over current baseline assignment algorithms (see, for example, Table 22.1). This was a valuable demonstration indeed, because it reminded us that differential prediction still has merit, even in light of a large body of research that notes that cognitive abilities generally predict a substantial proportion of performance in most jobs.

In order to make the results of Zeidner and Johnson even more powerful, several basic directions must be considered in the next round of thinking about classification. For example:

1. We should embed these results in psychological theory. My comment here is that we need to explain why the various results are as they are. Early in their chapter, the authors noted that researchers in industrial psychology have adopted different theoretical perspectives regarding an overall g factor versus specific factors, and so on. But we still need to know why the differential classification simulations provide the increased efficiency. What factors in the predictor space are providing the differential results? What factors in the criterion space are differentially predicted? What are the weights that are used in the classification-oriented composites?[2] What is the logical basis for the different groupings of jobs and job families used in this simulation? These are absolutely crucial questions, and work on classification algorithms needs to address them. Until we have a better understanding of what is going on, we will not be able to fully justify our actions, or make even further adjustments to the organizational system.

As an aside to this concern, Zeidner and Johnson listed several "insupportable beliefs or assumptions" that arose during an "initial hopeful period," including an assumption that "test composites tailored to jobs or job families would readily provide substantial improvement in predictive validity" compared to some unitary cognitive ability test. I would argue that there is some support for this. For example, Zeidner and Johnson did get improved power from their empirically driven classification algorithms. It seems quite possible that this increased efficiency can be related to some theoretical tailoring within the construction of job families and/or construction of selection test composites.

---

[2] There's a hint that some of these weights may be unexpectedly negative. If so, why are they negative?

2. A second need concerns the practical side of the resulting algorithms. What do these classification algorithms say we should do and what are the implications? As Wise noted in his chapter, "When individual performance is used as the criterion, optimal assignment algorithms usually lead to layering solutions where the most capable applicants are assigned to one job, the next most capable to another, and so on." I would expect that such "corner solutions" are probably not acceptable to the Armed Forces—for example, the Army requires "quality distributions" within each MOS.

In a related comment, several of the chapters discussed earlier suggested that the military can adopt (and has adopted) a social responsibility criterion as part of their selection and classification systems (e.g., an attempt at increasing minority participation in certain jobs). The question is, "How do the Zeidner and Johnson empirically based algorithms affect these corporate philosophical goals?" For example, Linn's chapter pointed out the disproportionate percentage of African Americans in jobs requiring lower technical skill. Linn further noted that there has been a trend to reverse these disproportionate percentages. Will the classification algorithms of Zeidner and Johnson continue this socially desirable trend? We simply don't know at this point.

Following are some specific comments about the Zeidner and Johnson chapter:

First, the gains in mean predicted performance (MPP) are impressive and, once again, can help motivate our field to consider more effective classification systems. In Table 22.2, the baseline MPP for classification is reported as .135. The gain from Stage 1 classification, using 16 operational job families, is .258; the percentage improvement is then computed as $(.258 - .135) / (.135) = .91$, for an increase of 91%. However, as the authors pointed out, such calculations are for classification effects only. Consistent with the focus of this conference, it is relevant to take an overall selection *and* classification view of the results. For example, the text indicated that there is already a gain in MPP (for Design A) because the Army has selected, based on AFQT scores, the top 75% of their applicants. This selection (not classification) effect results in an across-the-board increase in MPP of .225. Assuming such an increase holds for Design B, the baseline MPP is therefore $.225 + .135 = .360$, and the gain in MPP through better selection *and* classification for Stage 1 is $.225 + .258 = .483$. Thus, the percentage increase would be calculated as $(.483 - .360) / (.360) = .34$, for an increase of 34%. There is indeed an increase—but the suggestion is that incremental gains need to be considered relative to the entire selection and classification system.

Second, the utility analysis work in the military (Pritchard, Jones, Roth, Stuebing, & Ekeberg, 1988; Sadacca et al., 1990) has clearly shown that utility is not a linear function of performance. It would be instructive to conduct the

Zeidner and Johnson Differential Assignment Theory (DAT) analyses using utility as the criterion, rather than MPP. Indeed, Zeidner and Johnson stated, "the fourth concept of DAT maintains that utility analysis ... provides the best approach for evaluating alternative policies and procedures."

In sum, Zeidner and Johnson's chapter provided strong evidence that we may not be exploiting classification efficiency to the extent possible. The value in the exposition is to allow us to consider practical gains from classification (e.g., due to reconfigured job groupings), and focus our direction on explaining why, based on psychological theory, differential classification effects may be operating.

ALLEY'S CHAPTER

The chapter by Alley (24) was a practitioner-oriented summary of how one can statistically derive a classification system. He made the critical distinction that selection composites focus on performance payoff, whereas classification composites focus on decision index (DI) values. I think it would help the field's understanding of the selection versus classification controversy if this distinction is explored even further in future research.

Alley listed five stages in making classification decisions: from assembling the data, through deriving performance estimates and job clusters, through the operational development of measures. At each stage, he highlighted manuscripts and/or technical reports that would be useful for applying classification algorithms in the military.

Several statements were common to both the Alley and Wise chapters. For example, like Wise, Alley noted that precious little attention has been paid to the choice of a criterion measure in S&C decisions. In his conclusions, Alley called for a broadening of criterion measures beyond training and, in turn, a broadening of classification focus beyond initial job assignment. Wise's chapter provided an extensive taxonomy of how such thinking can be expanded.

Several specific comments about the Alley chapter follow.

First, early in the chapter, it was stated that "classification is broadly enough defined to include selection as a special case." Certainly, selection research typically considers a single job at a time, but I think it would be dangerous to subsume one concept within the other. In fact, in his discussion of the final stage in classification, Alley started with a set of classification composites and noted that, "If the intent is to select and classify with the same composites, the situation is a bit more complicated." That is, rather than derive composites from the decision index (DI) matrix, one needs to derive composites from the payoff matrix. These composites would probably then have higher intercorrelations (across job groupings), and this trade-off would be the price to pay "for having the composites serve both purposes."[3] I think it would be more correct to say that both "selection" and "classification" are special cases of "selection and classification."

Second, Alley made the interesting observation that selection researchers tend to focus on measuring task proficiency at fixed times, whereas personnel planners tend to measure the time to reach fixed proficiency levels. He said that the problem with the former approach is "trying to specify how much proficiency is enough." In my mind, the target of this criticism should be reversed. It should be toward the personnel planning approach and not the selection approach. That is, selection researchers tend to measure performance in a normative mode, with interval scales (at best). In contrast, personnel planning's "time to proficiency" assumes that everyone knows how to measure what is meant by "proficiency." This assumes a ratio scale of measurement (so we know precisely where the zero, or cut, point is). And in the social sciences, construction of ratio scales is quite problematic.

Third, note that the optimal allocation strategies were generated by linear programming algorithms. As with the Zeidner and Johnson chapter, these mathematical techniques told us very little, if anything, about what is going on or why particular allocations are being made. They were "simply" mathematical searches for points of maximization.

Alley also provided a summary list of five critical areas in need of future research. The research areas focus on the need for specifying predictors and criteria, and explicating cost-performance trade-off models. In my mind, these latter needs are consistent with what has been noted earlier in this review: the need for systematizing our S&C value judgments.

BLACK AND SMITH'S CHAPTER

The chapter by Black and Smith (23) provided an explanation, and computer simulations, of a cost-performance trade-off (CPT) model. This CPT model helps find the cost-effective level for the percentage of high-quality recruits needed to meet performance goals. The CPT model will estimate the required number of high-quality recruits only if one inputs the definition of performance, the required standard for performance across different jobs, and the assumed relations among model parameters (e.g., between performance and organizational utility; between quality of recruits and the cost of obtaining those recruits). As in the previous chapters, it again became clear that cost-performance trade-offs involve substantial value decisions.

---

[3] This trade-off was also noted by Zeidner and Johnson, who found that the choice of the best predictors depended on whether one was maximizing classification efficiency or predictive validity.

There was an explicit consideration of the limitations of the current CPT model in the Black and Smith chapter. To put these limitations in a positive light, it would prove useful to the field to consider these limitations as needs for future research. Thus, we need to expand CPT models to include other dimensions of performance (e.g., leadership), other predictors (e.g., motivational ones), a longer time period (reminiscent of Wise's statement), the minimum number of individuals required to operate a particular weapons system (regardless of the recruit quality), and so forth. Basic research on these factors would clearly enhance what we know about making selection and classification decisions. The chapter by Black and Smith was valuable in that it provided a good listing of these needs.

Following are some specific comments about the Black and Smith chapter.

First, these authors noted that the cost of obtaining higher quality recruits gets progressively more expensive (i.e., there's a nonlinear cost function), and that the CPT's "cost function correctly captures the increasing marginal cost nature of recruiting costs." However, it seems that there are two nonlinearities involved in recruiting costs. First is the one incorporated by the CPT: high-quality recruits are nonlinearly more expensive to obtain than recruits of less quality. The second is the possibility that, within the batch of high quality recruits, the first few high-quality recruits are less costly to obtain than later, equally qualified recruits. Such nonlinearities in recruiting costs can have substantial impact on overall utility, and it would be interesting to include them in the CPT model (see Martin & Raju, 1992, for a recent discussion of these factors).

Second, Black and Smith claimed that the CPT model operates "without using what must be arbitrary performance valuations." I think this sentence is misleading. As already noted, there are many value decisions about the parameters of such models that must be made before conducting the simulations. Although it may be true that performance isn't directly valued in the CPT model (e.g., no utility values are used), there are built-in valuations. For example, the use of a dichotomous performance criterion (e.g., qualified person-months) versus the use of a continuous performance measure implicitly reflects a choice between utility curves that are step functions and smooth, monotonic utility functions, respectively.

Third, the Black and Smith chapter generated results by applying the CPT model to a variety of scenarios. Rather than labeling these outcomes as "results," I would more cautiously label them as "manipulation checks." For example, the "results" are that higher unemployment rates reduce the cost of increased quality goals; or, as the number of new hires is reduced, it is more cost effective to set higher-quality goals. These results are, in some sense, built into the way in which the CPT model is constructed. Because they are a function of the initial assumptions of the CPT model, they are manipulation checks and care must be used in considering them in any prescriptive fashion.

Fourth, Black and Smith reported that the characteristics of jobs vary more within occupations than between occupations. This is consistent with Zeidner and Johnson's findings that classification efficiency can be increased by considering different groupings of jobs.

In sum, the CPT model is useful for understanding selection and classification. From my vantage, its usefulness is heuristic—by stating the parameters needed to operate such a model, focusing basic research on the limiting factors of the model, and delineating the value choices necessary in deciding about the characteristics of the model's parameters.

COMMONALITIES AND CONCLUSIONS

Although the titles of the chapters may indicate differences, there appear to be some fundamental commonalities across the chapters that lead to several overall conclusions. Although perhaps "obvious" on the surface, the conclusions are critical to thinking about selection and classification issues. Each conclusion implies that we have a way to go before we have a theoretical understanding of the practical implications of selection and classification systems in organizations:

1. *There is no inherent inconsistency between the psychometric concept of validity generalization and the potential for increased efficiency due to classification.* It is important to keep in mind two facets of validity generalization: transportability and situational specificity (cf. Kemery, Mossholder, & Roth, 1987). By transportability, it is meant that a test that has nonzero validity in one application will most likely (statistically speaking) have nonzero validity in another situation. By situational specificity, it is meant that these validities still have an underlying distribution with nonzero variance. Selection tests may be transportable. Indeed, other chapters in various sections of this conference suggest such findings (e.g., Ree & Earles, in this volume). However, the work of Zeidner and Johnson strongly suggests that there is sufficient situational specificity across jobs so that classification algorithms based on these differences can increase the overall operating efficiency of an organization.

2. *Selection and classification decisions are value decisions,* and its corollary, *Maximizing job performance may not be the only objective for selection and classification decisions.* These two conclusions clearly permeated the three chapters by Linn, Wise, and Alley. Is it mean predicted performance we want to maximize? How about the utility of that performance? But who's to make the utility judgments? At what level are these judgments to be made:

Are we interested in maximizing aggregated individual utility, group utility, or organizational effectiveness?[4]

Speaking of maximizing performance (or its value), when do we measure this performance? During training, early on the job, or late in a career? If we choose one time period, who decides? If we choose all three, utility analysts need to model how utility parameters change across a person's career and, at the same time, incorporate recent thinking about the changing patterns of validity coefficients across time (e.g., Ackerman, 1989; Henry & Hulin, 1987; Russell, Colella, & Bobko, 1993). Even if such models are available, how do we combine these different utility values (across career progression)? What are the weights and who determines them?

These already somewhat unanswerable, value-laden questions assume that some sort of performance (or its value) needs to be maximized. To complicate matters further, what about the trade-off between social obligations (i.e., issues of ethnic and gender balance) and performance maximization? In some cases there may not be a trade-off, but the literature on cognitive ability testing and selection indicates that these two criteria are not perfectly compatible.

It should be clear that any organization adopting a selection and classification system will have to ask very basic questions before it can apply statistical algorithms. The role of values in the system is inevitable, and we need to incorporate the thinking of organizational theorists in these areas. For example, Keeley (1983) summarized the role of values in organizational theorizing, and the existence of multiple constituencies in defining organizational effectiveness has been discussed by several researchers (e.g., Connolly, Conlon, & Deutsch, 1980; Zammuto, 1984). By acknowledging this multiplicity of structures, we can make the potential tensions explicit. Only then will we begin to have a fuller understanding of the implications of our selection and classification decisions. Wise's "criteria criteria" and description of the "goal space" are good first steps in this process.

3. *We need to know why things work the way they do.* I have already pointed this out in the context of the chapters by Zeidner and Johnson and Alley. Until we know where the incremental efficiency of classification is coming from, we won't know what its long-term implications are, it will be difficult to judge the acceptability of the system, and it will be nearly impossible to modify the system rationally. (I do mean rationally here, not empirically.)

The "why" question appears in other chapters. For example, Linn concluded that the topic of differential prediction should remain on our field's research

---

[4] And ecological validity considerations tell us that these are not necessarily simple transformations of one to the other.

agenda. There is good reasoning behind his statement. However, I suggest that, as social scientists, we all have a responsibility to look beyond dichotomous variables (Bartlett, Bobko, Mosier, & Hannan, 1978). Why does Linn's provocative finding of different results for hands-on and job knowledge tests happen? What are the underlying individual difference mechanisms? Why are there differences in statistical results across the dichotomous variables of gender or race? What components of the distinction between males and females cause these regression differences? Are these componential differences learned or innate? Are they "changeable" in the short period of time the military devotes to training? Should we try to change them (another value decision)? Only when we know what these components are can we make informed decisions about whether the regression differences are real or artifactual, whether the persons can or should be changed, whether the job should be restructured, and so forth. We need to keep in mind the statement attributed to Kurt Lewin: "There's nothing so practical as a good theory." With an increased understanding of why things happen, we will then be in a better position to tailor our organizational decisions and explicate any trade-offs inherent in the selection and classification process.

ACKNOWLEDGMENTS

A preliminary version of this manuscript was presented at the S&C Conference. I wish to thank F. Mark Schemmer for his helpful comments on an earlier draft of this thinking.

The author served as the discussant for Session Three, "Operational Models for Selection and Classification Decisions: Making Use of Predictor and Criterion Information," at the S&C Conference.

REFERENCES

Ackerman, P. (1989). Within-task intercorrelations of skilled performance: Implications for predicting individual differences? *Journal of Applied Psychology, 74,* 360-364.

Bartlett, C. J., Bobko, P., Mosier, S., & Hannan, R. (1978). Testing of fairness with a moderated multiple regression strategy: An alternative to differential analysis. *Personnel Psychology, 31,* 233-241.

Bobko, P. (1985). Removing assumptions of bipolarity: Towards variation and circularity. *Academy of Management Review, 10,* 99-108.

Bobko, P., & Donnelly, L. (1988). Identifying correlates of job-level, overall worth estimates: Application in a public sector organization. *Human Performance, 1,* 187-204.

Campbell, J. P. (1990). Modeling the performance prediction problem in industrial and organizational psychology. In M. Dunnette & L. Hough (Eds.), *Handbook of industrial & organizational psychology* (Vol. 1, 2nd ed., pp. 687-732). Consulting Psychologists Press: Palo Alto, CA.

Connolly, T., Conlon, E., & Deutsch, S. (1980). Organizational effectiveness: A multiple-constituency approach. *Academy of Management Review, 5,* 211-217.

Darlington, R. (1971). Another look at "cultural fairness." *Journal of Educational Measurement, 8,* 71-82.

Dunbar, S., & Novick, M. (1988). On predicting success in training for men and women: Examples from Marine Corps clerical specialties. *Journal of Applied Psychology, 73,* 545-550.

Goldstein, I. (1991). Training in work organizations. In M. Dunnette & L. Hough (Eds.), *Handbook of industrial and organizational psychology* (Vol. 2, 2nd ed., pp. 507-620). Palo Alto, CA: Consulting Psychologists Press.

Henry, R., & Hulin, C. (1987). Stability of skilled performance across time: Some generalizations and limitations on utilities. *Journal of Applied Psychology, 72,* 457-462.

Houston, W., & Novick, M. (1987). Race-based differential prediction in Air Force technical training programs. *Journal of Educational Measurement, 24,* 309-320.

Keeley, M. (1983). Values in organizational theory and management education. *Academy of Management Review, 8,* 376-386.

Kemery, E., Mossholder, K., & Roth, L. (1987). The power of the Schmidt and Hunter additive model of validity generalization. *Journal of Applied Psychology, 72,* 30-37.

Martin, S., & Raju, N. (1992). Determining cutoff scores that optimize utility: A recognition of recruiting costs. *Journal of Applied Psychology, 77,* 15-23.

Messick, S. (1989). Validity. In R. Linn (Ed.), *Educational measurement* (3rd ed., pp. 13-103). New York: Macmillan.

Nord, R., & White, L. (1987). *Optimal job assignment and the utility of performance.* Paper presented at the annual convention of the American Psychological Association, New York.

Pritchard, R., Jones, S., Roth, P., Stuebing, K., & Ekeberg, S. (1988). Effects of group feedback, goal setting, and incentives on organizational productivity. *Journal of Applied Psychology, 73,* 337-358.

Russell, C., Colella, A., & Bobko, P. (1993). Expanding the dimensions of utility: The financial and strategic impact of personnel selection. *Personnel Psychology, 46,* 781-801.

Sadacca, R., Campbell, J., DiFazio, A., Schultz, S., & White, L. (1990). Scaling performance utility to enhance selection and classification decisions. *Personnel Psychology, 43,* 367-378.

Zammuto, R. (1984). A comparison of multiple constituency models of organizational effectiveness. *Academy of Management Review, 9,* 606-616.

Part IV

Where Do We Go Now?

Toward a New Agenda

CHAPTER

26

THE FUTURE: A RESEARCH AGENDA

Michael G. Rumsey
Clinton B. Walker
U.S. Army Research Institute

The dramatic progress in selection and classification research over the past decade could well have led to complacency or a move to consolidation of recent gains. But as seen in this conference, the momentum of the recent past continues. The participants presented a host of new directions that formed two dominant themes: first, expanding our view of the person, the job, and the person-job match, and second, integrating research findings in new ways.

Previous sections of the book presented the topical papers and discussants' remarks. These sections were the core of this conference, but not the only original part. Discussion that concluded the conference provided further ideas and helped place earlier presentations in a richer context. This chapter summarizes these discussions and concludes with comments on prospects for the field. This rendering of the group discussion is the editors'; any liberties taken with the original material is unintended.

EXPANDING OUR VISION

Characteristics of the Person

The history of selection and classification research has closely paralleled the history of research on intelligence. Cognitive abilities have been shown to relate clearly and consistently to job performance (Barrett & Depinet, 1991; McHenry, Hough, Toquam, Hanson, & Ashworth, 1990). In the area of classification, researchers have been trying to make use of specific cognitive abilities; but whether specific abilities can add much to general cognitive ability is arguable (Ree & Earles, this volume).

Speakers at this conference strongly urged researchers to look beyond cognitive abilities. Sternberg identified a number of areas deserving closer examination. Many, including motivation, values, personality, creativity, and styles of thinking, were addressed earlier in his topical paper. However, the group discussion highlighted some other aspects of motivation and personality. The discussion on motivation emphasized the link between this group of constructs and Self Efficacy, as well as the importance of the environmental context in developing a meaningful measure. The discussion on personality emphasized Tolerance of Boredom, Conscientiousness, and Self-Monitoring.

A number of additional areas emerged in Sternberg's presentation, as summarized below:

1. Flexibility, both as an ability and as a disposition to use the ability. The role of teaching/training in encouraging or inhibiting flexibility was also noted.

2. Social Intelligence and the ability to be "group intelligent", or to work effectively with a team. In any organization, it is important to be able to get along with people, give a good talk, and interview successfully for a job. A negative example cited by Sternberg was a job applicant who not only was arrogant, but also lacked the social intelligence to hide that fact during the job interview. The New York Yankees under Steinbrenner provided an example of the difference between aggregate individual ability and team performance.

3. Motor ability. Recently, the media reported an incident where the six police shooting at a fleeing criminal all missed! Although tests of psychomotor abilities have not typically added much to predicting overall job performance, the criticality of some of the job components that they do predict makes them important.

4. Learning rate and asymptote. Although such measures have been suggested for years (Christal, 1976), the spread of computerized testing makes them newly important for two reasons. First, computers are making more types of tests practical in more settings (e.g., of spatial and psychomotor aptitudes). But unlike tests of reading and mathematics, such new tests have content and formats that are far from overlearned. Their novelty makes their scores highly susceptible to practice and coaching. By using within-examinee data on change in performance over trials, we may be able to neutralize differences in practice and coaching in estimating real aptitude. Second, computer technology makes it possible to gather and quickly process the data needed for using such statistics.

The Job

Clearly the speakers felt that our view of job performance, which underwent a quantum expansion in the 1980s, is still underdeveloped. They offered a view of the job as broader, more dynamic, and more interactive than the view traditionally underlying performance measurement research. The job is not just the list of tasks that the organization expects the individual to do, said Ilgen; it is also the unofficial roles that the individual uniquely takes on in the work setting. In addition to the work of the individual, noted Murphy, we must look at performance also in terms of its contribution to the group. We must consider trends in how work is structured to meet its changing environment, such as the trend toward semi-autonomous work teams. And we need to look beyond predicting performance at a point in time or even over an extended assignment—we need to develop concepts and methods for predicting performance over an entire career.

These points are compelling, but are they realistic? For example, can we learn enough about how to measure both team performance and the individual's contribution to team performance to target such constructs in our predictors of individual performance? Can our knowledge of the future be sufficient for us to conduct job analyses that reflect both the present and future realities of the job? And finally, if we have separate measurements of job performance over an entire career, how could or should we combine these into a single criterion? These questions are not meant to discourage expeditions along the paths described; they are simply challenges to anyone following these paths.

Classification

Participants also argued for a broader view of the information that could assist in matching persons with the right jobs. Bobko's summary of the small group discussion suggested that the issues in personnel decision making are much more complex than is generally acknowledged. He reported on the following research themes emerging from this discussion:

1. What should classification maximize? Four parts of this question identified:

   a. Choice of performance components. Given that performance consists of components, which of these should be maximized? Or, if combined into a composite, how should the components be weighted? These are questions partly of research method and partly of the values of the given organization.

   b. Career perspective. How can we maximize performance at more than one time in the future? In any organization, individuals may stay for more than one tour (or contract, assignment, level, or other unit of analysis). How can we aggregate performance over time to generate the best criterion to maximize? How can we best classify in a world where it is likely that many individuals will change their jobs over the course of their careers, but the timing and direction of changes are not (at least now) predictable?

c. Time horizon for classifying. What time perspective should we use in our maximization? Should the classification software work with positions that are open or opening on this day, during the coming week, during the coming month, or further? A model that works with a longer time horizon increases the gain in performance that is theoretically possible through better matching of persons and jobs. For example, it could assign individuals to jobs that are not yet open. In contrast, an assignment system that fills only the jobs that are open now has little flexibility. But taking the shorter view increases the likelihood that theoretically possible gains will indeed be realized.

d. Individual versus unit performance. For what level(s) of aggregating persons should we maximize performance? At the individual level, the team, or higher? And for what occupational unit should we maximize? Should we select persons for specific jobs, or for a particular unit that needs their particular strengths? In the context of this discussion, issues about cost-benefit trade-offs and classification fairness were also raised.

2. When should individuals be classified—at the time of selection or only after being introduced to the organization and some occupational options within it? How should individuals' job preferences affect classification? What are the impacts of reducing individuals' freedom to choose? How does choice by the employee (e.g., of a job for its location or hours) affect the gains in performance that might be realized from the optimal classification system?

3. How can we achieve fairness in classification? Up to now, selection—who gets into the organization and who does not—has been the issue for work on fairness. But a whole set of related issues may still need attention regarding how we classify selectees into jobs that vary in attractiveness.

4. How should entry standards be set? This was the one theme that did not focus exclusively on classification. It was expressed in terms of two underlying issues:

a. "Quality goals" used by the military. A minimum standard is set on the overall selection score, and then a desired distribution of scores above that level is set as the goal. How should these goals be set? To what extent does this forced "distribution of quality" reduce the gains in job performance that would be possible under optimal classification? If more powerful classification tools were implemented, would that make it possible to have different, more easily attained goals for quality in terms of the selector score?

b. Setting minimum entry standards. Such standards affect efforts to maximize performance, as discussed in the prior paragraph. If we try to maximize only entry-level performance, a low standard may suffice. But in an organization that grows its mid-level and senior ranks internally, like the military, we need to ensure that enough people are brought in initially who will later qualify for the higher-level jobs. This need complicates the process of setting minimum entry standards and ties in with setting goals for the distribution of quality.

INTEGRATION OF CONCEPTS

Integration Across Content Domains

We turn here to the other dominant theme—integration. Zeidner and others stressed that we cannot consider the person and the job independently of the person-job match if we are to have a truly effective classification system.

First consider the person. Individual differences are often examined solely to improve selection. Zeidner says that this practice limits the benefits that an organization can realize from tests. We should also look for personal characteristics that are differentially valid across jobs—that predict performance well in some jobs but not in others. By looking only for predictors that have comparable validity across jobs, we sacrifice efficiency of classification.

The point applies equally well to job analysis and performance measurement, as noted by both Zeidner and McCloy. We need to consider those aspects of performance that vary from job to job as well as those that are common across jobs. This point is not lost in most task-based job analyses, but has it been given adequate attention with respect to "soft skill" analysis? Why was it so difficult in Project A (*Personnel Psychology*, 1990), for example, to differentially predict performance across jobs using temperament measures? Were our methods of job analysis sufficiently sensitive to those less obvious dimensions of performance, such as organizational citizenship or performance in groups, that might have been differentially salient across jobs?

Strong sentiment was voiced in the conference for more attention to integrating selection and classification with other organizational functions. Murphy, in his summary of the job performance session, addressed the issue in terms of learning how to choose the best interventions for improving job performance. Given that performance is a function of several types of personnel-focused tactics—selection, classification, training, and leadership—can we develop principles to prescribe the best mix of those interventions?

Although the discussion recommended integrating selection and classification with other personnel functions generally, the function that was most frequently cited was training. Testing at initial entry was noted as an opportunity for educational diagnosis in addition to classifying persons into occupations.

In parallel, researchers were urged to look for attributes of individual difference that are trainable and important for success on the job. Bandura's Self-Efficacy (this volume) was invoked by numerous participants as an example. For Murphy, Self-Efficacy is a possible "noncognitive g" which, others observed, can be improved with training. Campion suggested that improving Self-Efficacy of junior enlisted soldiers is a major, perhaps unrecognized, responsibility of noncommissioned officers. Flexibility, an attribute that Major General Gorden noted will be increasingly important in the Army, was also suggested as target of training, as well as of selection.

Lohman proposed a comprehensive theoretical orientation that would link individual differences, organizational processes, and performance. This formulation breaks down boundaries that are traditionally drawn between the individual and the organization, between training and selection and classification, and between aptitude and performance. In this approach, the organization is not perceived as an external agent acting on a passive individual. Rather, the organization and the individual are viewed as forming a partnership in trying to maximize the benefit of the individual to the organization. In this model, controls for faking and coaching are not needed, because the individual and the organization have a mutual interest in accurately measuring the individual's true potential.

In Lohman's view, testing for selection and classification could well provide information for training purposes. Information about individual strengths and weaknesses can serve as a basis for building on strengths and remedying weaknesses, not merely matching the individual to a particular slot in an organization.

Finally, aptitude is tied to performance, not just in terms of particular validation results, but in terms of theory that precedes the conduct of the validation research. In fact, in Lohman's model, it is psychological theory about aptitudes and how these can be modified or molded by organizational interventions and linked to field achievements that is the glue binding the elements of his model together.

The call for integration across psychological disciplines and across organizational functions is reminiscent of a similar call by Uhlaner in a 1970 address. After decrying "fractionated approaches which have left the decision-maker less and less satisfied with the human factors systems impacts," Uhlaner (pp. 4, 6) recommended a more systematic approach:

Fundamental to the understanding of the human factors system is the recognition that the effective behavior and work performance desired in a particular situation may be achieved in a great variety of ways—

admittedly for varying costs. . . . If more talented applicants are selected, the treatment (training) accorded them may be simplified, but the equipment may require less human engineering attention. On the other hand, less capable individuals may require longer and more skillful treatment (training and experience) and better human-engineered equipment.

Not only are there interactions between selection variables and treatment variables (training and experience) and job design variables (equipment, environment, and organization), but there are interactions within a domain, such as between cognitive and noncognitive variables within the selection domain. Any of the above conditions and resulting performance may be further modified—one way or another—by the kind of supervision and leadership provided in the work situation and by many other variables too numerous to mention here.

In 1981, the need to link selection and classification research with a larger research program addressing needs within the Army personnel system was reflected in a paper by Shields and Baker. The needs were identified as follows:

The problem in selection and classification is how best to assign available personnel resources to meet the near term demands on the personnel system. The problem in force modernization is to predict if the long term personnel demands imposed by improved and new weapons systems requirements will exceed the available manpower and personnel resources.

Both of these problems were linked; hence, a coordinated research plan was developed "to join the fruits of present day selection, classification and accessioning R&D to their counterparts in personnel affordability efforts to provide a smooth and continuous linkage of the Army personnel systems to Army personnel requirements." From this concept came Project A (Campbell, 1990), which validated the existing selection and classification system and developed new predictors; Project B (Konieczny, Brown, Hutton, & Stewart, 1990), which developed a new personnel allocation system; and MANPRINT (Kaplan & Hartel, 1988), which developed new methods for determining personnel requirements of new weapons systems.

The concepts of Uhlaner, Shields, and Baker have inspired comprehensive, systematic research approaches to organizational problems, but Lohman's lament suggests that further integration is desirable, particularly of selection and training. The Air Force's Learning Abilities Measurement Program (LAMP; Kyllonen, in this volume), seems like a vehicle for realizing many of the gains from such integration.

Still, no single effort has incorporated all of the elements required to meet Lohman's challenge. Such an effort would require a vision sufficiently broad and insightful to integrate aptitudes, performance, selection, training, and other personnel management functions in a manner that reflects the theoretical vitality of LAMP; the organizational sensitivity shown by Uhlaner, Shields, and Baker; and a research execution plan as comprehensive and coordinated as Project A to translate vision and sensitivity into action. The investment needed for such an effort would be considerable but, given the potential gains, not at all unreasonable.

Integration and Implementation

The final conference discussion session gave participants an opportunity to raise other issues. This session was remarkable for the emphasis given to the implementation of research products rather than to the content of the research. There was a prevailing theme that the future of selection and classification research, at least within the military services, depends as much, if not more, on the researchers' ability to deal with implementation issues as on the quality of the research conducted. This issue is presented under its own heading because it involves the integration of selection and classification research with other components of the organization.

Participants raised a number of familiar points that bear repeating: take a "user-oriented" approach in identifying research issues, involve the user in the research process from the beginning, and explain benefits in terms the user can understand. Likewise, well-known dangers of an overeagerness to serve the user were raised: a focus on short-term goals at the expense of long-term goals, neglect of important scientific issues, and premature termination of research projects based on discouraging early findings. A delicate balance between the user's short-term needs and scientific and practical issues of longer-term significance must be maintained for a scientific program to remain viable— ignore either, and the research unit may soon find itself unsupported.

A balance must also be maintained between research efforts focused on narrowly defined objectives and those that encompass the entire organization. It is sometimes necessary to narrow the scope of the investigation to address problems of practical significance to the sponsor; yet, one may at other times need to examine the entire organizational context to understand the full dimensions of the user's problem. Knowing how to properly scope the problem is a constant challenge to the researcher's judgment, knowledge, and understanding.

The implementation process may itself be a proper object of the researcher's attention, particularly if the process is complex and cumbersome. The researcher must understand the process to make it work properly, and occasionally may need to suggest changes to the process to allow it to function more effectively. Here, researchers could benefit from the large, interdisciplinary literature on change strategies, technical assistance, and technology transfer (Berman, McLaughlin, Bass, Pauly, & Zellman, 1977; Stanford Research Institute, 1977).

Prospects

In the early 1980s, personnel researchers in all of the American military services set out to expand the set of well-grounded predictors beyond the construct of general aptitude. A host of new spatial, psychomotor, temperament, interest, and information-processing tests were developed and validated against both traditional and new criteria (Campbell, 1990; Kyllonen, this volume).

The results of these projects have converged on the conclusion that new aptitude tests make consistent but small gains over general aptitude in predicting composite criteria of skilled performance (Peterson, Oppler, Sager, & Rosse, in press), although larger gains were obtained for some specific measures against narrower performance measures (Busciglio, Silva, & Walker, 1990).

However, the criteria examined were not confined to new proficiency measures. An expansion of the criterion space to include "will-do" performance, as represented by ratings and administrative measures, helped unearth the large gains that many of the researchers had hoped for. These measures were found not to be merely low-fidelity representations of the proficiency measures, but to complement such measures, thus providing a more complete picture of individual performance.

With the present conference, the flowering of the performance space of the 1980s is continuing. Along with our growing understanding and more sophisticated measurement of job performance come opportunities to validate the recently expanded set of predictor measures and to push this expansion of the predictor space even further.

Hand in hand with the expansion of the predictor and criterion space come new challenges in the realm of classification. Zeidner and Johnson maintained that we have hardly begun to capitalize on the classification power of our existing predictors, much less of an expanded set of measures. These authors have brought classification research to the foreground and have made the case that the potential gains from improved classification are too dramatic to ignore.

Thus, the emerging research agenda will include further examination of the tests developed from the 1980s, as well as tests designed to cover new domains, against an ever-richer concept of job performance, with the greatest possible attention to the question of how best to use the full set of predictors to maximum effect in placing the right person in the right job.

REFERENCES

Barrett, G. R., & Depinet, R. L. (1991). A reconsideration of testing for competence rather than for intelligence. *American Psychologist, 46*, 1012-1024.

Berman, P., McLaughlin, M. W., Bass, G., Pauly, E., & Zellman, G. (1977). *Federal programs supporting educational change, Vol VII: Factors affecting implementation and continuation* (Report No. R-1589). Santa Monica, CA: RAND Corp. (NTIS No. 619951)

Busciglio, H. H., Silva, J., & Walker, C. B. (1990, June). *The potential of new Army tests to improve job performance.* Paper presented at the Army Science Conference, Durham, NC.

Christal, R. E. (1976, October). *What is the value of aptitude tests?* Paper presented at the annual conference of the Military Testing Association, Gulf Shores, AL.

Kaplan, J., & Hartel, C. (1988). MANPRINT methods: Development of HARDMAN III. *Proceedings of the 27th Annual Army Operations Research Symposium.*

Konieczny, F. B., Brown, G. N., Hutton, J., & Stewart, J. E. II. (1990). *Enlisted Personnel Allocation System: Final Report (TR902).* Alexandria, VA: U.S. Army Research Institute. (AD A229 095)

McHenry, J. J., Hough, L. M, Toquam, J. L., Hanson, M. A., & Ashworth, S. (1990). Project A validity results: the relationship between predictor and criterion domains. *Personnel Psychology, 43,* 335-354.

Personnel Psychology (1990, Summer). Project A: The U.S. Army Selection and Classification Project (Special Issue), 43, 2.

Peterson, N. G., Oppler, S. H., Sager, C. E., & Rosse, R. L. (in press). *Analysis of the Enhanced Computer Administered Test Battery: An Evaluation of Potential Revisions and Additions to the Armed Services Vocational Aptitude Battery.* Alexandria, VA: U.S. Army Research Institute.

Shields, J. L., & Baker, J. D. (1981, May). *The Army's personnel problems and the golden spike solution.* Paper presented at the National Security Industrial Association First Annual Conference on Personnel and Training Factors in System Effectiveness, San Diego.

Stanford Research Institute (1977). *Evaluation of the National Diffusion Network. Final Report, Vol. I: Findings and Recommendations.* Menlo Park, CA: Author. (ERIC No. ED147327)

Uhlaner, J. E. (1970, September). *Human performance, jobs and systems psychology—The systems measurement bed.* Presidential address to the Division of Military Psychology, American Psychological Association, Miami.

Author Index

Page numbers in *italics* denote complete bibliographical information.

467

Subject Index